Trials of the Century

Trials of the Century

AN ENCYCLOPEDIA OF POPULAR CULTURE AND THE LAW

Volume One

Scott P. Johnson

ABC-CLIO

Santa Barbara, California • Denver, Colorado • Oxford, England

Copyright 2011 by ABC-CLIO, LLC

Library of Congress Cataloging-in-Publication Data

Johnson, Scott Patrick.
   Trials of the century : an encyclopedia of popular culture and the law / Scott P. Johnson.
        p. cm.
   Includes bibliographical references and index.
   ISBN 978-1-59884-261-6 (hard copy : alk. paper) —
ISBN 978-1-59884-262-3 (ebook)   1. Trials—United States.   I. Title.
   KF220.J64   2010
   345.73'07—dc22   2010015948

ISBN: 978-1-59884-261-6
EISBN: 978-1-59884-262-3

15   14   13   12   11   1   2   3   4   5

This book is also available on the World Wide Web as an eBook.
Visit www.abc-clio.com for details.

ABC-CLIO, LLC
130 Cremona Drive, P.O. Box 1911
Santa Barbara, California 93116-1911

This book is printed on acid-free paper ∞

Manufactured in the United States of America

Contents

List of Entries

Acknowledgments

First and foremost, I would like to thank the editors at ABC-CLIO who provided wonderful support and assistance throughout the two years of researching and writing this encyclopedia. In particular, Holly Heinzer, Kim Kennedy White, and Lauren Thomas were instrumental in providing guidance and advice during the entire process. Their professionalism improved the quality of my work and it has been greatly appreciated.

I am indebted to the mentors who have been integral in my development as an instructor and researcher. Christopher E. Smith of Michigan State University, Thomas R. Hensley of Kent State University, and Stephen J. Simpson of Frostburg State University have greatly influenced my academic career through their advice, encouragement, and positive example.

I am fortunate to have colleagues in the Political Science Department at Frostburg State University who provide a healthy environment for conducting academic research. The professional relationships and friendships that I have made at Frostburg State have enhanced my academic career and personal life in such a way as to make "work" more enjoyable.

My wife, Phaiboon Ladkubon Johnson, has provided a strong foundation of love and support for the past 15 years. Throughout my academic career, she never doubted that I could become a university professor, even when I doubted myself at times. It has been a blessing to have a partner who has always remained confident that I would achieve my professional goals.

My wife and I have been fortunate enough to establish wonderful friendships that have enhanced my professional career as well as our personal lives. In particular, I would like to express my gratitude toward Jack and Ruth Armstrong and Dennis and Suzi Mills for their support and friendship over the years.

Finally, I would like to express my gratitude toward my mother and stepfather, Kathy and Dale Neely, who have provided unconditional love and support over the years. My mother always understood the importance of education, and I vividly remember her taking my brother and me on numerous visits to the public library in order to sharpen our reading skills, even before we started grade school. Because her concern and sacrifice ensured that I would succeed academically, I dedicate this encyclopedia to my mother.

Introduction

Trials of the Century: An Encyclopedia of Popular Culture and the Law focuses on the criminal, civil, religious, and political trials that have fascinated the American public over the course of five centuries. From colonial era trials to the modern-day legal dramas of the 21st century, this encyclopedia provides detailed information regarding each "trial of the century" and biographical information pertaining to persons involved in the trials as well as historical information related to events and other topics surrounding the legal controversy. The trials are also analyzed in order to understand their importance within popular culture as well as their larger impact on the American legal system. As noted below, the "trials of the century" have captured the attention of the nation based upon a variety of factors.

Politics and Crime

A significant number of the "trials of the century" discussed in this encyclopedia combine the forces of politics and crime. For example, the assassination of a political leader automatically produced the high-profile trials of the Lincoln conspirators, Clay Shaw and Sirhan Sirhan. Even an attempted assassination of a political leader generated public interest in the trials of Richard Lawrence, Arthur Bremer, and John W. Hinckley Jr. Political factors and criminal activity have also formed to bring about trials involving terrorist attacks committed on American soil. Domestic and foreign terrorist plots have produced trials related to the Haymarket Square bombing of the late 19th century, the Nazi Saboteurs captured during World War II, the Oklahoma City bombing, and, most recently, the 9/11 attacks. Politics was also at the foundation of the "trials of the century" involving the labor movement in the early 1900s where such individuals as Bill Haywood, Joe Hill, and Leon Czolgosz faced prosecution for crimes committed based upon their political beliefs. In addition, politics was a critical factor in the Cold War trials involving such accused communists as Alger Hiss and Julius and Ethel Rosenberg, and politics was clearly the basis for the Chicago Seven trial, involving antiwar protestors at the 1968 Democratic National Convention in Chicago. Finally, politics was the dominant force in such legal controversies as the treason trial of Aaron Burr, and the impeachment trials of a U.S. Supreme Court justice, Samuel Chase, and two presidents, Andrew Johnson and William Jefferson Clinton.

Race and Ethnicity

Race, particularly the struggle of African Americans, has served as a pervasive theme in many of the "trials of the century" discussed throughout the encyclopedia. Beginning with the Great Negro Plot Trials of the 18th century and the Nat Turner and Amistad slave trials of the 19th century, race played a critical role in generating public interest in legal cases in the early part of American history. In addition, the trials of Dred Scott and John Brown have been viewed as major factors in causing the outbreak of the Civil War and ending the practice of slavery in America. In the 20th century, racial discrimination also produced historical trials involving the practice of lynching, the policy of segregation, the civil rights movement, and police brutality against African Americans.

Race and ethnicity also were factors in creating an interest in trials involving other minority groups. For instance, Native Americans were the focus of the Dakota Conflict trials of the mid-19th century and the murder trial of Leonard Peltier in 1979, while prejudice against Asian Americans was evident in the Massie trials of 1931–1932. The discrimination against ethnic groups such as Jewish Americans was highlighted in the Leo Frank trial, while negative attitudes toward German and Italian immigrants played a critical role in the Bruno Hauptmann and Sacco and Vanzetti trials respectively.

Women's Rights

Gender, particularly the role of women in society and politics, has created legal controversies that have been transformed into "trials of the century." During the colonial era, the push for women's rights generated conflict in the trial of Anne Hutchinson who sought to become a practicing minister in the colony of Massachusetts. Women's rights were also at the heart of the pre–Civil War trial of Celia, a slave, who had murdered her slave master after he had sexually assaulted her. The trial of Susan B. Anthony during the women's suffrage era demonstrated the lack of equality given to women within the legal system after she stood trial for simply voting in a presidential election. The Lizzie Borden trial, the murder trials of Harry Thaw, and the Triangle Shirtwaist Fire trial also caused gender to influence the legal proceedings as stereotypes about women were emphasized and the lack of protections and rights afforded to women were clearly evident.

Religion

American culture also has become enthralled by legal disputes involving religion. The Salem Witchcraft trials were one of the first trials to invoke religion and the fear of evil into a legal proceeding. The slave revolt of Nat Turner in 1831 was based largely upon religion as was John Brown's raid at Harper's Ferry in 1859. The 19th century Carthage Conspiracy trial of 1844 highlighted the discrimination and violence against Mormons because of their religious beliefs but the Mountain Meadows Massacre trials of 1875–1876 also demonstrated how Mormons were motivated to commit violent acts of their own based upon religious beliefs and fears. Charles Guiteau's assassination of President James Garfield in 1881 was based largely upon his irrational religious views and the legal basis for the Scopes Monkey trial in 1925 centered upon the interpretation of the Bible in the battle between creationism and evolution. Finally, a legal battle between evangelical Christians and the world of pornography took center stage in 1984 when Reverend Jerry Falwell filed a civil lawsuit against Larry Flynt of *Hustler* magazine.

Celebrity and Wealth

American culture has always been fascinated by crimes involving celebrities and the wealthy, which serve as the basis for several of the "trials of the century." The trial of the professional baseball players of the Chicago White Sox in 1921 who were accused of throwing the 1919 World Series as well as the trial of Bruno Hauptmann who kidnapped and murdered the child of a national hero, Charles Lindbergh, probably matched the intensity of the criminal trials of modern-day celebrities such as O. J. Simpson and Michael Jackson. The O. K. Corral trial of 1881 involving such legendary figures as Wyatt Earp and Doc Holliday, the sexual assault trial of Hollywood film star, Fatty Arbuckle, in the 1920s, and the trial of Lenny Bruce, a 1960s comedian who pushed the boundaries of free speech, also exemplified the public's attraction toward celebrity. When wealthy and privileged individuals are accused of violent crimes such as Dr. Sam Sheppard in 1954, Patty Hearst in the 1970s, and the Menendez brothers and O. J. Simpson in the 1990s, the American media and public cannot help but fixate on every detail of the crime and subsequent trial pertaining to individuals who previously had appeared beyond the reach of the legal system.

Nature of the Crime

The nature of a crime itself has sometimes caused the American public to become captivated with a subsequent trial. The Leopold and Loeb trial in 1924 was closely followed by the American public because of the senseless and violent murder of a young boy who was killed simply for the thrill. The Charles Manson trial of 1970–1971 gained prominence largely because of the violent and brutal nature of the murders committed by the followers of the Manson cult. The Mountain Meadows massacre in 1857 and the My Lai massacre in 1970 are examples of crimes of murder on such a large scale that they demanded the attention of the American public and the world.

Legal controversies involving sex scandals such as the Harry Thaw trials, the Fatty Arbuckle trials, the Massie trials, and the Clinton impeachment trial have caused Americans to obsess over the lurid details related to accusations of seduction, sexual assault, and sexual harassment. The McMartin Preschool Abuse trials and the Michael Jackson trial also illustrate how the sexual nature of a crime can garner the attention of the public for better or worse. The fact that children were the apparent victims in sexual assault cases triggered a strong emotional reaction with many in the public demanding punishment for the alleged perpetrators.

Each of the "trials of the century" within the encyclopedia cannot be neatly categorized into the one of the areas described above. In fact, most of the trials overlap into multiple areas which probably accounts for why a legal controversy created such a strong interest among the American people in the first place. In sum, a "trial of the century" achieved its status based largely upon a mixture of political, social, religious, and economic factors as well as intangibles such as the role of the media, the nature of a crime, or legal controversy, and the personalities involved in the legal proceedings.

The Anne Hutchinson Trials (1637–1638)

Anne Hutchinson was tried in the colony of Massachusetts for challenging the belief system of the Puritan religion, particularly the issue of women as leaders within the church. The trial was significant because it highlighted the lack of rights and privileges afforded an accused person in the 17th century. In addition, the issues of religious freedom and equality within the colonies were important factors in determining the outcome of the trial. Today, Hutchinson is viewed as a courageous hero who challenged a system of tyranny that denied her basic protections of due process that are often taken for granted in the American justice system today (Morris 1967, 3–4).

Even though many persons came to the American colonies from European countries in search of religious freedom, the colonial governments had been known to force religious beliefs upon its citizens. For example, the colony of Massachusetts was considered Puritan, which favored more purity in terms of worship. Puritans were not tolerant of other belief systems (LaPlante 2005, 4–5). As a settler in Massachusetts, Anne Hutchinson began violating the values of the Puritan religion when she expressed openly that women should be treated with respect and dignity in society. Hutchinson began holding Bible studies at her home and informed her followers that she interpreted the Bible differently than the traditional ministers of the Puritan religion (Morris 1967, 6–7). Specifically, Hutchinson challenged the Puritan interpretation of the story of Adam and Eve where the woman was blamed for original sin which justified the domination of women by men in society. Hutchinson also interpreted the Bible to provide equal rights for women and to end racial discrimination against Native Americans (Ellsberg 1997, 367–368).

Probably the most controversial view expressed by Hutchinson was her belief in the "covenant of grace," or the idea that a person could be saved simply by having faith in God. Hutchinson argued that people could speak directly to God without the assistance of the church or the Bible. The Puritan clergy viewed Hutchinson's ideas as disrespectful because they believed in the "covenant of works," or the idea that a person must obey the moral laws of the church in order to be saved (Morris 1967, 7–8). Hutchinson even went further in offending the clergy by stating that she could recognize who would be saved by God and who would not be saved (LaPlante 2005, 45–48). As Hutchinson's following started to grow rapidly numbering nearly 100 people, men as well as women began to attend her Bible studies, including Sir Henry Vane, who was elected the governor of Massachusetts in 1636 (Morris 1967, 8–9).

The Puritan ministers and the government officials in Massachusetts became very concerned about Hutchinson because they feared that she was becoming too powerful within the religious and political communities. Initially, the religious clergy criticized Hutchinson for confusing the members of the Puritan Church with different interpretations of the Bible, but gradually the ministers began focusing on the issue of gender. The ministers began emphasizing specific verses from the Bible that, according to their interpretation, prohibited women from speaking about religious matters (Ellsberg 1997, 367–368). In the political arena, the opposition to Hutchinson was confirmed by the results of the 1637 election for governor of Massachusetts where John Winthrop defeated Sir Henry Vane. Winthrop had openly criticized Hutchinson and her views that contradicted the teachings of the Puritan ministers. Winthrop considered Hutchinson's interpretations of the Bible to be heretical, or a serious challenge to the traditional belief system of the Puritan religion. Hutchinson responded to Winthrop by stating that the Lord God had revealed himself to her in a vision and God told her not to be afraid because justice would be served in her dispute with the Puritan ministers. Winthrop considered her comments to be blasphemous and decided to hold a trial in order to judge her actions (Crawford 1970, 144–146).

The civil trial of Anne Hutchinson was scheduled for November 7–8, 1637 in Newtown (Cambridge), Massachusetts. The trial would be held at the Massachusetts General Court, which heard judicial cases during the colonial era. Hutchinson was 46 years old at the time of the trial, and she was pregnant with her 15th child. Governor Winthrop was in charge of the court proceedings with several government officials and religious ministers also seated as judges on the court. Winthrop not only served as the main judge but also performed the role of lead prosecutor during the trial. In the American justice system today, Winthrop would be expected to remove himself from the trial if the defendant happened to be one of his political opponents. Furthermore, a person would never be permitted to perform the dual role of judge and prosecutor in a case. Winthrop's participation as the judge in the trial of Anne Hutchinson created a serious conflict of interest and the fact that he also planned to assume the role of prosecutor guaranteed an unfair trial for Hutchinson (Morris 1967, 12–13).

For the most part, the trial was a political hearing mixed together with legal and religious elements with no consideration for separation of church and state. From the outset of the trial, Hutchinson's basic rights were violated by modern day standards. She was brought to trial without being informed of the charges against her and without any knowledge of the possible punishment that she faced if found guilty. Based upon the comments of Winthrop at the beginning of the trial, it has been assumed that she was charged with making false and reckless statements that harmed the reputation of the religious ministers. Hutchinson was not provided an attorney to represent her, but it should be noted that no defense attorneys actually practiced law in the colony of Massachusetts in 1637 (Morris 1967, 11–13).

For several days, Hutchinson was forced to stand trial as prosecutors tried to get her to confess to committing blasphemy against the Puritan religion. Prosecutors accused her of violating the Fifth Commandment, which held that a person must honor their father and mother, because she had encouraged people to challenge and disagree with the "fathers" of the colony of Massachusetts (Morris 1967, 16). Hutchinson was also accused of taking women away from their families so they could attend the Bible studies and discussion groups in her home (17).

A number of witnesses testified against Hutchinson by describing how she preached the "covenant of grace" to her followers and rejected the "covenant of works," which was taught by the Puritan ministers (Morris 1967, 19–20). Hutchinson denied that she preached in public about the covenant of grace, but it was well known that she discussed such matters in private conversations (21).

The few witnesses who testified in defense of Hutchinson were treated so harshly by the judges that they apologized for disagreeing with and offending the judges (Morris 1967, 23). The key witness for the defense was Reverend John Cotton, who was viewed as a radical follower of Hutchinson by the court and the only minister that Hutchinson approved of because he practiced the "covenant of grace." Cotton was pressed harshly by the judges to defend Hutchinson and he provided sympathetic testimony by discussing the technical differences between Hutchinson and the ministers in terms of their religious views. Cotton's testimony actually appeared to provide an opportunity for the judges to acquit Hutchinson. Unfortunately, Hutchinson's controversial statements to the judges during the trial would undo any sympathy created by Cotton's testimony (Law Library, "Anne Hutchinson Trial").

While Hutchinson defended herself skillfully throughout the two day trial, any chance of an acquittal ended when she informed the judges that they had no control over her and only God could judge her. Surprisingly, Hutchinson warned the judges that God would ruin them and the entire colony of Massachusetts if she was treated unfairly (Hutchinson, "The Trial"). Her comments caused many in the courtroom to become very angry with her and she was called "evil" and a "follower of the devil" by many observers (Morris 1967, 27–28). The religious ministers scolded her and stated that she had acted outside of her role as a woman in society and had attempted to act as if she was a man, a religious minister, and a judge. Clearly, the outcome of the trial had been determined even before it began. On November 8, 1637, the Court condemned her and ordered her banished from the colony of Massachusetts because she was worthless as a woman in society. Hutchinson was placed under house arrest until the church could hold its own religious trial to determine her status as a member of the congregation (Crawford 1970, 144–146).

On March 22, 1638, a religious trial was held at the First Church in Boston where Hutchinson was charged by the chief prosecutor, Reverend John Davenport, with disrespecting the Puritan religion and immoral conduct because she had allowed men and women together in her home for the Bible studies which were held every Sunday. The judges on the religious court consisted of John Wilson and clergy from the Church of Boston who found Hutchinson guilty of the charges (Law Library, "Anne Hutchinson Trial"). As punishment, the judges ruled that Hutchinson must leave the Puritan

Church because she had openly disagreed with the beliefs and traditions of the Puritan religion (LaPlante 2005, 174–207). Surprisingly, Reverend Cotton decided to testify against Hutchinson at the religious trial in order to save his reputation and escape any punishment that had been given to the defense witnesses who testified on behalf of Hutchinson. Cotton stated publicly that Hutchinson was immoral and a dangerous influence upon other women. Cotton even went as far as to question whether Hutchinson would remain loyal to her husband (Morris 1967, 24–31).

After the political and religious trials, Hutchinson was forced to leave Massachusetts and settled in Rhode Island (Morris 1967, 31). She had become the first female defendant to have been tried in the New World (LaPlante 2005, 12). Her political and religious trials inspired the American development of religious freedom, tolerance for the participation of women in society, and the basic freedoms of due process found in the Bill of Rights. In a symbolic gesture, Michael Dukakis, the governor of Massachusetts, pardoned Anne Hutchinson in 1987 (LaPlante 2005, 237).

References

Crawford, Deborah. *Four Women in a Violent Time.* New York: Crown Publishers, 1970.

Ellsberg, Robert. *All Saints: Daily Reflections on Saints, Prophets, and Witnesses From Our Time.* New York: Crossroad Publishing Company, 1997.

LaPlante, Eva. *American Jezebel: The Uncommon Life of Anne Hutchinson, the Woman Who Defied the Puritans.* New York: HarperCollins, 2005.

Law Library–American Law and Legal Information. "Anne Hutchinson: 1637 and 1638—General Court Summons Hutchinson." *Great American Trials.* Vol. 1. http://law.jrank.org/pages/2325/Anne-Hutchinson-Trials-1637–1638-General-Court-Summons-Hutchinson.html (accessed March 23, 2009).

Morris, Richard B. *Fair Trial: Fourteen Who Stood Accused, From Anne Hutchinson to Alger Hiss.* New York: Harper and Row, 1967.

"Trial at the Court of Newton. 1637." *Anne Hutchinson: The Trial.* http://www.annehutchinson.com/anne_hutchinson_trial_011.htm (accessed March 22, 2009).

Anne Hutchinson's Trial November 1637.

The Examination of Mrs. Ann Hutchinson at the court a Newtown.

Mr. Winthrop, governor. Mrs. Hutchinson, you are called here as one of those that have troubled the peace of the commonwealth and the churches here; you are known to be a woman that hath had a great share in the promoting and divulging of those opinions that are causes of this trouble, and to be nearly joined not only in affinity and affection with some of those the court had taken notice of and passed censure upon, but you have spoken divers things as we have been informed very prejudicial to the honour of the churches and ministers thereof, and you have maintained a meeting and an assembly in your house that hath been condemned by the general assembly as a thing not tolerable nor comely in the sight of God nor fitting for your sex, and notwithstanding that was cried down you have continued the same, therefore we have thought good to send for you to understand how things are, that if you be in an erroneous way we may reduce you that so you may become profitable member here among us, otherwise if you be obstinate in your course that then the court may take such course that you may trouble us no further, therefore I would intreat you to express whether you do not hold and assent in practice to those opinions and factions that have been handled in court already, that is to say, whether you do not justify Mr. Wheelwright's sermon and the petition.

Mrs. Hutchinson. I am called here to answer before you but I hear no things laid to my charge.

Gov. I have told you some already and more I can tell you.

(Mrs. H.) Name one Sir.

Gov. Have I not named some already?

Mrs. H. What have I said or done?

Gov. Why for your doings, this you did harbour and countenance those that are parties in this faction that you have heard of.

(Mrs. H.) That's matter of conscience, Sir.

Gov. Your conscience you must keep or it must be kept for you.

Mrs. H. Must not I then entertain the saints because I must keep my conscience.

Gov. Say that one brother should commit felony or treason and come to his other brother's house, if he knows him guilty and conceals him he is guilty of the same. It is his conscience to entertain him, but if his conscience comes into act in giving countenance and entertainment to him that hath broken the law he is guilty too. So if you do countenance those that are transgressor of the law you are in the same fact.

Mrs. H. What law do they transgress?

Gov. The law of God and of the state.

Mrs. H. In what particular?

Gov. Why in this among the rest, whereas the Lord doth say honour they father and they mother.

Mrs. H. Ey Sir in the Lord. *(Gov.)* This honour you have broke in giving countenance to them.

Mrs. H. In entertaining those did I entertain them against any act (for there is the thing) or what god hath appointed?

Gov. You knew that Mr. Wheelwright did preach this sermon and those that countenance him in this do break a law.

Mrs. H. What law have I broken?

Gov. Why the fifth commandment.

Mrs. H. I deny that for he saith in the Lord.

Gov. You have joined with them in the faction.

Mrs. H. In what faction have I joined with them?

Gov. In presenting the petition.

Mrs. H. Suppose I had set my hand to the petition what then? *(Gov.)* You saw that case tried before.

Mrs. H. But I had not my hand to the petition.

Gov. You have councelled them.

(Mrs. H.) Wherein?

Gov. Why in entertaining them.

Mrs. H. What breach of law if that Sir?

Gov. Why dishonouring of parents.

Mrs. H. But put the case Sir that I do fear the Lord and my parents, may I not entertain them that fear the Lord because my parents will not give me leave?

Gov. If they be the fathers of the commonwealth, and they of another religion, if you entertain them then you dishonour your parents and are justly punishable.

[. . .]

Mr. Weld. I then said to Mrs. Hutchinson when it was come to this issue, why did you let us go thus long and never tell us of it?

Gov. I should wonder why the elders should move the elders of our congregation to have dealth with her if they saw not some cause.

Mr. Cotton. Brother Weld and brother Shepard, I did then clear myself unto you that I understood her speech in expressing herself to you that you did hold forth some matter in your preaching that was not pertinent to the seal of the spirit—*Two lines defaced.*

Dep. Gov. They affirm that Mrs. Hutchinson did say they were not able ministers of the new testament.

Mr. Cotton. I do not remember it.

Mrs. H. If you please to give me leave I shall give you the ground of what I know to be true. Being much troubled to see the falseness of the constitution of the church of England, I had like to have turned separatist; whereupon I kept a day of solemn humiliation and pondering of the thing; this scripture was brought unto me—he that denies Jesus Christ to become in the flesh is antichrist—This I considered of and in considering found the papists did not deny him to become in the flesh, nor we did not deny him—who then was antichrist? Was the Turk antichrist only? The Lord knows that I could not open scripture; he must by his prophetical office open it unto me. So after that being unsatisfied in the thing, the Lord was pleased to bring this scripture out of the Hebrews. He that denies the testament denies the testator, and in this did open unto me and give me to see that those which did not teach the new covenant had the spirit of antichrist, and upon this he did discover the ministry unto me and ever since, I bless the Lord, he hath let me see which was the clear ministry and which the wrong. Since that time I confess I have been more choice and he hath let me to distinguish between the voice of my beloved and the voice of Moses, the voice of John Baptist and the voice of antichrist, for all those voices are spoken of in scripture. Now if you do condemn me for speaking what in my conscience I know to be the truth I must commit myself unto the Lord.

Mr. Nowell. How do you know that that was the spirit?

Mrs. H. How did Abraham know that it was God that bid him offer his son, being a breach of the sixth commandment?

Dep. Gov. By an immediate voice.

Mrs. H. So to me by an immediate revelation.

Dep. Gov. How! An immediate revelation.

Mrs. H. By the voice of his own spirit to my soul. I will give you another scripture, Jer. 46. 27, 28—out of which the Lord shewed me what he would do for me and the rest of his servants.—But after he was pleased to reveal himself to me I did presently like Abraham run to Hagar. And after that he did let me see the atheism of my own heart, for which I begged of the Lord that it might not remain in my heart, and being thus, he did shew me this (a twelvemonth after) which I told you of before. Ever since that time I have been confident of what he hath revealed unto me.

[. . .]

Salem Witchcraft Trials (1692)

The Salem Witchcraft trials occurred in the village of Salem, Massachusetts, during the spring and summer of 1692 and involved hundreds of individuals who were accused of witchcraft. The trials resulted in the conviction and execution of 19 men and women, and one elderly man was also executed after he refused to be tried for the charges of witchcraft made against him. As many as 13 other individuals who were accused of witchcraft also may have died in prison. The trials demonstrated how a lack of due process, poor economic conditions, a divided church congregation, an unsuccessful frontier war against the Native Americans, and hysteria over the fear of witchcraft combined to cause the unnecessary deaths of innocent people (Linder, "Salem Witchcraft Trials").

In 1688, John Putnam, a respected and important member of the Salem community, arranged for a new minister, Samuel Parris, to preach at the local church. Parris moved to Salem from Barbados with his family and a slave named Tituba. In February 1692, Parris's 10-year-old daughter, Betty, became very sick and exhibited strange behavior such as diving under furniture and twisting her body in pain. She also stated that she had a fever. Scientists have speculated that Betty Parris may have eaten cereal or bread contaminated with a certain type of fungus which caused such strange behavior as violent fits and hallucinations (Caporael 1976, 23–26). However, a book entitled *Memorable Providences* written by Cotton Mather in 1689 provided an alternative explanation for the behavior of Betty Parris and other young girls in the village who demonstrated the same types of behavior. Mather was the minister of Boston's Old North Church and he had investigated the strange behavior of four children in Boston, concluding in his book that an Irish woman who practiced witchcraft was responsible for the children's behavior. Mather's book was very popular at the time and influenced the people of Salem who frequently discussed the possibility of witchcraft affecting their community (Norton 2002, 34–48).

A doctor in the village named William Griggs provided medicine to Betty Parris and a number of other young girls with similar symptoms but, when the medicine failed, Dr. Griggs suggested that witchcraft may have caused the children's behavior. Members of the Salem village were convinced easily because it was believed that witches preyed upon children as their victims (Norton, 2002, 19–36).

A neighbor of the Parris family tried to develop a way to combat the witchcraft by having a dog eat a rye cake containing the victim's fluids. Supposedly, witches used dogs to fulfill their duties. When the attempt to combat the witchcraft with the cake failed, the people in the village began to suspect Tituba, the Parris' slave, of being a witch because she had helped the neighbor bake the cake and because she also had talked with the young girls about voodoo rituals from her homeland of Barbados. At the end of February 1692, arrest warrants were issued for Tituba and two other women, Sarah Good and Sarah Osborn, because Betty Parris and another young victim had listed the three women as the persons responsible for their illness. A key force behind the prosecutions was the Putnam family, a powerful family within the Salem community whose 11-year-old daughter had displayed the same behavior as Betty Parris (Yool 1992, 7–15).

The Putnam family filed a legal grievance against Tituba, Sarah Good, and Sarah Osborn with two local magistrates, John Hathorne and Jonathan Corwin. The magistrates conducted interrogations of the three women by asking leading questions which demonstrated that they assumed the women were guilty (Norton 2002, 27–30). Initially, Tituba denied that she was guilty but then, perhaps out of fear, confessed that she knew a man dressed in black from Boston who appeared to her as a dog or a pig and made her carry out his wishes. Tituba also stated that she and the other women, including Good and Osborn, were able to fly around with brooms. The magistrates assumed that the man in black was the devil and used her confession to expand the search for more witches (42–48).

When the prisons started to become filled with accused witches and the entire colony of Massachusetts was in an uproar, the governor of Massachusetts, Sir William Phips, returned from England and established a special court of criminal jurisdiction, called the Court of Oyer and Terminal, to hear the witchcraft cases (Norton 2002, 169–170). The court was composed of five judges, including three judges who strongly favored the prosecution of witches as they were influenced by their friendship with Cotton Mather. The chief justice of Massachusetts, William Stoughton, was one of the five judges who had a strong reputation for hunting witches. While Stoughton was the most powerful of the judges, he had no legal training (Hoffer 1997, 89–93).

In fact, the trials were lacking any of the due process associated with modern day trials. For example, the defendants were not represented by lawyers, were not allowed to bring witnesses to testify on their behalf, and were not allowed to appeal a guilty verdict from a jury. In addition, the judges admitted hearsay and gossip as evidence and also admitted into evidence testimony from witnesses that the persons accused of being witches had appeared to them in dreams and visions. The judges, at times, acted as prosecutors and asked interrogating questions of the witnesses and also allowed spectators to interrupt the trials with personal stories. Interestingly, the judges asked for advice from religious leaders in the community who had more knowledge about witchcraft than the judges (Hoffer 1997, 75–76).

By September 1692, the citizens within the community of Salem started raising questions about how so many intelligent and educated people could be guilty of witchcraft. An elite group of educated citizens began an attempt to end the witch hunts. The father of Cotton Mather, Increase Mather, wrote a book entitled *Cases of Conscience* where he argued that it was better for 10 persons suspected of witchcraft to escape prosecution than for one innocent person to be imprisoned. He also asked the courts to behave more professionally by excluding evidence such as hearsay and dreams. Because of Increase Mather's book, Governor Phips ordered the courts to utilize a rigorous standard of clear and convincing evidence in prosecuting witches. Because of the new standards, a large majority of the final 33 witchcraft trials resulted in acquittals and Governor Phips would eventually pardon and release from prison all of the convicted and accused witches (Norton 2002, 280–282).

As a result of the Salem Witchcraft trials, the following 19 persons, with their execution date listed in parentheses, were hanged on Gallows Hill during the summer of 1692: Bridget Bishop (June 10), Rebecca Nurse, Sarah Good, Susannah Martin, Elizabeth Howe, Sarah Wildes (June 19), George Burroughs, Martha Carrier, John Willard, George Jacobs Sr., John Proctor (August 19), Martha Corey, Mary Eastey, Ann Pudeator, Alice Parker, Mary Parker, Wilmott Redd, Margaret Scott, Samuel Wardwell (September 22). Giles Corey, an 80-year-old man, refused to be tried in court and was executed by having stones pressed upon him on September 19, 1692. The number of accused witches that died in prison ranged between 4 and 13 depending upon the source. Two dogs also were executed for allegedly assisting the witches in carrying out their tasks (Norton 2002, 229–278).

Scholars of the Salem Witchcraft trials have documented striking differences between the accused and the accusers. Those persons accused of witchcraft were wealthier than the accusers and, interestingly, the accusers stood to gain property from the imprisonment and conviction of these wealthier property owners. The accused and the accusers also were on opposite sides of a split in the church congregation. Many of the churchgoers that were accused of witchcraft had supported a former minister, George Burroughs, who was forced to resign by many of the persons who would become the accusers. Hence, scholars concluded that the desire for wealth and property as well as a congregation battle probably determined who would be accused, convicted, and executed for witchcraft. In addition to the property and religious issues, historians also point to the failure of the colony to defend itself in its frontier battles with the Indians. According to one historian, the judges' excitement in prosecuting witches can be traced to the judges' attempt to shift the blame for its military defeats on an alliance between the Indians and the devil (Norton 2002, 296–304). The judges had been leading figures in an ineffective war effort against the Indians.

While there were a myriad of reasons why the Salem Witchcraft trials occurred, the trials serve as a reminder that the American system of criminal justice has never been perfect, even in the modern era. Thus, it is important to protect the freedoms and rights of criminal defendants regardless of the fear and hysteria created by the political, social, and economic environment (Hoffer 1997, 145–147).

References

Caporael, Linda. "Ergotism: The Satan Loosed in Salem?" *Science* 192, no. 4234 (April 1976): 21–26.

Hoffer, Peter Charles. *The Salem Witchcraft Trials: A Legal History*. Lawrence: University Press of Kansas, 1997.

Linder, Douglas O. "The Witchcraft Trials in Salem: A Commentary." *Famous Trials.* http://www.law.umkc.edu/faculty/projects/ftrials/salem/SAL_ACCT.HTM (accessed March 1, 2009).

Norton, Mary Beth. *In the Devil's Snare: The Salem Witchcraft Crisis of 1692.* New York: Vintage, 2002.

Yool, George Malcolm. *1692 Witch Hunt: A Layman's Guide to the Salem Witchcraft Trials.* New York: Heritage Books, 1992.

John Peter Zenger Trial (1735)

The trial of John Peter Zenger, a German immigrant and publisher, stands as a great testament to the importance placed upon freedom in America during the colonial era. Zenger's successful attempt to demand his freedom of the press rights was one of the most courageous and inspiring acts during the early years of American history (Linder, "Peter Zenger").

The legal controversy began with the appointment of William Cosby by King George II of England to serve as British royal governor of New York in January 1732. Cosby quickly lived up to his reputation as a greedy, petty, and jealous person by demanding that the previous governor, Rip Van Dam, turn over half of his salary to Cosby. Van Dam had served as interim governor for roughly three months until Cosby arrived in America in April 1732. To his credit, Van Dam stated that he would give Cosby half of his salary earned if Cosby would, in turn, give Van Dam half of the salary that Cosby stood to earn over the next four years. Obviously, Van Dam was being sarcastic because he stood to profit immensely from half of Cosby's four-year salary as opposed to Cosby receiving only one half of his three-month salary as interim governor (Buranelli 1957, 12–13).

Governor Cosby knew that he did not have a good legal argument and a jury probably would not award him half of Van Dam's salary so he decided to have the case heard by a special court of judges who would sit without a jury. Van Dam appealed to the Supreme Court to challenge Cosby's attempt to have the case heard only by the judges on the newly created court. When the Supreme Court, fearful of being fired by the governor, voted 2–1 in favor of Cosby's special court, Cosby was angered by the dissenting vote cast against him by Chief Justice Lewis Morris and asked for Morris to justify his vote. Instead of explaining his vote privately to Cosby, Morris asked John Peter Zenger, a publisher, to print Morris's reasons for voting against the governor in a pamphlet that would be available to the public. Cosby responded with an attempt to solidify his power by firing Morris from his leadership post as chief justice of the Supreme Court and also hiring Francis Harison to perform the role of editor and censor of the *New York Gazette,* the only significant newspaper in New York. Harison printed only flattering stories of Cosby in order to repair Cosby's image within the colony (Buranelli 1957, 14–17).

In the meantime, political opposition led by Morris, Van Dam, and an attorney, James Alexander, had surfaced against Governor Cosby and a plan to start a rival newspaper was underway. James Alexander recruited John Peter Zenger to publisher the newspaper, which was to be called the *New York Weekly Journal*. It became the first independent newspaper to cover politics in America. Zenger was very important to the plan because he owned a printer, which was extremely rare in the colonies. In fact, the only other printer in the colonies belonged to the *New York Gazette*. Zenger agreed to publish the newspaper as a way to expose the biased views expressed in the *Gazette* (Linder, "Peter Zenger").

The first issue of the *New York Weekly Journal* produced a story about Morris's election to the local assembly despite Cosby's attempts to fix the election against Morris by having some of his supporters, mainly Quakers, deemed ineligible to vote. In addition to stories about the corrupt politics of Cosby, the *Journal* published editorials that strongly defended freedom of the press (Buranelli 1957, 22–30).

In 1734, Governor Cosby began to try and shut down the *Journal;* however, a grand jury would not indict the newspaper for libelous material, or presenting false information. Cosby responded by offering a reward to anyone who exposed the authors of the newspaper and he also demanded that the *Journal* be burned in public. Cosby proceeded to order the Supreme Court justices to issue a warrant for the arrest of John Peter Zenger. Zenger was arrested on November 18, 1734, and placed in jail by the sheriff (Buranelli 1957, 32–40).

Because the judge set Zenger's bail at such a high amount, he was forced to remain in jail. However, while serving his time in jail, Zenger was able to communicate through various letters to the public which turned him into a martyr, or a sympathetic person defending his rights. Zenger's legal defense was provided by Andrew Hamilton, the best lawyer in the colonies. In the usual fashion of a tyrant, Governor Cosby tried to get the judges in the trial to select favorable jurors who would vote against Zenger but the judges rejected Cosby's attempt to influence the jury selection (Putnam 1997, 68–82).

The trial began with a reading of the charges against Zenger. He was charged with printing false information against the Governor with the hope of ruining the reputation of Governor Cosby and his administration. Andrew Hamilton admitted that Zenger published the material and the trial moved quickly to the issue of whether the material was false against the governor. Hamilton argued that the libel law in England, which punished anyone who criticized government officials, should not be the libel law in the colonies of America. He argued passionately that citizens should have the right to speak and write freely if they are not being served well by their leaders, such as Governor Cosby. Hamilton stated that a person should not be charged with a crime of libel if a person spoke the truth against his government. Hamilton's argument was significant because no one had ever successfully challenged a charge of libel by simply maintaining that their expression was truthful. In short, throughout England and the colonies, it was impossible to win a libel case if it was determined a person published false material (Rutherfurd 1904, 198–241).

Overall, throughout the trial, Hamilton's strategy was to persuade the jury to reject the libel law as bad law. In effect, the jury could determine that Zenger was guilty of violating the law but, because the law was wrong, he should be declared innocent. Hamilton eloquently presented his strategy to the jury, but the judge stated that the law was clear and it was not their task to determine if the law was correct or wrong. The jurors were simply to decide whether Zenger printed the materials and the court would decide if the material was libelous. In effect, the judge's instructions to the jury were meant to ensure that Zenger would be convicted (Buranelli 1957, 55–59).

Surprisingly, the jury deliberated for a short period of time and decided to find Zenger not guilty of printing material against a government official in a false manner. Zenger had spent eight months in prison and his case created strong opposition against such laws that punished individuals for criticizing government officials. After Zenger's trial, prosecutors were hesitant to try anyone for libeling a government official. Although such libel laws were not declared unconstitutional until nearly two centuries later in the U.S. Supreme Court decision of *New York Times v. Sullivan* (1964), the trial of John Peter Zenger established a strong foundation for freedom of the press that greatly influenced the First Congress that drafted the First Amendment to the U.S. Constitution in 1790 (Putnam 1997, 142–149).

References

Buranelli, Vincent. *The Trial of Peter Zenger.* New York: NYU Press, 1957.

Linder, Douglas O. "The Trial of John Peter Zenger: An Account." *Famous Trials.* http://www.law.umkc.edu/faculty/projects/ftrials/zenger/zengeraccount.html (accessed March 1, 2009).

Morris, Richard. *Fair Trial: Fourteen Who Stood Accused, from Anne Hutchinson to Alger Hiss.* New York: Knopf, 1967, pp. 69–95.

Putnam, William Lowell. *John Peter Zenger and the Fundamental Freedom.* Jefferson, NC: McFarland and Company, 1997.

Rutherfurd, Livingston. *John Peter Zenger, His Press, His Trial, and a Bibliography of Zenger Imprints.* New York: Dodd, Mead and Company, 1904.

The Libel Case of John Peter Zenger

[. . .]

Mr. Hamilton. I thank your Honour. Then Gentlemen of the Jury, it is to you we must now appeal, for Witnesses, to the Truth of the Facts we have offered, and are denied the Liberty to prove; and let it not seem strange, that I apply my self to you in this Manner, I am warranted so to do both by Law and Reason. The Law supposes you to be summoned, *out of the Neighbourhood where the Fact is alledged to be committed*; and the Reason of your being taken out of the Neighbourhood is, *because you are supposed to have the best Knowledge of the Fact that is to be tried.* And were you to find a Verdict against my Client, you must take upon you to say, the Papers referred to in the Information, and which we acknowledge we printed and published, are *false, scandalous and seditious*; but of this I can have no Apprehension. You are citizens of *New York*, you are really what the Law supposes you to be, *honest and lawful Men*; and according to my Brief, the Facts which we offer to prove were not committed in a Corner; they are notoriously known to be true; and therefore in your Justice lies our Safety. And as we are denied the Liberty of giving Evidence, to prove the Truth of what we have published, I will beg Leave to lay it down as a standing Rule in such Cases: *That the suppressing of Evidence ought always to be taken for the strongest Evidence*; and I hope it will have that Weight with you. But since we are not admitted to examine our Witnesses, I will endeavour to shorten the Dispute with Mr. Attorney, and to that End, I desire he would favour us with some Standard Definition of a Libel, by which it may be certainly known, whether a Writing be a Libel, yea or not.

Mr. Attorney. The Books, I think, have given a very full Definition of a Libel; they say it is *in a strict Sense taken for a malicious Defamation, expressed either in Printing or Writing, and tending either to blacken the Memory of one who is dead, or the Reputation of one who is alive, and expose him to publick Hatred, Contempt or Ridicule. But it is said, That in a larger Sense the Notion of a Libel may be applied to any Defamation whatsoever, empressed either by Signs or Pictures, as by fixing up a Gallows against a Man's Door, or by painting him in a shameful and ignominious Manner. And since the chief Cause for which the Law so severely punishes all Offences of this Nature, is the direct Tendency of them to a Breach of Publick Peace, by provoking the Parties injured, their Friends and Families to Acts of Revenge, which it would be impossible to restrain by the severest Laws, were there no Redress from Publick Justice for Injuries of this kind, which of all others are most sensibly felt; and since the plain Meaning of such Scandal as is expressed by Signs or Pictures, is as obvious to common Sense, and as easily understood by every common Capacity, and altogether as provoking as that which is expressed by Writing or Printing, why should it not be equally criminal? And from the same Ground it seemeth also clearly to follow, That such Scandal as is expressed in a scoffing and ironical Manner, makes a Writing as properly a Libel, as that which is expressed in direct Terms; as where a Writing, in a taunting Manner reckoning up several Acts of publick charity done by one, says* You will not play the Jew, nor the Hypocrite, *and so goes on in a Strain of Ridicule to insinuate, that what he did was owing his Vain-Glory; or where a Writing, pretending to recommend to one the Characters of several great men for his Imitation, instead of taking Notice of what they are generally esteemed famous for, pitched on such Qualities only which their Enemies charge them with the Want of, as by proposing such a one to be imitated for his Courage, who is known to be a great Statesman, but no Soldier, and another to be imitated for his Learning, who is known to be a great General, but no Scholar, &c.* which *Kind of Writing is as well understood to mean only to upbraid the Parties with the Want of these Qualities, as if it had directly and expressly done so.*

Mr. *Hamilton.* Ay, Mr. Attorney; but what certain Standard Rule have the Books laid down, by which we can certainly know, whether the Words or the Signs are malicious? Whether they are defamatory? Whether they tend to the Breach of the Peace, and are sufficient Ground to provoke, a Man, his Family, or Friends to Acts of Revenge, especially those of the *ironical* sort words? And what Rule have you to know when I write *ironically?* I think it would be hard, when I say, *such a Man is a very worthy honest Gentleman, and of fine Understanding,* that therefore I meant *he was a Knave or a Fool.*

Mr. *Attorney.* I think the Books are very full; it is said in I *Hawk. p.* 193 just now read, *That such Scandal as is expressed in a scoffing and ironical Manner, makes a Writing as properly a Libel, as that which is expressed direct Terms; as where a Writing, in a taunting Manner says, reckoning up several Acts of Charity done by one, says,* You will not play the Jew or Hypocrite, *and so goes on to insinuate, that what he did was owing to his Vain-Glory &c. Which Kind of Writing is as well understood to mean only to upbraid the Parties with the Want of these Qualities, as if it had directly and expressly done so.* I think nothing can be plainer or more full that these Words.

Mr. *Hamilton.* I agree the Words are very plain, and I shall not scruple to allow (when we are agreed that the Words are *false and scandalous, and were spoken in an ironical and scoffing Manner, &c.*) that they are really *libellous;* but here still occurs the Uncertainty, which makes the Difficulty to know, what Words are *scandalous* and what are not; for you say, they may be *scandalous, true or false;* besides, how shall we know whether the Words were spoke in a *scoffing and ironical manner* or seriously? Or how can you know, whether the Man did not think as he wrote? For by your rule, if he did, it is no *Irony,* and consequently no *Libel.* But under Favour, Mr. Attorney, I think the same Book, and the same Section will shew us the only Rule by which all these things are to be known. The Words are these; *which Kind of Writing is as well UNDERSTOOD to mean only to upbraid the Parties with the Want of these Qualities, as if they had directly and expressly done so.* Here it is plain, the words are *scandalous, scoffing and ironical,* only as they are UNDERSTOOD. I know no rule laid down in the Books but his, I mean, as the Words are *understood.*

Mr. *Ch. Just.* That is certain. All Words are libellous or not, as they are *understood.* Those who are to judge of the Words, must judge whether they are *scandalous* or *ironical, tend to the Breach of the Peace,* or are *seditious:* There can be no Doubt of it.

Mr. *Hamilton.* I thank Your Honour; I am glad to find the Court of this Opinion. Then it follows that those twelve Men must Understand the Words in the Information to be *scandalous,* that is to say *false;* for I think it is not pretended they are of the *ironical* Sort; and when they understand the Words to be so, they will say we are guilty of publishing a *false Libel,* and not otherwise.

Mr. Ch. Just. No, Mr. *Hamilton*; the Jury may find that *Zenger* printed and published those papers, and leave it to the Court to judge whether they are libellous; you know this is very common; it is in the Nature of special Verdict, where the Jury leave the matter of Law to the Court.

Mr. Hamilton. I know, may it please Your Honour, the Jury may do so; but I do likewise know, they may do otherwise. I know they have the Right beyond all Dispute, to determine both the Law and the Fact, and where they do not doubt of the Law, they ought to do so. (This of leaving it to the Judgment of the Court, *whether the Words are libellous or not*, in Effect renders Juries useless to say no worse) in many Cases; but this I shall have Occasion to speak to by and by; and I will with the Court's Leave proceed to examine the Inconveniencies that must inevitably rise from the Doctrines Mr. Attorney has laid down; and I observe, in support of this Prosecution, he has frequently repeated the Words taken from the Case of *Libel, famous,* in *5 Co.* This is indeed the leading Case, and to which almost all the other Cases upon the Subject of Libels do refer; and I must insist upon saying, That according as this Case seems to be understood by the Court and Mr. Attorney, it is not Law at this Day: for tho' I own it to be base and unworthy to scandalize any Man, yet I think it is even villainous to scandalize a Person of publick Character, and I will go so far into Mr. Attorney's Doctrine as to agree, that if the Faults, Mistakes, nay even the Vices of such a Person be private and personal, and don't affect the Peace of the publick, or the Liberty or Property of our Neighbour, it is unmanly and unmannerly to expose them either by Word or Writing. But when a Ruler of a People brings his personal Failings, but much more his Vices, into his Administration, and the People find themselves affected by them, either in their Liberties or Properties, that will alter the Case mightily, and all the high Things that are said in Favour of Rulers, and of Dignities, and upon the side of Power, will not be able to stop People's Mouths when they feel themselves oppressed, I mean in a free government. It is true in Times past it was a Crime to speak Truth, and in that terrible Court of Star Chamber, many worthy and brave Men suffered for so doing; and yet even in that Court, and in those bad Times, a great and good Man durst say, what I hope will not be take amiss of me to say in this place, *to wit, The Practice of Informations for Libels is a Sword in the Hands of a wicked King, and an arrand Coward, to cut down and destroy the innocent; the one cannot, because of his high Station, and the other dares not, because of his Want of Courage, revenge himself in another Manner.*

Mr. Attorney. Pray Mr. *Hamilton*, have a Care what you say, don't go too far neither, I don't like those Liberties.

[. . .]

Mr. Hamilton. I hope to be pardon'e Sir for my Zeal upon this Occasion; it is an old and wise Caution. *That when our Neighbour's House is on Fire, we ought to take Care of our own.* For tho' Blessed be God, I live in a Government where Liberty is well understood, and freely enjoyed; yet Experience has shewn us all (I'm sure it has to me) that a bad Precedent in one Government, is soon set up for an Authority in another; and therefore I cannot but think it mine, and every Honest Man's duty, that (while we pay all due Obedience to Men in Authority) we ought at the same Time to be upon our Guard against Power, wherever we apprehend it may affect ourselves or our Fellow-Subjects.

I am truly very unequal to such an Undertaking on many Accounts. And you see I labour under the Weight of many Years, and am born down with great Infirmities of Body; yet Old and Weak as I am, I should think it my duty if required, to go to the utmost Part of the Land, where my Service cou'd be of any Use in assisting to quence the Flame of Prosecutions upon Informations, set on Foot by the Government, to deprive a People of the Right of Remonstrating, (and complaining too) of the arbitrary Attempts of Men in Power. Men who injure and oppress the People under their Administration, provoke them to cry out and complain; and then make that very Complaint the Foundation for new Oppressions and Prosecutions. I wish I could say there were no Instances of this Kind. But to conclude; the Question before the Court and you Gentlemen of the Jury, is not so small nor private Concern, it is not the Cause of a poor Printer, nor of *New-York* alone, which you are not trying: No! It may in its Consequence, affect every Freeman that lives under a British Government on the main of *America.* It is the best Cause. It is the Cause of Liberty; and I make no Doubt but your upright Conduct, this Day, will not only entitle you to the Love and Esteem of your Fellow-Citizens; but every Man who prefers Freedom to a Life of Slavery will bless and honour You, as Men who have baffled the Attempt of Tyranny; and by an impartial and uncorrupt Verdict, have laid a noble Foundation for securing to ourselves, our Posterity, and our Neighbours, That, to which Nature and the Laws of our Country have given us a Right,—The Liberty—both of exposing and opposing arbitrary Power (in these Parts of the World, at least) by speaking and writing Truth.

Mr. Ch. Just. Gentlemen of the Jury. The great Pains Mr. *Hamilton* has taken to shew how little Regard Juries ought to pay to the Opinion of the Judges; and his insisting so much upon the Conduct of some Judges in Tryals of this kind; is done no doubt, with a Design that you should take but very little Notice of what I might say upon this Occasion. I shall therefore only observe to you that as the Facts or Words in the Information are confessed, the only thing that can come in Question before you is, whether the Words as set forth in the Information made a Libel. And that is a Matter of Law, no doubt, an which you may leave to the Court. But I shall trouble you no further with any Thing more of my own, but read to you the Words of a learned and upright Judge in a Case of the like Nature.

'To say that corrupt Officers are appointed to administer Affairs, is certainly a Reflection on the Government. If People should not be called to account for possessing the People with an ill Opinion of the Government, no Government can subsist. For it is very necessary for all Governments that the People should have a good opinion it. And nothing can be worse to any Government, than to endeavour to procure Animosities; as to the Management of it, this has been always look'd upon as a Crime, and no Government can be safe without it be punished.'

'Now you are to consider, whether these Words I have read to you, do not tend to beget an ill Opinion of the Administration of the Government? To tell us, that those that are employed know nothing of the matter, and those that do know are not employed. Men are not adapted to Offices, but Offices to Men, out of a particular Regard to their Interest, and not to their Fitness for the Places; this is the Purport of these Papers.'

Mr. *Hamilton.* I humbly beg your Honours Pardon: I am very much misapprehended, if you suppose what I said was so designed.

Sir, you, know, I made an Apology for the Freedom I found my self under a Necessity of using upon this Occasion. I said, there was Nothing personal designed; it arose from the nature of our Defence.

The Jury withdrew, and in a small Time returned, and being asked by the Clerk whether they were agreed on their Verdict, and whether *John Peter Zenger* was guilty of Printing and Publishing the Libels in the Information mentioned? They answered by *Thomas Hunt*, their Foreman, *Not Guilty.* Upon which there were three Huzzas in the Hall which was crowded with People, and the next Day I was discharged from my Imprisonment.

New York Weekly Journal 12–17–1733

It is agreed on all Hands, that a Fool may ask more Questions than a wise Man can answer, or perhaps will answer if he could; but notwithstanding that, I would be glad to be satisfied in the following Points of Speculation that the above Affidavits afford. And it will be no great Puzile to a wife man to answer with a *Yea*, or a *Nay*, which is the most that will be required in most of those Questions.

Q.1. It is prudent in the French governours not to suffer an Englishman to view their Fortifications, sound their harbours, tarry in their country to discover their Strength?

Q.2. It is prudent in an English Governour to suffer a French man to view our Fortifications, sound our harbours? &c.

Q.3. If the above Affidavits be true, had the French a bad Harvest in Canada? Or do they want Provisions?

Q.4. Was the Letter from the Governour of Louisburg to our Governour true?

Q.5. Might not our Governour as easily have discovered the falsehood of it as any body else; if he would?

Q.6. Ought he not to have endeavored to do it?

Q.7. Did our governour endeavour to do it?

Q.8. Was it not known to the greatest Part of the town, before the Sloop *Le Caesar* left New-York, that the French in the Sloop *Le Caesar* had founded and taken the Land-Marks from without Sandyhook up to New-York? Had taken the View of the Town? Had been in the Fort?

Q.9. Might not the governour have known the same Thing, if he would?

Q.10. Is there not great Probability that he did know it?

Q.11. Was it four our Benefit or that of the French these soundings and Land-marks were taken, and View made?

Q.12. Could we not, by seizing their Papers, and confining their Persons, have prevented them in great Measure from making use of the Discoveries they made?

Q.13. Ought they not to have been so prevented?

Q.14. Was it prudent to suffer them to pass through Hellgate, and also to discover that Way of Access to us?

Q.15. If a French Governour had suffered an English Sloop and company to do what a French sloop and Company has done here, would he not have deserved to be _____?

Q.16. Since it appears by the Affidavits, there was no such scarcity of provisions as by the letter from the Governour of Louisburgh to our Governour, since the conduct of the French to the English that happen to go to Canada, shews they think it necessary to keep us ignorant of their State and Condition as much as they can. Since the Sounding our harbours, viewing our Fortifications, and the honourable Treatment they have received here (the reverse of what we receive in Canada) has let them into a perfect Knowledge of our State and Condition. And since their Voyage must appear to any Man of the least Penetration to have been made with an Intent to make that Discovery, and only with that Intent. Whether it would not be reasonable in us to provide as well and as soon as we can for our Defence?

Q.17. Whether that can be done any way so well and effectually as by calling the Assembly very together?

Q.18. If this be not done, and any dangerous consequences follow after so full Warning, Who is Blameable?

The "Great Negro Plot" Trials (1741)

The Great Negro Plot of 1741 involved an alleged conspiracy among black slaves and poor whites to set arson fires throughout New York City. The goal of the conspiracy was to burn New York City to the ground, murder the white men, and elect a new governor for the British colony of New York. The conspiracy supposedly grew out of the history of slave revolts in New York that began in the late 17th century and continued almost on an annual basis well into the 18th century. Such slave revolts occurred mainly because of the mistreatment of slaves by their masters, economic tensions between slaves and whites who competed for the same employment opportunities during an economic depression, and a war between England and Spain in which the Spanish government offered blacks freedom in exchange for spying for Spain and fighting against the British (Law Library, "Great Negro Plot").

Between 1687 and 1741, it was fairly common for slaves to revolt against slave owners. One of the more infamous slave revolts occurred in 1712 when 23 black slaves set out to murder as many white persons as possible by using guns, knives, and swords. In addition, a few slaves set fires to destroy the property of their masters. As a result of the New York Slave Revolt of 1712, the New York governor executed 21 slaves for murdering 9 white persons and injuring 6 and the colony of New York passed the Negro Slave Act of 1740, which sentenced to death any slave who committed murder or arson against whites (Hoffer 2003, 47–48).

In 1741, the New York colony was a difficult place for everyone. After a harsh winter during which food supplies were limited, an economic depression took hold and many slaves and poor whites were in jeopardy of starving to death. White persons were angered at the growing population of slaves who would work for less money than whites, thus causing unemployment among white citizens engaged in the trade businesses. Whites became very afraid that another slave revolt would occur as a result of the growing tensions between blacks and whites amidst the economic despair of the times. To make matters worse, British troops had been removed from New York City because of England's ongoing war with Spain called the War of Jenkins' Ear that lasted from 1739–1748. With desperate economic conditions, racial tensions, and a lack of a British military presence in New York City, many persons began anticipating a revolt similar to the Slave Revolt of 1712 (Lepore 2006, 52–58).

In the spring of 1741, a number of fires broke out in the Manhattan section of New York City. Inside the walls of Fort George, the governor's mansion also caught fire as did a church connected to the governor's residence. As the number of fires grew with every passing day, whites began to suspect that slaves were setting the fires. On April 6, 1741, a slave named Cuffee was seen running from one of the fires at a storehouse and he was arrested. The New York City government found it necessary to conduct an investigation and Daniel Horsmanden, a New York supreme court justice, was hired to lead the investigation. Horsmanden began focusing upon white men who sold alcohol to black slaves as a source of the conspiracy (Lepore 2006, 40–63).

A key suspect in the conspiracy was John Hughson, who owned a bar along the Hudson River. Hughson was poor and illiterate when he arrived in New York and could not find work as a shoemaker so he decided to open a bar. Hughson had a reputation for selling alcohol to free blacks, black slaves, and poor whites and for being involved in criminal activity, such as theft. In fact, Hughson had been arrested for receiving stolen property shortly before the fires began in New York City (Hoffer 2003, 72–85).

Through his investigation, Daniel Horsmanden was able to secure testimony from one of Hughson's servants, Mary Burton, who stated that she was involved with Hughson in the conspiracy. She testified in exchange for immunity from prosecution that Hughson was involved in a conspiracy with blacks and poor whites to destroy the city of New York by way of setting fires. She stated specifically that three black slaves, Caesar Vaarck, Prince Auboyneau, and Cuffee, had met regularly with Hughson at his bar to discuss the plot (Hoffer 2003, 7–8).

On May 2, 1741, a British court of law found Caesar Vaarck and Prince Auboyneau guilty and sentenced the two slaves to death (Lepore 2006, 85–90). In a separate trial, Cuffee also was found guilty and burned at the stake. After the verdicts, a number of barns were burned and, when two other black slaves were arrested for the fires, they confessed to the previous fire that destroyed the governor's mansion and named 50 other persons who also were involved in the conspiracy. The two slaves were burned at the stake, almost immediately after their confessions (Lepore 2006, 102–108).

After the public became aware of the conspiracy, a wave of arrests followed that included over 100 blacks and 20 whites. It has been estimated that between May and August 1741 over 30 of the persons arrested were eventually hanged or burned at the stake for their alleged part in the conspiracy (Davis 1990, ix).

On June 4, 1741, John Hughson and his wife, Sarah, were charged with encouraging the black slave, Cuffee, to set the fire that burned down the storehouse. In addition, the Hughsons were charged with bringing together Caesar Vaarck, Prince Auboyneau, and Cuffee into the conspiracy to start fires with intent to destroy the New York City government. The key witness who testified against the Hughsons was their servant, Mary Burton. John and Sarah Hughson were found guilty of advising black slaves to burn down the city of New York, for a conspiracy to murder white people, and for serving the slaves food and alcohol in the process. John and Sarah Hughson were executed by hanging on June 12, 1741 (Hoffer 2003, 72–85).

Perhaps in an attempt to make a name for his self, Horsmanden expanded the investigation into the conspiracy because he argued that the Hughsons were not smart enough to organize such a sophisticated plot. Horsmanden focused upon John Ury, a school teacher who also passed himself off as a Roman Catholic priest. Mary Burton had named Ury, in her deposition, as the power behind the conspiracy. Ury was arrested on June 24, 1741, and tried for the conspiracy (Hoffer 2003, 144–145). Ury defended himself with no lawyer and claimed to be innocent of all charges against him. However, at the time of the trial, the governor of Georgia had warned Horsmanden of Spanish spies who were on their way to destroy New York. Horsmanden argued forcefully that Ury was, in fact, one of these spies working for the Spanish government and his proof was that Ury could read Latin. Ury was convicted on the charges of conspiracy on July 29, 1741, and hanged on August 29, 1741 (Hoffer 2003, 145–151).

Horsmanden's investigation took a surprising turn when Mary Burton, the key witness for the prosecution, began naming conspirators who were from the higher levels of society, including family members of powerful government officials. Because of the sensitive nature of her testimony and the embarrassment that it could cause powerful individuals, Horsmanden's investigation was brought to a close and the remaining slaves and whites in prison awaiting their trials were released (Lepore 2006, 200–203).

Today, historians are divided in their explanations of the Great Negro Trials of 1741. Some historians argue that no conspiracy existed at all and the trials were the result of anxiety caused by the economic depression and racial tensions as well as the panic over the war with Spain and potential spies trying to destroy the British colonies. Others, however, are convinced that a conspiracy did exist, but that many of the persons tried, convicted, and executed were probably innocent and not involved in the conspiracy (Law Library, "Great Negro Plot").

References

Davis, Thomas J. *The "Great Negro Plot" in Colonial New York.* Amherst: University of Massachusetts Press, 1990.

Hoffer, Peter Charles. *The Great New York Conspiracy of 1741.* Lawrence: University Press of Kansas, 2003.

Johnson, Mat. *The Great Negro Plot: A Tale of Conspiracy and Murder in Eighteenth Century New York.* New York: Holtzbrinck Publishers, 2007.

Law Library–American Law and Legal Information. "The Great Negro Plot Trial: 1741." *American Law Encyclopedia.* Vol. 2. http://law.jrank.org/pages/2351/Great-Negro-Plot-Trial-1741.html (accessed March 1, 2009).

Lepore, Jill. *New York Burning: Liberty, Conspiracy, and Slavery in Eighteenth Century Manhattan.* New York: Knopf, 2006.

The Boston Massacre Trials (1770)

For many years prior to the Revolutionary War, the British military and the American colonists had become resentful of each other. British soldiers had occupied major cities in the American colonies for long periods of time and exploited the colonists to the point where British soldiers and colonists routinely began to engage in clashes with each other. In March 1770, a series of conflicts between British soldiers and American colonists in Boston, Massachusetts, resulted in the deaths of five colonists. The event has often been referred to as "the Boston Massacre" and was significant because historians considered the murders of the five colonists and the trial that followed a leading cause of the Revolutionary War and the subsequent independence of America (Linder, "Boston Massacre").

Under British law, it was common for British troops to occupy cities such as Boston during the colonial era. The quartering of British troops meant that soldiers could occupy households or businesses at their pleasure (Zobel 1996, 96–99). British soldiers had offended the colonists in Boston when they took jobs away from the colonists after they had agreed to work for lower wages as a way to supplement their military salaries. It was also common for British soldiers to refuse to pay for services rendered as well as to disrespect the colonists with personal insults. When conflict began to escalate in 1768 between the British soldiers and the colonists in Boston, the governor of Massachusetts, appointed by King George of England, ordered the British soldiers to restore peace to the city (100–107).

The Boston Massacre began simply enough on March 5, 1770, as a dispute between a British officer, named Captain John Goldfinch, and Edward Garrick, the apprentice of a wigmaker. Garrick accused Goldfinch on King Street of refusing to pay for services rendered on a wig that had been prepared for Goldfinch (Kidder 2005, 4). When a British soldier, Private Hugh White, intervened and told Garrick that Goldfinch was a "gentleman" and would pay his bill if it was owed to the wigmaker, Garrick responded by stating that there existed no "gentlemen" in the British military. Angered by the insult of all of the British soldiers, White struck Garrick with his rifle (Zobel 1996, 185–186).

A small group of colonists who noticed the confrontation between White and Garrick began yelling at White after he knocked Garrick to the ground. As the small crowd grew to nearly 50 people, they began to throw snow and ice at Private White. A few blocks away from White and Garrick another incident between British soldiers and colonists had started, and suddenly hundreds of colonists had entered into the streets to challenge the British soldiers who had joined together under the leadership of Captain Thomas Preston to decide how to protect Private White from the angry colonists (Zobel 1996, 184–205).

The colonists began to throw rocks, sticks, oyster shells, and pieces of coal at the soldiers and one colonist by the name of Crispus Attucks, who was a large man, grabbed a weapon from a British soldier, named Hugh Montgomery, and knocked him to the ground. With the British soldiers cornered by the angry mob of colonists, Montgomery yelled for the British soldiers to fire on the colonists (Zobel 1996, 194–199). Captain Preston knew that as the commanding officer he could not order the British soldiers to fire upon the civilians because colonial law stated that British soldiers could not fire upon civilians unless authorized by a court order from a judge. After many shots were fired into the crowd by British soldiers, five colonists were dead and six were seriously injured in the streets of Boston. As the British soldiers were reloading their weapons, Captain Preston yelled at the soldiers to stop firing their weapons (192–205).

When Governor Thomas Hutchinson of Massachusetts heard of the shooting, he ran down to King Street and confronted Captain Preston by asserting that Preston was not authorized by any judge to fire upon civilians. Governor Hutchinson then promised the crowd that the law would be applied and justice would be served. A warrant was issued for the arrest of Captain Preston who was then questioned by two judges, Richard Dania and John Tudor, for one hour (Zobel 1996, 202–205).

Captain Preston and the eight soldiers were represented by a young defense attorney named John Adams, who would later become the second president of the United States (Kidder 2005, 9–12). On March 12, 1770, a grand jury issued indictments for Captain Preston and eight British soldiers to be tried for the murders of the five colonists (Zobel 1996, 218–222). While Preston and the British soldiers waited in jail for their trials, many Bostonians, including John Hancock and Samuel Adams, asked Governor Hutchinson to remove all of the British troops from Boston. Governor Hutchinson honored the request because public opinion had turned strongly against the British military presence in Boston (206–209).

Captain Preston and Samuel Adams both had engaged in attempts to influence public opinion about the murders of the colonists by writing letters to the *Boston Gazette*. Preston's letters from prison praised the citizens of Boston who knew that he was innocent, while Adams published letters claiming that the British soldiers instigated the massacre with their aggressive behavior toward the colonists (Zobel 1996, 216–236).

Government officials decided that Preston would be tried separately from the eight soldiers, which was a concern for the soldiers who feared that Preston's legal defense would center upon the argument that he did not order the shooting of the civilians. If Preston was to be acquitted, then logic would dictate that the soldiers could more easily be found guilty because it would be assumed that they acted without orders from Preston, their commanding officer (Zobel 1996, 216–211; 241–243).

The trial of Captain Thomas Preston was held during the last week of October 1770. The key issue in the trial was based upon whether Preston ordered the soldiers to fire their weapons. Preston's defense attorney, John Adams, called three eyewitnesses who testified that Preston did not give an order to the soldiers to fire their weapons. However, Samuel Quincy, the solicitor general of Massachusetts and the prosecutor in the case, provided four witnesses who testified that Preston did, in fact, order the soldiers to fire their weapons at the crowd of civilians (Zobel 1996, 247–264).

A jury of 12 men acquitted Preston based largely upon Preston's deposition describing the details of the events leading up to the shooting of the five colonists. John Adams had been successful in his defense of Preston because he had raised reasonable doubt in the minds of the jurors (Zobel 1996, 265–266).

On November 27, 1770, John Adams began his second trial in defense of the eight British soldiers. The legal defense strategy of Adams centered on the argument that the soldiers had fired upon the mob because they feared for their lives (Zobel 1996, 268–293). Adams focused upon one of the victims, Patrick Carr, who had died from the shooting (211–215). Carr supposedly told his physician on his death bed that he was not angry at the British soldiers because they had simply shot at the colonists in self-defense. Adams presented more than 40 witnesses and then provided a closing argument where he powerfully stated that a person had the right to defend himself if his life was in jeopardy (285–287).

The jury returned a verdict of not guilty in favor of six of the eight soldiers. However, the prosecution had convincingly offered testimony from eyewitnesses that two of the soldiers, Hugh Montgomery and Matthew Kilroy, definitely fired upon the crowd with malice. Montgomery and Kilroy were convicted of man-slaughter. Instead of receiving the expected sentence of death, Adams used a loop-hole in the British law by having the two men read scripture from the Bible. This act of reading from the Bible allowed the judge to issue a lenient sentence and the two men simply had their thumbs branded by the sheriff as punishment for their crime (Linder, "Boston Massacre").

In December of 1770, Captain Thomas Preston returned to England and act-ually was awarded 200 pounds from the British government for his problems related to the Boston Massacre. The murder of the five colonists provided inspira-tion that the colonies should revolt from the British. As debates raged throughout the colonies about whether the British military overreacted or whether the angry crowd of civilians was to blame, the Boston Massacre brought the colonists one step closer to the Revolutionary War. American independence from Britain was formally declared less than five years after the trials of Preston and the British soldiers (Zobel 1996, 298–303). After the U.S. Constitution was ratified in 1789 by the 13 colonies, the First Congress of the United States drafted a Bill of Rights, which included the Third Amendment that prohibited the quartering of military troops in the homes of U.S. citizens. Clearly, James Madison, the author of the Third Amendment, and the other Founding Fathers drew from their experiences of the British troops occupying such cities as Boston during the colonial era (Amar 2000, 59–63).

References

Amar, Akhil Reed. *The Bill of Rights: Creation and Reconstruction.* New Haven, CT: Yale University Press, 2000.

Kidder, Frederic. *History of The Boston Massacre.* Highland Park, NJ: Gyphron Press, 2005.

Linder, Douglas O. "The Boston Massacre Trials: An Account." *Famous Trials.* http://www.law.umkc.edu/faculty/projects/ftrials/bostonmassacre/bostonaccount.html (accessed March 1, 2009).

Zobel, Hiller B. *The Boston Massacre.* New York: W. W. Norton and Company, 1996.

Impeachment Trial of Samuel Chase (1805)

The impeachment of Associate Justice Samuel Chase was a landmark event in American political history because it constituted the only time a U.S. Supreme Court justice was ever impeached. Justice Chase, who served on the U.S. Supreme Court from 1796 to 1811, was impeached in 1804 by the U.S. House of Representatives. The U.S. House of Representatives passed eight articles of impeachment against Justice Chase that involved his partisan and unfair conduct, including allegations that he denied a fair trial to defendants (Rehnquist 1993, 90–97). However, the U.S. Senate acquitted Chase on all of the charges and he continued to serve on the U.S. Supreme Court until his death (104–105). The acquittal of Chase by the U.S. Senate laid the groundwork for an independent federal judiciary as it sent a strong message that Supreme Court justices should not be impeached simply for their political views (114).

The impeachment charges against Chase were based largely upon his political conduct during trials where he served as a judge. In the early years of the U.S. political system, U.S. Supreme Court justices also served as trial judges at the lower circuit court level. This practice ended at the end of the 19th century (Rehnquist 1993, 21–23).

When Thomas Jefferson became president in 1800, he was angered by the opinions written by Chase that favored the Federalist Party. As a Democratic-Republican, Jefferson's political views were in tune with the latter day Anti-Federalists who disliked the idea of a stronger national government as well as a strong and independent federal judiciary with the power of judicial review. As Chase continued to express his Federalist philosophy and to criticize President Thomas Jefferson and his Democratic-Republican Party from the bench, Jefferson suggested that the U.S. House of Representatives, which was controlled by the Democratic-Republicans, impeach Chase for his lack of objectivity as a federal judge (Rehnquist 1993, 22–23).

The first impeachment article centered upon Chase's behavior as a judge in the treason trial of John Fries in 1799. As a supporter of Thomas Jefferson, Fries had organized an armed revolt against federal excise taxes in the state of Pennsylvania. In his capacity as the judge, Chase issued a controversial opinion, even before the start of the trial, in which he stated that Fries was guilty of treason. During the trial, Chase allegedly provided a false definition of treason to ensure a guilty verdict against Fries. Fries's defense lawyers resigned from the case because the outcome had been predetermined by Chase, and Fries basically had no legal representation, except for advice from Chase during the course of the trial. As expected, Fries was found guilty and sentenced to be executed by hanging. President Adams issued a pardon to Fries because of the blatant political bias that Chase demonstrated toward Fries throughout the trial. In fact, Chase admitted during the impeachment trial that he tried to prejudice the jury against Fries with his opinions of the law (Rehnquist 1993, 58–73).

A number of other articles of impeachment were filed against Chase in regard to his conduct as the trial judge in the libel case of James Callender. Callender had criticized the Federalist Party, President John Adams, and Alexander Hamilton in an Anti-Federalist publication entitled *The Prospect Before Us,* which was designed to challenge the Federalist Party publications. Callender was charged with crimes under the Sedition Act of 1798, which made it a crime to publish false and malicious information against the U.S. government or its officials. During the trial, Chase refused to allow a juror to be excused and also refused to allow a material witness to testify on behalf of Callender. Chase fined Callender $200 and gave him a lengthy prison sentence which was rare in cases involving sedition. Callender was eventually pardoned by President Thomas Jefferson in 1801 (Rehnquist 1993, 74–89).

A few of the remaining articles of impeachment were filed against Chase concerning errors of procedure committed by Chase in his capacity as a trial judge, and an eighth and final article was passed because of remarks that Chase had made before a Baltimore grand jury wherein he strongly criticized Jefferson and his policies (Rehnquist 1993, 76–99).

The impeachment trial of Justice Samuel Chase began in 1805 with Vice President Aaron Burr serving as the judge during the impeachment proceedings (Rehnquist 1993, 18–20). Chase argued that he did not deserve to be removed from office based upon the legal definitions of high crimes and misdemeanors (93–95). The U.S. Senate voted to acquit Chase on all of the eight charges with more than a few of the articles of impeachment defeated by a very large margin. While the Federalist Senators voted as expected to acquit Chase, many of the Senators from the Democratic-Republican Party even voted against removing Chase from office because he was viewed simply as a person with strong political opinions (108–109).

If President Jefferson had succeeded in removing Chase from the Supreme Court, it is quite possible that he would have attempted to remove other Federalist justices. Hence, the acquittal of Chase has been cited as precedent throughout American history that U.S. Supreme Court justices should not be removed from office simply because of their political beliefs. Chase's acquittal also has been used to put forth the argument that the federal judiciary should be independent of the other two branches of government within the U.S. political system, and especially free of any legislative interference (Rehnquist 1993, 134).

Samuel Chase

Samuel Chase was a significant figure during the colonial era as well as during the early years of the United States. Chase had a very successful law practice in Annapolis, Maryland, which served as the nation's capital from November 1783 until August 1784. Chase's political career began as a member of the Maryland colonial and state legislatures and he also served as a representative of Maryland at the Continental Congresses from 1774 to 1778. Chase was a strong personality who argued passionately for American independence from Great Britain and, in 1776, he was a signer of the Declaration of Independence. His earlier political leanings favored the Anti-Federalists who wanted less power for the federal government and more power for the states and individuals. Hence, he opposed the ratification of the U.S. Constitution because he feared that the document provided too much power for the federal government and weakened the position of the states. Chase's vote against the Constitution as part of the Maryland delegation caused voters to turn against him and he lost his seat in the Maryland legislature in 1788 (Rehnquist 1993, 20–22).

Chase had a number of business dealings that failed, which caused him to file for bankruptcy. He also was accused of attempting to use his political office for financial gain. When he tried to corner the flour market and benefit from inside information about the speculation of market prices, he was removed from the Continental Congress. Chase was simultaneously serving as a local judge and as a chief judge of the Maryland Court when George Washington appointed him to the U.S. Supreme Court in 1796. Despite Chase's financial failures and the corruption charges, President Washington was confident in Chase's legal abilities and admired his strong voice for American independence as well as his support of Washington during his years of service in the Continental Congress (Law Library, "Samuel Chase").

While serving on the U.S. Supreme Court, Chase altered his political views and became a supporter of the Federalist Party and began to favor a stronger national government at the expense of the states (Rehnquist 1993, 21). Chase was instrumental in establishing the federal courts as an independent and powerful branch of government in relation to the executive and legislative branches of government. Chase played a key role in handing down rulings that paved the way for the creation of judicial review, or the power of the federal courts to strike down governmental acts as unconstitutional. Chase also was influential in establishing the supremacy of federal treaties over state legislation (Law Library, "Samuel Chase").

 Impeachment

Article I, section 3 of the U.S. Constitution grants the power of impeachment to the U.S. House of Representatives. Impeachment was equivalent to being charged with an offense in a criminal court, except these charges were viewed as strictly political. After a government official was impeached by a majority vote in the House of Representatives, the U.S. Senate was then given the power to determine if the government official should be removed from his or her position by a two-thirds vote. The vice president of the United States, who serves as the president of the Senate, serves as the judge in impeachment trials (Black 1974, 5–14).

Article II, section 4 of the U.S. Constitution states that the president, vice president, and any federal official is subject to impeachment if he or she commits treason, bribery, or any high crimes and misdemeanors. In the case of the president's impeachment, the vice president would be replaced as the judge by the chief justice of the United States Supreme Court to avoid a conflict of interest (Black 1974, 5–14).

References

Black, Charles L. Jr. *Impeachment: A Handbook.* New Haven, CT: Yale University Press, 1974.

Haw, James. *Stormy Patriot: The Life of Samuel Chase.* Baltimore: Maryland Historical Society, 1980.

Law Library–American Law and Legal Information. "Samuel Chase: The Samuel Chase Impeachment Trial." *American Law Encyclopedia.* Vol. 2. http://law.jrank.org/pages/5152/Chase-Samuel.html (accessed March 1, 2009).

Rehnquist, William. *Grand Inquests: The Historic Impeachments of Justice Samuel Chase and President Andrew Johnson.* New York: Quill, 1993.

The Treason Trial of Aaron Burr (1807)

In 1803, President Jefferson and the United States purchased the Louisiana territory from France. The Louisiana Purchase added a large area of land west of the Mississippi River to the United States (Isenberg 2008, 283–286). Shortly thereafter, in 1805, Aaron Burr resigned from the vice presidency at the end of President Thomas Jefferson's first term in office. Because Burr's political career was at its end, Burr allegedly began an attempt to establish his own country by using a small military force to take control of the newly acquired Louisiana territory and invade parts of Mexico controlled by Spain (279–309). Burr's actions eventually resulted in his arrest and he was charged with treason (Melton 2001, 153–154). A trial was held to determine if Burr did, in fact, attempt to steal the Louisiana territory from the United States and, in the process, attempt to instigate an illegal war with Spain. The treason trial of Aaron Burr provided a constitutional challenge for the United States during its early years as it divided the executive branch, led by President Thomas Jefferson, and the federal judiciary and its leader, Chief Justice John Marshall (Linder, "Aaron Burr").

The idea for the Burr conspiracy began in 1804 with conversations between Burr and his close friend, General James Wilkinson, who had served in the military with Burr in Canada during the 1770s. Wilkinson had been named commander-in-chief of the U.S. Army by President Jefferson and also served as the governor of the newly purchased Louisiana territory. Burr and Wilkinson had corresponded in a series of coded messages in order to plan the military takeover of the Louisiana territory (Linder, "Aaron Burr").

In March of 1805, shortly after his resignation as vice president, Burr began traveling throughout the United States and the Louisiana territory to meet with military leaders, recruit volunteers for his operation, and arrange for the transportation of his military force. In addition to purchasing vessels and large quantities of food for his military expedition, Burr leased a large amount of land in Texas, which was technically still part of Mexico. Because the Louisiana territory and parts of Mexico were largely unsettled and numerous border disputes already existed between Spain and the United States, Burr thought that it would be easy to instigate a war between Spain and the United States. Once the military conflict began, Burr and his small military force would claim the Louisiana territory and parts of Mexico with New Orleans as the capital of his new country. In effect, the conspiracy would allow Burr to become the leader of a new empire that would provide him with an incredible amount of wealth and power that he could never attain if he simply retired from politics in the eastern part of the United States (Melton 2001, 51–99).

The conspiracy was spoiled when General Wilkinson decided to betray Burr by sending in military troops to New Orleans to prepare for an attack from Burr's men. Wilkinson sent one of Burr's secret letters that had been decoded to President Jefferson as well as a letter from one of Burr's conspirators, Senator Jonathan Dayton of Ohio. The two letters provided the strongest evidence of the Burr conspiracy and revealed Burr's intent to start his own country within the Louisiana territory and Mexico by instigating a war with Spain. President Jefferson issued an executive proclamation ordering military and government officials to arrest and punish all persons involved in the conspiracy (Melton 2001, 122–143).

After the vessels that Burr had purchased for the military operation had been confiscated by the federal government in Ohio, Burr's small military force was left in shambles as the plans for the takeover of the Louisiana territory began to unravel quickly (Melton 2001, 135–141). Burr was arrested for the first time in Mississippi after the governor of Mississippi convinced Burr to turn himself over to authorities (141–142). A grand jury acquitted Burr after hearing the evidence against him. After Burr's acquittal in Mississippi, he was alleged to have fled from federal authorities until he was arrested a second time in the Alabama territory and held at a military fort for two weeks (143–145). He was then taken by horseback to Richmond, Virginia, where he was to be tried for treason against the United States (159–161).

The judge that presided over the treason trial of Aaron Burr was Chief Justice John Marshall of the United States Supreme Court (Melton 2001, 195). The prosecutor, George Hay, introduced evidence at a grand jury hearing that Burr had planned to conduct a military takeover of New Orleans in order to establish the city as the national capital of his new country (167–178). Edmund Randolph and Luther Martin provided the legal defense for Burr by arguing that Burr had not committed treason against the United States because he had not engaged in an overt act of war against the United States. Burr's defense attorneys noted that Burr never fled from authorities and cooperated with investigators when Wilkinson accused Burr of the conspiracy to invade Mexico, a Spanish territory. Randolph and Luther also cited the fact that Burr was cleared on charges of treason by a grand jury in the Mississippi territory. Randolph and Luther concluded that Burr's actions were peaceful and he only acted in the best interests of the United States. Burr even made a statement during the trial where he reinforced the arguments presented by Randolph and Luther (196–213).

After the statements were issued by the prosecution and defense before the grand jury, John Marshall decided not to pursue a charge of treason against Burr because the evidence against Burr was not compelling enough (Isenberg 2008, 316). Instead, Marshall concluded that Burr would only stand trial for high misdemeanors (McCaleb and Beard 2006, 228). Prosecutors attempted to bring more evidence that Burr did indeed plan to separate the western territory from the United States and invade Mexico in order to establish his own country. The additional evidence had been gathered at the insistence of President Jefferson and General Wilkinson. However, again, Marshall ruled against the prosecution and refused to issue an indictment against Burr for treason. It was not until General Wilkinson finally was brought to testify before the grand jury that Marshall decided to bring charges of treason against Burr. Wilkinson's testimony was the centerpiece of the prosecution's case against Burr because their secret correspondence was the origin of the conspiracy (Melton 2001, 177–188).

The treason trial of Aaron Burr began on August 3, 1807, at the Virginia House of Delegates. During the trial, General Wilkinson and other witnesses provided compelling testimony for the prosecution that Burr had discussed carrying out the conspiracy. However, in order to find Burr guilty of treason under Article III, section 3 of the U.S. Constitution, the burden fell upon the prosecution to provide two persons who witnessed Burr committing an overt act of war against the United States. The only overt act of war that was introduced by the prosecution occurred at an island along the Ohio River where Burr's men had assembled with weapons and vessels, but the prosecution could not produce two witnesses to testify that Burr participated in this act. The prosecution's case was weakened further when Burr objected that he was approximately 100 miles away from the island when the overt act of treason had occurred. In sum, the prosecution was disadvantaged because it lacked the witnesses to prove that Burr was in a certain place, during a specific time period, with the intent to commit treason (McCaleb and Beard 2006, 258–274).

Chief Justice John Marshall delivered his opinion to the jury and declared that Burr should be found not guilty of treason because, under the law, he had not committed an overt act of war against the United States. After a few hours of deliberation, the jury also found that Burr was not guilty, but suggested that Marshall's opinion and instructions to the jury had left them with no alternative in the matter (McCaleb and Beard 2006, 290–291).

After the verdict, President Jefferson was angry with Chief Justice Marshall and contemplated whether he should instruct the House to impeach Marshall but, he chose not to take this course of action. Jefferson also considered introducing a constitutional amendment to limit the power of the federal courts because he thought that Burr had received favorable treatment from Marshall, who often had opposed Jefferson in the past on issues related to the federal judiciary (Melton 2001, 165–171). After the trial, Burr's reputation in American politics was ruined and he left the United States and spent four years in England and other parts of Europe before returning to the United States in 1812, where he lived the rest of his life in obscurity until his death in 1836 (Isenberg 2008, 367–386; 403–404).

References

Abernathy, Thomas. *The Burr Conspiracy*. New York: Oxford University Press, 1954.

Isenberg, Nancy. *Fallen Founder: The Life of Aaron Burr*. New York: Penguin, 2008.

Linder, Douglas O. "The Treason Trial of Aaron Burr," *Famous Trials*. http://www.law.umkc.edu/faculty/projects/ftrials/burr/burraccount.html (accessed March 1, 2009).

McCaleb, Walter F. and Charles A. Beard. *The Aaron Burr Conspiracy*. Whitefish, MT: Kessinger Publishing, 2006.

Melton, Buckner. *Aaron Burr: Conspiracy to Treason*. New York: Wiley, 2001.

The Trial of Nat Turner (1831)

Nat Turner led the largest slave revolt in the history of the United States when he and approximately 70 other slaves murdered roughly 60 white men, women, and children in Southampton County, Virginia, over a two-day period, specifically August 21–22, 1831. As a consequence of the revolt, white plantation owners throughout the southern states sought revenge by murdering hundreds of blacks, many of whom did not participate in the rebellion. The violence and brutality that occurred between blacks and whites during the revolt and its aftermath were unprecedented given the short duration of the conflict which lasted only a few weeks. In addition, the legal restrictions placed upon blacks after the uprising had serious consequences for the educational development of blacks. Today, many African

Americans and Africans regard Nat Turner as a significant historical figure who symbolizes the struggle for freedom around the world (French 2003, 1–6).

On February 12, 1831, Nat Turner observed a solar eclipse and believed that it was a message from God to revolt against all of the white slave owners and their families in Southampton, Virginia (Oates 1990, 51–56). On August 21, 1831, Turner began the revolt with a small number of slaves, probably five or six, and started by entering the home of his slave master, Joseph Travis, in the middle of the night and murdering Travis, his wife, and children with a hatchet. The rebellion continued over two days where Turner recruited somewhere between 50 and 100 hundred slaves to participate as they entered home after home in the countryside of Southampton murdering white slave owners and their families with hatchets, axes, and knives. Many of the victims were gruesomely mutilated and decapitated. After each of the murders, Turner and his followers would free any slaves that lived and worked on the plantations (70–79).

Within 24 hours of the beginning of the slave revolt, armed militias from various counties in Virginia and North Carolina joined with U.S. military forces out of Norfolk, Virginia. The military forces began murdering hundreds of black slaves throughout the southern states as panic and rumor spread suggesting that the slave rebellion had reached other parts of the country. Many of the victims murdered by the militias were not tried in a court of law or given any due process and most were probably not involved in the revolt by Turner and his followers. While the Turner slave revolt lasted only two days, the murdering of black slaves by the militias lasted two weeks until a military general finally issued an order for the military forces and white citizens to stop killing black slaves at random (Oates 1990, 79–100).

After Turner's band of followers was defeated by a much larger military force comprised of militia and U.S. military personnel, Turner was able to hide out and escape capture until two slaves reported his whereabouts to authorities. Turner had been hiding in a cave near his former master's home and fled after the two slaves had accidentally noticed him living in the makeshift dwelling. After a two-week chase, a white citizen farmer was able to capture Turner at gunpoint on October 31, 1831 (Gray 2004, 2).

After Turner was arrested, he was represented by a court-appointed attorney, Thomas Gray (Oates 1990, 120–121). While awaiting trial in the Southampton County Jail, Turner was interviewed for three days by Gray where Turner subsequently confessed to his leadership role in the revolt. During his confession, Turner discussed how God had revealed events to him that occurred before his birth and how easily he learned to read and write as a child. Turner stated that his parents told him that he was destined to serve a great purpose on earth. As a young adult, Turner said that he had experienced visions from the Holy Spirit who instructed him to destroy the white race. Turner described in detail how he and the other slaves murdered Joseph Travis and his family while they slept in their beds. Turner also told of the murders of several other slave owners and their families. Turner denied any knowledge or involvement in similar revolts that occurred simultaneously in other states, such as North Carolina (120–124).

Gray concluded from the confession that Turner was someone with little formal education but he knew how to read and write and was highly intelligent. Gray also concluded that Turner was a religious fanatic who considered himself a hero and a great liberator (Oates 1990, 120–124).

In the *Commonwealth of Virginia v. Nat Turner* (1831), Turner pled not guilty to charges of conspiracy to commit rebellion and make insurrection to take the lives of free white persons because he said that he did not "feel" guilty, even though he had confessed to the murders. Prosecutors introduced Turner's confession as evidence and Turner and his defense attorney did not introduce any evidence on his own behalf. The case was submitted without a legal argument to the judge who found Turner guilty of the charges (Oates 1990, 124–125).

During the sentencing phase of the trial, the judge addressed Turner by stating that, based upon the evidence, there was no doubt that Turner had taken the lives of innocent men, women, and children in a violent and brutal fashion. The judge noted that the only explanation for Turner's actions was his radical beliefs, and he felt sympathy and pity for Turner. However, the judge ruled that he must issue the harshest sentence possible under the law and Turner's only hope was in the next world. Turner's trial, conviction, and sentence occurred on the same day, November 5, 1831. Turner was sentenced to death by hanging and he was executed on November 11, 1831 (Oates 1990, 120–125).

In 1832, Turner's lawyer, Thomas Gray, published *The Confessions of Nat Turner,* which provided perhaps the best document toward understanding the motives for the murders committed by Turner and his followers, although some historians question whether Gray offered a fair portrayal in his writing of the Turner confession (Oates 1990, 144–145). In addition to his religious beliefs and visions, many Southerners believed that Turner was inspired by a newsletter entitled *The Liberator* published by Lloyd Garrison, a white abolitionist. In the newsletter of July 23, 1831, roughly one month before the revolt, Garrison published an entry entitled *Song, supposed to be sung by Slaves in Insurrection.* Within the song, Garrison publicly encouraged black slaves to seek vengeance and attack whites as part of God's will (Oates 1990, 129–135).

As a consequence of the Turner revolt, many southern states passed new laws prohibiting anyone from educating blacks to read and write and also restricting blacks from participating in religious activities without the assistance of a white religious leader. The new laws that ensured illiteracy for blacks caused many black families to move to the northern parts of the United States (American Heritage, "Nat Turner"). Opposition to the laws placed the issue of literacy for blacks on the national agenda after the Civil War when blacks were free to seek an education. During the post–Civil War period, many charitable organizations comprised of religious, military, and financial leaders were concerned about the lasting effects of the illiteracy laws and offered funding to provide educational opportunities for blacks. A number of black universities in the south were eventually created as a direct result of such funding (Franklin and Carter 2004, 1–81).

 ## Nat Turner

Nat Turner was born in 1800 and lived most of his life in Southampton, Virginia. At an early age, Turner was educated to read and write and became very interested in and inspired by the Bible. As a young adult, Turner began experiencing visions that he believed were messages from God. Turner would often perform the role of a Baptist minister preaching to other slaves, and he developed somewhat of a religious following within the Southampton community. In 1830, Turner was purchased by a plantation owner named Joseph Travis who, according to Turner himself, treated his slaves very well (Oates 1990, 7–52; Greenberg 2004, 6).

References

American Heritage.com: History's Homepage. "Nat Turner, Lightning Rod." *American Heritage People.* http://www.americanheritage.com/people/articles/web/20051111-nat-turner-slavery-rebellion-virginia-civil-war-thomas-r-gray-abolitionist.shtml (accessed March 7, 2009).

Franklin, V. P., and Julian Savage Carter. *Cultural Capital and Black Education: African American Communities and the Funding of Black Schooling.* Greenwich, CT: Information Age Publishing, 2004.

French, Scot. *The Rebellious Slave: Nat Turner in Memory.* Boston: Houghton Mifflin Harcourt, 2003.

Gray, Thomas R. *The Confessions of Nat Turner: The Leader of the Late Insurrection in Southampton, Virginia.* Whitefish, MT: Kessinger Publishing, 2004.

Greenberg, Kenneth S. *Nat Turner: A Slave Rebellion in History and Memory.* New York: Oxford University Press, 2004.

Johnson, F. Roy. *The Nat Turner Insurrection Together with Thomas R. Gray's the Confession, Trial and Execution of Nat Turner as a Supplement.* Chicago, IL: Johnson Publishing Company, 1966.

Oates, Stephen B. *The Fires of Jubilee: Nat Turner's Fierce Rebellion.* New York: Harper Perennial, 1990.

Nat Turner: *Confessions of Nat Turner* (1831)

In 1831, African American Nat Turner led a slave rebellion in southern Virginia that shocked the nation. He and his supporters killed over 60 whites in a single night but were ultimately hunted down and captured. Condemned in the Virginia courts, Turner dictated this book, an excerpt of which appears below, as he awaited execution. Despite the ultimate failure of Nat Turner's Rebellion, the event had significant repercussions on American society, as it brought the issue of slavery firmly to the attention of a group of Northern reformers that thereafter embraced abolitionism. It also stifled discussion in the South of the possibility of gradually emancipating some of its slaves.

. . . To a mind like mine, restless, inquisitive and observant of every thing that was passing, it is easy to suppose that religion was the subject to which it would be directed, and although this subject principally occupied my thoughts—there was nothing that I saw or heard of to which my attention was not directed—The manner in which I learned to read and write, not only had great influence on my own mind, as I acquired it with the most perfect ease, so much so, that I have no recollection whatever of learning the alphabet—but to the astonishment of the family, one day, when a book was shewn to me to keep me from crying, I began spelling the names of different objects—this was a source of wonder to all in the neighborhood, particularly the blacks—and this learning was constantly improved at all opportunities—when I got large enough to go to work, while employed, I was reflecting on many things that would present themselves to my imagination, and whenever an opportunity occurred of looking at a book, when the school children were getting their lessons, I would find many things that the fertility of my own imagination had depicted to me before. . . .

[A]ll my time, not devoted to my master's service, was spent either in prayer, or in making experiments in casting different things in moulds made of earth, in attempting to make paper, gun-powder, and many other experiments, that although I could not perfect, yet convinced me of its practicability if I had the means.

I was not addicted to stealing in my youth, nor have ever been—Yet such was the confidence of the negroes in the neighborhood, even at this early period of my life, in my superior judgment, that they would often carry me with them when they were going on any roguery, to plan for them. Growing up among them, with this confidence in my superior judgment, and when this, in their opinions, was perfected by Divine inspiration, from the circumstances already alluded to in my infancy, and which belief was ever afterwards zealously inculcated by the austerity of my life and manners, which became the subject of remark by white and black.

Having soon discovered to be great, I must appear so, and therefore studiously avoided mixing in society, and wrapped myself in mystery, devoting my time to fasting and prayer-by this time, having arrived to man's estate, and hearing the scriptures commented on at meetings, I was struck with that particular passage which says: "Seek ye the kingdom of Heaven and all things shall be added unto you." I reflected much on this passage, and prayed daily for light on this subject—As I was praying one day at my plough, the spirit spoke to me, saying "Seek ye the kingdom of Heaven and all things shall be added unto you."

Question—what do you mean by the Spirit? Ans.—The Spirit that spoke to the prophets in former days—and I was greatly astonished, and for two years prayed continually, whenever my duty would permit—and then again I had the same revelation, which fully confirmed me in the impression that I was ordained for some great purpose in the hands of the Almighty.

Several years rolled round, in which many events occurred to strengthen me in this my belief. At this time I reverted in my mind to the remarks made of me in my childhood, and the things that had been shewn me—and as it had been said of me in my childhood by those by whom I had been taught to pray, both white and black, and in whom I had the greatest confidence, that I had too much sense to be raised, and if I was, I would never be of any use to any one as a slave. Now finding I had arrived to man's estate, and was a slave, and these revelations being made known to me, I began to direct my attention to this great object, to fulfill the purpose for which, by this time, I felt assured I was intended.

Knowing the influence I had obtained over the minds of my fellow servants (not by the means of conjuring and such like tricks—for to them I always spoke of such things with contempt) but by the communion of the Spirit whose revelations I often communicated to them, and they believed and said my wisdom came from God. I now began to prepare them for my purpose, by telling them something was about to happen that would terminate in fulfilling the great promise that had been made to me. . . .

Richard Lawrence Trial (1835)

Richard Lawrence was a person who suffered from severe mental illness and was responsible for the first assassination attempt of a U.S. president. Fortunately, Lawrence was unsuccessful in his attempt to assassinate President Andrew Jackson in 1835 as Jackson attended the funeral of a congressman in Washington, D.C. The trial of Richard Lawrence was uneventful as the jury easily and quickly reached a verdict of guilty by reason of insanity. Lawrence spent the remainder of his life committed to mental institutions (Cole 1993, 221–222).

In preparation for the assassination attempt, Richard Lawrence purchased two pistols in 1835 and began to stalk President Andrew Jackson. On January 30, 1835, President Jackson was in attendance at the funeral of Warren R. Davis, a congressman from South Carolina. As President Jackson entered the service, Lawrence was unsuccessful at obtaining a close enough position to shoot Jackson. However, as Jackson left the funeral, Lawrence stepped out from behind a pillar and shot at Jackson's back with one of his two pistols. Lawrence's pistol misfired when the percussion cap exploded but the bullet did not release. Lawrence tried again with his second pistol but it also misfired. Investigators later determined that Lawrence's two pistols were extremely sensitive to damp conditions, and the humid weather at the time caused moisture that, in turn, caused the two pistols to misfire. Lawrence was brought under control by a large crowd who witnessed the assassination attempt. Among those present in the crowd was Congressman Davy Crockett who assisted in the capture of Lawrence. It also was reported that President Jackson played a role in subduing Lawrence by using his own walking stick to strike Lawrence several times (Clarke 2007 236).

Richard Lawrence's trial began on April 11, 1835, with Francis Scott Key, author of the U.S. national anthem, acting as the prosecutor. A jury found Lawrence guilty by reason of insanity after only a few minutes of deliberation. Lawrence spent the next two decades in a variety of mental institutions until the government placed him in a newly opened facility in 1855 called the Government Hospital for the Insane in Washington, D.C. (Clarke 2007, 239).

Lawrence's assassination attempt on President Andrew Jackson caused some to believe in a conspiracy. Jackson himself believed that his political enemies, the Whigs, may have been involved in the attempted assassination. Jackson sought to eliminate the Bank of the United States and this angered the Whigs. However, no evidence surfaced to indicate a conspiracy and history has recorded the assassination attempt as the act of one delusional man (Smith 1881, 26–80). After surviving the assassination attempt, Andrew Jackson completed his second term as president by appointing Roger Taney to be the chief justice of the Supreme Court in 1836. Taney supported states' rights and contributed to the regional divisions over slavery by authoring the Court's opinion in *Dred Scott v. Sanford* (1857) in which he proclaimed that blacks were not citizens under the Constitution. The *Dred Scott* decision was considered a major cause of the Civil War (Cole 1993, 253–254).

 ## Richard Lawrence

Richard Lawrence was born in England at the beginning of the 19th century and, by the time he became an adult, he was diagnosed as mentally insane (Clarke 2006, 236–237). He had worked as a painter and some historians argue that the chemicals from the paint may have caused or added to his mental illness. In the 1830s, Lawrence began to have delusions that he was the King of England. He also believed that the United States government and President Andrew Jackson owed him a large amount of money. Lawrence also believed that Jackson had murdered his father in 1832 but Lawrence's father, who died in England in 1823, had never even been to the United States. Lawrence was unemployed most of his life and he blamed President Jackson and the U.S. government for his personal condition (237).

References

Cole, Donald B. *The Presidency of Andrew Jackson.* Lawrence: University Press of Kansas, 1993.

Clarke, James A. "Richard Lawrence." in *Defining Danger: American Assassins and the New Domestic Terrorists.* New Brunswick, NJ: Transaction Publishers, 2007.

Dixon, Barbara. *Assassinations and Assassination Attempts on American Public Officials, 1835–1972.* Washington, D.C.: Congressional Research Service, Library of Congress, 1972.

Lawrence, Richard. *Shooting at the President!: The remarkable trial of Richard Lawrence, self-styled "King of the United States," "King of England and of Rome," . . . the event, not before known to the public.* London: W. Mitchell, 1835.

"Trial of Richard Lawrence." In *Assassination and Insanity: Guiteau's Case Examined and Compared with Analogous Cases From the Earlier to the Present Times*, ed. William R. Smith, Washington, D.C.: William R. Smith, 1881.

Amistad Trials (1839–1841)

The *Amistad* trials fascinated America and its citizens as it became a symbol of freedom across the United States and also produced inspired attempts by abolitionists to end slavery. When a slave ship, the *Amistad*, sailed from Cuba and landed by mistake in Long Island, New York, a historic legal battle began to decide the fate of a large number of African men who had allegedly committed murder and mutiny aboard the ship. Because the ship had been sailing in international waters, it was uncertain whether the U.S. government had jurisdiction over the legal matter concerning who owned the slaves and valuables aboard the *Amistad*. More importantly, because the Africans had been illegally transported from Africa to Cuba, a Spanish colony, in violation of international law, it was also uncertain whether the Africans were the slave property of the Spanish government or free men who should be returned to their homeland of Africa (Linder, "Amistad").

On June 28, 1839, two Spaniards, Jose Ruiz and Pedro Montes, had purchased 53 slaves in Havana, Cuba. Ruiz and Montes left Havana with the slaves in a black sailing vessel called the *Amistad* en route to Puerto Principe, Cuba, a small city roughly 500 miles southeast of Havana (Owens 1953, 48–51). During the trip, a mutiny occurred aboard the vessel some time in July 1839 because the black slaves believed that they were going to be killed when they arrived in Puerto Principe. The black slaves were able to get free from their chains and proceeded to murder all of the crew on board, except Ruiz and Montes whom they spared in order to have the two men sail the black slaves back to their homeland of Africa. In an attempt to deceive the black slaves, Ruiz and Montes steered the sailing vessel toward the United States in the hope of landing on the shore of one of the southern colonies where slavery was legal. However, the two men aimlessly steered the vessel toward the United States for six weeks until they anchored about one mile from the shore of Long Island, New York (72–91).

On August 26, 1839, several of the black slaves from the *Amistad* took a small rowboat to shore. Four of the black slaves were covered only with blankets when they approached two sea captains, Peletiah Fordham and Henry Green, who had been hunting on the beach. They led the two sea captains to a place on the beach where they could view the *Amistad* that had been damaged somewhat on the journey westward from Cuba. The black men were wearing gold jewelry and told Fordham and Green that the *Amistad* contained trunks of gold and silk that they could have in exchange for sailing the black men back to their homeland of Africa (Owens 1997, 94–96). As Fordham and Green started in the rowboat with some of the slaves toward the *Amistad,* a U.S. Navy ship, the *Washington,* seized the row boat. The commander of the *Washington,* Lieutenant Thomas Gedney, took control of the situation by ordering everyone below deck on the *Amistad.* Gedney spoke with Ruiz and Montes who told Gedney the story of how they purchased the slaves in Cuba and how the mutiny had then occurred on board the ship (100–104). The *Amistad* was then taken to New London, Connecticut, where it became a huge news story across the United States (105).

Ruiz and Montes filed criminal charges against the slaves for murder and piracy in the U.S. District Court of Connecticut in the courtroom of Judge Andrew T. Judson. Judge Judson heard testimony from Ruiz and Montes about the mutiny aboard the *Amistad* and how crew members were murdered by the slaves. Judge Judson ordered a criminal trial to be held in the Circuit Court and the slaves were taken into custody and placed in jail in New Haven, Connecticut (Owens 1997, 220–235). The black slaves attracted thousands of people every day to the jail to examine the Africans. A group of abolitionists formed a group called the *Amistad* Committee to assist in the legal battle on behalf of the black slaves (Osagie 2000, 17–18).

The country of Spain was angered by the actions of the U.S. government in regard to the *Amistad* and ordered the U.S. government to return the vessel, it contents, and the slaves to their rightful owners in Havana, Cuba. The gold, wine, and silk aboard the *Amistad* were valued at roughly $50,000 and the slaves were estimated to be worth about $25,000. Spain also criticized the U.S. government for claiming jurisdiction over the legal issue of the *Amistad* and the slaves (Linder, "Amistad").

Judge Smith Thompson presided over the Circuit Court trial of the slaves in Hartford, Connecticut. The trial began on September 14, 1839. The U.S. attorney for the state of Connecticut, William S. Holabird, requested that the Judge Thompson turn the slaves over to President Martin Van Buren who should decide by himself how to handle the matter because of the potential for international conflict with other countries, especially Spain (Jones 1987, 57–77). Roger Baldwin, the defense attorney for the Africans, argued forcefully that the U.S. government should not support slavery and should not capture slaves and return them to a country that supports slavery (74–75). Judge Thompson ruled that the U.S. government did not have the power to hear the case because the alleged murders committed by the Africans happened within international waters, outside the boundaries of the United States and its legal system. More importantly, the alleged crimes did not involve any citizens of the United States. Judge Thompson refused to decide whether the slaves were property and who should retain ownership of the slaves. Thompson stated that a civil trial at the district court level would be the best place to decide such issues (63–74).

In anticipation of the civil trial, the defense lawyers decided to find someone in Connecticut who could communicate with the Africans. A linguistics expert from Yale University, Dr. Josiah Gibbs, was able to conclude that the Africans spoke a language called Mende and they were from Sierra Leone (Osagie 2000, 9–11). Gibbs was able to locate a British sailor, James Covey, who was originally from a village in Sierra Leone, and he was able to translate the stories of the slaves who were on board the *Amistad* (63–64).

The entire story of the Africans was provided for the defense attorneys. Apparently, the Africans had been captured in Sierra Leone and taken to a slave factory by other Africans. They were then taken across the Atlantic Ocean on the famous Middle Passage where many of the slaves died along the way on the trip to Havana, Cuba. Once the slaves arrived in Havana, the surviving members of the group were purchased by Ruiz and Montes (Cable 1977; Osagie 2000, 85–96).

The civil trial in the federal district court began on November 19, 1839, in Hartford, Connecticut but, after only two days of the testimony, the trial was postponed until January 7, 1840. President Martin Van Buren was anticipating a ruling in the government's favor and he was prepared to place the Africans in chains and sail them back to Cuba in order to prevent any appeal of the district court ruling (Myers 2001).

When the civil trial commenced in January, the defense lawyers argued that according to the stories of the Africans aboard the *Amistad,* they had been illegally transported from Africa to Cuba. Ruiz, who purchased the slaves in Havana, even admitted that the Africans were illegally transported in violation of an 1817 treaty between Britain and Spain that prohibited the transporting of slaves from Africa to any Spanish colony, such as Cuba (Owens 1997, 161–168). The slave traders engaged in a corrupt business of falsifying documents and bribed Cuban officials in exchange for allowing the slave trade to prosper in Cuba. The U.S. attorney, Holabird, maintained his stance that the Africans should be returned to Cuba, a colony of Spain, and even introduced statements from Spanish government officials requesting the return of the slaves. On January 13, 1840, Judge Judson declared that all of the Africans were free men and they had been seized in violation of international law. Also, President Martin Van Buren should return all of the Africans to their homeland (237–238).

After the U.S. government appealed the case to the Circuit Court, Circuit Judge Thompson, who had heard the criminal trial, upheld the judgment of Judge Judson in the civil trial as constitutional (Owens 1997, 173–187). Then, the U.S. government decided to appeal the case to the United States Supreme Court (245). The legal arguments began in the Supreme Court chambers located within the U.S. Capitol building on February 22, 1841. The attorney general of the United States, Henry Gilpin, presented the case for the government, and John Quincy Adams, a former president (1825–1829), argued on behalf of the Africans (Jones 1987, 171–172).

Gilpin introduced as evidence legal documents stating that the Africans were, in fact, Spanish property. Because the Africans were indeed slaves according to the legal documents, the Spanish government owned the slaves as property (Jones 1987, 182–189). The defense argument presented by Adams was powerful. Adams stated that the Africans had every right to the freedoms contained within the Declaration of Independence. He criticized President Van Buren for supporting the transportation of the Africans back to Cuba and also criticized any defense of slavery by southerners who had testified in the trial. Adams concluded with a call for the Supreme Court justices to decide in favor of the Africans and their freedom because it was the right and moral choice. Adams stated that the justices would be judged in heaven based upon how they ruled in the *Amistad* case (Jones 1987, 183–195).

On March 9, 1841, Justice Joseph Story wrote the opinion for the U.S. Supreme Court and held that the Africans were illegally transported from Africa to Cuba in violation of the international treaty between Britain and Spain that prohibited the transporting of slaves from Africa to a Spanish colony. Therefore, the documents introduced as evidence by Gilpin were produced fraudulently by the Spanish government. As a result, the Africans were free persons who could stay in the United States or return to their homeland of Africa. Justice Story provided no commentary about the legality or morality of slavery, but he instead chose to stay close to the letter of law (Jones 1987, 188–200).

In November 1841, the *Amistad* Committee raised $2,000 to charter a ship to take the 35 surviving Africans of the *Amistad* back to Sierra Leone. A number of Christian missionaries accompanied the Africans to Sierra Leone in the hopes of converting many of their fellow Africans to Christianity (Jones 1987, 197–204). Spain demanded monetary compensation for the gold, silk, and wine aboard the *Amistad* as well as the value of the slaves, but John Quincy Adams fought every attempt in the U.S. Congress to pay the Spanish government for their alleged financial losses. After slavery ended in the U.S. with the Northern victory in the Civil War, the Spanish government discontinued any attempts to gain payment for their supposed losses (Linder, "Amistad").

The *Amistad* case was significant because the legal controversy placed slavery on to the national agenda and demonstrated for the first time that the issue needed to be addressed because Americans were passionately divided between abolitionists and those who supported slavery. The *Amistad* Committee eventually grew into the American Missionary Association (AMA) in 1846, which was an evangelical Christian group focused upon ending slavery, educating African-Americans, seeking equal protection for blacks, and emphasizing Christian values. The AMA founded several universities and colleges for freed slaves after the Civil War, including Atlanta University in 1865, Fisk University in 1866, and Howard University in 1867 (DeBoer, "Blacks and the American Missionary Association").

John Quincy Adams

John Quincy Adams was born in Braintree, Massachusetts, on July 11, 1767. After graduating from Harvard University, Adams began a law practice (Nagel 1999, 3–53). In 1794, he was appointed as U.S. minister to the Netherlands by President George Washington (75–83). When his father, John Adams, became the second president of the United States, John Quincy Adams was appointed as the minister to Prussia in 1797 (107–108). From 1803 to 1808, he served as a U.S. senator from the state of Massachusetts (138–140). In 1809, Adams was appointed as the first American minister to Russia by President James Madison (183–185).

During the presidency of James Monroe from 1817 to 1825, Adams was appointed to serve as secretary of state. Adams is considered to be one of the greatest secretaries of state based upon the fact that he obtained the Florida territory from Spain and was instrumental in developing the Monroe Doctrine, which prohibited European nations from establishing additional colonies in the Western Hemisphere (Nagel 1999, 232–271).

In 1824, Adams won a controversial election for president when he defeated Andrew Jackson. Because neither Adams nor Jackson received a majority of the electoral votes, the presidential election was decided by the U.S. House of Representatives. Adams won largely because the third place finisher in the election, Speaker of the House Henry Clay, encouraged his supporters in the House to vote for Adams. Adams was accused by his political opponents of corruption when he then appointed Clay to become secretary of state. Adams became the first person to win the presidency who was the son of a former president. During his term as president, Adams advocated a network of highways and canals to unite the country and also was instrumental in promoting the arts and sciences as he created the first national university. In 1828, Adams lost his bid for reelection to Andrew Jackson (Nagel 1999, 296–323). In 1830, Adams won election to the U.S. House of Representatives representing the Plymouth district. He is the only person to serve in the House after having served as president. Adams would serve in the House for the remainder of his life (334–337).

In 1841, Adams served as the lawyer for the African slaves in the famous *Amistad* case. Adams successfully argued before the U.S. Supreme Court that the defendants should not be sent back to Cuba to resume their lives of slavery but, instead, should be set free (Nagel 1999, 379–381). On February 21, 1848, Adams collapsed on the floor of the House and suffered a stroke, while he was expressing his opposition to the Mexican-American War. He died two days later inside the Capitol Building in Washington, D. C. (413–414).

Cinque

Cinque was born in 1813 in the West African village of Mani. Cinque's father was a leader of a Mendi village. As a young adult, Cinque was being trained to become the leader of the village. However, Cinque was taken into slavery by African tribesmen when he failed to pay a debt. He was sent to a slave factory in Gallinas and then sold to a slaver trader from Spain. After being sold a second time, he was placed on a slave ship, the *Tecora*, which sailed to Havana, Cuba. In Havana, Cinque was sold a third time along with several other slaves and placed on a Spanish ship, the *Amistad*, bound for Puerto Principe, Cuba. Cinque became convinced that he and other slaves would be killed in Puerto Principe. Therefore, he led a violent revolt on the *Amistad*, taking control of the ship by murdering the captain and the cook. Cinque instructed Montes, one of the ship's owners, to sail east toward Africa but Montes attempted to deceive Cinque by sailing northwest toward the United States. After reaching the shore of Long Island, New York, Cinque and the other slaves were taken aboard the U.S. *Washington* on August 26, 1839. Cinque was identified as the leader of the revolt and he and the other slaves were charged with committing murder aboard the *Amistad*. The slaves were then taken to New Haven, Connecticut, where they were held in jail to await a trial. In 1839, a criminal trial was held and a federal judge ruled that the Africans had been illegally taken from Africa to Cuba in violation of an international treaty. Cinque and the others were considered to be free men. In 1841, the U.S. Supreme Court upheld the ruling of the federal judge. Cinque returned to his homeland in Africa with Christian missionaries and a number of the survivors from the *Amistad*. Cinque returned to find that his family was gone and his village destroyed. It was assumed that his family members had been sold into slavery. In 1879, Cinque died at the age of 66 and was given a Christian burial by the missionaries (Linder, "Cinque"). In 1997, Stephen Spielberg's film, *Amistad*, was released and Cinque was portrayed by actor Djimon Hounsou (Linder, "Stephen Spielberg's 'Amistad'").

References

Cable, Mary. *Black Odyssey: The Case of the Slave Ship Amistad.* New York: Penguin, 2003.

DeBoer, Clara Merritt. "Blacks and the American Missionary Association." *United Church of Christ.* http://www.ucc.org/about-us/hidden-histories/blacks-and-the-american.html (accessed March 12, 2009).

Jones, Howard. *The Mutiny on the Amistad: The Saga of a Slave Revolt and its Impact on American Abolition, Law, and Diplomacy.* New York: Oxford University Press, 1987.

Linder, Douglas O. "The Amistad Case." *Famous Trials.* http://www.law.umkc.edu/faculty/projects/ftrials/amistad/AMI_ACT.HTM (accessed March 1, 2009).

Linder, Douglas O. "Cinque." *Famous Trials.* http://www.law.umkc.edu/faculty/projects/ftrials/amistad/AMI_BCIN.HTM (accessed August 25, 2009).

Linder, Douglas O. "Stephen Spielberg's 'Amistad' (1997)." *Famous Trials.* http://www.law.umkc.edu/faculty/projects/ftrials/amistad/AMI_MOVI.HTM (accessed August 25, 2009).

Myers, Walter Dean. *Amistad: A Long Road to Freedom.* New York: Puffin, 2001.

Nagel, Paul C. *John Quincy Adams: A Public Life, a Private Life.* Cambridge, MA: Harvard University Press, 1999.

Osagie, Iyunolu Folayan. *The Amistad Revolt: Memory, Slavery, and the Politics of Identity in the United States and Sierra Leone.* Athens: University of Georgia Press, 2000.

Owens, William. *Slave Mutiny: The Revolt on the Schooner Amistad.* Baltimore: Black Classic Press, 1997.

United States v. Amistad (1841)

Mr. Justice Story delivered the opinion of the Court.

This is the case of an appeal from the decree of the Circuit Court of the District of Connecticut, sitting in admiralty. The leading facts, as they appear upon the transcript of the proceedings, are as follows: On the 27th of June, 1839, the schooner *L'Amistad*, being the property of Spanish subjects, cleared out from the port of Havana, in the island of Cuba, for Puerto Principe, in the same island. On board of the schooner were the captain, Ransom Ferrer, and Jose Ruiz, and Pedro Montez, all Spanish subjects. The former had with him a negro boy, named Antonio, claimed to be his slave. Jose Ruiz had with him forty-nine negroes, claimed by him as his slaves, and stated to be his property, in a certain pass or document, signed by the Governor General of Cuba. Pedro Montez had with him four other negroes, also claimed by him as his slaves, and stated to be his property, in a similar pass or document, also signed by the Governor General of Cuba. On the voyage, and before the arrival of the vessel at her port of destination, the negroes rose, killed the captain, and took possession of her. On the 26th of August, the vessel was discovered by Lieutenant

Gedney, of the United States brig Washington, at anchor on the high seas, at the distance of half a mile from the shore of Long Island. A part of the negroes were then on shore at Culloden Point, Long Island; who were seized by Lieutenant Gedney, and brought on board. The vessel, with the negroes and other persons on board, was brought by Lieutenant Gedney into the district of Connecticut, and there libelled for salvage in the District Court of the United States. A libel for salvage was also filed by Henry Green and Pelatiah Fordham, of Sag Harbour, Long Island. On the 18th of September, Ruiz and Montez filed claims and libels, in which they asserted their ownership of the negroes as their slaves, and of certain parts of the cargo, and prayed that the same might be "delivered to them, or to the representatives of her Catholic majesty, as might be most proper." On the 19th of September, the Attorney of the United States, for the district of Connecticut, filed an information or libel, setting forth, that the Spanish minister had officially presented to the proper department of the government of the United States, a claim for the restoration of the vessel, cargo, and slaves, as the property of Spanish subjects, which had arrived within the jurisdictional limits of the United States, and were taken possession of by the said public armed brig of the United States; under such circumstances as made it the duty of the United States to cause the same to be restored to the true proprietors, pursuant to the treaty between the United States and Spain: and praying the Court, on its being made legally to appear that the claim of the Spanish minister was well founded, to make such order for the disposal of the vessel, cargo, and slaves, as would best enable the United States to comply with their treaty stipulations. But if it should appear, that the negroes were persons transported from Africa, in violation of the laws of the United States, and brought within the United States contrary to the same laws; he then prayed the Court to make such order for their removal to the coast of Africa, pursuant to the laws of the United States, as it should deem fit.

On the 19th of November, the Attorney of the United States filed a second information or libel, similar to the first, with the exception of the second prayer above set forth in his former one. On the same day, Antonio G. Vega, the vice-consul of Spain, for the state of Connecticut, filed his libel, alleging that Antonio was a slave, the property of the representatives of Ramon Ferrer, and praying the Court to cause him to be delivered to the said vice-consul, that he might be returned by him to his lawful owner in the island of Cuba.

On the 7th of January, 1840, the negroes, Cinque and others, with the exception of Antonio, by their counsel, filed an answer, denying that they were slaves, or the property of Ruiz and Montez, or that the Court could, under the Constitution or laws of the United States, or under any treaty, exercise any jurisdiction over their persons, by reason of the premises; and praying that they might be dismissed. They specially set forth and insist in this answer, that they were native born Africans; born free, and still of right ought to be free and not slaves; that they were, on or about the 15th of April, 1839, unlawfully kidnapped, and forcibly and wrongfully carried on board a certain vessel on the coast of Africa, which was unlawfully engaged in the slave trade, and were unlawfully transported in the same vessel to the island of Cuba, for the purpose of being there unlawfully sold as slaves; that Ruiz and Montez, well knowing the premises, made a pretended purchase of them: that afterwards, on or about the 28th of June, 1839, Ruiz and Montez, confederating with Ferrer, (captain of the *Amistad*) caused them, without law or right, to be placed on board of the *Amistad*, to be transported to some place unknown to them, and there to be enslaved for life; that, on the voyage, they rose on the master, and took possession of the vessel, intending to return therewith to their native country, or to seek an asylum in some free state; and the vessel arrived, about the 26th of August, 1839, off Montauk Point, near Long Island; a part of them were sent on shore, and were seized by Lieutenant Gedney, and carried on board; and all of them were afterwards brought by him into the district of Connecticut.

On the 7th of January, 1840, Jose Antonio Tellincas, and Messrs. Aspe and Laca, all Spanish subjects, residing in Cuba, filed their claims, as owners to certain portions of the goods found on board of the schooner *L'Amistad*.

On the same day, all the libellants and claimants, by their counsel, except Jose Ruiz and Pedro Montez, (whose libels and claims, as stated of record, respectively, were pursued by the Spanish minister, the same being merged in his claims,) appeared, and the negroes also appeared by their counsel; and the case was heard on their libels, claims, answers, and testimony of witnesses.

On the 23d day of January, 1840, the District Court made a decree. By that decree, the Court rejected the claim of Green and Fordham for salvage, but allowed salvage to Lieutenant Gedney and others, on the vessel and cargo, of one-third of the value thereof, but not on the negroes, Cinque and others; it allowed the claim of Tellincas, and Aspe and Laca with the exception of the above-mentioned salvage; it dismissed the libels and claims of Ruiz and Montez, with costs, as being included under the claim of the Spanish minister; it allowed the claim of the Spanish vice-consul for Antonio, on behalf of Ferrer's representatives; it rejected the claims of Ruiz and Montez for the delivery of the negroes, but admitted them for the cargo, with the exception of the above-mentioned salvage; it rejected the claim made by the Attorney of the United States on behalf of the Spanish minister, for the restoration of the negroes under the treaty; but it decreed that they should be delivered to the President of the United States, to be transported to Africa, pursuant to the act of 3d March, 1819.

From this decree the District Attorney, on behalf of the United States, appealed to the Circuit Court, except so far as related to the restoration of the slave Antonio. The claimants, Tellincas, and Aspe and Laca, also appealed from that part of the decree which awarded salvage on the property respectively claimed by them. No appeal was interposed by Ruiz or Montez, or on behalf of the representatives of the owners of the *Amistad*. The Circuit Court, by a mere pro forma decree, affirmed the decree of the District Court, reserving the question of salvage upon the claims of Tellincas, and Aspe and Laca. And from that decree the present appeal has been brought to this Court.

The cause has been very elaborately argued, as well upon the merits, as upon a motion on behalf of the appellees to dismiss the appeal. On the part of the United States, it has been contended: 1. That due and sufficient proof concerning the property has been made to authorize the restitution of the vessel, cargo, and negroes to the Spanish subjects on whose behalf they are claimed pursuant to the treaty with Spain, of the 27th of October, 1795. 2. That the United States had a right to intervene in the manner in which they have done, to obtain a decree for the restitution of the property, upon the application of the Spanish minister. These propositions have been strenuously denied on the other side. Other collateral and incidental points have been stated, upon which it is not necessary at this moment to dwell.

Before entering upon the discussion of the main points involved in this interesting and important controversy, it may be necessary to say a few words as to the actual posture of the case as it now stands before us. In the first place, then, the only parties now before the Court on one side, are the United States, intervening for the sole purpose of procuring restitution of the property as Spanish property, pursuant to the treaty, upon the grounds stated by the other parties claiming the property in their respective libels. The United States do not assert any property in themselves, or any violation of their own rights, or sovereignty, or laws, by the acts complained of. They do not insist that these negroes have been imported into the United States, in contravention of our own slave trade acts. They do not seek to have these negroes delivered up for the purpose of being transported to Cuba as pirates or robbers, or as fugitive criminals against the laws of Spain. They do not assert that the seizure, and bringing the vessel, and cargo, and negroes into port, by Lieutenant Gedney, for the purpose of adjudication, is a tortious act. They simply confine themselves to the right of the Spanish claimants to the restitution of their property, upon the facts asserted in their respective allegations.

In the next place, the parties before the Court on the other side as appellees, are Lieutenant Gedney, on his libel for salvage, and the negroes, (Cinque, and others,) asserting themselves, in their answer, not to be slaves, but free native Africans, kidnapped in their own country, and illegally transported by force from that country; and now entitled to maintain their freedom.

No question has been here made, as to the proprietary interests in the vessel and cargo. It is admitted that they belong to Spanish subjects, and that they ought to be restored. The only point on this head is, whether the restitution ought to be upon the payment of salvage or not? The main controversy is, whether these negroes are the property of Ruiz and Montez, and ought to be delivered up; and to this, accordingly, we shall first direct our attention.

It has been argued on behalf of the United States, that the Court are bound to deliver them up, according to the treaty of 1795, with Spain, which has in this particular been continued in full force, by the treaty of 1819, ratified in 1821. The sixth article of that treaty, seems to have had, principally, in view cases where the property of the subjects of either state had been taken possession of within the territorial jurisdiction of the other, during war. The eighth article provides for cases where the shipping of the inhabitants of either state are forced, through stress of weather, pursuit of pirates, or enemies, or any other urgent necessity, to seek shelter in the ports of the other. There may well be some doubt entertained, whether the present case, in its actual circumstances, falls within the purview of this article. But it does not seem necessary, for reasons hereafter stated, absolutely to decide it. The ninth article provides, "that all ships and merchandise, of what nature soever, which shall be rescued out of the hands of any pirates or robbers, on the high seas, shall be brought into some port of either state, and shall be delivered to the custody of the officers of that port, in order to be taken care of and restored entire to the true proprietor, as soon as due and sufficient proof shall be made concerning the property thereof." This is the article on which the main reliance is placed on behalf of the United States, for the restitution of these negroes. To bring the case within the article, it is essential to establish, First, That these negroes, under all the circumstances, fall within the description of merchandise, in the sense of the treaty. Secondly, That there has been a rescue of them on the high seas, out of the hands of the pirates and robbers; which, in the present case, can only be, by showing that they themselves are pirates and robbers; and, Thirdly, That Ruiz and Montez, the asserted proprietors, are the true proprietors, and have established their title by competent proof.

If these negroes were, at the time, lawfully held as slaves under the laws of Spain, and recognised by those laws as property capable of being lawfully bought and sold; we see no reason why they may not justly be deemed within the intent of the treaty, to be included under the denomination of merchandise, and, as such, ought to be restored to the claimants: for, upon that point, the laws of Spain would seem to furnish the proper rule of interpretation. But, admitting this, it is clear, in our opinion, that neither of the other essential facts and requisites has been established in proof; and the onus probandi of both lies upon the claimants to give rise to the causes foederis. It is plain beyond controversy, if we examine the evidence, that these negroes never were the lawful slaves of Ruiz or Montez, or of any other Spanish subjects. They are natives of Africa, and were kidnapped there, and were unlawfully transported to Cuba, in violation of the laws and treaties of Spain, and the most solemn edicts and declarations of that government. By those laws, and treaties, and edicts, the African slave trade is utterly abolished; the dealing in that trade is deemed a heinous crime; and the negroes thereby introduced into the dominions of Spain, are declared to be free. Ruiz and Montez are proved to have made the pretended purchase of these negroes, with a full knowledge of all the circumstances. And so cogent and irresistible is the evidence in this respect, that the District Attorney has admitted in open Court, upon the record, that these negroes were native Africans, and recently imported into Cuba, as alleged in their answers to the libels in the case. The supposed proprietary interest of Ruiz and Montez, is completely displaced, if we are at liberty to look at the evidence of the admissions of the District Attorney.

It, then, these negroes are not slaves, but are kidnapped Africans, who, by the laws of Spain itself, are entitled to their freedom, and were kidnapped and illegally carried to Cuba, and illegally detained and restrained on board of the *Amistad*; there is no pretence to say, that they are pirates or robbers. We may lament the dreadful acts, by which they asserted their liberty, and took possession of the *Amistad*, and endeavoured to regain their native country; but they cannot be deemed pirates or robbers in the sense of the law of nations, or the treaty with Spain, or the laws of Spain itself; at least so far as those laws have been brought to our knowledge. Nor do the libels of Ruiz or Montez assert them to be such.

This posture of the facts would seem, of itself, to put an end to the Whole inquiry upon the merits. But it is argued, on behalf of the United States, that the ship, and cargo, and negroes were duly documented as belonging to Spanish subjects, and this Court have no right to look behind these documents; that full faith and credit is to be given to them; and that they are to be held conclusive evidence in this cause, even although it should be established by the most satisfactory proofs, that they have been obtained by the grossest frauds and impositions upon the constituted authorities of Spain. To this argument we can, in no wise, assent. There is nothing in the treaty which justifies or sustains the argument. We do not here meddle with the point, whether there has been any connivance in this illegal traffic, on the part of any of the colonial authorities or subordinate officers of Cuba; because, in our view, such an examination is unnecessary, and ought not to be pursued, unless it were indispensable to public justice, although it has been strongly pressed at the bar. What we proceed upon is this, that although public documents of the government, accompanying property found on board of the private ships of a foreign nation, certainly are to be deemed prima facie evidence of the facts which they purport to state, yet they are always open to be impugned for fraud; and whether that fraud be in the original obtaining of these documents, or in the subsequent fraudulent and illegal use of them, when once it is satisfactorily established, it overthrows all their sanctity, and destroys them as proof. Fraud will vitiate any, even the most solemn transactions; and an asserted title to property, founded upon it, is utterly void. The very language of the ninth article of the treaty of 1795, requires the proprietor to make due and sufficient proof of his property. And how can that proof be deemed either due or sufficient, which is but a connected, and stained tissue of fraud? This is not a mere rule of municipal jurisprudence. Nothing is more clear in the law of nations, as an established rule to regulate their rights, and duties, and intercourse, than the doctrine, that the ship's papers are but prima facie evidence, and that, if they are shown to be fraudulent, they are not to be held proof of any valid title. This rule is familiarly applied, and, indeed, is of every-days occurrence in cases of prize, in the contests between belligerents and neutrals, as is apparent from numerous cases to be found in the Reports of this Court; and it is just as applicable to the transactions of civil intercourse between nations in times of peace. If a private ship, clothed with Spanish papers, should enter the ports of the United States, claiming the privileges, and immunities, and rights belonging to bona fide subjects of Spain, under our treaties or laws, and she should, in reality, belong to the subjects of another nation, which was not entitled to any such privileges, immunities, or rights, and the proprietors were seeking, by fraud, to cover their own illegal acts, under the flag of Spain; there can be no doubt, that it would be the duty of our Courts to strip off the disguise, and to look at the case according to its naked realities. In the solemn treaties between nations, it can never be presumed that either state intends to provide the means of perpetrating or protecting frauds; but all the provisions are to be construed as intended to be applied to bona fide transactions. The seventeenth article of the treaty with Spain, which provides for certain passports and certificates, as evidence of property on board of the ships of both states, is, in its terms, applicable only to cases where either of the parties is engaged in a war. This article required a certain form of passport to be agreed upon by the parties, and annexed to the treaty. It never was annexed; and, therefore, in the case of the Amiable Isabella . . . it was held inoperative.

It is also a most important consideration in the present case, which ought not to be lost sight of, that, supposing these African negroes not to be slaves, but kidnapped, and free negroes, the treaty with Spain cannot be obligatory upon them; and the United States are bound to respect their rights as much as those of Spanish subjects. The conflict of rights between the parties under such circumstances, becomes positive and inevitable, and must be decided upon the eternal principles of justice and international law. If the contest were about any goods on board of this ship, to which American citizens asserted a title, which was denied by the Spanish claimants, there could be no doubt of the right of such American citizens to litigate their claims before any competent American tribunal, notwithstanding the treaty with Spain. A fortiori, the doctrine must apply where human life and human liberty are in issue; and constitute the very essence of the controversy. The treaty with Spain never could have intended to take away the equal rights of all foreigners, who should contest their claims before any of our Courts, to equal justice; or to deprive such foreigners of the protection given them by other treaties, or by the general law of nations. Upon the merits of the case, then, there does not seem to us to be any ground for doubt, that these negroes ought to be deemed free; and that the Spanish treaty interposes no obstacle to the just assertion of their rights.

There is another consideration growing out of this part of the case, which necessarily rises in judgment. It is observable, that the United States, in their original claim, filed it in the alternative, to have the negroes, if slaves and Spanish property, restored to the proprietors; or, if not slaves, but negroes who had been transported from Africa, in violation of the laws of the United States, and brought into the United States contrary to the same laws, then the Court to pass an order to enable the United States to remove such persons to the coast of Africa, to be delivered there to such agent as may be authorized to receive and provide for them. At a subsequent period, this last alternative claim was not insisted on, and another claim was interposed, omitting it; from which the conclusion naturally arises that it was abandoned. The decree of the District Court, however, contained an order for the delivery of the negroes to the United States, to be transported to the coast of Africa, under the act of the 3d of March, 1819, ch. 224. The United States do not now insist upon any affirmance of this part of the decree; and, in our judgment, upon the admitted facts, there is no ground to assert that the case comes within the purview of the act of 1819, or of any other of our prohibitory slave trade acts. These negroes were never taken from Africa, or brought to the United States in contravention of those acts. When the *Amistad* arrived she was in possession of the negroes, asserting their freedom; and in no sense could they possibly intend to import themselves here, as slaves, or for sale as slaves. In this view of the matter, that part of the decree of the District Court is unmaintainable, and must be reversed.

The view which has been thus taken of this case, upon the merits, under the first point, renders it wholly unnecessary for us to give any opinion upon the other point, as to the right of the United States to intervene in this case in the manner already stated. We dismiss this, therefore, as well as several minor points made at the argument.

As to the claim of Lieutenant Gedney for the salvage service, it is understood that the United States do not now desire to interpose any obstacle to the allowance of it, if it is deemed reasonable by the Court. It was a highly meritorious and useful service to the proprietors of the ship and cargo; and such as, by the general principles of maritime law, is always deemed a just foundation for salvage. The rate allowed by the Court, does not seem to us to have been beyond the exercise of a sound discretion, under the very peculiar and embarrassing circumstances of the case.

Upon the whole, our opinion is, that the decree of the Circuit Court, affirming that of the District Court, ought to be affirmed, except so far as it directs the negroes to be delivered to the President, to be transported to Africa, in pursuance of the act of the 3d of March, 1819; and, as to this, it ought to be reversed: and that the said negroes be declared to be free, and be dismissed from the custody of the Court, and go without day.

MR. JUSTICE BALDWIN dissented.

This cause came on to be heard on the transcript of the record from the Circuit Court of the United States, for the District of Connecticut, and was argued by counsel. On consideration whereof, it is the opinion of this Court, that there is error in that part of the decree of the Circuit Court, affirming the decree of the

District Court, which ordered the said negroes to be delivered to the President of the United States, to be transported to Africa, in pursuance of the act of Congress, of the 3d of March, 1819; and that, as to that part, it ought to be reversed: and, in all other respects, that the said decree of the Circuit Court ought to be affirmed. It is therefore ordered adjudged, and decreed by this Court, that the decree of the said Circuit Court be, and the same is hereby, affirmed, except as to the part aforesaid, and as to that part, that it be reversed; and that the cause be remanded to the Circuit Court, with directions to enter, in lieu of that part, a decree, that the said negroes be, and are hereby, declared to be free, and that they be dismissed from the custody of the Court, and be discharged from the suit and go thereof quit without day.

The Carthage Conspiracy Trial (1844)

The Carthage Conspiracy trial involved the 1844 murders of Joseph Smith, a Mormon prophet, and his brother, Hyrum, in Carthage, Illinois. The Smith brothers were being held in the Carthage jail awaiting trial on charges of treason when they were attacked by a mob of assassins (Oaks and Hill 1979, 6–29). The trial of the five persons who allegedly ordered the mob to attack the Smith brothers highlighted the tension between the Mormon and non-Mormon cultures in the state of Illinois at the time (103–108). The trial also was played out within the context of an anti-Mormon environment that perhaps caused the murders to be politically inspired and supported by a majority of the public. Many leaders within the community wanted to drive Mormons from Illinois because of their controversial religious beliefs (31–32). In retrospect, the criminal trial raised interesting questions about the ability to achieve justice using the jury system when a large segment of the population within a community supported a criminal act against a discriminated group (210–214).

In the early 1840s, after Smith and his followers were driven out of Missouri, Mormons began to arrive in Illinois in large numbers. In order to gain political support from the Mormons who had suddenly become a strong voting bloc, the Democratic and Whig parties in Illinois granted a liberal charter to allow Smith and his followers to settle in the city of Commerce, Illinois, which the Mormons renamed Nauvoo. Nauvoo was given an independent military force as well as their own court system. Nauvoo grew to become one of the largest cities in Illinois, second only to Chicago in terms of population (Oaks and Hill 1979, 11–19).

As Nauvoo became powerful economically and politically, it became more competitive with other parts of the state such as Carthage, the county seat, and Warsaw, the largest port in Illinois. As was the situation in Missouri, non-Mormons became angered at the power accumulated by the Mormons within the state of Illinois, and tensions between Mormons and non-Mormons escalated. The conflict between the two cultures focused almost exclusively upon Joseph Smith who, in addition to serving as the mayor of Navuoo, was also the leader of the Navuoo state militia, a local judge, and leader of the university. Non-Mormons were especially concerned that Smith wanted to become a king who would bring together religious, political, and economic aspects of society into his Mormon religion (Flanders, 1975, 32–56). Smith was so concerned about the potential for conflict that he met with President Martin Van Buren and started to petition the federal government to declare Nauvoo a federal territory to allow federal troops to protect the Mormons against any violence from anti-Mormons. When President Van Buren, a Democrat, told Smith that he could do nothing to help the Mormons, Smith returned to his followers in Illinois and told them that he would now support the Whig party (Oaks and Hill 1979, 10–17).

In addition to the conflicts outside of the church, serious problems also started to develop within Smith's church when a number of his followers decided that Smith had too much power as mayor of Nauvoo and as President of the Mormon Church. Smith's critics, who had left the church, published a newspaper entitled the *Nauvoo Expositor* which produced only one issue on June 7, 1844. The newspaper criticized Smith as a fallen prophet because he practiced polygamy and accused Smith of marrying and attempting to marry the wives of many church members. The newspaper even went as far as stating that Smith had forced women into marriage with him. As a response to the newspaper, the Nauvoo city council passed an ordinance that acknowledged the criticisms of Smith as slanderous. As mayor of Nauvoo, Smith, along with the city council, ordered the printing press that produced the newspaper to be destroyed. The destruction of the printing press caused the anti-Mormon forces to join together with the former members of Smith's church in order to destroy Smith and his church (Oaks and Hill 1979, 14–33).

An anti-Mormon newspaper, the *Warsaw Signal*, accused Smith of violating the freedom of the press and encouraging riots and treason by instructing his members to destroy the printing press. The *Warsaw Signal* cautioned that war between the Mormons and non-Mormons was inevitable (Oaks and Hill 1979, 14–15).

When Illinois authorities issued arrest warrants for Smith and the city council on the charge of inciting a riot, Smith declared martial law and called upon the Nauvoo militia to protect the city from any outside threats. Eventually, Smith and his brother, Hyrum, as well as the 15 city council members surrendered to authorities on the charge of inciting a riot. While most of the city council members were released after posting bond. Smith, his brother, and two other church members were denied bail and held in the jail on an additional charge of treason because Joseph Smith had declared martial law as mayor of Nauvoo (Oaks and Hill 1979, 18).

On June 27, 1844, Joseph and Hyrum Smith were in the Carthage jail awaiting their trial when a mob of 200 men with faces painted black with gunpowder and armed with weapons stormed the jailhouse (Hill 2004, 107). In the ensuing battle inside the jail cell,

Joseph and Hyrum Smith were murdered by gunfire, while the two church members, Willard Richards and John Taylor, survived the attacks by the mob (Oaks and Hill 1979, 102–103). While many were suspicious that the governor of Illinois, Thomas Ford, had ordered the men to murder the Mormons, Ford denied any involvement. Governor Ford initially had promised to protect Smith while he was awaiting trial, but instead he ordered most of the Illinois militia to abandon their posts at the jailhouse which left Smith and the others virtually unprotected from the mob. In his later writings, Ford supposedly expressed his belief that the Mormons should have been driven from Illinois because of their radical belief system (Hill 2004, 115–124).

On October 22, 1844, a grand jury assembled in Hancock County to determine who should be indicted for the murder of Joseph Smith. In determining the responsibility for the murder, 60 possible assassins were named before the grand jury, but only nine individuals were indicted (Oaks and Hill 1979, 51). In an attempt to gain a pre-trial advantage, anti-Mormons sought to influence the witnesses scheduled to testify on behalf of the state and to sway public opinion in their favor. The Mormons' goal was simply to protect their current leaders from being murdered while planning a move out of Illinois to the western part of the country (64).

Of the nine persons indicted for the murder, five individuals (Thomas Sharp, William Grover, Jacob Davis, Levi Williams, and Mark Aldrich) were officially charged with ordering the mob to storm the jailhouse and murder Joseph and Hyrum Smith, while the other four defendants supposedly fled and left the state of Illinois (79). The five defendants charged in the murders were all opponents of Joseph Smith, and they also were prominent political leaders of their time (Hill 2004, 118).

The trial of the five defendants charged with ordering the murder of Joseph Smith lasted from May 24, 1845, until May 30, 1845, in Carthage, Illinois (Oaks and Hill 1979, 80). The initial jury was comprised of all Mormons because the jurors were selected by a county commission elected by Mormons. But, at the request of the attorneys for the five defendants, Judge Richard M. Young dismissed the jury and a second jury of non-Mormons selected by appointed officials was seated for the trial (105–106). Judge Young agreed with the defense attorneys that the five defendants could not receive a fair trial before a prejudiced jury of Mormons (97). After hearing word of Judge Young's decision, the Mormon leadership decided not to assist the prosecutors in the trial because they knew that justice would not be served with a jury composed of non-Mormons. The leadership decided that they only wanted peace until they could leave Illinois and settle in the western part of the United States (102–103).

After the jury of 12 non-Mormons was seated, the five defendants pled not guilty to the charges of murdering Joseph Smith (105). The state prosecutor, Josiah Lamborn, presented the legal theory that the five men instigated a mob of assassins to murder Joseph Smith. Therefore, it was not necessary to prove that the five defendants entered the jail and directly caused the murder of the victim, but only that they caused the murder based upon their influence upon the mob. Lamborn's theory was based upon a conspiracy to murder, or an agreement among the men to commit the crime. Lamborn admitted that he had a difficult task in prosecuting the five defendants because so many people within the community wanted the five defendants to be found not guilty. However, Lamborn tried to appeal to the jury's sense of fairness and justice by asking the jurors to send a strong message that mob murder should not be permitted in the United States (114–115).

The witnesses called by the prosecution were not forthcoming in providing details about the involvement of the five defendants in the murder. Lamborn could only establish that one of the five defendants spoke vaguely of murdering Smith at the jail and that the other defendants were seen with a group of roughly 100 men a few hours before the murder. Lamborn was clearly at a disadvantage because most of his witnesses were reluctant to provide details about the role of the five men in the murder because of the hostile anti-Mormon community in which they lived. When Lamborn tried to force witnesses to answer vital questions, Judge Young sensed the anger from the people in the courtroom and ruled that witnesses did not have to answer such questions. Lamborn was so unsuccessful with his witnesses that the defense attorneys did not have to cross-examine most of them (Oaks and Hill 1979, 122–125). Even with the reluctance displayed by most of the witnesses, Lamborn was able to secure testimony from a three witnesses that provided sufficient evidence that four of the defendants (Aldrich, Grover, Sharp, and Williams) conspired to murder Joseph Smith. However, there seemed to be insufficient evidence against Davis (155–156).

The defense lawyers led by Orville H. Browning attempted to discredit the key witnesses for the prosecution during cross-examination and again when the defense attorneys presented 16 witnesses of their own who highlighted inconsistencies in the testimony of the prosecution witnesses. Interestingly, the defense team did not provide any alibis for the defendants or any testimony from the accused murderers (Oaks and Hill 1979, 166–169).

During the prosecution's closing arguments, Lamborn surprisingly admitted that his key witnesses had been discredited by the defense attorneys. He also decided to drop the charges against two of the defendants, Davis and Grover, because there was no solid evidence to convict them. With the prosecutor admitting that his best witnesses were unreliable, his case against the three remaining defendants, Aldrich, Sharp, and Williams, was circumstantial at best (Oaks and Hill 1979, 172–173).

Why would Lamborn apparently surrender the case? Court observers speculated that he had to throw out the testimony of the key witnesses because they were Mormons and the jury probably viewed their testimony as biased. In deciding not to rely upon the testimony of Mormons to convict defendants who had allegedly murdered a leader of the Mormon community, Lamborn was hoping to appear impartial and fair in presenting his case against the defendants. Another theory maintained that Lamborn was afraid of how the crowded courtroom of angry anti-Mormons would react to a guilty verdict. Clearly, it is possible that his life would be in danger if he was successful in prosecuting the defendants. Finally, it has been suggested that Lamborn was corrupt and decided to lose the case in exchange for money or political favors. It is interesting to note that Lamborn was only being paid $100 for his services as the state prosecutor. Whatever the reason for his surrender, the advantage shifted dramatically in favor of an acquittal for the defendants (Oaks and Hill 1979, 173–176).

In their closing arguments, the defense attorneys asserted that the five defendants must be acquitted because the prosecutor had no specific evidence that the men were involved in the murder. In fact, the prosecutor had admitted as much in his closing arguments that the state's case was weak. If the prosecutor was dropping charges for lack of evidence against Davis and Grover, then the charges must be dropped against the other three defendants as well. It seemed inconsistent for Lamborn to dismiss the charges against Davis and Grover when the same amount of evidence existed against the other three men. The defense team then followed with an appeal to the anti-Mormon sympathies of the jury by suggesting that the law should simply represent public opinion. Hence, it was implied that no person should be held accountable for the murder of Joseph Smith because the mob of assassins was acting on behalf of the interests of the people of Illinois (Oaks and Hill 1979, 177–183).

On May 30, 1845, after two and a half hours of deliberation, the jury returned a verdict of not guilty because of inadequate evidence against the five defendants. In the end, the verdict was a combination of a weak attempt to prosecute, a jury who favored an acquittal regardless of the evidence, a fear of civil war if a guilty verdict was issued, and a public who approved of the murder of the Mormon leader (Oaks and Hill 1979, 185).

On June 24, 1845, Judge Young attempted to hold a trial to try the five defendants for the murder of Hyrum Smith, the brother of Joseph, but no one showed up for the prosecution so the case was dismissed. It was assumed that the state of Illinois did not want another trial that might cause violence within the community (Oaks and Hill 1979, 191–192).

Legal theorists have suggested that the role of the jury is based historically on the power to ignore the law at times to produce a verdict consistent with the "moral sense of the community" (Oaks and Hill 1979, 211). In short, a jury might have to apply legal rules flexibly or ignore them to achieve justice. The Carthage conspiracy trial was an example of jury nullification where the jurors ignored the written law and instead chose to recognize the will of the community. Historically, however, jury nullification had not been accepted for murder, but only lesser offenses. In addition, jury nullification is only justified if the jury represents the entire community. However, in the Carthage conspiracy trial, Mormons were excluded from the jury. As a minority group, the Mormons were forced to accept the popular will of the majority of citizens (210–214).

The United States would also experience similar instances of jury nullification in the 20th century when southern juries composed of whites acquitted persons who committed murder against blacks and civil rights workers (Oaks and Hill 1979, 210–214). In *Batson v. Kentucky* (1986), the U.S. Supreme Court attempted to address the issue of racial discrimination and jury nullification by prohibiting the removal of jurors based upon race (Starr and McCormick 2000, 22). Today, judges also have the option of sequestering a jury to prevent biased news reports or public opinion from adversely affecting jurors or a judge could move the trial to a different location where citizens are unfamiliar with the crime of the defendant (121–122). In the Carthage conspiracy trial, the governor of Illinois, Thomas Ford, had prevented Judge Young from moving the trial to a different location (62–92).

Joseph Smith

Joseph Smith was born in Sharon, Vermont, on December 23, 1805. His parents were poor farmers. Smith grew up in an era of great religious activity, referred to as the Second Great Awakening, where Christian evangelism spread throughout the United States. In 1820, as a teenager living in western New York, Smith said that he walked into the woods to pray to God about which religion he should follow and God the Father and Jesus appeared to him and told him not to follow any particular religion. In 1823, Smith told his followers that he had a vision where an angel, Moroni, allowed him to view Golden Plates that contained information about a visit by Jesus to visit the native peoples of the Americas during ancient times. Smith translated the words on the Golden Plates and this became the Book of Mormons which was published in 1830 (PBS, "Joseph Smith").

Smith began to seek converts in New York but many Christians questioned his credibility and he was actually arrested for disturbing the peace. Smith was acquitted in court on such charges on more than one occasion. Smith's family moved out of New York because they were facing persecution and he and his followers moved west and set up operation in Kirtland, Ohio, and also in Missouri. In Ohio, Smith established a small church of about 2,000 members. Smith published a book of revelations and built a temple to prepare for the second coming of Jesus Christ (Oaks and Hill 1979, 6–8).

While living in Independence, Missouri, Smith began the first Mormon newspaper called the *Evening and Morning Star*. Many traditional Christians considered Smith to be guilty of blasphemy because Smith and his followers considered themselves to be modern day saints of Christ in the tradition of the Apostles. Because Smith spoke about visions and messages that he received directly from God, his critics maintained that he was being untruthful because God had not revealed himself or his message to anyone since the time of the Apostles. Another controversial aspect of Mormonism was the idea that men had failed to establish a moral government in America. Therefore, God must take over religious, political, social, and economic aspects of life in America. In 1838, Smith and his church members were forced to leave Missouri because of tensions between Mormons and non-Mormons that resulted in the Mormon War of 1838. Mormons had been purchasing a great deal of property and the non-Mormons feared that they would become too powerful economically and politically (Oaks and Hill 1979, 6–8).

In the 1840s, Smith moved his church to Illinois and established the city of Nauvoo where he became the mayor and a powerful economic, religious, and political force. When critics of Smith published a newspaper called the *Nauvoo Expositor* and claimed that he practiced polygamy, Smith ordered his followers to destroy the printing press and he was subsequently arrested for violating freedom of the press and rioting. While awaiting a trial in the county jail, Smith and his brother, Hyrum, were murdered on June 27, 1844, by an angry mob who acted upon the orders of Smith's political opponents (Oaks and Hill 1979, 6–23).

The deaths of Joseph and Hyrum Smith and the acquittal in the Carthage conspiracy trial of their opponents who ordered their murders caused Smith and his brother to become martyrs in the Mormon Church, also known today as The Church of Jesus Christ of Latter Day Saints. The Church of Jesus Christ of Latter Day Saints has been based in Salt Lake City, Utah, since 1847 and the number of person belonging to the church is estimated at 14 million (Ostling and Ostling 2007, 1–19).

References

Baum, Frank. *Minutes of Trial of Members of Mob Who Helped Kill Joseph Smith, the Prophet.* Handwritten manuscript of the trial proceedings. Bountiful, UT: Wilford C. Wood Museum, 1845.

Flanders, Robert. *Nauvoo: Kingdom on the Mississippi.* Urbana: University of Illinois Press, 1975.

Hill, Marvin S. "Carthage Conspiracy Reconsidered: A Second Look at The Murder of Joseph and Hyrum Smith." *Journal of the Illinois State Historical Society* 97, no. 2 (Summer 2004): 107–134.

Oaks, Dallin H., and Marvin S. Hill. *Carthage Conspiracy: The Trial of the Accused Assassins of Joseph Smith.* Urbana: University of Illinois Press, 1979.

Ostling, Richard, and Joan K. Ostling. *Mormon America.* New York: HarperOne, 2007.

PBS. "Joseph Smith." *American Prophet.* http://www.pbs.org/americanprophet/joseph-smith.html (accessed March 11, 2009)

Sharp, Thomas C. *Trial of the Persons Indicted in the Hancock Circuit Court for the Murder of Joseph Smith.* June 27th, 1844.

Starr, V. Hale, and Mark McCormick. *Jury Selection.* New York: Aspen Publishers, 2000.

Dr. John W. Webster Trial (1850)

The 1850 murder trial of Dr. John Webster, a professor at Harvard Medical College, was a sensational event that gained a large amount of publicity because the accused murderer and the victim had strong connections to the wealthy and social elites of Boston, Massachusetts. The Webster murder trial was also one of the first trials in which medical professionals were asked to provide expert testimony and forensic evidence was involved in the legal proceedings. Finally, in a controversial decision, the judge allowed circumstantial evidence, as opposed to concrete evidence, to be used by the jury to produce a verdict of guilty beyond a reasonable doubt against Webster (Dershowitz 2004, 101–108).

On November 23, 1849, Dr. George Parkman was last seen walking toward the Harvard Medical College where he was going to visit Dr. John Webster about collecting on a debt. Webster had borrowed more than $400 from Parkman, a Boston medical physician. Because Parkman was from the wealthiest family in Boston, Webster was extremely embarrassed that he could not repay the debt and allegedly became distraught that he would be publicly humiliated over the debt. When Parkman supposedly confronted Webster in his office laboratory about the debt, Webster struck Parkman in the head with a piece of firewood. After Webster realized that he had fractured Parkman's skull and could not revive Parkman, Webster locked his laboratory door and decided to dismember Parkman with the instruments in his medical laboratory. Webster then used a furnace in the lab to burn the remains of Parkman. Parkman was reported missing by his family who offered a reward of $3,000 for information concerning his disappearance (Morris 1967, 156–170).

Approximately one week later, Ephraim Littlefield, a janitor at the college, found body parts in the medical laboratory of Webster. Littlefield had become suspicious because he had witnessed a previous argument between Webster and Parkman, and Littlefield also had noticed Webster's laboratory door was locked on the exact day that Parkman disappeared. When Littlefield noticed the advertisements displayed by Parkman's family about his disappearance, Littlefield began searching Webster's laboratory for evidence (Schama 1992, 115–138).

On November 30, 1849, Webster was taken from his home in Cambridge by police without being told that he was under arrest for the murder of Parkman. Webster provided a large amount of information for the police but he was unaware that he was the main suspect in the murder. The police officers let Webster assume that he was simply a potential witness in the murder case before they arrested him and charged him with the crime (Morris 1967, 164).

The murder trial of John Webster was held from March 19, 1850, until April 1, 1850. Because Webster had allegedly dismembered Parkman's body, the prosecutors were forced to conduct the trial without Parkman's body as proof of the murder. Judge Lemuel Shaw allowed the prosecutors to introduce expert testimony from medical professionals such as Parkman's dentist to identify parts of the false teeth of Parkman that were found in Webster's laboratory. The Webster murder trial was the first trial to utilize dental evidence to identify a murder victim as well as one of the first trials to allow for the use of forensic evidence (PBS, "Parkman").

Webster's defense attorneys presented a number of witnesses who supposedly saw Parkman after the time period that Webster allegedly murdered Parkman. While such witnesses were designed to provide an alibi for Webster, Judge Shaw provided commentary that an alibi was difficult to prove and eyewitnesses were often mistaken (Morris 1967, 189–190).

Webster's attorneys also raised the issue that much of the evidence was circumstantial against Webster because it was not absolutely certain whether the remains found in the laboratory were of Parkman and, even if they were Parkman's remains, it was unknown how he was murdered. In addition, many people, including the janitor, had access to Webster's laboratory and could have planted the evidence to frame Webster. However, in a controversial statement to the jury, Judge Shaw asserted that circumstantial, or indirect, evidence could be used to prove that Webster was guilty beyond a reasonable doubt (Morris 1967, 189–193).

Critics of the murder trial have raised concerns that Webster's defense attorneys failed to introduce hundreds of pages of notes taken by the police officers while Webster was in custody. The notes supposedly provided a detailed account of Webster claiming his innocence after the police officers accused him of the murder. The notes also revealed Webster contesting much of the evidence found in his laboratory. Defense attorneys also failed to rigorously cross-examine Littlefield, the janitor, when he testified against Webster. The janitor supposedly had complete access to Webster's office during any hour or day of the week and also admitted to searching Webster's office prior to the date when Parkman had gone missing. Webster even complained at the sentencing stage of his trial about the weak effort provided by his defense attorneys. If Webster had been represented by modern-day lawyers, many legal scholars believe that he easily would have been acquitted of the murder charges (Morris 1967, 156–193).

On April 1, 1850, the jury found Webster guilty of murder and sentenced him to death by hanging. After the trial, Webster supposedly confessed to the crime, even though many social elites refused to believe that such a mild-mannered person was capable of committing such a horrible murder. Many prominent people within Boston society appealed to Massachusetts governor George Briggs for sympathy on behalf of Webster, but the governor refused to reduce Webster's sentence from death to life in prison. On August 30, 1850, Webster was hanged at Leverett Square in Boston, Massachusetts (Morris 1967, 194–203).

Today, legal scholars have drawn similarities between the murder trials of Dr. John Webster and O. J. Simpson. While millions of viewers watched the Simpson trial on television in 1995, the Webster trial was viewed by more than 50,000 spectators who visited the courtroom over the course of the two-week trial. Clearly, a sensationalism and celebrity surrounded both trials and the reliance upon forensic evidence was critical in both cases, although the Webster case involved a more primitive and undeveloped era of forensic science (PBS, "Parkman"). A key difference in the trials was obviously the fact that Simpson was provided with an effective legal defense as opposed to the court-appointed attorneys who provided a weak defense for Webster (Morris 1967, 156–166).

 Dr. John W. Webster

John W. Webster was born on May 20, 1793, in Boston, Massachusetts. Dr. Webster was a professor of chemistry and mineralogy at Harvard Medical College and had even earned his medical degree from Harvard in 1815. Webster's family was connected to many wealthy and educated elites within Boston society in the 19th century. Webster's grandfather made a great deal of money as a merchant but the family fortune was gone by the time that Webster had started his private practice as a physician. In order to provide a living for his family, Webster ended his medical practice and took employment as an instructor of chemistry at Harvard Medical College in 1824 where he earned roughly $1,000 a year (PBS, "Webster").

Webster's financial problems began when he built a mansion that he could not afford for his wife and daughters in Cambridge, Massachusetts. After Webster lost the mansion, he moved his family into a more modest house in Cambridge. Webster always seemed to be borrowing money from his friends and he accumulated a large amount of debt over the years, which became a source of embarrassment for the family (Morris 1976, 163–166). Webster was quoted as saying that he blamed his debt on his father who never gave him a proper allowance so he never understood how to manage money; his chemistry lectures which, at the time, required instructors to pay for supplies and materials out of their own pockets; and his wife and daughters whom he constantly spoiled with extravagant items (PBS, "Webster").

References

Cozzens, James Gould. *A Rope for Dr. Webster.* Columbia: Bruccoli-Clark Layman, 1976.

Dershowitz, Alan. *America on Trial: Inside the Legal Battles that Transformed Our Nation—From the Salem Witches to the Guantanamo Detainees.* New York: Warner Books, 2004.

Morris, Richard. *Fair Trial: Fourteen Who Stood Accused, from Anne Hutchinson to Alger Hiss.* New York: Harper and Row, 1967, pp. 156–203.

PBS. "People & Events: John White Webster (1793–1850)." *Murder at Harvard.* http://www.pbs.org/wgbh/amex/murder/peopleevents/p_webster.html (accessed February 27, 2009).

PBS. "People & Events: The Murder of Dr. Parkman." *Murder at Harvard.* http://www.pbs.org/wgbh/amex/murder/peopleevents/e_murder.html (accessed February 27, 2009).

Schama, Simon. *Dead Certainties: Unwarranted Speculations.* New York: Vintage, 1992.

Sullivan, Robert. *The Disappearance of Dr. Parkman.* Boston: Little, Brown and Company, 1971.

Thomson, Helen. *Murder at Harvard.* New York: Houghton Mifflin, 1971.

Missouri v. Celia, a Slave (1855)

In 1855, a slave named Celia in Missouri was charged with murdering her master who had consistently raped her over a number of years. The murder trial of *Missouri v. Celia,* a Slave, demonstrated that black slave women in the United States in the pre–Civil War era had no protection under the law from sexual assault by their masters. Even though Missouri law supposedly protected all women from rape, a black woman raped by her slave owner could not defend herself because she was considered the property of her master. The Celia murder trial was conducted within the United States when the country was on the verge of a civil war over the issue of slavery (Gordon-Reed 2002, 48–60).

In 1850, Robert Newsom purchased a 14-year-old slave girl named Celia. Because Newsom's wife had recently died, he decided that the slave girl could assist his daughters with some of the household chores (McLaurin 1999, 21–24). Newsom purchased Celia in Audrain County, Missouri, and raped Celia for the first time as he was transporting her back to his farm in Calloway County, Missouri. Newsom had Celia live in a small cabin near his farm, and he fathered two children with Celia over a five-year period (24–35).

Celia fell in love with a fellow slave named George and when she became pregnant again she was uncertain whether George or Newsom was the father of her unborn child. George then told Celia that he would no longer stay in a relationship with her if she continued to allow Newsom to have sexual relations with her (McLaurin 1999, 29–33). At this time, Celia asked Newsom's two daughters to talk to their father about leaving her alone (Gordon-Reed 2002, 51).

On June 23, 1855, Celia asked Newsom to leave her alone but he stated that he would be visiting her in the cabin that evening. When Newsom arrived at the cabin and approached Celia, she hit him twice in the head with a heavy stick and he fell dead to the floor. Celia then spent the rest of the night burning Newsom's body in the fireplace and hiding the remaining bones under the floor of the cabin (McLaurin 1999, 34–37).

On the day after the murder, Newsom's family and friends questioned George, the slave involved in the relationship with Celia, about the whereabouts of Robert Newsom. George told them that Celia was involved in the disappearance of Newsom. Celia eventually signed a confession that she unintentionally committed the murder of Newsom when he made sexual advances toward her. Celia was arrested on June 25, 1855, and taken to the Calloway County jail (McLaurin 1999, 42–52).

When the murder trial of Celia began on October 9, 1855, she was represented by three court-appointed attorneys. Because slaves were not allowed to testify in criminal court in the 19th century, Celia's story was told to the court by persons who had interviewed Celia about her relationship with Robert Newsom. Celia's attorneys tried to convey to the jury that Celia had acted in self-defense in the murder of Newsom; however, the witnesses provided vague testimony about the relationship of Celia and Newsom, and prosecutors were fairly effective at preventing the motive of self-defense from being considered by the jury (McLaurin 1999, 92–122).

Under a Missouri statute of 1845, a woman had the right to defend herself if she was being sexually assaulted, even if she murdered her assailant (PBS, "Missouri statute of 1845"). However, when one of Celia's attorneys attempted to have Judge William Hall inform the jury that a black slave woman should be treated equally as a free white woman under the Missouri law, Judge Hall refused to provide these instructions to the jury (PBS, "Missouri v. Celia").

Under the Missouri Slave Code of 1804, there was no difference between a slave and personal property (PBS, "Missouri Slave Code"). Therefore, Judge Hall instructed the jury that Newsom could not have raped Celia because she was his property and the owner of property could not intrude upon his own property (PBS, "Missouri v. Celia").

On October 10, 1855, the jury of 12 white men returned a verdict of guilty against Celia, and Judge Hall sentenced her to be hanged for the crime of murder. Under Missouri law, a pregnant woman could not be executed so the hanging was scheduled for November 16, 1855, when Celia would have already given birth to her child. The court records indicate that Celia gave birth to a stillborn child while awaiting her execution (McLaurin 1999, 118–122).

Celia's case was appealed to the Missouri Supreme Court based upon her attorneys' claims that Judge Hall had exercised prejudice in his rulings and also because he failed to instruct the jury about Celia's motive of self-defense (McLaurin 1999, 123–127). While the Missouri Supreme Court agreed to hear Celia's appeal, they refused to issue a stay of execution for Celia to prevent her hanging before the Missouri Supreme Court could actually hear her case. A number of citizens from Calloway County helped Celia escape temporarily from the jail in order to prevent her execution on November 16, 1855; however, she was later returned to authorities and a new execution date was scheduled. The Missouri Supreme Court finally ruled against the appeal of Celia and she was hanged on December 21, 1855, at the age of 19 (McLaurin 1999, 124–136).

The decision in the case of *Missouri v. Celia,* a Slave, was significant because, at the time, the entire country was forcefully engaged in a debate over the issue of slavery. Celia and her attorneys courageously challenged a system where the law had a limited effect over the behavior of paternalistic slave owners who routinely forced female slaves into sexual relationships (Gordon-Reed 2002, 54–55). Interestingly, the Missouri Supreme Court also ruled in favor of slavery in the infamous *Dred Scott v. Sanford* (1857) case that was eventually appealed to the U.S. Supreme Court. The U.S. Supreme Court upheld the Missouri Supreme

Court's decision in the *Dred Scott* case by holding that Congress could not force states to be "free states" and blacks could not sue for their freedom in federal court because they were not citizens under the U.S. Constitution. The *Dred Scott* decision has been cited by historians and legal scholars as one of the main causes of the Civil War (26–47).

References

Brownmiller, Susan. *Against Our Will: Men, Women, and Rape.* New York: Ballantine Books, 1993.

Fox-Genovese, Elizabeth. *Within the Plantation Household: Black and White Women of the Old South.* Chapel Hill: University of North Carolina Press, 1988.

Gordon-Reed, Annette, ed. *Race on Trial: Law and Justice in American History.* New York: Oxford University Press, 2002.

McLaurin, Melton A. *Celia: A Slave.* New York: Avon Books, 1999.

PBS. "Legal Rights and Government: Missouri v. Celia." *Slavery and the Making of America.* http://www.pbs.org/wnet/slavery/experience/legal/feature2c.html (accessed March 1, 2009).

PBS. "Missouri Slave Code of 1804." *Slavery and the Making of America.* http://www.pbs.org/wnet/slavery/experience/legal/p_feature2_law1.html (accessed March 1, 2009).

PBS. "Missouri Statute of 1845, article 2, section 29." *Slavery and the Making of America.* http://www.pbs.org/wnet/slavery/experience/legal/p_feature2_law1.html (accessed March 1, 2009).

Smith, Clay J., ed. *Rebels in Law: Voices in History of Black Women Lawyers.* Ann Arbor: University of Michigan Press, 2000.

Dred Scott Trials (1847–1857)

The case of Dred Scott involved two state trials in 1847 and 1850 and ended with a landmark decision by the U.S. Supreme Court, *Dred Scott v. Sanford* (1857). Dred Scott was a slave who sought his freedom because he had lived for a significant period of time within free territory where slavery was prohibited. However, while the case concerned the important issue of Scott's freedom, it also dealt with the U.S. Supreme Court striking down for the first time a major federal law as unconstitutional and definitely contributed to the conflict over slavery and the onset of the Civil War in the United States (Maltz 2007, 2–3).

Dred Scott was born around 1800 and immediately became a slave because his parents were the property of the Blow family in Virginia (Maltz 2007, 60). In 1830, Scott moved to St. Louis, Missouri, with the Blow family, but was eventually sold to a U.S. Army doctor named John Emerson (Fehrenbacher 2001, 239–241). Scott traveled frequently with Dr. Emerson to military facilities in Illinois and Wisconsin where slavery was prohibited according to the Missouri Compromise of

1820 (240–249). The U.S. Congress passed the Missouri Compromise as part of an agreement because of a split between the proslavery and antislavery members of Congress. According to the agreement, Missouri could enter into the Union as a slave state and Maine could enter into the Union as a free state but all of the western territory north of the 36 degree parallel, with the exception of Missouri, had to be free territory (107–113).

Because Dred Scott was illiterate, he was not aware that he could claim his freedom, even though he lived for nine years in free territories, such as Illinois and Wisconsin (Maltz 2007, 61–63). During his stay in the free territories, Scott met his wife, Harriet, who was also a slave (Finkelman 1997, 15–16). When Scott and his wife returned to St. Louis in 1842 with the Emerson family, Dr. Emerson passed away and Emerson's wife, Irene, decided to contract out Scott, his wife, and their two children to provide manual labor to another family who owned a grocery store (Maltz 2007, 63).

In 1846, Scott decided to file a lawsuit in court to sue for his family's freedom. It is uncertain exactly why Scott decided to sue for his freedom at this time. Scott may have been encouraged by antislavery groups in Missouri to sue for his freedom because he had lived in free territory or perhaps he was unhappy with being hired out to work for another family. One story also suggests that Scott did try to buy his freedom from Irene Emerson for $300 but she declined the offer, and the refusal most likely angered Scott (Fehrenbacher 2001, 249–252).

Because Scott had virtually no money, he and his family were supported financially in his lawsuit by a family minister as well as his previous owners, the Blow family. Scott filed his lawsuit initially in state court claiming that he should be granted freedom because he lived for an extended period in Illinois and Wisconsin (Fehrenbacher 2001, 128–129).

The first trial was held in the St. Louis circuit court in 1847. Scott lost the case because important testimony was dismissed as hearsay that would have proven that Scott was owned by the Emerson family. Even though it was clear by law that Scott had lived in free territory and should be granted his freedom, the jury had to rule against Scott because the legal issue of ownership of Scott as a slave was not resolved. However, the judge presiding in the first trial ruled in favor of granting a second trial because he felt that the important issue of a Scott's freedom should not be decided based upon a legal technicality, such as inadmissible testimony (PBS, "Dred Scott"; Blue and Naden 2005, 18–22).

The second trial was also held in the St. Louis Circuit Court in 1850. In the second trial, Scott's attorneys introduced evidence that he had, in fact, lived in free territory and additional testimony was introduced to prove that Scott was owned by the Emerson estate. The jury ruled in favor of Scott and he was to be granted his freedom (PBS, "Dred Scott").

However, because slaves were valuable property, Irene Emerson appealed the ruling to the Missouri Supreme Court. The three justices on the Missouri Supreme

Court had been looking for a case that would reinforce their proslavery positions because the issue of slavery had become such a divisive issue in the state of Missouri. Therefore, the Missouri Supreme Court issued a unanimous decision against Scott and held that he should be returned to slavery. In the 1851 state elections, Missouri voters replaced two of the three justices on the Missouri Supreme Court and Scott's attorneys resubmitted the lawsuit but the Missouri Supreme Court again ruled against Scott by a vote of 2–1 (Maltz 2007, 67–75).

In 1853, Scott's supporters provided legal and financial assistance and encouraged him to file his lawsuit in federal district court (Fehrenbacher 2001, 140–142). At this time, the ownership of Scott had been transferred to Irene Emerson's brother, John Sanford, a wealthy businessman who held strong views in favor of slavery. The lawsuit filed in federal district court was almost identical to the state cases, but Scott did ask for $9,000 in civil damages, and Sanford's attorneys introduced the legal argument that Scott should not have his claim heard in federal court because, as an African American, he was not a citizen under the U.S. Constitution. The federal district court ruled in favor of Sanford, and Scott remained a slave for the time being (Fehrenbacher 2001, 127–146).

In 1854, Scott's attorneys appealed the case to the U.S. Supreme Court (Maltz 2007, 75). In February 1856, the justices heard legal arguments from the attorneys and, finally, the U.S. Supreme Court ruled in favor of Sanford in 1857 by holding that Scott was not a free citizen with rights under the U.S. Constitution (Blue and Naden 2005, 7–8; see also entry below).

After the decision was handed down in *Dred Scott v. Sanford* (1857), Irene Emerson's second husband, Calvin Chafee, a Massachusetts' congressman, received an enormous amount of bad publicity because, oddly enough, he was an antislavery member of Congress. Chafee transferred ownership of Scott and his family back to the Blow family immediately after the U.S. Supreme Court ruling. At her request, Irene Emerson was given some financial compensation for agreeing to the transfer of ownership (Fehrenbacher 140–143; 231–232). Under Missouri law, the Blow family, as citizens of Missouri, had the legal authority to grant the Scott family their freedom. On May 26, 1857, Dred Scott and his family appeared in the St. Louis Circuit Court and were declared free persons under the law (Finkelman 1997, 3).

The *Dred Scott v. Sanford* decision stands today as perhaps the most embarrassing ruling ever handed down by the U.S. Supreme Court. The decision clearly harmed the image and power of the judiciary in its attempt to become a respectable branch of government within the developmental years of the U.S. political system. Most notably, it contributed significantly to the tension surrounding the issue of slavery and helped the country move one step closer to a civil war. The case has been cited repeatedly by legal scholars as an example of how the courts should exercise judicial restraint, particularly where political questions are involved or else risk damaging the reputation of the courts, judges, and the law itself (Finkelman 1997, 4–7; Blue and Naden 2005, 70–91).

 ### Dred Scott v. Sanford (1857)

In 1857, Chief Justice Roger Taney issued his ruling in a written opinion for the U.S. Supreme Court in the case of *Dred Scott v. Sanford*. Chief Justice Taney held that Scott had no right to file the claim in federal court because African Americans did not have citizenship under the U.S. Constitution. In addition, Taney ruled that Scott could not claim his freedom due to the fact that he had lived in Illinois and Wisconsin because Congress lacked the power to ban slavery in these territories. Therefore, the Missouri Compromise of 1820 was struck down as unconstitutional. In effect, Scott's freedom depended only upon the state law of Missouri which endorsed slavery as legal. In his opinion, Taney actually discussed the inferiority of African Americans compared to white persons and noted that African Americans deserved no respect from whites (Blue and Naden 2005, 7–8).

References

Blue, Rose, and Corrine J. Naden. *Dred Scott: Person or Property?* Tarrytown, NY: Benchmark Books, 2005.

Ehrlich, Walter. *They Have No Rights: Dred Scott's Struggle For Freedom.* Westport, CT: Greenwood Press, 1979.

Fehrenbacher, Don E. *Slavery, Law, & Politics: The Dred Scott Case in Historical Perspective.* New York: Oxford University Press, 2001.

Finkelman, Paul. *Dred Scott v. Sanford: A Brief History With Documents.* New York: Bedford/St. Martin's, 1997.

January, Brendan. *Dred Scott Decision.* New York: Children's Press, 1998.

Kaufman, Kenneth C. *Dred Scott's Advocate: A Biography of Roswell M. Field.* Columbia: University of Missouri Press, 1996.

Maltz, Eric. M. *Dred Scott and the Politics of Slavery.* Lawrence: University Press of Kansas, 2007.

PBS. "People and Events: Dred Scott's Fight for Freedom (1846–1857)." *Africans in America.* http://www.pbs.org/wgbh/aia/part4/4p2932.html (accessed February 28, 2009).

Scott v. Sandford (1857)*

Mr. Chief Justice Taney delivered the opinion of the court. . . .

The plaintiff in error, who was also the plaintiff in the court below, was, with his wife and children, held as slaves by the defendant in the State of Missouri, and

---

*Note to reader: Sanford was misspelled in this final report issued by the Supreme Court.

he brought this action in the Circuit Court of the United States for that district to assert the title of himself and his family to freedom.

The declaration is in the form usually adopted in that State to try questions of this description, and contains the averment necessary to give the court jurisdiction; that he and the defendant are citizens of different States; that is, that he is a citizen of Missouri, and the defendant a citizen of New York.

The defendant pleaded in abatement to the jurisdiction of the court, that the plaintiff was not a citizen of the State of Missouri, as alleged in his declaration, being a negro of African descent, whose ancestors were of pure African blood and who were brought into this country and sold as slaves.

To this plea the plaintiff demurred, and the defendant joined in demurrer. The court overruled the plea, and gave judgment that the defendant should answer over. And he thereupon put in sundry pleas in bar, upon which issues were joined, and at the trial the verdict and judgment were in his favor. Whereupon the plaintiff brought this writ of error . . .

The words "people of the United States" and "citizens'" are synonymous terms, and mean the same thing. They both describe the political body who, according to our republican institutions, form the sovereignty and who hold the power and conduct the Government through their representatives. They are what we familiarly call the "sovereign people," and every citizen is one of this people, and a constituent member of this sovereignty. The question before us is whether the class of persons described in the plea in abatement compose a portion of this people, and are constituent members of this sovereignty? We think they are not, and that they are not included, and were not intended to be included, under the word "citizens" in the Constitution, and can therefore claim none of the rights and privileges which that instrument provides for and secures to citizens of the United States. On the contrary, they were at that time considered as a subordinate and inferior class of beings who had been subjugated by the dominant race, and, whether emancipated or not, yet remained subject to their authority, and had no rights or privileges but such as those who held the power and the Government might choose to grant them . . .

. . . Each State may still confer [rights and privileges] upon an alien, or anyone it thinks proper, or upon any class or description of persons, yet he would not be a citizen in the sense in which that word is used in the Constitution of the United States, nor entitled to sue as such in one of its courts, nor to the privileges and immunities of a citizen in the other States. The rights which he would acquire would be restricted to the State which gave them. The Constitution has conferred on Congress the right to establish an uniform rule of naturalization, and this right is evidently exclusive, and has always been held by this court to be so. Consequently, no State, since the adoption of the Constitution, can, by naturalizing an alien, invest him with the rights and privileges secured to a citizen of a State under the Federal Government, although, so far as the State alone was concerned, he would undoubtedly be entitled to the rights of a citizen and clothed with all the rights and immunities which the Constitution and laws of the State attached to that character.

It is very clear, therefore, that no State can, by any act or law of its own, passed since the adoption of the Constitution, introduce a new member into the political community created by the Constitution of the United States. It cannot make him a member of this community by making him a member of its own. And, for the same reason, it cannot introduce any person or description of persons who were not intended to be embraced in this new political family which the Constitution brought into existence, but were intended to be excluded from it. . . .

In the opinion of the court, the legislation and histories of the times, and the language used in the Declaration of Independence, show that neither the class of persons who had been imported as slaves nor their descendants, whether they had become free or not, were then acknowledged as a part of the people, nor intended to be included in the general words used in that memorable instrument. . . .

But so far as mere rights of person are concerned, the provision in question is confined to citizens of a State who are temporarily in another State without taking up their residence there. It gives them no political rights in the State as to voting or holding office, or in any other respect. For a citizen of one State has no right to participate in the government of another. But if he ranks as a citizen in the State to which he belongs, within the meaning of the Constitution of the United States, then, whenever he goes into another State, the Constitution clothes him, as to the rights of person, with all the privileges and immunities which belong to citizens of the State. And if persons of the African race are citizens of a State, and of the United States, they would be entitled to all of these privileges and immunities in every State, and the State could not restrict them, for they would hold these privileges and immunities under the paramount authority of the Federal Government, and its courts would be bound to maintain and enforce them, the Constitution and laws of the State to the contrary notwithstanding. And if the States could limit or restrict them, or place the party in an inferior grade, this clause of the Constitution would be unmeaning, and could have no operation, and would give no rights to the citizen when in another State. He would have none but what the State itself chose to allow him. This is evidently not the construction or meaning of the clause in question. It guarantees rights to the citizen, and the State cannot withhold them. And these rights are of a character and would lead to consequences which make it absolutely certain that the African race were not included under the name of citizens of a State, and were not in the contemplation of the framers of the Constitution when these privileges and immunities were provided for the protection of the citizen in other States. . . .

No one, we presume, supposes that any change in public opinion or feeling, in relation to this unfortunate race, in the civilized nations of Europe or in this country, should induce the court to give to the words of the Constitution a more liberal construction in their favor than they were intended to bear when the instrument was framed and adopted. Such an argument would be altogether inadmissible in any tribunal called on to interpret it. If any of its provisions are deemed unjust, there is a mode prescribed in the instrument itself by which it may be amended; but while it remains unaltered, it must be construed now as it was understood at the time of its adoption. It is not only the same in words, but the same in meaning, and delegates the same powers to the Government, and reserves and secures the same rights and privileges to the citizen; and as long as it continues to exist in its present form, it speaks not only in the same words, but with the same meaning and intent with which it spoke when it came from the hands of its framers and was voted on and adopted by the people of the United States. Any other rule of construction would abrogate the judicial character of this court, and make it the mere reflex of the popular opinion or passion of the day. This court was note created by the Constitution for such purposes. Higher and graver trusts have been confided to it, and it must not falter in the path of duty. . . .

Upon these considerations, it is the opinion of the court that the act of Congress which prohibited a citizen from holding and owning property of this kind in the territory of the United States north of the line therein mentioned is not warranted by the Constitution, and is therefore void, and that neither Dred Scott himself nor any of his family were made free by being carried into this territory, even if they had been carried there by the owner with the intention of becoming a permanent resident. . . .

. . . As Scott was a slave when taken into the State of Illinois by his owner, and was there held as such, and brought back in that character, his status as free or slave depended on the laws of Missouri, and not of Illinois. . . .

Mr. Justice Curtis dissenting. . . .

I can find nothing in the Constitution which, *proprio vigore,* deprives of their citizenship any class of persons who were citizens of the United States at the time of its adoption, or who should be native-born citizens of any State after its adoption, nor any power enabling Congress to disfranchise persons born on the soil of any State, and entitled to citizenship of such State by its Constitution and laws. And my opinion is that, under the Constitution of the United States, every free person born on the soil of a State, who is a citizen of that State by force of its Constitution or laws, is also a citizen of the United States. . . .

It has been often asserted that the Constitution was made exclusively by and for the white race. It has already been shown that, in five of the thirteen original States, colored persons then possessed the elective franchise, and were among those by whom the Constitution was ordained and established. If so, it is not true, in point of fact, that the Constitution was made exclusively by the white race. And that it was made exclusively for the white race is, in my opinion, not only an assumption not warranted by anything in the Constitution, but contradicted by its opening declaration that it was ordained and established by the people of the United States, for themselves and their posterity. And as free colored persons were then citizens of at least five States, and so in every sense part of the people of the United States, they were among those for whom and whose posterity the Constitution was ordained and established. . . .

The Trial of John Brown (1859)

Virginia v. John Brown was a case heard in October 1859 to prosecute abolitionist John Brown for his involvement in a plan to start an armed slave revolt by raiding a federal arsenal at Harper's Ferry, Virginia. The event resulted in the deaths of 7 people and injuries to 10 others. John Brown was tried and executed in 1859 for attempting to inspire the slave revolt in northern Virginia and his death ultimately increased the divisions of the North and South over the issue of slavery and helped Abraham Lincoln win the 1860 presidential election. Most importantly, Brown took a strong moral stand against slavery at a time when most political leaders lacked the courage to deal with the issue and he felt justified in using violence and risking his own life to force the country to confront the evils of slavery. In the end, Brown became probably the most controversial individual in America in the 19th century (Linder, "John Brown").

Brown began to develop his plan to inspire a slave revolt in the late 1840s. His plan involved using roughly 25 men to rescue slaves from plantations and take them into hiding in the Appalachian Mountains of Virginia. Brown's goal was to establish a colony of slaves in the mountains and motivate persons opposed to slavery in the North to take similar action (Linder, "John Brown").

In 1854, Brown and three of his sons traveled to the Kansas territory to try and make certain that Kansas did not turn into a slave state after Congress passed the Kansas-Nebraska Act of 1854 that permitted slavery to exist in the western territories. The battle over slavery in Kansas was viewed as critical because it would supposedly influence whether other western territories decided to adopt slavery (Peterson 2004, 5–9). Brown's experience in Kansas caused him to become even more radical. Proslavery supporters engaged in political corruption to try and turn Kansas into a slave state and many proslavery proponents committed acts of violence against any person who opposed slavery (Linder, "John Brown").

Brown decided to take matters into his own hands and, on May 26, 1856, he led six other men with weapons into proslavery territory in Pottawatomie, Kansas, and murdered five leaders of the proslavery movement. The murders made Brown a national figure in the antislavery movement and, for the first time, instilled fear into the proslavery leaders who had previously viewed persons in the antislavery movement as pacifists (Morris 1967, 262–263).

In May 1858, Brown traveled to an antislavery convention in Ontario, Canada, where he introduced a draft of an antislavery constitution that would be used to replace the existing U.S. Constitution that supported slavery. At the convention, Brown also proposed raising an army of African American men who would fight a war to end slavery (Morris 1967, 263–264).

On December 20, 1858, Brown and 20 other men participated in a legendary invasion of two farms in Missouri where they helped 12 black men escape slavery by taking them on a 1,000-mile trip during the winter into Canada. Brown quickly became a mythical figure who inspired persons opposed to slavery and caused concern among slave owners throughout the country (Linder, "John Brown").

Finally, Brown decided that it was time to enact his plan of inspiring a slave revolt. The specifics of the plan involved attacking Harper's Ferry, a small town in Virginia (modern-day West Virginia) where thousands of weapons were manufactured and stored by the U.S. government. Brown and roughly 25 men would take the weapons and give them to freed slaves and retreat to the mountains where they would plan repeated invasions to free more slaves who would also be provided with weapons (Linder, "John Brown"; Morris 1967).

On October 16, 1859, the operation to invade Harper's Ferry began but the plan did not go as well as Brown and his recruits had hoped. The slaves became confused when Brown and his followers provided them with weapons and didn't quite believe that he was trying to free them. Amidst the confusion, President James Buchanan and the governor of Virginia received word of the attack on Harper's Ferry from a train that had passed through the area. U.S. soldiers and state militias were ordered to the area and they responded by killing and wounding most of Brown's men. After being cornered by Colonel Robert E. Lee and his military company, Brown was wounded when he was stabbed in a last stand at a fire engine house where he had taken hostages. Brown was arrested with four of his men on the morning of October 18, 1859, and taken to Charles Town, Virginia, where he was charged with treason, encouraging slaves to revolt, and murder (Morris 1967, 264–269).

On October 26, 1859, John Brown's trial began in Charles Town with Brown pleading not guilty to the charges. Because he had been injured during his capture, Brown asked that his trial be delayed, but Judge Andrew Parker denied his request. Therefore, Brown would be required to lie down on a folding bed throughout most of the trial (Linder, "John Brown").

Reporters for the newspapers quickly noted that the trial took on an absurd quality with over 600 spectators yelling and screaming at Brown throughout the trial.

The initial prosecutor in the trial, Charles Harding, had to be replaced because he was an alcoholic and kept showing up drunk at the trial where he often fell asleep. Judge Parker quickly replaced Harding with a new prosecutor, Andrew Hunter (Peterson 2004, 13–30).

Brown's defense attorneys tried to persuade Brown to plead insanity in order to reduce any punishment if he was found guilty of the charges; however, Brown refused to allow his attorneys to pursue the insanity defense. In fact, Brown showed none of the typical symptoms of insanity. Brown appeared calm and connected to reality during the trial as he concentrated completely on the legal proceedings (Linder, "Brown").

Hunter called witnesses to testify before the jury about the actions of Brown and his men on October 16–18 at Harper's Ferry. A train conductor testified how Brown and his men used rifles to take control of the train and made the conductor move the train away from a bridge. One of the train's baggage handlers was apparently shot during the seizure of the train. The conductor also testified about the details of Brown's revolt because he had witnessed an interview with Brown by authorities after he was captured (Linder, "John Brown").

Another witness for the prosecution, Colonel Lewis W. Washington, described how he was taken hostage by Brown and his men. On cross-examination by Brown's attorney, Lawson Botts, Washington did concede that, while Brown and his men took slave owners and their families as prisoners, they treated everyone with respect and promised not to harm any of them. Brown's defense attorneys were trying to establish that, while Brown was obviously guilty of organizing and participating in the raid, he did so in a manner that lacked cruelty and recklessness. Brown's attorneys hoped that this tactic would spare Brown the death penalty (Linder, "John Brown").

However, a few of the witnesses did testify that Brown threatened bodily harm to persons if they did not cooperate. For example, a slave owner, John Allstadt, testified that he had been threatened by Brown's men and he also saw Brown fire upon military soldiers prior to his capture in the engine house where the hostages, including Allstadt, were being held. Allstadt went as far as saying that he thought Brown had murdered at least one soldier. Under cross-examination, Allstadt noted that he was not absolutely certain whether Brown killed the soldier. However, while Brown may not have murdered anyone himself, Brown's men did murder 7 persons and wounded 10 in the raid on Harper's Ferry. The prosecution concluded by using Brown's draft of the antislavery Constitution as proof that he had a larger plan to cause a revolution and argued that his words and actions did constitute treason and resulted in the deaths of several citizens of Virginia (Linder, "John Brown"; Peterson 2004, 272–278).

The defense attorneys for Brown also called witnesses who described how Brown treated the prisoners kindly. For instance, Joseph A. Brewer was one hostage who found Brown to be an honest and respectable person. Brewer noted that Brown even allowed Brewer to leave the engine house to carry an injured person into town for medical attention. Brewer promised Brown that he would return to the engine house as a hostage and he actually honored the promise. Another witness for the defense told of how Brown instructed his men not to shoot anyone unless they were forced to act in self-defense Finally, Captain Simms of the Frederick, Maryland, volunteer unit noted that Brown treated his hostages with respect even though some attempted to antagonize him (Linder, "John Brown").

The most powerful moment of the trial occurred when a soldier named Henry Hunter described how he murdered one of Brown's men, William Thompson. Brown had a very close friendship with Thompson and was visibly shaken by Hunter cruelly bragging about his accomplishment. Brown blurted out in the courtroom that he was not being provided a fair trial and also was denied the testimony of several witnesses because the court had failed to deliver a number of subpoenas. Brown ended his outburst by stating that he was not confident in his defense lawyers. Botts and Green subsequently withdrew as Brown's legal counsel and they were replaced by a 21-year-old lawyer from Boston, George Hoyt, who had no knowledge of the case. Judge Parker decided to postpone the trial for one day in order for two additional lawyers to arrive in town to assist Hoyt in the legal defense of Brown (Linder, "John Brown").

On October 30, 1859, one of Brown's new defense attorneys, Hiram Griswold, presented closing arguments by introducing a technical argument that Brown should not be tried for treason against the state of Virginia because he was a citizen of New York. Griswold also argued that Brown only tried to free the slaves and did not attempt to inspire a revolt as suggested by the prosecution. Finally, Griswold suggested that any deaths that occurred at Harper's Ferry were not murders in the traditional sense of criminal law because the raid at Harper's Ferry was a military conflict (Linder, "John Brown).

The prosecutor, Andrew Hunter, offered closing arguments by stating that Brown had come into the state of Virginia with the intent to murder its citizens. In addition, Brown's antislavery constitution, drafted in Ontario in 1858 to replace the existing U.S. Constitution, proved that he had every intention of creating a revolution and, therefore, he committed treason. Even if Brown did not intend to murder the citizens of Virginia, Hunter stated that it was important for the jury to understand that deaths had occurred in the process of Brown committing a felony. According to the criminal laws of Virginia, Brown's actions still constituted murder (Linder, "John Brown").

On the same day that the closing arguments were delivered, the jury deliberated for less than an hour and returned a verdict of guilty against John Brown. At his sentencing hearing on November 2, 1859, Brown gave an eloquent statement where he asserted that his Christian religion had taught him that it was right and just to take such a strong stance against slavery. Brown ended his statement by noting that, if giving his life would further the cause of ending slavery, he would accept his death along with the millions of slaves who have suffered and died in the United States. Judge Andrew Parker then sentenced Brown to death and he was hanged in Charles Town on December 2, 1859 (Morris 1967, 290–294).

After Brown's execution, Henry David Thoreau and Ralph Waldo Emerson praised Brown and used their literary skills to transform him into a legendary figure (Peterson 2004, 7–16). John Brown's life and death made him a hero and martyr in the eyes of many people who opposed slavery. Brown's actions inspired Northerners to take a stronger stance against slavery and probably caused the Civil War to begin earlier than it would have otherwise. Because of the principled and courageous behavior of John Brown, an entire generation of African Americans probably did not have to experience slavery, and the seeds were planted much earlier in the push for civil rights (Linder, "John Brown").

John Brown

John Brown was born in 1800 in Connecticut to a family that was strongly opposed to slavery. His family practiced a form of Christianity called Calvinism and they did not believe that white people were superior to persons of other races. In fact, when his family moved to Ohio when Brown was a young child, they lived among a large population of Native Americans and Brown had many close friends who were Native Americans. While Brown was traveling with his family in Michigan, he met a slave boy at a home where his family spent the night and he witnessed the cruel treatment of the slave owners toward the young boy. Brown called the experience a defining moment in his life, and it caused him to become very passionate about ending slavery in the United States (Linder, "John Brown").

As a teenager, Brown became even more devoted to his Christian religion and began helping fugitive slaves escape through the Underground Railroad. As Brown grew into adulthood, married, and fathered a large number of children, he and his family were committed to ending slavery and living in African American communities and embracing their culture. Brown was also quoted as saying that he would die for African Americans if necessary (Linder, "John Brown").

During the pre–Civil War era, John Brown was viewed by many people as radical in his antislavery viewpoints. For example, he was kicked out of his church because he demanded that blacks be allowed to sit with him during church services and he continually hid fugitive slaves in his barn as they made their way north through the Underground Railroad (Linder, "John Brown).

Interestingly, Brown admired Nat Turner who led a slave revolt in Virginia in 1831 where many white slave owners and their families were murdered and he also supported the slaves who engaged in mutiny aboard the slave ship, *Amistad,* in 1839. While most people who wanted to end slavery were content to use proper legal channels, Brown was extreme in the sense that he felt it was necessary to use violence to end slavery in America (Morris 1967, 259–260; Linder, "John Brown").

References

Carton, Evan. *Patriotic Treason: John Brown and the Soul of America.* New York: Free Press, 2006.

DeCaro, Lou Jr. *John Brown: The Cost of Freedom.* New York: International Publishers, 2007.

Linder, Douglas O. "The Trial of John Brown: A Commentary." *Famous Trials.* http://www.law.umkc.edu/faculty/projects/FTRIALS/johnbrown/brownaccount.html (accessed March 1, 2009).

Morris, Richard. *Fair Trial: Fourteen Who Stood Accused, from Anne Hutchinson to Alger Hiss.* New York: Harper and Row, 1967, pp. 259–295.

Peterson, Merrill D. *John Brown: The Legend Revisited.* Charlottesville: University of Virginia Press, 2004.

Reynolds, David S. *John Brown Abolitionist: The Man Who Killed Slavery, Sparked The Civil War and Seeded Civil Rights.* New York: Vintage, 2006.

The Dakota Conflict Trials (1862)

In August 1862, the Sioux Indian tribes located in Minnesota were on the brink of starvation because the U.S. government had violated treaties and cheated the Indians out of money and goods that were promised in exchange for the use of their land. In response to their depressed situation, the Sioux tribes began to attack and murder white settlers in order to steal food and supplies as well as to drive whites from Minnesota. The attacks by the Sioux tribes started the Dakota War of 1862 which lasted from August to September of 1862. The war ended with the surrender of the Sioux Indians and a victory for the U.S. military (Linder, "Dakota Conflict"). The subsequent trials of Sioux Indians charged with murdering white citizens were held before a military commission and resulted in the execution of 38 Native Americans. Legal scholars have severely criticized the U.S. government for using the military commission and denying basic rights and due process to the Sioux Indians (Chomsky 1990, 13–98).

On September 28, 1862, Colonel Sibley appointed a military commission to try Sioux tribe members for murder and violence against white settlers (Anderson 1988, 220). The military commission initially was composed of five members: Captain Grant, Colonel Crooks, Lieutenant Colonel Marshall, Lieutenant Olin, Captain Grant, and Captain Bailey. Major Bradley was substituted for Lieutenant Colonel Marshall after only a handful of trials had been held because Marshall had to attend to other military duties (Heard, "Trials of The Prisoners").

Reverend S. R. Riggs provided information to the military commission regarding the crimes committed by the Sioux Indians. He interrogated a number of the half-breeds who were witnesses to the criminal acts. Riggs was very acquainted with the language, culture, and habits of the Indians and he served as a grand jury for the military commission. After Riggs provided the information for the military authorities, the Sioux prisoners were arraigned based upon written charges signed by Colonel Silbey (Heard, "Trials of The Prisoners").

The first person charged by the commission was an African American named Godfrey who had joined with the Sioux Indians in the war effort against the United States. Godfrey was charged with murdering seven whites who were citizens of the United States at New Ulm, Minnesota, on August 19, 1862. After the charges were read, evidence would be introduced to prove the charges, unless a defendant admitted guilt. Several witnesses testified against Godfrey in order to provide evidence that he was guilty of the charges. Godfrey was sentenced to death by the military commission (Heard, "Trials of The Prisoners"). Interestingly, Godfrey testified as a witness against Sioux Indians in 55 of the military trials. The military commission held nearly 400 such trials over the course of several weeks and each proceeded along the same pattern as the Godfrey trial. Over 300 Sioux Indians were found guilty of war crimes and sentenced to death. Even if a tribe member only participated in a battle with a weapon, the defendant was often found guilty and issued a death sentence (Linder, "Dakota Conflict").

Legal scholars have questioned the fairness of the military trials. Defendants were clearly denied due process as some trials were conducted in less than five minutes and insufficient evidence was often used to establish guilt in many cases. The defendants were not allowed legal representation because Colonel Sibley argued that the right to an attorney was not guaranteed in a military trial. The military leaders seated on the military commission also demonstrated prejudice against the Sioux Indians because they had recently fought against the same Indians in the military conflict. Many critics also argued that the trials should have been held at the state level using basic rules of criminal procedure instead of the military trial procedures. The decision to hold military trials was made by Colonel Silbey who lacked the necessary authority. Silbey's decision was based upon the use of a military commission after the Mexican-American War in 1847. However, the Mexican-American War trials were held in a hostile area where martial law had been imposed and the United States did not have a civil court system that was functioning in the occupied area (Linder, "How Fair Were The Dakota Conflict Trials").

As the 303 Sioux Indians convicted of war crimes were about to be executed by hanging, President Abraham Lincoln became concerned about the fairness of the military trials, so he intervened and had his legal assistants review the trial records to determine how many were actually guilty of murder. The review of the court transcripts found that the large majority of the Sioux Indians did not commit murder or violent crimes against the white settlers. In the end, President Lincoln recommended only 39 of the defendants for execution, but later postponed the execution of one of them. President Lincoln had most likely prevented the execution of 265 persons who did not deserve such punishment (Chomsky 1990, 13–14; Gilman 1991, 115–123). On December 26, 1862, 38 Sioux Indians were hanged in public on a single platform in a mass execution (Schultz 1993, 259–264). The remaining Sioux Indians were held in prison for four years where many of them died from disease. The remaining survivors were eventually sent to Nebraska with their families when President Andrew Johnson expelled the Sioux tribes from Minnesota (Linder, "Dakota Conflict").

The Dakota Conflict Trials produced the largest mass execution in the history of the United States (Schultz 1993, 5–6). Many of the Sioux tribes were relocated to parts of South Dakota, while others fled to Canada. Those Sioux that remained in the United States continued to be treated unfairly based upon the broken treaties signed between the Sioux tribes and the American government. Over the next three decades, the U.S. government attempted to assimilate the Sioux into American culture, but most of the Sioux were resistant to the government proposals as they wanted to retain their own history and culture. Military conflicts continued between the Sioux tribes and U.S. military forces such as the Great Sioux War of 1876–1877 where the Sioux and Cheyenne tribes joined together to defeat General Custer at the Battle of Little Bighorn in Montana territory (Gibbon 2002, 124–127). However, the Sioux were finally conquered in the massacre at Wounded Knee, South Dakota, in 1890 (1–14).

 ### Dakota War of 1862

The Dakota War of 1862 was an armed conflict between the United States military and several tribes of Sioux Indians. The war began in August 1862 in the southwestern part of Minnesota near the Minnesota River and was caused by the failure of the U.S. government to honor treaties and agreements with the Indians. The war lasted roughly one month and ended with the surrender of the Indians (Linder, "Dakota Conflict").

The United States government had entered into treaties with the Sioux Indians of Minnesota in 1851 and 1858. In exchange for the U.S. government providing regular payments to Sioux Indians, the Indians would hand over large parts of their land in Minnesota and move to two small reservations in southwestern Minnesota along the Minnesota River. However, a sizable portion of the money and goods promised to the Sioux tribes by the U.S. government was never given to the Indians (Anderson 1988, 19–21). In addition, corruption within the Bureau of Indian Affairs, an executive governmental agency, resulted in part of the money being stolen. Traders and agents who conducted business with Indians also took advantage of the Sioux tribes by overcharging them for goods and supplies. As a result of the debt owed by the Sioux tribes to the traders and agents, the U.S. government often would simply hand over regular payments intended for the Sioux tribes to the traders and agents (Linder, "Dakota Conflict").

To make matters worse, the Native American culture began to break down because, on the rare occasion that payments were handed out, the U.S. government provided payments to individual tribe members. The emphasis upon individual payments and the dependence upon the U.S. government for their livelihood reduced the leadership role of the tribal chiefs and also ended the community lifestyle of the Native Americans where members had worked together on the land to provide food and supplies for the entire tribe. As tensions and conflict increased among the thousands of Indians living on the small congested reservations, the food supply became scarce and starvation and disease were widespread among the Sioux tribes. Consequently, the Sioux Indians turned their anger and resentment toward the white settlers who, for the most part, were insensitive to the conditions on the reservations. For example, a white trader told the Sioux Indians to eat grass when he refused to provide a line of credit in exchange for food until government payments arrived (Carley 2001, 1–7).

On August 17, 1862, when payments from the U.S. government had not arrived on time as usual, four young Sioux Indians went on a hunting trip for food and came across some eggs. One of the young Indians warned that the eggs were the property of a white settler and should be left alone. This angered one of the young Indians who dared the others to join him in attacking the home of the white settler. After the four young Indians murdered five white settlers, they returned to their reservation to tell others about the revenge that they had taken against the whites who were responsible for their circumstances (Carley 2001, 7–10).

The leader of the Sioux tribe, Little Crow, warned that the payments from the government would definitely end because of the bloodshed, and war was certain now that whites had been killed. The tribal council decided to declare war on the white settlers and drive them from the Minnesota territory. Over the course of a few days, the Sioux Indians killed hundreds of white settlers and their families and attacked Fort Ridgley and the community of New Ulm, Minnesota (Carley 2001, 25–32).

On August 23, 1862, Governor Alexander Ramsey of Minnesota organized American military troops under the direction of Colonel Henry Sibley in an attempt to suppress the revolt of the Sioux tribes but, the Sioux tribes had some success in battling roughly 1,500 U.S. military soldiers throughout the early part of September 1862. However, the conflict turned in favor of the U.S. military by the end of September when the Sioux lost over 1,000 Dakota tribe members in the Battle of Wood Lake (Carley 2001, 59–63).

The Sioux tribes were divided about the war and many Sioux Indians, known as "friendlies," assisted in rescuing white settlers who had been captured by the Sioux Indians who favored the war. As the Sioux tribes suffered more and more casualties, the divisions over the war intensified (Schultz 1993, 183–236). When the Sioux tribes fighting against the U.S. forces ran out of food and supplies, most of the Sioux Indians involved in the conflict decided to surrender on September 26, 1862 (Linder, "Dakota Conflict").

References

Anderson, Gary C. *Through Dakota Eyes: Narrative Accounts of the Minnesota Indian War of 1862*. St. Paul: Minnesota Historical Society Press, 1988.

Carley, Kenneth, *The Dakota War of 1862*. St. Paul: Minnesota Historical Society Press, 2001.

Chomsky, Carol, "The United States—Dakota War Trials: A Study in Military Injustice." *Stanford Law Review* 43 (1990): 13–98.

Cox, Hank H. *Lincoln and the Sioux Uprising of 1862*. Nashville, TN: Cumberland House Publishing, 2005.

Gibbon, Guy. *The Sioux: The Dakota and Lakota Nations*. Malden, MA: Wiley-Blackwell, 2002.

Gilman, Rhoda. *The Story of Minnesota's Past*. St. Paul: Minnesota Historical Society Press, 1991.

Heard, Issac. "Trials of the Prisoners." *History of the Sioux War and Massacre*. http://www.law.umkc.edu/faculty/projects/ftrials/dakota/Trials_of_Prisoners.html#Trials%20of%20The (accessed March 17, 2009).

Linder, Douglas O. "The Dakota Conflict Trials." *Famous Trials*. http://www.law.umkc.edu/faculty/projects/ftrials/dakota/Dak_account.html (accessed March 1, 2009).

Linder, Douglas O. "How Fair Were The Dakota Conflict Trials." *Famous Trials*. http://www.law.umkc.edu/faculty/projects/ftrials/dakota/dakfairness.html (accessed March 13, 2009).

Meyer, Roy. *History of the Santee Sioux: United States Indian Policy on Trial*. Lincoln: University of Nebraska Press, 1967.

Schultz, Duane, *Over The Earth I Came: The Great Sioux Uprising of 1862*. New York: St. Martin's Griffin, 1993.

Zabelle-Derounian-Stodola, Kathryn, *The War in Words: Reading the Dakota Conflict Through the Captivity Literature*. Lincoln: University of Nebraska Press, 2009.

The Trial of Lambdin P. Milligan (1864)

The trial of Lambdin P. Milligan who was tried, convicted, and sentenced to death before a military commission during the Civil War resulted in a landmark case before the U.S. Supreme Court. In *Ex parte Milligan* (1866), the U.S. Supreme Court sought to define the powers of the president and Congress during wartime in relation to the basic freedoms of an individual placed in prison without any evidence used to justify his incarceration (Nevins, "Copperhead Conspirator").

Lambdin P. Milligan was an attorney who lived in Huntington, Indiana. Milligan was part of a political group in the North known as "the Copperheads" who supported the Confederate cause at any price. During the Civil War, Milligan was an outspoken critic of the Lincoln administration and its controversial policies (Nevins, "Copperhead Conspirator"). For example, in 1862, Lincoln ordered that any person who was disloyal to the United States would be subject to a trial and punishment by a military commission. Military commissions, also known as military courts, are necessary when a war or revolt has occurred and witnesses, judges, jurors, and prosecutors need to be protected from an enemy attack (Neely 1992, 161–175). Lincoln also decided to suspend the writ of habeas corpus which meant that any disloyal citizen could be imprisoned without any evidence being presented to justify such a detention. The writ of habeas corpus is guaranteed as a basic freedom in the U.S. Constitution. Habeas corpus is Latin for "produce the corpse" in reference to the key piece of evidence in a murder case. Therefore, the government must produce evidence as a justification for imprisoning any citizen. Under the U.S. Constitution, a citizen cannot be arrested, tried, and convicted without the government producing evidence to justify a criminal prosecution (9–11).

In 1864, Milligan and four other individuals were arrested and charged with planning to steal weapons from the Union army and raid Union prison camps in an attempt to free Confederate soldiers. After the liberation of the Confederate prisoners, Milligan allegedly planned to start a revolt to take over the state government of Indiana (Irons 2005, 81).

In the fall of 1864, a military commission tried and convicted Milligan for conspiring to overthrow the government, even though President Lincoln and the federal government had not introduced any evidence against him. Milligan was then sentenced to be hanged for his crimes. Fortunately, Milligan's execution was scheduled for May 1865 and this allowed his case to be argued before the U.S. Supreme Court after the Civil War had ended. One of the three attorneys who argued on behalf of Milligan before the U.S. Supreme Court was James Garfield who would later become the president of the United States in 1881. The main constitutional issue involved in the case of *Ex parte Milligan* was the fact that President Lincoln had suspended the writ of habeas corpus and ordered defendants to be tried in military court beginning in 1862 and Congress had supported these actions by the president during the Civil War, even though the civil courts in Indiana were in operation. In *Ex parte Milligan* (1866), the U.S. Supreme Court ruled that the conviction and death sentence of Lambdin P. Milligan was illegal under the U.S. Constitution (Nevins, "Copperhead Conspirator"; see entry below).

The U.S. Supreme Court decision freed Milligan after he had served 18 months in prison and spared him from being executed. Milligan sued the U.S. military in civil court for false imprisonment and a jury ruled in his favor and awarded him $5. Legal scholars have argued that, because the *Ex parte Milligan* ruling was notably handed down after the end of the Civil War, President Lincoln still had been successful in imprisoning citizens unlawfully during the war (Neely 1992, 160–184). While some scholars viewed the *Ex parte Milligan* as a largely symbolic ruling that proved the weakness of the Supreme Court in confronting a president during wartime, the justices did establish a rule to govern future circumstances and affirmed clearly that civil law was supreme over military authority whenever the civil courts were functioning. The U.S. Supreme Court held firmly that the rights and protections of U.S. citizens must be absolute and are indisputable, unless the courts are in a state of disarray because of a war and martial law has been declared (Nevins, "Copperhead Conspirator").

 ## Summary of *Ex parte Milligan* (1866)

In *Ex parte Milligan* (1866), the U.S. Supreme Court ruled unanimously that the president or Congress did not have the power to establish military courts and suspend the writ of habeas corpus if the civilian courts were operating and functioning within a state. Therefore, Milligan's conviction and death sentence were unconstitutional because Indiana was not in a state of revolt during the Civil War and the Indiana court system was functioning properly. In short, Milligan should have been tried in a normal court of law, not in front of military officers (Nevin, "Copperhead Conspirator").

The justices of the Supreme Court added that, while the federal government does have the power to suspend the writ of habeas corpus during a military revolt when the courts are not functioning, a person can only be placed in prison. The suspension of the writ of habeas corpus does not allow for charges to be filed nor can a citizen be tried, convicted, and executed by a military court without the introduction of credible evidence. Even if Milligan's imprisonment had been lawful, the federal government had no power to hold a trial and issue a death sentence while the writ of habeas corpus was suspended (Irons 2005, 81–86).

Even though the Supreme Court's ruling was unanimous, four of the nine justices joined a concurring opinion where they agreed with the outcome of the Court's decision, but parted with the other five justices in terms of the legal basis for the ruling. The four justices in concurrence argued that Congress should have the authority to suspend the writ of habeas corpus and try citizens before a military court, even in a state where the courts were operating properly. However, the concurring opinion argued that the president should not possess this power. Because five justices are necessary for a majority ruling, the concurring opinion signed by the four justices did not carry any weight as an official holding of the Court (Epstein and Walker 2007, 294–300).

References

Burton, Harold H. *Ex Parte Milligan and Ex Parte McCardle: The Story of a Dramatic Case and its Sequel in the Field of Judicial Review.* s.n., 1954.

Epstein, Lee, and Thomas Walker. *Constitutional Law for a Changing America: Institutional Powers and Constraints.* Washington, D.C.: CQ Press, 2007.

Fisher, Louis. *Military Tribunals and Presidential Power: American to the War on Terrorism.* Lawrence: University Press of Kansas, 2005.

Irons, Peter. *War Powers: How the Imperial Presidency Hijacked the Constitution.* New York: Metropolitan Books, 2005.

Kelley, Darwin N. *Milligan's Fight Against Lincoln.* Hicksville, NY: Exposition Press, 1973.

Neely, Mark E. *The Fate of Liberty: Abraham Lincoln and Civil Liberties.* New York: Oxford University Press, 1992.

Nevins, Allen, "The Case of the Copperhead Conspirator." *Joel Samaha, University of Minnesota: Cases and Other Sources.* http://www.soc.umn.edu/~samaha/cases/milligan_copperhead_conspirator.htm (accessed March 18, 2009).

Justice Davis's opinion for the U.S. Supreme Court in *Ex parte Milligan* (1866)

JUSTICE DAVIS delivered the opinion of the Court:

On the 10th day of May, 1865, Lambden P. Milligan presented a petition to the Circuit Court of the United States for the District of Indiana, to be discharged from an alleged unlawful imprisonment . . .

Milligan insists that said military commission had no jurisdiction to try him upon the charges preferred, or upon any charges whatever; because he was a citizen of the United States and the State of Indiana, and had not been, since the commencement of the late Rebellion, a resident of any of the States whose citizens were arrayed against the government, and that the right of trial by jury was guaranteed to him by the Constitution of the United States . . .

The importance of the main question presented by this record cannot be over-stated; for it involves the very framework of the government and the fundamental principles of American liberty.

During the late wicked Rebellion, the temper of the times did not allow that calmness in deliberation and discussion so necessary to a correct conclusion of a purely judicial question. Then, considerations of safety were mingled with the exercise of power; and feelings and interests prevailed which are happily terminated. Now that the public safety is assured, this question, as well as all others, can be discussed and decided without passion or the admixture of any element not required to form a legal judgment. We approach the investigation of this case, fully sensible of the magnitude of the inquiry and the necessity of full and cautious deliberation . . .

The controlling question in the case is this: Upon the facts stated in Milligan's petition, and the exhibits filed, had the military commission mentioned in it jurisdiction, legally, to try and sentence him? Milligan, not a resident of one of the rebellious states, or a prisoner of war, but a citizen of Indiana for twenty years past and never in the military or naval service, is, while at his home, arrested by the military power of the United States, imprisoned, and, on certain criminal charges preferred against him, tried, convicted, and sentenced to be hanged by a military commission, organized under the direction of the military commander of the military district of Indiana. Had this tribunal the legal power and authority to try and punish this man?

No graver question was ever considered by this court, nor one which more nearly concerns the rights of the whole people; for it is the birthright of every American citizen when charged with crime, to be tried and punished according to law. The power of punishment is, alone through the means which the laws have provided for that purpose, and if they are ineffectual, there is an immunity from punishment, no matter how great an offender the individual may be, or how much his crimes may have shocked the sense of justice of the country, or endangered its safety. By the protection of the law human rights are secured; withdraw that protection, and they are at the mercy of wicked rulers, or the clamor of an excited people. If there was law to justify this military trial, it is not our province to interfere; if there was not, it is our duty to declare the nullity of the whole proceedings. The decision of this question does not depend on argument or judicial precedents, numerous and highly illustrative as they are. These precedents inform us of the extent of the struggle to preserve liberty and to relieve those in civil life from military trials. The founders of our government were familiar with the history of that struggle; and secured in a written constitution every right which the people had wrested from power during a contest of ages. By that Constitution and the laws authorized by it this question must be determined. The provisions of that instrument on the administration of criminal justice are too plain and direct, to leave room for misconstruction or doubt of their true meaning. Those applicable to this case are found in that clause of the original Constitution which says, "That the trial of all crimes, except in case of impeachment, shall be by jury"; and in the fourth, fifth, and sixth articles of the amendments . . .

Have any of the rights guaranteed by the Constitution been violated in the case of Milligan? and if so, what are they?

Every trial involves the exercise of judicial power; and from what source did the military commission that tried him derive their authority? Certainly no part of the judicial power of the country was conferred on them; because the Constitution expressly vests it "in one supreme court and such inferior courts as the Congress may from time to time ordain and establish," and it is not pretended that the commission was a court ordained and established by Congress. They cannot justify on the mandate of the President; because he is controlled by law, and has his appropriate sphere of duty, which is to execute, not to make, the laws; and there is "no unwritten criminal code to which resort can be had as a source of jurisdiction."

But it is said that the jurisdiction is complete under the "laws and usages of war."

It can serve no useful purpose to inquire what those laws and usages are, whence they originated, where found, and on whom they operate; they can never be applied to citizens in states which have upheld the authority of the government, and where the courts are open and their process unobstructed. This court has judicial knowledge that in Indiana the Federal authority was always unopposed, and its courts always open to hear criminal accusations and redress grievances; and no usage of war could sanction a military trial there for any offence whatever of a citizen in civil life, in nowise connected with the military service. Congress could grant no such power; and to the honor of our national legislature be it said, it has never been provoked by the state of the country even to attempt its exercise. One of the plainest constitutional provisions was, therefore, infringed when Milligan was tried by a court not ordained and established by Congress, and not composed of judges appointed during good behavior. . . .

It is claimed that martial law covers with its broad mantle the proceedings of this military commission. The proposition is this: that in a time of war the commander of an armed force (if in his opinion the exigencies of the country demand it, and of which he is to judge), has the power, within the lines of his military district, to suspend all civil rights and their remedies, and subject citizens as well as soldiers to the rule of his will; and in the exercise of his lawful authority cannot be restrained, except by his superior officer or the President of the United States.

If this position is sound to the extent claimed, then when war exists, foreign or domestic, and the country is subdivided into military departments for mere convenience, the commander of one of them can, if he chooses, within his limits, on the plea of necessity, with the approval of the Executive, substitute military force for and to the exclusion of the laws, and punish all persons, as he thinks right and proper, without fixed or certain rules.

The statement of this proposition shows its importance; for, if true, republican government is a failure, and there is an end of liberty regulated by law. Martial law, established on such a basis, destroys every guarantee of the Constitution, and effectually renders the "military independent of and superior to the civil power"— the attempt to do which by the King of Great Britain was deemed by our fathers such an offence, that they assigned it to the world as one of the causes which impelled them to declare their independence. Civil liberty and this kind of martial law cannot endure together; the antagonism is irreconcilable; and, in the conflict, one or the other must perish.

This nation, as experience has proved, cannot always remain at peace, and has no right to expect that it will always have wise and humane rulers, sincerely attached to the principles of the Constitution. Wicked men, ambitious of power, with hatred of liberty and contempt of law, may fill the place once occupied by Washington and Lincoln; and if this right is conceded, and the calamities of war again befall us, the dangers to human liberty are frightful to contemplate. If our fathers had failed to provide for just such a contingency, they would have been false to the trust reposed in them. They knew—the history of the world told them—the nation they were founding, be its existence short or long, would be involved in war; how often or how long continued, human foresight could not tell; and that unlimited power, wherever lodged at such a time, was especially hazardous to freemen. For this, and other equally weighty reasons, they secured the inheritance they had fought to maintain, by incorporating in a written constitution the safeguards which time had proved were essential to its preservation. Not one of these safeguards can the President, or Congress, or the Judiciary disturb, except the one concerning the writ of habeas corpus.

It is essential to the safety of every government that, in a great crisis, like the one we have just passed through, there should be a power somewhere of suspending the writ of habeas corpus. In every war, there are men of previously good character, wicked enough to counsel their fellow-citizens to resist the measures deemed necessary by a good government to sustain its just authority and overthrow its enemies; and their influence may lead to dangerous combinations. In the emergency of the times, an immediate public investigation according to law may not be possible; and yet, the peril to the country may be too imminent to suffer such persons to go at large. Unquestionably, there is then an exigency which demands that the government, if it should see fit in the exercise of a proper discretion to make arrests, should not be required to produce the persons arrested in answer to a writ of habeas corpus. The Constitution goes no further. It does not say after a writ of habeas corpus is denied a citizen, that he shall be tried otherwise than by the course of the common law; if it had intended this result, it was easy by the use of direct words to have accomplished it. The illustrious men who framed that instrument were guarding the foundations of civil liberty against the abuses of unlimited power; they were full of wisdom, and the lessons of history informed them that a trial by an established court, assisted by an impartial jury, was the only sure way of protecting the citizen against oppression and wrong. Knowing this, they limited the suspension to one great right, and left the rest to remain forever inviolable. But, it is insisted that the safety of the country in time of war demands that this broad claim for martial law shall be sustained. If this were true, it could be well said that a country, preserved at the sacrifice of all the cardinal principles of liberty, is not worth the cost of preservation. Happily, it is not so.

It will be borne in mind that this is not a question of the power to proclaim martial law, when war exists in a community and the courts and civil authorities are overthrown. Nor is it a question what rule a military commander, at the head of his army, can impose on states in rebellion to cripple their resources and quell the insurrection. The jurisdiction claimed is much more extensive. The necessities of the service, during the late Rebellion, required that the loyal states should be placed within the limits of certain military districts and commanders appointed in them; and, it is urged, that this, in a military sense, constituted them the theatre of military operations; and, as in this case, Indiana had been and was again threatened with invasion by the enemy, the occasion was furnished to establish martial law. The conclusion does not follow from the premises. If armies were collected in Indiana, they were to be employed in another locality, where the laws were obstructed and the national authority disputed. On her soil there was no hostile foot; if once invaded, that invasion was at an end, and with it all pretext for martial law. Martial law cannot arise from a threatened invasion. The necessity must be actual and present; the invasion real, such as effectually closes the courts and deposes the civil administration.

It is difficult to see how the safety of the country required martial law in Indiana. If any of her citizens were plotting treason, the power of arrest could secure them, until the government was prepared for their trial, when the courts were open and ready to try them. It was as easy to protect witnesses before a civil as a military tribunal; and as there could be no wish to convict, except on sufficient legal evidence, surely an ordained and established court was better able to judge of this than a military tribunal composed of gentlemen not trained to the profession of the law.

It follows, from what has been said on this subject, that there are occasions when martial rule can be properly applied. If, in foreign invasion or civil war, the courts are actually closed, and it is impossible to administer criminal justice according to law, then, on the theatre of active military operations, where war really prevails, there is a necessity to furnish a substitute for the civil authority, thus overthrown, to preserve the safety of the army and society; and as no power is left but the military, it is allowed to govern by martial rule until the laws can have their free course. As necessity creates the rule, so it limits its duration; for, if this government is continued after the courts are reinstated, it is a gross usurpation of power. Martial rule can never exist where the courts are open, and in the proper and unobstructed exercise of their jurisdiction. It is also confined to the locality of actual war.

Lincoln Conspiracy Trial (1865)

The Civil War was an extremely divisive period in the history of the United States. President Abraham Lincoln was forced to take controversial measures to end slavery, win the war for the North, and unite the country. To name a few of his tactics, Lincoln imprisoned citizens who were suspected of being sympathetic to the southern states, even if evidence was lacking. Lincoln also authorized the illegal searches of homes and seizure of private property. Within this political environment, a wide conspiracy developed among supporters of the Confederacy to assassinate Lincoln and high-ranking officials within his administration. The conspirators viewed Lincoln as a tyrant who was forcing the South to bring about major changes in their culture and way of life. In the end, the conspiracy resulted in the deaths of a president and his assassin as well as the military trial and execution of four conspirators involved in the plot (Hanchett 1989, 25–33).

On April 14, 1865, less than a week after the end of the Civil War, John Wilkes Booth assassinated President Abraham Lincoln while the president was attending a play at the Ford Theatre in downtown Washington, D.C. (Hanchett 1989, 53–56). At the same time that Booth was firing the fatal shot that killed President Lincoln, two other conspirators, Lewis Powell and David Herold, attempted to assassinate Secretary of State William Seward. Two additional conspirators, Michael O'Laughlen and George Atzerodt, had been assigned separately to assassinate Secretary of War Edwin Stanton and Vice President Johnson, respectively. However, O'Laughlen and Atzerodt both failed to carry out their individual roles in the plot. Edman Spangler, a theatre stagehand who held a door for Booth as he left the Ford Theatre, was also charged as a conspirator as well as Samuel Arnold who was arrested by authorities after a letter was found in Booth's hotel room containing Arnold's name. The most controversial suspects arrested in the conspiracy were probably Mary Surratt, who was arrested when it was discovered that her boarding house in Washington, D.C. was frequented by the conspirators, and Dr. Samuel Mudd, who was accused of involvement in the conspiracy because he had fixed Booth's leg that had been broken when Booth jumped from the theatre box after shooting Lincoln. In total, eight conspirators were arrested and charged with participating in the assassination plot against Lincoln and his Cabinet members (43–58).

On May 1, 1865, President Andrew Johnson ordered the eight conspirators to be tried before a military commission. A military commission, or military court, is used by the U.S. government during times of war or emergency when a normal civilian trial might be too dangerous because the supporters of the enemy might try to sabotage the trial by rescuing defendants or executing witnesses, prosecutors, or the judge. Therefore, military courts are recommended where military officers conduct the trial in a closed environment with less protection for the rights of the defendants. In the Lincoln conspiracy trial, only a simple majority of the military officers was needed to impose a verdict of guilty and a two-thirds vote was required for a death sentence. President Johnson and Secretary of War Stanton named nine military officers to judge the conspirators involved in the Lincoln assassination plot (Hanchett 1989, 67–68).

The decision to use a military commission was not supported by many high-ranking officials at the time. Gideon Welles, secretary of the navy, and Edward Bates, who served as attorney general under Lincoln, maintained that the use of the military commission to try the conspirators was unconstitutional because it violated the basic principle of due process and provided little protection for the rights of criminal defendants. However, Edwin Stanton, secretary of war, argued for the use of the military commission mainly because he wanted the trial to end quickly with the execution of the conspirators. Stanton felt strongly that the trial and execution should be completed before President Lincoln was buried (Linder, "Assassination Conspirators"). In addition to the eight conspirators, Stanton also wanted to use the military trial as a chance to expose the evils of the Confederacy (Hanchett 1989, 64). Therefore, the military commission also decided to prosecute Booth, who had already been killed by military soldiers in Virginia, as well as President Jefferson Davis of the Confederacy, and other Confederate intelligence leaders. Allegedly, the Confederacy had supported acts of terrorism against the United States, especially towards the end of the war when the Union troops appeared to be close to victory (Linder, "Assassination Conspirators").

President Andrew Johnson realized that the decision to use a military commission was a very sensitive issue, so he asked Attorney General James Speed to draft a legal opinion on the matter. In his opinion, Speed held that the use of the military commission, instead of a civil court, was constitutional because the assassination of Lincoln had occurred prior to the official end of the Civil War. Therefore, the assassination of Lincoln must be considered as an "act of war" against the United States which provided jurisdiction for the War Department to conduct a military trial of the conspirators (Linder, "Assassination Conspirators").

At the beginning of the trial, evidence was introduced by military officers that intelligence agents of the Confederacy, in coordination with Booth and the conspirators, had begun the plot to assassinate Lincoln and members of his Cabinet in the summer of 1864 in order to leave the United States without any leadership.

Witnesses also testified that, in November 1864, John Wilkes Booth and the conspirators had planned to kidnap President Lincoln, take him to Richmond, Virginia, and eventually exchange him for Confederate prisoners being held by the Union military (43–50). Political historians have suggested that, if Booth and the conspirators had carried out the kidnapping or assassination of Lincoln during the Civil War in 1864, it may have turned the tide in favor of the Confederacy. However, because the assassination plot was implemented after the war in 1865 when the country was clearly exhausted from the casualties of four years of bloodshed, Booth and his followers were viewed simply as murderers and criminals (Linder, "Assassination Conspirators").

In regard to the eight conspirators, witness testimony easily established the involvement of Lewis Powell and David Herold in the conspiracy. Powell was identified as the person who stabbed Secretary of State Seward in his home, according to one of Seward's servants (Steers 2001, 126–130). Herold had accompanied Powell to Seward's home on the night of the attack and was also in the company of Booth in Virginia when both were cornered by U.S. soldiers. Herold ended up surrendering prior to the killing of Booth who refused to give in to military authorities (130, 202–209).

Edward Spangler was the employee of the Ford Theatre who held a door for Booth as he escaped after the assassination. Witnesses testified that Spangler had spoken with Booth just hours before the assassination and told other employees at the theatre not to tell anyone in what direction that Booth left on his horse (Steers 2001, 226). While he clearly assisted in Booth's get away, Spangler was viewed by the military commission as having only a minor role, if any, in the overall conspiracy (Hanchett 1989, 66–70).

Samuel Arnold admitted involvement in the aborted plan to kidnap Lincoln in 1864, but Arnold's attorneys denied his participation in the assassination plot (Steers 2001, 218–226). Prosecutors introduced a number of telegrams that connected Michael O'Laughlen to Booth as well as a number of witnesses who testified that O'Laughlen was seen at the home of Secretary of War Stanton on the night prior to the assassination. O'Laughlen allegedly had asked someone where he could find Stanton. Prosecutors also presented evidence that George Atzerodt had been inquiring about the whereabouts of Vice President Johnson two days before the assassination and also met frequently with Booth in Washington, D.C., prior to the assassination (Linder, "Assassination Conspirators").

Critics of the military trial have stated that Mary Surratt's role in the conspiracy was based simply upon guilt by association. A number of witnesses testified that Booth, Herold, and Powell were seen frequently at Mary Surratt's boarding house, and some evidence was introduced to show that Surratt seemed to have some knowledge about the storage of weapons and the escape plan of Booth and the conspirators. Finally, witnesses testified that Surratt had lied about knowing the conspirators when she was initially questioned by authorities (Hanchett 1989, 61–71).

The testimony against Dr. Samuel Mudd was based upon establishing that Mudd knew Booth prior to the assassination and had a close friendship with the assassin. Prosecutors argued that Mudd had lied when he stated to authorities that the first time he met Booth was when he treated his broken leg. Witnesses also testified that Mudd and Booth had been seen together on a number of occasions in the past and that Mudd seemed to know in advance that Lincoln was going to be killed (Linder, "Assassination Conspirators;" Steers 2001, 147–154).

The military trial of the eight conspirators lasted seven weeks, from May 1, 1865, until June 29, 1865. The military commission found all of the eight defendants guilty of conspiracy. Mary Surratt, George Atzerodt, David Herold, and Lewis Powell were sentenced to death by hanging. Samuel Arnold, Michael O'Laughlen, and Dr. Samuel Mudd were given life sentences in a hard labor camp and Edman Spangler was sentenced to six years in prison. President Johnson reviewed the military records of the trial and approved all of the verdicts. On July 7, 1865, the four conspirators who received the death sentence were hanged together, despite attempts by Surratt's lawyers to gain a stay of execution for her. Mary Surratt was the first woman to be executed in the United States (Linder, "Assassination Conspirators").

Mudd, O'Laughlen, Arnold, and Spangler were taken to a military facility in Florida to serve out their prison sentences. In 1867, O'Laughlen died of yellow fever that he contracted while in prison. In March 1869, Mudd, Arnold, and Spangler were pardoned by President Johnson who was leaving office after losing the 1868 presidential election to Ulysses S. Grant (Hanchett 1989, 88–89).

Legal scholars have criticized the actions of the 1865 military commission over the last century and a half. The military commission clearly did not meet the modern-day standards of due process. For example, the defense attorneys for the alleged conspirators were given very little time to prepare a defense. In addition, circumstantial evidence was relied upon to imply guilt; some important evidence was withheld during the trial; all of the defendants were prohibited from testifying on their own behalf; and there was no appeal process. Perhaps the most offensive feature of the military trials in the Lincoln assassination plot was the two-thirds vote that was necessary to impose a death sentence. In the post–Civil War era, the United States changed the requirements for a death sentence to a unanimous vote by the military commission (Steers 2001, 222–223).

John Wilkes Booth

John Wilkes Booth was born on May 10, 1838. He was the 9th of 10 children born to Junius Brutus Booth and his mistress, Mary Ann Holmes.

Booth's father, a nationally recognized Shakespearean actor, was not able to marry his mistress until 1851 because a divorce had not been granted from his first wife whom he had married in England in 1815. The Booth family lived on a large farm in Bel Air, Maryland (History.com, "John Wilkes Booth").

After his father's death in 1852, John Wilkes Booth left military school and became an actor. He made his debut in a Shakespeare play, *Richard III,* at the Charles Street Theatre in Baltimore, Maryland (History.com, "John Wilkes Booth"). Later, Booth signed a contract with a Shakespearean theatre company in Richmond, Virginia and enjoyed a very successful acting career by delivering performances all over the United States. On November 9, 1863, Booth took part in a play called *Marble Heart* at the Washington Ford theatre with President Abraham Lincoln in attendance. During the performance, Lincoln sat in the same theatre box at the Ford theatre where Booth would eventually assassinate him in 1865 (Linder, "John Wilkes Booth").

Booth supported slavery and enlisted in the Virginia militia to assist in the capture of John Brown who had conducted a violent raid on Harper's Ferry in an attempt to rescue slaves. In 1859, Booth witnessed the execution of John Brown (Linder, "John Wilkes Booth"). During the Civil War, Booth worked for the Confederate military as a secret agent smuggling weapons, food, medical supplies, and information from the northern part of the country. Because Booth was a nationally renowned actor, he had been awarded the privilege of traveling throughout the United States without restrictions during the war (Clarke 2006, 20). In 1864, Booth developed a plan to kidnap President Lincoln and trade him for Confederate prisoners of war but, the plan was unsuccessful. After Lincoln won reelection in 1864 and the Civil War ended with a Union victory, Booth plotted the assassination of the president. On April 14, 1865, Booth shot and killed President Lincoln at the Ford Theatre. After the assassination, Booth fled the theatre and went to Virginia where he was tracked down by authorities. Booth was surrounded by government soldiers as he hid in a barn at Garrett's tobacco farm in Port Royal, Virginia. When Booth refused to surrender, he was shot and killed on April 26, 1865 (Linder, "John Wilkes Booth").

Lewis Powell

Lewis Powell was born on April 22, 1844, in Randolph County, Alabama. His father was a Baptist minister, teacher, and farmer. He was the youngest of eight children. He lived the early part of his life in rural Georgia and Live Oak, Florida. As a young boy, he earned the nickname "Doc" because he liked to care for sick animals (Linder, "Lewis Powell").

In 1861, at the age of 17, he enlisted in the Confederate army and joined the 2nd Infantry out of Florida. Powell was wounded and captured by Union soldiers at the Battle of Gettysburg on July 2, 1863. After being transferred from Gettysburg to West Baltimore Hospital, Powell escaped to Virginia with assistance from a volunteer nurse. While in Virginia, he joined a Confederate militia known as Mosby's Rangers and also began work with the Confederate Secret Service (Linder, "Lewis Powell").

In the early months of 1865, Powell supposedly deserted the Confederacy and settled in Baltimore, Maryland. In Baltimore, Powell was arrested for assaulting a maid and was forced to claim allegiance to the Union forces. At this time, Powell also changed his name to "Lewis Paine." In March 1865, a confederate intelligence agent introduced Powell to John Surratt who, in turn, introduced Powell to John Wilkes Booth. Booth had been planning a kidnapping of President Abraham Lincoln and asked Powell to participate. The conspiracy to kidnap Lincoln evolved into the assassination conspiracy. On April 14, 1865, while Booth was committing the assassination of Lincoln, Powell was supposed to assassinate Secretary of State William Seward at his home where he was recovering from an accident in a carriage ride. Powell's attempt to kill Seward failed as he was only able to wound the secretary of state with a knife before Seward's bodyguards intervened to stop the attack (Linder, "Lewis Powell").

Powell was arrested by authorities at Mary Surratt's house on April 17, 1865. At the military trial, Powell's attorney attempted to argue that he was insane but the military commission found him guilty and sentenced him to death. Powell was hanged on July 7, 1865 (Linder, "Lewis Powell").

David E. Herold

David Herold was born in 1842 in Maryland. He was the 6th of 11 children to Adam and Mary Porter Herold (Linder, "David E. Herold"). Herold's father was the chief clerk of the Navy yard store in Washington, D.C. David Herold became a pharmacist and clerked at a number of stores in Washington (Lawson and Howard 1917, 106). While studying at Charlotte Hall Academy, Herold met John Surratt who introduced him to John Wilkes Booth in 1863. Booth asked Herold to join him in the kidnapping of President Abraham Lincoln which turned into an assassination conspiracy. It has been alleged that Herold was supposed to assassinate Vice President Andrew Johnson but Herold did not carry out his part of the assassination conspiracy (Linder, "David E. Herold").

On April 14, 1865, Herold accompanied Lewis Powell to the home of Secretary of State William Seward and he stood outside Seward's home while

Powell attempted to kill the secretary. Herold fled the scene at the Seward house and met up with Booth who had already assassinated Lincoln. Herold assisted Booth in his escape to the Maryland home of Dr. Samuel Mudd where Booth had his broken leg set by the physician. When Herold and Booth were discovered and surrounded at Garrett's farm in northern Virginia by Union soldiers, Herold surrendered to authorities. At the military trial, Herold's attorney tried to convince the military officers that Herold was an immature and simple man who was greatly influenced by John Wilkes Booth to take part in the assassination conspiracy. However, the military commission viewed Herold as a key figure in the assassination plot. He was found guilty and sentenced to death. Herold was hanged along with his fellow conspirators, Mary Surratt, Lewis Powell, and George Atzerodt, on July 7, 1865, in Washington, D.C. (Linder, "David E. Herold").

Michael O'Laughlen

Michael O'Laughlen was born into a family of respected Catholics in Baltimore, Maryland, in 1840. O'Laughlen and John Wilkes Booth were childhood friends who grew up across the street from each other. O'Laughlen was employed as a craftsman of ornamental plaster until he joined the Confederate army in 1861. In June 1862, he was discharged from the military for health reasons and returned to Baltimore to work for his brother's feed and produce company (Leonard 2004, 50).

In August 1864, Booth recruited O'Laughlen to assist in the kidnapping of President Abraham Lincoln. On March 15, 1865, O'Laughlen attended a meeting with Booth and fellow conspirators at the Gautier restaurant in Washington, D.C. At the meeting, a detailed plan was designed to kidnap Lincoln from his carriage as he rode to a matinee performance of a play. However, Lincoln altered his plans and chose to make a speech before some Union soldiers from Indiana (Leonard 2004, 51–53). Another kidnapping plan involved Booth capturing Lincoln at the Ford Theatre while O'Laughlen put out the lights in the theatre but they later determined that the plan was not practical (Linder, "Michael O'Laughlen").

O'Laughlen was arrested by federal authorities three days after the Lincoln assassination and charged with stalking General Ulysses S. Grant with intent to murder him. At the military trial, prosecutors introduced as evidence vague telegrams between O'Laughlen and Booth in an attempt to establish that O'Laughlen was involved in the plan to kidnap Lincoln. While O'Laughlen was in Washington at the time of the Lincoln assassination, historians are divided concerning whether he figured into the assassination conspiracy. Military prosecutors argued that O'Laughlen had planned to assassinate General

Grant by searching for him at the home of Secretary of War Edwin Stanton. On the evening prior to the Lincoln assassination, O'Laughlen was seen at the home of Stanton at approximately 10:30 p.m. by Major Kilburn Knox and two other witnesses. Knox testified that O'Laughlen was wearing dark clothing and a hat when he inquired about Stanton (Linder, "Michael O'Laughlen").

Defense attorney Walter Cox argued that O'Laughlen was innocently walking the streets of Washington to observe the celebration of the Union victory over the Confederate army. Several witnesses also testified to having seen O'Laughlen walking the streets of Washington on the night prior to the assassination of the president. Cox concluded based upon the alibis that the prosecution witnesses must have been mistaken when they testified that O'Laughlen was at the Stanton residence. According to Cox, O'Laughlen contributed nothing to the planning of the conspiracy (Linder, "Michael O'Laughlen").

The military commission returned a verdict of guilty against O'Laughlen and he was sentenced to life in prison. After serving two years in prison at Fort Jefferson in Florida, O'Laughlen died of yellow fever virus in 1867 (Linder, "Michael O'Laughlen").

Mary Surratt

Mary Surratt was born "Mary Jenkins" in 1823 in Waterloo, Maryland. She was educated at a Catholic seminary for girls. At the age of 17, she married John Surratt. In 1853, John and Mary Surratt purchased a large piece of land in Prince George's County, Maryland, roughly 20 miles from Washington, D.C. After her husband built a saloon and post office on their property, it was named Surrattsville. During the Civil War, the Surratt's property was used as a safe haven for Confederate soldiers. John and Mary Surratt had two sons, John Jr., and Issac, and one daughter, Anna. John Jr., the oldest son of Mary Surratt, served as an intelligence agent for the Confederacy. John Surratt Jr. worked closely with John Wilkes Booth, David Herold, Lewis Powell, and George Atzerodt in assisting the Confederacy (Linder, "Mary Surratt").

In 1864, two years after her husband's death, Mary Surratt purchased a home in Washington, D.C., and rented her Prince George's home to a retired policeman, John Lloyd. While living in her new house in Washington, Mary Surratt met frequently with Booth, Powell, and other conspirators involved in the plot to assassinate President Lincoln (Linder, "Mary Surratt").

On April 14, 1865, the day of the assassination, Mary Surratt rented a carriage in the early afternoon and traveled from Washington to Surrattsville with Lewis Weichmann, a friend who had rented a room from her. At Surrattsville, Weichmann saw her speaking with John Wilkes Booth at the Surratt's saloon.

After she returned to Washington in the evening, Weichmann witnessed a second meeting between Surratt and Booth when Booth visited at her home. On April 17, 1865, federal investigators interviewed Surratt at her home and arrested her after discovering evidence linking her to Booth (Linder, "Mary Surratt").

The military commission relied mostly upon the testimony of Lewis Weichmann and John Lloyd in their prosecution of Surratt. Weichmann had witnessed previous meetings between Surratt, Booth, and the other conspirators as well as the two meetings on the day of the assassination between Surratt and Booth. Lloyd, the retired policemen who rented the Surratt home in Surrattsville, had witnessed suspicious events as well. Lloyd testified that Mary Surratt, David Herold, and George Atzerodt had hidden weapons and ammunition inside the Surratt saloon about six weeks prior to the assassination. A few days before the assassination, Surratt told Lloyd that the weapons and ammunition would be needed shortly. On the day of the assassination, Surratt asked Lloyd to get the weapons and ammunition ready because someone would be coming for them later in the evening. After Booth assassinated Lincoln, David Herold and Booth rode on horseback from Washington to Surrattsville to pick up the weapons and ammunition at midnight. Lloyd noted that Booth stayed on his horse because he had a broken leg (Linder, "Mary Surratt").

Frederick Aiken, the defense attorney for Mary Surratt, tried to discredit Lloyd's testimony by maintaining that the retired policeman was an alcoholic and was simply trying to escape conviction himself by blaming Surratt. However, the evidence against Surratt was overwhelming and the military commission found her guilty of conspiracy and sentenced her to death. Five of the nine military officers on the commission recommended that President Andrew Johnson reduce her sentence to life in prison because she was a 42-year-old woman. President Johnson refused to commute Surratt's sentence to life in prison and stated that she was instrumental in devising the plot to assassinate Lincoln. On July 7, 1865, Mary Surratt was hanged along with her fellow conspirators, David Herold, Lewis Powell, and George Atzerodt. She was the first woman to be executed in the United States (Linder, "Mary Surratt").

Samuel Arnold

Samuel Arnold was born on September 6, 1834, in the Georgetown area of Washington, D.C. Arnold's father, George Arnold, was a respected baker. His family later moved to Baltimore, Maryland, where Arnold spent most of his youth. Arnold was a classmate of John Wilkes Booth at the St. Timothy's Military Academy in the early 1850s. Booth and Arnold frequently were in trouble at school. During one episode, Booth and Arnold stole some guns and threatened the teachers at the school. During the Civil War, Arnold enlisted in the Confederate army and served with the Maryland Infantry. He was discharged from the military in November 1861 for health reasons (Leonard 2004, 48–49).

In August 1864, Booth recruited Arnold to take part in the kidnapping of President Abraham Lincoln. At the time, Arnold was out of work and looking for adventure. On March 15, 1865, Arnold, Booth, and the other conspirators planned the kidnapping at Gautier's Restaurant in Washington. The kidnapping was scheduled to take place on March 17, 1865, while Lincoln was traveling by carriage to see a matinee play at the Campbell Hospital. However, Lincoln changed his plans and decided to give a speech to Union soldiers from Indiana and the kidnapping plot could not be carried out by Booth and his conspirators (Leonard, 2004, 51–53).

After the assassination of Lincoln by Booth on April 14, 1865, a search by investigators of Booth's hotel room produced a letter that Arnold had written to Booth on March 27, 1865. On April 17, 1865, authorities arrested Arnold in Old Point Comfort, Virginia, where he was employed as a clerk (Linder, "Samuel Arnold").

During the conspiracy trial, prosecutors introduced Arnold's letter from March 27 as evidence against Arnold. Arnold had written vaguely in the letter that no one was "more in favor of the enterprise" than himself. Prosecutors interpreted the letter as proof that Arnold was involved with Booth in the conspiracy to assassinate Lincoln. Defense attorney Walter Cox argued that Arnold had decided not to participate in the kidnapping of Lincoln by the end of March of 1865 and left Washington for Maryland. Cox maintained that there was absolutely no evidence connecting Arnold to the assassination. Cox argued that, even if Arnold had been involved in a kidnapping plan that never occurred, it was no reason to find him guilty of conspiracy to murder the president (Linder, "Samuel Arnold").

The military commission found Arnold guilty of conspiracy and ordered that he be given a life sentence in prison at Fort Jefferson, Florida. On March 2, 1869, President Andrew Johnson pardoned Arnold. After Arnold was released from prison, he published his confession regarding the kidnapping conspiracy in a book entitled *Samuel Bland Arnold: Memoirs of a Lincoln Conspirator,* written by Michael W. Kauffman. On September 21, 1906, Arnold died of tuberculosis (Linder, "Samuel Arnold").

John Surratt

John Surratt was born in the Congress Heights district of Washington, D.C., on April 13, 1844 to John Surratt Sr. and Mary Surratt. John Surratt had initially planned to join the priesthood by studying at St. Charles College, a seminary school in Catonsville, Maryland. After his father's death in 1862, John Surratt was assigned to operate the post office in Surrattsville, Maryland, a town named after his family (Linder, "John Surratt").

In 1863, Surratt began working as a spy for the Confederate State Department. Surratt provided information for Confederate vessels traveling on the Potomac River and also relayed messages about the movements of Union troops to leaders of the Confederacy in Richmond, Virginia (Linder, "John Surratt").

After Surratt moved to Washington, D.C, with his mother, he was introduced to John Wilkes Booth by Dr. Samuel Mudd on December 24, 1863. Surratt met with Booth and the other conspirators on March 15, 1865, at Gautier's Restaurant to plan the kidnapping of President Lincoln. At the time of the assassination, Surratt was supposedly in the state of New York on an intelligence operation for the Confederacy. After Surratt heard that Booth had murdered the president, he left the country for Canada. After his mother, Mary Surratt, was executed on July 7, 1865, for her part in the conspiracy, Surratt left Canada and traveled to Europe and then to Egypt. Surratt was finally identified as one of the conspirators in the assassination as he was traveling through Alexandria, Egypt. He was arrested in November of 1866 and sent back to the United States to stand trial. Unlike the other conspirators who were tried before a military court, Surratt was tried by a civilian court of law (Linder, "John Surratt").

The trial of John Surratt began on June 10, 1867, in criminal court in Washington, D.C., where Surratt was charged as an accomplice in the assassination of the president. The trial lasted for two months with 80 witnesses testifying for the prosecution and 90 witnesses called for the defense. However, the trial ended in a mistrial with the jury voting eight to four in favor of an acquittal. The federal government planned upon a second trial, but eventually dismissed the charges against Surratt in the summer of 1868 (Heidler, Heidler, and Coles 2002, 1909).

After his release from prison, Surratt worked as a teacher at the Rockville Female Academy in Maryland for a short period of time before settling in Baltimore to work for a freight company. In 1870, Surratt began a lecture tour speaking about the Lincoln conspiracy in an effort to tell his side of the story. He admitted that he was involved in the conspiracy to abduct Lincoln on March 17, 1865, but denied any involvement in the assassination. Most importantly, he emphasized that the Confederate government was not involved in the kidnapping or assassination conspiracy (Heidler, Heidler, and Coles 2002, 1909). On April 21, 1916, John Surratt passed away at the age of 72 after contracting pneumonia. He was the last surviving person with a direct connection to the conspiracy involving President Lincoln (Linder, "John Surratt").

Edman Spangler

Edman Spangler was born on August 10, 1825, in York, Pennsylvania, to William and Ann Marie Spangler. Edman's father, William, was the Sheriff of York County and the Spangler family was viewed as respectable within the community. His mother died when he was only five years old and his father remarried to Sarah Lightener. Spangler was not well educated based upon his writing and spelling abilities (Steers 2003, xlvii). He began working as a carpenter and met John Wilkes Booth when he was hired to work for the Booth family in Bel Air, Maryland. (Kimmel 1940, 76).

Throughout the Civil War, Spangler was employed at the Ford Theatre as a carpenter and stagehand where he was known as a heavy drinker of alcohol. While working at the theatre, Spangler became reacquainted with John Wilkes Booth, who worked as an actor. Spangler often took care of Booth's horse when he attended plays or performed at the theatre. Spangler also had agreed to convert a shed in the back of the theatre into a stable for Booth to keep a few horses (Steers 2003, xlviii–xlix).

When Booth arrived at the Ford Theatre on the evening of the assassination, he asked Spangler to watch his horse. Spangler, in turn, asked another employee, Joseph "Peanuts" Burroughs, to tend to the horse. After Booth shot Lincoln in the theatre, Jacob Ritterspaugh, another employee at the theatre, followed Booth out of the theatre and witnessed him ride away on his horse. Spangler allegedly slapped Ritterspaugh across the mouth and told him not to tell anyone which direction Booth left on his horse. On April 17, 1865, three days after the assassination, Spangler was arrested and charged as Booth's accomplice in the assassination (Linder, "Edman Spangler").

At the military trial, Ritterspaugh testified against Spangler, but other witnesses interpreted the slap by Spangler as a way to calm down Ritterspaugh who was yelling about having seen Booth commit the assassination. Other witnesses for the prosecution observed Booth in the back entrance of the theatre calling for Spangler to hold his horse prior to the assassination. Spangler allegedly was heard telling Booth that he would help him all that he could. Another witness testified that Spangler had an opportunity to stop Booth from leaving the theatre but, instead, he allowed the assassin to escape (Linder, "Edman Spangler").

Thomas Ewing provided legal representation for Spangler and maintained that Spangler agreed to assist Booth on the evening of the assassination but he did not know that Booth intended to murder the president. The military commission concluded that Spangler was guilty of serving as Booth's accomplice and he was ordered to spend six years in prison. After serving only 18 months of his sentence at Fort Jefferson in Florida, Spangler was pardoned by President Andrew Johnson on March 2, 1869 (Linder, "Edman Spangler"). After leaving prison, Spangler returned to work at the Ford Theatre until 1873 when his poor health forced him to retire. Spangler was given some farmland by Dr. Samuel Mudd in Maryland and lived on the farm for six years until his death on February 7, 1875 at the age of 49 (Steers 2003, l–li).

George Atzerodt

George Atzerodt was born in Germany on June 12, 1835. He came to the United States with his family when he was eight years old. The Atzerodt family settled on a farm in Germantown, Maryland, roughly 20 miles from Washington, D.C. In 1846, George's father, Johann, sold the farm and moved the family to Westmoreland, Virginia. After his father's death in 1857, George moved to Port Tobacco, Maryland, with his brother and started painting carriages for a living. After the business venture failed, George Atzerodt began working for the Confederacy by taking soldiers and supplies across the Potomac River in a ferry (Steers 2003, lxvi). Atzerodt actually helped John Surratt, a Confederate spy, cross the Potomac River (Linder, "George Atzerodt").

John Surratt introduced Atzerodt to John Wilkes Booth who convinced Atzerodt to join the conspiracy to kidnap President Lincoln which was planned for March 17, 1865. Atzerodt's role in the plot was to help Booth get the abducted president across the Potomac River by hiring a ferryman and using his connections with Confederate spies throughout Maryland who worked along the river (Steers 2003, lxvi).

On the morning of the assassination, Atzerodt met with Booth, David Herold, and Lewis Powell at the Herndon House near the Ford Theatre. Atzerodt was assigned by Booth to assassinate Vice President Andrew Johnson, while Powell and Herold were assigned to murder Secretary of State William Seward. Atzerodt rented a room at the Kirkwood House near the room occupied by the vice president, but was unable to carry out his part in the conspiracy. After having a few drinks at a bar, he wandered around Washington, D.C., until he arrived in the Georgetown district. Atzerodt proceeded to rent a room at the Kimmel House where he went to sleep at 2:00 a.m. Atzerodt left Washington on the following morning and returned to Germantown, Maryland, to hide out at the family farm, which was now owned by his uncle (Steers 2003, lxvii).

On April 20, 1865, Atzerodt was arrested by authorities after an employee of the Kirkwood House reported a suspicious person in a gray coat who had rented a room adjacent to the vice president's room. A search of Atzerodt's room produced a bank book with the name of John Wilkes Booth. Because Atzerodt signed in at the Kirkwood House using his real name, he was quickly connected to the conspiracy (Linder, "George Atzerodt").

At the military trial, Atzerodt's defense attorney, Captain William E. Doster, argued that Atzerodt did not possess the courage to carry out the assassination of Vice President Johnson and Booth was aware of his cowardice. Therefore, it is reasonable to assume that Booth would not have assigned such an important task to Atzerodt. Several witnesses were called by the defense to persuade the military commission that Atzerodt was indeed a coward (Linder, "George Atzerodt").

In order to prove that Atzerodt was part of the conspiracy, the prosecution called John Lee, a detective, to testify about his search of Atzerodt's room which produced Booth's bank book. Other witnesses testified to having seen Atzerodt meeting with Booth on a number of occasions at the Pennsylvania House in Washington, D.C. Finally, John Fletcher testified that Atzerodt invited him out for a drink at the Union hotel on the evening of the assassination and Atzerodt acted in a very excited manner (Linder, "George Atzerodt").

The military commission concluded that Atzerodt was guilty of conspiracy to assassinate the president and sentenced him to be hanged. After the trial, Atzerodt confessed to a minister that he was involved in planning the kidnapping of Lincoln but he was not assigned the role of assassinating the vice president. Atzerodt said that he was only given the task of backing up David Herold who was actually assigned by Booth to assassinate the vice president. On July 7, 1865, Atzerodt was hanged with three other conspirators, Mary Surratt, David Herold, and Lewis Powell (Linder, "George Atzerodt").

Dr. Samuel Mudd

Samuel Mudd was born on December 20, 1833, on a large tobacco plantation in Charles County, Maryland. Mudd was a student at Georgetown College and then graduated with a medical degree from the Baltimore Medical College (McHale 2000, 7–11). Mudd supported the Confederacy and slavery and often expressed his hatred for President Abraham Lincoln (Linder, "Dr. Samuel Mudd").

Immediately after John Wilkes Booth assassinated Lincoln, Booth and David Herold rode their horses to Mudd's home near Bryantown, Maryland, where Mudd had set up his medical practice. After Booth shot Lincoln, he suffered a broken leg when he jumped from Lincoln's theatre box to the stage below. Mudd set Booth's broken leg and secured a pair of crutches for him as well. Booth shaved off his moustache and left with Herold after spending one night at Mudd's residence (Linder, "Dr. Samuel Mudd").

When military authorities tracked Booth's escape path to Mudd's home on April 18, 1865, Lieutenant Alexander Lovett questioned Mudd who claimed that he fixed the broken leg of a man who was a stranger to him. When Lovett asked to search Mudd's home, the wife of Dr. Mudd gave Lovett the boot taken from the broken leg of the stranger. Lovett noticed that Booth's name had been written on the inside of the boot. After Lovett presented a photograph of Booth, Mudd said that he did not recognize him. Mudd was arrested six days later and charged with assisting Booth in his escape after authorities concluded that Mudd's answers to Lovett's questions were not convincing (Linder, "Dr. Samuel Mudd").

During the conspiracy trial, several witnesses testified that Mudd knew Booth before he came to the doctor's home to have his leg treated. This allowed prosecutors to establish that Mudd had lied to investigators about fixing the broken leg of a stranger. Mudd was also easily connected to other conspirators, such as Mary Surratt and her son, John, based upon eyewitness accounts of having seen Mudd in their company on a number of occasions. Lieutenant Lovett testified that Mudd seemed suspicious when he arrived at Mudd's home and began questioning the physician. The prosecution ended its case by calling witnesses, including two slaves from Mudd's home, who heard Mudd make unpleasant statements concerning Lincoln (Linder, "Dr. Samuel Mudd").

Defense attorneys for Mudd tried to argue that most of the prosecution witnesses were lying because Mudd had only met Booth on one occasion before he treated the leg of the assassin. Therefore, it was reasonable to assume that Mudd would not have recognized Booth based on one previous meeting. Mudd's lead attorney, Thomas Ewing, had a difficult time explaining how, after hearing about the assassination, Mudd was not suspicious of a man with a broken leg who arrived at his home in the middle of the night and then shaved his moustache to alter his appearance.

In his closing statement in defense of Mudd, Ewing held that it was not a crime to fix a man's broken leg, even if Mudd knew that Booth was the assassin. Most importantly, Ewing maintained that there was no evidence to suggest that Mudd was part of the conspiracy. Prosecutors countered that Mudd had assisted in the conspiracy by providing directions for Booth and Herold before they left his home (Linder, "Dr. Samuel Mudd").

The military commission found Mudd guilty of conspiracy and issued a life sentence as punishment for the conviction. On route to the federal prison at Fort Jefferson in Florida, Mudd confessed that he knew Booth prior to fixing his broken leg but said that he had lied in an attempt to protect his family. One conspirator, George Atzerodt, claimed in his confession that Mudd was supposed to play an important role in the plan to kidnap Lincoln in March of 1865 (Linder, "Dr. Samuel Mudd").

In 1867, an epidemic of yellow fever swept the federal prison at Fort Jefferson causing the death of Michael O'Laughlen, who was also convicted of conspiracy in the death of Lincoln. In addition, the yellow fever caused the death of the prison doctor and, as a result, Mudd became the new doctor at the prison. In February 1869, Mudd was pardoned by President Andrew Johnson. On January 10, 1883, Mudd died in Waldorf, Maryland, after contracting pneumonia. Mudd was 49 years old at the time of his death (Linder, "Dr. Samuel Mudd").

References

Bishop, Jim. *The Day Lincoln was Shot.* New York: Greenwich House, 1984.

Chamlee, Roy Z. Jr. *Lincoln's Assassins: A Complete Account of Their Capture, Trial, and Punishment.* Jefferson, NC: McFarland and Company, 2008.

Clarke, James W. *Defining Danger: American Assassins and the New Domestic Terrorists.* New Brunswick, NJ: Transaction Publishers, 2007.

Hanchett, William. *The Lincoln Murder Conspiracies.* Urbana-Champaign: University of Illinois Press, 1989.

Harris, T. M. *Assassination of Lincoln: A History of the Great Conspiracy Trial of the Conspirators by a Military Commission.* Boston: William Press, 2008.

Heidler, David Stephen, Jeanne T. Heidler, and David J. Coles. *Encyclopedia of the American Civil War: A Political, Social, and Military History.* New York: W. W. Norton and Company, 2002.

History.com. "Hunt for Abraham Lincoln's Assassin, John Wilkes Booth." *The American Civil War.* http://www.history.com/content/civilwar/the-hunt-for-john-wilkes-booth/john-wilkes-booth-biography (accessed July 29, 2009).

Kimmel, Stanley. *The Mad Booths of Maryland.* Indianapolis: Bobbs-Merrill, 1940.

Lawson, John Davison and Robert Lorenzo Howard. *American State Trials: A Collection of the Important and Interesting Trials Which Have Taken Place in the United States from the Beginning of Our Government to the Present Day.* St. Louis, MO: Thomas Law Books, 1917.

Leonard, Elizabeth D. *Lincoln's Avengers: Justice, Revenge, and Reunion after the Civil War.* New York: W. W. Norton and Company, 2004.

Linder, Douglas O. "Lincoln Assassination Conspirators: David E. Herold." *Famous Trials.* http://www.law.umkc.edu/faculty/projects/ftrials/lincolnconspiracy/herold.html (accessed July 29, 2009).

Linder, Douglas O. "Lincoln Assassination Conspirators: Dr. Samuel Mudd." *Famous Trials.* http://www.law.umkc.edu/faculty/projects/ftrials/lincolnconspiracy/mudd.html (accessed July 31, 2009).

Linder, Douglas O. "Lincoln Assassination Conspirators: Edman Spangler." *Famous Trials*. http://www.law.umkc.edu/faculty/projects/ftrials/lincolnconspiracy/spangler.html (accessed July 31, 2009).

Linder, Douglas O. "Lincoln Assassination Conspirators: George Atzerodt." *Famous Trials*. http://www.law.umkc.edu/faculty/projects/ftrials/lincolnconspiracy/atzerodt.html (accessed July 31, 2009).

Linder, Douglas O. "Lincoln Assassination Conspirators: John Surratt." *Famous Trials*. http://www.law.umkc.edu/faculty/projects/ftrials/lincolnconspiracy/surrattj.html (accessed July 30, 2009).

Linder, Douglas O. "Lincoln Assassination Conspirators: John Wilkes Booth." *Famous Trials*. http://www.law.umkc.edu/faculty/projects/ftrials/lincolnconspiracy/booth.html (accessed July 29, 2009).

Linder, Douglas O. "Lincoln Assassination Conspirators: Lewis Powell." *Famous Trials*. http://www.law.umkc.edu/faculty/projects/ftrials/lincolnconspiracy/powell.html (accessed July 29, 2009).

Linder, Douglas O. "Lincoln Assassination Conspirators: Mary Surratt." *Famous Trials*. http://www.law.umkc.edu/faculty/projects/ftrials/lincolnconspiracy/surrattm.html (accessed July 30, 2009).

Linder, Douglas O. "Lincoln Assassination Conspirators: Michael O'Laughlen." *Famous Trials*. http://www.law.umkc.edu/faculty/projects/ftrials/lincolnconspiracy/olaughlin.html (accessed July 29, 2009).

Linder, Douglas O. "Lincoln Assassination Conspirators: Samuel Arnold." *Famous Trials*. http://www.law.umkc.edu/faculty/projects/ftrials/lincolnconspiracy/arnold.html (accessed July 30, 2009).

Linder, Douglas O. "The Trial of the Lincoln Assassination Conspirators." *Famous Trials*. http://www.law.umkc.edu/faculty/projects/ftrials/lincolnconspiracy/lincolnaccount.html (accessed March 1, 2009).

McHale, John. Dr. *Samuel A. Mudd and the Lincoln Assassination*. Southampton, NY: Heritage Books, 2000.

Roscoe, Theodore. *The Web of Conspiracy*. Englewood Cliffs, NJ: Prentice Hall, 1960.

Steers, Edward. *The Trial: The Assassination of President Lincoln and the Trial of the Conspirators*. Lexington: University Press of Kentucky, 2003.

Steers, Edward Jr. *Blood on the Moon: The Assassination of Abraham Lincoln*. Lexington: University Press of Kentucky, 2001.

Swanson, James and Daniel Weinberg. *Lincoln's Assassins: Their Trial and Execution*. New York: Harper Perennial, 2008.

Lincoln conspirators trial, Charge and Specification (1865)

Charge and Specification against David E. Herold, George A. Atzerodt, Lewis Payne, Michael O'Laughlin, Edward Spangler, Samuel Arnold, Mary E. Surratt, and Samuel A. Mudd.

CHARGE—For maliciously, unlawfully, and traitorously, and in aid of the existing armed rebellion against the United States of America, on or before the 6th day of March, A.D. 1865, and on divers other days between that day and the 15th day of April, A.D. 1865, combining, confederating, and conspiring together with one John H. Surratt, John Wilkes Booth, Jefferson Davis, George N. Sanders, Beverly Tucker, Jacob Thompson, William C. Cleary, Clement C. Clay, George Harper, George Young, and others unknown, to kill and murder, within the Military Department of Washington, and within the fortified and intrenched lines thereof, Abraham Lincoln, late, and at the time of said combining, confederating, and conspiring, President of the United States of America, and Commander-in-Chief of the Army and Navy thereof; Andrew Johnson, now Vice-President of the United States aforesaid; William H. Seward, Secretary of State of the United States aforesaid; and Ulysses S. Grant, Lieutenant-General of the Army of the United States aforesaid, then in command of the Armies of the United States, under the direction of the said Abraham Lincoln; and in pursuance of in prosecuting said malicious, unlawful and traitorous conspiracy aforesaid, and in aid of the said rebellion, afterward, to wit, on the 14th day of April, A.D. 1865, within the Military Department of Washington, aforesaid, and within the fortified and intrenched lines of said Military Department, together with said John Wilkes Booth and John H. Surratt, maliciously, unlawfully, and traitorously murdering the said Abraham Lincoln, then President of the United States and Commander-in-Chief of the Army and Navies of the United States, as aforesaid; and maliciously, unlawfully, and traitorously assaulting, with intent to kill and murder, the said William H. Seward, then Secretary of State of the United States, as aforesaid; and lying in wait with intent maliciously, unlawfully, and traitorously to kill and murder the said Andrew Johnson, then being Vice-President of the United States; and the said Ulysses S. Grant, then being Lieutenant-General, and in command of the Armies of the United States, as aforesaid.

SPECIFICATION.—In this: that they, the said David E. Herold, Edward Spangler, Lewis Payne, Michael O'Laughlin, Samuel Arnold, Mary E. Surratt, George A. Atzerodt, and Samuel A. Mudd, together with the said John H. Surratt and John Wilkes Booth, incited and encouraged thereunto by Jefferson Davis, George N. Sanders, Beverly Tucker, Jacob Thompson, William C. Cleary, Clement C. Clay, George Harper, George Young, and others unknown, citizens of the United States aforesaid, and who were then engaged in armed rebellion against the United States of America, within the limits thereof, did, in aid of said rebellion, on or before the 6th day of March, A.D. 1865, and on divers other days and times between that day and the 15th day of April, A.D. 1865, combine, confederate, and conspire together, at Washington City, within the Military Department of Washington, and within the intrenched fortifications and military lines of the United States, there being, unlawfully, maliciously, and traitorously to kill and murder Abraham Lincoln, then President of the United States aforesaid, and Commander-in-Chief of the Army and Navy thereof; and unlawfully, maliciously, and traitorously to kill and murder Andrew Johnson, now Vice-President of the said United States, upon whom, on the death of said Abraham Lincoln, after the fourth day of March, A.D. 1865, the office of President of the said United States, and Commander-in-Chief of the Army and Navy thereof, would devolve; and to unlawfully, maliciously, and traitorously kill and murder Ulysses S. Grant, then Lieutenant-General, and, under the direction of the said Abraham Lincoln, in command of the Armies of the United States, aforesaid; and unlawfully, maliciously, and traitorously kill and murder William H. Seward, then Secretary of the United States aforesaid, whose duty it was, by law, upon the death of said President and Vice-President of the United States aforesaid, to cause an election to be held for electors of President of the United States: the conspirators aforesaid designing and intending, by the killing and murder of the said Abraham Lincoln, Andrew Johnson, Ulysses S. Grant, and William H. Seward, as aforesaid to deprive the Army and Navy of the said United States of a constitutional Commander-in-Chief; and to deprive the Armies of the United States of their lawful commander; and to prevent a lawful election of President and Vice-President of the United States aforesaid; and by the means aforesaid to aid and comfort the insurgents engaged in armed rebellion against the said United States, as aforesaid, and thereby to aid in the subversion and overthrow of the Constitution and laws of said United States.

And being so combined, confederated, and conspiring together in the prosecution of said unlawful and traitorous conspiracy, on the night of the 14th day of April, A.D. 1865, at the hour of about 10 o'clock and 15 minutes P.M., at Ford's Theater, on Tenth Street, in the City of Washington, and within the military department and military lines aforesaid, John Wilkes Booth, one of the conspirators aforesaid, in pursuance of said unlawful and traitorous conspiracy, did, then and there, unlawfully, maliciously, and traitorously, and with intent to kill and murder the said Abraham Lincoln, discharge a pistol then held in the hands of him, the said Booth, the same being then loaded with powder and a leaden ball, against and upon the left and posterior side of the head of said Abraham Lincoln; and did thereby, then and there, inflict upon him, the said Abraham Lincoln, then President of the said United States, and Commander-in-Chief of the Army and Navy thereof, a mortal wound, whereof, afterward, to-wit, on the 15th day of April, A.D. 1865, at Washington City aforesaid, the said Abraham Lincoln died; and thereby, then and there, and in pursuance of said conspiracy, the said defendants, and the said John Wilkes Booth and John H. Surratt did unlawfully, traitorously, and maliciously, and with the intent to aid the rebellion, as aforesaid, kill and murder the said Abraham Lincoln, President of the United States, as aforesaid.

And in further prosecution of the unlawful and traitorous conspiracy aforesaid, and of the murderous and traitorous intent of said conspiracy, the said Edward Spangler, on said 14th day of April, A.D. 1865, at about the same hour of that day, as aforesaid, within said military department and the military lines aforesaid, did aid and assist the said John Wilkes Booth to obtain entrance to the box in said theater, in which said Abraham Lincoln was sitting at the time he was assaulted and shot, as aforesaid, by John Wilkes Booth; and also did, then and there, aid said Booth in barring and obstructing the door of the box of said theater, so as to hinder and prevent any assistance to or rescue of the said Abraham Lincoln against the murderous assault of the said John Wilkes Booth; and did aid and abet him in making his escape after the said Abraham Lincoln had been murdered in manner aforesaid.

And in further prosecution of said unlawful, murderous and traitorous conspiracy, and in pursuance thereof, and with the intent as aforesaid, the said David E. Herold did, on the night of the 14th of April, A.D. 1865, within the military department and military lines aforesaid, aid, abet, and assist the said John Wilkes Booth in the killing and murder of the said Abraham Lincoln, and did, then and there, aid and abet and assist him, the said John Wilkes Booth, in attempting to escape through the military lines aforesaid, and did accompany and assist the said John Wilkes Booth in attempting to conceal himself and escape from justice, after killing and murdering said Abraham Lincoln as aforesaid.

And in further prosecution of said unlawful and traitorous conspiracy, and of the intent thereof, as aforesaid, the said Lewis Payne did, on the same night of the 14th day of April, A.D. 1865, about the same hour of 10 o'clock and 15 minutes P.M., at the City of Washington, and within the military department and the military lines aforesaid, unlawfully and maliciously make an assault upon the said William H. Seward, Secretary of State, as aforesaid, in the dwelling-house and bed-chamber of him, the said William H. Seward, and the said Payne did, then and there, with a large knife held in his hand, unlawfully, traitorously, and in pursuance of said conspiracy, strike, stab, cut, and attempt to kill and murder the said William H. Seward, and did thereby, then and there, with intent aforesaid, with said knife, inflict upon the face and throat of the said William H. Seward divers grievous wounds. And the said Lewis Payne, in further prosecution of said conspiracy, at the same time and place last aforesaid, did attempt, with the knife aforesaid, and a pistol held in his hand, to kill and murder Frederick W. Seward, Augustus H. Seward, Emrick W. Hansell, and George F. Robinson, who were then striving to protect and rescue the said William H. Seward from murder by the said Lewis Payne, and did, then and there, with said knife and pistol held in his hands, inflict upon the head of said Frederick W. Seward, and upon the persons of said Augustus H. Seward, Emrick W. Hansell, and George F. Robinson, divers grievous and dangerous wounds, with intent, then and there, to kill and murder the said Frederick W. Seward, Augustus H. Seward, Emrick W. Hansell, and George F. Robinson.

And in further prosecution of said conspiracy and its traitorous and murderous designs, the said George A. Atzerodt did, on the night of the 14th of April, A.D. 1865, an about the same hour of the night aforesaid, within the military department and the military lines aforesaid, lie in wait for Andrew Johnson, then Vice-President of the United States aforesaid, with the intent unlawfully and maliciously to kill and murder him, the said Andrew Johnson.

And in the further prosecution of the conspiracy aforesaid, and of its murderous and treasonable purposes aforesaid, on the nights of the 13th and 14th of April, A.D. 1865, at Washington City, and within the military department and military lines aforesaid, the said Michael O'Laughlin did, then and there, lie in wait for Ulysses S. Grant, then Lieutenant-General and Commander of the Armies of the United States, as aforesaid, with intent, then and there, to kill and murder the said Ulysses S. Grant.

And in further prosecution of said conspiracy, the said Samuel Arnold did, within the military department and the military lines aforesaid, on or before the 6th day of March A.D. 1865, and on divers other days and times between that day and the 15th day of April, A.D. 1865, combine, conspire with, and aid, counsel, abet, comfort, and support, the said John Wilkes Booth, Lewis Payne, George A. Atzerodt, Michael O'Laughlin, and their confederates in said unlawful, murderous, and traitorous conspiracy, and in the execution thereof, as aforesaid.

And in further prosecution of said conspiracy, Mary E. Surratt did, at Washington City, and within the military department and military lines aforesaid, on or before the 6th day of March, A.D. 1865, and on divers other days and times between that day and the 20th day of April, A.D. 1865, receive, entertain, harbor, and conceal, aid and assist the said John Wilkes Booth, David E. Herold, Lewis Payne, John H. Surratt, Michael O'Laughlin, George A. Atzerodt, Samuel Arnold, and their confederates, with the knowledge of the murderous and traitorous conspiracy aforesaid, and with the intent to aid, abet, and assist them in execution thereof, and in escaping from justice after the murder of the said Abraham Lincoln, as aforesaid.

And in further prosecution of said conspiracy, the said Samuel A. Mudd did, at Washington City, and within the military department and military lines aforesaid, on or before the 6th day of March, A.D. 1865, and on divers other days and times between that day and the 20th day of April, A.D. 1865, advise, encourage, receive, entertain, harbor, and conceal, aid and assist the said John Wilkes Booth, David E. Herold, Lewis Payne, John H. Surratt, Michael O'Laughlin, George A. Atzerodt, Mary E. Surratt, and Samuel Arnold, and their confederates, with knowledge of the murderous and traitorous conspiracy aforesaid, and with the intent to aid, abet, and assist them in the execution thereof, and in escaping from justice after the murder of the said Abraham Lincoln, in pursuance of said conspiracy in manner aforesaid.

By order of the President of the United States.

Henry Wirz Trial (1865)

Captain Henry Wirz was the only soldier of the Confederacy found guilty and sentenced to death for war crimes committed during the Civil War. Wirz was the commander of Camp Sumter, also known as "Andersonville," a Confederate prison located in Georgia. Wirz was tried before a military commission on charges of conspiracy and murder related to his duties as the person in charge of the prison. Even today, his trial remains a point of controversy with historians. Wirz was viewed by his accusers as a brutal murderer who destroyed the lives of Union soldiers held as prisoners of war at Andersonville. However, his supporters argued that Wirz was a martyr deprived of due process by a military commission which presented biased testimony and evidence against Wirz that may have resulted in the conviction and execution of an innocent man (Carnes and Drew, "Henry Wirz").

The military commission led by the Judge Advocate General of the Union Army charged Wirz with conspiring to destroy the lives of Union soldiers by allowing a horrible environment to exist among the Andersonville prisoners that included starvation, disease, overcrowding, and unsanitary conditions. Wirz was also charged with causing the murder of 13 prisoners through actions of his own or by way of issuing orders to Confederate prison guards (Carnes and Drew, "Henry Wirz").

Prior to the trial, defense attorneys argued that the charges against Wirz should be dismissed for a variety of reasons. For instance, the terms of surrender agreed upon by the Union and Confederate forces stated that, if Confederate soldiers agreed to put down their weapons, then they were, in effect, pardoned by the United States and could return to their homes without prosecution. Prosecutors, however, maintained that the terms of the surrender did not include the war crimes allegedly committed by Wirz (Carnes and Drew, "Henry Wirz").

Wirz's defense attorneys also asserted that the military commission did not have jurisdiction because the war had ended and any such trial should be conducted in a normal civil court of law where Wirz would be guaranteed his due process rights. However, prosecutors noted that the southern states were still in a state of rebellion and the war could resume at any moment. Finally, Wirz's attorneys argued that the charges against Wirz for murdering 13 prisoners was vague because the documents presented by prosecutors did not include the name of even one victim. Prosecutors decided not to respond to the vagueness argument. In every attempt made by defense attorneys to have the charges against Wirz dismissed, the military commission sided with the prosecutors and the military trial of Henry Wirz began on August 23, 1865, in Washington, D.C., at the U.S. Capitol (Carnes and Drew, "Henry Wirz").

The strategy of the prosecutors led by Colonel N. P. Chipman was to prove that Wirz had knowledge of the terrible conditions at Andersonville. However, while the prosecution proved that Wirz knew about the poor conditions at the prison based upon Wirz's letters to the Confederate Department of Prisons, the letters also revealed that he tried to convince Confederate authorities to improve the situation of the Union soldiers held at the prison (Carnes and Drew, "Henry Wirz").

Nearly all of the 160 witnesses called to testify against Wirz had no knowledge of any murders committed by Wirz at the prison. The few witnesses who said that Wirz had murdered prisoners based their testimony on hearsay evidence that could not be confirmed (Page and Haley 2006, 207). The key witness for the prosecution was Felix de la Baume, a prisoner held at Andersonville. De la Baume stated that he saw Wirz murder prisoners. However, after the trial and execution of Wirz, de la Baume admitted that he had lied in his testimony before the military commission (Carnes and Drew, "Felix de la Baume").

Colonel Chipman, the lead prosecutor, maintained complete control over the legal proceedings and only allowed witnesses to take the stand if their testimony was approved in advance by the prosecution. Even though defense attorneys complained about this tactic used by the prosecutors, the military commission supported this unfair practice used by the prosecutors (Carnes and Drew, "Henry Wirz").

Over the course of the trial, the defense attorneys produced 68 witnesses consisting mainly of Andersonville prisoners and their relatives who testified that Wirz was a compassionate person who was very concerned about the suffering of the prisoners and the overall condition of the prison (Chipman 2008, 301–322). Defense attorneys also tried to introduce statistics to show that Andersonville was no different than any other prison camp during the war. In fact, the harsh conditions of Andersonville were most likely a product of the South experiencing severe food shortages. The Confederacy had a difficult time feeding their soldiers let alone Union prisoners of war. It was also shown that the Confederacy repeatedly tried to exchange prisoners with the Union Army, even allowing a large number of prisoners from Andersonville to return to the North when they had become seriously ill. The military commission deemed such evidence as useless and refused to admit the information (Page and Haley 2006, 205–216).

On October 24, 1865, the military commission found Wirz guilty of conspiring to destroy the lives of prisoners by allowing conditions to become worse and also causing the murder of 13 soldiers of the Union army held as prisoners at Andersonville. The military commission ordered the execution of Wirz by hanging. On the night before the scheduled execution, President Andrew Johnson informed Wirz that he would grant him a pardon in exchange for his testimony that the president of the Confederacy, Jefferson Davis, was responsible for the deaths of prisoners at Andersonville. Wirz refused to accept the agreement because his pardon would have been based upon a lie. Wirz was hanged outside the U.S. Capitol building in the Old Capitol Prison yard on November 10, 1865, before nearly 300 Union soldiers who had been given tickets by the federal government to view the execution (Page and Haley 2006, 217–233).

While it is uncertain whether Wirz was guilty of the charges filed against him, it is certain that he was denied a fair trial by the military commission and his trial, conviction, and execution are yet another reminder that criminal defendants' rights are often sacrificed during wartime when military commissions are used instead of a civil court of law. The defense attorneys were clearly disadvantaged in their attempt to present their case before the military authorities, and Wirz was also denied a proper appeal of his conviction. Ultimately, the public's desire for revenge fueled by newspaper reports of the conditions at Andersonville was satisfied by the execution of Wirz. However, it is unsatisfying and disturbing to imagine that an unfair trial quite possibly may have resulted in the execution of an innocent man (Page and Haley 2006, 234–242).

References

Carnes, Bill and Troy Drew. "Felix de la Baume." *Famous Trials*. http://www.law.umkc.edu/faculty/projects/ftrials/Wirz/cont1.htm (accessed March 18, 2009).

Carnes, Bill and Troy Drew. "The Trial of Henry Wirz: A Brief Summary." *Famous Trials*. http://www.law.umkc.edu/faculty/projects/ftrials/Wirz/INTRO.HTM (accessed March 18, 2009).

Chipman, Norton P. *The Tragedy of Andersonville: Trial of Captain Henry Wirz (1911).* Whitefish, MT: Kessinger Publishing, 2008.

Harper, Frank. *Andersonville: The Trial of Captain Henry Wirz.* Greeley: University of Northern Colorado, 1986.

La Force, Glen W. "The War-Crimes Trial of Major Henry Wirz, C.S.A.: Justice Served or Justice Denied?" *Journal of Confederate History* (Fall 1988): 287–312.

Page, James Madison, and Michael Joachim Haley. *The True Story of Andersonville Prison: A Defense of Major Henry Wirz.* Scituate, MA: Digital Scanning, 2006.

Ruhlman, R. Fred. *Captain Henry Wirz and Andersonville Prison: A Reappraisal.* Knoxville: University of Tennessee Press, 2006.

Rutherford, Mildred Lewis. *Andersonville Prison and Captain Henry Wirz's Trial.* Plains, GA: United Daughter's of the Confederacy, 1983.

WAR DEPARTMENT, ADJUTANT-GENERAL'S OFFICE, Washington, November 6, 1865.

I. Before a military commission which convened at Washington, D.C., August 23, 1865, pursuant to paragraph 3, Special Orders, No. 453, dated August 23, 1865, and paragraph 13, Special Orders, No. 524, dated October 2, 1865, War Department, Adjutant-General's Office, Washington, and of which Maj. Gen. Lewis Wallace, U.S. Volunteers, is president, was arraigned and tried—

Henry Wirz.

CHARGE I: Maliciously, willfully, and traitorously, and in aid of the then existing armed rebellion against the United States of America, on or before the let day of March, A.D. 1864, and on divers other days between that day and the 10th day of April, 1865, combining, confederating, and conspiring, together with John H. Winder, Richard B. Winder, Joseph [Isaiah H.] White, W. S. Winder, R. R. Stevenson, and others unknown, to injure the health and destroy the lives of soldiers in the military service of the United States, then held and being prisoners of war within the lines of the so-called Confederate States, and in the military prisons thereof, to the end that the armies of the United States might be weakened and impaired, in violation of the laws and customs of war.

Specification.—In this, that he, the said Henry Wirz, did combine, confederate, and conspire with them, the said John H. Winder, Richard B. Winder, Joseph [Isaiah H.] White, W. S. Winder, R. R. Stevenson, and others whose names are unknown, citizens of the United States aforesaid, and who were then engaged in armed rebellion against the United States, maliciously, traitorously, and in violation of the laws of war, to impair and injure the health and to destroy the lives—by subjecting to torture and great suffering; by confining in unhealthy and unwholesome quarters; by exposing to the inclemency of winter and to the dews and burning sun of summer; by compelling the use of impure water; and by furnishing insufficient and unwholesome food—of large numbers of Federal prisoners, to wit, the number of 30,000 soldiers in the military service of the United States of America, held as prisoners of war at Andersonville, in the State of Georgia, within the lines of the so-called Confederate States, on or before the 1st day of March, A.D. 1864, and at divers times between that day and the 10th day of April, A.D. 1865, to the end that the armies of the United States might be weakened and impaired and the insurgents engaged in armed rebellion against the United States might be aided and comforted. And he, the said Henry Wirz, an officer in the military service of the so-called Confederate States, being then and there commandant of a military prison at Andersonville, in the State of Georgia, located, by authority of the so-called Confederate States, for the confinement of prisoners of war, and, as such commandant, fully clothed with authority, and in duty bound to treat, care, and provide for such prisoners held as aforesaid as were or might be placed in his custody according to the law of war, did, in furtherance of such combination, confederation, and conspiracy, and incited thereunto by them, the said John H. Winder, Richard B. Winder, Joseph [Isaiah H.] White, W. S. Winder, R. R. Stevenson, and others whose names are unknown, maliciously, wickedly, and traitorously confine a large number of such prisoners of war, soldiers in the military service of the United States, to the amount of 30,000 men, in unhealthy and unwholesome quarters, in a close and small area of ground wholly inadequate to their wants and destructive to their health, which he well knew and intended; and, while there so confined during the time aforesaid, did, in furtherance of his evil design, and in aid of the said conspiracy, willfully and maliciously neglect to furnish tents, barracks, or other shelter sufficient for their protection from the inclemency of winter and the dews and burning sun of summer; and with such evil intent did take, and cause to be taken, from them their clothing, blankets, camp equipage, and other property of which they were possessed at the time of being placed in his custody; and, with like malice and evil intent, did refuse to furnish, or cause to be furnished, food either of a quality or quantity sufficient to preserve health and sustain life; and did refuse and neglect to furnish wood sufficient for cooking in summer and to keep the said prisoners warm in winter; and did compel the said prisoners to subsist upon unwholesome food, and that in limited quantities entirely inadequate to sustain health, which he well knew; and did compel the said prisoners to use unwholesome water, reeking with the filth and garbage of the prison and prison guard, and the offal and drainage of the cookhouse of said prison, whereby the prisoners became greatly reduced in their bodily strength, and emaciated and injured in their bodily health; their minds impaired and their intellects broken; and many of them, to wit, the number of 10,000, whose names are unknown, sickened and died by reason thereof, which he, the said Henry Wirz, then and there well knew and intended; and, so knowing and evilly intending, did refuse and neglect to provide proper lodgings, food, or nourishment for the sick, and necessary medicine and medical attendance for the restoration of their health; and did knowingly, willfully, and maliciously, in furtherance of his evil designs, permit them to languish and die from want of care and proper treatment. And the said Henry Wirz, still pursuing his evil purpose, did permit to remain in the said prison, among the emaciated sick and languishing living, the bodies of the dead, until they became corrupt and loathsome and filled the air with fetid and noxious exhalations, and thereby greatly increased the unwholesomeness of the prison, insomuch that great numbers of said prisoners, to wit, the number of 1,000. whose names are unknown, sickened and died by reason thereof. And the said Henry Wirz, still pursuing his wicked and cruel purpose, wholly disregarding the usages of civilized warfare, did, at the time and place aforesaid, maliciously and willfully subject the prisoners aforesaid to cruel, unusual, and infamous punishment upon slight, trivial, and fictitious pretenses, by fastening large balls of iron to their feet, and binding large numbers of the prisoners aforesaid closely together with large chains around their necks and feet, so that they walked with the greatest difficulty—and, being so confined, were subjected to the burning rays of the sun, often without food or drink for hours, and even days—from which said cruel treatment large numbers, to wit, the number of 100, whose names are unknown, sickened, fainted, and died. And he, the said Wirz, did further cruelly treat and injure said prisoners by maliciously confining them within an instrument of torture called the "stocks," thus depriving them of the use of their limbs, and forcing them to lie, sit, and stand for many hours without the power of changing position, and being without food or drink, in consequence of which many, to wit, the number of thirty, whose names are unknown, sickened and died. And he, the said Wirz, still wickedly pursuing his evil purpose, did establish and cause to be designated within the prison inclosure containing said prisoners, a "dead-line," being a line around the inner face of the stockade or wall inclosing said prison, and about twenty feet distant from and within said stockade; and having so established said dead-line, which was in many places an imaginary line, and in many other places marked by insecure and shifting strips of boards nailed upon the top of small and insecure stakes or posts, he, the said Wirz, instructed the prison guard stationed around the top of said stockade to fire upon and kill any of the prisoners aforesaid who might touch, fall upon, pass over or under or across the said "dead-line." Pursuant to which said orders and instructions, maliciously and needlessly given by said Wirz, the said prison guard did fire upon and kill a large number of said prisoners, to wit, the number of about 300. And the said Wirz, still pursuing his evil purpose, did keep and use ferocious and bloodthirsty beasts, dangerous to human life, called bloodhounds, to hunt down prisoners of war aforesaid who made their escape from his custody, and did then and there willfully and maliciously suffer, incite, and encourage the said beasts to seize, tear, mangle, and maim the bodies and limbs of said fugitive prisoners of war, which the said beasts, incited as aforesaid, then and there did, whereby a large number of said prisoners of war, who, during the time aforesaid, made their escape and were recaptured, and were, by the said beasts then and there cruelly and inhumanly injured, insomuch that many of said prisoners, to wit, the number of about fifty died. And the said Wirz, still pursuing his wicked purpose, and still aiding in carrying out said conspiracy, did use and cause to be used, for the pretended purposes of vaccination, impure and poisonous vaccine matter, which said impure and poisonous matter was then and there, by the direction and order of said Wirz, maliciously, cruelly, and wickedly deposited in the arms of many of said prisoners, by reason of which large numbers of them, to wit, 100, lost the use of their arms, and many of them, to wit, about the number of 200, were so injured that they soon thereafter died. All of which he, the said Henry Wirz, well knew and maliciously intended, and in aid of the then existing rebellion against the United States, with the view to assist in weakening and impairing the armies of the United States, and in furtherance of the said conspiracy and with the full knowledge, consent, and connivance of his co-conspirators aforesaid, he, the said Wirz, then and there did.

CHARGE 2: Murder, in violation of the laws and customs of war.

Specification 1.—In this, that the said Henry Wirz, an officer in the military service of the so-called Confederate States of America, at Andersonville, in the State of Georgia, on or about the 8th day of July, A.D. 1864, then and there being commandant of a prison there located, by the authority of the said so-called Confederate States, for the confinement of prisoners of war taken and held as such from the armies of the United States of America, while acting as said commandant, feloniously, willfully, and of his malice aforethought, did make an assault, and he, the said Henry Wirz, a certain pistol called a revolver then and there loaded and charged with gunpowder and bullets, which said pistol the said Henry Wirz in his hand then and there had and held to, against, and upon a soldier belonging to the Army of the United States, in his, the said Henry Wirz's, custody, as a prisoner of war, whose name is unknown, then and there feloniously, and of his malice aforethought, did shoot and discharge, inflicting upon the body of the soldier aforesaid a mortal wound with the pistol aforesaid, in consequence of which said mortal wound, murderously inflicted by the said Henry Wirz, the said soldier thereafter, to wit, on the 9th day of July, A.D. 1864, died.

Specification 2.—In this, that the said Henry Wirz, an officer in the military service of the so-called Confederate States of America, at Andersonville, in the State of Georgia, on or about the 20th day of September, A.D. 1864, then and there being commandant of a prison there located, by the authority of the said so-called Confederate States, for the confinement of prisoners of war taken and held as such from the armies of the United States of America, while acting as said commandant, feloniously, willfully, and of his malice aforethought, did jump upon, stamp, kick, bruise, and otherwise injure with the heels of his boots, a soldier belonging to the Army of the United States, in his, the said Henry Wirz's, custody as a prisoner of war, whose name is unknown, of which said stamping, kicking, and bruising, maliciously done and inflicted by the said Wirz, he, the said soldier, soon thereafter, to wit, on the 20th day of September, A.D. 1864, died.

Specification 3.—In this, that the said Henry Wirz, an officer in the military service of the so-called Confederate States of America, at Andersonville, in the State of Georgia, on or about the 13th day of June, A.D. 1864, then and there being commandant of a prison there located, by the authority of the said so-called Confederate States, for the confinement of prisoners of war, taken and held as such from the armies of the United States of America, while acting as said commandant, feloniously, and of his malice aforethought, did make an assault, and he, the said Henry Wirz, a certain pistol called a revolver then and there loaded and charged with gunpowder and bullets, which said pistol the said Henry Wirz, in his hand then and there had and held to, against, and upon a soldier belonging to the Army of the United States, in his, the said Henry Wirz's, custody as a prisoner of war, whose name is unknown, then and there feloniously, and of his malice aforethought, did shoot and discharge, inflicting upon the body of the soldier aforesaid a mortal wound with the pistol aforesaid, in consequence of which said mortal wound, murderously inflicted by the said Henry Wirz, the said soldier immediately, to wit, on the day aforesaid, died.

Specification 4.—In this, that the said Henry Wirz, an officer in the military service of the so-called Confederate States of America, at Andersonville, in the

State of Georgia, on or about the 30th day of May, A.D. 1864, then and there being commandant of a prison there located, by the authority of the said so-called Confederate States, for the confinement of prisoners of war, taken and held as such from the armies of the United States of America, while acting as said commandant, feloniously, and of his malice aforethought, did make an assault, and he, the said Henry Wirz, a certain pistol called a revolver then and there loaded and charged with gunpowder and bullets, which said pistol the said Henry Wirz in his hand then and there had and held to, against, and upon a soldier belonging to the Army of the United States, in his, the said Henry Wirz's, custody as a prisoner of war, whose name is unknown, then and there feloniously, and of his malice aforethought, did shoot and discharge, inflicting upon the body of the soldier aforesaid a mortal wound with the pistol aforesaid, in consequence of which said mortal wound, murderously inflicted by the said Henry Wirz, the said soldier, on the 30th day of May, A.D. 1864, died.

Specification 5.—In this, that the said Henry Wirz, an officer in the military service of the so-called Confederate States of America, at Andersonville, in the State of Georgia, on or about the 20th day of August, A.D. 1864, then and there being commandant of a prison there located, by the authority of the said so-called Confederate States, for the confinement of prisoners of war, taken and held as such from the armies of the United States of America, while acting as said commandant, feloniously, and of his malice aforethought, did confine and bind with an instrument of torture called "the stocks," a soldier belonging to the Army of the United States, in his, the said Henry Wirz's, custody as a prisoner of war, whose name is unknown, in consequence of which such cruel treatment, maliciously and murderously inflicted as aforesaid, he, the said soldier, soon thereafter, to wit, on the 30th day of August, A.D. 1864, died.

Specification 6.—In this, that the said Henry Wirz, an officer in the military service of the so-called Confederate States of America, at Andersonville, in the State of Georgia, on or about the 1st day of February, 1865, then and there being commandant of a prison there located, by the authority of the said so-called Confederate States, for the confinement of prisoners of war, taken and held as such from the armies of the United States of America, while acting as said commandant, feloniously, and of his malice aforethought, did confine and bind within an instrument of torture called "the stocks," a soldier belonging to the Army of the United States, in his, the said Henry Wirz's, custody as a prisoner of war, whose name is unknown, in consequence of which said cruel treatment, maliciously and murderously inflicted as aforesaid, he, the said soldier, soon thereafter, to wit, on the 6th day of February, A.D. 1865, died.

Specification 7.—In this, that the said Henry Wirz, an officer in the military service of the so-called Confederate States of America, at Andersonville, in the State of Georgia, on or about the 20th day of July, A.D. 1864, then and there being commandant of a prison there located, by the authority of the said so-called Confederate States, for the confinement of prisoners of war, taken and held as such from the armies of the United States of America, while acting as said commandant, feloniously, and of his malice aforethought, did fasten and chain together several persons, soldiers, belonging to the Army of the United States, in his, the said Henry Wirz's, custody as prisoners of war, whose names are unknown, binding the necks and feet of said prisoners closely together, and compelling them to carry great burdens, to wit, large iron balls chained to their feet, so that, in consequence of the said cruel treatment inflicted upon them by the said Henry Wirz as aforesaid, one of said soldiers, a prisoner of war as aforesaid, whose name is unknown, on the 25th day of July, A.D. 1864, died.

Specification 8.—In this, that the said Henry Wirz, an officer in the military service of the so-called Confederate States of America, at Andersonville, in the State of Georgia, on or about the 15th day of May, A.D. 1864, then and there being commandant of a prison there located, by the authority of the said so-called Confederate States, for the confinement of prisoners of war, taken and held as such from the armies of the United States of America, while acting as said commandant, feloniously, willfully, and of his malice aforethought, did order a rebel soldier, whose name is unknown, then on duty as a sentinel or guard to the prison of which said Henry Wirz was commandant as aforesaid, to fire upon a soldier belonging to the Army of the United States, in his, the said Henry Wirz's, custody as a prisoner of war, whose name is unknown; and in pursuance of said order, so as aforesaid maliciously and murderously given as aforesaid, he, the said rebel soldier, did, with a musket loaded with gunpowder and bullet, then and there fire at the said soldier so as aforesaid held as a prisoner of war, inflicting upon him a mortal wound with the musket aforesaid, of which he, the said prisoner, soon thereafter, to wit, on the day aforesaid, died.

Specification 9.—In this, that the said Henry Wirz, an officer in the military service of the so-called Confederate States of America, at Andersonville, in the State of Georgia, on or about the 1st day of July, A.D. 1864, then and there being commandant of a prison there located, by the authority of the said so-called Confederate States, for the confinement of prisoners of war, taken and held as such from the armies of the United States of America, while acting as said commandant, feloniously, and of his malice aforethought, did order a rebel soldier, whose name is unknown, then on duty as a sentinel or guard to the prison of which said Wirz was commandant as aforesaid, to fire upon a soldier belonging to the Army of the United States, in his, the said Henry Wirz's, custody as a prisoner of war, whose name is unknown; and in pursuance of said order, so as aforesaid maliciously and murderously given as aforesaid, he, the said rebel soldier, did, with a musket loaded with gunpowder and bullet, then and there fire at the said soldier so as aforesaid held as a prisoner of war, inflicting upon him a mortal wound with the said musket, of which he, the said prisoner, soon thereafter, to wit, on the day aforesaid, died.

Specification 10.—In this, that the said Henry Wirz, an officer in the military service of the so-called Confederate States of America, at Andersonville, in the State of Georgia, on or about the 20th day of August, A.D. 1864, then and there being commandant of a prison there located, by the authority of the said so-called Confederate States, for the confinement of prisoners of war, taken and held as such from the armies of the United States of America, while acting as said commandant, feloniously, and of his malice aforethought, did order a rebel soldier, whose name is unknown, then on duty as a sentinel or guard to the prison of which said Wirz was commandant as aforesaid, to fire upon a soldier belonging to the Army of the United States, in his, the said Henry Wirz's, custody as a prisoner of war, whose name is unknown; and in pursuance of said order, so as aforesaid maliciously and murderously given as aforesaid, he, the said rebel soldier, did, with a musket loaded with gunpowder and bullet, then and there fire at the said soldier so as aforesaid held as a prisoner of war, inflicting upon him a mortal wound with the said musket, of which he, the said prisoner, soon thereafter, to wit, on the day aforesaid, died.

Specification 11.—In this, that the said Henry Wirz, an officer in the military service of the so-called Confederate States of America, at Andersonville, in the State of Georgia, on or about the 1st day of July, A.D. 1864, then and there being commandant of a prison there located, by, the authority of the said so-called Confederate States, for the confinement of prisoners of war, taken and held as such from the armies of the United States of America, while acting as said commandant, feloniously, and of his malice aforethought, did cause, incite, and urge certain ferocious and bloodthirsty animals, called bloodhounds, to pursue, attack, wound, and tear in pieces a soldier belonging to the Army of the United States, in his, the said Henry Wirz's, custody as a prisoner of war, whose name is unknown; and in consequence thereof the said bloodhounds did then and there, with the knowledge, encouragement, and instigation of him, the said Wirz, maliciously and murderously given by him, attack and mortally wound the said soldier, in consequence of which said mortal wound he, the said prisoner, soon thereafter, to wit, on the 6th day of July, A.D. 1864, died.

Specification 12.—In this, that the said Henry Wirz, an officer in the military service of the so-called Confederate States of America, at Andersonville, in the State of Georgia, on or about the 27th day of July, A.D. 1864, then and there being commandant of a prison there located, by the authority of the said so-called Confederate States, for the confinement of prisoners of war, taken and held as such from the armies of the United States of America, while acting as said commandant, feloniously, and of his malice aforethought, did order a rebel soldier, whose name is unknown, then on duty as a sentinel or guard to the prison of which said

Wirz was commandant as aforesaid, to fire upon a soldier belonging to the Army of the United States, in his, the said Henry Wirz's, custody as a prisoner of war, whose name is unknown; and in pursuance of said order, so as aforesaid maliciously and murderously given as aforesaid, he, the said rebel soldier, did, with a musket loaded with gunpowder and bullet, then and there fire at the said soldier so as aforesaid held as a prisoner of war, inflicting upon him a mortal wound with the said musket of which said mortal wound he, the said prisoner, soon thereafter, to wit, on the day aforesaid, died.

Specification 13.—In this, that the said Henry Wirz, an officer in the military service of the so-called Confederate States of America, at Andersonville, in the State of Georgia, on or about the 3d day of August, 1864, then and there being commandant of a prison there located, by the authority of the said so-called Confederate States, for the confinement of prisoners of war, taken and held as such from the armies of the United States of America, while acting as said commandant, feloniously, and of his malice aforethought, did make an assault upon a soldier belonging to the Army of the United States, in his, the said Henry Wirz's, custody as a prisoner of war, whose name is unknown, and with a pistol called a revolver, then and there held in the hands of the said Wirz, did beat and bruise said soldier upon the head, shoulders, and breast, inflicting thereby mortal wounds, from which said beating and bruising aforesaid, and mortal wounds caused thereby, the said soldier soon thereafter, to wit, on the 4th day of August, A.D. 1864, died.

To which charges and specifications the accused, Henry Wirz, pleaded not guilty.

Finding.

The court, having maturely considered the evidence adduced, finds the accused, Henry Wirz, as follows:

Charge I.

Of the specification, guilty, after amending said specification to read as follows:

In this, that he, the said Henry Wirz, did combine, confederate, and conspire with them, the said Jefferson Davis, James A. Seddon, Howell Cobb, John H. Winder, Richard B. Winder, Isaiah H. White, W. S. Winder, W. Shelby Reed, R. R. Stevenson, S. P. Moore, [W. J. W.] Kerr (late hospital steward at Andersonville), James W. Duncan. Wesley W. Turner, Benjamin Harris, and others whose names are unknown, citizens of the United States aforesaid, and who were then engaged in armed rebellion against the United States, maliciously, traitorously, and in violation of the laws of war, to impair and injure the health and to destroy the lives—by subjecting to torture and great suffering; by confining in unhealthy and unwholesome quarters; by exposing to the inclemency of winter and to the dews and burning sun of summer; by compelling the use of impure water, and by furnishing insufficient and unwholesome food—of large numbers of Federal prisoners, to wit, the number of about 45,000 soldiers in the military service of the United States of America, held as prisoners of war at Andersonville, in the State of Georgia, within the lines of the so-called Confederate States, on or before the 27th day of March, A.D. 1864, and at divers times between that day and the 10th day of April, A.D. 1865, to the end that the armies of the United States might be weakened and impaired, and the insurgents engaged in armed rebellion against the United States might be aided and comforted. And he, the said Henry Wirz, an officer in the military service of the so-called Confederate States, being then and there commandant of a military prison at Andersonville, in the State of Georgia, located by authority of the so-called Confederate States for the confinement of prisoners of war, and as such commandant, fully clothed with authority, and in duty bound to treat, care, and provide for such prisoners, held as aforesaid, as were or might be placed in his custody, according to the law of war, did, in furtherance of such combination, confederation, and conspiracy, maliciously, wickedly, and traitorously confine a large number of prisoners of war, soldiers in the military service of the United States, to the number of about 45,000 men, in unhealthy and unwholesome quarters, in a close and small area of ground wholly inadequate to their wants and destructive to their health, which he well knew and intended; and, while there so confined during the time aforesaid, did, in furtherance of his evil design, and in aid of the said conspiracy, willfully and maliciously neglect to furnish tents, barracks, or other shelter sufficient for their protection from the inclemency of winter and the dews and burning sun of summer; and with such evil intent did take, and cause to be taken, from them, their clothing, blankets, camp equipage, and other property of which they were possessed at the time of being placed in his custody; and, with like malice and evil intent, did refuse to furnish, or cause to be furnished, food either of a quality or quantity sufficient to preserve health and sustain life; and did refuse and neglect to furnish wood sufficient for cooking in summer and to keep the said prisoners warm in winter; and did compel the said prisoners to subsist upon unwholesome food, and that in limited quantities, entirely inadequate to sustain health, which he well knew; and did compel the said prisoners to use unwholesome water, reeking with the filth and garbage of the prison and prison guard and the offal and drainage of the cook-house of said prison, whereby the prisoners became greatly reduced in their bodily strength, and emaciated and injured in their bodily health; their minds impaired and their intellects broken; and many of them, to wit, about the number of 10,000, whose names are unknown, sickened and died by reason thereof, which he, the said Henry Wirz, then and there well knew and intended; and, so knowing and evilly intending, did refuse and neglect to provide proper lodgings, food, or nourishment for the sick, and necessary medicine and medical attendance for the restoration of their health; and did knowingly, willfully, and maliciously, in furtherance of his evil designs, permit them to languish and die from want of care and proper treatment. And the said Henry Wirz, still pursuing his evil purposes, did permit to remain in the said prison among the emaciated sick and languishing living, the bodies of the dead until they became corrupt and loathsome, and filled the air with fetid and noxious exhalations, and thereby greatly increased the unwholesomeness of the prison, insomuch that great numbers of said prisoners, whose names are unknown, sickened and died by reason thereof. And the said Henry Wirz, still pursuing his wicked and cruel purpose, wholly disregarding the usages of civilized warfare, did, at the time and place aforesaid, maliciously and willfully subject the prisoners aforesaid to cruel, unusual, and infamous punishment, upon slight trivial, and fictitious pretenses, by fastening large balls of iron to their feet, and binding numbers of the prisoners aforesaid closely together with large chains around their necks and feet, so that they walked with the greatest difficulty, and being so confined were subjected to the burning rays of the sun, often without food or drink for hours, and even days, from which said cruel treatment numbers, whose names are unknown, sickened, fainted, and died. And he, the said Wirz, did further cruelly treat and injure said prisoners by maliciously tying them up by the thumbs, and willfully confining them within an instrument of torture called "the stocks," thus depriving them of the use of their limbs, and forcing them to lie, sit, and stand for many hours without the power of changing position, and being without food or drink, in consequence of which many, whose names are unknown, sickened and died. And he, the said Wirz, still wickedly pursuing his evil purpose, did establish, and cause to be designated within the prison inclosure containing said prisoners, a "dead-line," being a line around the inner face of the stockade or wall inclosing said prison, and about twenty feet distant from and within said stockade; and having so established said dead-line, which was in some places an imaginary line, and in other places marked by insecure and shifting strips of boards, nailed upon the top of small and insecure stakes or posts, he, the said Wirz, instructed the prison guard stationed around the top of said stockade to fire upon and kill any of the prisoners aforesaid who might fall upon, pass over or under or across the said dead-line; pursuant to which said orders and instructions, maliciously and needlessly given by said Wirz, the said prison guard did fire upon and kill a number of said prisoners. And the said Wirz, still pursuing his evil purpose, did keep and use ferocious and bloodthirsty dogs, dangerous to human life, to hunt down prisoners of war aforesaid who made their escape from his custody; and did then and there willfully and maliciously suffer, incite, and encourage the said dogs to seize, tear, mangle, and maim the bodies and limbs of said fugitive prisoners of war, which the said dogs, incited as aforesaid, then and there did, whereby a number of said prisoners of war, who, during the time aforesaid, made their escape and were recaptured, died. And the said Wirz, still pursuing his wicked purpose, and still aiding in carrying out said conspiracy, did cause to be used for the pretended purposes of vaccination, impure and poisonous vaccine matter, which said impure and poisonous matter was then and there, by the direction and order of said Wirz, maliciously, cruelly, and wickedly deposited in the arms of many of said prisoners, by reason of which large numbers of them lost the use of their arms, and many of them were so injured that they soon thereafter died. All of which he, the said Henry Wirz, well knew and maliciously intended, and in aid of the then existing rebellion against the United States, with a view to assist in weakening and impairing the armies of the United States, and in furtherance of the said conspiracy, and with the full knowledge, consent, and connivance of his co-conspirators aforesaid, he, the said Wirz, then and there did,

Of the charge, guilty, after amending said charge to read as follows:

Maliciously, willfully, and traitorously, and in aid of the then existing armed rebellion against the United States of America, on or before the 27th day of March, A.D. 1864, and on divers other days between that day and the 10th day of April, A.D. 1865, combining, confederating, and conspiring, together with Jefferson Davis, James A. Seddon, Howell Cobb, John H. Winder, Richard B. Winder, Isaiah H. White, W. S. Winder, W. Shelby Reed, R.R. Stevenson, S. P. Moore, [W. J. W.] Kerr (late hospital steward at Andersonville), James W. Duncan, Wesley W. Turner, Benjamin Harris, and others unknown, to injure the health and destroy the lives of soldiers in the military service of the United States, then held and being prisoners of war within the lines of the so-called Confederate States, and in the military prisons thereof, to the end that the armies of the United States might be weakened and impaired, in violation of the laws and customs of war.

Charge II.

Of the first specification, guilty, adding the words "or about" immediately before the phrase "the 9th day of July."

Of the second specification, guilty.

Of the third specification, guilty, after striking out "June" and inserting instead "September."

Of the fourth specification, not guilty.

Of the 5th specification, guilty, after striking out the phrase "on the 30th day" and inserting instead the phrase "on or about the 25th day."

Of the sixth specification, guilty, after striking out the word "1st" and inserting "15th," and also striking out the phrase "on the 6th day" and inserting instead the phrase "on or about the 16th day.

Of the seventh specification, guilty, after striking out the word "20th" and inserting instead the word "1st," and also after inserting" or about "immediately before the phrase" the 25th day."

Of the eighth specification, guilty.

Of the ninth specification, guilty.

Of the tenth specification, not guilty.

Of the eleventh specification, guilty, after striking out the word "1st" and inserting instead the word "6th;" after striking out also the phrase "incite and urge" and the phrase "encouragement and instigation" and by adding the words "or about" after the word "on," where it occurs in the specification; and also after striking out the phrase "animals called bloodhounds" and inserting the word "dogs;" and also striking out the word "bloodhounds" where it afterward occurs and insert the word "dogs;" and also striking out the words "given by him."

Of the twelfth specification, guilty.

Of the thirteenth specification, not guilty.

Of the charge, guilty.

Sentence.

And the court does therefore sentence him, Henry Wirz, to be hanged by the neck till he be dead at such time and place as the President of the United States may direct, two-thirds of the members of the court concurring herein.

And the court also finds the prisoner, Henry Wirz, guilty of having caused the death, in manner as alleged in specification 11, to charge 2, by means of dogs, of three prisoners of war in his custody, and soldiers of the United States, one occurring on or about the 15th day of May, 1864; another occurring on or about the 11th day of July, 1864; another occurring on or about the 1st day of September, 1864; but which finding, as here expressed, has not and did not enter into the sentence of the court as before given.

II. The proceedings, finding, and sentence in the foregoing case having been submitted to the President of the United States, the following are his orders:

Executive Mansion, November 3, 1865.

The proceedings, finding, and sentence of the court in the within case are approved, and it is ordered that the sentence be carried into execution by the officer commanding the Department of Washington on Friday the 10th day of November, 1865, between the hours of 6 o'clock a.m. and 12 o'clock noon.

ANDREW JOHNSON,
President.

Source: U.S. War Department, War of the Rebellion: A Compilation of the Official Records of the Union and Confederate Armies, Ser. II, Vol. VIII.

Andrew Johnson Impeachment Trial (1868)

The first impeachment trial of a U.S. president occurred in 1868 and involved President Andrew Johnson, a Democrat from Tennessee. Johnson had served as vice president under President Abraham Lincoln and assumed the power of the presidency after the assassination of Lincoln on April 14, 1865. Johnson's impeachment trial was based largely upon the political motives of the radical Republicans in Congress who wanted Johnson removed from office because they were angered that Johnson was too forgiving in his policies toward the southern states in the aftermath of the Civil War (Rehnquist 1993, 143–150).

The post–Civil War era, often referred to as Reconstruction, was a difficult period in the history of the United States. During the Reconstruction period, political leaders had different ideas about how to deal with the southern states that had broken away from the United States and established their own government, the Confederate States of America, in an attempt to preserve slavery. The radical Republicans in Congress wanted the southern states to be treated as traitors defeated by the United States military. Under the policies of the radical Republicans, federal troops would occupy the southern territories and admit the states based upon federal rules prohibiting slavery and recognizing basic rights for the newly freed slaves (Linder, "Andrew Johnson").

President Johnson took a more lenient approach toward the southern states. Johnson proposed a plan to treat the southern states as sovereign and independent from the federal government and wanted the states readmitted to the United States with new leaders and their own free government. Under Johnson's plan, the southern states would most likely deny basic rights to the newly freed slaves and establish a new state constitution and government that was discriminatory toward African Americans (Linder, "Andrew Johnson").

In addition to Johnson's policies toward Reconstruction, the radical Republicans were also angered because Johnson had vetoed two bills passed by Congress in support of the newly freed slaves. The first bill dealt with providing more support for an executive agency known as the Freedmen's Bureau that was basically a federal welfare agency to assist the 4 million blacks in transition from slavery to freedom. The second bill was the Civil Rights Act of 1866 that was designed to provide fundamental rights to the newly freed slaves such as the right to own private property, make contracts, and testify in a court of law. Congress eventually overrode both of Johnson's vetoes with a two-thirds vote of each house of Congress. When Congress overrode Johnson's veto of the Civil Rights Act of 1866, it was the first time in the history of the United States that Congress had checked the veto power of a president (Benedict 1999, 8–14).

The argument presented by the House of Representatives to impeach Johnson from office ultimately was based upon Johnson's violation of the Office and

Tenure Act of 1867 which required Johnson to gain approval from the United States Senate prior to removing a Cabinet member (Ross 2008, 68–79). Johnson had decided to remove the secretary of war, Edwin Stanton, because Stanton had spoken out publicly against Johnson's Reconstruction policies; however, the U.S. Senate voted against Johnson's decision to remove Stanton. When Johnson went ahead and ordered Major General Lorenzo Thomas to replace Stanton, the radical Republicans who controlled the House of Representatives had had enough of President Johnson (Benedict 1999, 95–106). The House of Representatives impeached Johnson on February 24, 1868, by the necessary majority vote. An impeachment trial was scheduled to be held in the U.S. Senate with Chief Justice Salmon Chase serving as the judge. A two-thirds vote of the U.S. Senate would be required to remove Johnson from the presidency (Ross 1999, 78–79).

On March 30, 1868, members of the House of Representatives presented evidence and witnesses before the U.S. Senate to support the articles of impeachment against Johnson. The evidence centered on Johnson's violation of the Office and Tenure Act as well as harsh speeches that Johnson made around the country in which he described as treasonous those members of Congress who opposed his Reconstruction policies (Benedict 1999, 143–145).

The attorneys for President Johnson asserted that the Office and Tenure Act was an unconstitutional violation of presidential power under Article II of the U.S. Constitution. The attorneys also noted that Johnson's removal of a Cabinet member without the consent of the Senate did not meet the standard for an impeachable offense, such as violating the freedoms of U.S. citizens or the national security interests of the country. Johnson's attorneys concluded that the only offense committed by the president was his attempt to reconcile the differences between the northern and southern states by showing kindness to the southern states in the aftermath of the Civil War (Benedict 1999, 146–167).

Thirty-six of the 54 senators needed to vote in favor of the impeachment charges against President Johnson to remove him from office. Most observers of the impeachment trial assumed that the vote would be extremely close. In the end, 35 senators voted against Johnson and his presidency was saved by one single vote (Rehnquist 1993, 234–235).

Many historians have viewed the impeachment trial of Andrew Johnson as an unfair attempt to remove a president for political reasons. If Johnson had been removed from office, it may have set a dangerous precedent that presidents could be impeached and removed from office for political differences as opposed to the constitutional requirement of "high crimes and misdemeanors" (Ross 1999, 203–211) However, others have argued that if Johnson had been removed from office, the southern states may not have been able to establish racist policies such as the black codes and Jim Crow laws that ensured "separate but equal" would dominate the South for the next 100 years (Packard 2003, 45–51).

In the 1868 presidential election, President Andrew Johnson was defeated handily by Republican Ulysses S. Grant (Rehnquist 1993, 249–259). Prior to leaving office, Johnson granted pardons to all Confederates on Christmas Day, December 25, 1868, and further secured his legacy as a sympathizer of the southern states during the Reconstruction era (Hearn 2007, 200–211).

References

Benedict, Michael Les, *The Impeachment and Trial of Andrew Johnson*. New York: W. W. Norton and Company, 1999.

Gerson, Noel B, *The Trial of Andrew Johnson*. Nashville, TN: T. Nelson, 1977.

Hearn, Charles G. *Impeachment of Andrew Johnson*. Jefferson, NC: McFarland and Company, 2007.

Linder, Douglas O. "The Impeachment Trial of Andrew Johnson." *Famous Trials*. http://www.law.umkc.edu/faculty/projects/ftrials/impeach/imp_account2.html (accessed March 1, 2009).

Packard, Jerrold M. *American Nightmare: The History of Jim Crow*. New York: St. Martin's Griffin, 2003.

Rehnquist, William. *Grand Inquests: The Historic Impeachments of Justice Samuel Chase and President Andrew Johnson*. New York: Quill, 1993.

Ross, Edmund Gibson. *History of the Impeachment of Andrew Johnson: And His Trial by the Senate for High Crimes and Misdemeanors in Office*. Charleston: Forgotten Books, 2008.

Smith, Gene, *High Crimes and Misdemeanors: The Impeachment Trial of Andrew Johnson*. New York: William Morrow and Company, 1977.

Trefousse, Hans L. *Impeachment of a President: Andrew Johnson, the Blacks, and Reconstruction*. Bronx: Fordham University Press, 1999.

Lyman Trumbull: Speech in Defense of Andrew Johnson (1868)

During Andrew Johnson's impeachment trial in 1868, U.S. senator Lyman Trumbull defends the president in a speech excerpted here.

In coming to the conclusion that the President is not guilty of any of the high crimes and misdemeanors with which he stands charged, I have endeavored to be governed by the case made, without reference to other acts of his not contained in the record, and without giving the least heed to the clamor if intemperate zealots who demand the conviction of Andrew Johnson as a test of part faith, or seek to identify with and make responsible for his acts those who from convictions of duty feel compelled, on the case made, to vote for his acquittal.

His speeches and the general course of his administration have been as distasteful to me as to anyone, and I should consider it the great calamity of the age if the disloyal element, so often encouraged by his measures, should gain political ascendancy. If the question was, Is Andrew Johnson a fit person for President? I should answer, no; but it is not a party question, nor upon Andrew Johnson's deeds and acts, except so far as they are made to appear in the record, that I am to decide.

Painful as it is to disagree with so many political associates and friends whose conscientious convictions have led them to a different result, I must, nevertheless, in the discharge of the high responsibility under which I act, be governed by what my reason and judgment tell me is the truth, and the justice and law of this case. . . .

Once set the example of impeaching a President for what, when the excitement of the hour shall have subsided, will be regarded as insufficient causes, as several of those now alleged against the President were decided to be by the House of Representatives only a few months since, and no future President will be safe who happens to differ with a majority of the House and two-thirds of the Senate on any measure deemed by them important, particularly if of a political character. Blinded by partisan zeal, with such an example before them, they will not scruple to remove out of the way any obstacle to the accomplishment of their purposes, and what then becomes of the checks and balances of the Constitution, so carefully devised and so vital to its perpetuity? They are all gone.

In view of the consequences likely to flow from this day's proceedings, should they result in conviction on what my judgment tells me are insufficient charges and proofs, I tremble for the future of my country. I cannot be an instrument to produce such a result; and at the hazard of the ties even of friendship and affection, till calmer times shall do justice to my motives, no alternative is left me but the inflexible discharge of duty.

Susan B. Anthony Trial (1873)

Susan B. Anthony was a prominent leader of the women's civil rights movement in the 19th century who helped to establish the National Women's Suffrage Association (NSWA) in 1869 with Elizabeth Cady Stanton. The main purpose of the NWSA was to gain voting rights for women in the United States (Ward and Burns 1999, 179–189). When the U.S. Constitution was ratified in its original form in 1789, it did not recognize the right to vote for women. When Anthony decided to vote in the presidential election of 1872, she was subsequently arrested and tried in criminal court. The trial of Susan B. Anthony was a historic event because it provided an opportunity for Anthony to express her views about gender discrimination and women suffrage to the entire country (Sherr 1996, 107–117).

When Anthony registered to vote on November 1, 1872, in her hometown of Rochester, New York, along with a group of 50 women at a barbershop, election officials refused to allow Anthony to register to vote. She subsequently engaged in a debate with election officials for roughly an hour. Anthony began by citing the Fourteenth Amendment to the U.S. Constitution which guaranteed privileges, such as voting, to all U.S. citizens. While the Fourteenth Amendment, ratified in 1868, was designed to provide legal protections for African Americans after the Civil War, Anthony argued that the amendment did not mention that its privileges were limited strictly to men. Anthony also threatened to sue the election officials in civil court for large monetary damages. The election officials decided to allow Anthony to register to vote in the upcoming 1872 election. While election officials were concerned that they could be arrested for allowing a woman to register to vote, they also realized that Anthony was a powerful figure with important connections, both financially and politically. Hence, the election officials would probably have encountered legal troubles regardless of their decision (Linder, "Susan B. Anthony").

On November 5 1872, Susan B. Anthony and eight other women cast their ballots in the eighth ward of Rochester. Anthony voted for the incumbent Republican candidate for president, Ulysses S. Grant, because his party had promised to listen to her arguments in favor of allowing women the right to vote. In fact, Anthony voted for every Republican on her ballot, or what is called "straight-ticket" voting. Election officials voted 2–1 to accept her ballot (Linder, "Susan B. Anthony").

After a complaint was filed against Anthony by an election poll watcher, U.S. commissioner, William Storrs, issued an arrest warrant for Anthony on November 14, 1872, charging her with unlawfully voting in a federal election in violation of the Enforcement Act passed by Congress in 1870. Anthony was facing a maximum fine of $500 or three years in prison (Linder, "Susan B. Anthony").

When a federal marshal showed up at Anthony's home to arrest her, he stated that the U.S. commissioner would like to see her. Anthony was insulted by the preferential treatment of the marshal and demanded that she be arrested, similar to how a man would be arrested, so the federal marshal placed her in handcuffs and took her to the commissioner's office. In addition to Anthony being arrested, several other women who had voted were arrested as well as the election officials who had registered the women to vote (Harper 2007, 480–502).

Anthony's attorney, Henry Selden, argued at a preliminary hearing on November 29, 1872, that Anthony had not violated the Enforcement Act because she believed that she had the right to vote. Under the federal law, a person could only be arrested and prosecuted if he or she knowingly cast an illegal ballot. However, the commissioner concluded that Anthony probably did violate the federal law. When Anthony refused to pay the bail of $500, the commissioner ordered a federal marshal to take her into custody until a grand jury could decide if Anthony would be indicted on the federal charges. On January 24, 1873, a grand jury comprised entirely of men indicted Anthony for knowingly voting in a federal election as an individual of the female sex. Anthony's criminal trial was set for May 1873 in federal district court (Linder, "Susan B. Anthony").

After Anthony's attorney posted bail with his own personal finances, Anthony went on a lecture tour in the months leading up to her trial by speaking in every town in Monroe County, New York, in an attempt to educate citizens about women's suffrage. Her lecture tour was titled, "Is It a Crime for a Citizen of the U.S. to Vote"? Her lecture tour was so influential that federal prosecutors were forced to move her trial from Monroe County to Ontario County because they feared that potential jurors who had heard her lecture would not vote to convict her (Harper 2007, 503–521).

During the criminal trial, the witnesses for the prosecution included election officials who testified that Anthony had cast a ballot in the 1872 election in violation of a federal law prohibiting a person from knowingly casting an illegal ballot. Defense attorneys for Anthony argued that she was being prosecuted solely because of her gender and that women must be given the right to vote in order to receive impartial treatment from elected representatives in the legislature. The basis of Anthony's legal argument presented by her attorney was centered on the privileges and immunities clause of the Fourteenth Amendment which prohibited states from enforcing laws that violated the privileges and immunities of all persons who possessed citizenship within the United States. Even if the Fourteenth Amendment could not be used to protect Anthony's right to vote, she should not be prosecuted because she truly believed that she had the legal right to vote. Technically, Anthony would not be in violation of the federal law that allowed for the prosecution of persons who "knowingly" voted illegally (Linder, "Susan B. Anthony").

After the prosecution and defense rested in their arguments before the jury, the federal judge in the trial, Ward Hunt, issued a statement ordering the jury to issue a verdict of guilty because the Fourteenth Amendment did not protect a woman's right to vote and Anthony knew that she was breaking a federal law when she voted in the 1872 federal election. Apparently, Judge Ward had prepared his statement to the jury even before the trial began (Linder, "Susan B. Anthony").

Prior to the sentencing of Anthony, Judge Ward asked her if she had anything to say before sentencing was imposed. Anthony then engaged in a heated exchange with Judge Ward where she asserted that her right to a trial by jury had been violated, women all over the United States were second class citizens dominated by men, and each woman has been denied participation in our democratic society without the right to vote. Judge Ward finally sentenced Anthony to a fine of $100 and also ordered her to pay the court costs of the prosecution. As expected, Anthony refused to pay the fine and did not pay the fine for the rest of her life. Judge Ward did not pursue payment of the fine because he wanted to prevent an appeal of his ruling (Linder, "Susan B. Anthony").

Susan B. Anthony became a martyr in the eyes of her supporters, while her opponents viewed her simply as a criminal. Anthony printed 3,000 copies of the trial transcript and had the copies circulated to government officials, libraries, and political activists. Susan B. Anthony died in 1906 and it was not until 14 years after her death in 1920 that the Nineteenth Amendment to the U.S. Constitution was ratified to ensure women the right to vote across the entire United States (Sherr 1996, 324). She was honored by the U.S. government when she became the first woman to appear on U.S. coinage. Anthony appeared on the one dollar coin minted from 1979 to 1999 (226).

References

Barry, Kathleen. *Susan B. Anthony: A Biography of a Singular Feminist.* Bloomington, IN: AuthorHouse, 2000.

Harper, Ida Husted. *The Life and Work of Susan B. Anthony.* Vol. 1. New York: BiblioLife, 2007.

Linder, Douglas O. "The Trial of Susan B. Anthony for Illegal Voting." *Famous Trials.* http://www.law.umkc.edu/faculty/projects/ftrials/anthony/sbaaccount.html (accessed March 1, 2009).

Sherr, Lynn. *Failure Is Impossible: Susan B. Anthony in Her Own Words.* New York: Three Rivers Press, 1996.

Ward, Geoffrey, and Ken Burns. *Not For Ourselves Alone: The Story of Elizabeth Cady Stanton and Susan B. Anthony.* New York: Knopf, 1999.

Henry Ward Beecher Trial (1875)

The adultery trial of Henry Ward Beecher has been called the biggest sex scandal of the 19th century. Within American culture, the civil trial raised important issues related to the institution of marriage and traditional morality (Fox 1999, 1–10). From a legal perspective, the trial exposed a flaw in the common law system of justice where a husband or wife was prohibited from testifying against his or her spouse. The common law rule of inter-spousal immunity proved to be a significant obstacle in establishing the truth about the relationship between Reverend Beecher and a woman within his congregation (Law Library, "Tilton v. Beecher").

Henry Ward Beecher was a revolutionary figure in the 19th century. He was a respected preacher at the Plymouth Congregational Church in Brooklyn, New York, and he also was actively involved in terms of progressive reform. Beecher was ahead of his time as a leader who opposed slavery, favored voting rights for women, and expressed a strong belief in Charles Darwin's theory of evolution (Law Library, "Tilton v. Beecher").

A local newspaper, the *New York Independent,* often published Beecher's sermons which referenced his political and social views. In 1861, Beecher had become an influential figure at the *New York Independent* when he recommended that his assistant, Theodore Tilton, be hired as an editor. Throughout the 1860s,

Beecher developed a very close relationship with Tilton and his family, including his wife, Elizabeth (Law Library, "Tilton v. Beecher").

In the late 1860s, Tilton began writing editorials in the *New York Independent* that were considered controversial. He advocated free love and also became critical of the idea of marriage and traditional values. At the same time, Beecher started providing spiritual counseling and guidance for Elizabeth Tilton, in part, because of her husband's radical viewpoints (Law Library, "Tilton v. Beecher").

In July 1870, Elizabeth Tilton told her husband that Beecher had attempted to seduce her during their private meetings together. However, while Elizabeth Tilton initially confessed to the affair in a letter to her husband, she would later recant her confession in a letter that Beecher encouraged her to write (Fox 1999, 171–174).

In 1874, four years after his wife's initial confession, Theodore Tilton announced to the public that Beecher had made sexual advances toward his wife. The accusation became a national scandal, and Beecher responded by expelling Tilton from the congregation of the Plymouth Church (Fox 1999, 125–134).

In June 1874, Beecher asked the most respected members of the Plymouth Church to conduct an investigation in order to determine whether he had attempted to seduce Elizabeth Tilton (Law Library, "Tilton v. Beecher"). On August 27, 1874, the committee concluded that, as a result of her husband's extremist views about free love, it was expected that Elizabeth Tilton would seek counseling from the reverend of her church. During the private sessions, Elizabeth Tilton developed a strong emotional attachment to Beecher. However, the committee emphasized that Beecher did not make any sexual advances toward Elizabeth Tilton based upon the evidence presented by her. In addition, the committee praised Beecher as a devout Christian who was respected and admired by his congregation (Fox 1999, 54).

Tilton accused the committee of issuing a biased report and filed a lawsuit against Beecher in civil court in Brooklyn, New York. While Tilton previously had only maintained that Beecher had attempted to seduce his wife, his lawsuit went further and accused Beecher and Elizabeth Tilton of actually engaging in a sexual relationship. On January 4, 1875, the civil trial of *Tilton v. Beecher* began in the courtroom of Judge Joseph Neilson with Tilton charging Beecher with adultery. Tilton hired three lawyers, W. Fullerton, Samuel D. Morris, and Roger Pryor, to represent him in the lawsuit, while Beecher was defended by five lawyers, William Evarts, John L. Hill, John Porter, Thomas Sherman, and Benjamin Tracy (Law Library, "Tilton v. Beecher").

During the trial, Theodore and Elizabeth Tilton were not allowed to testify because, under common law, husbands and wives were prohibited from testifying for or against their spouses. The justification for inter-spousal immunity within criminal and civil cases was based upon the idea that marriage was a sacred institution, and husbands or wives might be tempted to commit perjury to protect their spouse or themselves. In addition, it was possible that testimony from a spouse could negatively affect the relationship between husband and wife (Law Library, "Tilton v. Beecher").

Judge Neilson, however, did permit Theodore Tilton to testify based upon an exception to the common law rule of inter-spousal immunity. During his testimony, Tilton was not allowed to reveal anything about his relationship with his wife that was considered to be confidential. Therefore, Tilton was not permitted to discuss any conversations with his wife that related directly to the alleged adultery. Ultimately, Tilton's testimony simply concerned his own observations of the relationship between his wife and Beecher which provided little evidence that adultery had been committed (Law Library, "Tilton v. Beecher").

Two former members of Beecher's congregation, Francis and Emma Moulton, were called to testify by Tilton's attorneys. The husband and wife swore that Beecher had confessed to them about his affair with Elizabeth Tilton. The Moultons also stated that they encouraged Beecher to confess his sins publicly to the church but he said that he would rather die than admit his relationship with Elizabeth Tilton. Emma Moulton also added that Elizabeth Tilton had decided to deny the affair regardless of the fact that it might cause her husband to lose the case against Beecher ("Mr. Beecher On Trial").

Beecher eventually took the witness stand and, during direct testimony, he emphatically denied committing adultery with Elizabeth Tilton. However, on cross-examination by Tilton's attorneys, his testimony seemed puzzling to many court observers who noted that he contradicted himself and often claimed a loss of memory or provided vague answers when asked specific questions about his relationship with Elizabeth Tilton. Tilton's attorneys also confronted Beecher about the statements made by the Moultons and about his own letters which suggested that he asked for forgiveness from Theodore Tilton and even discussed the fault of Tilton's wife, implying she had done something wrong. However, Beecher stated that Tilton and the Moultons were simply trying to blackmail him, and he also denied that his letters implied he had committed adultery with Elizabeth Tilton (Beecher 1875, 21–32).

In defense of Beecher, his attorneys relied largely upon a number of character witnesses who testified to Beecher's integrity. The defense also attempted to destroy the character of Theodore Tilton who was portrayed as an adulterer as well as someone who was intensely jealous of Beecher (Law Library, "Tilton v. Beecher").

After attorneys for both sides rested, the jury deliberated for roughly one week and, on July 1, 1875, announced that they could not reach a decision. While the 12 jurors failed to reach a unanimous verdict, they did vote 9–3 in favor of acquitting Beecher. Judge Neilson declared a mistrial which was a victory for Beecher since a second trial was not planned for the future (Law Library, "Tilton v. Beecher"). Interestingly, three years after the adultery trial in 1878, Elizabeth Tilton changed her story yet again and confessed to having had a sexual relationship with Beecher (Fox 1999, 4–5).

On June 24, 1883, at Beecher's 70th birthday party, Judge Neilson spoke publicly about the trial and expressed his sincere belief that Beecher was innocent of the charges. However, the scandal had an effect on the reputation of Beecher who never retained his previous status as a leading spokesperson on issues related to progressive reform (Law Library, "Tilton v. Beecher").

The Henry Ward Beecher trial was a national scandal that involved celebrity, sex, religion, politics, and marriage. Because Beecher was an important voice for the voting rights of women, legendary figures of the suffrage movement, such as Susan B. Anthony and Elizabeth Stanton, were forced into the awkward position of commenting publicly about Beecher's activities ("The Scandal: Susan B. Anthony's Statement Contradicted"). In terms of its effect on the American legal system, the trial resulted in the elimination of the common law rule of inter-spousal immunity. Today, the communications between spouses within a marriage remain protected, and a husband or wife cannot be forced to testify against each other; however, a husband or wife may waive this privilege of confidentiality in order to testify against a spouse in a criminal case (Law Library, "Tilton v. Beecher").

References

Beecher, Henry Ward. "The Beecher Trial: A Review of the Evidence." *New York Times.* July 3, 1875, pp. 1–34.

Fox, Richard Wightman. *Trials of Intimacy: Love and Loss in the Beecher-Tilton Scandal.* Chicago: University of Chicago Press, 1999.

Law Library–American Law and Legal Information. "Tilton v. Beecher: 1875—Plymouth Church Clears, Mrs. Tilton Never Testifies." http://law.jrank.org/pages/2629/Tilton-v-Beecher-1875.html. *Notable Trials and Court Cases—1833 to 1882* (accessed January 12, 2010).

"Mr. Beecher On Trial; Remarkable Testimony from Mrs. Moulton." *New York Times: Archives.* February 20, 1875. http://query.nytimes.com/gst/abstract.html?res=9505EED A133EE43BBC4851DFB466838E669FDE (accessed January 13, 2010).

"The Scandal: Susan B. Anthony's Statement Contradicted." *Brooklyn Daily Eagle.* July 27, 1874. http://eagle.brooklynpubliclibrary.org/Repository/getFiles.asp?Style=OliveXLib: ArticleToMailGifMSIE&Type=text/html&Path=BEG/1874/07/31&ID=Ar00201&Locale=&ChunkNum=0 (accessed January 13, 2010).

The Mountain Meadows Massacre Trials (1875–1876)

On September 11, 1857, 120 people, including many women and children, were murdered by Mormons at Mountain Meadows in the southern part of the Utah territory. The victims had been traveling in wagons from Arkansas through Utah on their way to California. The tragedy of the Mountain Meadows massacre had its origins in the history of persecution against Mormons and the controversial teachings of Brigham Young, the 19th-century leader of the Mormon religion, who encouraged a culture of violence as a way to save his followers. While it took 20 years before anyone was convicted for the murders, the prosecution of John D. Lee in 1877 highlighted the "politics" of the American criminal justice system as federal authorities attempted to achieve, at least, a semblance of justice for the victims of the Mountain Meadows massacre (Linder, "The Mountain Meadows Massacre of 1857").

In 1851, the territorial government of Utah was established when Brigham Young was appointed as its first governor by President Milliard Fillmore. Young imposed upon his followers a controversial version of the Mormon religion which permitted men to have several wives and tied religion and government together. However, the most controversial idea of the Mormon religion in the 19th century promoted by Young was the doctrine of "blood atonement," which encouraged the murder of persons who sinned against God as a way to save their souls (Walker, Turley, and Leonard 2008, 20–25).

Throughout the 1850s, Brigham Young and the Mormons maintained tense relations with the federal government. The Mormon Church had grown resentful toward the federal government because of the decades of discrimination and persecution faced by its followers. From the federal government's perspective, Brigham Young was a dangerous leader who encouraged violence among his followers (Linder, "The Mountain Meadows Massacre of 1857").

When economic conditions worsened for the Mormons because of a drought in 1856, Young blamed the problems on the sins of Mormons who had lost their way with God. In order to restore the purity of the Mormon religion, Young ordered a "Reformation," where he demanded the murder of Mormons who had committed serious sins. Young's inspirational speeches to his congregation produced a culture of violence. As federal officials fled the area in fear for their lives, Mormons activated their own militia because they were concerned that the federal government would send military troops into the Utah territory (Bagley 2004, 48–54).

During this time period, several families in Arkansas had loaded up their wagons and were headed westward on a planned trip through Utah to California. The Arkansas families were referred to as the Fancher Party, and they were set to arrive at a campsite roughly 70 miles north of Mountain Meadows in early September of 1857. When rumors began to spread through the Mormon community that members of the Fancher Party may have been involved in the murders of two Mormon apostles, Parley Pratt in eastern Arkansas and Joseph Smith in Illinois, Issac Haight, commander of the Utah militia, held a meeting to discuss the course of action against the Fancher Party (Linder, "The Mountain Meadows Massacre of 1857").

The assault on the Fancher families began as a battle on Sunday, September 6, 1857, when approximately 50 Native American Indians and Mormons dressed as Indians attacked the campsite. Brigham Young had convinced the Indians that the non-Mormons passing through Utah were a threat to everyone in Utah and gave the Indians permission to take the cattle of the families. By encouraging the Indians to engage in violence with non-Mormons, Young was sending a strong message to the federal government that outsiders were not welcome in the Utah territory (Linder, "The Mountain Meadows Massacre of 1857").

Over the next three days, a stand-off occurred in the battle between the Mormon forces, who had been joined by an additional 100 men, and the Fancher families who were well armed. By this time, the Indian forces had left the battle and were no longer participating in the assault on the families. On September 11, 1857, the Mormons then used two of its members, John D. Lee and William Batemen, to pretend as if they were surrendering by walking toward the campsite with white flags. The families, who were desperate for an end to the conflict, came out from behind the security of their wagons and agreed to give up their weapons and cattle in an exchange for a promise that they would not be harmed by either the Mormons or any Indians. The Mormons began walking the Fancher families in the direction of Cedar City, Utah, about 35 miles away (Linder, "The Mountain Meadows Massacre of 1857").

As the men of the Fancher families walked behind the wagons with one Mormon guard next to each man, the Mormons took their guns and shot and killed each of the men walking next to them. Next, the women and children who had been riding in the wagons were murdered. Of the 140 members of the Fancher Party, 120 were massacred by the Mormon forces. The 20 surviving members of the Fancher Party were all six years of age or younger and were later placed in Mormon households (Bagley 2004, 4–5).

When California newspapers began publishing reports of the massacre from mail carriers who had traveled through the area and witnessed the 120 dead bodies of the Fancher families, the public demanded that the federal government take military action against the persons involved in the murders. Brigham Young and other Mormon leaders decided to deny the involvement of Mormons in the massacre and attempted to blame the Indians. On March 18, 1858, Congress began an official investigation into the deaths of the Fancher Party at Mountain Meadows (Linder, "The Mountain Meadows Massacre of 1857").

On June 26, 1858, federal troops entered Utah and took control of the territory under an agreement with Brigham Young, which included a pardon for any Mormon who committed violent acts as part of "the rebellion." In November 1858, a U.S. federal district court judge, John Cradlebaugh, decided to investigate the massacre at Mountain Meadows and sought the arrest of John D. Lee, Issac Haight, and John Higbee for the murders of the Fancher families. However, a federal marshal refused to make the arrests because he feared the reaction from the local population, and the federal government refused to instruct federal troops to protect him. Once the Civil War started in 1861, there was little interest in prosecuting the persons responsible for the murders and, when the war ended, a new governor of Utah, Alfred Cumming, refused to prosecute because he knew that it would be futile, given the fact that Brigham Young remained in control of the Utah criminal justice system (Linder, "The Mountain Meadows Massacre of 1857").

In the early 1870s, a writer for the *Utah Reporter,* Charles W. Wandell, published a series of stories on the massacre which sparked a renewed interest in the tragedy. Wandell confronted Brigham Young's explanation of the murders and even provided a confession from a former Mormon, Philip Klingensmith, who had participated in the crimes (Bagley 2004, 268–269). In addition to Wandell's stories, Congress passed a law called the Poland Act which redefined the jurisdiction of the criminal justice system in Utah and allowed for juries to be composed of non-Mormons. Since Brigham Young would have less control over the jury system, it was reasonable to think that a criminal trial could be held in Utah and justice might be served for the victims of the Mountain Meadows massacre (283–288).

Arrests warrants were issued for nine men supposedly involved in the massacre, but the federal government decided to try John D. Lee first because they felt that he provided the best chance for a conviction. On July 23, 1875, John D. Lee went on trial in Beaver, Utah, in the courtroom of U.S. district judge Jacob Boreman. The federal prosecutors, William C. Carey and Robert Baskin, would argue the case against Lee, while Brigham Young paid for four lawyers to provide the legal defense (Linder, "The Mountain Meadows Massacre of 1857"). Lee's defense attorneys quickly became divided about whether implicating high-ranking officials within the Mormon community in the massacre would provide the best defense for Lee (Brooks 1991, 191).

The 12-man jury was composed of eight Mormons, three non-Mormons, and one person who had left the Mormon Church. The trial began amidst rumors that violence might be committed against prosecution witnesses by a local mob, so a federal marshal had to issue a public threat to anyone who might be thinking about disrupting the judicial proceedings (Bagley 2004, 291–293).

The opening statement for the prosecution was made by William Carey who described in detail the massacre of September 11, 1857. The prosecution then called several witnesses who testified how officials within the Mormon community sought to cause problems for any non-Mormons traveling through Utah in 1857. For example, witnesses told how they were instructed not to sell food or supplies to the Fancher families when they arrived in southern Utah. Witnesses also relayed stories of people being assaulted or kicked out of the church if they tried to assist any non-Mormons traveling through the territory. In 1857, witnesses portrayed the Utah territory as a place of anger and resentment against outsiders who were viewed as a danger to the Mormon community (Linder, "The Mountain Meadows Massacre of 1857").

The star witness for the prosecution was Philip Klingensmith, who described in detail the attack on the Fancher families at Mountain Meadows, the false surrender and negotiations with the families orchestrated by John D. Lee, and, finally, the execution of the men, women, and children. Klingensmith also stated that he thought Lee had received orders to murder the families from high-ranking Mormon officials such as Higbee and Haight. Klingensmith concluded his testimony by recalling a meeting where Brigham Young and other officials discussed how to divide up the personal possessions of the victims. At the meeting, Young also instructed his followers not to talk to anyone about the massacre (Bagley 2004, 292).

Defense attorney Wells Spicer argued that Lee was reluctant to take part in the attack on the Fancher families. According to Spicer, the Fancher Party was to blame because they instigated the attack. Spicer also claimed that Lee was threatened by Mormon officials, such as Haight and Higbee, as well as the Indians who said that they would kill Lee if he didn't participate in the killing. In a puzzling move, Spicer returned after a recess and asked that his previous comments about Lee acting upon orders from Mormon officials be withdrawn from the court record. Apparently, some Mormon officials were displeased with the Spicer's legal strategy to connect high ranking members to the massacre (Bagley 2004, 294–295).

Overall, the defense attorneys were disorganized in their presentation before the court. For example, the defense called witnesses who accused the Fancher Party of poisoning spring water which led to the death of an Indian and this supposedly explained the massacre of the families by the Indians. However, even though the story was discredited on cross-examination by the prosecution, the defense continued to rely on the story during closing arguments (Linder, "The Mountain Meadows Massacre of 1857").

In the end, the jury voted in a predictable fashion with the eight Mormons and the former Mormon voting not guilty and the three non-Mormons voting for a conviction. On August 5, 1875, Judge Boreman was forced to declare a mistrial because of the hung jury. However, as a result of the first trial, the American public lost respect for the Mormon Church as their reputation was severely damaged by the information presented in court about their role in the massacre (Brooks 1991, 191–193).

After Sumner Howard replaced William Carey as the federal prosecutor in Utah in April 1876, Howard came to the conclusion that a deal had to be struck with Brigham Young to secure a conviction against John D. Lee. As pressure from the federal government and the American public began to intensify, Brigham Young realized that someone would have to be sacrificed or else the status of the Mormon Church would continue to deteriorate throughout the country (Linder, "The Mountain Meadows Massacre of 1857").

It has been speculated that Howard entered into an agreement with Young to try Lee before an all-Mormon jury and present prosecution witnesses who would only testify about Lee's role in the massacre. Hence, the high-ranking officials within the Mormon community would be absolved of any blame for the massacre, including Young whose deposition from the first trial would be introduced. In the deposition, Young stated that he ordered safe passage for the Fancher Party through Utah, although historians remain divided over the truthfulness of Young's testimony. After trying Lee, Howard promised that no one else would be prosecuted in the future for the murders. In exchange, Young was required to produce witnesses to testify against Lee and also guarantee a guilty verdict from the all-Mormon jury (Linder, "The Mountain Meadows Massacre of 1857").

The second trial of John D. Lee began on September 14, 1876. Lee was represented by defense attorney, William Bishop, who was immediately surprised and confused to find that the Mormon leadership was assisting in the prosecution of the case. Prior to the trial, Bishop had expected the Mormon leadership to defend Lee against the accusations of murder at Mountain Meadows. Beginning with the opening statement to the jury, Sumner Howard made it perfectly clear that John Lee was the person responsible for the massacre and the leadership within the Mormon community had nothing to do with the tragedy. Howard exaggerated the role of Lee in the massacre by describing how Lee encouraged other Mormons and the Indians to attack the Fancher Party. Howard also claimed that Lee had invented the plan concerning the fake surrender that lured the families out from behind their wagons and Lee personally murdered a large number of men, women, and children at Mountain Meadows. Unlike the first trial, several witnesses testified to the fact that they saw Lee commit the murders, but the witnesses conveniently could not remember anyone else besides Lee who committed a murder on the day of the massacre (Bagley 2004, 301–310).

When Lee realized that he was doomed to be offered as a scapegoat for the massacre, he instructed his defense attorneys to provide no defense in his favor after the prosecution finished its case. In his closing statement, Bishop simply told the jury that Lee obviously was being sacrificed by the Mormon Church. After a brief trial that lasted only six days and a few hours of deliberation by the all-Mormon jury, Lee was found guilty of first-degree murder (Linder, "The Mountain Meadows Massacre of 1857").

Three weeks after the second trial, Judge Boreman sentenced Lee to be executed. After the sentence was issued, Lee told Judge Boreman that he preferred to be shot. After several months of appeals, Lee's execution was scheduled for March 23, 1877 (Bagley 2004, 315–317). Lee made a statement prior to his execution where he maintained that he did not intend to do anything wrong and did not believe in the teachings of Brigham Young. He concluded his statement by declaring that he had been sacrificed by cowards. Lee was then executed near the site of the massacre at Mountain Meadows by a firing squad (Walker, Turley, and Leonard 2008, 230–231).

During his time in prison awaiting his execution, Lee wrote about the history of the Mormon Church and his interpretation of the causes of the Mountain Meadows massacre. Lee's defense attorney, William Bishop, sent the manuscript to a St. Louis publishing company in 1877 and the book became a best-seller entitled *Mormonism Unveiled or the Life and Confession of John D. Lee* (Bagley 2004, 311–319).

The history of discrimination against Mormons, the economic conditions in the 1850s in Utah, and the controversial teachings of Brigham Young created a culture of fear and violence that ultimately led to the tragedy at Mountain Meadows. The conviction and execution of John D. Lee in 1877 provided some closure for the American public, but the massacre of 120 members of the Fancher Party in 1857 will always rank as one of the largest mass killings of American civilians and perhaps the darkest moment of the 19th century (Linder, "The Mountain Meadows Massacre of 1857").

References

Bagley, Will. *Blood of the Prophets: Brigham Young and the Massacre at Mountain Meadows.* Norman: University of Oklahoma Press, 2004.

Brooks, Juanita. *The Mountain Meadows Massacre.* Norman: University of Oklahoma Press, 1991.

Linder, Douglas O. "The Mountain Meadows Massacre of 1857 and the Trials of John D. Lee: An Account." *Famous Trials.* http://www.law.umkc.edu/faculty/projects/FTRIALS/mountainmeadows/leeaccount.html (accessed July 20, 2009).

Walker, Ronald W., Richard E. Turley, and Glen M. Leonard. *Massacre at Meadows Mountain.* New York: Oxford University Press, 2008.

The O. K. Corral Trial (1881)

The most famous gunfight in the Old West involved a showdown in Tombstone, Arizona, between Wyatt Earp, his two brothers, and Doc Holliday against four outlaws. In the aftermath of shooting, three of the outlaws were killed and a pretrial hearing was held to determine if the Earp brothers and Doc Holliday should be tried for murder. The gunfight and subsequent trial was a legendary event in the history of the American West and transformed Wyatt Earp into a heroic figure throughout the world (Law Library, "Wyatt Earp Trial").

At 3:00 p.m. on Wednesday, October 26, 1881 in Tombstone, Arizona, four lawmen and four outlaws engaged in a shootout near the O. K. Corral. The four lawmen represented the Tombstone Marshal's Office and consisted of the Earp brothers, Wyatt, Virgil, and Morgan, and their close friend, Doc Holliday. The four outlaws were known as the Clanton and McLaury clans and consisted of Ike and Billy Clanton and Tom and Frank McLaury. The gunfight resulted from a long-standing feud between the two groups and ended in the deaths of three of the outlaws, Billy Clanton and Tom and Frank McLaury (Linder, "The Earp-Holliday Trial").

The sheriff of Tombstone, Johnny Behan, was uncertain whether he should arrest the Earp brothers and Doc Holliday for the murder of the three cowboys because most people in the town were split about whether the lawmen had acted properly in instigating a gun battle with the cowboys. On October 29, 1881, Ike Clanton took the unusual step of filing first-degree murder charges against the four lawmen. Ordinarily, Sheriff Behen would have filed the charges but Clanton was allowed to file the charges because Behen knew that, as sheriff, he would be required to testify as a witness at the trial (Linder, "The Earp-Holliday Trial").

The Preliminary Hearing ("The Murder Trial")

Justice of the Peace Wells W. Spicer presided over the preliminary hearing where Spicer would be forced to decide whether enough evidence existed to try the defendants for murder. Under normal circumstances, a preliminary hearing is a routine step toward a criminal trial and the prosecutor would present evidence to justify a criminal trial with hardly any resistance from the defense. However, because Spicer was considered to be supportive of the Earp brothers, the defendants thought that they had a better chance of having the charges dismissed at the preliminary hearing than securing an acquittal after a criminal trial before a jury of 12 men. Therefore, the preliminary hearing took on the form of a regular trial with both sides fighting hard for a victory as dozens of witnesses were called and cross-examined by the prosecution and defense teams. It would last almost one month and stands today as the longest preliminary hearing in the history of the state of Arizona (Linder, "The Earp-Holliday Trial").

The Earps and Holliday were represented by Thomas Fitch, a former member of Congress from Nevada with a reputation as a brilliant strategist in the courtroom. The prosecution team would consist of Lyttleton Price, Ben Goodrich, and Will McLaury, the brother of the McLaurys killed in the shootout. A key obstacle for the prosecution was the fact that the three prosecutors each had different goals in mind. Price favored a less aggressive approach during the hearing because he was part of the Tombstone establishment, which included the Earps. Goodrich was Ike Clanton's personal attorney and wanted the Earps and Holliday eventually to be convicted but he understood that a moderate approach was necessary because the defendants were lawmen and part of the establishment. Finally, as expected, McLaury took the most extreme approach because he wanted to avenge the murder of his two brothers (Linder, "The Earp-Holliday Trial").

On October 31, 1881, the preliminary hearing officially began with testimony from the coroner who spoke about the specific gunshot wounds of the three men who were killed. The coroner refused to assign blame to either party (Lubet 2006, 86).

Next, Billy Allen testified as the first witness for the prosecution. Allen stated that Frank McLaury simply wanted to get his brother and Ike Clanton out of town after he heard of the problems that they had encountered with the four lawmen. Allen also said that he witnessed the gunfight and the Earps and Doc Holliday began firing first at the Clanton and McLaury brothers who were not given a chance to surrender their weapons. On cross-examination, Allen's credibility was damaged when he exercised his right to remain silent after Thomas Fitch asked Allen if he recently had fled Colorado to avoid prosecution on robbery charges (86–89).

On November 2, 1881, Sheriff Behen testified that he had heard about the trouble between the two parties and tried to disarm the Clanton and McLaury brothers at the O. K. Corral but was unsuccessful for the most part. Behen then told how the Earps and Holliday arrived for the showdown and he ordered the lawmen not to enter into a gun battle with the cowboys. Behen concluded his testimony by providing details of the exchange of words between the two groups prior to the shooting. Wyatt Earp allegedly told the cowboys that they had been looking for a fight. Virgil Earp then supposedly told the cowboys to raise their hands. Behen believed that the shooting began when Holliday fired the first shot at Billy Clanton (Linder, "The Earp-Holliday Trial").

During cross-examination, Thomas Fitch asked Behen about his competition with Wyatt Earp for the job of sheriff as a way to demonstrate the likelihood of bias in his testimony against his rival. Fitch also pointed out the errors in Behen's description of the gunfight. Behen had stated that Holliday fired the first shot with a pistol, but other eyewitnesses had testified that Holliday had a shotgun during the entire battle. The most successful part of the cross-examination occurred when Fitch asked Behen if he had visited Virgil Earp in the hospital and told him that he was right to have engaged in the gunfight with the cowboys (Lubet 2006, 92–100).

Entering the preliminary hearing, the prosecution's goal had been to establish that the killing of the three cowboys was premeditated based upon comments overheard by witnesses at the gunfight. However one witness, Martha King, could not identify which Earp brother said, "Let them have it" before the shooting began. Another witness, Wesley Fuller, testified that Billy Clanton shouted, "Don't shoot me!" But, Fuller was discredited by Fitch under cross-examination because he had admitted publicly that he wanted to "cinch" Doc Holliday with his testimony (Linder, "The Earp-Holliday Trial"). Finally, Billy Claiborne testified that the lawmen had their guns in their hands as they approached the Clanton and McLaury brothers. Once again, however, Fitch was successful at discrediting a witness during cross-examination when, after he asked Claiborne whether he was currently facing murder charges in South Carolina, Claiborne refused to answer (Lubet 2006, 111–117).

Ike Clanton's testimony for the prosecution tried to establish that the Earp brothers and Holliday were simply looking for a fight, but he neglected to talk about the series of confrontations that led to the showdown. During cross-examination, Fitch easily got Clanton to acknowledge that he also had been looking for a fight by insulting and challenging the lawmen. During his questioning of Clanton, Fitch also revealed the secret deals that Clanton had discussed with Wyatt Earp to improve Earp's campaign for sheriff. Fitch suggested that Earp could have used the secret deals against Clanton by exposing him to his fellow cowboys, and this served as motivation to engage in a fight with Wyatt Earp. In response to Fitch's suggestion, Clanton started making outrageous claims that the Earps and Holliday had been involved in a stagecoach robbery and murder which significantly harmed the prosecution's case. After the cross-examination, Fitch had established that Clanton was as much to blame for the gunfight as the defendants and turned the cowboy into an unreliable witness (Lubet 2006, 117–131).

The defense team began the presentation of its case on November 16, 1881. Wyatt Earp provided testimony in narrative form to take advantage of the fact that cross-examination was not permitted during a preliminary hearing if a defendant simply provided an account of the event. Earp told about the history of conflict between the Earps and the McLaury brothers who had been arrested for stealing mules in the past. Earp speculated that the McLaury brothers had been looking for a chance to even the score and used the Earps' trouble with Ike Clanton as an opportunity (Lubet 2006, 137–140).

Wyatt Earp placed part of the blame for the shootout on Sheriff Behen who misled Earp into thinking the cowboys did not have any guns at the O. K. Corral. When the lawmen approached the cowboys, they saw that the cowboys had guns in their possession. Earp maintained that, as an officer of law, he acted in self-defense when he realized the Clanton and McLaury brothers had weapons and were in violation of a Tombstone ordinance prohibiting the possession of guns in a public place (Lubet 2004, 143–148).

On November 19, 1881, Virgil Earp gave testimony from his bed at a local hotel because he was still recovering from a gunshot wound to the leg. Virgil Earp spoke about how he had been warned that Ike Clanton was planning upon killing him. In addition, several other threats had been made against the Earp brothers by the Clanton and McLaury brothers. Virgil Earp stated that the cowboys would have been left alone if they had not left the O. K. Corral but, when they walked out into the street toward the vacant lot, they had violated the gun possession law and were subject to arrest (Lubet 2006, 157–164).

The defense concluded by calling a number of witnesses, such as H. F. Sills and Ned Boyle, who testified to the threats made by Ike Clanton against the Earps. The prosecution case was also damaged by Winfield Williams' testimony for the defense when Williams testified that he overheard Sheriff Behen praise Virgil Earp for having done the right thing in engaging in the gunfight (Lubet 2006, 165–172).

After hearing testimony from 30 witnesses, Judge Spicer finally handed down his ruling on November 30, 1881. Spicer ruled in favor of the defense and stated that there would not be a criminal trial for the Earps and Doc Holliday. While the decision of the lawmen to approach the Clanton and McLaury brothers was unwise, their actions did not constitute a criminal offense. Spicer laid the blame for the shootout on Ike Clanton and the three men who were killed because they refused to surrender their weapons to Sheriff Behen initially and then later to the Earps and Holliday. Spicer added that if the Earps and Holliday were truly seeking revenge, Clanton would not have survived the gunfight. According to Spicer, the actions of the defendants were justified and there was no reason to believe that they were guilty of committing murder (Law Library, "Wyatt Earp Trial").

In the aftermath of the preliminary hearing, Ike Clanton and the outlaws in Tombstone plotted revenge against the Earp brothers. On December 28, 1881, Virgil Earp was ambushed by several cowboys who shot him twice in the arm. Virgil Earp survived, but the attack left his arm permanently damaged for the remainder of his life. Ike Clanton was charged with the attempted murder of Virgil Earp, but the charges were thrown out of court because of insufficient evidence. On March 18, 1882, Morgan Earp was shot and killed while playing pool. Apparently, someone had fired a rifle through a window of the pool hall. The attacks on the two Earp brothers led to Wyatt Earp's legendary "Vendetta Ride" where he tracked down and murdered the three men suspected in the two shootings (Linder, "The Earp-Holliday Trial").

The preliminary hearing in the Earp brothers and Holliday "trial" demonstrated that the performance of the attorneys and the preferences of the judge often determine the outcome of a case. In short, the truth can be subject to interpretation and manipulation. Thomas Fitch clearly outperformed the prosecuting attorneys by exploiting their errors, strategically manipulating the judicial process, and effectively cross-examining witnesses. Judge Spicer also played a critical role in the outcome as he obviously favored the defendants and chose to downplay any evidence of their guilt. Ultimately, the gunfight at the O. K. Corral and subsequent "trial" made a hero of Wyatt Earp who, in reality, was a controversial figure who engaged in unethical and, perhaps, illegal activities in performing his duties as a lawman (Law Library, "Wyatt Earp Trial").

Doc Holliday

Doc Holliday, also known as John Henry Holliday, was born on August 14, 1851, in Spalding County, Georgia. His father was a major in the Confederate army. Holliday went to dental school in Philadelphia, Pennsylvania (Barra 2009, 286–289). In 1872, he received a degree from the Pennsylvania College of Dental Surgery and opened a dental office in Atlanta.

Holliday was diagnosed with tuberculosis soon after he started practicing as a dentist and decided to move to Texas where the drier and warmer weather might improve his health (Tanner and Dearment 2001, 61–82).

In 1873, Holliday opened a dental office in Dallas, Texas, but he quickly took to the various saloons where he could engage in illegal gambling. Holliday's intelligence and education made him a skilled gambler who was able to earn a significant amount of money. Because gambling was illegal, Holliday was arrested on occasion and, because it was dangerous, it required him to become very skilled with a gun and knife. Holliday started to get involved in shootouts in saloons and, eventually, the altercations led to Holliday gaining a reputation as someone who had killed men, usually in self-defense. It is uncertain how much of Holliday's reputation was real or mythical (Tanner and Dearment 2001, 83–100).

In 1877, Holliday met Wyatt Earp in Fort Griffin, Texas, and the two men formed a friendship. At this time, Holliday also met a woman named Mary Catherine Haroney, or "Big Nose Kate," who worked at a saloon in Fort Griffin. Holliday would start a long relationship with the dance-hall girl. After Holliday stabbed a gambler, Ed Bailey, who had threatened him with a pistol during a card game, he was arrested. As a vigilante group was about to exact revenge against Holliday, "Big Nose Kate" helped Holliday escape, and they fled to Dodge City, Kansas, where Wyatt Earp was employed as the assistant marshal (Barra 2009, 288). While living in Dodge City, Holliday saved Earp's life at the Long Branch Saloon where a group of Texas cowboys had plotted revenge against Earp (Tanner and Dearment 2001, 124–126).

In 1880, Holliday and Earp met again in Tombstone, Arizona, where they entered into conflict with several outlaws (Tanner and Dearment 2001, 137–160). The conflict resulted in the famous O. K. Corral shootout in 1881 where Earp, his two brothers, and Holliday emerged victorious (161–182). After the battle at the O. K. Corral, Holliday moved to Colorado where he was forced to do battle with lawmen who tried to arrest him for illegal gambling or for murders he had allegedly committed. Holliday also had to beware of outlaws seeking revenge against him (183–200). On November 8, 1887, Doc Holliday died of tuberculosis in Glenwood Springs, Colorado, at the age of 36 (216–223).

Wyatt Earp

Wyatt Earp was born on March 19, 1848, in Monmouth, Illinois. Wyatt had four brothers, James, Virgil, Morgan, and Warren. The Earp brothers spent most of their childhood in Illinois and Iowa but, in 1864, the family moved to San Bernardino, California. At the age of 20, Wyatt and his brother, Virgil, worked on the Union Pacific Railroad and eventually moved back to Illinois in 1868. Throughout the 1870s, Wyatt worked as a constable and assistant marshal in such places as Lamar, Missouri; Wichita, Kansas; and, finally, in Dodge City, Kansas. During this time period, he gained notoriety as a lawman and a gambler. While traveling through Texas in search of a fugitive, Wyatt met Doc Holliday and the two men developed a close friendship, especially after Holliday saved Wyatt's life in the Long Branch Saloon in Dodge City where outlaws were seeking revenge against Earp (Tefertiller 1999, 3–31).

In the late 1870s, Wyatt left Dodge City and was employed as a security guard for Wells Fargo bank in California. In 1878, he settled with other members of the Earp family in Tombstone, Arizona, where he worked as a security guard for the Oriental Saloon. Wyatt's brother, Virgil, eventually became the marshal of Tombstone. In 1881, a dispute between the Earp brothers and a gang of outlaws resulted in the famous gun battle at the O. K. Corral on October 26, 1881. The Earp brothers and Doc Holliday were charged with the murder of three outlaws but, after a preliminary hearing, the charges were dismissed based upon the judge ruling that the murders were committed in an act of self-defense (Tefertiller 1999, 114–162).

In 1882, Virgil Earp was shot and badly injured and, soon thereafter, Morgan Earp was shot and murdered in a pool hall. The shootings were believed to be acts of revenge for the murders committed at the O. K. Corral (Tefertiller 1999, 174–201). Wyatt tracked down and killed the three men suspected in the shootings of his brothers during a three week "vendetta ride" through the Arizona Territory from March 20 until April 15, 1882 (263–264).

Wyatt finally settled in California where he lived out the rest of his life as a lawman and gambler while engaging in mining and real estate investments (Tefertiller 1999, 281–305). He died on January 13, 1929, in Los Angeles, California at the age of 80. The cause of death was determined to be an infection of the bladder (327–328).

Virgil Earp

Virgil Earp was born on July 18, 1843, in Hartford, Kentucky. He later moved with his family to Illinois and then to Iowa. In 1861, he enlisted in the Union army with two of his older brothers and fought against the Confederate forces for four years. In the early 1870s, Virgil moved to Dodge City, Kansas, where he worked as a police officer. He then moved to Prescott, Arizona, where he worked as a farmer, delivered mail, and mined for gold (O'Neal 1991, 97–98).

In 1879, Virgil was hired as the deputy marshal in Tombstone, Arizona. In June of 1881, he was chosen to serve as the marshal of Tombstone and one month later was involved in the famous O. K. Corral shootout with his brothers and Doc Holliday who fought successfully against outlaws from the Clanton gang. As a result of the O. K. Corral gunfight where three members of the Clanton gang were killed, Virgil lost his position as marshal and was charged with murder. After a preliminary hearing, Virgil, two of his brothers, and Doc Holliday had the murder charges dismissed when the judge ruled that the men had acted in self-defense (Linder, "The Earp-Holliday Trial").

In December 1881, Virgil was shot by assailants as an act of revenge for the murders committed at the O. K. Corral. While Virgil survived, his left arm was permanently disabled by the ambush. In 1882, after his brother, Morgan, was shot and killed in a pool hall as further revenge for the incident at the O. K. Corral, Virgil decided to leave Tombstone and moved to California to live with his parents (Linder, "The Earp-Holliday Trial"). While living in California, Virgil was hired as a security guard by the Southern Pacific Railroad. In 1886, Virgil opened a private detective business in Colton, California, and was also elected as the first marshal of Colton city in 1887. In the latter part of his life, Virgil traveled throughout the western part of the country in such places as Colorado, Arizona, and Nevada where he continued his work as a lawman, saloonkeeper, and miner. After a six-month bout with pneumonia, Virgil Earp died on October 19, 1905, in Goldfield, Nevada at the age of 62 (O'Neal 1991, 98).

Morgan Earp

Morgan Earp was born in Pella, Iowa, on April 24, 1851. Morgan grew up in Iowa but moved with his family to California when he was 13. Morgan had a close relationship with his brother, Wyatt, because they were the two youngest of the Earp brothers. In 1875, Morgan became a deputy sheriff in Dodge City, Kansas. From 1877 to 1880, Morgan served as the marshal of Butte, Montana. In 1880, Morgan joined his brothers in Tombstone, Arizona, where he initially worked as a security guard for Wells Fargo but then was appointed to serve as deputy marshal under his brother, Virgil, who was the marshal of Tombstone (O'Neal 1991, 96).

After a conflict developed between the Earp brothers and a number of outlaws, Morgan participated in the famous gunfight near the O. K. Corral on October 26, 1881, with his two brothers, Wyatt and Virgil, and Doc Holliday who did battle against the Clanton and McLaury brothers. Morgan allegedly fired the first shot of the shootout at Billy Clanton. While three of the outlaws were killed in the gunfight, the Earp brothers and Holliday survived; however, Morgan was seriously injured by a bullet to his left shoulder (Linder, "The Earp-Holliday Trial").

After murder charges against the Earp brothers and Holliday were dismissed, Morgan was assassinated while he was playing a game of billiards on March 18, 1882, when two men fired gunshots from the back door of the pool hall. The murder of Morgan Wyatt was considered to be an act of revenge for Morgan's part in the gunfight at the O. K. Corral (O'Neal 1991, 97). Wyatt Earp obtained vengeance for the murder of his brother when he went on his legendary "Vendetta Ride" and killed the three men considered to be responsible for the assassination of Morgan as well as the assassination attempt on his brother, Virgil (Linder, "The Earp-Holliday Trial").

The O. K. Corral Gunfight

In the early 1880s, Tombstone, Arizona, was a town located in the southern Arizona territory about 30 miles from the Mexican border. The town of 7,000 epitomized the "Old West" with its saloons, gambling houses, and prostitution. Tombstone had become one of the largest towns in the southwestern part of the United States after silver was discovered in the Huachuca Mountains in the late 1870s (Linder, "The Earp-Holliday Trial").

After serving as a lawman in Dodge City, Kansas, for a number of years, Wyatt Earp arrived in Tombstone in 1879 and assumed the role of deputy marshal. Wyatt Earp and his three brothers, James, Virgil, and Morgan, worked together with a friend, Doc Holliday, to try and maintain order in the town. The Earp brothers and Doc Holliday had to deal with men who were involved in such illegal activities as stealing horses, robbing stagecoaches, and committing murder in the process. Such men in the Old West were considered outlaws and thieves and were often referred to as "cowboys" (Lubet 2006, 7–16).

At this time, Wyatt Earp had entered into a rivalry within another lawman, Johnny Behan, as both men pursued the same woman, Josephine Marcus, and both men sought to become the sheriff of Tombstone. Wyatt Earp eventually won over Josephine Marcus who would become his wife, but Behan was appointed to be the sheriff by the governor of Arizona, John C. Fremont (Linder, "The Earp-Holliday Trial").

When a Tombstone stagecoach was robbed of $26,000 and the driver and a passenger were murdered in March of 1881, Wyatt Earp saw an opportunity to steal the sheriff's job from Behan by hunting down the bandits and increasing his popularity in the process. A posse led by the Earp brothers and Doc Holliday captured one of the bandits but, when the criminal escaped from the jail, Wyatt Earp suspected that Sheriff Behan may have allowed for the prisoner to escape because he wanted his own posse of lawmen to make the arrests and gain the publicity (Linder, "The Earp-Holliday Trial").

Wyatt Earp decided to enter into a secret deal with a known outlaw, Ike Clanton. In exchange for information leading to the arrest of the stagecoach robbers, Earp promised Clanton the $6,000 in reward money offered by Wells Fargo. However, the fugitives of the stagecoach robbery and murder were killed in a gunfight in New Mexico before Clanton could set a trap for Wyatt Earp to capture them. Therefore, the secret deal could not be completed (Linder, "The Earp-Holliday Trial").

Afterward, Wyatt Earp again tried to use Clanton to increase his popularity by having the cowboy stage a fake robbery where Earp and his posse would scare off the fake "outlaws." However, Clanton refused because he suspected that he was being setup by Earp. The two men then entered into a tense relationship after Clanton turned down the offer to stage the robbery (Law Library, "Wyatt Earp Trial"). Clanton also started to become concerned that Earp would reveal to his fellow outlaws that he was working with the lawman as a "snitch." In September 1881, when Wyatt Earp's posse arrested two men in the connection with another stagecoach robbery and the men arrested were friends of Ike Clanton, the bad feelings between Clanton and Wyatt Earp intensified even more (Linder, "The Earp-Holliday Trial").

Beginning on the evening of October 25, 1881, Ike Clanton and his friend, Tom McLaury, encountered Doc Holliday and Wyatt Earp in the saloons and at "all-night" card games where insults were exchanged between the men. After threats from Ike Clanton continued into the next day, Virgil Earp located Clanton on the street and proceeded to punch him (Lubet 2006, 3–4). Then, Virgil and Morgan Earp arrested Ike Clanton for carrying a rifle in a public place and took him to the Tombstone courthouse. Clanton paid a $25 fine but continued to threaten the Earp brothers and Doc Holliday. After Wyatt Earp arrived at the courthouse, he entered into a heated argument with Ike Clanton and both men exchanged threats with each other. As Wyatt Earp exited the courthouse in an angry mood, he ran into Ike Clanton's friend, Tom McLaury, and struck him in the head and shoulder with the butt of his revolver. When Billy Clanton and Frank McLaury arrived in Tombstone and heard about the treatment of their brothers by the Earps, they loaded up on weapons and bullets at a local gun store and headed for the O. K. Corral to discuss with their brothers how they would settle matters with the lawmen (Linder, "The Earp-Holliday Trial").

Sheriff Behen attempted to prevent the Earps and Doc Holliday from meeting up at the O. K. Corral with the four outlaws by misleading them into thinking he had disarmed the cowboys. However, the lawmen ignored Behen's plea. On October 26, 1881, at a vacant lot near the O. K. Corral, the three Earp brothers and Doc Holliday entered into a showdown against the Clanton and McLaury brothers. After Wyatt Earp asked the cowboys to turn over their weapons, several shots of gunfire were exchanged between the "lawmen" and "cowboys" who were roughly 10 feet apart. When the smoke cleared, Tom and Frank McLaury lay dead in the vacant lot along with their fellow cowboy, Billy Clanton. Ike Clanton escaped any injury and fled into a nearby house. Three of the lawmen, Virgil and Morgan Earp and Doc Holliday, were seriously injured but survived. Wyatt Earp was unharmed. The most legendary gun battle in the history of the Old West had lasted roughly 30 seconds (Linder, "The Earp-Holliday Trial").

References

Barra, Allen. *Inventing Wyatt Earp: His Life and Many Legends.* Lincoln: University of Nebraska Press, 2009.

Law Library–American Law and Legal Information. "Wyatt Earp Trial: 1881—A Mysterious Stagecoach Robbery, Trouble Brewing, Shootout, The Hearing, Aftermath." *Notable Trials and Court Cases—1833 to 1882.* http://law.jrank.org/pages/2659/Wyatt-Earp-Trial-1881.html (accessed July 17, 2009).

Linder, Douglas O. "The Earp-Holliday Trial: An Account." *Famous Trials.* http://www.law.umkc.edu/faculty/projects/FTRIALS/earp/earpaccount.html (accessed July 17, 2009).

Lubet, Steven. *Murder in Tombstone: The Forgotten Trial of Wyatt Earp.* New Haven, CT: Yale University Press, 2006.

O'Neal, Bill. *Encyclopedia of Western Gunfighters.* Norman: University of Oklahoma Press, 1991.

Tanner, Karen Holliday, and Robert K. Dearment. *Doc Holliday: A Family Portrait.* Norman: University of Oklahoma Press, 2001.

Tefertiller, Casey. *Wyatt Earp: The Life Behind the Legend.* New York: Wiley, 1999.

Charles Guiteau Trial (1881–1882)

Charles Guiteau was a disturbed individual who was responsible for the assassination of President James Garfield in 1881. Guiteau's background and psychology was a mix of religion, politics, and law (Clarke 2006, 240–244). Many scholars have written in government textbooks that Guiteau assassinated President Garfield because he was denied a government appointment and was simply a "disappointed office-seeker." However, Guiteau was clearly an insane person who was detached from reality believing that God instructed him to murder President Garfield (Clarke 2006, 244–250). Guiteau's trial was an example of the lack of due process in the 19th century and the problems that persist even today in presenting an insanity defense and determining whether a criminal defendant should be held responsible for an unlawful act because of mental illness (Clarke 2006, 250–254).

After several failures in his life as a religious figure and an attorney, Charles Guiteau was working as a bill collector in New York City when he turned to politics and became active in the Republican Party during the presidential campaign of 1880. He was part of the Stalwart faction of the Republican Party that wanted Ulysses S. Grant for a third term as their nominee. The Stalwarts were a part of the Republican Party that favored the traditional political machine where patronage was practiced. Patronage involved appointing party loyalists to political office as opposed to the civil service system based upon merit. After a long convention battle, the Republican Party eventually settled on James Garfield as their candidate. Guiteau had given public speeches in support of Grant; however, when Garfield received the nomination, Guiteau simply substituted Garfield's name for Grant. Guiteau's public speeches were a mix of politics and religion and were mostly incoherent babblings at train stations where people would routinely make fun of him (Clarke 2006, 244–246).

As further evidence of his psychological problems, Guiteau truly believed that a speech he wrote and delivered in support of Garfield in New York City had helped Garfield defeat Democrat Winfield Scott Hancock in the 1880 presidential election (Ackerman 2003, 177–179). Even though Guiteau had never met Garfield, he began to bother Garfield's staff for an appointment within the administration. Guiteau was confident that he would receive an appointment overseas as an ambassador to France, Austria, or some other European country (Clarke 2006, 245).

After Garfield's inauguration in March 1881, Guiteau kept bothering Secretary of State James Blaine for the diplomatic appointment (Ackerman 2003, 265–269). Blaine became so frustrated by all of Guiteau's letters requesting an appointment that he finally told Guiteau to quit bothering him (Clarke 2006, 245–246).

At the same time that Guiteau was failing in his desperate and unrealistic attempt for an appointment, the newspapers were covering a conflict between President Garfield and the Republican Party bosses within the Stalwart faction. The Stalwart faction had been angered because Garfield had refused to appoint enough Stalwarts within his administration. Even though Garfield had selected a Stalwart, Chester Arthur, as his running mate, the Stalwart faction was angered by Garfield's other appointments (Clarke 2006, 246).

Charles Guiteau had been greatly influenced by the media coverage of the battle between Garfield and the Stalwarts and he felt that it was his duty to assassinate Garfield in order to put a Stalwart, Chester Arthur, in the White House. Garfield fantasized that he would be acquitted of the murder charges and would then travel to Europe where he would publish a book of his theological writings, give lectures to large audiences, and return to the United States where he would run for president in 1884 (Clarke 2006, 251–252).

Guiteau purchased a .45 handgun revolver for $15 and planned to shoot Garfield on June 30, 1881. The newspapers had printed that, on this date, Garfield was scheduled to catch a train at the Baltimore and Potomac station in order to travel to his alma mater, Williams College, to give a commencement address and then take a vacation. Guiteau shot Garfield twice, once in the arm and once in the back, as he entered the train station. In his mind, Guiteau's decision to shoot Garfield would unite all of his interests of religion, law, and politics and bring the Republican Party and the nation together once and for all. Guiteau really believed that he would be viewed as a hero by the nation and he even had a note in his pocket asking that military troops be dispatched to the prison to protect him after his assassination of Garfield (Clarke 2006, 248–250).

Garfield was treated by physicians who did not practice proper sterilization techniques, and he suffered severe infections as the physicians searched inside his body for the bullet that entered his back. It is believed that Garfield would have survived the shooting today with modern medical practices. Instead, President Garfield lingered for months on his death bed where he finally died on September 19, 1881. The fact that Garfield suffered for such a long period of time caused the public to have little sympathy for Guiteau and his alleged mental illness (Rosenberg 1995, 3–9).

The trial of Charles Guiteau began on November 14, 1881, in the old criminal court building in Washington, D.C. The prosecutors introduced witnesses at the train station who saw Guiteau shoot President Garfield and also presented the physician who conducted the autopsy on the president. The defense attorneys for Guiteau argued that their client was insane and deserved sympathy. Guiteau testified at his trial and discussed the time that he spent at a religious commune and also how God had instructed him to assassinate Garfield. During his trial, Guiteau displayed the behavior of someone who was clearly delusional, and all of the psychiatrists confirmed this fact, but the insanity defense by his lawyers failed because it was very difficult at this time to acquit by reason of insanity (Dershowitz 2004, 183–186). In the 19th century, the American legal system applied the M'Naughten Rule from English common law in cases involving the insanity defense. Under the M'Naughten Rule at the time, the government only had to prove that Guiteau understood the consequences of his actions and knew that his behavior was illegal. The jury deliberated for one hour and found Guiteau guilty of murder, and he was sentenced by Judge Walter Cox to die by hanging on June 30, 1882 (Clark 1994; Rosenberg 1995, 63–67; 111–154).

While in prison awaiting execution, Guiteau ate and slept comfortably, convinced in the knowledge that his appeals would succeed or he would be pardoned by President Chester Arthur. He showed no anger when he was hanged and simply believed he was a martyr similar to Jesus and believed that God would take care of him in the afterlife. He consistently stated during the trial that God had killed Garfield and he did not have any say in the matter. He mistook the public onlookers during his trial in the packed courtroom as evidence of respect and admiration. When some people played jokes on Guiteau by sending him phony checks in the amount of $1 million for his legal defense or when women would jokingly send marriage proposals to him, he took such gestures seriously. When his appeals failed and he was awaiting execution, Guiteau said God would punish the jury, prosecuting attorneys, and the new president, Chester Arthur, who refused to issue a pardon (Clarke 2006, 252–254).

An autopsy of Guiteau's brain revealed severe degeneration of cells and blood vessels. As a result of the autopsy, public opinion shifted about Guiteau's mental state, and the general consensus was that Guiteau suffered from a severe mental illness and was legally insane (Rosenberg 1995, 238–240). While the courts began to value the testimony of psychiatrists in cases involving the insanity defense, the legal definition of insanity did not change. In the 20th century, the legal definition of insanity was altered to make it easier for individuals to gain an acquittal based upon an insanity defense. In 1954, the Durham rule was established by the U.S. Court of Appeals for the D.C. Circuit which maintained that a person could not be held responsible for an illegal act if the act was a result of mental illness (Clarke 2006, 375–376). However, after the acquittal of John Hinckley for his assassination attempt on President Ronald Reagan in 1981, Congress passed the Insanity Reform Act of 1984 which basically changed the legal definition back to the 19th century M'Naughten Rule. Hence, if Guiteau was tried for murder in the 21st century, the outcome of his insanity defense most likely would have been the same as in the 19th century (Clarke 2006, 3).

In the aftermath of the Garfield assassination, Congress passed the Pendleton Act of 1883, also known as the Civil Service Reform Act, which established the Civil Service Commission. The Civil Service Commission shifted the hiring process of federal government employees toward a merit-based system where persons were hired based upon their performance on competitive examinations. The Pendleton Act officially ended the "spoils system," also known as patronage, where, upon assuming office, presidents would fire all of the federal employees and replace them with party loyalists (Ackerman 2003, 437). Because the Pendleton Act was enacted almost immediately after the assassination of Garfield, it created the misconception that Guiteau acted rationally and committed the assassination because he was denied a government appointment that he deserved. In reality, the patronage system had become problematic prior to the assassination and a strong movement had already developed to replace it with a merit-based system (408–409).

Charles Guiteau

Charles Guiteau was born in Freeport, Illinois, in 1841 and is best known as the person who assassinated President James Garfield in 1881 (Hayes and Hayes 2007). There was overwhelming evidence to suggest that Guiteau was mentally ill and detached from reality because, during the course of his life, he demonstrated symptoms of insanity. Guiteau's mother died when he was seven years old. It was believed that his mother also was psychotic which has led some scientists to argue that Guiteau's mental illness was hereditary. Guiteau's father, who was intensely religious, gave him up to be raised by his sister, Frankie. Guiteau also was raised, in part, by his stepmother who married his father when Guiteau was 12. Guiteau was a bright and gifted young man and actually attended the University of Michigan for a short period of time. It was extremely rare for any young man to attend college in the 19th century because such education was usually reserved for only the wealthy and the privileged. Hence, Guiteau clearly was above average in intelligence (Clarke 2006, 240; Rosenberg 1995, 13–42).

While attending the University of Michigan, he became inspired by the religious writings of John Noyes who founded a religious commune in Oneida, New York. Noyes practiced what he called "Bible Communism." After one year at Michigan, Guiteau left college and went straight for the Oneida commune. In the Oneida commune, Guiteau received religious instruction and also enjoyed the fact that men and women practiced "free love" (Clarke 2006, 240).

During his time at the commune, Guiteau began a behavioral pattern of failure that would continue throughout the rest of his life. When Guiteau attempted to become a leader within the commune, he was quickly rejected by the other members. Guiteau fantasized that God had ordained him to lead the commune and he believed he was the only one capable of leading the group. Psychiatrists have stated that his unrealistic desire to lead the commune was an example of his many delusions of grandeur (Clarke 2006, 240–241).

In addition to his failed attempt at leadership in the commune, Guiteau was rejected by all of the women in the commune who nicknamed him "Charles Git Out." Guiteau left the commune because he did not enjoy the labor tasks that he was assigned and moved to New York City where he lived a very lonely and poor existence (Clarke 2006, 241).

While living in New York City, Guiteau tried to start a religious newspaper which he called the *Daily Theocrat*. However, it failed when he could not secure any financial support. Guiteau truly felt that his newspaper would be the first religious newspaper in the country and that it would bring about a spiritual awakening across the United States (Clarke 2006, 242).

After Guiteau failed with his newspaper idea, he returned to the Oneida commune but again found himself frustrated and left a second time on bad terms. Guiteau filed a frivolous civil lawsuit for $9,000 against the commune because the members had wasted six years of his life. When Guiteau wrote letters to various newspapers as well as national and state officials complaining about the commune and how it ruined his life by causing all of his personal problems, the commune filed a counter lawsuit for slander (Clarke 2006, 242–243).

Guiteau was known to borrow money from family members and creditors who would be forced to pester him in order to receive repayment. The correspondence between Guiteau and those to whom he owed money produced some comical exchanges that demonstrated an odd arrogance and unintentional humor. Clearly, Guiteau had a tenuous grasp of reality (Clarke 2006, 243–244).

Guiteau practiced law briefly in Chicago, but his attempt at the legal profession also failed miserably. During this time, he married a woman, a librarian named Annie Bunn. However, the marriage ended in divorce after five years because Guiteau was physically abusive to his wife and also committed adultery with a prostitute (Clarke 2006, 243).

References

Ackerman, Kenneth. *The Dark Horse: The Surprise Election and Political Murder of President James A. Garfield.* New York: Da Capo Press, 2003.

Clark, James C. *The Murder of James A. Garfield: The President's Last Days and the Trial and Execution of his Assassin.* Jefferson, NC: McFarland and Company, 1994.

Clarke, James W. *Defining Danger: American Assassins and the New Domestic Terrorists.* New Brunswick, NJ: Transaction Publishers, 2006.

Dershowitz, Alan. *America on Trial: Inside the Legal Battles that Transformed Our Nation-From the Salem Witches to the Guantanamo Detainees.* New York: Warner Books, 2004.

Hayes, Henry G., and Charles J. Hayes. *A Complete History of the Life and Trial of Charles Julius Guiteau, Assassin of President Garfield.* Whitefish, MT: Kessinger Publishing, 2007.

Rosenberg, Charles. *The Trial of the Assassin Guiteau: Psychiatry and the Law in the Gilded Age.* Chicago: University of Chicago Press, 1995.

The Haymarket Riot Trial (1886)

The most legendary trial involving the battle of organized labor against corporate and government leaders occurred in the late 19th century. When seven police officers were killed by an explosion at a labor rally, the murder trial of eight labor activists caused public support for workers and unions to decline rapidly. Even though the eight defendants were probably innocent and the identity of the person responsible for the bombing was never discovered, the trial was a significant setback for labor leaders in their attempt to improve conditions within the industrial workplace (Law Library, "Haymarket Trial").

The Haymarket Square riot of 1886 resulted from tensions between the labor movement seeking an eight-hour workday and police who supported the employers in the labor dispute. On May 4, 1886, a bomb exploded when police tried to break up a labor rally in Haymarket Square in Chicago, Illinois. The explosion caused the deaths of seven police and an unknown number of union workers who were fired upon by police after the blast (Linder, "The Haymarket Riot and Subsequent Trial").

On May 5, 1886, police arrested August Spies, George Engel, Albert Parsons, Samuel Fielden, Oscar Neebe, Adolf Fischer, and Michael Schwab, who were leaders and supporters of the labor movement. The individuals had allegedly encouraged the violence against the police through speeches, rallies, and publications such as a German language newspaper, the *Arbeiter-Zeitung*. On May 14, 1886, Louis Lingg also was arrested by police as a key suspect in the bombing. Lingg was an expert in explosives, and police believed that he may have been the person responsible for throwing the bomb near the police officers (Law Library, "Haymarket Trial").

On May 27, 1886, a grand jury indicted the eight defendants on the charge of conspiracy to commit the murder of Officer Mathias Degen, the first police officer to die in the bombing. The Haymarket Riot Trial was scheduled to begin on June 21, 1886, in front of Judge Joseph Gray in Chicago, Illinois. The eight defendants were to be represented by defense lawyer William Black, who had served as a captain in the Union army during the Civil War, and three other defense attorneys, William Foster, Moses Salomon, and Sigismund Zeisler. The defense team quickly experienced a setback as the jury did not include one worker or immigrant, which clearly favored the prosecution. It has been alleged that Judge Gary influenced the bailiff during the jury selection process to avoid any potential jurors who had worked in factories (Law Library, "Haymarket Trial"). At the outset of the trial, Judge Gary also provided questionable instructions to the jury that clearly favored a conviction. The judge stated that the jurors only had to be convinced beyond a reasonable doubt that the defendants were guilty of wanting to attack the police and overthrow the government in order to convict the defendants of murder (Green 2006, 215–216).

Julius Grinnell provided the opening remarks for the prosecution and emphasized how August Spies often gave speeches to large crowds of workers where he claimed that violence was the only way to achieve the goals of the labor movement. Grinnell also described a meeting of labor activists at a saloon on the day prior to the bombing where George Engel and others approved the use of explosives at the Haymarket Square rally. Supposedly, Louis Lingg was to deliver the explosives. While Grinnell admitted that the person who actually threw the bomb toward the police was unknown, the eight defendants had participated in the bombing through their assistance and encouragement (Linder, "The Haymarket Riot and Subsequent Trial").

Gottfried Waller, a labor leader who testified for the prosecution to avoid criminal charges, discussed the meeting at the saloon where the Haymarket rally was planned but he denied that there was any discussion of explosives because they had not anticipated any problem from the police (Green 2006, 216).

The key testimony for the prosecution came from M. M. Thompson who told how he overheard Michael Schwab and August Spies discussing the police presence at the Haymarket rally. Thompson interpreted a vague conversation between Schwab and Spies to mean that bombs were about to be set off to deal with the police officers. Thompson also suggested that Spies used certain German words printed in the *Arbeiter-Zeitung* newspaper as signals for labor activists to commit violent acts against authorities. Another witness, H. L. Gilmer, claimed to have seen Spies light the fuse of the bomb that exploded near the police, although the credibility of his testimony was seriously questioned. The remainder of the prosecution's case consisted of radical newspapers, pamphlets, and leaflets introduced as evidence as well as the raw materials used to make explosives (Green 2006, 219–221).

The mayor of Chicago, Carter Harrison, proved to be the strongest witness for the defense. Harrison testified that the Haymarket rally was always planned as a nonviolent gathering, and he relayed to Police Chief John Bonfield that a police presence was not necessary at the event. Several other defense witnesses confirmed the testimony of Mayor Harrison. Other defense witnesses testified that the bomb had been thrown from an area far from Spies's location, which discredited Gilmer's testimony for the prosecution (Linder, "The Haymarket Riot and Subsequent Trial").

On August 7, 1886, two of the defendants, Samuel Fielden and August Spies, testified in their own defense. Fielden read portions of his speech made at the Haymarket rally to illustrate the peaceful nature of his words, and Spies told how he initially circulated flyers on the day prior to the rally where he asked workers to take up arms but, in an attempt to discourage violence, he removed the phrase in the leaflets that were circulated later in the day (Linder, "The Haymarket Riot and Subsequent Trial").

In his summary argument for the defense, Sigismund Ziesler laid the blame for the riot on the police, especially Police Chief Bonfield, who should not have ordered his officers to disperse a peaceful rally. Defense attorney William Foster followed Ziesler by criticizing the weak evidence put forth by police that failed to connect any of the defendants to the bombing. For example, Oscar Neebe was arrested because he had a few flyers in his saloon, Spies was arrested for a German word printed in his newspaper, and Lingg was not directly connected to the bomb that exploded in any way. Foster concluded by arguing that the prosecution's case was built entirely upon the prejudice against immigrant workers and the need to provide a scapegoat for the deaths of the police officers (Linder, "The Haymarket Riot and Subsequent Trial").

William Black provided the closing arguments for the defense. Black emphasized that the two key eyewitnesses for the prosecution, Thompson and Gilmer, had failed to connect any of the defendants to the bombing because they were easily contradicted and discredited by several defense witnesses. In fact, six of the eight defendants were nowhere near Haymarket Square at the time of the explosion. The two defendants who were at the rally, Spies and Fielden, were sitting on the speaker's stage which was in the opposite direction from where the bomb was thrown. Black concluded by pleading with the jury not to convict the defendants simply because their political beliefs and actions were unpopular (Linder, "The Haymarket Riot and Subsequent Trial").

Three prosecutors, Francis W. Walker, George Ingham, and Julius Grinnell, presented the final arguments for the state of Illinois. Walker stated that the bombing was the result of a conspiracy within the labor movement to start a revolt. According to Walker, the revolt had caused the death of Officer Mathias Degen. Ingham accused the defendants of trying to promote anarchy at the expense of a government ruled by law and order. Finally, Grinnell offered a powerful closing statement where he told the jury that a not-guilty verdict would increase the violent acts committed by militant labor activists around the country and result in the deaths of innocent people (Green 2006, 222–231).

After a few hours of deliberations, the jury rendered its verdict on August 20, 1886. All of the eight defendants were found guilty of conspiracy to murder Officer Degen. Seven of the defendants were issued death sentences, while Oscar Neebe, the saloon owner arrested for possessing controversial leaflets, was sentenced to 15 years in prison (Law Library, "Haymarket Trial").

The convictions were appealed to the Illinois Supreme Court based upon the prejudice exhibited by the judge, prosecution and jury, the introduction of illegally seized evidence at trial, and procedural errors committed by the judge. On September 14, 1886, the Illinois Supreme Court rejected the arguments of the defense and reaffirmed the convictions and death sentences (Green 2006, 247–248). The defendants appealed to the U.S. Supreme Court, but the justices delivered an opinion on October 27, 1886 which stated that they refused to hear the case because no federal issues had been raised in the trial. Even though the constitutional rights of the defendants had been violated, such as their search and seizure rights within the Fourth Amendment and their trial rights within the Sixth Amendment, the federal courts refused to review such violations in the late 19th century because the legal rights found in the Bill of Rights had not yet been nationalized upon the states. Therefore, during this era, the U.S. Supreme Court simply would defer to a state court to decide if a defendant's rights had been violated within their criminal justice system (252–254).

Due to a strong outcry from the public where thousands of letters were sent to Governor Richard Oglesby of Illinois, the sentences of Fielden and Schwab were reduced to life in prison on November 10, 1887. Governor Oglesby selected Fielden and Schwab for clemency because the two defendants had made a request in writing to the governor. The other five defendants facing execution refused to ask for clemency (Green 2006, 252–264).

On November 11, 1887, Spies, Parsons, Fischer, and Engel were executed by hanging in front of 250 newspaper reporters, the 12 jurors, and several other witnesses (Green 2006, 268–271). A fifth defendant, Louis Lingg, was also supposed to have been hanged, but he committed suicide on the day prior to the date of the executions (264). After serving only six years of their prison sentences, Neebe, Schwab, and Fielden were pardoned by Governor John P. Altgeld on June 26, 1893 (287–294).

The Haymarket Riot Trial demonstrated how a tragic event was used to prosecute innocent persons simply because they held unpopular beliefs and were considered guilty by association. The reputation of the labor movement and its agenda was clearly damaged by the Haymarket Square bombing and subsequent trial because of its connection to socialists, communists, and anarchists. The trial and conviction of the eight defendants in the Haymarket trial further radicalized persons within the labor movement and even influenced a young man by the name of Leon Czolgosz to assassinate President William McKinley in 1901 in an attempt to strike a blow for the working man (Green 2006, 301–303).

 ## The Haymarket Square Bombing

At the end of the Civil War, leaders of organized labor began focusing on the rights of workers. Labor groups demanded that the 10-hour workdays be reduced to 8 without a decline in daily wages. The movement toward establishing an 8-hour work day inspired the creation of more unions and rallies that pressured government leaders. As states, such as Illinois in 1867, passed legislation to ensure an 8-hour workday, employers in the city of Chicago argued that the law violated the "liberty of contract" clause in the U.S. Constitution. The liberty of contract prohibited any government interference in the relationship between employers and employees in the workplace. Large businesses in Chicago simply ignored the legislation and refused to recognize the 8-hour workday and even forced some employees to work as many as 12 hours a day. Such businesses used their huge profits to bribe police who suppressed any revolt by the workers. Corrupt politicians also were bought and they simply refused to implement the 8-hour law (Linder, "The Haymarket Riot and Subsequent Trial").

As conditions grew worse for workers in the 1870s, Albert Parsons and August Spies, leaders of organized labor, encouraged immigrants from the European socialist countries to join a new political party, the Social Democratic Workermen's Party. As police increased their violence against striking workers who tried to establish the 8-hour workday, Parsons and Spies became more radical and militant in their tactics to protect the rights of workers (Green 2006, 54–73).

In the economic depression of 1883–1886, organized labor became more aggressive as wealthy businessmen lived a life of luxury, while unemployment increased dramatically. Even when a business made a profit, workers would have their pay reduced. As the number of union strikes increased, police exercised more violence against workers. Parsons and Spies decided to form an armed militia to protect workers and also started training anarchists to develop explosives to use against the police and wealthy business leaders (Avrich 1986, 181–186).

By 1886, membership in the militant unions was increasing at a rapid pace and socialist and anarchist publications were encouraging violent action on behalf of workers' rights. The militant union members created thousands of dynamite bombs to use in their war against the capitalists. As the labor movement gained support nationwide, the leaders of organized labor planned for the largest strike in the history of the city of Chicago when 60,000 workers would walk away from their jobs on May 1, 1886. Because of the threat of the large strike, referred to as "Emancipation Day," thousands of workers secured a shorter workday without having their wages reduced and the Chicago City Council passed the 8-hour workday for all city employees. On May 1, 1886, the entire city of Chicago saw business activity reduced to a standstill. The largest strike in Chicago history was a success as workers celebrated with parades throughout the city and parties began at saloons. Most importantly, no violence was reported on the day of the strike (Green 2006, 145–161).

Unfortunately, some employers at Chicago factories decided to lock out the union strikers and hired replacement workers which caused severe tension to build. At McCormick Reaper Works, the owner of the factory, Cyrus McCormack Jr., hired replacement workers and used 400 armed police to protect the new workers who were referred to as "scabs" by union members. As an insult to the striking union workers, McCormick granted the replacement workers an 8-hour day. Two days later, on May 3, 1886, hundreds of striking workers gathered near the McCormick plant to hear speeches from Albert Parsons and August Spies. The tension between the opposing sides resulted in violence when police shot and killed two union workers and injured several others who had been harassing replacement workers as they left the McCormick plant at the end of the workday (Green 2006, 1 62–170).

After the killing of the two workers, August Spies published a leaflet distributed to the working-class areas of Chicago. The leaflet encouraged union members to take up arms as a result of the murders committed by the police. After a number of German socialists and anarchists received the leaflets at a local saloon, they planned a rally for the following day in Haymarket Square where speakers planned to condemn the recent violence by police (Linder, "The Haymarket Riot and Subsequent Trial").

On May 4, 1886, 3,000 workers attended the rally at Haymarket Square. August Spies and Albert Parsons both spoke at the rally. The final speaker, Samuel Fielden, provided the most controversial speech of the evening when he allegedly remarked that the police should be attacked for the crimes that they had committed against McCormick workers. When Police Chief John Bonfield heard about the remark, he ordered his police officers to Haymarket Square to put an end to the rally. When Police Captain William Ward ordered the crowd to disperse, Fielden agreed to end his speech and the crowd started to scatter. Suddenly, a bomb exploded in direction of the police officers killing and wounding several of them. As workers ran from the scene, police officers fired shots at the crowd. After five minutes of chaos, the Haymarket Square riot ended, causing the deaths of seven police officers and several workers (Green 2006, 174–191).

References

Avrich, Paul. *The Haymarket Tragedy.* Princeton: Princeton University Press, 1986.

Green, James. *Death in the Haymarket: A Story of Chicago, the First Labor Movement, and the Bombing that Divided Gilded Age America.* New York: Pantheon, 2006.

Law Library–Law and Legal Information. "Haymarket Trial: 1886—Chicago: Hotbed of Radicalism, Police Arrest Eight Anarchists." *Great American Trials.* Vol. 1. http://law.jrank.org/pages/2683/Haymarket-Trial-1886.html (accessed July 16, 2009).

Linder, Douglas O. "The Haymarket Riot and Subsequent Trial." *Famous Trials.* http://www.law.umkc.edu/faculty/projects/FTRIALS/haymarket/haymktaccount.html (accessed July 16, 2009).

Pardon of the Haymarket anarchists (1893) [excerpt]

On the night of May 4, 1886, a public meeting was held on Haymarket Square, in Chicago; there were from 800 to 1,000 people present, nearly all being laboring men. There had been trouble, growing out of the effort to introduce an eight-hour day, resulting in some collisions with the police, in one of which several laboring people were killed, and this meeting was called as a protest against alleged police brutality.

The meeting was orderly and was attended by the mayor, who remained until the crowd began to disperse, and then went away. As soon as Capt. John Bonfield, of the Police Department, learned that the mayor had gone, he took a detachment of police and hurried to the meeting for the purpose of dispersing the few that remained, and as the police approached the place of meeting a bomb was thrown by some unknown person, which exploded and wounded many and killed several policemen, among the latter being one Mathias Degan. A number of people were arrested, and after a time August Spies, Albert R. Parsons, Louis Lingg, Michael

Schwab, Samuel Fielden, George Engle, Adolph Fischer, and Oscar Neebe were indicted for the murder of Mathias Degan. The prosecution could not discover who had thrown the bomb and could not bring the really guilty man to justice, and as some of the men indicted were not at the Haymarket meeting and had nothing to do with it, the prosecution was forced to proceed on the theory that the men indicted were guilty of murder, because it was claimed they had, at various times in the past, uttered and printed incendiary and seditious language, practically advising the killing of policemen, of Pinkerton men, and others acting in that capacity, and that they were, therefore, responsible for the murder of Mathias Degan. The public was greatly excited and after a prolonged trial all of the defendants were found guilty; Oscar Neebe was sentenced to fifteen years' imprisonment and all of the other defendants were sentenced to be hanged. The case was carried to the Supreme Court and was there affirmed in the fall of 1887. Soon thereafter Lingg committed suicide. The sentence of Fielden and Schwab was commuted to imprisonment for life, and Parsons, Fischer, Engle and Spies were hanged, and the petitioners now ask to have Neebe, Fielden and Schwab set at liberty.

The several thousand merchants, bankers, judges, lawyers and other prominent citizens of Chicago, who have by petition, by letter and in other ways urged executive clemency, mostly base their appeal on the ground that, assuming the prisoners to be guilty, they have been punished enough; but a number of them who have examined the case more carefully, and are more familiar with the record and with the fact disclosed by the papers on file, base their appeal on entirely different grounds. They assert:

First—That the jury which tried the case was a packed jury selected to convict.

Second—That according to the law as laid down by the Supreme Court, both prior to and again since the trial of the case, the jurors, according to their own answers, were not competent jurors, and the trial was, therefor, not a legal trial.

Third—That the defendants were not proven to be guilty of the crime charged in the indictment.

Fourth—That as to the defendant Neebe, the State's Attorney had declared at the close of the evidence that there was no case against him, and yet he has been kept in prison all these years.

Fifth—That the trial judge was either so prejudiced against the defendants, or else so determined to win the applause of a certain class in the community, that he could not and did not grant a fair trial.

Upon the question of having been punished enough, I will simply say that if the defendants had a fair trial, and nothing has developed since to show that they were not guilty of the crime charged in the indictment, then there ought to be no executive interference, for no punishment under our laws could then be too severe. Government must defend itself; life and property must be protected, and law and order must be maintained; murder must be punished, and if the defendants are guilty of murder, either committed by their own hands or by some one else acting on their advice, then, if they have had a fair trial, there should be in this case no executive interference. The soil of America is not adapted to the growth of anarchy. While our institutions are not free from injustice, they are still the best that have yet been devised, and therefore must be maintained. . . .

. . . It is shown here that the bomb was, in all probability, thrown by someone seeking personal revenge; that a course had been pursued by the authorities which would naturally cause this; that for a number of years prior to the Haymarket affair there had been labor troubles, and in several cases a number of laboring people, guilty of no offense, had been shot down in cold blood by Pinkerton men, and none of the murderers were brought to justice. The evidence taken at coroners' inquests and presented here, shows that in at least two cases men were fired on and killed when they were running away, and there was consequently no occasion to shoot, yet nobody was punished; that in Chicago there had been a number of strikes in which some of the police not only took sides against the men, but without any authority of law invaded and broke up peaceable meetings, and in scores of cases brutally clubbed people who were guilty of no offense whatever. . . .

. . . It is further charged, with much bitterness, by those who speak for the prisoners, that the record of this case shows that the judge conducted the trial with malicious ferocity, and forced eight men to be tried together; that in cross-examining the State's witnesses, he confined counsel to the specific points touched on by the State, while in the cross-examination of the defendants' witnesses he permitted the State's Attorney to go into all manner of subjects entirely foreign to the matters on which the witnesses were examined in chief; also, that every ruling throughout the long trial on any contested point, was in favor of the State; and further, that page after page of the record contains insinuating remarks of the judge, made in the hearing of the jury, and with the evident intent of bringing the jury to his way of thinking; that these speeches, coming from the court, were much more damaging than any speeches from the State's Attorney could possibly have been; that the State's Attorney often took his cue from the judge's remarks; that the judge's magazine article recently published, although written nearly six years after the trial, is yet full of venom; that, pretending to simply review the case, he had to drag into his article a letter written by an excited woman to a newspaper after the trial was over, and which therefore had nothing to do with the case, and was put into the article simply to create a prejudice against the woman, as well as against the dead and the living; and that, not content with this, he, in the same article, makes an insinuating attack on one of the lawyers for the defense, not for anything done at the trial, but because more than a year after the trial, when some of the defendants had been hung, he ventured to express a few kind, if erroneous, sentiments over the graves of his dead clients, whom he at least believed to be innocent. It is urged that such ferocity of subserviency is without a parallel in all history; that even Jeffries in England contented himself with hanging his victims, and did not stoop to berate them after death.

These charges are of a personal character, and while they seem to be sustained by the record of the trial and the papers before me, and tend to show the trial was not fair, I do not care to discuss this feature of the case any farther, because it is not necessary. I am convinced that it is clearly my duty to act in this case for the reasons already given, and I, therefore, grant an absolute pardon to Samuel Fielden, Oscar Neebe and Michael Schwab, this 26th day of June, 1893.

Lizzie Borden Trial (1893)

The trial of Lizzie Borden fascinated the nation and produced a controversial verdict that divides people to this day. Police and prosecutors arrested and tried Lizzie Borden for the murders of her father and stepmother on the basis of circumstantial, or indirect, evidence. Because prosecutors had a weak case against Lizzie Borden, they attempted to sway the all-male jury by drawing upon the stereotypes of women, in particular the idea that women were more cunning and shrewd than men. The trial revealed the unprofessional behavior of police and prosecutors and the discrimination that existed against women in the late 19th century (Law Library, "Lizzie Borden Trial").

On August 4, 1892, Andrew and Abby Borden were murdered at their home in Fall River, Massachusetts. Apparently, the Bordens were killed in a brutal fashion with an axe or hatchet. Police investigators initially did not suspect the Borden's daughter, Lizzie, as the murderer. However, five days after the murders, she became the main suspect in the investigation after she provided confusing answers to a prosecutor and judge during questioning at the courthouse. For example, Lizzie gave different answers regarding what she was doing around the time of the murders. Lizzie initially stated that she was looking for fishing equipment in the barn, but then changed her story by suggesting she may have been in the yard or perhaps she was picking fruit. The prosecutor and judge interpreted her inconsistent statements as a sign that she was guilty of the murders. However, it was very possible that she was experiencing shock and trauma from the murders of her parents. Police suspected that Lizzie harbored resentment based upon her natural mother's death when she was a child or perhaps she wanted access to her father's estate valued at between $300,000 and $500,000. Interestingly, police did not focus on Lizzie's sister, Emma, who theoretically could have possessed the same motives as her sister (Law Library, "Lizzie Borden Trial").

On August 11, 1892, police arrested Lizzie Borden for the murders of her parents. Lizzie Borden pled not guilty to the charges and was placed in jail to await judicial proceedings. On August 22, 1892, Lizzie Borden appeared in court for a pretrial hearing where the judge stated that she was most likely guilty of murdering her father and stepmother. The judge scheduled her to appear before a grand jury where she was indicted after one witness testified that Lizzie wore a blue dress on the day of the murders and a separate witness, who was a family friend by the name of Alice Russell, testified that she saw Lizzie burn a blue dress a few days after the murders because it supposedly had been ruined by "paint" (Linder, "Lizzie Borden Trial").

The trial of Lizzie Borden began on June 5, 1893. The trial was held in the courthouse in New Bedford, Massachusetts, where a three-judge panel presided over the case and 12 men were selected as jurors. Lizzie Borden was represented by two defense lawyers, Andrew Jennings and George Robinson. Robinson had served previously as the governor of Massachusetts and was considered to be a criminal defense attorney with exceptional skills. The prosecution was led by Hosea Knowlton and William H. Moody (Linder, "Lizzie Borden Trial").

In his opening statement, Moody asserted that the prosecution would show that she was the only person with the motive and opportunity to commit the murders. Moody dramatically made a point of emphasizing how Lizzie probably destroyed blood evidence when she burned the blue dress. Then, Moody presented four axes and hammers taken from the Borden residence (Law Library, "Lizzie Borden Trial").

Andrew Jennings, who had served as a family attorney for the Borden's in the past, opened for the defense by claiming the prosecution had no concrete evidence against Lizzie Borden. Jennings emphasized that there was no weapon or blood from the crime scene that could be connected to his client (Law Library, "Lizzie Borden Trial").

One of the key witnesses called by the prosecution was Bridget Sullivan who had been working at the Borden's home as a maid at the time of the murders. Sullivan testified that Lizzie was the only person at the home during the time that Andrew and Abby Borden were murdered. Although Lizzie supposedly did not have a good relationship with her stepmother, Sullivan testified that she never saw any signs that there were any problems between the two family members. Other witnesses, however, did testify that Lizzie did not get along well with her stepmother (Linder, "Lizzie Borden Trial").

Another key witness for the prosecution was Alice Russell who was a family friend who came to stay with Lizzie and her sister, Emma, in the days after the murders. Russell stated in her testimony that Lizzie visited her on the evening prior to the murders and expressed concern to Russell that something bad was going to happen at the home. Then, Russell described how Lizzie burned the blue dress in front of her and Lizzie told Russell that she needed to dispose of the dress because it was covered in old paint. On cross-examination for the defense, George Robinson questioned Russell about the blue dress by suggesting that Lizzie would not have burned the dress in front of her if she was guilty of the murders. Instead, if Lizzie was guilty, she would have wisely destroyed the evidence secretly (Linder, "Lizzie Borden Trial").

A critical witness for the defense was Lizzie's sister, Emma, who testified that Lizzie had a good relationship with her father and stepfather, although there had been some bitterness between Lizzie and her stepmother when her father had given a piece of property to the stepmother (Linder, "Lizzie Borden Trial"). Emma also testified that the blue dress burned by Lizzie was, in fact, old and worn and needed to be destroyed (Law Library, "Lizzie Borden Trial").

The defense attorneys called only a few other witnesses to the stand for the purpose of establishing that someone other than Lizzie probably committed the murders. These defense witnesses attempted to establish that suspicion men were seen near the Borden house on the night before and the morning of the murders. The defense attorneys had the most success during the trial when Robinson was cross-examining the prosecution witnesses. Robinson was praised by the media for his skillful cross-examination that highlighted contradictions made by the key witnesses for the prosecution (Linder, "Lizzie Borden Trial").

The defense also succeeded in raising serious questions about the prosecution's case. For example, the defense asked why the four axes and hatchets taken from the Borden home did not have any blood on them (Law Library, "Lizzie Borden Trial"). The defense also disputed the prosecution's timeline which provided roughly 10 minutes between Andrew Borden's death and Lizzie notifying the maid of the murder. Given this timeline, Lizzie could not have committed the murder because she would not have been able to clean her clothes and hide the murder weapon in such a short period of time (Linder, "Lizzie Borden Trial").

A key moment at the trial occurred when the three-judge panel ruled that Lizzie's confusing testimony before the judge and prosecutor in the days after the murders could not be admitted as evidence by the prosecution. The judge argued that her testimony must be considered coerced because she did not have an attorney present at the time of the questioning (Linder, "Lizzie Borden Trial"). The inquest conducted by the government officials represented the unethical tactics used by police and prosecutors during this era. The authorities clearly were insensitive to the stress and trauma experienced by Lizzie Borden in the aftermath of the murders (Law Library, "Lizzie Borden Trial").

On the last day of the trial, the prosecutors tried to admit evidence regarding Lizzie's attempt to purchase poison from a pharmacist on the day prior to the murders. However, the judges ruled that the testimony of the pharmacist would not be heard by the jury. Supposedly, Andrew and Abby Borden had experienced stomach pains on the day before they were murdered. Prosecutors were trying to imply that Lizzie may have attempted to poison her parents and, when she failed, decided to murder them the following day with an axe or hatchet (Linder, "Lizzie Borden Trial").

Defense attorneys summed up their case by repeating to the jury that there was no direct evidence whatsoever against Lizzie Borden. The prosecution had not connected any blood evidence or weapon to their client. Such a crime could not have been committed by a woman with such a good reputation but, instead, must have been committed by an insane and evil person. In short, the prosecution did not prove that the defendant was guilty beyond a reasonable doubt (Linder, "Lizzie Borden Trial").

Hosea Knowlton provided the closing statement for the prosecution where he detailed the circumstantial case against Lizzie Borden. In attempt to turn the all-male jury against Lizzie Borden, the prosecution tried to compensate for their lack of real evidence against the defendant by drawing upon the negative stereotypes of women perpetuated during the late 19th century. Knowlton described women as physically weak, but emotionally and psychologically manipulative and shrewd. Knowlton also noted how women were prone to extreme swings of emotion that caused them to love and hate with more passion than men (Law Library, "Lizzie Borden Trial").

One of the three judges, Judge Dewey, provided instructions to the jury and seemed to emphasize that the case against Lizzie Borden was weak and based largely upon indirect evidence. As predicted by most court observers who viewed the case against Lizzie Borden as weak, the jury found Lizzie Borden not guilty on June 20, 1893, after deliberating slightly more than one hour (Law Library, "Lizzie Borden Trial"). Interestingly, if Lizzie Borden had been found guilty of the murders, she would have been executed by way of the electric chair, which had just been invented and put into use by the state of Massachusetts (Law Library, "Lizzie Borden Trial").

In the aftermath of the Lizzie Borden trial, the *New York Times* praised the verdict of the jury. The *Times* also criticized the Fall River police officials, who charged Borden with the murders, as symbolic of the incompetence of law enforcement in small towns across the country (Linder, "Lizzie Borden Trial"). In the end, the rule of law prevailed over the prejudices displayed by the police and prosecution who tried to portray Lizzie Borden as an evil and vindictive woman who represented the worst attributes of her gender (Law Library, "Lizzie Borden Trial").

References

Axelrod-Contrada, Joan. *The Lizzie Borden "Axe-Murder" Trial: A Headline Court Case.* Berkeley Heights, NJ: Enslow Publishers, 2000.

Brown, Arnold R. *Lizzie Borden: The Legend, the Truth, the Final Chapter.* Nashville, TN: Rutledge Hill Press, 1991.

Law Library-American Law and Legal Information. "Lizzie Borden Trial: 1893." *Great American Trials.* Vol. 1. http://law.jrank.org/pages/2708/Lizzie-Borden-Trial-1893.html (accessed April 8, 2009).

Linder, Douglas O. "The Trial of Lizzie Borden." *Famous Trials.* http://www.law.umkc.edu/faculty/projects/ftrials/LizzieBorden/bordenaccount.html (accessed April 8, 2009).

Herman Mudgett (alias "Henry Holmes") Trial (1895)

At the same time that Jack the Ripper was committing his infamous murders in London, England, Herman Mudgett was becoming the first serial killer in America. While Jack the Ripper has attained a far greater status as a legendary figure, Mudgett operated over a longer period of time and probably murdered 10 times as many men, women, and children than his English counterpart. The murder trial of Mudgett became a national obsession with newspapers and the American public at the end of the 19th century simply because of the gravity of the evil committed by Mudgett (Pawlak, "American Gothic: The Strange Life of H. H. Holmes").

Herman Mudgett, also known as Dr. Henry Howard Holmes or H. H. Holmes, was a brilliant and educated con artist who had studied at the medical school of the University of Michigan. Holmes made the bulk of his money by stealing from wealthy people and creditors. In addition to his career as a con artist, he was also responsible for several murders which he usually committed for profit (Ramsland, "H. H. Holmes: Master of Illusion").

His murder spree began in the summer of 1886 when he was hired to work at the drugstore of Dr. E. S. Holton in Edgewood, Illinois. After Holton died of cancer, Holmes offered to buy the drugstore from Holton's widow. She agreed to sell him the drugstore as long as she could continue to reside in the upstairs area of the building. When Holmes failed to pay Mrs. Holton for the drugstore, she decided to take him to court. However, Holmes then murdered Mrs. Holton and told everyone in town that she had moved to California (Larson 2004, 35–47).

Holmes used the financial profits derived from his fraudulent activities to buy property across the street from the drugstore where he constructed an elaborate castle in 1888 containing 71 bedrooms as well as secret mazes, hallways, and closets. The bedrooms were soundproof with pipes that allowed Holmes to pump gas into the rooms from a control panel. The bedrooms also only locked from the outside. In the basement of the castle, Holmes built a crematorium where he also kept a tank full of acid and a table used to dissect bodies (Larson 2004, 66–93).

Holmes's first murder victims at the castle were Julia Conner, his personal bookkeeper, and her young daughter. When Holmes and Julia Conner started having an affair, she decided to leave her husband who had operated a jewelry store on the first floor of Holmes's drugstore. After murdering Conner and her daughter, Holmes started a relationship with another one of his employees, Emmaline Cigrand, whom he also eventually murdered. While people in the neighborhood wondered about the disappearance of the two women, Holmes sold the skeletons of both women to medical schools. Holmes also cashed in their life insurance policies which they were required to purchase as part of their employment with him. Holmes had paid the premiums for the life insurance policies which listed him as the beneficiary (Pawlak, "American Gothic: The Strange Life of H. H. Holmes").

In 1893, Holmes decided to rent rooms in his castle to tourists who were visiting the Chicago World's Fair. Holmes rented the rooms mainly to young women. It is unknown how many people died at the castle but it is estimated that roughly 50 tourists disappeared during the World's Fair. While Holmes's guests were asleep inside the castle, Holmes would simply turn on the gas pipes connected to the bedrooms and the guests would die from asphyxiation. Holmes would then transport the dead bodies to the basement where he would dispose of his victims through cremation or by dissolving the bodies in the acid tank (Pawlak, "American Gothic: The Strange Life of H. H. Holmes").

After the World's Fair, Holmes convinced one of his assistants, Benjamin Pietzel, to take out a $10,000 insurance policy with Fidelity Mutual Life Association. Pietzel and Holmes entered into an agreement to split the money from the insurance policy after they faked the death of Pietzel in a laboratory explosion. Prior to the explosion, Holmes would substitute a corpse resembling Pietzel in order to swindle the insurance company. Holmes and Pietzel's wife, Carrie, would divide the money between themselves, while Pietzel remained in hiding. Before the plan could be carried out, however, Holmes was arrested in St. Louis and placed in prison on charges of fraud. While serving his brief sentence in prison, Holmes met Marion Hedgepeth, a legendary bank robber who agreed to connect Holmes with a corrupt lawyer to help with the life insurance scam. Hedgepeth simply asked for $500 of the policy once the scam was completed (Ramsland, "H. H. Holmes: Master of Illusion").

After he was released from prison, Holmes took Pietzel to Philadelphia where they rented a house that would be used to fake Pietzel's death in the laboratory explosion. However, it is believed that Holmes murdered Pietzel and placed his dead body in the laboratory prior to the explosion. Holmes then went to Pietzel's wife in St. Louis and convinced her to allow him to take her 15-year-old daughter, Alice, to identify the body. Carrie Pietzel was aware of the scam and believed Holmes when he said that her husband was in hiding. In fact, Holmes was afraid that Carrie Pietzel might actually recognize her husband's corpse if he took her to identify the body so he persuaded her to let him take her daughter to make the trip to Philadelphia to participate in the fraud (Ramsland, "H. H. Holmes: Master of Illusion").

After the initial trip to Philadelphia with Pietzel's daughter, Holmes actually returned to St. Louis and convinced Carrie Pietzel to allow him to take two more of her children, Howard and Nellie, on a trip. Holmes assured Carrie Pietzel that it was necessary to move her and the three children around the country as part of the plan to swindle the insurance company. Holmes took the three Pietzel children, Alice, Howard, and Nellie, to Toronto where he murdered the two girls, Alice and Nellie, and buried the children in the basement of a home that he had rented. Later on, he murdered the young boy, Howard, near Indianapolis, Indiana, and stuffed the child in a chimney. In order to appease Carrie Pietzel, Holmes told her that the three children were staying with a wealthy woman, Millie William, in England. It is believed that Holmes murdered the Pietzel children and had eventually planned upon murdering Carrie Pietzel as well so he would not have to split the insurance money with the Pietzel family (Ramsland, "H. H. Holmes: Master of Illusion").

After Hedgepeth, Holmes's former cellmate, did not receive his $500 cut from the insurance policy, he reported to Fidelity Life Insurance that Holmes was involved in the scam. The insurance company hired the Pinkertons, a legendary detective agency, who tracked Holmes down and arrested him on charges of insurance fraud in Boston on November 17, 1894. Holmes admitted to the insurance fraud but lied when he told the investigators that he had substituted a corpse to fake the death of Pietzel. In December 1894, as investigators and the press began asking more questions about the whereabouts of Pietzel and his three children, Holmes concocted a story of how Pietzel had committed suicide by poisoning himself with chloroform. Therefore, it was, in fact, Pietzel's body that was found in the laboratory after the explosion. Holmes continued to tell Carrie Pietzel and the police that the Pietzel children were in England; however, authorities remained unaware that Holmes had actually murdered Pietzel and his three children as well as several other people over the years (Martin, "The Master of the Murder Castle").

In order to avoid a trial, which might reveal information about the various murders that he had committed and to receive a reduced sentence, Holmes entered a plea of guilty on May 28, 1895, on charges of insurance fraud. While Holmes was serving his time in prison for the insurance scam, the Philadelphia and Chicago police forces began their own investigations into the activities of Holmes (Ramsland, "H. H. Holmes: Master of Illusion").

The Philadelphia investigation was led by Detective Frank Geyer who traveled throughout the United States and Canada in an attempt to find clues that would lead him to the Pietzel children. Geyer eventually discovered the bodies of the three Pietzel children after a two-month journey where he painstakingly tracked the past travels of Holmes and the three children. During this time, the Chicago police searched Holmes's castle in Englewood and found evidence of human remains as well as his elaborate system for disposing of his victims. It is estimated that the number of persons murdered by Holmes ranged somewhere between 20 and 250 victims. Holmes denied that he had murdered anyone despite the several body parts and human remains found in his castle. He even went as far as to publish a memoir during his time in prison which told the story of his life and how he had been falsely accused of the murders (Ramsland, "H. H. Holmes: Master of Illusion").

On October 28, 1895, the murder trial of Henry Holmes, also known as Herman Mudgett, began in Philadelphia, Pennsylvania. Judge Michael Arnold was selected to direct the courtroom where Holmes faced a charge of first-degree murder in the death of his assistant, Benjamin Pietzel. District Attorney George S. Graham was assigned as the lead prosecutor for the state of Pennsylvania (Fuller, Wrightington, Spencer, and Baldwin 1902, 176).

At the outset of the trial, Holmes fought constantly with his attorneys so he decided to dismiss his legal counsel and represent himself as his own attorney. Interestingly, Holmes was the first person ever in the United States to represent himself in a murder trial. During the jury selection process, Holmes tried to remove potential jurors who had read anything in the newspapers about the alleged murder, but Judge Arnold ruled that this was not sufficient cause to reject someone as a juror (Ramsland, "H. H. Holmes: Master of Illusion").

The *Philadelphia Inquirer* initially praised Holmes for his performance in the courtroom as he seemed familiar with various aspects of the law. For example, Holmes asked for an analysis of the liquid poison that he allegedly used to murder the Pietzel children and requested that toxicology reports be provided as well. However, Holmes presented an inadequate defense for the most part. For instance, Holmes did not take the witness stand in his own defense and failed to call any witnesses to support his innocence. Furthermore, during the questioning of expert witnesses who testified that Pietzel did not commit suicide, Holmes failed to make any points that might suggest he did not murder Pietzel. Holmes also made a mistake during the trial when he asked for a recess to eat lunch immediately after the corpse of Benjamin Pietzel was described during the proceedings. Courtroom observers stated that Holmes appeared insensitive to the discussion of his partner's body who, according to Holmes, had committed suicide. By the end of the first day of the trial, Holmes asked that his two attorneys be brought back into the courtroom to provide legal representation (Ramsland, "H. H. Holmes: Master of Illusion").

The prosecution made its case by presenting to the jury how Pietzel's body was identified at the laboratory and they used physicians as expert witnesses to prove that Pietzel was already dead when someone introduced chloroform into his body in order to fake the suicide. Since Holmes had admitted to being with Pietzel at the laboratory prior to the explosion, it was easy for the jury to draw the logical conclusion that Holmes had murdered Pietzel (Ramsland, "H. H. Holmes: Master of Illusion").

In terms of a motive for the murder, District Attorney Graham introduced as evidence the $10,000 insurance policy taken out by Pietzel and emphasized to the jury that Holmes had been paying the premiums on the policy. By murdering Pietzel, Holmes would no longer be required to pay the premiums and would be able to collect the money on behalf of Pietzel's wife (Fuller, Wrightington, Spencer, and Baldwin 1902, 181).

During the trial, District Attorney Graham also made reference to Holmes's shameful behavior demonstrated throughout his life as a way to influence the jurors. For example, in addition to having been charged with insurance fraud and murder, Holmes also was guilty of polygamy. It was revealed during the trial that Holmes was simultaneously married to three women. Holmes's third wife, Georgie Anna Yoke, was called by the prosecution to describe Holmes's behavior on the day that Pietzel was supposedly murdered. According to Yoke, Holmes behaved in a very nervous and excited manner on the day that Pietzel was allegedly murdered and, when Holmes returned from Pietzel's rented house, he wanted to leave the city quickly. Holmes decided to cross-examine Yoke himself, but he failed to persuade her to change her story (Fuller, Wrightington, Spencer, and Baldwin 1902, 182).

After Yoke's testimony, Carrie Pietzel took the witness stand and provided the most emotional part of the trial. She told the jury how she was informed of the deaths of her three children and how she had to identify their remains, which were decomposed (Ramsland, "H. H. Holmes: Master of Illusion").

In his closing statement for the prosecution, Graham spoke for two hours and referred to Holmes as a dangerous man who deserved to be sentenced to death for the murder of Pietzel. Holmes's defense attorneys attempted to argue during their closing statements that Pietzel had committed suicide, but the jurors had already made up their minds (Ramsland, "H. H. Holmes: Master of Illusion").

The five-day trial had been a national sensation as the newspapers covered every detail and people crowded into the courtroom simply to catch a glimpse of the defendant who had allegedly murdered Pietzel and several other people in a gruesome fashion. On November 2, 1895, after the jury deliberated for two and a half hours, Holmes was found guilty of first-degree murder in the death of Benjamin Pietzel and sentenced to death. After the conviction, Holmes's attorneys filed an appeal for a new trial, but it was denied. When the Hearst newspaper organization offered Holmes $7,500 for a confession, Holmes admitted to the murder of Pietzel as well as 26 other men, women, and children. His entire confession was published in the *Philadelphia Inquirer* where Holmes stated that he felt that his life was controlled by the devil and the act of murder had come naturally to him (Ramsland, "H. H. Holmes: Master of Illusion").

Holmes was executed by hanging at the Philadelphia County Prison on May 7, 1896. At Holmes's request, his body was buried with cement surrounding his coffin in order to prevent anyone from digging up his body and dissecting it (Larson 2004, 386–387).

Today, criminal-justice scholars who have studied the case of Henry Holmes (i.e., Herman Mudgett) remain unsatisfied. While he was found guilty of murdering Benjamin Pietzel, authorities failed to conduct a complete investigation into the horrible crimes that he supposedly committed at his castle in Englewood, Illinois. In addition, Holmes made statements and admissions before, during, and after the murder trial that provided inconsistencies in terms of the actual number of persons that he murdered. Finally, the behavior of Holmes seemed remarkable in its complexity. While he initially seemed to focus upon young women as his victims, he also murdered several men and children. Furthermore, it is uncertain whether he was motivated primarily by money or whether he was an evil and disturbed person who simply enjoyed the act of murder. In the end, however, most legal researchers tend to agree that justice was served in the conviction and execution of Henry Holmes (Martin, "The Master of Murder Castle").

References

Fuller, Horace Williams, Sydney Russell Wrightington, Arthur Weightman Spencer, and Thomas Tileston Baldwin. *The Green Bag.* Vol. 14. Boston: Boston Book Company, 1902.

Geary, Rick. *The Beast of Chicago: An Account of the Life and Crimes of Herman W. Mudgett, Known to the World as H. H. Holmes.* New York: NBM Publishing, 2003.

Larson, Erik. *The Devil in the White City: Murder, Magic, and Madness at the Fair that Changed America.* New York: Vintage Books, 2004.

Martin, John Barlow. "The Master of Murder Castle: A Classic of Chicago Crime." *Harper's Weekly.* December 1943, 76–85.

Pawlak, Debra. "American Gothic: The Strange Life of H. H. Holmes." *The Media Drome.* http://www.themediadrome.com/content/articles/history_articles/holmes.htm (accessed December 31, 2009).

Ramsland, Katherine. "H. H. Holmes: Master of Illusion." *TruTV Crime Library: Criminal Minds and Methods.* http://www.trutv.com/library/crime/serial_killers/history/holmes/index_1.html (accessed December 31, 2009).

Leon Czolgosz Trial (1901)

Leon Czolgosz lived during a period in the history of the United States when industrialists concentrated great wealth by exploiting the large mass of workers who lived in extreme poverty. Czolgosz witnessed firsthand the political and economic oppression of his family and friends during the latter part of the 19th century and decided that he must strike a blow against the enemy of the good working people of America. Czolgosz focused his attention upon the most powerful man in the United States, President William McKinley, who represented the interests of the wealthy and provided no relief for poor workers suffering throughout the country (Clarke 2006, 32–45).

In the 1896 presidential election between Republican William McKinley and Democrat William Jennings Bryan, McKinley represented the wealthy industrialists and Bryan represented the working poor. Czolgosz believed that money from the wealthy industrialists swayed the election to McKinley (Clarke 2006, 38). In 1897, the Lattimer Mines Massacre occurred in Pennsylvania where police killed Slavic miners who were peacefully demonstrating. Later on, the police officers were acquitted. This caused Czolgosz to have a nervous breakdown in the fall of 1897 (39–41). Czolgosz absorbed the radical literature of his day and was obsessed with the need for radical social change. Czolgosz was a follower of Emma Goldman, an anarchist and feminist who was a great speaker. Czolgosz heard her speak on a number of occasions and also had brief conversations with her. Anarchists thought that Czolgosz might be a government spy and sent out a warning to others to watch out for him. He often used an alias, Fred C. Nieman (43–50).

In 1900, King Humbert I of Italy was assassinated by an anarchist named Gaetano Bresci. Bresci killed the king for the sake of the common man. Czolgosz found in Bresci his hero, a man who had the courage to sacrifice himself for a cause (Clarke 2006, 43). Inspired by Bresci, Czolgosz sought to assassinate President McKinley because he was wealthy and indifferent to the working class (MacDonald 1902, 375–384). Czolgosz heard McKinley speak in Buffalo at the Pan-American Exposition about the prosperity of America, while so many of the working poor suffered. On September 6, 1901, Czolgosz went to the exposition with a pistol concealed in a handkerchief bandaged around his right hand. McKinley was standing in a receiving line greeting people when Czolgosz shot McKinley twice at point-blank range. McKinley died eight days later. When Czolgosz was arrested, police found a folded newspaper clipping about Bresci in Czolgosz's pocket (Johns 1970, 90–94).

The trial of Leon Czolgosz began on September 23, 1901, at the Buffalo Supreme Court. The judge in the trial was Truman C. White. Czolgosz was given court-appointed attorneys who spent most of the trial apologizing for having to represent an assassin. Czologosz tried to have his attorneys removed, but he was denied this request by the judge. Czologosz was clearly denied an adequate legal defense during the short trial (Clarke 2006, 47–49).

A variety of witnesses testified to the shooting of President McKinley by Czolgosz. Then, Czolgosz himself took the stand and was briefly interrogated by District Attorney Thomas Penney at which time Czolgosz answered basic questions about himself quietly and nervously. While Czolgosz admitted to the murder of President McKinley and pled guilty expressing no regret. Judge Truman C. White did not accept Czolgosz's plea of guilty and forced the clerk to enter a not guilty plea (Buffalo History Works, "Leon Czolgosz").

The trial lasted less than eight hours and resulted in a conviction of first-degree murder for which Czolgosz was sentenced to death. Prior to his execution, Czolgosz made several statements claiming responsibility for the assassination of McKinley and stating that he murdered McKinley because the president kept giving speeches in which he talked about the prosperity of America yet was insensitive to the plight of working people who lived in poverty (Clarke 2006, 48). Witnesses said that Czolgosz was calm and collected as he entered the execution room at the Auburn prison. Czolgosz was executed by electrocution at approximately 7:00 a.m. on October 29, 1901, in the Auburn prison (Seibert 2002, 247–314).

Scholars continue to debate whether Czolgosz was sane or suffered from mental illness. Prior to the execution of Czolgosz, five psychiatrists examined the assassin and found that he did not suffer from any mental illness. However, two psychiatrists, Walter Channing and L. Vernon Briggs, challenged the results of the five psychiatrists by closely examining the personal history of Czolgosz (Clarke 2006, 30). Channing concluded that Czolgosz suffered from a mental disorder based upon the fact that he spent a great deal of time alone and refused to eat food prepared by his stepmother for fear of being poisoned by her. Channing also pointed to the "nervous breakdown" of Czolgosz after the Lattimer Mines Massacre in 1897 as an event of great significance in establishing the mental condition of Czolgosz (Channing 1902, 261–266). Briggs also arrived at the same conclusion as Channing when he argued that Czolgosz suffered from mental illness, specifically paranoid schizophrenia (Briggs 1921, 321–338). More recently, however, James Clarke provided a strong argument that the assassination of McKinley by Czolgosz was a rational act given the political and economic context of 19th century America (Clarke 2006, 30–32).

After the assassination, the government sought to eliminate anarchists who were blamed for McKinley's death. While some anarchists condemned Czolgosz, others such as Emma Goldman praised him as a brave martyr (Clarke 2006, 49). Oddly enough, the McKinley assassination provided America with a more progressive leader in Theodore Roosevelt who was more sympathetic to the working class. Roosevelt pushed for the creation of the Departments of Labor and Commerce and also weakened the power of large corporations (Rauchway 2004, 185–189).

 ## Leon Czolgosz

In May 1873, Leon Czolgosz was born into brutal poverty to parents who were Polish immigrants. His mother died during child birth when Czolgosz was 12. At the age of 14, Czolgosz began working in the steel and glass factories of Cleveland and Pittsburgh. Because he was earning only $4 a day, Czolgosz joined a union and went on strike, but this resulted in him being fired. Czolgosz and his family usually had little money left for housing and medical care. As a young man, he only had one girlfriend who broke up with him and afterward he was too shy to talk to women. Czolgosz was always fairly quiet and withdrawn. He was known to sleep a lot and he refused to eat food prepared by his stepmother because he feared that she might poison him. Czolgosz's political views were greatly influenced by the Haymarket Square bombing in 1886, which involved a labor rally in Chicago where a bomb exploded killing 11 persons. Anarchists were arrested for the crime, although there was little evidence against them. Czolgosz was angry that five anarchists were executed for the bombing and saw this as an injustice against the labor movement. Incidents such as the Haymarket Square bombing caused Czolgosz to reject religion because he believed that God had abandoned the working man (Clarke 2006, 32–37).

References

Briggs, L. Vernon. *The Manner of Man That Kills.* Boston: Gorham Press, 1921.

The Buffalo History Works. "The Trial and Execution of Leon Czolgosz." http://www.buffalohistoryworks.com/panamex/assassination/executon.htm (accessed March 2, 2009).

Channing, W. "The Mental State of Czolgosz, the Assassin of President McKinley." *American Journal of Insanity* 59 (1902): 233–278.

Clarke, James A. *Defining Danger: American Assassins and the New Domestic Terrorists.* New Brunswick, NJ: Transaction Publishers, 2007.

Johns, A. Wesley. *The Man Who Shot McKinley.* South Brunswick, NJ: A. S. Barnes, 1970.

MacDonald, Carlos F. "The Trial, Execution, Autopsy, and Mental Status of Leon F. Czolgosz, Alias Fred Nieman, the Assassin of President McKinley." *The American Journal of Insanity* 58 (January 1902): 369–386.

Rauchway, Eric. *Murdering McKinley: The Making of Theodore Roosevelt's America.* New York: Hill and Wang, 2004.

Seibert, Jeffrey W. *"I Done My Duty": The Complete Story of the Assassination of President McKinley.* Bowie, MD: Heritage Books, 2002.

The Trial of William "Big Bill" Haywood (1907)

Although the murder trial of William "Big Bill" Haywood has received little attention historically compared to other trials, it clearly ranks as one of the greatest trials in American legal history because it has come to symbolize the class warfare between the interests of powerful mining companies in the western states and the labor movement at the turn of the 20th century. The trial was ultimately viewed as a victory for organized labor and a defeat for the mining companies and marked the end of a violent period in the western part of the United States (Law Library, "William Haywood Trial").

On December 30, 1905, the former governor of Idaho, Frank Steunenberg, was killed by an explosion in his front yard as he returned to his home in Caldwell, Idaho, after a walk in the snow. The explosion was alleged to have been the work of the Western Federation of Miners (WFM), a union of silver mine workers angered at Steunenberg for calling upon federal troops to break a labor strike in the northern region of Idaho known as the Coeur d'Alene territory. During Steunenberg's term as governor of Idaho in the 1890s, he had appealed for the use of federal troops a number of times to violate the rights of the union by imprisoning workers without bail. The federal troops also tried to prevent violent acts of revenge committed by the WFM against persons and property connected to the Western Mine Owners' Association (Dubofsky 1987, 39–40).

On the day after the assassination of Steunenberg, a waitress at the Saratoga hotel in Caldwell reported that she had waited on a person by the name of "Thomas Hogan" shortly after the explosion. The waitress recalled that Hogan acted very nervously based upon the fact that his hands were trembling and he would not look the waitress in the eye. Police conducted a search of Hogan's hotel room and found material used to make explosives. Hogan was questioned by police and finally arrested on January 1, 1906, at the hotel bar and charged with first-degree murder. After repeated interrogations, Hogan stated that his real name was "Harry Orchard." Orchard admitted to police that he knew persons associated with the WFM but refused to confess to the murder of Steunenberg (Linder, "The Trial of William Haywood").

Because authorities in Idaho did not believe that Orchard acted alone in the murder of Steunenberg, they hired the Pinkerton Detective Agency to investigate. The agency sent its best detective, James McParland, to Idaho. McParland had become famous for working to uncover criminal acts such as kidnapping and murder committed by labor activists in Pennsylvania in the 1870s (Dubofsky 1987, 40).

McParland began by questioning Orchard at the state prison in Boise, Idaho. McParland told Orchard that he might be given a reduced sentence if he cooperated with authorities and testified against WFM leaders who were involved in the assassination of Steunenberg. Orchard provided a detailed confession concerning his involvement in the murder of Steunenberg and also admitted to being involved in 17 other murders ordered by WFM officials. Specifically, Orchard named WFM Secretary-Treasurer William Haywood, President Charles Moyer, and the president's advisor, George Pettibone, as the key figures in the conspiracy to murder Steunenberg and other individuals targeted by the union leaders (Dubofsky 1987, 40–42).

McParland was concerned that it would be difficult to arrest the three union leaders who were stationed at the WFM headquarters in Denver, Colorado, because they would most likely use their lawyers to resist extradition to Idaho. Therefore, McParland secured arrest warrants secretly on February 15, 1906, from Colorado authorities and, two days later, transported the three men to Idaho quickly by train so they could not contact their family members or attorneys (Linder, "The Trial of William Haywood").

Edmund Richardson, the attorney for the WFM, traveled to Idaho and filed a legal petition claiming that the WFM leaders were denied an opportunity to challenge their arrest and transfer to Idaho within the Colorado court system. The WTM leaders lost their legal challenge in the Idaho state courts and also lost their appeal to the U.S. Supreme Court when the justices ruled in *Pettibone v. Nichols* (1906) that their constitutional rights had not been violated by their forcible removal from Colorado (Linder, "The Trial of William Haywood").

After the decision was handed down by the U.S. Supreme Court, the WFM hired Clarence Darrow, a legendary defense attorney from Chicago, to work with Edmund Richardson in preparing the legal defense for William Haywood who would be the first of the three union leaders tried for conspiracy to commit first-degree murder (Linder, The Trial of William Haywood). Darrow and Richardson were concerned, not only with the testimony of Orchard, but also with a miner named Steve Adams who confirmed Orchard's testimony when he confessed to his role in one of the bombings that killed 13 people. Like Orchard, Adams had decided to testify against the WFM leaders in the hopes of receiving a reduced punishment. Fortunately for Haywood, Darrow was able to get Adams to take back his confession in exchange for a promise from Darrow to represent Adams in his murder trial. Therefore, the murder trial of Haywood would be based largely upon the credibility of Orchard's testimony which would lack support from a second witness such as Adams (Carlson 1984, 102–118).

The trial of William Haywood began on May 9, 1907. The two key prosecutors representing the state of Idaho would be William Borah and James Hawley. Borah and Hawley were two of the most celebrated trial lawyers in Idaho. Judge Fremont Wood presided over the murder trial which was held in the Ada County Courthouse in Boise, Idaho. The newspapers in Boise described the trial as a battle between labor and capital that would be observed by the entire world (Law Library, "William Haywood Trial").

Haywood's defense attorneys and prosecutors battled over jury selection for six weeks as both sides investigated potential jurors in an attempt to gain a favorable jury for the trial. Ultimately, the jury consisted of mostly older men and all were or had been farmers which clearly favored the defense lawyers. Nine of the 12 jurors were currently farmers, while the other 3 jurors were a construction foreman, a real estate agent, and a contractor (Lukas, 1997, 525–528).

Hawley provided the opening remarks for the prosecution. While Hawley told the jury about the assassination of Steunenberg and the prison confession of Orchard, Darrow strategically interrupted with objections and effectively caused Hawley to lose his confidence. Most court observers judged Hawley's opening statement to be ineffective (Linder, "The Trial of William Haywood").

The prosecution then proceeded to call a number of witnesses to describe what happened on the day of the assassination. A person who lived in Steunenberg's neighborhood testified to hearing the explosion, and a physician who attended to the former governor while he was dying also provided dramatic testimony. Two additional witnesses testified to having seen Orchard looking at Steunenberg's house with binoculars and leaving the Saratoga hotel immediately before the explosion. Finally, Julian Steunenberg, the son of the former governor, recalled Orchard inquiring about the possibility of purchasing some livestock from Frank Steunenberg (Linder, "The Trial of William Haywood").

Obviously, the star witness for the prosecution would be Harry Orchard who had been placed in protective custody for fear that he would be murdered by WFM officials. Orchard testified about his career as a terrorist for the WFM, which began in 1903. Orchard told how the WFM targeted men working in the silver mines who refused to join the union and also described how he failed in his attempts to assassinate such prominent individuals as the governor of Colorado, two justices who served on the Colorado Supreme Court, and corporate executives of the mining company. Orchard concluded his testimony by stating that Steunenberg was murdered in order to intimidate politicians who might be inclined to oppose the goals of the WFM (Lukas 1997, 553–559).

The cross-examination of Orchard was conducted by Edmund Richardson, who treated Orchard as a hostile witness by insulting and verbally attacking him. Richardson's strategy was designed to discredit Orchard by portraying him as a person of immoral character who lied and cheated throughout his entire life. Richardson ended the cross-examination by suggesting that Orchard had no remorse for the murders he committed and only agreed to testify for the prosecution in order to avoid the death penalty. Overall, most court observers viewed Orchard's testimony as effective and Richardson's cross-examination as unsuccessful (Carlson 1984, 116–128).

The prosecution concluded its case against Haywood by introducing evidence from *Miner's Magazine*, a publication created by the WFM. Several articles within the magazine expressed hatred for Steunenberg and delight over his assassination (Linder, "The Trial of William Haywood"). After the prosecution rested its case, Darrow and Richardson asked Judge Wood to declare an acquittal, also known as a directed verdict, for Haywood, but Wood ruled that the case should be decided by the jury (Lukas 1997, 565–567).

The defense team for Haywood called over 80 witnesses in their attempt to discredit Orchard's testimony. Orchard was portrayed by the defense as someone who made a habit of lying throughout his entire life (Law Library, "William Haywood Trial"). Another witness was Morris Friedman, who worked as a secretary for the Pinkerton Detective Agency. Friedman testified that Pinkerton often used undercover operatives to gain access to the WFM in an attempt to destroy the union financially. The purpose of Friedman's testimony was to create reasonable doubt in the minds of the jurors by suggesting that perhaps Pinkerton's undercover people may have committed some of the crimes described by Orchard in an attempt to destroy the reputation of the WFM. In short, the defense wanted the jury to think Pinkerton may have tried to frame the WFM for the various murders. In addition to Friedman, the two other WFM leaders arrested with Haywood, Charles Moyer and George Pettibone, were called by the defense attorneys to deny the criminal allegations made against them by Orchard (Linder, "The Trial of William Haywood").

On July 11, 1907, after two months of testimony from prosecution and defense witnesses, Clarence Darrow finally called the defendant, William Haywood, to the witness stand. Haywood denied all of the allegations made by Orchard against him such as ordering Orchard to murder various political officials, including Steunenberg, and to bomb railroads and mines in an effort to kill nonunion miners. William Borah conducted the cross-examination of Haywood but was ineffective at challenging Haywood, who appeared as a very imposing figure during five hours of questioning (Linder, The Trial of William Haywood).

James Hawley provided the first summary of the prosecution's case for the jury. Hawley asked the jurors to do justice by finding Haywood guilty of conspiracy to commit first-degree murder. Hawley also praised Orchard for his confession and referred to the WFM as one of the worst criminal organizations that ever existed within the United States (Linder, "The Trial of William Haywood").

In the first summary for the defense team, Edmund Richardson tried to justify the hatred that WFM and Haywood must have felt for Steunenberg, the former governor who called upon federal troops to imprison silver miners in northern Idaho in 1899. However, according to Richardson, the murder of Steunenberg was not ordered by Haywood, but instead committed by Orchard and the Pinkerton Detective Agency, who plotted strategically to destroy the WFM (Linder, "The Trial of William Haywood").

The second summary for the defense came from Clarence Darrow. Darrow provided an impressive summary for the jury. Darrow argued dramatically that Orchard had lied in his confession and testimony, and tried to excuse the violence committed by labor organizations by arguing that their wrongdoings were outweighed by the fact that they represented a just cause in supporting poor working families devoted to God. Darrow wisely appealed to the fact that the majority of jurors were Idaho farmers who had working class backgrounds (Carlson 1984, 129–132).

Darrow concluded by asserting that Orchard's murder of Steunenberg was personal in the sense that the former governor had caused Orchard to lose his investments in the silver mines when the federal government took control of the mines. In other words, Orchard acted alone in the assassination and did not receive orders from WFM leaders. Darrow's conclusion also included a powerful endorsement of Haywood as a good man as well as a plea to the jury to find Haywood not guilty because he represented thousands of workers who would be weaker and poorer if such a great union leader as Haywood was convicted and executed (Carlson 1984, 130–132).

The final address to the jury was made by William Borah, who made the second summary for the prosecution. Like Darrow, Borah also provided a dramatic and impressive performance for the court. Borah reminded the jury that the trial of William Haywood was a murder trial, not a judgment on the organized labor movement. Borah also tried to connect Haywood to radical elements within the labor movement such as anarchists and revolutionary socialists who wanted to overthrow the U.S. government. Finally, Borah asked the jurors to consider why Orchard consistently made trips from Idaho to Denver. Borah suggested that Orchard had to make the frequent trips to Denver because the WFM and Haywood were providing financial support and legal protection for him (Carlson 1984, 131–133).

Judge Wood provided jury instructions, which included a statement that Haywood could only be found guilty if he could be connected to the assassination beyond a reasonable doubt based upon the evidence presented. Wood also noted that a person could not be convicted on the testimony of an accomplice unless the accomplice had his testimony verified by a second witness. Clearly, Judge Wood's instructions were made to criticize the prosecution for failing to provide a second witness or other evidence to corroborate the testimony of Orchard (Law Library, "William Haywood Trial).

On the morning of Saturday, July 28, 1907, the 12 jurors entered the jury conference room to begin their deliberations. On the morning of the next day, July 29, 1907, the jury informed Judge Wood that they had reached an outcome in the murder trial of William Haywood. The clerk of the court announced that the jury had found Haywood not guilty of conspiracy to murder Frank Steunenberg (Law Library, "William Haywood Trial").

A number of jurors who were interviewed after the trial claimed that Judge Wood's instructions to the jury emphasizing confirmation of Haywood's involvement in the murder beyond a reasonable doubt played a critical role in the verdict. Because Orchard's testimony could not be backed up by a second witness, such as Steve Adams, who withdrew his confession, the jurors were uncomfortable in convicting Haywood based upon the testimony of only one person. In addition, other factors such as Haywood's strong performance as a witness in his own defense and Darrow's emotional summation also seemed to persuade the jury. The media and members of the Pinkerton Detective Agency suggested another possibility. They speculated that the WFM may have bribed or threatened bodily harm to the jurors (Linder, "The Trial of William Haywood").

After the Haywood trial, George Pettibone was also tried for the murder of Steunenberg in January 1908. Prosecutors again used Orchard as its main witness. At the Pettibone trial, Darrow provided the cross-examination of Orchard and successfully caused the jury to view him as a witness who lacked credibility. Eventually, Pettibone would be found not guilty in less time than the jury deliberated in the Haywood case. As a result of the acquittals in the Haywood and Pettibone trials, prosecutors chose not to try Charles Moyer for his role in the assassination (Carlson 1984, 138–154).

Even though Harry Orchard attempted to gain the favor of prosecutors by providing critical testimony in the Haywood and Pettibone trials, he was ultimately convicted in March 1908 for his role in the murder of Frank Steunenberg. Orchard was initially sentenced to death, but his sentence was later reduced to life in prison (Linder, "The Trial of William Haywood").

The trial of William Haywood represented a huge victory for organized labor and a significant defeat for the federal government, the state government of Idaho, and corporate mining organizations. The forces of government and big business had been attempting to use the courts and the military to weaken the labor movement by connecting it to violent acts, such as the assassination of Steunenberg. However, the effort failed because of a lack of prosecutorial evidence and a legendary performance by defense attorney Clarence Darrow, who swayed a jury consisting mainly of working class farmers (Law Library, "William Haywood Trial").

 William "Big Bill" Haywood

William "Big Bill" Haywood is viewed historically as a radical leader of the labor movement who successfully organized unions, intimidated government officials and business leaders, and consistently faced prosecution by the law for his alleged actions. Haywood was born in 1869 in Salt Lake City, Utah territory, and his father, a rider for the Pony Express, died when Haywood was a young child. At the age of nine, Haywood accidentally injured his right eye while making a slingshot with a knife and lived the rest of his life with only one eye (Dubofsky 1987, 10–12). As a young boy, Haywood began to work in the mines, and he saw firsthand how workers were mistreated by the mining companies and left unprotected by government authorities. Miners often worked long hours for low wages in unsafe working environments (Law Library, "William Haywood Trial").

The Haymarket Square riots in 1886, which involved a labor rally in Chicago where a bomb killed 11 persons, had a great influence on Haywood's radicalism. Haywood failed to believe that the conviction and execution of several members of the labor movement for the Haymarket Square bombing were justified because of a lack of evidence against the defendants (Dubofsky 1987, 13). Haywood was also inspired to join the labor movement because of the Pullman railroad strikes of 1893 where Eugene V. Debs and the American Railway Union led thousands of workers to strike because of a significant cut in wages (Carlson 1984, 44–58).

While working in the silver mines of Idaho in 1896, Haywood attended a speech given by Ed Boyce, the president of the Western Federation of Miners (WFM). Haywood was so inspired by Boyce's speech that he joined the WFM and, four years later, became a leading member of its executive board. After Boyce retired in 1902, Haywood became one of the key leaders of the WFM along with Charles Moyer (Dubofsky 1987, 15–23). Unfortunately, Haywood and Moyer differed greatly on how to achieve the goals of the labor movement. Haywood favored strikes and violence, while Moyer favored negotiation and compromise. Haywood's most important goal was to unite all workers regardless of their trade and to achieve an eight-hour workday for laborers. Haywood used his skills as a powerful speaker to rally union members toward this cause (Linder, "William D. Haywood").

From 1902 to 1904, the WFM was engaged in "The Colorado Labor Wars" with the mining business officials and the state government of Colorado. During this time period, 33 deaths resulted from violence committed by both sides against union and nonunion workers. On one particular occasion, 13 nonunion workers were killed at a train station by an explosion in Independence, Colorado. Mining officials and government leaders suspected that Haywood had ordered the bombing, and they sought revenge against union workers for the violence (Carlson 1984, 57–77).

In 1906, Haywood was arrested for ordering the assassination of Frank Steunenberg, a former governor of Idaho. Haywood was acquitted on charges of conspiracy to commit murder in 1907 (see entry above). While in prison awaiting trial, Haywood ran for governor of Colorado as a member of the Socialist party in 1906 and received 16,000 votes, continued working as a leader of the WFM, and began his legal education by completing law courses through the mail (Linder, "The Trial of William Haywood").

After Moyer forced Haywood out of the WFM in 1908, Haywood decided to become actively involved with an international labor organization known as the Industrial Workers of the World (IWW), also known as the "Wobblies" (Carlson 1984, 83–84). In 1915, Haywood was chosen as the president of IWW. Haywood led strikes throughout the United States and was able to enroll over 3 million factory workers to join the IWW. Haywood was convicted in 1918 of interfering with U.S. industries producing materials for the military after he encouraged workers to go on strike (Linder, "The Trial of William Haywood"). Haywood was sentenced to 30 years in jail but when he was released on bail pending an appeal of his conviction, he fled to the Soviet Union where he worked as an advisor to the Russian government until his death in 1928 (Carlson 1984, 313–328).

References

Carlson, Peter. *Roughneck: The Life and Times of Big Bill Haywood*. New York: W. W. Norton and Co., Inc. 1984.

Dubofsky, Melvyn. *"Big Bill" Haywood*. New York: St. Martin's Press, 1987.

Law Library–American Law and Legal Information. "William "Big Bill" Haywood Trial: 1907—The Coeur D'alene Strike, Haywood's Fate Rests on Orchard's Credibility." *Great American Trials*. Vol. 1. http://law.jrank.org/pages/2760/William-Big-Bill-Haywood-Trial-1907.html (accessed July 5, 2009).

Linder, Douglas O. "The Trial of William "Big Bill" Haywood." *Famous Trials*. http://www.law.umkc.edu/faculty/projects/ftrials/haywood/HAY_ACCT.HTM (accessed July 5, 2009).

Linder, Douglas O. "William D. Haywood." *Famous Trials*. http://www.law.umkc.edu/faculty/projects/ftrials/haywood/HAY_BHAY.HTM (accessed July 7, 2009).

Lukas, J. Anthony. *Big Trouble: A Murder in a Small Western Town Sets Off a Struggle for the Soul of America*. New York: Simon and Schuster, 1997.

The Harry Thaw Murder Trials (1907–1908)

The two murder trials of Harry K. Thaw, an emotionally unstable millionaire, are considered by many legal scholars as the first "trial of the century" of the 20th century. Thaw's murder of Stanford White was based largely upon his obsession with the fact that White had allegedly taken advantage of Thaw's wife, Evelyn Nesbit, prior to their marriage when she was just a teenage girl. Thaw's defense attorneys developed an extreme version of the temporary insanity defense by arguing that Thaw had a mental disorder associated only with American men referred to as "dementia Americana." The mental disorder supposedly caused American men to act uncontrollably once they discovered that their wives or daughters had been disrespected by another man (Law Library, "Harry Thaw Trials").

Harry Thaw was a Pittsburgh millionaire who had inherited his wealth from his father who was a coal and railroad baron. On June 25, 1906, Thaw murdered Stanford White, a famous architect from New York City. Thaw shot White three times with a revolver during a musical at the Madison Square Garden theatre. The theatre had an open-air rooftop so the murder of White by Thaw has been referred to as *The Rooftop Murder.* The crime occurred in front of approximately one thousand witnesses. Thaw's motive for the murder was the fact that his wife, Evelyn Nesbit, had been taken advantage of by White when she was just a 16-year-old girl who had arrived in New York City looking for work as a model, actress, and singer (Uruburu 2008, 269–289).

At 3:00 a.m. on June 26, 1906, Thaw was charged with the murder of White and placed in prison. Thaw immediately proclaimed his innocence because White had had a reputation for seducing young teenage girls. Thaw viewed himself as a hero who was justified in murdering White because he wanted to save young girls from a pervert who deserved to die (Linder, "The Trials of Harry Thaw").

The First Trial (1907)

In January 1907, a jury of 12 men was selected to hear the trial of Harry Thaw for the murder of Stanford White. Thaw's several defense attorneys, paid for by his wealthy family, consisted of Delphin Delmas, John Gleason, Clifford Hartridge, Hugh McPike, and George Peabody. The defense team planned to argue that Thaw was sane, except for the night of the murder when he had experienced temporary insanity based upon severe anxiety brought about by the thought of another man taking advantage of his wife. The prosecution team led by William Jerome would simply argue that Thaw committed the murder based upon the motive of jealousy. In fact, according to the prosecution, Thaw was not a hero but a jealous husband who could not control his emotions (Law Library, "Harry Thaw Trials").

Judge James Fitzgerald presided over the murder trial which began on February 4, 1907, in New York City. The prosecution presented its case by calling Warner Paxon to the witness stand. Paxon had witnessed the murder of White and described how he walked Thaw out of the theatre to a police officer who placed him under arrest. Paxon also testified about a conversation that he overheard in which Thaw told his wife, Evelyn Nesbit, that he had murdered White because he wanted to protect her. Nesbit responded by informing her husband that he was going to be in a great deal of trouble because of the murder. After Paxon's testimony, a coroner testified to the fact that White died quickly from a bullet wound to the head that caused severe blood loss. The prosecutors' case lasted roughly only two hours by basically providing the jury with the specifics of the murder (Linder, "The Trials of Harry Thaw").

Harry Thaw's defense began with John Gleason arguing that Thaw had suffered from an extreme form of temporary insanity when he became obsessed with Stanford White after he learned that White had taken advantage of his wife when she was a teenager. Gleason told the jurors that Thaw's behavior could be attributed to mental instability passed down from family members as well as stress-related factors (Linder, "The Trials of Harry Thaw").

Gleason then called Dr. C. C. Wiley as the first witness for the defense. Wiley, who had served as a psychiatrist for the Thaw family, told the jurors that Thaw was detached from reality at the time of the White murder. Wiley testified that, immediately after the murder, Thaw told his wife that he was trying to save her life. According to Wiley, Thaw's statement to his wife was evidence of his delusion (Linder, "The Trials of Harry Thaw").

A second witness was an employee at the Madison Square Garden theatre named Benjamin Bowman. Bowman testified that he heard Stanford White say in December 1903 that he would shoot Thaw with a pistol after he heard Thaw had left the theatre with his former mistress, Evelyn Nesbit. Bowman supposedly had informed Thaw of the threat from White (Linder, "The Trials of Harry Thaw").

The bulk of the Thaw's defense was presented by Delphin Delmas, a San Francisco lawyer who supposedly had never lost a case. Delmas decided to move away from the initial strategy of temporary insanity and decided instead to try and win an acquittal for Thaw by attacking the murder victim, Stanford White. Because White had a reputation as a sexual pervert, Delmas knew that he could make the jurors feel contempt for someone who preyed on young girls. Delmas's plan was ultimately to get the jurors to forgive Thaw for the murder by using Evelyn Nesbit as a key witness who would testify about her relationship with White when she was just a young girl. In short, the murder trial of Thaw would be transformed into a judgment about the character of Stanford White (Law Library, "Harry Thaw Trials").

In her testimony, Evelyn Nesbit often cried as she described to the jurors how Stanford White used champagne to seduce her when she was only 16 years old. Nesbit also told a story about how White tried to get her to meet with an attorney who could help keep her away from Thaw. When Harry Thaw discovered how White tried to use an attorney to keep Nesbit away from him, he became extremely agitated. Finally, Nesbit told the jury how White was rumored to have had sexual relationships with many teenage girls at his wild parties ("Beauty as Evidence," *Life*).

During cross-examination, the prosecutors tried to discredit Nesbit's testimony. District Attorney Jerome asked Nesbit if she had ever posed in the nude during her modeling assignments. Nesbit answered by denying that she had ever posed nude for photographers or painters. Next, Jerome asked Nesbit if she thought that it was immoral for a young teenage girl to have a sexual relationship with an older married man. Nesbit stated that while she knew it was wrong, she didn't completely understand how White had taken advantage of her until years later when she told her husband, Harry Thaw, about the relationship. The jury was shocked to hear about how White provided financial support for Nesbit and her mother in exchange for a sexual relationship with the young girl. In the end, Nesbit said that Thaw began to view White as an evil person when he learned White had used his money to manipulate and control her (Linder, "The Trials of Harry Thaw").

A leading conservative activist, Reverend Anthony Comstock, provided a sworn statement for the defense team which detailed how Comstock told Thaw that he must stop White. A letter written from Thaw to Comstock described the New York City studio apartment of White as a place where young women were taken advantage of on a regular basis. Thaw included in the letter a drawing of White's home which contained a red velvet swing and mirrors throughout the bedroom (Linder, "The Trials of Harry Thaw").

Dr. Charles Wagner, a psychiatrist, also testified for the defense when he stated that Thaw's murder of White was an act of rage based upon poor impulse control. Wagner told the jury that Thaw never intended to murder White and only carried the revolver with him because he feared that he might need the weapon to defend himself from White and his bodyguards. Wagner ended his testimony by asserting that Thaw simply wanted White to stand trial for his immoral behavior with young women and never planned upon murdering him. The final witness for the defense team was Harry Thaw's mother, Mrs. William Thaw, who testified that White had caused her son an enormous amount of emotional distress and went as far as to say that White had ruined her son's life (Linder, "The Trials of Harry Thaw").

When the prosecutors sensed that the jurors seemed to be leaning toward an acquittal based upon the temporary insanity defense, District Attorney Jerome decided to pursue a different strategy. The prosecution would try to prove that Thaw was not just temporarily insane at the time of the murder but permanently and criminally insane. An acquittal based upon temporary insanity would provide Thaw with his freedom, but an acquittal based upon permanent and criminal insanity would at least require Thaw to be committed to a mental facility.

In pursuing the new strategy, Jerome produced a sworn statement filed by Evelyn Nesbit against Thaw in which she stated that he had attacked her while the two spent the night together in a German castle while vacationing in Europe. Nesbit also claimed that Thaw was addicted to cocaine. In addition to Nesbit's sworn statement, the prosecution called a number of psychiatrists who testified that Thaw was a dangerous and insane person (Linder, "The Trials of Harry Thaw").

As a result of the prosecution's shift in strategy to try and get Thaw declared criminally insane and committed to an institution, Judge Fitzgerald appointed a committee of neutral psychiatrists to evaluate Thaw. On April 4, 1907, the committee concluded that Thaw was not insane and the trial continued (Linder, "The Trials of Harry Thaw").

On April 8, 1907, Delphin Delmas offered a closing statement for the jury in which he described the horrible acts committed by White against Evelyn Nesbit. Delmas also asserted that Thaw had done God's work in murdering White, and Thaw should be seen as a hero by the jurors. Finally, Delmas noted that Thaw was only insane based upon a phenomenon that he referred to as "dementia Americana." According to Delmas, this type of insanity makes a man hold his home and family sacred. Thaw was only trying to protect his wife against an evil man and any American man would have acted in the same way. In sum, White deserved to die because of a higher law that allows a man to murder another person who is viewed as a threat to his home and family (Uruburu 2008, 303–317).

In his closing statements for the prosecution, William Jerome accused Thaw of committing the murder of White because of his own jealous rage. Jerome ended by stating that Thaw was worse than White in terms of his own evil nature and quoted from the 10 Commandments when he stated that "dementia Americana" is not an excuse for violating the Bible's commandment of "Thou Shalt not Kill" (Linder, "The Trials of Harry Thaw").

The jury began its deliberations on April 10, 1907. After more than two days of debate, the jurors informed Judge Fitzgerald that they were deadlocked with seven votes for conviction and five votes for acquittal. Judge Fitzgerald then chose to declare a mistrial in the first murder trial of Harry Thaw (Law Library, "Harry Thaw Trials").

The Second Trial (1908)

The second murder trial of Harry Thaw began on January 6, 1908, and was presided over by Judge Victor Dowling in New York City. Thaw's new defense team was led by Martin Littleton and included Daniel O'Reilly and Russell Peabody (Law Library, "Harry Thaw Trials"). Based upon the transcripts from the first trial, Thaw's defense attorneys concluded that they would not be able to secure an acquittal based upon the "dementia Americana" theory. Therefore, they decided to try and prove that Thaw was completely insane and simply have him placed in a mental institution rather than risk the real possibility of a guilty verdict for first-degree murder and prison time or perhaps even a death sentence. After the trial, the defense attorneys figured that they would fight in court to have Thaw declared sane and released from the mental institution (Linder, "The Trials of Harry Thaw").

Martin Littleton spent the second trial presenting evidence to the jury to prove that Thaw was insane based upon a history of emotional instability within the Thaw family. Harry Thaw's mother testified about a number of relatives in the family who had been placed in mental institutions. A nurse for the Thaw family as well as grade school teachers also testified about Thaw's odd behavior as a young child where he often would act in a strange and violent manner. Finally, Evelyn Nesbit as well as a number of psychiatrists testified about a suicide attempt by Thaw and the paranoia and depression he experienced throughout his life (Linder, "The Trials of Harry Thaw").

District Attorney William Jerome attempted to prove that Thaw was guilty of first-degree murder by establishing that Thaw was sane because he knew the act of murder was wrong. According to Jerome, Thaw was not insane but merely a person who was spoiled by his family's wealth and someone who exhibited temper tantrums throughout his life (Linder, "The Trials of Harry Thaw").

On February 1, 1908, the jury returned a verdict of not guilty by reason of insanity in the murder of Stanford White. Judge Dowling declared that Thaw was criminally insane and was not to be released because he posed a danger to the public safety. Dowling ordered that Thaw be placed in the Matteawan Mental Hospital in Fishkill, New York (Law Library, "Harry Thaw Trials").

The murder trials of Harry Thaw received worldwide attention because of the prominent status of the victim, the wealth of the murderer's family, the drama surrounding the crime, and the decadent lifestyles of the rich and famous in New York City. In addition, the murder trials saw the insanity defense taken to an extreme level with the "dementia Americana" strategy used by Delmas in the first trial (Law Library, "Harry Thaw Trials").

 Harry K. Thaw

Harry K. Thaw was born in Pittsburgh, Pennsylvania, in 1871. His family was extremely wealthy as his father, William Thaw, made $40 million in the coal and railroad business in Pittsburgh. Thaw was extremely spoiled by his mother and his dysfunctional relationship with her supposedly caused Thaw to behave violently whenever he did not have his way as a child. Thaw's strange behavior continued into his adult life. Thaw was admitted to Harvard University but was expelled because he did not attend classes and spent all of his time playing poker. After Thaw moved to New York City, he depended upon his mother for money as he lived the life of a playboy. During his stay in New York City, Thaw spent most of his time taking drugs such as cocaine and morphine, attending Broadway shows, and pursuing chorus girls. Thaw's mother was forced to pay off large gambling debts that Thaw had accumulated and also bailed him out of trouble several times when he was arrested by police (Law Library, "Harry Thaw Trials").

Thaw met Stanford White, a famous architect, while the two men were both seeking the attention of chorus girls in New York City. After White made some negative comments about Thaw to a group of chorus girls, Thaw became angry because he was convinced that White's remarks caused the girls to lose interest in him. As an act of revenge, Thaw began pursuing Evelyn Nesbit, a beautiful and popular model in New York City, after Thaw heard that White had become interested in her (Linder, "The Trials of Harry Thaw").

White tried to discourage Nesbit from seeing Thaw, but when Nesbit was hospitalized with appendicitis, Thaw was able to visit her frequently at the hospital and brought expensive gifts to Nesbit and her mother. Thaw eventually took Nesbit and her mother on a European vacation where he spent large amounts of money in an attempt to persuade Nesbit to marry him. Nesbit told Thaw that she could not marry him because she was not a virgin, and she then described to Thaw how Stanford White had taken advantage of her when she was a young teenage girl. Thaw was extremely agitated by Nesbit's story about White taking advantage of her but continued to ask Nesbit for her hand in marriage. Thaw decided to take Nesbit to a German castle where he also took advantage of her sexually. Nesbit stayed with Thaw either because she feared for her life or wanted to be the wife of a wealthy man. Eventually, Thaw and Nesbit married on April 4, 1905 (Linder, "The Trials of Harry Thaw").

Thaw never could get over Nesbit's story about White taking advantage of his wife when she was just a young teenager, and he became increasingly obsessed with seeking revenge against White. On June 25, 1906, while attending a musical at the Madison Square Garden theatre with his wife, Thaw shot and murdered White, who was also in attendance at the theatre. The murder resulted in two criminal trials with the second trial ending in a not-guilty verdict by reason of insanity (see entry above). The judge ruled that Thaw should be committed to a mental institution in Fishkill, New York, because he posed a danger to society (Linder, "The Trials of Harry Thaw").

In June 1915, a jury assembled in the Supreme Court of New York to judge whether Thaw could be released from the mental institution. Harry Thaw testified for five hours on his own behalf, and the jury concluded he was sane. Immediately upon his release from the mental institution, Harry Thaw and Evelyn Nesbit were granted a divorce (Linder, "The Trials of Harry Thaw").

In 1917, Thaw was arrested for kidnapping and assaulting a teenage boy named Fred Gump. After the assault trial, Thaw was committed a second time to another mental institution in Pennsylvania. Even after his release from the Pennsylvania facility in 1924, Thaw was often accused of violent behavior throughout the remainder of his life. However, Thaw's family always supported him with legal and financial assistance. In 1947, Thaw died of a heart attack at the age of 76 in Miami, Florida (Law Library, "Harry Thaw Trials").

Thaw left $10,000 to Evelyn Nesbit in his will, which amounted to less than 1 percent of his entire estate (AP, "Harry Thaw Will").

Evelyn Nesbit

Evelyn Nesbit was born in the village of Tarentum, Pennsylvania, in 1884. In 1893, Nesbit's family moved to nearby Pittsburgh, Pennsylvania, when she was a young child. Almost immediately upon the family's arrival in Pittsburgh, Nesbit's father died. After her father's death, Nesbit lived in extreme poverty because her father, who had an unsuccessful law practice, left the family with a large amount of financial debt (Mooney 1976, 25–30).

As Nesbit reached her teenage years, her physical beauty was noticed by local artists who hired her as a model. In 1901, at the age of 16, Nesbit and her mother moved to New York City where she gained employment as a model for various artists who were well known throughout the world. Nesbit modeled for painters, sculptors, and photographers which allowed her to support her entire family with her financial earnings. During the height of her modeling career, Evelyn Nesbit was considered one of the most beautiful women in the world as she appeared in such publications as *Cosmopolitan, Harper's Bazaar,* and *Ladies' Homes Journal* (Uruburu 2008, 53–78).

When Evelyn began work as a chorus girl on Broadway, she was introduced to Stanford White, a famous architect who designed many buildings in New York City. White, who was 47 years old and married at the time, had a reputation as a playboy who seduced young teenage girls. White took Nesbit to his apartment where he pushed her on a red velvet swing that hung in his bedroom. After giving champagne to Nesbit, who was 16 years old, White allegedly had sex with her after she had passed out from the alcohol (Uruburu 2008, 79–130).

After her encounter with White, Nesbit began dating a young man by the name of John Barrymore, an actor from a famous theatrical family. Nesbit's mother disapproved of the relationship because she thought that the young Barrymore was not yet wealthy enough for her daughter. When Nesbit became serious with Barrymore, her mother and Stanford White supposedly arranged for her to be sent to a boarding school where she could be kept away from Barrymore (Mooney 1976, 61–65).

In 1903, Nesbit met Harry K. Thaw who used his wealth to convince Nesbit's mother that he was the proper man for her daughter. Thaw was an unstable millionaire who was violent and obsessive with women. Thaw took Nesbit and her mother on a European vacation where he proposed marriage after taking advantage of Nesbit while they spent the night in a German castle (Linder, "The Trials of Harry Thaw").

After Nesbit confessed to Thaw that she also had been taken advantage of by Stanford White, Thaw became obsessed with protecting her from White. Even after Nesbit and Thaw married on April 4, 1905, Thaw carried a pistol with him at all times to protect his wife from White whom he viewed as evil. While attending a musical with his new wife at the Madison Square Garden theatre in June 1906, Thaw shot White in the head and murdered him in front of hundreds of onlookers. The two murder trials of Harry Thaw were scandalous because they introduced the public to the lifestyles of the rich and famous in New York City as the jury heard that Nesbit was taken advantage of by both White and Thaw (Linder, "The Trials of Harry Thaw").

In 1915, Nesbit divorced Thaw after he was released from a mental institution where he had been committed as punishment for the verdict in the second murder trial. Nesbit resumed her career as an entertainer by appearing in vaudeville acts and silent films but with only limited success. In 1916, she entered into a short marriage with her dancing partner, Jack Clifford. She was known to have attempted suicide a number of times during the remainder of her life (Linder, "The Trials of Harry Thaw").

The sensational interest surrounding Evelyn Nesbit influenced popular culture with the release of a celebrated film entitled, "The Girl in the Red Velvet Swing" in 1955. The part of Evelyn Nesbit was portrayed by a popular actress named Joan Collins. Toward the end of Nesbit's life, she worked as a sculptor in Los Angeles, California. She died in 1967 at the age of 82 of natural causes (Linder, "The Trials of Harry Thaw").

References

Associated Press. "Harry Thaw Leaves $10,000 To Evelyn Nesbit." *Washington Post.* March 30, 1947.

"Beauty as Evidence." *Life.* (June 1981): 10–13.

Langford, Gerald. *The Murder of Stanford White.* London: V. Gollancz, 1963.

Law Library–American Law and Legal Information. "Harry Thaw Trials: 1907–08—Evelyn Nesbit Comes to New York, Thaw Is Tried For Murder, Suggestions for Further Reading" *Great American Trials.* Vol. 1. http://law.jrank.org/pages/2751/Harry-Thaw-Trials-1907–08.html (accessed June 23, 2009).

Linder, Douglas O. "The Trials of Harry Thaw for the Murder of Stanford White." *Famous Trials.* http://www.law.umkc.edu/faculty/projects/ftrials/thaw/Thawaccount.html (accessed June 23, 2009).

Mooney, Michael M. *Evelyn Nesbit and Stanford White: Love and Death in the Gilded Age.* New York: William Morrow and Company, 1976.

Uruburu, Paula. *American Eve: Evelyn Nesbit, Stanford White: The Birth of the "It" Girl and the Crime of the Century.* New York: Riverhead, 2008.

The Trial of Sheriff Joseph Shipp et al. (1907–1909)

The trial of Sheriff Joseph F. Shipp et al. was the first and last criminal trial in the history of the U.S. Supreme Court. The trial involved Shipp and several other defendants who were charged with contempt of court for ignoring an order by the U.S. Supreme Court to delay the execution of a black man convicted of raping a white woman. The trial also involved significant issues of federalism concerning the powers of the federal courts in relation to the states. In the end, the U.S. Supreme Court sent a strong message that its orders could not be ignored and the rule of law must be respected (Law Library, "United States v. Shipp").

The Rape Trial of Ed Johnson

The origins of the trial of Sheriff Joseph F. Shipp can be traced to the rape of Nevada Taylor, a 21-year-old white woman, who resided in Chattanooga, Tennessee. Taylor had been walking home from her job as a bookkeeper on the evening of January 23, 1906, when she was attacked by an assailant. When Taylor arrived at her home and told her father, William Taylor, that she had been assaulted, Sheriff Joseph Shipp was notified of the crime (Linder, "The Trial of Joseph Shipp et al.").

Sheriff Shipp asked Nevada Taylor if she could identify her attacker and she responded that he may have been black, but she was not completely certain. Sheriff Shipp's investigation of the crime scene revealed a black leather belt that seemed to match the size of marks found around the neck of Taylor. Two days after the crime, Will Hixon, who owned a store near the crime scene, reported to police that, on the day of the crime, he had seen a black man swinging a black leather belt around the time of the assault. Shipp located the suspect, Ed Johnson, riding on an ice wagon and placed Johnson under arrest for the sexual assault of Nevada Taylor (Curriden and Phillips 2001, 27–40).

Shipp interrogated Johnson who continued to deny that he had raped Taylor, even though Hixon identified Johnson as the man that he had seen with the black belt. When the public gained knowledge of the arrest, a large crowd of over a thousand people with guns and ropes, led by the younger brother of Nevada Taylor, gathered around the Hamilton County Jail and demanded that Johnson be handed over to be lynched. When the crowd tried to get inside the jail, Governor Cox of Tennessee ordered the National Guard to prevent the lynching of Johnson. While the crowd was unsuccessful at capturing Johnson, the jail ended up being severely damaged by the raid. As a result of the attempt on his life, Johnson was transferred to a jail in Nashville, Tennessee (Linder, "The Trial of Joseph Shipp et al.").

On January 27, 1906, Nevada Taylor traveled to Nashville and identified Johnson as the man who had attacked her (Curriden and Phillips 2001, 54–56). Later in the day, Judge Samuel McReynolds and Matt Whitaker, prosecutor for Hamilton County, presided over a grand jury that quickly indicted Johnson (56–59). On the following day, Judge McReynolds appointed legal representation for Johnson. Three lawyers from Chattanooga would defend Johnson at his trial which was scheduled to begin in roughly one week. One of the lawyers, Lewis Sheppard, was considered to be the best defense attorney in Chattanooga. Within two weeks of the alleged crime, Johnson had been arrested, indicted, and would stand trial for the sexual assault of Nevada Taylor (60–63).

On February 6, 1906, Prosecutor Whitaker called Nevada Taylor as the first witness. Taylor described the sexual assault and told the jury about the black leather belt that had been wrapped around her neck by the assailant. Taylor then proceeded to identify her attacker as Ed Johnson who sat with his lawyers in the courtroom. Next, the physician who examined Taylor after the crime testified for the court. Will Hixon followed the physician and testified about having seen Johnson near the crime scene with the black leather belt. Finally, Sheriff Shipp and two of his deputies concluded the case for the prosecution by testifying about the investigation and eventual arrest of Johnson (Law Library, "United States v. Shipp").

On the second day of the trial, the first witness called by the defense attorneys was Ed Johnson, who took the stand on his own behalf. Under oath, Johnson denied that he committed the crime and testified that he had been working at a saloon on the evening of the attack. In addition to Johnson's testimony, the defense team called several witnesses to support Johnson's alibi (Linder, "The Trial of Joseph Shipp et al.").

On the third and last day of the trial, the jury asked that Nevada Taylor return to the witness stand to confirm that Johnson was the person who assaulted her. Taylor appeared a bit uncertain when she stated that she would not swear Johnson was the person who assaulted her but she believed that he was the assailant. After Taylor's second testimony, a juror attempted to attack Johnson but was restrained by other jurors (Linder, "The Trial of Joseph Shipp et al.").

On February 9, 1906, after slightly more than one day of deliberations, the jury found Johnson guilty of one count of rape. Johnson's defense lawyers convinced him to waive his appeal because, if he delayed his death sentence with an appeal, then a lynch mob would probably raid the jail and execute Johnson immediately. Therefore, Johnson accepted the verdict and Judge McReynolds ordered that Johnson be hanged on March 13, 1906 (Linder, "The Trial of Joseph Shipp et al.").

Johnson's Appeal to the Federal Courts

A few hours after the sentence was issued, Ed Johnson changed his mind and decided that he did not want to be executed. Johnson then asked his father,

"Skinbone" Johnson, to speak with Noah Parden, a respected African American attorney, about getting a new trial through the appellate process. Parden appealed the verdict but, on March 3, 1906, the Tennessee Supreme Court denied a new trial for Johnson based upon their conclusion that no serious errors occurred during the court proceedings. Parden decided to file a writ of habeas corpus petition in federal court. A habeas corpus petition is an attempt by a defendant to force authorities to prove to the federal courts that sufficient evidence exists to justify imprisonment. The term "habeas corpus" is Latin for "produce corpse" in a murder trial which is used as an example to illustrate that prosecutors must provide credible evidence to justify the denial of freedom and imprisonment (Curriden and Phillips 2001, 142–145).

Parden argued before U.S. District Court Judge Charles Clark on March 10, 1906, that Johnson's constitutional rights had been violated throughout the trial such as when black jurors were excluded from serving on the jury or when Johnson's attorneys had abandoned him at the sentencing stage by convincing him not to file an appeal. Judge Clark ruled that Johnson had received a fair trial, but he did postpone the execution of Johnson for 10 days so he could appeal to the U.S. Supreme Court (Curriden and Phillips 2001, 150–168). Surprisingly, the U.S. Supreme Court in an opinion by Justice John Marshall Harlan ruled that Johnson was entitled to an appeal of the guilty verdict and the execution would be delayed until the appeal process was completed. The U.S. Supreme Court sent telegrams of its order to delay the execution to all of the parties involved, including Sheriff Shipp (3–19; 168–170).

The Lynching of Ed Johnson

When the news of the Supreme Court's decision reached the citizens of Chattanooga, a group of 20 men with guns walked to the Hamilton County Jail on March 19, 1906. The men proceeded to break into the jail and search for Johnson. As a crowd of two hundred men and women screamed and yelled in the prison courtyard, Johnson was removed from his cell and taken to a nearby bridge where a noose was placed around his neck. The man holding the rope asked Johnson if he had anything to say before he was executed by the lynch mob. Johnson again denied that he raped Nevada Taylor. Johnson's body was found hanging from the bridge with bullet holes in his body and a note containing a racial slur addressed to Justice Harlan (Linder, "The Trial of Joseph Shipp et al.").

When word of the lynching reached Justice Harlan in Washington, D.C., he met with Chief Justice Melville Fuller and Justice Oliver Wendell Holmes, and the justices decided to take action against the citizens of Chattanooga for blatantly disregarding a Supreme Court order. President Theodore Roosevelt even got involved by demanding that action was required by the federal government.

President Roosevelt met with his attorney general, William Moody, to decide upon an appropriate response to the lynching of Johnson. President Roosevelt ordered two Secret Service agents to Chattanooga to begin an investigation but little evidence was collected because most people in the community refused to talk with federal officials. Finally, Noah Parden and Reverend Howard Jones, a minister of a local Baptist church, were able to locate witnesses who would speak with the federal agents. During the course of the investigation, the two federal agents were threatened and assaulted and Reverend Jones had his house burned down for assisting in the investigation (Curriden and Phillips 2001, 238–249).

On April 20, 1906, the Secret Service agents filed their report concerning the lynching of Johnson. In the report, it was revealed that Sheriff Joseph Shipp deliberately ordered a number of deputies to vacate their duties at the Hamilton County Jail, which left only one prison guard to protect Johnson. Sheriff Shipp had stood near the crowd of people in the courtyard of the prison, but he refused to identify any participant in the lynching. In addition, Judge McReynolds and Prosecutor Whitaker knew the lynch mob was breaking into the jail and did nothing to prevent the capture of Johnson. In fact, McReynolds and Whitaker watched the entire event from their office windows in the courthouse (Linder, "The Trial of Joseph Shipp et al.").

United States v. Shipp et al.

In May 1906, Attorney General Moody met with Chief Justice Fuller and Justice Harlan and they decided to file contempt charges against 26 residents of Chattanooga, including Sheriff Shipp and a number of his deputies, because they had ignored the Supreme Court order to delay the execution. The criminal case would be the first and last criminal trial by the U.S. Supreme Court (Curriden and Phillips 2001, 254–257). The trial would be prosecuted by the Office of the Solicitor General within the Justice Department. The Solicitor General is considered a ranking member of the Justice Department within the executive branch, and always serves as the attorney for the federal government in disputes involving the United States as a party. In the case of *United States v. Shipp et al.,* Solicitor General Henry Hoyt would serve as the prosecutor along with other members of the Justice Department who would represent the federal government (258–263).

After lawyers for Shipp and the other defendants entered a plea of not guilty, the Supreme Court heard pretrial arguments concerning the jurisdiction of the case. Specifically, the issue of whether the Supreme Court had the power to hear such a unique case needed to be resolved. Hoyt argued that Johnson had a right to apply for the habeas corpus petition in federal court which was a constitutional right afforded every prisoner, and the Supreme Court was within its power to order a delay of the execution. Judson Harmon, arguing for Shipp and the other defendants, argued that Johnson's federally protected rights, such as the right to a fair trial, had not been violated because the trial was held in a state court. Harmon's legal argument was based upon the fact that the Bill of Rights had not been nationalized yet by the Supreme Court and, therefore, did not apply to the states. In 1906, Harmon noted that each state decided the constitutional rights of defendants according to its own state constitution and state court decisions. The criminal case of Ed Johnson should not have involved the federal government but, instead, it was a legal matter to be resolved within the state of Tennessee. According to Harmon, the defendants in the current case could not have violated the order because the federal courts did not have the power to issue such an order (Curriden and Phillips 2001, 258–275).

At this point in the defense's argument, Justice Holmes interrupted and asked Harmon whether the Supreme Court had the power to force states to respect the right to a fair trial. In the early part of the 20th century, it was unheard of for the justices to consider applying any part of the Bill of Rights to the states because, during this era of federalism, the federal government deferred such matters to the states. In fact, the majority of the freedoms in the Bill of Rights would not be nationalized until the 1960s. Justice Holmes's comment revealed how angry the justices were at the defendants for defying the Supreme Court order and for taking the law into their own hands. On December 24, 1906, the justices of the Supreme Court issued a unanimous decision that the high court had jurisdiction to try the criminal case against Shipp and the other conspirators (Curriden and Phillips 2001, 275–284).

U.S. Supreme Court Criminal Trial

On February 12, 1907, the trial of Joseph Shipp and 26 other defendants officially began in the United States Custom House in Chattanooga, Tennessee. The greater part of the trial would be held in Chattanooga so local witnesses would not have to travel to Washington, D.C., to testify in the criminal trial. The justices did not travel to Chattanooga to attend the trial but instead appointed James D. Maher, a deputy clerk, to serve as the administrator at the trial. Maher would maintain a complete record of the proceedings which the justices could review (Law Library, "United States v. Shipp").

The prosecution led by Terry Sanford, assistant attorney general of the Justice Department, called its first witness, J. L. Chivington, a reporter for a local newspaper. Chivington testified that he witnessed the lynching of Johnson and also told the jury that the Hamilton County Jail normally had seven deputies guarding the jail but, on the night that Johnson was lynched, only one guard was on duty (Curriden and Phillips 2001, 293–294). Another witness, Edward Chaddick, an employee of the Western Union, took the witness stand and testified that he personally delivered a telegram to Sheriff Shipp containing the order by the Supreme Court to delay the execution of Johnson (294). The most dramatic testimony came from a female prisoner, Ellen Baker, who testified that all of the prisoners were moved from the third floor of the jail, with the exception of Johnson and herself (294–297). Finally, John Stonecipher provided key testimony for the prosecution as he recalled a conversation at a saloon with Frank Ward who asked Stonecipher to join the others in the lynching of Johnson. When Stonecipher told Ward that Sheriff Shipp would not allow the lynching, Ward replied that the sheriff and deputies had agreed to allow the lynching. Afterward, a number of conspirators harassed Stonecipher for not taking part in the lynching and threatened to blow up his house if he testified in a criminal trial (300–306).

After Maher issued a recess in the trial until June 1907, Terry Sanford called a Chattanooga judge, A. J. Ware, to the witness stand, and Ware identified one of the defendants, Nick Nolan, as the person who secured the noose around Johnson's neck. Ware also identified Luther Williams as the person who shot Johnson five times after Johnson did not die immediately from the hanging (Curriden and Phillips 2001, 306–308).

On June 15, 1907, the defense attorneys presented their case by having witnesses offer alibis for some of the defendants as well as attest to the good character of those accused in the lynching. Luther Williams testified on his own behalf, denied shooting Johnson five times, and stated that he only observed the lynching from a distance. The defense attorneys also tried to discredit a number of the witnesses who testified for the prosecution (Linder, "The Trial of Joseph Shipp").

Sheriff Joseph Shipp provided the final testimony for the defense. Shipp denied conspiring to allow the lynching of Johnson and testified that he ran to the jail when he heard about the attempt to lynch Johnson but a number of men with guns prevented him from stopping the lynching. On cross-examination, Shipp was unable, or unwilling, to identify any of the persons who detained him or any of the persons involved in the lynching. Shipp also claimed that he only had one gun in his possession and would have been unable to stop the large mob that possessed several weapons. The defense attorneys rested their case on June 29, 1907, and the trial entered into a long recess (Linder, "The Trial of Joseph Shipp").

The final part of the trial was moved to the U.S. Supreme Court in Washington, D.C., in order for the justices to hear closing arguments and issue a ruling in the case. Prior to the closing statements, the Supreme Court decided in November 1908 to drop charges against 17 of the defendants charged with contempt because of a lack of evidence. However, the justices would decide the fate of the nine defendants that remained, including Sheriff Shipp, after the closing arguments (Law Library, "United States v. Shipp").

In March 1909, Attorney General Charles Bonaparte offered closing statements for the prosecution which signified the importance of the trial. Bonaparte had replaced William Moody as attorney general as of December 17, 1906. In his six-hour summary of the evidence, Bonaparte argued for the guilt of the defendants who took the law into their own hands and, in doing so, ignored an order from the most powerful court in the country. For the defense, Judson Harmon maintained that, while Sheriff Shipp was negligent in providing security at the jail for Johnson, he simply displayed poor judgment in failing to plan ahead for an attack on the jail by the lynch mob. Therefore, Shipp could not be found guilty of ignoring the order of the Supreme Court (Curriden and Phillips 2001, 318–324).

On May 24, 1909, by a vote of 6–3, the Supreme Court found Shipp guilty of contempt of court for disobeying an order of the Supreme Court and, in the process, assisting the lynch mob by failing to provide adequate security at the jail. The Supreme Court also found Jeremiah Gibson, Nick Nolan, Luther Williams, Henry Padgett, and William Mayes guilty of criminal contempt. Deputy Sheriff Matthew Galloway, Alf Handman, and Bart Justice were acquitted by the justices. The three justices who cast the dissenting votes in the trial argued that all of the defendants should have been acquitted (Curriden and Phillips 2001, 327–334).

On November 15, 1909, Shipp and the other defendants appeared before the nine justices of the Supreme Court to receive their punishment. Chief Justice Fuller sentenced Shipp, Williams, and Nolan to 90 days in a federal jail, while Padgett, Mayes, and Gibson received a lesser sentence of 60 days (Curriden and Phillips 2001, 334–338).

The trial of Sheriff Joseph Shipp and his conspirators was the first successful attempt by the federal courts to address the "lynching laws" in the southern states which permitted lynch mobs to carry out the executions of black men accused of raping white women. The trial and conviction of Shipp and the five other defendants had a great impact on the southern states. Beginning in 1909, the United States experienced a steady decline in the number of lynchings in the South. The U.S. Supreme Court had confronted mob rule by reinforcing the rule of law, which has always been the goal of the American criminal justice system (Lief and Caldwell 2007, 64–65).

 ## Sheriff Joseph F. Shipp

Joseph F. Shipp was born on February 3, 1845, in Jasper County, Georgia. As a teenager, he left school to join the Confederate Army, serving as a private in Virginia during the Civil War. At the battle of Malvern Hill, he was wounded and subsequently promoted to captain for demonstrating bravery in action. After the war, Shipp moved back to Georgia where he worked in his family's cotton gin business. In 1874, Shipp moved to Chattanooga, Tennessee, and worked as a furniture manufacturer. His business was quite profitable and, by 1896, he owned several homes and properties. In 1900, he was elected as the tax collector in Hamilton County, Tennessee, and, in 1904, was elected to a two-year term as sheriff of Hamilton County. In 1906, he was reelected to another two-year term (Armstrong 1992, 462).

In 1907, Sheriff Shipp was charged with contempt of court by the U.S. Supreme Court. Shipp had ignored a stay of execution order and allowed the execution of an African American man accused of raping a white woman. In 1908, Shipp lost his reelection bid for sheriff in part due to a large turnout by African American voters. In 1909, the U.S. Supreme Court found Shipp guilty of contempt in the only criminal trial conducted by the Supreme Court. Shipp was sentenced to 90 days in the federal jail in Washington, D.C. After his release from jail, Shipp returned to Chattanooga and received a hero's welcome from a crowd of 10,000 people. He lived the remainder of his life in Chattanooga where he worked to promote the history of the Confederacy. Shipp passed away on September 18, 1925, in Chattanooga at the age of 80 (Linder, "Sheriff Joseph F. Shipp").

References

Armstrong, Zella. *The History of Hamilton County and Chattanooga, Tennessee.* Vol. 1. Johnson City, TN: The Overmountain Press, 1992.

Curriden, Mark, and Leroy Phillips Jr., *Contempt of Court: The Turn-of-the-Century Lynching that Launched a Hundred Years of Federalism.* New York: Anchor, 2001.

Law Library–American Law and Legal Information. "et al. United States v. Shipp: 1907–09—An Arrest Is Made, A Near Lynching and a Trial, A Guilty Verdict and Lynching, A Long Road to Justice." *Great American Trials.* Vol. 1. http://law.jrank.org/pages/2756/United-States-v-Shipp-et-al-1907–09.html (accessed July 15, 2009).

Lief, Michael S., and H. Mitchell Caldwell. *The Devil's Advocate: Greatest Closing Arguments in Criminal Law.* New York: Scribner, 2007.

Linder, Douglas O. "Sheriff Joseph F. Shipp." *Famous Trials.* http://www.law.umkc.edu/faculty/projects/ftrials/shipp/shippbiog.html (accessed August 25, 2009).

Linder, Douglas O. "The Trial of Joseph Shipp et al.: An Account." *Famous Trials.* http://www.law.umkc.edu/faculty/projects/ftrials/shipp/trialaccount.html (accessed July 15, 2009).

The Triangle Shirtwaist Fire Trial (1911)

The Triangle Shirtwaist Fire trial involved immigrant workers who were treated horribly within their work environment and unjustly within the criminal justice system. The deaths of 146 persons working for the Triangle Shirtwaist factory were caused by the negligence of powerful businessmen who owned the factory and refused to provide a safe working environment for their employees. During the trial, a highly skilled defense attorney for the defendants was able to discredit honest testimony from key prosecution witnesses and also used false testimony from defense witnesses who were either bribed or intimidated by the factory owners. The jury was unable to convict because they were confused by the witnesses from both sides concerning who was telling the truth and who was lying. The acquittal of the wealthy defendants created such a public outcry that significant changes were eventually brought about in terms of safety standards and an overall improvement of working conditions for labor employees (Morris 1967, 358–383).

On Saturday, March 25, 1911, a fire started on the 8th floor of the Asch building in New York City where employees of the Triangle Shirtwaist Factory were ending their work day. Most of the immigrant employees working at the factory were teenage girls and children who spoke hardly any English. The fire quickly spread to the 9th and 10th floors. While most of the 600 employees were able to escape down either the building's only fire escape or elevator, 145 people, mostly young girls, on the 9th floor and one person on the 10th floor died in the fire. The 146 victims either died from being burned alive or from falling to the street below when they were forced to jump out of a nearby window to avoid the flames (Linder, "Triangle Shirtwaist Factory Trial"). According to the fire marshal, the fire most likely began when a lit match was thrown in a waste basket near flammable material such as oil cans or cloth. Although smoking was prohibited in the factory, cigarette cases were found by investigators throughout the work environment. Employees later stated that cigarette smoking was widespread throughout the factory because employers were concerned that an enforcement of the smoking ban would harm the morale of the workers and decrease productivity (Morris 1967, 361).

Most people began to blame the New York City's Building Department for improper inspection of the factory. Serious questions were raised about whether the factory met the city's safety standards. For example, the Asch building with its 10 stories had only one fire escape and it did not meet safety rules. The elevator doors and lighting also were cited as violations of state law. In addition, flammable materials such as paper, cloth, and cardboard boxes were littered around the factory while large numbers of people were crammed together on to the floor of the workplace (Morris, 1967, 360–361).

The public anger also was directed toward the owners of the Triangle Shirtwaist Company, Issac Harris and Max Blanck, who were accused of operating a profitable garment business where young immigrants worked on sewing machines for long hours and received very little money. Many leaders within the labor movement argued that Harris and Blanck symbolized the capitalist greed in Industrial America in the early 20th century where employers would hire women and children because they did not have to pay them as much as adult male workers. The owners also would tax workers for the use of chairs and lockers at the factory and would also charge the workers for using electricity and work supplies such as needles. Most disturbingly, Harris and Blanck allegedly refused to cut into their profits to provide the necessary safety precautions such as a sprinkler system, proper ventilation, or emergency exits that would have prevented deaths in the case of a fire. Instead, the young immigrants faced inhumane and unsafe working conditions. On April 11,

1911, Harris and Blanck were indicted by a grand jury on manslaughter charges in the deaths of their 146 employees (Morris 1967, 362–364).

Judge Thomas Crain presided over the trial that began on December 4, 1911. Charles Bostick and J. Robert Rubin, assistant district attorneys of New York City, led the prosecution team, while Harris and Blanck were represented by Max D. Steuer, a famous and skilled New York defense attorney. The courtroom was packed with emotional onlookers who had lost loved ones in the fire. Harris and Blanck would often make their way to the courtroom amidst chants of "Murderer! We want justice!" (Morris 1967, 364–365).

Bostick opened for the prosecution and stated how he would prove that Harris and Blanck were guilty of manslaughter by simply establishing that one of victims, Margaret Schwartz, died in the fire as a result of the negligence of the factory owners. Prosecution witnesses were called to testify that the owners kept the ninth floor door locked to prevent employees from leaving their work stations or stealing materials from the workplace. Employees also locked the doors to keep labor representatives from entering to speak with the workers about joining a union. If the door had been unlocked, the 145 victims who perished in the fire on the ninth floor may have been able to escape down the stairway (Morris 1967, 363–365).

Two witnesses, Kate Gartman and Kate Alterman, provided compelling testimony regarding how the locked door on the ninth floor directly caused the death of Margaret Schwartz, whom they saw burned to death in the fire. During cross-examination, Steuer tried to convince the jury that Alterman had been coached in her testimony by asking her to repeat her testimony several times. Unfortunately, while Alterman was honest in her testimony, Steuer had demonstrated that she was overcoached by the prosecution which allowed Steuer to discredit Alterman successfully in front of the jury (Linder, "Triangle Shirtwaist Factory Trial").

In defense of Harris and Blanck, Steuer called several witnesses such as customers, salesmen, and employees who testified that they often entered and exited through the ninth-floor door that was supposed to have been locked at the time of the fire. Apparently, a key was usually inside the lock or attached to the door at all times. A critical witness for the defense named Mary Levantini maintained that she had used the key to open the ninth-floor door only to find that the fire prevented her from exiting down the stairwell. Bostick accused Levantini of lying during his cross-examination for the prosecution. Bostick reminded the jury that countless witnesses had testified previously to using the stairwell below the ninth floor, and none of the witnesses recalled any fire that could have prevented anyone from exiting the building (Linder, "Triangle Shirtwaist Factory Trial").

The prosecution introduced evidence that most of the testimony from the defense witnesses was untruthful. In fact, several employees who initially made preliminary statements to authorities that the door was always locked suddenly changed their stories on the witness stand. The prosecution argued that their stories had changed because they had been contacted by Harris and Blanck and given an increase in pay in exchange for lying or were threatened by the supervisor of the factory to lie during the trial (Morris 1967, 378).

On December 27, 1911, Judge Crain read instructions to the jury, which included the state of New York's labor law requiring all doors within a factory to be built so as to open easily and prohibiting the locking of doors during hours when employees were at work. Crain told the jury that Harris and Blanck were to be found guilty of manslaughter if it was proven that the door on the ninth floor was locked during the fire and if Harris and Blanck possessed knowledge that the door was locked (Linder, "Triangle Shirtwaist Factory Trial").

In slightly over an hour, the jury returned a verdict of not guilty against the two defendants. Jurors stated publicly that they felt that the ninth-floor door was locked at the time of the fire but concluded that prosecutors failed to prove that Harris and Blanck had knowledge that the door was locked. In 1912, Bostick attempted to prosecute Harris and Blanck for a second time using different victims, but a judge dismissed the case because it violated double jeopardy to prosecute someone twice for the same offense (Law Library, "Triangle Shirtwaist Factory Trial"). In 1914, a series of civil lawsuits were settled between family members of the victims and Harris and Blanck with the average settlement equal to $75 for each person who died in the fire (Linder, "Triangle Shirtwaist Factory Trial").

The public demand for governmental action resulted in the Factory Investigating Commission, which examined working conditions in factories throughout New York City. The commission's recommendations led to a complete overhaul of safety conditions for workers as a number of state labor regulations were passed into law (Linder, "Triangle Shirtwaist Factory Trial"). The Bureau of Fire Prevention was created in New York City to implement and enforce the safety regulations. Ultimately, Franklin D. Roosevelt's administration pushed for safety measures across the United States for all workers. FDR's agencies served as a foundation for Congress creating the Occupational Safety and Health Administration (OSHA) in 1970. Today, workers are protected from the greed and negligence that caused the Triangle Shirtwaist fire (Law Library, "Triangle Shirtwaist Fire Trial").

References

Greene, Jacqueline Dembar, and Dave Von Drehle. *Triangle Shirtwaist Factory Fire*. New York: Bearport Publishing, 2007.

Law Library–American Law and Legal Information. "Triangle Shirtwaist Fire Trial: 1911—Harris and Blanck Go Free." *Great American Trials*. Vol. 1. http://law.jrank.org/pages/2772/Triangle-Shirtwaist-Fire-Trial-1911-Blanck-Harris-go-Free.html (accessed April 6, 2009).

Linder, Douglas O. "The Triangle Shirtwaist Factory Trial." *Famous Trials*. http://www. law.umkc.edu/faculty/projects/ftrials/triangle/triangleaccount.html (accessed April 5, 2009).

Morris, Richard B. *Fair Trial: Fourteen Who Stood Accused, from Anne Hutchinson to Alger Hiss.* New York: Harper and Row, 1967.

Leo Frank Trial (1913)

The trial and conviction of Leo Frank in Atlanta for the rape and murder of a young girl was based largely upon southern prejudice against Jews. The Frank trial revealed the unequal treatment of minorities (blacks and Jews) within the American criminal justice system, particularly in the South. In addition to the anti-Semitism faced by Frank, the jury viewed him as a northern capitalist who used his education and wealth to exploit southerners. After the jury conviction, Frank was sentenced to death but his sentence was reduced by the governor to life in prison to remedy an obvious injustice. As a result of the governor's decision, Frank was kidnapped from prison and lynched by an angry mob convinced of his guilt. Because of the racism and hatred that had developed during the Leo Frank trial, many southerners expressed a renewed interest in the Ku Klux Klan, which saw its membership increase dramatically in the aftermath of this national scandal (Law Library, "Leo Frank Trial").

At 3:00 a.m. on April 27, 1913, the body of a 13-year-old girl, Mary Phagan, was discovered in the basement of the National Pencil Factory in Atlanta, Georgia. Mary Phagan had gone to the factory on the previous day to receive her paycheck from Leo Frank, a superintendent. Apparently, she had been sexually assaulted and then murdered. The young girl's skull was covered in blood and a rope had been placed around her neck (Dinnerstein 2008, 2–3).

The city of Atlanta was in turmoil during this time period. Atlanta was one of the worst cities in the United States for crime, violence, and racial tension. To make matters worse, Atlanta had one of the worst records for child labor where young children worked in factories for only a few pennies a day. Within this difficult climate, Atlanta's citizens became outraged when they heard about the murder of Mary Phagan. After thousands of people attended her funeral, local politicians and police were pressured to find the murderer quickly (Dinnerstein 2008, 7–16).

Police investigators collected two notes written on yellow paper at the crime scene. The two notes seemed to identify the murderer as an African American man. In terms of physical evidence, police found human feces at the bottom of an elevator shaft in the basement as well as bloody fingerprints on a basement door and also on the coat of Mary Phagan. Unfortunately, police lost a piece of board taken from the basement door which contained the fingerprints and never tested the fingerprints on the young girl's coat (Dinnerstein 2008, 3–4).

Although the evidence seemed to point elsewhere, investigators focused upon the second floor of the factory where red stains and hair were found near a wood-cutting machine outside the office of Leo Frank (Lawson and Howard 1918, 183–184). On April 29, 1913, police arrested Leo Frank for suspicion of murder based largely upon circumstantial evidence. Frank was the last person to see Mary Phagan alive, acted nervously when questioned by police, and suspiciously telephoned the night watchman from his home to check on the factory during the evening after the murder had occurred (Dinnerstein 2008, 4).

Factory workers also told police that Leo Frank had flirted with young girls at the factory, including Mary Phagan, and a landlady swore to prosecutors that Frank had called her several times to reserve a room for himself and a young girl on the day of the murder. As a result of the police investigation, District Attorney Hugh Dorsey decided to seek an indictment against Frank on murder charges. On May 24, 1913, a grand jury indicted Frank for the rape and murder of Mary Phagan (Linder, "The Trial of Leo Frank").

As Frank was being indicted, Jim Conley, a 27-year-old African American janitor at the factory, came forward and admitted writing the two notes left at the crime scene. Initially, Conley told authorities that he wrote the notes at the request of Frank prior to the murder. Conley later produced a different version of the story wherein Frank asked Conley to watch the door while he engaged in a sexual act with Mary Phagan. Conley told police that Phagan was accidentally killed by Frank when she fell against a machine. Conley and Frank carried the body of the young girl to the basement and then Frank asked Conley to write the two notes. Interestingly, Conley also admitted depositing the human feces prior to the death of Mary Phagan (Lawson and Howard 1918, 184–185).

Prosecutors considered charging Conley with murder as well, but District Attorney Dorsey thought that it might weaken the case against Frank to have two murder suspects blaming each other for the crime. Dorsey also calculated that Frank was a better target for prosecution because he was Jewish and wealthy, and a conviction in such a high-profile case would launch Dorsey's political career. In fact, Dorsey would later serve two terms as governor of Georgia from 1917 to 1921 (Law Library, "Leo Frank Trial").

Citizens in the state of Georgia expressed hatred for Frank, who was a wealthy Jew from the North, while Mary Phagan was a local southerner. The fact that Frank was the supervisor at the factory, apparently preying upon young girls, produced even more hostility from southerners who viewed Frank as a symbol of how northern capitalists had traditionally exploited their southern women (Melnick 2000, 45–51).

The trial began on July 28, 1913, and was presided over by Judge Leonard Roan in Atlanta. During the first day of the trial, the night watchman from the factory testified about Frank calling him on the evening of April 26 to ask him if everything at the factory was alright. Lee said that Frank had never called him before to ask about the factory and also seemed nervous during the conversation. Prosecutors then presented testimony from investigators who told how Frank seemed nervous during questioning by police (Law Library, "Leo Frank Trial").

District Attorney Dorsey questioned police detectives who testified about the blood spots found at the murder scene near Frank's office, how Frank may have been able to obtain a rope similar to the rope found around Mary Phagan's neck, and, finally, how Frank may have blocked off access to the second floor where the murder was alleged to have been committed (Linder, "The Trial of Leo Frank").

Luther Rosser, the defense attorney for Frank, countered Dorsey by effectively cross-examining the police detectives. Rosser was able to get detectives to doubt whether the red spots near the work area of the second floor were, in fact, blood stains. Rosser also was able to obtain statements from police that the basement area had been blocked off by someone suggesting that the crime was committed there rather than on the second floor. Finally, Rosser was able to establish on cross-examination that the type of rope around the young girl's neck could have been found at a number of places at the factory (Linder, "The Trial of Leo Frank").

On August 4, 1913, the star witness for the prosecution, Jim Conley, took the stand before a packed courtroom. Conley told his story about how Frank asked him to serve as a "lookout" for him as he met with Mary Phagan. Frank allegedly told Conley that he struck the girl after she refused his advances and she accidentally hit her head and was killed. Conley then testified that Frank offered him $200 to help move the body of the young girl to the basement. Afterward, Frank supposedly told Conley to write the two notes and leave them in the basement. Frank also asked Conley to return to the factory later to burn the body. Conley said he didn't return to the factory that evening because he got drunk and fell asleep. Conley ended his testimony by informing the jury that prior to Frank's encounter with Mary Phagan, he had seen Frank engaged in sexual activity with other young women at the factory (Melnick 2000, 70–86).

On cross-examination, Rosser was able to get Conley to admit that he had not always told police investigators the truth based upon his different versions of what happened on the day of the murder. However, for the most part, Rosser was unsuccessful in his attempt to discredit Conley who had rehearsed his testimony with prosecutors prior to the trial (Linder, "The Trial of Leo Frank").

In presenting their case for acquittal, Frank's defense team sought to create reasonable doubt concerning the timeline established by Conley's testimony. Conley had indicated in his testimony that Frank committed the murder at a specific time during the day. However, defense attorneys used several witnesses to prove that Frank was most likely at home when the murder of Mary Phagan occurred at the factory (Linder, "The Trial of Leo Frank").

The defense team also sought to use various witnesses to prove that Frank was a person of good character, while Conley was a person of questionable character. On August 18, 1913, Frank testified for four hours about his life story and his responsibilities as a supervisor at the factory. On the day of the murder, Frank said that he was busy checking payroll accounts and barely had time to notice Mary Phagan when she stopped by his office to collect her paycheck. Frank said that he did not see her again until the body was discovered in the basement. Frank ended his testimony by stating that he was very upset because of the young girl's death and called Conley's story a complete lie (Lawson and Howard 1918, 186).

The prosecution countered Frank's testimony by calling young women from the factory to testify that Frank had behaved improperly with young girls. During closing statements before the jury, Prosecutor Frank Hooper compared Frank's personality to that of "Dr. Jekyll and Mr. Hyde." At one moment, Frank appeared to be a respectable person, but he could quickly transform himself into an immoral person who preyed on young women. Hooper also drew on racial stereotypes to try and convince the jury that Conley, an African American man with little education, could not have written the two notes by himself (Linder, "The Trial of Leo Frank").

In closing statements for the defense, Reuben Arnold accused prosecutors of anti-Semitism. Arnold asserted that Frank became the focus of the investigation when it was discovered that he was a Jew and a person of wealth. Arnold claimed that the young girls who testified against Frank were simply disgruntled workers who no longer were employed at the factory. Finally, Arnold said that Conley was the real murderer who had created an exaggerated story about Frank to save himself. Luther Rosser ended the closing statements for the defense by making racist remarks about Conley whom he believed to be the person who murdered Mary Phagan (Linder, "The Trial of Leo Frank").

In his closing statements for the prosecution, Hugh Dorsey accused the defense team of resorting to racial prejudice against Conley to gain an acquittal. Dorsey dramatically argued before the jury that Frank had made sexual advances toward Mary Phagan and, when she refused, Frank sexually assaulted her. Dorsey theorized that Frank murdered the young girl to silence her in order to save his reputation and avoid prosecution (Linder, "The Trial of Leo Frank").

After a short deliberation, the jury found Frank guilty of murder. Judge Roan had not allowed Frank to be present during the reading of the verdict because he feared a riot in the courtroom if the jury had decided to acquit Frank. The citizens of Atlanta who believed that justice had been served by the guilty verdict began celebrating in the streets. At the sentencing phase of the trial on October 10, 1913, Judge Roan ordered that Frank be executed by hanging (Lawson and Howard 1918, 188).

Frank's attorneys filed a motion for a new trial. Among the many reasons for a new trial was the fact that Judge Roan should not have allowed Conley's testimony about Frank's sexual behavior toward women at the factory. In addition, two of the jurors made anti-Semitic remarks about Frank during the trial. Finally, defense attorneys maintained that Conley's story was illogical because, according to Conley, Frank instructed him to write the two notes, while simultaneously telling him to burn the body. Judge Roan denied the motion for a new trial but, in his ruling, stated that he was not convinced about Frank's guilt. Nevertheless, Judge Roan concluded that he must respect the decision of the jury (Linder, "The Trial of Leo Frank").

On February 17, 1913, the Georgia Supreme Court voted 4–2 to deny Frank's appeal for a new trial. The two dissenting judges argued that Frank was denied a fair trial because Judge Roan had allowed Conley's explicit statements about Frank's sexual activities into the court record which influenced the jury in favor of a conviction (Linder, "The Trial of Leo Frank").

After the Georgia Supreme Court decision, the possibility of Frank's innocence was bolstered by the fact that an examination of the hair found near Frank's office did not match the hair of Mary Phagan. The hair had been a key piece of physical evidence used to justify the prosecution's case for conviction. Furthermore, a number of witnesses for the prosecution recanted their testimony given at the trial. The landlady who recalled Frank trying to reserve a room on the day of the murder said that she had been coerced into lying by police. Similarly, another witness also recanted his testimony when he said that investigators encouraged him to testify that Frank had made advances toward Mary Phagan in the past. Finally, evidence started to point toward Conley as the real murderer. For instance, a young woman who worked at the factory came forward and told a story of how Conley had attempted to sexually assault her. In addition, two persons had come forward to say that Conley had confessed to them that he committed the murder (Dinnerstein 2008, 102–104). As the public and newspaper media debated the guilt or innocence of Frank, Conley was finally tried and convicted for aiding and assisting in the murder of Mary Phagan and was sentenced to one year in prison (Linder, "The Trial of Leo Frank").

After a second denial by the Georgia Supreme Court for a new trial, Frank's lawyers filed a petition in federal court arguing that Frank's due process rights were violated because the courtroom environment was prejudicial and Judge Roan did not allow Frank to be present when the jury's verdict was read. Unfortunately, the federal district court and the U.S. Supreme Court both ruled that Frank's case could not be reviewed in federal court because the errors committed at his trial did not qualify under the writ of habeas corpus petition, which was designed only to release someone from prison who was being held illegally (Melnick 2000, 129–130).

Governor John M. Slaton of Georgia was the last chance for Frank as his lawyers sought a pardon from the governor. When Conley's lawyer came forward and admitted that his client had murdered Mary Phagan, thousands of letters were delivered to the governor's office requesting clemency for Frank. Conley's lawyer knew that his client had been convicted once for aiding in the murder and could not be tried a second time so he wanted to save Frank from being wrongfully executed. On June 21, 1915, Governor Slaton reduced Leo Frank's sentence to life in prison. Slaton felt that he could not issue a full pardon to Frank because the public reaction would be too violent. In fact, after Frank's sentence was simply commuted to life in prison, the state militia had to be called upon to resist a mob of angry people throwing stones and bottles at the governor's house (Dinnerstein 2008, 114–135).

While Frank was serving his life sentence at a prison farm in Milledgeville, Georgia, a gang of 25 men raided the prison on August 16, 1915, overpowering the prison warden and guards. Frank was kidnapped by the men and driven to Marietta, Georgia, where was he was hanged from an oak tree (Dinnerstein 2008, 136–148). Leo Frank remains the only known Jewish person to have been lynched in the history of the United States. On March 11, 1986, the Georgia State Board of Pardons and Paroles granted a pardon to Leo Frank to establish his innocence posthumously (Law Library, "Leo Frank Trial").

References

Dinnerstein, Leonard. *The Leo Frank Case.* Athens: University of Georgia Press, 2008.

Law Library–American Law and Legal Information. "Leo Frank Trial: 1913—Little Mary Phagan Murdered, Prosecutors Emphasize Frank's Nervousness, Prosecution Clinches Their Case, Frank Convicted, Commuted, and Lynched." *Great American Trials.* Vol. 1. http://law.jrank.org/pages/2793/Leo-Frank-Trial-1913.html (accessed May 27, 2009).

Lawson, John Davison, and Robert Lorenzo Howard. *American State Trials.* St. Louis, MO: Thomas Law Books, 1918.

Linder, Douglas O. "The Trial of Leo Frank: An Account." *Famous Trials.* http://www.law.umkc.edu/faculty/projects/ftrials/frank/frankaccount.html (accessed May 27, 2009).

Melnick, Jeffrey. *Black-Jewish Relations on Trial: Leo Frank and Jim Conley in the New South.* Oxford: University of Mississippi Press, 2000.

Frank v. Mangum (1915)

MR. JUSTICE PITNEY, after making the foregoing statement, delivered the opinion of the Court.

The points raised by the appellant may be reduced to the following:

(1) It is contended that the disorder in and about the court room during the trial and up to and at the reception of the verdict amounted to mob domination, that not only the jury, but the presiding judge, succumbed to it, and that this in effect wrought a dissolution of the court, so that the proceedings were coram non judice.

(2) That Frank's right to be present during the entire trial until and at the return of the verdict was an essential part of the right of trial by jury, which could not be waived either by himself or his counsel.

(3) That his presence was so essential to a proper hearing that the reception of the verdict in his absence, and in the absence of his counsel, without his consent or authority, was a departure from the due process of law guaranteed by the 14th Amendment, sufficient to bring about a loss of jurisdiction of the trial court, and to render the verdict and judgment absolute nullities.

(4) That the failure of Frank and his counsel, upon the first motion for a new trial, to allege as a ground of that motion the known fact of Frank's absence at the reception of the verdict, or to raise any jurisdictional question based upon it, did not deprive him of the right to afterwards attack the judgment as a nullity, as he did in the motion to set aside the verdict.

(5) And that the ground upon which the supreme court of Georgia rested its decision affirming the denial of the latter motion . . . ,—viz., that the objection based upon Frank's absence when the verdict was rendered was available on the motion for new trial, and under proper practice ought to have been then taken, and because not then taken could not be relied upon as a ground for setting aside the verdict as a nullity, was itself in conflict with the Constitution of the United States because equivalent in effect to an ex post facto law, since, as is said, it departs from the practice settled by previous decisions of the same court.

In dealing with these contentions, we should have in mind the nature and extent of the duty that is imposed upon a Federal court on application for the writ of habeas corpus. . . . Under the terms of that section, in order to entitle the present appellant to the relief sought, it must appear that he is held in custody in violation of the Constitution of the United States. *Rogers v. Peck.* . . . Moreover, if he is held in custody by reason of his conviction upon a criminal charge before a court having plenary jurisdiction over the subject-matter or offense, the place where it was committed, and the person of the prisoner, it results from the nature of the writ itself that he cannot have relief on habeas corpus. Mere errors in point of law, however serious, committed by a criminal court in the exercise of its jurisdiction over a case properly subject to its cognizance, cannot be reviewed by habeas corpus. That writ cannot be employed as a substitute for the writ of error. *Ex parte Parks* . . . ; *Ex parte Siebold* . . . ; *Ex parte Royall* . . . ; *Re Frederich* . . . ; *Baker v. Grice* . . . ; *Tinsley v. Anderson* . . . ; *Markuson v. Boucher*. . . .

As to the "due process of law" that is required by the 14th Amendment, it is perfectly well settled that a criminal prosecution in the courts of a state, based upon a law not in itself repugnant to the Federal Constitution, and conducted according to the settled course of judicial proceedings as established by the law of the state, so long as it includes notice and a hearing, or an opportunity to be heard, before a court of competent jurisdiction, according to established modes of procedure, is "due process" in the constitutional sense. *Walker v. Sauvinet* . . . ; *Hurtado v.*

California . . .; *Andrews v. Swartz* . . .; *Bergemann v. Backer* . . .; *Rogers v. Peck* . . .; *United States ex rel. Drury v. Lewis* . . .; *Felts v. Murphy* . . .; *Howard v. Kentucky*. . . .

It is therefore conceded by counsel for appellant that, in the present case, we may not review irregularities or erroneous rulings upon the trial, however serious, and that the writ of habeas corpus will lie only in case the judgment under which the prisoner is detained is shown to be absolutely void for want of jurisdiction in the court that pronounced it, either because such jurisdiction was absent at the beginning, or because it was lost in the course of the proceedings. And since no question is made respecting the original jurisdiction of the trial court, the contention is and must be that by the conditions that surrounded the trial, and the absence of defendant when the verdict was rendered, the court was deprived of jurisdiction to receive the verdict and pronounce the sentence.

But it would be clearly erroneous to confine the inquiry to the proceedings and judgment of the trial court. The laws of the state of Georgia (as will appear from decisions elsewhere cited) provide for an appeal in criminal cases to the supreme court of that state upon divers grounds, including such as those upon which it is here asserted that the trial court was lacking in jurisdiction. And while the 14th Amendment does not require that a state shall provide for an appellate review in criminal cases (*McKane v. Durston* . . .; *Andrews v. Swartz* . . .; *Rogers v. Peck* . . .; *Reetz v. Michigan* . . .), it is perfectly obvious that where such an appeal is provided for, and the prisoner has had the benefit of it, the proceedings in the appellate tribunal are to be regarded as a part of the process of law under which he is held in custody by the state, and to be considered in determining any question of alleged deprivation of his life or liberty contrary to the 14th Amendment.

In fact, such questions as are here presented under the due process clause of the 14th Amendment, though sometimes discussed as if involving merely the jurisdiction of some court or other tribunal, in a larger and more accurate sense involve the power and authority of the state itself. The prohibition is addressed to the state; if it be violated, it makes no difference in a court of the United States by what agency of the state this is done; so, if a violation be threatened by one agency of the state, but prevented by another agency of higher authority, there is no violation by the state. It is for the state to determine what courts or other tribunals shall be established for the trial of offenses against its criminal laws, and to define their several jurisdictions and authority as between themselves. And the question whether a state is depriving a prisoner of his liberty without due process of law, where the offense for which he is prosecuted is based upon a law that does no violence to the Federal Constitution, cannot ordinarily be determined, with fairness to the state, until the conclusion of the course of justice in its courts. *Virginia v. Rives* . . .; *Civil Rights Cases* . . .; *McKane v. Durston* . . .; *Dreyer v. Illinois* . . .; *Reetz v. Michigan* . . .; *Carfer v. Caldwell* . . .; *Waters-Pierce Oil Co. v. Texas* . . .; *Re Frederich* . . .; *Whitten v. Tomlinson* . . .; *Baker v. Grice* . . .; *Minnesota v. Brundage* . . .; *Urquhart v. Brown*. . . .

It is indeed, settled by repeated decisions of this court that where it is made to appear to a court of the United States that an applicant for habeas corpus is in the custody of a state officer in the ordinary course of a criminal prosecution, under a law of the state not in itself repugnant to the Federal Constitution, the writ, in the absence of very special circumstances, ought not to be issued until the state prosecution has reached its conclusion, and not even then until the Federal questions arising upon the record have been brought before this court upon writ of error. *Ex parte Royall* . . .; *Re Frederich* . . .; *Whitten v. Tomlinson* . . .; *Baker v. Grice* . . .; *Tinsley v. Anderson* . . .; *Markuson v. Boucher* . . .; *Urquhart v. Brown* . . . And see *Henry v. Henkel*. . . . Such cases as *Re Loney* . . . and *Re Neagle* . . . are recognized as exceptional.

It follows as a logical consequence that where, as here, a criminal prosecution has proceeded through all the courts of the state, including the appellate as well as the trial court, the result of the appellate review cannot be ignored when afterwards the prisoner applies for his release on the ground of a deprivation of Federal rights sufficient to oust the state of its jurisdiction to proceed to judgment and execution against him. This is not a mere matter of comity, as seems to be supposed. The rule stands upon a much higher plane, for it arises out of the very nature and ground of the inquiry into the proceedings of the state tribunals, and touches closely upon the relations between the state and the Federal governments. As was declared by this court in *Ex parte Royall* . . . , applying in a habeas corpus case what was said in *Covell v. Heyman* . . . , a case of conflict of jurisdiction: "The forbearance which courts of co-ordinate jurisdiction, administered under a single system, exercise towards each other, whereby conflicts are avoided by avoiding interference with the process of each other, is a principle of comity, with perhaps no higher sanction than the utility which comes from concord; but between state courts and those of the United States, it is something more. It is a principle of right and of law, and therefore, of necessity." And see *Re Tyler*. . . .

It is objected by counsel for appellee that the alleged loss of jurisdiction cannot be shown by evidence outside of the record; that where a prisoner is held under a judgment of conviction passed by a court having jurisdiction of the subject-matter, and the indictment against him states the case and is based upon a valid existing law, habeas corpus is not an available remedy, save for want of jurisdiction appearing upon the face of the record of the court wherein he was convicted. The rule at the common law . . . , and other acts of Parliament prior to that of July 1, 1816 . . . , seems to have been that a showing in the return to a writ of habeas corpus that the prisoner was held under final process based upon a judgment or decree of a court of competent jurisdiction closed the inquiry. So it was held, under the judiciary act of 1789 . . . , in *Ex parte Watkins* . . . And the rule seems to have been the same under the act of March 2, 1833 . . . , and that of August 29, 1842 . . . But when Congress, in the act of February 5, 1867 . . . , extended the writ of habeas corpus to all cases of persons restrained of their liberty in violation of the Constitution or a law or treaty of the United States, procedural regulations were included . . . These require that the application for the writ shall be made by complaint in writing, signed by the applicant and verified by his oath, setting forth the facts concerning his detention, in whose custody he is detained, and by virtue of what claim or authority, if known; require that the return shall certify the true cause of the detention; and provide that the prisoner may, under oath, deny any of the facts set forth in the return, or allege other material facts, and that the court shall proceed in a summary way to determine the facts by hearing testimony and arguments, and thereupon dispose of the party as law and justice require. The effect is to substitute for the bare legal review that seems to have been the limit of judicial authority under the common-law practice, and . . . a more searching investigation, in which the applicant is put upon his oath to set forth the truth of the matter respecting the causes of his detention, and the court, upon determining the actual facts, is to "dispose of the party as law and justice require."

There being no doubt of the authority of the Congress to thus liberalize the com-monlaw procedure on habeas corpus in order to safeguard the liberty of all persons within the jurisdiction of the United States against infringement through any viola-tion of the Constitution or a law or treaty established thereunder, it results that under the sections cited a prisoner in custody pursuant to the final judgment of a state court of criminal jurisdiction may have a judicial inquiry in a court of the United States into the very truth and substance of the causes of his detention, although it may become necessary to took behind and beyond the record of his conviction to a sufficient extent to test the jurisdiction of the state court to proceed to judgment against him. *Re Cuddy . . . ; Re Mayfield . . . ; Whitten v. Tomlinson . . . ; Re Watts. . . .*

In the light, then, of these established rules and principles: that the due process of law guaranteed by the 14th Amendment has regard to substance of right, and not to matters of form or procedure; that it is open to the courts of the United States, upon an application for a writ of habeas corpus, to look beyond forms and inquire into the very substance of the matter, to the extent of deciding whether the prisoner has been deprived of his liberty without due process of law, and for this purpose to inquire into jurisdictional facts, whether they appear upon the record or not; that an investigation into the case of a prisoner held in custody by a state on conviction of a criminal offense must take into consideration the entire course of proceedings in the courts of the state, and not merely a single step in those proceedings; and that it is incumbent upon the prisoner to set forth in his application a sworn statement of the facts concerning his detention and by virtue of what claim or authority he is detained,—we proceed to consider the questions presented.

I. And first, the question of the disorder and hostile sentiment that are said to have influenced the trial court and jury to an extent amounting to mob domination.

The district court having considered the case upon the face of the petition, we must do the same, treating it as if demurred to by the sheriff. There is no doubt of the jurisdiction to issue the writ of habeas corpus. The question is as to the propriety of issuing it in the present case. . . . [I]t was the duty of the court to refuse the writ if it appeared from the petition itself that appellant was not entitled to it. And see *Ex parte Watkins* . . .; *Ex parte Milligan* . . .; *Ex parte Terry.* . . .

Now the obligation resting upon us, as upon the district court, to look through the form and into the very heart and substance of the matter, applies as well to the averments of the petition as to the proceedings which the petitioner attacks. We must regard not any single clause or paragraph, but the entire petition, and the exhibits that are made a part of it. Thus, the petition contains a narrative of disorder, hostile manifestations, and uproar, which, if it stood alone, and were to be taken as true, may be conceded to show an environment inconsistent with a fair trial and an impartial verdict. But to consider this as standing alone is to take a wholly superficial view. The narrative has no proper place in a petition addressed to a court of the United States except as it may tend to throw light upon the question whether the state of Georgia, having regard to the entire course of the proceedings, in the appellate as well as in the trial court, is depriving appellant of his liberty and intending to deprive him of his life without due process of law. Dealing with the narrative, then, in its essence, and in its relation to the context, it is clearly appears to be only a re-iteration of allegations that appellant had a right to submit, and did submit, first to the trial court, and afterwards to the supreme court of the state, as a ground for avoiding the consequences of the trial; that the allegations were considered by those courts, successively, at times and places and under circumstances wholly apart from the atmosphere of the trial, and free from any suggestion of mob domination, or the like; and that the facts were examined by those courts not only upon the affidavits and exhibits submitted in behalf of the prisoner which are embodied in his present petition as a part of his sworn account of the causes of his detention, but also upon rebutting affidavits submitted in behalf of the state, and which, for reasons not explained, he has not included in the petition. As appears from the prefatory statement, the allegations of disorder were found by both of the state courts to be groundless except in a few particulars as to which the courts ruled that they were irregularities not harmful in fact to defendant, and therefore insufficient in law to avoid the verdict . . . And it was because the defendant was concluded by that finding that the supreme court, upon the subsequent motion to set aside the verdict, declined to again consider those allegations. . . .

Whatever question is raised about the jurisdiction of the trial court, no doubt is suggested but that the supreme court had full jurisdiction to determine the matters of fact and the questions of law arising out of this alleged disorder; nor is there any reason to suppose that it did not fairly and justly perform its duty. It is not easy to see why appellant is not, upon general principles, bound by its decision. It is a fundamental principle of jurisprudence, arising from the very nature of courts of justice and the objects for which they are established, that a question of fact or of law distinctly put in issue and directly determined by a court of competent jurisdiction cannot afterwards be disputed between the same parties. *Southern P. R. Co. v. United States* . . . The principle is as applicable to the decisions of criminal courts as to those of civil jurisdiction. As to its application, in habeas corpus cases, with respect to decisions by such courts of the facts pertaining to the jurisdiction over the prisoner, see *Ex parte Terry* . . .; *Ex parte Columbia George*. . . .

However, it is not necessary, for the purposes of the present case, to invoke the doctrine of res judicata; and, in view of the impropriety of limiting in the least degree the authority of the courts of the United States in investigating an alleged violation by a state of the due process of law guaranteed by the 14th Amendment, we put out of view for the present the suggestion that even the questions of fact bearing upon the jurisdiction of the trial court could be conclusively determined against the prisoner by the decision of the state court of last resort.

But this does not mean that that decision may be ignored or disregarded. To do this, as we have already pointed out, would be not merely to disregard comity, but to ignore the essential question before us, which is not the guilt or innocence of the prisoner, or the truth of any particular fact asserted by him, but whether the state, taking into view the entire course of its procedure, has deprived him of due process of law. This familiar phrase does not mean that the operations of the state government shall be conducted without error or fault in any particular case, nor that the Federal courts may substitute their judgment for that of the state courts, or exercise any general review over their proceedings, but only that the fundamental rights of the prisoner shall not be taken from him arbitrarily or without the right to be heard according to the usual course of law in such cases.

We, of course, agree that if a trial is in fact dominated by a mob, so that the jury is intimidated and the trial judge yields, and so that there is an actual interference with the course of justice, there is, in that court, a departure from due process of law in the proper sense of that term. And if the state, supplying no corrective process, carries into execution a judgment of death or imprisonment based upon a verdict thus produced by mob domination, the state deprives the accused of his life or liberty without due process of law.

But the state may supply such corrective process as to it seems proper. Georgia has adopted the familiar procedure of a motion for a new trial, followed by an appeal to its supreme court, not confined to the mere record of conviction, but going at large, and upon evidence adduced outside of that record, into the question whether the processes of justice have been interfered with in the trial court. Repeated instances are reported of verdicts and judgments set aside and new trials granted for disorder or mob violence interfering with the prisoner's right to a fair trial. *Myers v. State* . . .; *Collier v. State.* . . .

Such an appeal was accorded to the prisoner in the present case (*Frank v. State* . . .), in a manner and under circumstances already stated, and the supreme court, upon a full review, decided appellant's allegations of fact, so far as matters now material are concerned, to be unfounded. Owing to considerations already adverted to (arising not out of comity merely, but out of the very right of the matter to be decided, in view of the relations existing between the states and the Federal government), we hold that such a determination of the facts as was thus made by the court of last resort of Georgia respecting the alleged interference with the trial through disorder and manifestations of hostile sentiment cannot, in this collateral inquiry, be treated as a nullity, but must be taken as setting forth the truth of the matter; certainly until some reasonable ground is shown for an inference that the court which rendered it either was wanting in jurisdiction, or at least erred in the exercise of its jurisdiction; and that the mere assertion by the prisoner that the facts of the matter are other than the state court, upon full investigation, determined them to be, will not be deemed sufficient to raise an issue respecting the correctness of that determination; especially not, where the very evidence upon which the determination was rested in withheld by him who attacks the finding.

It is argued that if in fact there was disorder such as to cause a loss of jurisdiction in the trial court, jurisdiction could not be restored by any decision of the supreme court. This, we think, embodies more than one error of reasoning. It regards a part only of the judicial proceedings, instead of considering the entire process of law. It also begs the question of the existence of such disorder as to cause a loss of jurisdiction in the trial court, which should not be assumed, in the face of the decision of the reviewing court, without showing some adequate ground for disregarding that decision. And these errors grow out of the initial error of treating appellant's narrative of disorder as the whole matter, instead of reading it in connection with the context. The rule of law that in ordinary cases requires a prisoner to exhaust his remedies within the state before coming to the courts of the United States for redress would lose the greater part of its salutary force if the prisoner's mere allegations were to stand the same in law after as before the state courts had passed judgment upon them.

We are very far from intimating that manifestations of public sentiment, or any other form of disorder, calculated to influence court or jury, are matters to be lightly treated. The decisions of the Georgia courts in this and other cases show that such disorder is repressed, where practicable, by the direct intervention of the trial court and the officers under its command; and that other means familiar to the common-law practice, such as postponing the trial, changing the venue, and granting a new trial, are liberally resorted to in order to protect persons accused of crime in the right to a fair trial by an impartial jury. The argument for appellant amounts to saying that this is not enough; that by force of the "due process of law" provision of the 14th Amendment, when the first attempt at a fair trial is rendered abortive through outside interference, the state, instead of allowing a new trial under better auspices, must abandon jurisdiction over the accused, and refrain from further inquiry into the question of his guilt.

To establish this doctrine would, in a very practical sense, impair the power of the states to repress and punish crime; for it would render their courts powerless to act in opposition to lawless public sentiment. The argument is not only unsound in principle, but is in conflict with the practice that prevails in all of the states, so far as we are aware. The cases cited do not sustain the contention that disorder or other lawless conduct calculated to overawe the jury or the trial judge can be treated as a dissolution of the court, or as rendering the proceedings coram non judice, in any such sense as to bar further proceedings. In *Myers v. State* . . .; *Collier v. State* . . .; *Sanders v. State* . . .; *Massey v. State* . . .; and *State v. Weldon* . . . ,—in all of which it was held that the prisoner's right to a fair trial had been interfered with by disorder or mob violence,—it was not held that jurisdiction over the prisoner had been lost; on the contrary, in each instance a new trial was awarded as the appropriate remedy. So, in the cases where the trial judge abdicated his proper functions or absented himself during the trial (*Hayes v. State* . . .; *Blend v. People* . . .; *Shaw v. People* . . .; *Hinman v. People* . . .; *McClure v. State* . . .; *O'Brien v. People* . . .; *Ellerbe v. State* . . .) the reviewing court of the state in each instance simply set aside the verdict and awarded a new trial.

The Georgia courts, in the present case, proceeded upon the theory that Frank would have been entitled to this relief had his charges been true, and they refused a new trial only because they found his charges untrue save in a few minor particulars not amounting to more than irregularities, and not prejudicial to the accused. There was here no denial of due process of law.

2. We come, next, to consider the effect to be given to the fact, admitted for present purposes, that Frank was not present in the court room when the verdict was rendered, his presence having been waived by his counsel, but without his knowledge or consent. No question is made but that at the common law and under the Georgia decisions it is the right of the prisoner to be present

throughout the entire trial, from the commencement of the selection of the jury until the verdict is rendered and jury discharged. *Wade v. State* . . .; *Martin v. State* . . .; *Nolan v. State* . . .; *Smith v. State* . . .; *Bonner v. State* . . .; *Barton v. State* . . .; *Cawthon v. State* . . .; *Bagwell v. State* . . .; *Lyons v. State* . . . But the effect of these decisions is that the prisoner may personally waive the right to be present when the verdict is rendered, and perhaps may waive it by authorized act of his counsel; and that where, without his consent, the verdict is received in his absence, he may treat this as an error, and by timely motion demand a new trial, or (it seems) he may elect to treat the verdict as a nullity by moving in due season to set it aside as such. But we are unable to find that the courts of Georgia have in any case held that, by receiving a verdict in the absence of the prisoner and without his consent, the jurisdiction of the trial court was terminated. In the *Nolan* Case . . . , the verdict was set aside as void on the ground of the absence of the prisoner; but this was not held to deprive the trial court of its jurisdiction. On the contrary, the jurisdiction was treated as remaining, and that court proceeded to exercise it by arraigning the prisoner a second time upon the same indictment, when he pleaded specially, claiming his discharge because of former jeopardy; the trial court overruled this plea, the defendant excepted, and the jury found the defendant guilty; and, upon review, the supreme court reversed this judgment, not for the want of jurisdiction in the trial court, but for error committed in the exercise of jurisdiction. To the same effect is *Bagwell v. State.* . . .

In most of the other states, where error is committed by receiving a verdict of guilty during the involuntary absence of the accused, it is treated as merely requiring a new trial. In a few cases, the appellate court has ordered the defendant to be discharged, upon the ground that he had been once in jeopardy and a new trial would be futile.

However, the Georgia supreme court in the present case . . . held, as pointed out in the prefatory statement, that because Frank, shortly after the verdict, was made fully aware of the facts, and he then made a motion for a new trial upon over 100 grounds, without including this as one, and had the motion heard by both the trial court and the supreme court, he could not, after this motion had been finally adjudicated against him, move to set aside the verdict as a nullity because of his absence when the verdict was rendered. There is nothing in the 14th Amendment to prevent a state from adopting and enforcing so reasonable a regulation of procedure. *Dreyer v. Illinois.* . . .

It is insisted that the enforced absence of Frank at that time was not only a deprivation of trial by jury, but was equally a deprivation of due process of law within the meaning of the Amendment, in that it took from him at a critical stage of the proceeding the right or opportunity to be heard. But repeated decisions of this court have put it beyond the range of further debate that the "due process" clause of the 14th Amendment has not the effect of imposing upon the states any particular form or mode of procedure, so long as the essential rights of notice and a hearing, or opportunity to be heard, before a competent tribunal, are not interfered with. Indictment by grand jury is not essential to due process (*Hurtado v. California* . . .; *Lem Woon v. Oregon* . . . , and cases cited). Trial by jury is not essential to it, either in civil cases (*Walker v. Sauvinet*. . .), or in criminal (*Hallinger v. Davis* . . .; *Maxwell v. Dow*. . .).

It is argued that a state may not, while providing for trial by jury, permit the accused to waive the right to be heard in the mode characteristic of such trial, including the presence of the prisoner up to and at the time of the rendition of the verdict. But the cases cited do not support this contention. In *Hopt v. Utah* . . . (principally relied upon), the court had under review a conviction in a territorial court after a trial subject to the local Code of Criminal Procedure, which declared: "If the indictment is for a felony, the defendant must be personally present at the trial." The judgment was reversed because of the action of the trial court in permitting certain challenges to jurors, based upon the ground of bias, to be tried out of the presence of the court, the defendant, and his counsel. The ground of the decision of this court was the violation of the plan mandate of the local statute; and the power of the accused or his counsel to dispense with the requirement as to his personal presence was denied on the ground that his life could not be lawfully taken except in the mode prescribed by law. No other question was involved. See *Diaz v. United States*. . . .

The distinction between what the common law requires with respect to trial by jury in criminal cases, and what the states may enact without contravening the "due process" clause of the 14th Amendment, is very clearly evidenced by *Hallinger v. Davis* . . . and *Lewis v. United States* . . . , which were under consideration by the court at the same time, both opinions being written by Mr. Justice Shiras. In the *Lewis Case*, which was a conviction of murder in a circuit court of the United States, the trial practice being regulated by the common law, it was held to be a leading principle, pervading the entire law of criminal procedure, that after indictment nothing should be done in the absence of the prisoner; that the making of challenges is an essential part of the trial, and it was one of the substantial rights of the prisoner to be brought face to face with the jurors at the time the challenges were made; and that in the absence of a statute, this right as it existed at common law must not be abridged. But in the *Hallinger Case*, where a state by legislative enactment had permitted one charged with a capital offense to waive a trial by jury and elect to be tried by the court, it was held that this method of procedure did not conflict with the 14th Amendment. So in *Howard v. Kentucky* . . . ,—a case closely in point upon the question now presented,—this court, finding that by the law of the state an occasional absence of the accused from the trial, from which no injury resulted to his substantial rights, was not deemed material error, held that the application of this rule of law did not amount to a denial of due process within the meaning of the 14th Amendment.

In fact, this court has sustained the states in establishing a great variety of departures from the common-law procedure respecting jury trials. Thus, in *Brown v. New Jersey* . . . , a statute providing for the trial of murder cases by struck jury was sustained, notwithstanding it did not provide for twenty peremptory challenges. *Simon v. Craft* . . . , while not a criminal case, involved the property of a person alleged to be of unsound mind, and it was held that an Alabama statute, under which the sheriff determined that Mrs. Simon's health and safety would be endangered by her presence at the trial of the question of her sanity, so that while served with notice she was detained in custody and not allowed to be present at the hearing of the inquisition, did not deprive her of property without due process of law. In *Felts v. Murphy* . . . , where the prisoner was convicted of the crime of murder, and sentenced to imprisonment for life, although he did not hear a word of the evidence given upon the trial because of his almost total deafness, his inability to hear being such that it required a person to speak through an eartrumpet close to his ear in order that such person should be heard by him, and the trial court having failed to see to it that the testimony in the case was repeated to him through his ear trumpet, this court said that this was "at most an error, which did not take away from the court its jurisdiction over the subject-matter and over the person accused." In *Twining v. New Jersey* . . . , it was held that the exemption of a prisoner from compulsory self-incrimination in the state courts was not included in the guaranty of due process of law contained in the 14th Amendment. In *Jordan v. Massachusetts* . . . , where one of the jurors was subject to reasonable doubt as to his sanity, and the state court, pursuant to the local law of criminal procedure, determined upon a mere preponderance of the evidence that he was sane, the conviction was affirmed. In *Garland v. Washington* . . . , it was held that the want of a formal arraignment, treated by the state as depriving the accused of no substantial right, and as having been waived, and thereby lost, did not amount to depriving defendant of his liberty without due process of law.

Our conclusion upon this branch of the case is, that the practice established in the criminal courts of Georgia that a defendant may waive his right to be present when the jury renders its verdict, and that such waiver may be given after as well as before the event, and is to be inferred from the making of a motion for new trial upon other grounds alone, when the facts respecting the reception of the verdict are within the prisoner's knowledge at the time of making that motion, is a regulation of criminal procedure that it is within the authority of the state to adopt. In adopting it, the state declares in effect, as it reasonably may declare, that the right of the accused to be present at the reception of the verdict is but an incident of the right of trial by jury; and since the state may, without infringing the 14th Amendment, abolish trial by jury, it may limit the effect to be given to an error respecting one of the incidents of such trial. The presence of the prisoner when the verdict is rendered is not so essential a part of the hearing that a rule of practice permitting the accused to waive it, and holding him bound by the waiver, amounts to a deprivation of "due process of law."

3. The insistence that the decision of the supreme court of Georgia in affirming the denial of the motion to set aside the verdict . . . on the ground that Frank's failure to raise the objection upon the motion for a new trial amounted to a waiver of it was inconsistent with the previous practice as established in *Nolan v. State* . . . , and therefore amounted in effect to an ex post facto law in contravention of 10 of article 1 of the Federal Constitution, needs but a word. Assuming the inconsistency, it is sufficient to say that the constitutional prohibition: "No state shall . . . pass any bill of attainder, ex post facto law, or law impairing the obligation of contracts," as its terms indicate, is directed against legislative action only, and does not reach erroneous or inconsistent decisions by the courts. *Calder v. Bull* . . . ; *Fletcher v. Peck* . . . ; *Kring v. Missouri* . . . ; *Thompson v. Utah* . . . ; *Cross Lake Shooting & Fishing Club v. Louisiana* . . . ; *Ross v. Oregon*. . . .

4. To conclude: Taking appellant's petition as a whole, and not regarding any particular portion of it to the exclusion of the rest,—dealing with its true and substantial meaning, and not merely with its superficial import,—it shows that Frank, having been formally accused of a grave crime, was placed on trial before a court of competent jurisdiction, with a jury lawfully constituted; he had a public trial, deliberately conducted, with the benefit of counsel for his defense; he was found guilty and sentenced pursuant to the laws of the state; twice he has moved the trial court to grant a new trial, and once to set aside the verdict as a nullity; three times he has been heard upon appeal before the court of last resort of that state, and in every instance the adverse action of the trial court has been affirmed; his allegations of hostile public sentiment and disorder in and about the court room, improperly influencing the trial court and the jury against him, have been rejected because found untrue in point of fact upon evidence presumably justifying that finding, and which he has not produced in the present proceeding; his contention that his lawful rights were infringed because he was not permitted to be present when the jury rendered its verdict has been set aside because it was waived by his

failure to raise the objection in due season when fully cognizant of the facts. In all of these proceedings the state, through its courts, has retained jurisdiction over him, has accorded to him the fullest right and opportunity to be heard according to the established modes of procedure, and now holds him in custody to pay the penalty of the crime of which he has been adjudged guilty. In our opinion, he is not shown to have been deprived of any right guaranteed to him by the 14th Amendment or any other provision of the Constitution or laws of the United States; on the contrary, he has been convicted, and is now held in custody, under "due process of law" within the meaning of the Constitution.

The final order of the District Court, refusing the application for a writ of habeas corpus, is affirmed.

Joe Hill Trial (1914)

The murder trial of Joe Hill, and his subsequent conviction and execution, created a legendary figure for the labor movement. Today, Hill remains a powerful source of inspiration for workers and revolutionaries across the globe. It has been noted that the songs and ideas of Joe Hill played an important role in the civil rights protests and the progressive movements of the modern era. While the life and death of Joe Hill continue to influence labor activists, folk singers, and poets, legal analysts have failed to reach an agreement concerning whether Hill received a fair trial and whether he was a murderer or a heroic martyr (Smith 1984, 1–15).

In 1905, the International Workers of the World (IWW), also known as the Wobblies, was created as an international union to promote the rights of workers. The IWW often would use songs as a way to communicate with workers from all over the world. The songs often were derived from popular, or religious, music with new lyrics that promoted the prolabor agenda. Beginning in 1909, the songs were published in the *Little Red Song Book,* which achieved a circulation of 50,000 and successfully united workers from different cultures. The songs assisted the IWW in participating in over 100 labor strikes prior to World War I (Law Library, "Joe Hill Trial").

In 1911, the *Little Red Song Book* included lyrics from Joe Hill, a laborer who became an important spokesman for the IWW. Hill was born in Sweden and came to the United States in 1902 at the age of 23. Hill soon became a popular folk hero as he traveled around the United States looking for work and performing songs using various musical instruments such as a guitar, piano, banjo, and violin. In addition to his songwriting, Hill also made political speeches and wrote satirical poems as a way to encourage workers to join unions and become active politically (Law Library, "Joe Hill Trial").

In January 1914, Hill was living with friends in Salt Lake City, Utah, while he was working as a laborer in the silver mines. On January 10, 1914, Hill went out for the evening and returned with a bullet wound to his chest that required the attention of a physician. Hill told the doctor that he had received the gunshot wound because of an argument with another man over a woman. On the same evening, John G. Morrison and his son, Arling, were working in their grocery store in Salt Lake City when two men wearing red handkerchiefs as masks entered the store and fired pistols killing the father and son. However, prior to being shot and killed, Arling Morrison was able to use a handgun from behind the counter to shoot one of the intruders. A witness supposedly saw one of the men running away from the store holding his chest (Law Library, "Joe Hill Trial").

Initially, police investigators thought that the killings were an act of revenge because Morrison had worked as a police officer in the past and had recently been attacked by men whom he had arrested during his law-enforcement career. After dismissing a dozen suspects, investigators focused upon Hill when police found a red handkerchief in his room. In addition, the doctor who treated Hill said that he had a pistol in his possession at the time that he was being treated, but Hill later disposed of the pistol and it was never recovered by authorities. When he was arrested, Hill suspiciously refused to say much about the shooting, except that it occurred because of a dispute over a woman. However, Hill did state that his hands were over his head when he was shot and the bullet hole in his coat, which was four inches below the wound in his back, seemed to support his story (BBC, "Joe Hill-Murderer or Martyr?").

The murder trial of Joe Hill began on June 17, 1914. Judge Morris L. Ritchie presided over the trial and E. O. Leatherwood served as the lead prosecutor. Hill was represented by four defense lawyers, Soren X. Christensen, Orrin N. Hilton, E. D. McDougall, and F. B. Scott. While the prosecution presented several eyewitnesses to the murders who testified that Hill resembled one of the intruders, E. O. Leatherwood admitted that he had only circumstantial, or indirect, evidence connecting Hill to the murders (Law Library, "Joe Hill Trial"). One of the eyewitnesses was Merlin Morrison who was the 13-year-old son and brother of John and Arling Morrison, respectively. Merlin Morrison initially stated that he could not positively identify Hill as one of the intruders but, later on, changed his mind. Another witness testified that one of the intruders had scars on his face similar to marks on the face of Hill. In addition to the eyewitnesses, prosecutors attempted to establish a motive for the murders by arguing that it was a case of a robbery gone wrong, although no money was taken from the grocery store. The fact that one of the intruders was heard to have yelled, "We've got you now," prior to shooting Morrison, seemed to suggest that the murderers were not motivated by money (Smith 1984, 79–93).

Hill's defense attorneys argued that the prosecutors could not establish a motive to explain why Hill committed the murders. The fact that Hill did not know Morrison and because money was not taken from the store created serious questions concerning why Hill would commit such a murder. Hill's lawyers, Orrin Hilton and Soren Christensen, also noted that four other people besides Hill were treated for bullet wounds in Salt Lake City on the night of the murders. The prosecution's case was further weakened by the fact that none of Hill's blood was found inside the grocery store and the bullet that caused the wounds to Hill's chest and back and passed through his body was not found inside the store (BBC, "Joe Hill-Murderer or Martyr?").

Even though Hill denied that he was involved in the murders, he refused to testify during the trial and his lawyers, Hilton and Christensen, were frustrated because Hill would not reveal his whereabouts on the night of the murder. Hill's refusal to testify and his lack of an alibi raised suspicions with the jury, but it was rumored that Hill had spent the evening with a woman who was married and he simply wanted to protect her. Such a scandal would have destroyed the reputation of a married woman in Utah in the early part of the 20th century. Others speculated that Hill was advised by IWW leaders not to testify because the prosecution's case was weak or perhaps because he would have been unable to explain himself during cross-examination by the prosecution (BBC, "Joe Hill-Murderer or Martyr?").

On June 28, 1914, Hill was found guilty and sentenced to die. Apparently, the circumstantial evidence such as the eyewitnesses, Hill's chest wound, and the red handkerchief combined with the lack of an alibi and the biased newspaper coverage of Hill as a member of the IWW led the jury to conclude that Hill was guilty of murder (Smith 1984, 100–102).

In his appeal to the Utah Supreme Court, Hill was represented by Orrin Hilton who argued that eyewitnesses to the shootings were not entirely positive in their identification of Hill, and the prosecution never established a motive for the killings. Hilton also cited numerous errors committed by Judge Ritchie such as his decision to allow a newspaper reporter to testify as an expert on guns and his refusal to allow the defense lawyers to introduce testimony regarding assailants who had previously attempted to murder John Morrison. Unfortunately, Hill's chances for a successful appeal decreased when he wrote a letter to the court arguing that the state of Utah had no right to ask him about how he acquired the bullet wound to his chest. The Utah Supreme Court subsequently upheld the conviction of Joe Hill and his execution was scheduled for October 1, 1915 (Smith 1984, 105–111).

As the execution date approached, an international effort to save the life of Joe Hill began as thousands of letters were written, rallies were held, and money was raised. As the Utah State Board of Pardons heard an appeal from Hill's lawyer to reduce his sentence to life in prison, prominent individuals such as American Federation of Labor President Samuel Gompers, Helen Keller, and high-ranking officials in the Swedish government pressured President Woodrow Wilson to urge Governor William Spry of Utah to grant clemency to Hill. However, the Board of Pardons and Governor Spry refused to act unless Hill explained his whereabouts on the evening of the murders and how he obtained the bullet wound (Smith 1984, 139–169).

Because of the international media attention, the execution was repeatedly moved back to a later date. Hill sat in prison for nearly two years during the appeals process but continued to write songs, poems, and letters that would further enhance his status as a legendary figure within the labor movement. In one of his final letters to William "Big Bill" Haywood, an IWW leader, Hill wrote that he would die as a "true blue rebel" and told Haywood not to mourn his death but to continue organizing workers around the world. Hill was finally executed before a firing squad on November 19, 1915, in the Utah State Prison (Smith 1984, 171–177).

At Hill's request, he was cremated in Chicago, and thousands of mourners attended a ceremony in his honor. Hill's ashes were sent to every state chapter of the IWW, with the exception of Utah (Rosemont 2003, 139–150). In 1930, Alfred Hayes paid tribute to Hill in a poem entitled "I Dreamed I Saw Joe Hill Last Night." The poem was turned into a song written by Earl Robinson in 1936. The impact of Joe Hill on the popular culture of America cannot be measured. Joe Hill had a significant influence upon such authors as Upton Sinclair, Eugene O'Neill, and Carl Sandburg as well as such songwriters and performers as Paul Robeson, Pete Seeger, Woody Guthrie, Steve Earle, Joan Baez, and Bob Dylan. The legend of Joe Hill will forever serve as a symbol of the working man's fight for justice in a capitalist society (150–203).

References

BBC.com. "Joe Hill—Murderer or Martyr?" February 19, 2002. http://www.bbc.co.uk/dna/h2g2/A676361 (accessed August 14, 2009).

Law Library–American Law and Legal Information. "Joe Hill Trial: 1914—Circumstantial Evidence But No Motive." *Great American Trials.* Vol. 1. http://law.jrank.org/pages/2799/Joe-Hill-Trial-1914.html (accessed August 14, 2009).

Rosemont, Franklin. *Joe Hill: The IWW & the Making of a Revolutionary Working Class Counterculture.* Chicago: Charles H. Kerr, 2003.

Smith, Gibbs M. *Joe Hill.* Layton, UT: Gibbs Smith Publishing, 1984.

The Chicago Black Sox Trial (*The State of Illinois v. Eddie Cicotte et al.*, 1921)

The Chicago Black Sox trial was the first American trial involving criminal charges against professional athletes. The eight players from the Chicago White Sox accused of purposely losing the 1919 World Series against the Cincinnati Reds either approached, or were approached by, a variety of professional gamblers to throw the World Series in exchange for financial gain. Because the owner of the White Sox, Charles Comiskey, had underpaid many of the players on the team, the eight players were vulnerable to accepting bribes in exchange for fixing the series (Linder, "Black Sox"). Interestingly, legal scholars at the time were unsure if a trial would even occur because the charge of conspiracy to fix a professional game for money had never before been tried in an American court of law (Carney 2006, 136). Technically, it was not a crime to fix the outcome of a professional sport in 1919, and it was considered doubtful whether the prosecution could meet the burden of proving a charge of fraud committed by the players against the American public and Comiskey (Chermak and Bailey 2007, 10).

After the World Series ended with the Reds defeating the White Sox by 5 games to 3, rumors began to spread. Many people openly questioned how a heavily favored team such as the White Sox could lose to the underdog Cincinnati Reds. Comiskey publicly stated that his players had not thrown the World Series, but privately he hired an investigator to look into the finances of seven of his players. The conspiracy of the 1919 World Series was exposed by a number of leaks. An associate of Arnold Rothstein, a powerful sports gambler, told the manager of the White Sox, Kid Gleason, that some of his players had thrown the series. Prior to the series, a player for the New York Giants also had seen a telegram sent to one of his teammates by Bill Burns indicating that the White Sox were about to fix the 1919 World Series. Finally, Eddie Cicotte, a pitcher for the White Sox, decided to testify before a grand jury about his part in fixing the World Series. "Shoeless" Joe Jackson, one of the best players on the White Sox, was the second person to come forward and provide testimony about his involvement in the scandal. Comiskey subsequently suspended eight of the players mentioned in the testimony of Cicotte and Jackson. The suspension came at the end of the 1920 baseball season when the White Sox had been poised to win the championship. However, after the suspension, the White Sox were given no chance of winning the World Series in 1920 (Linder, "Black Sox").

On October 22, 1920, a grand jury indicted eight players (Chick Gandil, Eddie Cicotte, "Swede" Risberg, Claude Williams, Oscar Felsch, Fred McMullin, Joe Jackson, and Buck Weaver) of the White Sox and five professional gamblers on conspiring to defraud a variety of people and organizations by throwing the 1919 World Series. Among the professional gamblers indicted were Abe Attell, Bill Burns, and "Sport" Sullivan. However, the professional gamblers did not show up for the trial because they had fled Chicago. Arnold Rothstein, the most powerful gambler of his time, was not mentioned in the indictment by the grand jury, even though he supposedly was integral in providing money for the scandal. Shortly after the indictments were delivered, the original confessions of some of the White Sox players were stolen allegedly by Rothstein, Comiskey, or perhaps both (Linder, "Black Sox"). Years later, the confessions would surface mysteriously in the possession of an attorney who had worked for Comiskey (Asinof and Gould 2000, 289–291).

The trial began on June 27, 1921, in front of Judge Hugo Friend in Chicago, Illinois. The eight players and five professional gamblers were officially charged with the following crimes: 1) conspiracy to commit fraud against the American public, 2) conspiracy to commit fraud against the owner of the White Sox, Charles Comiskey, 3) conspiracy to commit fraud against Ray Schalk, a player on the White Sox who was not involved in the scandal, 4) conspiracy to commit fraud against the industry of professional baseball, and 5) conspiracy to gain the confidence of various victims and then commit fraud (Ginsburg 2004, 143).

In delivering the opening statement to the jury on July 18, 1921, the prosecution, led by George Gorman, attempted to quote from a copy of the confession of Eddie Cicotte but one of the defense attorneys, Michael Ahearn, objected (Linder, "Black Sox"). The defense attorneys, led by Ahearn, were some of the best legal counsel in the state of Illinois and probably were hired by Comiskey to represent the players. Oddly enough, even though the players allegedly had conspired against him, Comiskey secretly wanted the players to be acquitted, which would allow them to play baseball again for his team (Carney 2006, 146). Initially, Judge Friend ruled in favor of the defense by stating that the prosecution could not refer to any of the confessions. Because the original confessions had been stolen, the prosecution had to show that the confessions were provided voluntarily without a promise of immunity offered to the defendants in order to admit them as evidence. During the trial, the stolen confessions would pose difficulty for the prosecution team. In the end, Judge Friend ruled that the prosecutors were allowed to admit copies of the confessions from three of the defendants, Cicotte, Jackson, and Williams, who had signed a waiver regarding immunity. However, Judge Friend held that the evidence could only be used in determining the guilt of Cicotte, Jackson, and Williams and not the other five defendants (Chermak and Bailey 2007, 10).

The prosecution decided to use Bill Burns, one of the professional gamblers charged in the indictment, as its key witness. Gorman promised Burns immunity from prosecution if he would testify against the players. Burns provided three days of testimony and described how the players had come to him with the idea of fixing the World Series. Specifically, Burns identified Eddie Cicotte as the person whom he met in a New York hotel one month prior to the World Series. Burns then described in detail a later meeting with some of the other professional gamblers and seven of the White Sox players. Shoeless Joe Jackson was the only player absent from the meeting. At the meeting, the gamblers and players discussed the financing of the operation. The defense attorneys attempted to discredit Burns on cross-examination by claiming that the players did not initiate the meeting but, instead, the gamblers had sought out the players. In the end, the testimony of Bill Burns was viewed as a success for the prosecution (Chermak and Bailey 2007, 10).

Charles Comiskey also provided testimony for the prosecution and discussed how he was harmed financially by the conspiracy to throw the World Series. In their cross-examination of Comiskey, the defense team attempted to disprove the prosecution's argument that Comiskey was damaged financially by introducing evidence that Comiskey had made more money in the year after the 1919 World Series than ever before in his life (Chermak and Bailey 2007, 10).

In presenting their case for the players, the defense attorneys called Kid Gleason, the manager of the White Sox; several players who were not involved in the alleged conspiracy; and a chief financial accountant for the White Sox. Gleason testified that the eight players charged with conspiracy were practicing with the team at the time they were supposedly meeting with Bill Burns and the other professional gamblers. Therefore, Gleason tried to provide an alibi for the players. Then, the White Sox players who were not involved in the scandal testified that they thought the eight players tried their best during the World Series and showed no indication that they were trying to lose the games. Finally, the chief financial officer testified that Comiskey had made more profit during the 1920 baseball season than in the 1919 season (Linder, "Black Sox").

On July 29, 1921, Edward Prindeville delivered the closing statement for the prosecution by asserting that the baseball players had defrauded the American public of their favorite pastime. Prindeville closed by stating that all of the fans in America had been cheated by the players for $20,000, a relatively small amount of cash. The prosecution asked the jury to find the defendants guilty and sentence each player to five years in prison and a $5,000 fine (Linder, "Black Sox").

The closing arguments for the defense team were delivered by Ben Short and Morgan Frumberg. Short noted that there was an agreement between the gamblers and the players but it was a secret agreement. The players did not intend to hurt the game of baseball or Comiskey because they never wanted the agreement to be made public. Frumberg questioned how Arnold Rothstein, a wealthy professional gambler at the center of the controversy, had escaped prosecution, while the White Sox players who had very little money were forced to take the blame for the scandal (Linder, "Black Sox").

In his instructions to the jury, Judge Friend probably determined the outcome of the trial by informing the jury that they had to find the White Sox players guilty of, not only throwing the World Series, but conspiring to defraud the American public.

On August 2, 1921, the jury deliberated for two hours and returned a verdict of not guilty against all of the White Sox players. Ultimately, the prosecution could not meet the burden of proof necessary to prove that any of the players committed fraud. While the testimony of the professional gamblers and the copies of the confessions may have shown that the players fixed professional baseball games, there was no hard evidence that the players intended to commit fraud against the American public in the process (Chermak and Bailey 2007, 11).

Despite their acquittal in the criminal trial, the newly appointed commissioner of baseball, Kenesaw Landis, issued a lifetime ban against the eight White Sox players for throwing a baseball game and for associating with known gamblers who discussed throwing baseball games. None of the eight players ever played major league baseball again (Asinof and Gould 2000, 279–292).

Even though the Black Sox scandal gained national attention, the federal government did not begin regulating sports gambling until the 1950s when congressional investigations revealed that gambling was connected to organized crime. Congress finally addressed the issue of fixing sporting contests by passing into law the Racketeer Influenced and Corrupt Organizations Act (RICO) of 1970 which enabled the federal government to prosecute organized criminals who attempt to use bribery as a way to influence sporting events. In 1979, Congress also passed the Bribery in Sporting Contests Act, which makes it a federal crime to bribe a person in order to affect the outcome of a sporting event (Cotton and Wolohan 2006, 272).

Charles Comiskey

Charles Comiskey was born on August 15, 1859, in Chicago, Illinois. He was a professional baseball player and manager for the St. Louis Brownies, the Chicago Pirates, and the Cincinnati Reds during the latter part of the 1800s. Comiskey is one of only two players in the history of the game to have 200 hits, 100 runs scored, 100 runs batted in, and 100 stolen bases in a single season (Reference.com, "Charles A. Comiskey"). Comiskey was instrumental in the development of the American League. Eventually, Comiskey went on to become the owner of the Chicago White Sox from 1901 to 1931. Comiskey died at the age of 72 on October 26, 1931, in Eagle River, Wisconsin. In 1939, Comiskey was elected into the Baseball Hall of Fame and, today, the baseball stadium used by the Chicago White Sox is named after Comiskey as a way to honor him (Linder, "President of the White Sox: Charles Comiskey").

"Shoeless" Joe Jackson

Joe Jackson was born in Pickens County, South Carolina, on July 16, 1888. Jackson had very little education because he was forced to help support his family as a child by working in a textile factory. At the age of 13, Jackson joined the Brandon Mill baseball team and was the youngest member of the squad (Fleitz 2001, 6–7).

In 1908, Jackson began playing professional baseball with a minor league team, the Greenville Spinners of the Carolina Association. He earned his nickname when he acquired a blister on his foot from a new pair of shoes and decided to play a baseball game in his socks. While he was running the bases in his socks, a fan yelled at him, "You shoeless son of a gun," and the nickname stayed with him during his entire baseball career (Fleitz 2001, 16–17).

Later, in 1908, Jackson signed a contract to play with the Philadelphia Athletics and their manager, Connie Mack. Jackson did not adjust well to life in the big city of Philadelphia and played only five games for the Athletics before being sent to the minor leagues. He was eventually traded to the Cleveland Naps in 1910. In 1911, Jackson played his first full season in the major leagues and set a record for rookies with a .408 batting average (Fleitz 2001, 21–40).

After three successful years in Cleveland, Jackson was traded to the Chicago White Sox in 1915 where he led the White Sox to a World Series victory against the New York Giants in 1917. Jackson enjoyed a .307 batting average during the series (Fleitz 2001, 113–146). In 1919, the White Sox were heavily favored to defeat the Cincinnati Reds but lost the World Series. Jackson and seven of his teammates were charged with conspiracy to fix the World Series in exchange for money from organized crime figures (Linder, "Black Sox").

In 1921, a jury in Chicago found the eight members of the Chicago White Sox not guilty of purposely losing the World Series (Fleitz 2001, 234–248). However, after the trial, major league baseball appointed a commissioner who banned Jackson and the other players allegedly involved in the scandal from playing professional baseball. The commissioner, Kenesaw Mountain Landis, stated that, despite the verdict of the jury, professional baseball was tainted by the scandal and needed to remove any players associated with organized gambling (Linder, "Black Sox").

Jackson spent the next 20 years as a player and manager for minor league teams based in Georgia and South Carolina. In 1922, Jackson owned a dry cleaning business in Savannah, Georgia and, 11 years later, opened a barbecue restaurant and a liquor store in Greenville, South Carolina. Jackson died of a heart attack on December 5, 1951, in Greenville, South Carolina, at the age of 63 (Sagart 2004, 146–152).

Throughout the latter part of his life, Jackson proclaimed his innocence concerning the conspiracy to take part in fixing the 1919 World Series. In the modern era, a movement has developed to remove Jackson's name from the list of players ineligible to be inducted into the professional baseball hall of fame in Cooperstown, New York. In 1988, a dramatic film about the Black Sox Scandal of 1919 entitled *Eight Men Out* was released and actor D. B. Sweeney played the part of Joe Jackson (Sagart 2004, 154–165).

Buck Weaver

George Daniel "Buck" Weaver was born in Pottstown, Pennsylvania, on August 8, 1890. Weaver began playing semiprofessional baseball in the Connecticut State League. In 1910, at the age of 20, Weaver signed with the Chicago White Sox and was sent to the minor leagues to develop his skills (Ginsburg 2004, 108). In 1912, Weaver's mother passed away and he had to make the tough decision to forgo his mother's funeral in Pennsylvania in order to attend spring training and compete for a spot on the White Sox's roster. Weaver earned rave reviews from the sports writers of the *Chicago Tribune* who wrote about a heartbroken youngster with great character and grit who attended spring training without mentioning his mother's death to anyone (Biography, "George Daniel 'Buck' Weaver").

Weaver played shortstop for the first five years of his career with the White Sox. However, in 1917, he switched to third base when the team signed Swede Risberg to play at shortstop. At this time, Weaver had improved his game significantly and was considered the leader of the team. He was named to the American League All-Star team and led the White Sox in hitting and fielding. In the 1917 World Series, the White Sox defeated the New York Giants, and Weaver had the second best average on his team during the series with a .333 batting average (Biography, "George Daniel 'Buck' Weaver").

In the 1919 World Series, the White Sox lost to the Cincinnati Red Legs, and Weaver again performed exceptionally with a .324 batting average and no fielding errors during the series. After another successful season in 1920, Weaver and seven other players from the White Sox were charged in criminal court with conspiring to fix the 1919 World Series in exchange for payments from organized gamblers. Weaver was the only one of the eight players who did not accept any money from the gamblers and was also the only player to proclaim his innocence directly to Charles Comiskey, the owner of the Chicago White Sox. However, Weaver apparently knew about the fix because he met twice with White Sox players and the gamblers where he told everyone at the meetings that it was impossible to fix the World Series (Biography, "George Daniel 'Buck' Weaver").

While Weaver demanded that he receive a separate trial, he was forced to sit with the other seven White Sox players during the 1921 conspiracy trial. The eight players for the White Sox were eventually acquitted by a Chicago jury on the conspiracy charges but Weaver, along with the other players, received a lifetime ban from the newly appointed commissioner, Kenesaw Mountain Landis. In Landis's statement in which he issued the lifetime bans, he directed one sentence specifically toward Weaver by asserting that anyone who even discusses the possibility of throwing a game with gamblers will not be allowed to play professional baseball. Therefore, even though Weaver probably did not participate in the fix and refused to take money from the gamblers, he should have come forward with the information about players and gamblers discussing the possibility of throwing the World Series (Linder, "Black Sox"). Weaver obviously paid a price for refusing to snitch on his teammates, and his loyalty cost him his career in professional baseball (The Baseball Page.com, "Buck Weaver").

Throughout the remainder of his life, Weaver applied six times to gain reinstatement to major league baseball but he was denied each time. Weaver was reduced to playing semiprofessional baseball for the rest of his career. He also worked as a day painter and was employed in the drugstore business with a family member. On January 31, 1956, Buck Weaver died of a heart attack in Chicago, Illinois, at the age of 65. In 1988, a dramatic film, *Eight Men Out,* was released and the story of the film was told largely from the perspective of Buck Weaver whose character was played by a popular actor, John Cusack (Biography, "George Daniel 'Buck' Weaver").

Arnold Rothstein

Arnold Rothstein was born in New York City on January 17, 1882. At the age of 16, Rothstein dropped out of school and began working as a gambler specializing in horse races, professional baseball, and boxing matches. He also made money as a "loan shark" by lending money at very high interest rates. In 1914, Rothstein became heavily involved in bookmaking and made a fortune, for the most part, by fixing sporting events (Linder, "Arnold Rothstein").

Rothstein became famous for his involvement with the 1919 World Series when he provided the money to pay off players from the Chicago White Sox to lose to the Cincinnati Red Legs. It was estimated that Rothstein bet over a quarter of a million dollars on Cincinnati to win the World Series. Rothstein wisely used an intermediary, Joseph "Sport" Sullivan, to pay off the players and, therefore, he was able to remain behind the scenes during the conspiracy (Pietrusza 2004, 153–154).

On October 1, 1920, Rothstein testified before a Cook County grand jury investigating the fixing of the World Series and he swore under oath that he had nothing to do with the scandal. Instead, Rothstein blamed the conspiracy on one of his gambling associates. Three weeks later, Rothstein was cleared by the grand jury of any involvement in the fixing of the series. Because

Rothstein never had any direct contact with the White Sox players, prosecutors failed to find any evidence that connected him to the scandal (Pietrusza 2004, 171–192).

After the "Black Sox" conspiracy trial in 1921, Rothstein attempted to improve his reputation by proclaiming that he was leaving the world of gambling but, instead, continued operating gambling houses and even ventured into bootlegging and drug trafficking. On November 6, 1928, Rothstein was shot and killed during a poker game in a hotel in New York City (Pietrusza 2004, 291–318).

After Rothstein was murdered, an investigation by the federal government revealed that Rothstein had bribed an attorney to obtain the sworn statements of four gamblers who had named Rothstein as the person responsible for the Black Sox scandal of 1919 (Linder, "Arnold Rothstein"). In the modern era, Rothstein has been portrayed in popular films about organized crime figures, including the 1991 film *Mobsters,* starring Christian Slater (Tucker 2008, 182). Rothstein was even mentioned in the famous film, *Godfather II,* when a character by the name of Hyman Roth tells Michael Corleone, the Godfather, that a statue should be built in honor of Rothstein because he was able to fix the 1919 World Series (Asinof and Gould 2000, xv).

1919 World Series: The Black Sox Scandal

The 1919 World Series between the Chicago White Sox and Cincinnati Reds resulted in one of the greatest scandals in the history of professional sports. Often referred to as "the Black Sox Scandal," the fixing of the 1919 World Series involved a group of talented and underpaid players, an owner who cheated his players out of a proper salary, professional gamblers seeking to capitalize on the situation, and an American public deceived by their favorite pastime (Linder, "Black Sox").

Charles Comiskey, owner of the Chicago White Sox in 1919, had a reputation for being very tight with his money. For example, despite the fact that he owned the best team in baseball, he refused to pay a decent salary to some of the best players ever to play the game. Two of the greatest players of the game, "Shoeless" Joe Jackson and Buck Weaver, were paid only $6,000 per year by Comiskey, while players with lesser talent were paid nearly twice as much on other teams. At the end of 1917 season, Comiskey actually went as far as benching his star pitcher, Eddie Cicotte, to prevent him from winning 30 games which would have forced Comiskey to pay him a $10,000 bonus. To make matters worse for the best team in baseball, the players for the Chicago White Sox received less allowance money than other teams while traveling on the road. Because free agency was prohibited by professional baseball in the early part of the 20th century, a player was forced to accept a contract with his current team and was prevented from negotiating a contract with any other professional team. Eight of the players for the Chicago White Sox began to feel such resentment toward their owner that they decided to enter into a conspiracy to throw the World Series of 1919 in exchange for large sums of cash from professional gamblers (Linder, "Black Sox").

The idea of a conspiracy to throw the World Series allegedly began with a conversation toward the end of the 1919 baseball season between the first baseman for the White Sox, Chick Gandil, and a professional gambler named "Sport" Sullivan. It is not known who initially suggested the idea of losing the World Series on purpose but, by the end of the conversation, Gandil had agreed to recruit several players who would throw the World Series in exchange for $80,000 each (Asinof and Gould 2000, 6–9).

Gandil spoke first with Eddie Cicotte, the star pitcher for the White Sox, who had been cheated out of the bonus by Comiskey. Because Cicotte hated Comiskey and also had financial troubles, he agreed to participate in the conspiracy but he wanted $10,000 from Sullivan before the World Series began. After Cicotte agreed to take part in the scheme, Gandil quickly recruited "Swede" Risberg, the team's shortstop and Fred McMullin, a reserve player. Because another starting pitcher was critical to the success of the conspiracy, Gandil persuaded Claude "Lefty" Williams to join as well. Finally, Gandil asked the three best hitters on the team, Buck Weaver, "Shoeless" Joe Jackson, and Oscar Felsch to have a discussion about throwing the World Series with the five players that had already signed on to the deal. Gandil's version of events detailed how all of the players agreed to participate in the fix of the World Series and perhaps even double cross the gamblers by getting the money up front and then winning the World Series anyway (Asinof and Gould 2000, 16–38).

When Gandil met with the professional gambler, Sullivan, to inform him that the players had agreed to lose the World Series and also that they wanted $80,000 in advance, Sullivan did not think that he could raise this much cash so quickly. When another gambler, Bill Burns, heard about the possible conspiracy, he approached Cicotte and stated that he would advance the players $100,000 to beat Sullivan's potential offer. Gandil and Cicotte agreed to take the $100,000 after Burns secured the finances for the fix from the most important sports gambler of his time, Arnold Rothstein. However, Rothstein had serious concerns about whether the World Series could be thrown successfully by the recruited players. When Rothstein refused to provide the money for the conspiracy, one of his assistants, Abe Attell, a former professional boxer, decided to deceive Burns and the players for the White Sox by telling them that Rothstein would provide the money. Attell was hoping that his lie would provide an opportunity to make some cash for himself (Asinof and Gould 2000, 26–44).

Meanwhile, "Sport" Sullivan separately approached Rothstein about providing the money for the initial plan between Sullivan and the players participating in the fix. Because Sullivan was more respected than Burns, Rothstein agreed to provide the advance money. Hence, two different gamblers had approached Rothstein about bankrolling the conspiracy with only Sullivan acquiring the money from Rothstein. However, both Burns and Sullivan independent of each other told the players that Rothstein would provide the money in advance. Burns actually believed that he would receive the money from Rothstein to give to the players but he was, in fact, being deceived by Attell, acting as an intermediary between Burns and Rothstein (Linder, "Black Sox").

Rothstein agreed to provide the $80,000 to the players through "Sport" Sullivan, but only $40,000 would distributed among the players in advance, while the other half of the money would be placed in a safe in Chicago and given to the players after the White Sox lost the World Series to the Cincinnati Reds. Instead of giving the $40,000 to the White Sox players, Sullivan performed a double cross by only giving $10,000 of the money to the players and betting the remaining $30,000 for himself on the Reds. Rothstein then placed $270,000 worth of his own bets in favor of the Reds to defeat the White Sox in the 1919 World Series (Linder, "Black Sox").

On October 1, 1919, in the first inning of Game 1, Cicotte, the starting pitcher for the White Sox, hit the first batter for the Reds as a sign to Rothstein that the White Sox were going to throw the World Series. Prior to the first game of the World Series, Eddie Cicotte had found $10,000 under the pillow in his hotel room. The Reds easily won the first game of the series, 9–1. Several suspicious plays were noticed by Comiskey, the team's owner, including a ball thrown high to second base by Cicotte on what should have been an easy double play. After the game, Comiskey asked the White Sox manager, Kid Gleason, if he thought that his team was about to lose the World Series on purpose (Linder "Black Sox").

In Game 2, the Cincinnati Reds defeated the White Sox 4–2 to take a 2–0 lead in the best-of-nine-games series. Again, a number of suspicious plays were evident, such as Gandil grounding out weakly twice at critical times in the game with runners in scoring position and less than one out. In addition, the starting pitcher for the White Sox, Lefty Williams, walked several Reds' batters even though he had demonstrated great control of his pitches during the season and also would not throw his curve ball when the White Sox catcher, Ray Schalk, had called for the pitch consistently throughout the game. After the second game, Gandil found $10,000 in his hotel room that had been placed there by Bill Burns (Linder, Black Sox").

Game 3 saw the White Sox defeat the Reds 3–0 based upon the fact that Gandil and the other players recruited into the fix were supposedly angered by the fact that they had only received a small portion of the money promised by the gamblers. Gandil played a key part in the victory by driving in two runs for the White Sox (Linder, "Black Sox").

Prior to the fourth game of the series, Gandil told Sullivan that he wanted $20,000 or else the players would end the conspiracy and try to win the World Series. Sullivan provided the money and Gandil divided the money between Risberg, Felsch, Williams, and Jackson. In Game 4, Cicotte, starting his second game of the series, suspiciously threw a ball away to first base and even stepped in front of a ball on its way to home plate that would have prevented a Reds' player from scoring. In Game 5, Felsch made critical errors when he misplayed two fly balls and Risberg made another error when he let a throw from Felsch get by him. Cincinnati won 2–0 in Game 4 and 5–0 in Game 5 to take a 4–1 lead in the series (Linder, "Black Sox").

When the gamblers did not provide any more money for the players after Game 5, the White Sox players decided that they would try to win the World Series after all. Games 6 and 7 provided no suspicious plays as the White Sox won Game 6 by a score of 5–4 and Game 7 by a 4–1 margin. Rothstein became worried that he would lose his $270,000 bet on the Reds so he instructed Sullivan to hire a thug to intimidate the Game 8 starting pitcher for the White Sox, "Lefty" Williams, into making certain that a Game 9 was not necessary. The thug threatened Williams with physical harm if he did not throw Game 8. Williams did not last one inning of Game 8 and was removed after the Reds built a 4–0 lead. The Cincinnati Reds won Game 8 with a 10–5 victory and captured the 1919 World Series (Linder, "Black Sox").

References

Asinof, Eliot, and Stephen Jay Gould. *Eight Men Out: The Black Sox and the 1919 World Series.* New York: Holt, 2000.

The Baseball Page.com. "Buck Weaver." *Player Pages.* http://www.thebaseballpage.com/players/weavebu01.php (accessed August 11, 2009).

Biography. "George Daniel 'Buck' Weaver." *ClearBuck.com.* http://www.clearbuck.com/bio.htm (accessed August 11, 2009).

Carney, Gene. *Burying the Black Sox: How Baseball's Cover-up of the 1919 World Series Fix Almost Succeeded.* Washington, D.C.: Potomac Books, 2006.

Chermak, Stephen M., and Frankie Y. Bailey. *Crimes and Trials of the Century.* Westport, CT: Greenwood Press, 2007.

Cotton, Doyice J., and John Wolohan, eds. *Law for Recreation and Sport Managers.* Dubuque, IA: Kendall/Hunt Publishing Company, 2006.

Encyclopedia Topics. "Charles A. Comiskey." *Reference.com.* http://www.reference.com/browse/Charles+A+Comiskey (accessed August 10, 2009).

Fleitz, David L. *Shoeless: The Life and Times of Joe Jackson.* Jefferson, NC: McFarland and Company, 2001.

Ginsburg, Daniel E. *The Fix Is In: A History of Baseball Gambling and Game Fixing Scandals.* Jefferson, NC: McFarland and Company, 2004.

Linder, Douglas O. "The Big Money Behind the Fix: Arnold Rothstein." *The Black Sox Trial: Biographies of Key Figures.* http://www.law.umkc.edu/faculty/projects/ftrials/blacksox/biographies.html (accessed August 12, 2009).

Linder, Douglas O. "The Black Sox Trial: An Account." *Famous Trials.* http://www.law.umkc.edu/faculty/projects/ftrials/blacksox/blacksoxaccount.html (accessed March 2, 2009).

Linder, Douglas O. "President of the White Sox: Charles Comiskey." *The Black Sox Trial: Biographies of Key Figures.* http://www.law.umkc.edu/faculty/projects/ftrials/blacksox/biographies.html (accessed August 10, 2009).

Pietrusza, David. *Rothstein: The Life and Times, and Murder of the Criminal Genius Who Fixed the 1919 World Series.* New York: Carroll and Graf Publishers, 2004.

Sagart, Kelly Boyer. *Joe Jackson: A Biography.* Westport, CT: Greenwood Publishing Group, 2004.

Stein, Irving. *The Ginger Kid: The Buck Weaver Story.* Dubuque, IA: Brown and Benchmark, 1992.

Tucker, Ken, *Scarface Nation: The Ultimate Gangster Movie and How It Changed America.* New York: St. Martin's Griffin, 2008.

Sacco and Vanzetti Trial (1921)

The trial of Nicola Sacco and Bartolomeo Vanzetti, in 1921, was historic in the sense that a mystery continues to surround the truth about the murder trial of the two Italian immigrants who may have been wrongfully convicted and executed for a crime that they did not commit. The Sacco and Vanzetti trial raised serious issues concerning due process and fair trial rights for European immigrants who faced discrimination in America. In addition, the early part of the 20th century saw the Bolshevik Revolution of 1917 in Russia create an environment of fear in the United States where anarchists, socialists, and communists became the focus of criminal investigations (Chermak and Bailey 2007, 19–20).

On April 15, 1920, Frederick Parmenter, a paymaster, and Alessandro Berardelli, his security guard, were in the process of delivering envelopes of payroll money to workers at a shoe manufacturing company in Braintree, Massachusetts. As Parmenter and Berardelli were walking down the street toward the shoe factory, two gunmen shot and murdered the paymaster and his guard and stole two boxes containing the envelopes with approximately $30,000 worth of cash. According to witnesses, the two gunmen proceeded to enter the backseat of a blue car with the two boxes and drove away from the murder scene (Linder, "Trial of Sacco and Vanzetti").

A few days after the murder, police located a blue Buick with no license plates that had been abandoned in a wooded area in West Bridgewater, Massachusetts, several miles south of the crime scene. Police discovered that the vehicle had been stolen and may have been the blue car involved in the murders of Parmenter and Berardelli (Linder, "Trial of Sacco and Vanzetti").

On May 5, Sacco and Vanzetti were arrested by Brockport police after witnesses in Bridgewater observed the two men acting suspiciously while boarding a streetcar headed for Brockport. Sacco and Vanzetti both were carrying loaded revolvers at the time of their arrests. Vanzetti also had in his possession information regarding an anarchist meeting. District Attorney Frederick Katzmann questioned the two men and grew suspicious when they failed to provide a legitimate reason about why they had been in Bridgewater with loaded weapons. Katzmann also discovered that Sacco had not reported to work on April 15, the day of the murders. Therefore, it appeared that Katzmann may have found at least two of the persons responsible for the murders in Braintree (Linder, "Trial of Sacco and Vanzetti").

Carlo Tresca, a leader within the anarchist movement, worked with a defense legal committee to hire a well-known lawyer, Fred Moore, and the goal was to build political support for the idea that Sacco and Vanzetti were being tried because they were immigrants and connected to the anarchist movement, not necessarily because they had actually committed the murders. Leading up to the trial, Tresca and Moore attempted to gain publicity by informing the anarchist and immigrant populations that Sacco and Vanzetti were unjustly accused of the murder charges (Russell 1986, 24–25).

The Sacco and Vanzetti trial officially began on May 31, 1921, in Dedham, Massachusetts, presided over by Judge Webster Thayer. The prosecutor, Frederick Katzmann, introduced his case before the jury by presenting several witnesses who testified that they saw Sacco and Vanzetti near the Braintree area around the time of the murder. A few other witnesses testified that Sacco resembled one of the gunmen, but they refused to say whether they were absolutely certain in their identification. Other circumstantial evidence introduced by the prosecution included Sacco's absence from work on the day of the murders, a gray cap found at the crime scene that was similar to a cap Sacco used to wear and, prior to their arrest, Sacco and Vanzetti had visited an automobile repair shop that was connected to the stolen Buick used as a getaway car (Linder, "Trial of Sacco and Vanzetti").

Sacco and Vanzetti also produced suspicious information when they were questioned by investigators. For example, the two defendants lied about their connections to socialists and anarchists and denied their friendship with the owner of the automobile repair shop (Russell 1986, 62–64). They also provided confusing statements regarding the handguns in their possession at the time of their arrest. Sacco had in his possession a Colt revolver, and a third bullet ("bullet #3") found in one of the victims had been fired from a Colt (101). Vanzetti told two different stories about where he purchased his handgun and how many bullets fit into the chamber. The prosecution speculated that Vanzetti was lying because his weapon was very similar to the one taken from the security guard after he was murdered (98–99).

The only piece of physical evidence against one of the defendants involved the prosecution's use of a ballistics expert to show that "bullet #3" probably was fired from Sacco's Colt handgun based upon the unique markings on bullets produced from Sacco's weapon (Russell 1986, 98–102). A medical expert compared hairs found in the gray cap discovered at the crime scene and concluded that they matched Sacco's hair but the prosecution chose not to introduce this physical evidence because this type of forensic science was not well developed and was viewed as unreliable in 1921 (Linder, "Trial of Sacco and Vanzetti").

The defense attorneys countered with witnesses that testified Sacco was in Boston and Vanzetti was in Plymouth at the time of the murders. The defense also attempted to disprove the testimony of the ballistics expert by calling two ballistics experts of their own who argued that "bullet #3" could not have come from Sacco's weapon (Russell 1986, 101–102). In regard to the gray cap, the defense maintained that the cap could have been owned by someone in the crowd who gathered around the crime scene after the murder. Finally, the inconsistent statements made by Sacco and Vanzetti to investigators after their arrest were based upon the fact that the two defendants were afraid that they would be deported once it was revealed that they were associated with socialists and anarchists (Russell 1986, 102).

The most dramatic part of the trial involved testimony from Sacco and Vanzetti who spoke in broken English about their belief in socialism and anarchism as well as their hatred of capitalism. Sacco specifically repeated how wealthy people had all of the advantages in society such as education and better living conditions, while working class people suffered with no opportunity for advancement (Linder "Trial of Sacco and Vanzetti").

In the end, the ballistics expert who testified for the prosecution seemed to have the most impact on the jury of 12 men who found Sacco and Vanzetti guilty of murder in the first degree on July 14, 1921 (Frankfurter 2003, 8). After the guilty verdict, international protests occurred around the world with the largest demonstrations held in Italy and France. Anarchists set off a bomb at the U.S. embassy in Paris, France, and a second bomb intended for U.S. officials in Portugal was intercepted by authorities. Defense attorneys filed several motions for a new trial but Judge Thayer rejected all of the motions (Linder, "Trial of Sacco and Vanzetti").

When a prisoner named Celestino Madeiros, who was serving time in the Dedham jail with Sacco, confessed to having committed the murders with four other individuals, it appeared that Sacco and Vanzetti might be able to receive a new trial (Russell 1986, 127–128). However, Madeiros's statements to authorities supposedly contradicted some basic facts about the murders. For instance, Madeiros said that he and the others didn't arrive in Braintree until the afternoon when, in fact, witnesses testified that the individuals who committed the crime had been seen in Braintree throughout the morning on the day of the murders. Madeiros also described the money stolen from the paymaster as having been inside a black bag, but it was common knowledge that the money was being carried in a metal container (129–130).

The Madeiros confession produced more outrage from working-class people around the world who believed that Sacco and Vanzetti had been unjustly tried and convicted (Russell 1986, 132–133). The public response caused Governor Alvan Fuller of Massachusetts to appoint A. Lawrence Lowell, the president of Harvard University, to head a three-person committee to investigate the possibility that Sacco and Vanzetti were wrongfully convicted. The Lowell Committee concluded that Sacco and Vanzetti were both guilty beyond a reasonable doubt, although the committee seemed to imply that it was less confident in Vanzetti's guilt. On August 3, 1927, Governor Fuller decided against clemency for the two defendants (136).

Sacco and Vanzetti were executed in the electric chair on August 23, 1927, at Charlestown State prison. Prior to the executions, Sacco proclaimed his loyalty to the anarchist movement, while Vanzetti asserted his innocence. After the executions, thousands of people demonstrated all over the globe, and violent protests occurred in such countries as Germany, France, and Switzerland (Linder, "Trial of Sacco and Vanzetti").

Francis Russell, a historian who is considered the leading expert on the Sacco-Vanzetti trial, produced a classic analysis entitled *Sacco & Vanzetti: The Case Resolved* (1986). Russell examined the trial transcripts and physical evidence and also conducted countless interviews with persons involved in the proceedings. Russell concluded that Sacco was guilty, while Vanzetti was innocent (Russell 1986, 1–10). The Harvard University president, A. Lawrence Lowell, also admitted that the case against Vanzetti was mostly circumstantial, or based upon indirect evidence, which usually creates enough doubt to produce a not guilty verdict from a jury. Furthermore, leaders within the anarchist movement, such as Carlo Tresca, revealed to investigators in the early 1940s that it was common knowledge among their members that Sacco committed the murders, but Vanzetti spoke the truth about his innocence (Russell 1986, 27–31). In 1961, advanced ballistics tests were conducted on the Colt revolver owned by Sacco, and the results confirmed that "bullet #3" was fired from Sacco's weapon (Linder, "Trial of Sacco and Vanzetti").

Regardless of the various theories surrounding the guilt or innocence of the defendants, Sacco and Vanzetti probably did not receive a fair trial. Katzmann, the lead prosecutor, often referred to the defendants' radical beliefs during the trial and appealed to the jury's sense of patriotism in asking them to return a verdict of guilty. In addition, Judge Thayer supposedly referred to the defendants as "anarchist bastards" privately. In the modern era, the pretrial publicity emphasizing the radical beliefs of the defendants may have forced the trial to be moved outside of Massachusetts and the defendants today would have attracted criminal defense attorneys with exceptional skills who may have been able to secure an acquittal, even for Sacco. Unfortunately, the lead defense attorney, Fred Moore, provided ineffective legal representation when he decided not to emphasize the weak case against Vanzetti because he feared that, by comparison, it would have guaranteed a guilty verdict for Sacco. In addition to a questionable legal strategy, the fact that Sacco and Vanzetti faced prejudice because they were uneducated immigrants connected to political groups with controversial views made it highly unlikely that the two defendants could have received a fair trial in New England in the early 20th century (Frankfurter 2003, 46). On August 23, 1977, the 50th anniversary of the executions, Governor Michael Dukakis of Massachusetts issued a proclamation to remove the disgrace attached to the names of the defendants when he stated that "the high standards of justice" were not met in the trial (Russell 1986, 8–10).

References

Chermak, Steven M., and Frankie Y. Bailey. *Crimes and Trials of the Century.* Westport, CT: Greenwood Publishing Group, 2007.

Frankfurter, Felix. *The Case of Sacco and Vanzetti: A Critical Analysis for Lawyers and Laymen.* Buffalo, NY: William S. Hein and Company, 2003.

Linder, Douglas O. "The Trial of Sacco and Vanzetti." *Famous Trials.* http://www.law.umkc.edu/faculty/projects/ftrials/SaccoV/s&vaccount.html (accessed March 26, 2009).

Russell, Francis. *Sacco & Vanzetti: The Case Resolved.* New York: Harper and Row, 1986.

Bartolomeo Vanzetti: Court Statement (1927)

Italian immigrants and self-professed anarchists, Nicola Sacco and Bartolomeo Vanzetti were tried and convicted for murder in Massachusetts in the early 1920s. The case proved a controversial one, as many Americans grew to suspect that the two men had been condemned for their political beliefs rather than their supposed crime. Such suspicions received confirmation from the shaky evidence used to incriminate them. Nevertheless, in the face of criticism from high-profile figures around the world, Sacco and Vanzetti were executed on August 23, 1927. Vanzetti made this statement, an excerpt of which appears below, shortly before his death.

Now, I should say that I am not only innocent of all these things, not only have I never committed a real crime in my life—though some sins but not crimes—not only have I struggled all my life to eliminate crimes, the crimes that the officials and the official moral condemns, but also the crime that the official moral and the official law sanctions and sanctifies—the exploitation and the oppression of the man by the man, and if there is a reason why I am here as a guilty man, if there is a reason why you in a few minutes can doom me, it is this reason and none else. . . .

We were tried during a time that has now passed into history. I mean by that, a time when there was a hysteria of resentment and hate against the people of our principles, against the foreigner, against slackers. . . .

Well, I have already said that I not only am not guilty . . . but I never commit a crime in my life—I have never stole and I have never killed and I have never spilt blood, and I have fought against crime and I have fought and have sacrificed myself even to eliminate the crimes the law and the church legitimate and sanctify.

This is what I say: I would not wish to a dog or to a snake, to the most low and misfortunate creature of the earth—I would not wish to any of them what I have had to suffer for things that I am not guilty of. But my conviction is that I have suffered for things I am guilty of. I am suffering because I am a radical and indeed I am a radical; I have suffered because I was an Italian, and indeed I am an Italian; I have suffered more for my family and for my beloved than for myself; but I am so convinced to be right that if you could execute me two times, and if I could be reborn two other times, I would live again to do what I have done already.

I have finished. Thank you.

Fatty Arbuckle Trials (1921–1922)

The three criminal trials of Roscoe Conkling "Fatty" Arbuckle for rape and manslaughter were sensationalized by the tabloid newspapers, which emphasized the lack of morality in the lifestyles of film celebrities as a means toward increasing their circulation. Unfortunately, the lurid details about the lifestyles of the Hollywood celebrities overshadowed the fact that an innocent man was unjustly tried for a serious crime because of one woman's attempt to extort money. In the end, the trials destroyed the character and professional career of "Fatty" Arbuckle and also brought about the self-regulation of the Hollywood movie industry (Law Library, "'Fatty' Arbuckle Trials").

"Fatty" Arbuckle was the most popular comedian of his time who starred in silent films. In 1918, he signed an unprecedented contract to make $3 million per year (Law Library, "'Fatty' Arbuckle Trials"). In 1921, Arbuckle held a party in three rooms at the St. Francis Hotel in San Francisco on Labor Day weekend. A young actress named Virginia Rappe attended the party with her friend, Maude Delmont. Supposedly, Rappe drank too much alcohol at the party and became ill, suffering terrible stomach pains. Rappe was taken to a hospital where she died three days later of an inflammation of the stomach tissue caused by a ruptured bladder (Yallop 1976, 108–116).

Rappe's friend, Maude Delmont, filed a complaint against Arbuckle accusing him of sexually assaulting Rappe at the party and eventually causing her death. The district attorney for San Francisco, Matthew Brady, asked a grand jury to charge Arbuckle with rape or attempted rape in a hotel room based upon the complaint filed by Delmont. Because Arbuckle weighed over 260 pounds, Brady maintained that the actor's weight on top of Rappe's body caused the ruptured bladder which led to her death (Yallop 1976, 150–154). Unfortunately, Brady had disregarded an autopsy report that concluded Rappe's body showed no signs of rape or violence. The report also stated that she died of a ruptured bladder as a result of natural causes (Law Library, "'Fatty' Arbuckle Trials").

Another problem for District Attorney Brady was the fact that he was unaware that, prior to Rappe's death, Delmont wrote a telegram to two attorneys describing how she was going to blackmail Arbuckle. Delmont's plan was to withdraw the complaint against Arbuckle in exchange for money. The complaint filed by Delmont was a complete lie. When the media published Brady's statement of the criminal charges, Brady knew that the trial of manslaughter against Arbuckle would create an international scandal to ensure the publicity necessary to launch his political career. Ironically, while Delmont was the key source of information in the decision to prosecute Arbuckle, Brady could not call her as a witness because she would be easily discredited since the extortion telegrams had been obtained by Arbuckle's attorneys. Delmont also had a history of criminal activity, including fraud and extortion. Since Brady could not rely upon his star witness, he made public statements to the tabloid newspapers that Arbuckle was guilty and supposedly pressured witnesses into lying about Arbuckle's behavior at the party (Law Library, "'Fatty' Arbuckle Trials").

Regardless of the fact that Arbuckle was probably innocent of the charges, movie theatres and film organizations as well as entire states banned the showing of Arbuckle's films. Arbuckle had been convicted in the court of public opinion due to the newspaper and tabloid coverage of the scandal led by the *Los Angeles Examiner*. The *Examiner* was owned by William Randolph Hearst, who was largely responsible for starting the trend of "yellow journalism" in the United States in the late 19th century. "Yellow journalism" was a term used to describe news coverage that was exaggerated, sensational, and unprofessional. Hearst's news publications sacrificed integrity in favor of boosting circulation to increase profits (Yallop 1976, 138–142). As a result of the biased news coverage destroying the character of

Arbuckle, he became a target for women's rights groups and religious ministers and symbolized the decline of moral values in society (Law Library, "'Fatty' Arbuckle Trials").

When a judge issued his statement regarding whether to hold Arbuckle over for trial, he remarked that there was little evidence against Arbuckle to justify a trial but, in the interests of judging the morality of America and its institutions, Arbuckle should be tried for manslaughter. Therefore, the trial became a judgment on the guilt or innocence of society, as opposed to one individual (Law Library, "'Fatty' Arbuckle Trials").

The first trial of Fatty Arbuckle began on November 14, 1921, in front of Judge Harold Louderback and saw 60 witnesses testify, including several physicians. The prosecutor's case was based largely upon circumstantial, or indirect, evidence. For example, prosecutors called upon Betty Campbell, a model who attended the party, to testify that she saw Arbuckle smiling after the alleged rape. Campbell would later recant her testimony by stating that Brady threatened to file perjury charges against her if she refused to testify. Next, a nurse from the hospital who examined Rappe testified that Arbuckle probably killed Rappe by bruising her body with his weight. Finally, a criminologist claimed that he discovered Arbuckle's bloody fingerprints on the bathroom door of the hotel room, and a physician from the hotel also testified that Rappe's bladder appeared to have been injured by physical force. However, a maid testified that she cleaned the hotel room prior to the investigation, which called into question the fingerprint, and the hotel doctor also stated on cross-examination that Rappe never mentioned to him that she had been sexually assaulted. Obviously, the prosecution had no real, or direct, evidence against Arbuckle (Law Library, "'Fatty' Arbuckle Trials").

Defense attorneys, led by Gavin McNab, could have easily destroyed the credibility of the alleged victim, Virginia Rappe, by introducing as evidence her promiscuous lifestyle, which included heavy drinking, dancing naked at parties, sexually transmitted diseases, abortions, and an illegitimate child. However, the defense team refused to pursue this strategy in the first trial because it thought that the jury might react negatively toward Arbuckle if they tried to destroy the credibility of Rappe. Arbuckle also refused to allow his defense attorneys to proceed with this strategy during the first trial out of respect for the alleged victim (Yallop 1976, 223).

Arbuckle testified in his own defense by telling the jury that he attempted to help Rappe when he found her ill and vomiting in the hotel bathroom. Arbuckle said that he carried her to the bed until a doctor arrived and concluded that Rappe was simply intoxicated (Yallop 1976, 225–231). Medical doctors also testified for the defense by maintaining that inflammation in Rappe's bladder caused the rupture which led to her death (Law Library, "'Fatty' Arbuckle Trials").

The jury deliberated for nearly two days but was dismissed by Judge Louderback on December 4, 1921, after it failed to produce a unanimous verdict. The deadlock was supposedly caused by one woman, Helen Hubbard. Hubbard's husband was a lawyer who conducted legal business with the prosecutor's office, which should have automatically excluded her from serving on the jury. Hubbard expressed her bias openly when she told the other jurors that she believed Arbuckle was guilty on the day of his arrest. Hubbard was able to convince only one other juror to vote with her prior to the judge declaring a mistrial (Yallop 1976, 239–241).

Surprisingly, the district attorney tried Arbuckle a second time in the courtroom of Judge Louderback with the trial beginning on January 11, 1922. The same witnesses were presented in the second trial, but two witnesses for the prosecution did come forward and state that they were coerced by Brady to testify against Arbuckle. Another victory for the defense team occurred when the alleged fingerprint of Arbuckle on the bedroom door of the hotel room was excluded as evidence because the criminologist who found the fingerprint reversed himself in the second trial and stated that it was probably a fake. The defense team made a mistake, however, in deciding not to allow Arbuckle to testify in the second trial. Most of the jurors assumed that Arbuckle was guilty because he refused to testify. Arbuckle's sincere testimony in the first trial had been viewed by the jurors as a critical reason for voting 10–2 in favor of acquittal. On February 3, 1922, the jury in the second trial also deadlocked by a vote of 9–3 in favor of conviction (Law Library, "'Fatty' Arbuckle Trials").

A third trial started on March 13, 1922, again with Judge Louderback presiding over the proceedings. In the third trial, the defense attorneys wisely decided to let Arbuckle testify to provide his account of what transpired in the San Francisco hotel room on Labor Day in 1921. Gavin McNab also finally provided the details about the immoral lifestyle of Rappe and made his strongest reference to date about the fraudulent complaint filed by Maude Delmont. McNab referred to Delmont as "the complaining witness that never witnessed" (Yallop 1976, 252–253).

On April 12, 1922, the jury deliberated for five minutes, returning with an acquittal for Arbuckle on the manslaughter charges. The jury foreman read a statement compiled by all of the jurors that tried to go further than a simple acquittal. The jury apologized for the injustice that had been done to Arbuckle who could not have committed the crime because there was no evidence to support a conviction. The jury concluded their statement by emphasizing that Arbuckle was entirely believable in his testimony and completely innocent of the charges filed against him (Yallop 1976, 252–254).

Many legal scholars consider the Fatty Arbuckle trials to be the most important celebrity trials of the 20th century. The trials resulted in the creation of the Production, or Hays, Code in 1930 where the Hollywood movie industry began self-regulation to determine morally acceptable content of films for the American public. The trials also told the story of unethical prosecutors and the irresponsible media who took a complaint from a witness with no credibility and used her complaint to manipulate public opinion and the criminal justice system for their own purposes. While justice was finally served after the three trials, Arbuckle's personal reputation and film career were ruined. With mounting legal debts, he was forced to work behind the scenes as a movie producer under a different name. In 1933, Arbuckle was on the verge of a comeback after he signed a deal to make several films for Warner Brothers. However, he suffered a heart attack two months later and died (Law Library, "'Fatty' Arbuckle Trials").

References

Law Library–American Law and Legal Information. "'Fatty' Arbuckle Trials: 1921– 1922." *Great American Trials.* Vol. 1. http://law.jrank.org/pages/2839/-Fatty-Arbuck le-Trials-1921–22.html (accessed April 12, 2009).

Oderman, Stuart. *Roscoe "Fatty" Arbuckle: A Biography of the Silent Film Comedian, 1887–1933.* Jefferson, NC: McFarland and Company, 2005.

Yallop, David A. *The Day the Laughter Stopped.* New York: St. Martin's Press, 1976.

Nathan F. Leopold Jr. and Richard Loeb Trial (1924)

The trial of Nathan F. Leopold Jr. and Richard Loeb was sensational in the sense that it involved two teenage defendants from wealthy families facing the death penalty for kidnapping and murder. The murder and subsequent trial captured the attention of the nation for two months and became one of the first "trials of the century" in the 20th century. The trial of the two defendants from privileged backgrounds revealed the bias in the American criminal justice system that continues even today. The wealthy and socially connected families of the defendants were able to hire the best defense attorney in the United States in an attempt to save the lives of their children. As a result, Leopold and Loeb were spared the death penalty. If the young men had been raised in poverty and represented by lesser attorneys, they most certainly would have been executed for their horrible crime (Law Library, "Leopold and Loeb Trial").

Richard Loeb, age 18, and Nathan Leopold, age 19, were gay lovers from upper-class families in Chicago, Illinois. Loeb and Leopold also were young men with a college education and extraordinary intelligence. However, they both maintained a fascination with crime. Leopold and Loeb decided to kidnap and murder a high school student from a wealthy family and demand a ransom by telling the parents that the child was still alive. The crime was basically an intellectual exercise for the two men who sought to challenge the moral values of society by committing the perfect crime simply for the thrill and excitement (Linder, "Leopold and Loeb Trial").

On May 21, 1924, Leopold and Loeb abducted 14-year-old Bobby Franks, who was someone that they knew only as an acquaintance. When Leopold and Loeb saw Franks walking home from his private school in the Hyde Park district, Loeb talked Franks into coming over to their rented automobile. Loeb asked Franks about a tennis racquet because the two had played tennis together and then invited Franks into the car for a ride around the block. When Franks entered the vehicle, one of the two men struck Franks in the head with a heavy chisel. Franks was then suffocated to death with a gag by one of the two men (Chermak and Bailey 2007, 76).

Leopold and Loeb drove to the Illinois-Indiana border and burned Franks's face with acid to prevent identification of the victim and placed his body in a drainage sewer near the Pennsylvania Railroad tracks. Franks's personal items such as his belt and shoes were discarded in Indiana and his clothes were later burned in the basement of Loeb's home. After telephone calls were made to the parents of Bobby Franks, a ransom note was delivered asking for $10,000 in unmarked bills. Before the father of Bobby Franks could deliver the ransom money, however, the body of Bobby Franks was discovered when a railroad worker noticed a foot sticking out of the drainage sewer (Linder, "Leopold and Loeb Trial").

Fortunately, police investigators found a pair of horn-rimmed eyeglasses near the body of Bobby Franks. Apparently, the eyeglasses had fallen out of Leopold's pocket as he was disposing of the body. Because the eyeglasses were unique, they were easily traced to a Chicago optometrist who had ordered the eyeglasses for Leopold. Leopold told the police that he must have dropped the eyeglasses when he was bird watching (Chermak and Bailey 2007, 78–79). Leopold told police that he was driving around in his car with Loeb looking for girls at Lincoln Park on the day of Franks's murder. Both young men confirmed each other's alibi (Linder, "Leopold and Loeb Trial").

Police were almost convinced that Loeb and Leopold were not involved in the murder, but then the *Chicago Daily News* discovered in their own investigation that Leopold had typed notes on a typewriter for a law-school study group. A typewriter expert matched the type on the law school notes with the type on the ransom note sent to the parents of Bobby Franks. Additional information also surfaced when police questioned Sven Englund, the chauffeur for the Leopold family, who revealed that Leopold's car was being repaired on the day of the murder (Chermak and Bailey 2007, 79). Englund had also seen the two young men cleaning a strange car on the same day. The chauffeur had unwittingly implicated Leopold in the murder because, if the car was being repaired, Leopold could not have been driving around in his car with Loeb on the day of the murder (Law Library, "Leopold and Loeb Trial").

Police were able to secure a confession from Loeb first, and then Leopold also confessed. However, each of the young men said that the other committed the murder. Leopold and Loeb appeared to take great pride in showing the police and media where they hid the physical evidence such as Franks's personal items, the chisel, and the rubber boots used by the defendants to walk through mud in order to dispose of the body in the sewer. At one point during the investigation, Leopold compared the murder of Franks to a scientist killing an insect. Neither Leopold nor Loeb expressed any remorse for the murder of the young boy (Chermak and Bailey 2007, 81).

The wealthy families of the two young men hired Clarence Darrow for $100,000 to provide legal representation (Law Library, "Leopold and Loeb Trial"). Darrow was the most famous defense attorney in the United States and an opponent of the death penalty. Benjamin Bachrach, an attorney who was a cousin to Leopold, also provided legal counsel for the defense (Chermak and Bailey 2007, 80).

The state of Illinois decided to charge Leopold and Loeb with kidnapping and murder. Both crimes made the young men eligible for death by hanging. Initially, the two defendants entered pleas of not guilty, but Darrow convinced the young men to change their pleas to guilty so that a judge would decide the sentence, instead of a jury of 12 persons. Darrow knew that Judge John R. Caverly could be convinced to issue a life sentence, not a death sentence, because he had a history of treating young offenders with sympathy. Because public opinion was strongly in favor of executing Leopold and Loeb, Darrow did not want to face a jury that would most likely impose a death sentence for both defendants. The decision to impose a death sentence would more likely come from a jury where the responsibility was divided between 12 persons. However, a judge was less likely to order an execution because the weight of the decision rested heavily on one person (Linder, "Leopold and Loeb Trial").

While the guilt of the two defendants was a settled issue because of the confessions, the issue of whether Leopold and Loeb should receive the death penalty would be determined by the expert testimony of psychiatrists. The defense strategy was designed to prove that both young men were mentally unstable in order to avoid a death sentence (Linder, "Leopold and Loeb Trial"). Darrow planned upon calling the president of the American Psychiatric Association to testify for the defense as well as other famous psychiatrists who developed a profile of his clients that showed serious psychological problems and conflicted personalities. Prosecutors, in turn, would present the best psychiatrists in the city of Chicago who would argue that the young men were relatively normal in terms of their mental function and, therefore, deserved to be executed for committing such a horrible crime (Law Library, "Leopold and Loeb Trial").

The trial, which was basically a sentencing hearing, began on July 23, 1924, with prosecutors presenting several witnesses who provided details of how Leopold and Loeb murdered Bobby Franks. The defense attorneys then used a parade of psychiatrists, regarded as the best in the country, to explain the psychological problems of the two defendants. The psychiatrists discussed how Leopold and

Loeb were extremely immature and insecure, almost childlike in their behavior, and were fascinated by the idea of criminal behavior (Linder, "Leopold and Loeb Trial"). The two young men had committed a variety of lesser offenses such as shoplifting, stealing automobiles, and burglary. Their minds were a combination of reality and fantasy with no emotional reaction to any of the crimes that they committed (Law Library, "Leopold and Loeb Trial"). Other psychiatrists detailed Leopold and Loeb's obsession with Friedrich Nietzsche, a philosopher whose ideas had been used to justify criminal behavior. Some scholars argued that Nietzsche actually encouraged persons of superior intelligence, referred to as "supermen," to behave as if the laws of good and evil did not apply to them. The prosecutors responded with their own psychiatrists who presented their diagnosis that Leopold and Loeb were sane in terms of their emotional responses and showed no signs of mental illness (Linder, "Leopold and Loeb Trial").

The most dramatic moment of the trial involved Darrow's closing statement where he pleaded for 12 hours with Judge Caverly to spare the lives of the two young men. Darrow emphasized the youth of Leopold and Loeb and argued that they had acted upon impulses predetermined by hereditary and environmental factors beyond their control. Darrow concluded by telling Judge Caverly that the death penalty was immoral, and the state of Illinois should not commit murder or else it was no better than Leopold and Loeb. Instead of vengeance, a progressive justice system should show mercy and issue a life sentence where the defendants would live within a depressing environment for the remainder of their years. According to court observers, Judge Caverly was emotionally moved by the passionate defense of Darrow who was trying courageously to save the lives of the two young men (Chermak and Bailey 2007, 86).

Robert Crowe, the state's attorney for Cook County, issued the closing statement for the prosecution by belittling Darrow's attempt to save the lives of the defendants. Crowe accused Darrow of making a career out of protecting murderers by using emotional speeches to disguise the facts of a case (Chermak and Bailey 2007, 87). Crowe made fun of Darrow's claim that Nietzsche, hereditary factors, or immoral influences from society were responsible for the murder. Crowe asserted that no one else was responsible for the murder, except for the defendants. The death penalty was the only just punishment for the premeditated murder of a young boy by two "cowardly perverts" (Linder, "Leopold and Loeb Trial").

On August 22, 1924, Judge Caverly ruled that Leopold and Loeb would not receive the death penalty but instead would serve a life sentence for murder and 99 years for the kidnapping. Judge Caverly based his decision upon the young age of the defendants and because the field of criminology could gain knowledge from studying the two subjects. After the verdict, Loeb and Leopold were taken to the Illinois State prison in Joliet, Illinois, to begin serving their life sentences (Linder, "The Leopold and Loeb Trial").

In 1936, Loeb was murdered by another prison inmate who slashed his throat with a razor. Loeb allegedly made sexual advances toward the inmate who was subsequently tried for murder in criminal court. A jury found the inmate not guilty and concluded that he murdered Loeb in self-defense (Linder, "Leopold and Loeb Trial"). Leopold became eligible for parole after the governor of Illinois, Adlai Stevenson, reduced his sentence in 1949 because Leopold participated in a medical experiment where he volunteered to be infected with malaria. Leopold was paroled in 1958 after 33 years in prison and moved to Puerto Rico to escape any publicity in the United States (Law Library, "Leopold and Loeb Trial").

While the Leopold and Loeb trial highlighted the advantage provided to wealthy defendants who could afford the best legal defense, it also provided the American legal system with one of the most passionate and eloquent arguments against capital punishment. Darrow's closing statement before Judge Caverly is considered to be his most famous speech. Throughout his career as a criminal defense attorney, Darrow's skills in the courtroom were so extraordinary that none of his defendants facing the death penalty were ever executed (Chermak and Bailey 2007, 81–86).

References

Chermak, Steven M., and Frankie Y. Bailey. *Crimes and Trials of the Century.* Westport, CT: Greenwood Press, 2007.

Higdon, Hal. *Leopold & Loeb: The Crime of the Century.* Urbana: University of Illinois Press, 1979.

Law Library–American Law and Legal Information. "Leopold and Loeb Trial: 1924." *Great American Trials.* Vol. 1. http://law.jrank.org/pages/2852/Leopold-Loeb-Trial-1924.html (accessed April 11, 2009).

Linder, Douglas O. "The Leopold and Loeb Trial: A Brief Account." *Famous Trials.* http://www.law.umkc.edu/faculty/projects/ftrials/leoploeb/Accountoftrial.html (accessed April 10, 2009).

Clarence Darrow: Mercy for Leopold and Loeb Speech (1924)

One of the most brilliant trial lawyers of his time, Clarence Darrow used his remarkable abilities in the courtroom to defend the common person. In the 1924 Leopold and Loeb trials, Darrow represented Nathan Leopold and Richard Loeb, the young sons of two wealthy and distinguished Chicago families, in "the crime of the century." Leopold and Loeb, who had murdered 14-year-old Bobby Franks, pleaded guilty to the crime. In order to avoid the death penalty for his clients, Darrow used psychiatric evidence to prove that Leopold and Loeb had been temporarily insane and won them sentences of life imprisonment. This was the first time an insanity plea had been successfully employed as a defense in a murder case in the United States.

Now, your Honor, I have spoken about the war. I believed in it. I don't know whether I was crazy or not. Sometimes I think perhaps I was. I approved of it; I joined in the general cry of madness and despair. I urged men to fight. I was safe because I was too old to go. I was like the rest. What did they do? Right or wrong, justifiable or unjustifiable—which I need not discuss to-day—it changed the world. For four long years the civilized world was engaged in killing men. Christian against Christian, barbarian uniting with Christians to kill Christians; anything to kill. It was taught in every school, aye in the Sunday schools. The little children played at war. The toddling children on the street. Do you suppose this world has ever been the same since then? How long, your Honor, will it take for the world to get back the humane emotions that were slowly growing before the war? How long will it take the calloused hearts of men before the scars of hatred and cruelty shall be removed?

We read of killing one hundred thousand men in a day. We read about it and we rejoiced in it—if it was the other fellows who were killed. We were fed on flesh and drank blood. Even down to the prattling babe. I need not tell your Honor this, because you know; I need not tell you how many upright, honorable young boys have come into this court charged with murder, some saved and some sent to their death, boys who fought in this war and learned to place a cheap value on human life. You know it and I know it. These boys were brought up in it. The tales of death were in their homes, their playgrounds, their schools; they were in the newspapers that they read; it was a part of the common frenzy—what was a life? It was nothing. It was the least sacred thing in existence and these boys were trained to this cruelty.

It will take fifty years to wipe it out of the human heart, if ever. I know this, that after the Civil War in 1865, crimes of this sort increased, marvelously. No one needs to tell me that crime has no cause. It has as definite a cause as any other disease, and I know that out of the hatred and bitterness of the Civil War crime increased as America had never known it before. I know that growing out of the Napoleonic wars there was an era of crime such as Europe had never seen before. I know that Europe is going through the same experience to-day; I know it has followed every war; and I know it has influenced these boys so that life was not the same to them as it would have been if the world had not been made red with blood. I protest against the crimes and mistakes of society being visited upon them. All of us have a share in it. I have mine. I cannot tell and I shall never know how many words of mine might have given birth to cruelty in place of love and kindness and charity.

Your Honor knows that in this very court crimes of violence have increased growing out of the war. Not necessarily by those who fought but by those that learned that blood was cheap, and human life was cheap, and if the State could take it lightly why not the boy? There are causes for this terrible crime. There are causes, as I have said, for everything that happens in the world. War is a part of it; education is a part of it; birth is a part of it; money is a part of it—all these conspired to compass the destruction of these two poor boys. Has the court any right to consider anything but these two boys? The State says that your Honor has a right to consider the welfare of the community, as you have. If the welfare of the community would be benefited by taking these lives, well and good. I think it would work evil that no one could measure. Has your Honor a right to consider the families of these two defendants? I have been sorry, and I am sorry for the bereavement of Mr. and Mrs. Frank, for those broken ties that cannot be healed. All I can hope and wish is that some good may come from it all. But as compared with the families of Leopold and Loeb, the Franks are to be envied—and everyone knows it.

I do not know how much salvage there is in these two boys. I hate to say it in their presence, but what is there to look forward to? I do not know but what your Honor would be merciful if you tied a rope around their necks and let them die; merciful to them, but not merciful to civilization, and not merciful to those who would be left behind. To spend the balance of their days in prison is mighty little to look forward to, if anything. Is it anything? They may have the hope that as the years roll around they might be released. I do not know. I do not know. I will be honest with this court as I have tried to be from the beginning. I know that these boys are not fit to be at large. I believe they will not be until they pass through the next stage of life, at forty-five or fifty. Whether they will then, I cannot tell. I am sure of this; that I will not be here to help them. So far as I am concerned, it is over.

I would not tell this court that I do not hope that some time, when life and age have changed their bodies, as they do, and have changed their emotions, as they do—that they may once more return to life. I would be the last person on earth to close the door of hope to any human being that lives, and least of all to my clients. But what have they to look forward to? Nothing. And I think here of the stanza of Housman:

Now hollow fires burn out to black,
And lights are fluttering low:
Square your shoulders, lift your pack
And leave your friends and go.
O never fear, lads, naught's to dread,
Look not left nor right:
In all the endless road you tread
There's nothing but the night.

I care not, your Honor, whether the march begins at the gallows or when the gates of Joliet close upon them, there is nothing but the night, and that is little for any human being to expect.

But there are others to consider. Here are these two families, who have led honest lives, who will bear the name that they bear, and future generations must carry it on.

Here is Leopold's father—and this boy was the pride of his life. He watched him, he cared for him, he worked for him; the boy was brilliant and accomplished, he educated him, and he thought that fame and position awaited him, as it should have awaited. It is a hard thing for a father to see his life's hopes crumble into dust.

Should he be considered? Should his brothers be considered? Will it do society any good or make your life safer, or any human being's life safer, if it should be handed down from generation to generation, that this boy, their kin, died upon the scaffold?

And Loeb's, the same. Here are the faithful uncle and brother, who have watched here day by day, while Dickie's father and his mother are too ill to stand this terrific strain, and shall be waiting for a message which means more to them than it can mean to you or me. Shall these be taken into account in this general bereavement?

Have they any rights? Is there any reason, your Honor, why their proud names and all the future generations that bear them shall have this bar sinister written across them? How many boys and girls, how many unborn children will feel it? It is bad enough as it is, God knows. It is bad enough, however it is. But it's not yet death on the scaffold. It's not that. And I ask your Honor, in addition to all that I have said, to save two honorable families from a disgrace that never ends, and which could be of no avail to help any human being that lives.

Now, I must say a word more and then I will leave this with you where I should have left it long ago. None of us are unmindful of the public; courts are not, and juries are not. We placed our fate in the hands of a trained court, thinking that he would be more mindful and considerate than a jury. I cannot say how people feel. I have stood here for three months as one might stand at the ocean trying to sweep back the tide. I hope the seas are subsiding and the wind is falling, and I believe they are, but I wish to make no false pretense to this court. The easy thing and the popular thing to do is to hang my clients. I know it. Men and women who do not think will applaud. The cruel and thoughtless will approve. It will be easy to-day; but in Chicago, and reaching out over the length and breadth of the land, more and more fathers and mothers, the humane, the kind and the hopeful, who are gaining an understanding and asking questions not only about these poor boys, but about their own—these will join in no acclaim at the death of my clients. These would ask that the shedding of blood be stopped, and that the normal feelings of man resume their sway. And as the days and the months and the years go on, they will ask it more and more. But, your Honor, what they shall ask may not count. I know the easy way. I know your Honor stands between the future and the past. I know the future is with me, and what I stand for here; not merely for the lives of these two unfortunate lads, but for all boys and all girls; for all of the young, and as far as possible, for all of the old. I am pleading for life, understanding, charity, kindness, and the infinite mercy that considers all. I am pleading that we overcome cruelty with kindness and hatred with love. I know the future is on my side. Your Honor stands between the past and the future. You may hang these boys; you may hang them by the neck until they are dead. But in doing it you will turn your face toward the past. In doing it you are making it harder for every other boy who in ignorance and darkness must grope his way through the mazes which only childhood knows. In doing it you will make it harder for unborn children. You may save them and make it easier for every child that sometime may stand where these boys stand. You will make it easier for every human being with an aspiration and a vision and a hope and a fate. I am pleading for the future; I am pleading for a time when hatred and cruelty will not control the hearts of men. When we can learn by reason and judgment and understanding and faith that all life is worth saving, and that mercy is the highest attribute of man.

I feel that I should apologize for the length of time I have taken. This case may not be as important as I think it is, and I am sure I do not need to tell this court, or to tell my friends that I would fight just as hard for the poor as for the rich. If I should succeed in saving these boys' lives and do nothing for the progress of the law, I should feel sad, indeed. If I can succeed, my greatest reward and my greatest hope will be that I have done something for the tens of thousands of other boys, for the countless unfortunates who must tread the same road in blind childhood that these poor boys have trod—that I have done something to help human understanding, to temper justice with mercy, to overcome hate with love.

I was reading last night of the aspiration of the old Persian poet, Omar Khayyam. It appealed to me as the highest that I can vision. I wish it was in my heart, and I wish it was in the hearts of all.

So I be written in the Book of Love,
I do not care about that Book above.
Erase my name or write it as you will,
So I be written in the Book of Love.

The Court-Martial Trial of General William Mitchell (1925)

The court-martial trial of General William Mitchell was the longest and most controversial military trial in American history. Mitchell was a visionary who predicted the Pearl Harbor attack of December 7, 1941, and tried to warn military leaders that the United States was unprepared for war, unless it developed its military aircraft. Mitchell's court-martial trial is a testament to the fact that military leaders do not receive criticism well and often are inflexible to changing technology. Today, Mitchell is regarded as the father of the modern U.S. Air Force as well as a revolutionary figure in the history of the American military (Law Library, "Billy Mitchell Court-Martial").

At the age of 19, William Mitchell joined the army in 1898 during the Spanish-American War. During World War I, Mitchell earned a reputation as a legendary and fearless pilot. By the end of the war in 1918, he had been promoted to colonel and then to brigadier general in command of the U.S. air combat units in France. During his service, Mitchell had become convinced that the U.S. military must invest in air power in order to provide adequate defense for its citizens and defeat its enemies in future wars. Mitchell failed to understand why the army had not considered using airplanes to drop men behind enemy lines or bomb enemy targets during World War I. Mitchell proposed the idea to General John J. Pershing, but the military commander rejected the plan (Law Library, "Billy Mitchell Court-Martial").

Mitchell remained undeterred and, as chief of the U.S. Air Service, began training paratroopers and using airplanes for aerial mapping. While Mitchell was involved in designing new technology for military aircraft, he also became a harsh critic of the Navy and War Departments, which ignored his advice to develop the Air Service (Law Library, "Billy Mitchell Court-Martial").

In February 1921, the House Appropriations Committee approved Mitchell's plan, entitled Project B, to demonstrate how airplanes could be used to sink captured German battleships, which the United States was required to destroy under the armistice treaty signed at the end of World War I (Law Library, "Billy Mitchell Court-Martial"). During the demonstration, Mitchell's aircraft, operating under strict rules of engagement defined by the navy, bombed and sunk old American battleships and a number of the German World War I battleships, including the *Ostfriesland,* which was considered indestructible. Even though Mitchell's demonstration was considered a success, the army and navy announced that battleships, not aircraft, would remain the foundation of U.S. military strength (Waller 2004, 142–155).

Mitchell began speaking publicly about the need for the development of air power and predicted that other countries, such as Russia, Germany, and Japan, would build up their military aircraft in the near future. In his testimony before the Lampert Committee in the U.S. House of Representatives, Mitchell accused military leaders of lying to the American public and jeopardizing national security by failing to develop a national air force. In 1924, Mitchell was given assignments in Hawaii and Asia, in part, to keep him away from news media in Washington, D.C. Mitchell produced a 324-page report based upon his experiences in the Far East which predicted that U.S. military bases in the Philippines and Hawaii, including Pearl Harbor, would be attacked in the near future by Japan (Law Library, "Billy Mitchell Court-Martial").

In 1925, when the old naval airship, the *Shenandoah,* crashed in a storm over Ohio, killing 14 crew members, and three naval seaplanes crashed on a trip from California to Hawaii, Mitchell told news reporters that the navy and army leaders were guilty of incompetence and treason in failing to improve military aircraft.

President Calvin Coolidge responded to the comments by issuing orders for Mitchell to be court-martialed (Waller 2004, 16–31).

On October 28, 1925, the military trial of Brigadier General William Mitchell began in Washington, D.C. Mitchell was charged with insubordination and behavior that dishonored military service under the 96th Article of War (Maksel 2009). Major Allen Gullion, Lieutenant Joseph McMullen, and Colonel Sherman Moreland served as prosecutors, while Mitchell's legal defense team consisted of Frank Plain, Frank Reid, and Colonel Herbert White. The trial was presided over by Major General Robert Howze as well as several military leaders, including General Douglas MacArthur, who served simultaneously as judges and jurors as was required under military law (Law Library, "Billy Mitchell Court-Martial").

Defense attorney Frank Reid presented 41 witnesses who testified that Mitchell was only exercising his freedom of speech in trying to raise awareness of the need to investigate and study air defense as a way to enhance American security (Maksel 2009). Among the defense witnesses, Major Carl Spaatz discussed the significant weakness of U.S. airpower in relation to other countries, Major Hap Arnold detailed the number of soldiers whose lives were lost due to outdated military equipment being used by the Air Service, and Captain Eddie Rickenbacker testified that the U.S. military must be able to fight airpower with airpower in future wars because antiaircraft weapons used from the ground would be insufficient (Law Library "Billy Mitchell Court-Martial").

Because the right to remain silent does not apply to military trials, Mitchell testified in his own defense by asserting that the function of the War and Navy Departments was to protect the citizens of the United States. Hence, according to Mitchell, their failure to provide safety for the American people was the same as a criminal act (Waller 2004, 239–252).

The prosecution, however, argued that Mitchell's free speech must be subject to limitations within the military establishment or else discipline and order would be abandoned with subordinates routinely criticizing their superiors (Maksel 2009). Prosecutors asserted that it did not matter if Mitchell was even telling the truth. Under military law, a person could still be convicted of insubordination, even if he or she spoke the truth (Waller 2004, 117).

In his closing remarks for the prosecution, Major Gullion portrayed Mitchell as an egomaniac and demagogue who had weakened the safety of the American people by openly criticizing the military of his country (Waller 2004, 318–322). According to Gullion, Mitchell was similar to Aaron Burr, who allegedly attempted to commit treason against his country for personal gain. Gullion added, however, that Mitchell lacked the grace and intelligence of Burr (Maksel 2009).

On December 17, 1925, after three hours of deliberation, a secret ballot of the military judges convicted Mitchell on all counts related to his insubordination and dishonorable conduct. The judges sentenced Mitchell to a five-year suspension from active duty and required him to forfeit his allowances and salary during this time period. The judges expressed in their opinion that Mitchell was given a lenient sentence because of the extraordinary leadership that he demonstrated during World War I (Waller 2004, 323–325).

Because of Mitchell's popularity with the American public, Congress debated whether to pass a joint resolution to restore his military status and pay. As was customary with military trials, President Coolidge reviewed the suspension but declined to overturn the verdict. However, Coolidge decided to restore his allowances and half of Mitchell's pay during the five years of suspension. On February 1, 1926, Mitchell resigned as an officer in the U.S. Army because he viewed the verdict as an injustice (Waller 2004, 327–331).

Mitchell died of pneumonia in 1936 but, five years after his death, Japan used air strikes to bomb Pearl Harbor as well as U.S. military bases in the Philippines. As Mitchell had predicted, the United States was unprepared for war as it lost numerous battleships to air attack during World War II. When the military finally developed the B-25 bomber in 1942, it was named the "Mitchell" after General William Mitchell and was used successfully to bomb enemy targets during World War II. The B-25 bomber is the only military aircraft in U.S. history named after a person. President Franklin Roosevelt honored Mitchell by posthumously increasing his rank to two-star general, and he also lobbied Congress to award Mitchell the Congressional Gold Medal (Waller 2004, 350–362).

Although General William Mitchell has been given less attention compared to other historical figures, the court-martial trial of Mitchell was a legendary event in American history. Mitchell was a national hero based upon his exploits in World War I, but he had gone rogue against the military establishment, creating a national scandal which resulted in his military trial and conviction. In the end, Mitchell was redeemed by history as a prophet whose warnings should have been heeded by American political and military leaders (Law Library, "Billy Mitchell Court-Martial").

References

Law Library–American Law and Legal Information. "Billy Mitchell Court-Martial: 1925." *Notable Trials and Court Cases—1918 to 1940.* http://law.jrank.org/pages/2858/Billy-Mitchell-Court-Martial-1925.html (accessed January 4, 2010).

Maksel, Rebecca. "The Billy Mitchell Court-Martial" *Air & Space* 24, no. 2 (July 1, 2009): 46–49.

Waller, Douglas C. *A Question of Loyalty: Gen. Billy Mitchell and the Court-Martial that Gripped the Nation.* New York: HarperCollins, 2004.

The Scopes Monkey Trial (1925)

On July 10, 1925, the *State of Tennessee v. John Scopes* trial began in Dayton, Tennessee. The trial is more famously known as the Scopes Monkey trial because it involved Charles Darwin's theory of evolution which argued that human beings descended from apes. The trial centered upon the legal issue of whether the state of Tennessee could prohibit the teaching of evolution within the public school system because evolution denied the story of creation told in the Bible. The Scopes Monkey trial has become legendary for highlighting a fundamental battle between the modern values of science versus the traditional values of religion that still exists today in American society (Linder, "Scopes Monkey Trial").

John Scopes was a high school teacher who taught biology at Clark County High School in Tennessee. Scopes had assigned readings on evolution to his students in violation of an antievolution law passed by the Tennessee state legislature (Larson 2006, 89–91). The antievolution law prohibited a teacher from instructing students using a theory that contradicted the Bible's story of creation and instead relied upon the idea that humans descended from animals (48–59). The American Civil Liberties Union (ACLU) had announced that it would provide legal services to anyone willing to challenge the antievolution law in Tennessee. Scopes volunteered to be arrested for violating the antievolution law and became part of a test case where legal action was created to test whether a law was in violation of the Constitution. Interest groups have relied upon test cases throughout the history of the United States to bring about changes in the meaning and interpretation of the law (80–92).

William Jennings Bryan offered to participate as part of the prosecution team representing the state of Tennessee (Larson 2006, 96–100). Bryan, who had run for president three times as a Democrat and lost each time, was a Fundamentalist Christian who inspired his political supporters to introduce antievolution bills in 15 state legislatures (Olasky and Perry 2005, 19–21). Scopes would be defended by John Neal, the dean of the law school at the University of Tennessee and Clarence Darrow, the most famous defense attorney in the United States in 1925 (Larson 2006, 100–106). The ACLU also hired Arthur Garfield Hays, an expert on issues related to free speech, as part of the defense team (68–69).

On the first day of the trial, a crowd of 1,000 people crowded into the Rhea County Courthouse to witness the legal battle over evolution that would be fought out by persons considered to be legends in the fields of politics and law. Judge John T. Raulston presided over the Scopes Trial, and he encouraged the publicity over the legal proceedings by permitting the trial to be broadcast live over the radio. Prior to the Scopes trial, a judicial proceeding had never been broadcast live over the radio. The jury selected for the trial was composed of 12 men who were mostly farmers and conservative Christians from Tennessee (Linder, "Scopes Monkey Trial").

The defense attorneys quickly moved to have the charges against Scopes dismissed based upon the argument that the antievolution law was a violation of basic freedom found in the state and federal constitutions; however, Judge Raulston refused to dismiss the charges. The opening statement from the prosecution was made by Bryan, who argued that if evolution was accepted in society, then it would be the end of Christianity. Clarence Darrow's opening statement for the defense was equally as dramatic as he compared Bryan and the prosecutors to ignorant bigots from the Middle Ages whose objective was to judge everyone according to the teachings of the Bible (Linder, "Scopes Monkey Trial").

The lead prosecutor, Tom Stewart, called several high school students as witnesses to testify that Scopes had taught the theory of evolution in the classroom. Then, Stewart called the owner of a local drugstore who sold the high school textbooks for the biology class. The owner of the drugstore testified that Scopes had commented he knew that he could be arrested under the laws of the state of Tennessee for using the textbooks which contained information about evolution (Linder, "Scopes Monkey Trial").

The defense attorneys called a zoologist from John Hopkins University as their first witness. The zoologist discussed the theory of evolution before the court. Upon cross-examination, Bryan ridiculed the scientist for his belief that man descended from apes. One of the defense attorneys, Dudley Malone, argued that Bryan's cross-examination was based upon ignorance and was the basis for religious persecution thousands of years ago. After both Bryan and Malone provided their emotional and inspirational speeches, Judge Raulston declared that the testimony of the zoologist could not be admitted as evidence because it was unrelated to the guilt or innocence of Scopes (Olasky and Perry 2005, 76–96). Clarence Darrow openly criticized Judge Raulston for his ruling concerning the zoologist's testimony, and his criticism caused the judge to hold him in contempt of court. Judge Raulston eventually dropped the contempt charges after Darrow apologized for his remarks (Olasky and Perry 2005, 115–117).

During the trial, the size of the crowd inside the courtroom had grown so large that the proceedings were ordered by Judge Raulston to be held outside. On the courthouse lawn, the defense attorneys called Bryan, one of the prosecuting attorneys, to take the stand as an expert witness who could provide knowledge about the teachings of the Bible. Clarence Darrow proceeded to question Bryan about various stories from the Bible that contradicted logic and reason. For example, it would have been impossible for Jonah to live inside a whale or Noah to have survived the great flood with various animals aboard his ark or a snake to have actually tempted Adam and Eve in the Garden of Eden. Darrow's strategy was to force Bryan to admit that the Bible could not be interpreted in a literal fashion. Bryan did admit that the words in the Bible were not always meant to be taken literally. The exchanges between Bryan and Darrow made for great theatre as each frustrated the other at different times, although the newspapers reported that Bryan lost out to Darrow in the war of words. On the following day, Judge Raulston ruled that Bryan would not take the witness stand for a second day and his testimony would not be admitted as evidence (Larson 2006, 3–8; 187–190).

In his closing statements, Darrow asked the jury to issue a guilty verdict against Scopes because the defense team's overall strategy was to have a guilty verdict appealed to a higher court in order to allow the Tennessee Supreme Court or perhaps the U.S. Supreme Court to declare the antievolution law unconstitutional. The jury found Scopes guilty of violating the antievolution law, and he was fined $100 by Judge Raulston (Linder, "Scopes Monkey Trial"). In 1926, the Tennessee Supreme Court reversed the decision of the court but failed to discuss the constitutionality of the antievolution law. Instead, the Tennessee Supreme Court ruled that the fine against Scopes should have been issued by the jury, not the judge. Hence, the Tennessee Supreme Court simply dismissed the case based upon a technicality (Larson 2006, 212–221). The U.S. Supreme Court finally struck down the antievolution laws passed by the states in *Epperson v. Arkansas* (1968). The antievolution laws were declared unconstitutional because they violated the Establishment Clause of the First Amendment which prohibited the advancement of religion by any state government (Larson 2006, 253–255).

The Scopes Monkey Trial illustrated how politics, law, and religion were often intertwined during the early part of the 20th century. For example, a prayer was conducted by Judge Raulston at the beginning of the Scopes trial and a sign actually hung outside the courtroom that read "Read Your Bible." During the trial, Clarence Darrow objected to both of these forms of religious expression (Linder, "Scopes Monkey Trial"). Beginning with the U.S. Supreme Court's decision in *Everson v. Board of Education of Ewing Township of New Jersey* (1947), the federal courts have forced the 50 states to recognize separation of church and state under the Establishment Clause of the First Amendment. More recently, the U.S. Supreme Court has reinforced the need for government to remain neutral in matters related to religion in such cases as *Engel v. Vitale* (1962), which prohibited prayer in the public schools, and *Edwards v. Aguillard* (1987), which barred states from requiring public school teachers to present the idea that God created the Earth. Today, evolution is widely accepted as a scientific theory in public schools across the country (Irons 2007, 28–43).

Clarence Darrow

On April 18, 1857, Clarence Darrow was born in Kinsman, Ohio. His father, Amirus Darrow, made furniture for a living and was a strong opponent of slavery. His mother, Emily Darrow, was an early supporter of women's rights. Darrow's parents instilled in him a strong belief in education. After attending Allegheny College and the University of Michigan School of Law, Darrow entered the practice of law in 1878 (Vile 2001, 178–179).

He began his legal practice in Youngstown, Ohio, but then moved to Chicago, Illinois, in 1888 where he practiced law for the next 40 years. Initially, he practiced as a corporate lawyer for the railroad companies but decided to switch sides in favor of labor. In 1894, he represented Eugene Debs, the leader of the American Railway Union, in the famous Pullman strike for which Debs was charged with conspiracy to obstruct interstate commerce. While Darrow lost the case, he established himself as a champion of the labor movement. In 1907, Darrow was called upon to represent William "Big Bill" Haywood and other union leaders when they were accused of assassinating the former governor of Idaho, Frank Steunenberg. Darrow won an acquittal for Haywood and the labor leaders by defining the case as poor laborers versus rich capitalists in order to gain sympathy from the jury (Vile 2001, 179–80).

In 1911, the president of the American Federation of Labor, Samuel Gompers, asked Darrow to represent two brothers, James and John McNamara, who were union leaders charged with killing 20 people when they allegedly set off a bomb at the *Los Angeles Times* building. However, Darrow disappointed labor leaders when he persuaded the McNamara brothers to plead guilty after he realized they were responsible for the murders. In the 1920s, Darrow gained notoriety for defending Benjamin Gitlow, a communist arrested under a New York law that prohibited revolutionary speech. While Gitlow's conviction was upheld on appeal, the case became a landmark ruling by the U.S. Supreme Court because it forced states to broaden the free speech rights of citizens (Vile 2001, 181).

Darrow is best known for serving as a criminal defense attorney in two cases. In 1924, he defended two murderers, Nathan Leopold and Richard Loeb, who were from wealthy Chicago families. Leopold and Loeb had murdered a 14-year-old boy simply for the thrill of trying to commit the perfect crime. While Leopold and Loeb were found guilty of murder, Darrow presented a passionate argument against the death penalty during the sentencing phase and convinced the judge to issue only life sentences to the defendants. In Darrow's most famous case, he defended John T. Scopes, a school teacher, who had violated a Tennessee law by teaching evolution in the classroom in the 1920s. The case was as much about the interpretation of the Bible as it was about teaching evolution. Darrow dramatically called the prosecuting attorney, William Jennings Bryan, to the witness stand to challenge his fundamentalist beliefs about the Bible. While Scopes was convicted and Darrow technically lost the case, many observers maintained that he had destroyed the literal interpretation of the Bible with his cross-examination of Bryan (Vile 2001, 181–184).

In 1925, Darrow defended an African American physician, Ossian Sweet, and 10 other black defendants who were accused of murdering a white man after a mob of white people threatened to throw the Sweet family out of a neighborhood in Detroit, Michigan. After the first trial resulted in a mistrial for the 11 defendants, the prosecution decided to try the defendants separately. Darrow proceeded to win an acquittal on grounds of self-defense for Henry Sweet, the brother of Ossian Sweet. Darrow won the case despite having to argue in front of an all-white jury. Darrow's closing statement in the Henry Sweet case lasted seven hours and has been called one of the greatest speeches of the civil rights movement. The charges were eventually dismissed against the other 10 defendants (Linder, "The Sweet Trials: An Account").

In 1927, Darrow retired but, five years later, briefly came out of retirement due to financial difficulties to defend Thomas Massie, and three others defendants, charged with committing an "honor killing" of a Hawaiian man who had allegedly raped Massie's wife. While the murder trial was controversial because of the racial divide between elite whites and nonwhites in Hawaii, Darrow was praised by the prosecuting attorney for his professional behavior during the trial. Massie and the other defendants were convicted of manslaughter and sentenced to 10 years in prison, but the Governor of Hawaii reduced the sentences to only one hour (Linder, "The Massie Trials: A Commentary"). Darrow gained national attention one last time in 1934 when he was called upon by the federal government to evaluate the National Industrial Recovery Act, a key feature of President Franklin Roosevelt's New Deal plan, which established public works and union protections for workers (Vile 2001, 184).

Darrow was the first trial lawyer in the United States to become a national celebrity. He is regarded as one of the greatest trial lawyers in American history. Darrow was renowned for his defense of workers' rights, his opposition to the death penalty, and his passionate and lengthy speeches delivered during the closing arguments of a trial (Vile 2001, 178). On March 13, 1938, Darrow passed away at his home in Chicago at the age of 80. In 1960, the *Scopes* trial was depicted in the successful film, *Inherit the Wind,* and Spencer Tracy was cast to play Darrow. Tracy's portrayal of Darrow as a heroic figure in the film has contributed to the popular view of Darrow as a legendary trial lawyer (184).

William Jennings Bryan

William Jennings Bryan was born on March 19, 1860, in Salem, Illinois. Bryan's father was a lawyer who served in the Illinois State Senate and also was elected as a state circuit judge (Cherny 1994, 1–23). Bryan dreamed of becoming a Baptist minister but changed his mind after witnessing a baptism which caused him to develop a fear of water. As a young child, he was home schooled with strict religious values and taught to believe that gambling and alcohol were evil. At the age of 14, Bryan was baptized as a Presbyterian (Linder, "William Jennings Bryan").

Bryan was educated at Illinois College where he graduated at the top of his class in 1881. Bryan earned his law degree from Northwestern University School of Law and practiced law in Jacksonville, Illinois, from 1883 to 1887. He then moved to Lincoln, Nebraska, where he was elected to the U.S. House of Representatives in 1890 and became the first Democratic congressman elected by the state of Nebraska (Cherny 1994, 19–50).

In 1896, Bryan won the Democratic nomination for president after he delivered his famous "Cross of Gold" speech at the convention in which he criticized the wealthy for using only the gold standard to back the U.S. dollar. Bryan supported using both the gold and silver standards which would have brought about inflation and made it easier for the working poor to pay off their debts. At 36 years of age, Bryan remains the youngest person ever to win the presidential nomination of a major party. In the 1896 presidential election, Republican William McKinley, supported by wealthy industrialists, would defeat Bryan, the populist candidate (Cherny 1994, 50–63).

In 1900, Bryan again received the Democratic nomination by adding such issues as anti-imperialism, campaign finance reform, and consumer protection to his candidacy. Bryan, however, lost a second time to McKinley, the incumbent president. In 1908, Bryan made a third attempt at the presidency when he secured the Democratic nomination but lost the general election to Republican William Howard Taft whose party benefited from eight years of success under President Theodore Roosevelt. In 1912, Democrat Woodrow Wilson won the presidency and appointed Bryan to serve as secretary of state, but Bryan resigned after Wilson decided to get the United States involved in World War I (Linder, "William Jennings Bryan").

After leaving the Wilson administration, Bryan drew from his Christian beliefs in fighting for a woman's right to vote and prohibition. Bryan also became interested in how science and modernism had weakened moral standards in the United States. Bryan wrote and spoke often about how scientific ideas such as evolution had permeated the American educational system and caused students to turn away from God. In 1925, he was asked by the World's Christian Fundamentals Association to assist in the prosecution of a school teacher in Tennessee who had violated a state law by teaching students about evolution. In one of the most famous trials in American history, Bryan battled Clarence Darrow, who served as the defense attorney for the school teacher, John T. Scopes. In a dramatic maneuver, Darrow called Bryan as a witness to challenge his fundamentalist view of the Bible. In the end, Bryan was victorious in the Scopes Monkey Trial as he won a conviction and Scopes was ordered to pay a $100 fine (Linder, "William Jennings Bryan").

On July 26, 1925, six days after the verdict in the *Scopes* trial, Bryan died in his sleep. Bryan's death was caused by his diabetes which was exacerbated by severe fatigue brought upon by the stress of the trial as well as the summer heat (Linder, "William Jennings Bryan").

References

Cherny, Robert W. *A Righteous Cause: The Life of William Jennings Bryan.* Norman: University of Oklahoma Press, 1994.

Irons, Peter H. *God on Trial: Dispatches from America's Religious Battlefield.* New York: Viking, 2007.

Larson, Edward J. *Summer of the Gods: The Scopes Monkey Trial and America's Continuing Debate over Science and Religion.* New York: Basic Books, 2006.

Linder, Douglas O. "The Massie Trials: A Commentary." *Famous Trials.* http://www.law. umkc.edu/faculty/projects/ftrials/massie/massietrialsaccount.html (accessed July 25, 2009).

Linder, Douglas O. "State v. John Scopes (The Monkey) Trial." *Famous Trials.* http://www. law.umkc.edu/faculty/projects/ftrials/scopes/evolut.htm (accessed March 23, 2009).

Linder, Douglas O. "The Sweet Trials: An Account." *Famous Trials.* http://www.law.umkc. edu/faculty/projects/FTRIALS/sweet/sweetaccount.HTM (accessed July 13, 2009).

Linder, Douglas O. "William Jennings Bryan (1860–1925)." *Famous Trials.* http:// www.law.umkc.edu/faculty/projects/ftrials/scopes/bryanw.htm (accessed August 18, 2009).

Olasky, Marvin and John Perry. *Monkey Business: The True Story of the Scopes Trial.* Nashville, TN: Broadman and Holman Publishing Group, 2005.

Vile, John R. *Great American Lawyers: An Encyclopedia.* Santa Barbara, CA: ABC-CLIO, 2001.

Scopes Trial: Clarence Darrow's Examination of William Jennings Bryan (1925)

The most dramatic scene of the Scopes Monkey Trial, in which high school teacher John T. Scopes was charged with illegally teaching the theory of evolution in violation of Tennessee law, Clarence Darrow's examination of William Jennings Bryan, who testified as an expert on the Bible, marked the high point of several months of national attention in mid-July 1925. Although his cross-examination held on the courthouse lawn was far from the drubbing publicized by the press, Darrow was able to get Bryan to concede that he did not believe the seven days mentioned in the Genesis account of creation were literal days. Not only did this concession put distance between Bryan and other believers in Biblical creation, but it also suggested that the Bible required interpretation. Moreover, Darrow ridiculed

Bryan's simple faith in the accounts of such Biblical miracles as Jonah being swallowed by a whale and Joshua commanding the sun to stand still as unscientific and suggested that Bryan had not thought deeply about the relationship between his faith and science. Nevertheless, the jury found against Scopes. Tennessee left its antievolution law on the books until May 1967.

Hays—The defense desires to call Mr. Bryan as a witness, and, of course, the only question here is whether Mr. Scopes taught what these children said he taught, we recognize what Mr. Bryan says as a witness would not be very valuable. We think there are other questions involved, and we should want to take Mr. Bryan's testimony for the purpose of our record, even if your honor thinks it is not admissible in general, so we wish to call him now.

The Court—Do you think you have a right to his testimony or evidence like you did these others?

McKenzie—I don't think it is necessary to call him, calling a lawyer who represents a client.

The Court—If you ask him about any confidential matter, I will protect him, of course.

Darrow—On scientific matters, Col. Bryan can speak for himself.

Bryan—If your honor please, I insist that Mr. Darrow can be put on the stand, and Mr. Malone and Mr. Hays.

The Court—Call anybody you desire. Ask them any questions you wish.

Bryan—Then, we will call all three of them.

Darrow—Not at once?

Bryan—Where do you want me to sit?

The Court—Mr. Bryan, you are not objecting to going on the stand?

Bryan—Not at all.

The Court—Do you want Mr. Bryan sworn?

Darrow—No.

Bryan—I can make affirmation; I can say "So help me God, I will tell the truth."

Darrow—No, I take it you will tell the truth, Mr. Bryan.

Darrow—You have given considerable study to the Bible, haven't you, Mr. Bryan?

Bryan—Yes, sir, I have tried to.

Darrow—Then you have made a general study of it?

Bryan—Yes, I have; I have studied the Bible for about fifty years, or sometime more than that, but, of course, I have studied it more as I have become older than when I was but a boy.

Darrow—You claim that everything in the Bible should be literally interpreted?

Bryan—I believe everything in the Bible should be accepted as it is given there: some of the Bible is given illustratively. For instance: "Ye are the salt of the earth." I would not insist that man was actually salt, or that he had flesh of salt, but it is used in the sense of salt as saving God's people.

Darrow—But when you read that Jonah swallowed the whale—or that the whale swallowed Jonah—excuse me please—how do you literally interpret that?

Bryan—When I read that a big fish swallowed Jonah—it does not say whale. That is my recollection of it. A big fish, and I believe it, and I believe in a God who can make a whale and can make a man and make both what He pleases.

Darrow—Now, you say, the big fish swallowed Jonah, and he there remained how long—three days—and then he spewed him upon the land. You believe that the big fish was made to swallow Jonah?

Bryan—I am not prepared to say that; the Bible merely says it was done.

Darrow—You don't know whether it was the ordinary run of fish, or made for that purpose?

Bryan—You may guess; you evolutionists guess. . .

Darrow—You are not prepared to say whether that fish was made especially to swallow a man or not?

Bryan—The Bible doesn't say, so I am not prepared to say.

Darrow—But do you believe He made them—that He made such a fish and that it was big enough to swallow Jonah?

Bryan—Yes, sir. Let me add: One miracle is just as easy to believe as another.

Darrow—Just as hard?

Bryan—It is hard to believe for you, but easy for me. A miracle is a thing performed beyond what man can perform. When you get within the realm of miracles; and it is just as easy to believe the miracle of Jonah as any other miracle in the Bible.

Darrow—Perfectly easy to believe that Jonah swallowed the whale?

Bryan—If the Bible said so; the Bible doesn't make as extreme statements as evolutionists do. . .

Darrow—The Bible says Joshua commanded the sun to stand still for the purpose of lengthening the day, doesn't it, and you believe it.

Bryan—I do.

Darrow—Do you believe at that time the entire sun went around the earth?

Bryan—No, I believe that the earth goes around the sun.

Darrow—Do you believe that the men who wrote it thought that the day could be lengthened or that the sun could be stopped?

Bryan—I don't know what they thought.

Darrow—You don't know?

Bryan—I think they wrote the fact without expressing their own thoughts.

Darrow—Have you an opinion as to whether or not the men who wrote that thought—

Gen. Stewart—I want to object, your honor; it has gone beyond the pale of any issue that could possibly be injected into this lawsuit, expect by imagination. I do not think the defendant has a right to conduct the examination any further and I ask your honor to exclude it.

Bryan—It seems to me it would be too exacting to confine the defense to the facts; if they are not allowed to get away from the facts, what have they to deal with?

The Court—Mr. Bryan is willing to be examined. Go ahead.

Mr. Darrow—I read that years ago. Can you answer my question directly? If the day was lengthened by stopping either the earth or the sun, it must have been the earth?

Bryan—Well, I should say so.

Darrow—Now, Mr. Bryan, have you ever pondered what would have happened to the earth if it had stood still?

Bryan—No.

Darrow—You have not?

Bryan—No; the God I believe in could have taken care of that, Mr. Darrow.

Darrow—I see. Have you ever pondered what would naturally happen to the earth if it stood still suddenly?

Bryan—No.

Darrow—Don't you know it would have been converted into molten mass of matter?

Bryan—You testify to that when you get on the stand, I will give you a chance.

Darrow—Don't you believe it?

Bryan—I would want to hear expert testimony on that.

Darrow—You have never investigated that subject?

Bryan—I don't think I have ever had the question asked.

Darrow—Or ever thought of it?

Bryan—I have been too busy on things that I thought were of more importance than that.

Darrow—You believe the story of the flood to be a literal interpretation?

Bryan—Yes, sir.

Darrow—When was that Flood?

Bryan—I would not attempt to fix the date. The date is fixed, as suggested this morning.

Darrow—About 4004 B.C.?

Bryan—That has been the estimate of a man that is accepted today. I would not say it is accurate.

Darrow—That estimate is printed in the Bible?

Bryan—Everybody knows, at least, I think most of the people know, that was the estimate given.

Darrow—But what do you think that the Bible, itself says? Don't you know how it was arrived at?

Bryan—I never made a calculation.

Darrow—A calculation from what?

Bryan—I could not say.

Darrow—From the generations of man?

Bryan—I would not want to say that.

Darrow—What do you think?

Bryan—I do not think about things I don't think about.

Darrow—Do you think about things you do think about?

Bryan—Well, sometimes.

(Laughter in the courtyard.)

Policeman—Let us have order . . .

Stewart—Your honor, he is perfectly able to take care of this, but we are attaining no evidence. This is not competent evidence.

Bryan—These gentlemen have not had much chance—they did not come here to try this case. They came here to try revealed religion. I am here to defend it and they can ask me any question they please.

The Court—All right.

(Applause from the court yard.)

Darrow—Great applause from the bleachers.

Bryan—From those whom you call "Yokels."

Darrow—I have never called them yokels.

Bryan—That is the ignorance of Tennessee, the bigotry.

Darrow—You mean who are applauding you? (Applause.)

Bryan—Those are the people whom you insult.

Darrow—You insult every man of science and learning in the world because he does not believe in your fool religion.

The Court—I will not stand for that.

Darrow—For what he is doing?

The Court—I am talking to both of you . . .

Darrow—Wait until you get to me. Do you know anything about how many people there were in Egypt 3,500 years ago, or how many people there were in China 5,000 years ago?

Bryan—No.

Darrow—Have you ever tried to find out?

Bryan—No, sir. You are the first man I ever heard of who has been in interested in it.

(Laughter.)

Darrow—Mr. Bryan, am I the first man you ever heard of who has been interested in the age of human societies and primitive man?

Bryan—You are the first man I ever heard speak of the number of people at those different periods.

Darrow—Where have you lived all your life?

Bryan—Not near you. (Laughter and applause.)

Darrow—Nor near anybody of learning?

Bryan—Oh, don't assume you know it all.

Darrow—Do you know there are thousands of books in our libraries on all those subjects I have been asking you about?

Bryan—I couldn't say, but I will take your word for it . . .

Darrow—Have you any idea how old the earth is?

Bryan—No.

Darrow—The Book you have introduced in evidence tells you, doesn't it?

Bryan—I don't think it does, Mr. Darrow.

Darrow—Let's see whether it does; is this the one?

Bryan—That is the one, I think.

Darrow—It says B.C. 4004?

Bryan—That is Bishop Usher's calculation.

Darrow—That is printed in the Bible you introduced?

Bryan—Yes, sir . . .

Darrow—Would you say that the earth was only 4,000 years old?

Bryan—Oh, no; I think it is much older than that.

Darrow—How much?

Bryan—I couldn't say.

Darrow—Do you say whether the Bible itself says it is older than that?

Bryan—I don't think it is older or not.

Darrow—Do you think the earth was made in six days?

Bryan—Not six days of twenty-four hours.

Darrow—Doesn't it say so?

Bryan—No, sir . . .

The Court—Are you about through, Mr. Darrow?

Darrow—I want to ask a few more questions about the creation.

The Court—I know. We are going to adjourn when Mr. Bryan comes off the stand for the day. Be very brief, Mr. Darrow. Of course, I believe I will make myself clearer. Of course, it is incompetent testimony before the jury. The only reason I am allowing this to go in at all is that they may have it in the appellate court as showing what the affidavit would be.

Bryan—The reason I am answering is not for the benefit of the superior court. It is to keep these gentlemen from saying I was afraid to meet them and let them question me, and I want the Christian world to know that any atheist, agnostic, unbeliever, can question me anytime as to my belief in God, and I will answer him.

Darrow—I want to take an exception to this conduct of this witness. He may be very popular down here in the hills . . .

Bryan—Your honor, they have not asked a question legally and the only reason they have asked any question is for the purpose, as the question about Jonah was asked, for a chance to give this agnostic an opportunity to criticize a believer in the world of God; and I answered the question in order to shut his mouth so that he cannot go out and tell his atheistic friends that I would not answer his questions. That is the only reason, no more reason in the world.

Malone—Your honor on this very subject, I would like to say that I would have asked Mr. Bryan—and I consider myself as good a Christian as he is—every question that Mr. Darrow has asked him for the purpose of bring out whether or not there is to be taken in this court a literal interpretation of the Bible, or whether, obviously, as these questions indicate, if a general and literal construction cannot be put upon the parts of the Bible which have been covered by Mr. Darrow's questions. I hope for the last time no further attempt will be made by counsel on the other side of the case, or Mr. Bryan, to say the defense is concerned at all with Mr. Darrow's particular religious views or lack of religious views. We are here as lawyers with the same right to our views. I have the same right to mine as a Christian as Mr. Bryan has to his, and we do not intend to have this case charged by Mr. Darrow's agnosticism or Mr. Bryan's brand of Christianity. (A great applause.)

Darrow—Mr. Bryan, do you believe that the first woman was Eve?

Bryan—Yes.

Darrow—Do you believe she was literally made out of Adams's rib?

Bryan—I do.

Darrow—Did you ever discover where Cain got his wife?

Bryan—No, sir; I leave the agnostics to hunt for her.

Darrow—You have never found out?

Bryan—I have never tried to find.

Darrow—You have never tried to find?

Bryan—No.

Darrow—The Bible says he got one, doesn't it? Were there other people on the earth at that time?

Bryan—I cannot say.

Darrow—You cannot say. Did that ever enter your consideration?

Bryan—Never bothered me.

Darrow—There were no others recorded, but Cain got a wife.

Bryan—That is what the Bible says.

Darrow—Where she came from you do not know. All right. Does the statement, "The morning and the evening were the first day," and "The morning and the evening were the second day," mean anything to you?

Bryan—I do not think it necessarily means a twenty-four-hour day.

Darrow—You do not?

Bryan—No.

Darrow—What do you consider it to be?

Bryan—I have not attempted to explain it. If you will take the second chapter—let me have the book. (Examining Bible.) The fourth verse of the second chapter says: "These are the generations of the heavens and of the earth, when they were created in the day that the Lord God made the earth and the heavens," the word "day" there in the very next chapter is used to describe a period. I do not see that there is any necessity for construing the words, "the evening and the morning," as meaning necessarily a twenty-four-hour day, "in the day when the Lord made the heaven and the earth."

Darrow—Then, when the Bible said, for instance, "and God called the firmament heaven. And the evening and the morning were the second day," that does not necessarily mean twenty-four hours?

Bryan—I do not think it necessarily does.

Darrow—Do you think it does or does not?

Bryan—I know a great many think so.

Darrow—What do you think?

Bryan—I do not think it does.

Darrow—You think those were not literal days?

Bryan—I do not think they were twenty-four-hour days.

Darrow—What do you think about it?

Bryan—That is my opinion—I do not know that my opinion is better on that subject than those who think it does.

Darrow—You do not think that?

Bryan—No. But I think it would be just as easy for the kind of God we believe in to make the earth in six days as in six years or in 6,000,000 years or in 600,000,000 years. I do not think it important whether we believe one or the other.

Darrow—Do you think those were literal days?

Bryan—My impression is they were periods, but I would not attempt to argue as against anybody who wanted to believe in literal days.

Darrow—I will read it to you from the Bible: "And the Lord God said unto the serpent, because thou hast done this, thou art cursed above all cattle, and above every beast of the field; upon thy belly shalt thou go and dust shalt thou eat all the days of thy life." Do you think that is why the serpent is compelled to crawl upon its belly?

Bryan—I believe that.

Darrow—Have you any idea how the snake went before that time?

Bryan—No, sir.

Darrow—Do you know whether he walked on his tail or not?

Bryan—No, sir. I have no way to know. (Laughter in audience).

Darrow—Now, you refer to the cloud that was put in heaven after the flood, the rainbow. Do you believe in that?

Bryan—Read it.

Darrow—All right, Mr. Bryan, I will read it for you.

Bryan—Your Honor, I think I can shorten this testimony. The only purpose Mr. Darrow has is to slur at the Bible, but I will answer his question. I will answer it all at once, and I have no objection in the world, I want the world to know that this man, who does not believe in a God, is trying to use a court in Tennessee—

Darrow—I object to that.

Bryan—(Continuing) to slur at it, and while it will require time, I am willing to take it.

Darrow—I object to your statement. I am exempting you on your fool ideas that no intelligent Christian on earth believes.

The Court—Court is adjourned until 9 o'clock tomorrow morning.

The Sweet Trials (1925–1926)

The Sweet murder trials were the consequence of racial tension that existed between African Americans and whites at the beginning of the 20th century. During World War I, African Americans from the South began migrating to industrial cities in the northern and Midwestern parts of the United States in search of wartime employment. The racial violence that occurred as a result of African American attempts to rent or purchase homes in white neighborhoods during this time period served as an introduction to the complex legal issues that the United States would encounter in the battle over civil rights in the 1960s. Fortunately, the Sweet trials involved a judge, prosecutors, defense attorneys, and jurors who performed their roles with integrity which increased respect for the American criminal justice system at a critical moment in its history (Law Library, "Sweet Trials").

From 1915 to 1925, Detroit, Michigan, experienced economic prosperity with the introduction of the automobile and manufacturing industry. As a result, the population of African Americans arriving from the economically depressed areas of the South in search of jobs grew dramatically from 7,000 to 82,000. Because Detroit's black district could not accommodate all of the new arrivals, some African Americans attempted to buy or rent homes in all-white neighborhoods. Intimidation and violence from groups, such as the Ku Klux Klan, caused most African Americans to avoid the white neighborhoods or sell their property that had been purchased back to white families (Linder, "The Sweet Trials").

In July 1925, a black physician named Ossian Sweet bought a home at 2905 Garland in a middle-class white district of Detroit. Despite threats of possible violence from whites, Sweet decided to move his family into their new home on September 8, 1925. Sweet brought several guns and ammunition into his new home along with his two brothers and a number of friends in anticipation of mob violence from whites in the neighborhood. Sweet also notified police of the threats made against his family and asked for protection (Linder, "The Sweet Trials").

On the evening of September 9, 1925, a large crowd of whites stood outside the Sweets' home, and some members of the crowd started throwing rocks at the house. Other people in the crowd yelled racial slurs at Dr. Sweet and his family as they turned off the lights inside their home and pulled down the blinds over the windows. Suddenly, a number of gun shots were fired from the Sweet house. One of the shots fired caused the death of Leon Breiner, a 33-year-old white man, standing across the street from the Sweet home. Breiner had been shot once in the back. Another shot fired from the Sweet home wounded Eric Houghberg in the leg (McRae 2009, 251–252).

Six police officers, who were present at the time the shots were fired, entered the Sweet residence and arrested the 11 people occupying the home at the time of the shooting. Each of the 11 persons was interviewed at the police station with each providing different interpretations of what happened at the time of the shootings. After Dr. Sweet told police that he had given a gun to each of the men inside the home on the evening of the shootings, an assistant district attorney informed the 11 persons who had been arrested that he would be recommending they be charged with murder. On September 16, 1925, each of the 11 defendants was denied bail at a pretrial hearing and eventually charged with first-degree murder and conspiracy to commit murder. The murder trial would be presided over by Judge Frank Murphy, who scheduled the court proceedings to begin on October 30, 1925 (Law Library, "Sweet Trials").

The National Association for the Advancement of Colored People (NAACP) hired Arthur Garfield Hays and Clarence Darrow, two of the best defense attorneys in the United States, to represent the defendants in the Sweet case (McRae 2009, 252–262). Hays was considered one of the best civil rights attorneys in America, and Darrow was known as the best defense attorney of his generation.

Hays and Darrow knew that, even though the crowd had been abusive toward the black family, it would be difficult for the defense to prove that the defendants acted in self-defense because no one had attempted to use force to enter the Sweet home. Under Michigan law, the forcible entry of the Sweet home would be the only justification for murdering Breiner in self-defense. Furthermore, the gunfire from the Sweet home appeared to be unprovoked and, because Breiner was shot in the back, he could not be considered someone who was threatening the Sweet family (Law Library, "Sweet Trials").

After an all-white jury was selected for the murder trial, Lester S. Moll began his opening statement for the prosecution by telling the courtroom how the all-white neighborhood had been changed forever by the gunfire that came from the Sweet home. Moll stated that African Americans had every right to move into the neighborhood, but Leon Breiner also had a right to live. Moll concluded his opening statement by emphasizing that the case was not about race but, instead, it was about a premeditated conspiracy to murder (Linder, "The Sweet Trials").

The prosecution would present 70 witnesses to make their case that the crowd outside the Sweet home was not violent prior to the shooting. Some prosecution witnesses admitted that they were not in favor of blacks moving into the white neighborhood, but they also emphasized that the crowd outside of the Sweet house was small and orderly (Linder, "The Sweet Trials"). Under cross-examination from Darrow, however, it became apparent that the prosecution witnesses had been coached in their testimony to stress that the crowd was small and nonviolent (Law Library, "Sweet Trials").

The biggest obstacle for the prosecution in presenting their case was the confusion concerning where the gunshots came from within the house and who actually fired the gunshots. While some prosecution witnesses testified that they thought the gunshots had been fired from the back porch of the Sweet home, others maintained that gunshots were fired from a bedroom window on the second floor. The fact that prosecutors could not prove which of the 11 defendants actually fired a weapon created a problem toward securing a conviction. Because the prosecutors were uncertain who fired the bullet that killed Breiner, they were left with using the vague charge of conspiracy against the defendants. Darrow was effective at criticizing the prosecutors by referring to the use of the conspiracy charge as an abuse of authority which had assumed that all of the defendants were involved in the murder (Law Library, "Sweet Trials").

The opening statement for the defense team was provided by Arthur Garfield Hays. Hays argued that the defendants were not murderers. The defendants instead acted out of fear based upon the history of discrimination against persons of their race. Hays and Darrow then called a number of witnesses who testified that the crowd outside the Sweet home was large, numbering nearly 1,000 people, with members of the crowd throwing rocks and yelling racial slurs and threats at the Sweet family (Linder, "The Sweet Trials").

The most important witness for the defense would be Dr. Ossian Sweet, whom Darrow used to show how the murder of Breiner was an act of self-defense committed by someone in the house who feared for his life. Sweet testified that, when he saw the large crowd outside of his home, he saw the same people who had been enslaving and murdering black people for hundreds of years in the United States. When prosecutors objected that the history of racism in the United States could not be used to justify a crime of murder, Darrow emphasized that the defendant's state of mind and psychology were critical to understanding how behavior could be influenced by the history of violence against blacks in the United States. Judge Murphy sided with the defense in ruling that Sweet's "state of mind" could be regarded as a factor by the jury (Vine 2005, 253–257).

Dr. Sweet ended his testimony by describing in detail the events of September 9, 1925. Sweet retold the story of how the large crowd threw rocks and broke the windows of his home, while shouting racial slurs at his family. Sweet stated that his family and friends hid inside the home and feared for their lives. Sweet then concluded by telling the jury how he suddenly heard gunfire coming from the upstairs of his house, but he was uncertain who fired the weapon (McRae 2009, 285–288).

In his closing statement for the prosecution, Lester Moll ridiculed the defense's theory that the murder of Leon Breiner was justified because of the fear developed over time in the minds of African Americans who had been victims of violence for centuries (Linder, "The Sweet Trials"). Clarence Darrow provided an emotional response to Moll's statement by asking the jurors to put aside their prejudices and imagine themselves in the place of the defendants. Darrow asked the jurors how they would feel if one of them had shot a black person and had to be tried by an all-black jury. Darrow concluded by maintaining that the Sweet family had been confronted with a dangerous situation on the night of the murder of Leon Breiner. The large crowd that had gathered outside the Sweet home had every intention of committing violence against a black family simply because of their race (McRae 2009, 288–292).

District Attorney Robert Toms issued the final closing statement of the trial for the prosecution. Toms reminded the jurors that their task was not to resolve the race issue in America. Toms also stated that the trial was about a crime of premeditated murder and not about racial discrimination. Finally, Toms disagreed with the defense's claim made by Darrow that the crowd intended to commit violence against the Sweet family (Linder, "The Sweet Trials").

Over the course of three days, November 25–27, 1925, the jury debated the fate of the 11 defendants. After 46 hours of debate, the jury told Judge Murphy that they were unable to reach a decision. Judge Murphy was forced to declare a mistrial and dismiss the charges against the 11 defendants (McRae 2009, 294–296). Interviews with the jurors after the trial suggested that the jury was leaning toward convicting Dr. Ossian Sweet and his younger brother, Henry Sweet, of manslaughter, but they could only muster 7 of 12 votes in favor of a guilty verdict. The jury appeared to be strongly in favor of a not guilty verdict for the remaining nine defendants. However, the closest that the jury came to a unanimous decision was a 10–2 vote in favor of an acquittal. After the trial, in December 1925, each of the defendants was released on bail by Judge Murphy (Linder, "The Sweet Trials").

Prosecutor Robert Toms chose to move ahead with a second trial, but he decided upon a strategy to try the 11 defendants separately. Toms proceeded to retry Henry Sweet first. Henry Sweet provided the strongest case for conviction because he had finally come forward and confessed to firing a gun through the front window of the house toward the murder victim, Leon Breiner (McRae 2009, 282–293).

The second trial of Henry Sweet began on April 19, 1926. Judge Frank Murphy again presided over the trial with Robert Toms and Clarence Darrow representing the prosecution and defense, respectively. The legal strategies were virtually identical from the first trial. Toms attempted to show that the crowd of people outside the Sweet home did not intend to commit any violence against the Sweet family, while Darrow again presented the self-defense argument as well as the idea that the psychological fear caused by the history of violence against blacks explained the behavior that caused the murder.

Similar to the first trial, Darrow provided a passionate argument for the defense with his closing statement. However, Darrow's summary in the second trial became memorable for its length as he spoke to the jury for eight hours. Although Darrow had argued more celebrated cases during his legal career, he often would refer to his closing statement in the Henry Sweet trial as the most satisfying of his legendary career (McRae 2009, 301–319). On May 13, 1926, after deliberating only four hours, an all-white jury of 12 men returned a verdict of not guilty in the case of *The People of Michigan v. Henry Sweet* (1926). After the acquittal of Henry Sweet, Prosecutor Toms chose not to enter into a second trial with any of the other individuals accused of conspiracy to murder in the first trial. On July 21, 1927, Toms formally decided to drop all of the charges against the other 10 defendants (Law Library, "Sweet Trials").

The Sweet trials stand as an example of how the American criminal system can operate with integrity, even when such emotional issues as racial tension and violence complicate the proceedings. Judge Frank Murphy was praised by legal observers for appointing himself to sit as the judge in the Sweet trials when other judges were too afraid to deal with such an explosive case. In assigning himself to the case, Judge Murphy was quoted as saying that he wanted a chance to demonstrate the integrity of the judicial process. Murphy would eventually be appointed to the U.S. Supreme Court by President Franklin Roosevelt in 1940. Clarence Darrow, perhaps the greatest defense attorney in the history of the United States, gave his best performances in the Sweet trials. Interestingly, Darrow held the prosecutors in the Sweet trials in such high esteem that he praised Robert Toms as "one of the fairest and most humane prosecutors" he had ever met. Finally, juries composed entirely of white men put aside any prejudices and sought to judge the African American defendants in a neutral manner. Overall, regardless of any opinions about the outcome, the best aspects of the American criminal justice system were on display in the Sweet trials (Linder, "The Sweet Trials").

References

Law Library–American Law and Legal Information. "Sweet Trials: 1925–26—Menacing Crowd Gathers, Darrow for the Defense." *Great American Trials*. Vol. 1. http://law.jrank.org/pages/2866/Sweet-Trials-1925–26.html (accessed July 13, 2009).

Linder, Douglas O. "The Sweet Trials: An Account." *Famous Trials*. http://www.law.umkc.edu/faculty/projects/FTRIALS/sweet/sweetaccount.HTM (accessed July 13, 2009).

McRae, Donald. *The Last Trials of Clarence Darrow*. New York: William Morrow and Company, 2009.

Vine, Phyllis. *One Man's Castle: Clarence Darrow in Defense of the American Dream*. New York: Harper, 2005.

Al Capone Trial (1931)

Throughout the decade of the 1920s, Chicago police authorities had failed to gain any control over the organized crime figures that used murder, violence, and bribery to protect their illegal businesses of bootlegging, gambling, and prostitution. However, in 1931, the federal government entered the battle with a creative strategy when it decided to try Al Capone, the most powerful leader in the world of organized crime, using federal tax laws. The trial would result in a conviction and the harshest penalty to date for a person who had avoided paying income tax to the federal government (Law Library, "Al Capone Trial").

In 1925, Alphonse Capone, commonly known as Al Capone, was 26 years old and operated an organized crime syndicate with 1,000 employees and a $300,000 financial network connected to gambling, prostitution, and bootlegging. During the era of prohibition when alcohol was illegal, Capone controlled a large system of distributorships in which alcohol was produced and processed for sale throughout the country. Capone was alleged to have ordered the deaths of hundreds of people to eliminate competition and maintain control of his bootleg operation. Capone also used the profits from his illegal endeavors to bribe local politicians and law-enforcement authorities who protected him from the law as well as from his rivals (Law Library, "Al Capone Trial").

In 1929, on St. Valentine's Day, Capone ordered the murder of "Bugs" Moran, a rival gangster. The murder was an act of revenge because Moran and his men had shot up Capone's headquarters. Capone's men disguised themselves as police officers and murdered seven of Moran's men in a Chicago warehouse. However, Moran was not murdered. Capone's men had thought that Moran was in the warehouse prior to the attack but they were mistaken. The murders came to be known as "the St. Valentine's Day Massacre," and the public demanded that the government take action to stop the violence that permeated their city (Law Library, "Al Capone Trial").

Frank Knox, the publisher of the *Chicago Daily News,* appealed to President Herbert Hoover for help in gathering information that could lead to the arrest and conviction of Capone. The federal government focused upon two areas in its attempt to monitor Capone's illegal activities, prohibition and income taxes. The Volstead Act had been passed by Congress in 1919 to reinforce the Eighteenth Amendment to the U.S. Constitution which had given the federal government the authority to prosecute anyone who was engaged in the sale and distribution of alcohol. President Hoover appointed Eliot Ness, a legendary federal agent, to gather information related to Capone's illegal breweries and supply routes. In terms of the investigation into tax evasion, President Hoover ordered the Internal Revenue Service (IRS) to analyze Capone's financial transactions (Law Library, "Al Capone Trial").

Frank J. Wilson, a special agent with the IRS, was dispatched to Chicago to begin his investigation into Capone's financial worth and expenditures; however, the gangster had cleverly hidden the vast majority of his financial transactions by always using cash, never using checks or a bank account, and placing property in someone else's name. Special Agent Wilson spent two years researching the financial purchases of Capone, which included luxurious items such as automobiles, boats, homes in Florida, and expensive suits (Law Library, "Al Capone Trial").

Special Agent Wilson assigned another special agent with the IRS, Michael Malone, to infiltrate Capone's organization as an undercover agent in an attempt to gather information and find witnesses who might agree to testify against Capone. Unfortunately, most of the members of Capone's syndicate were hostile toward the government and were willing to lie for Capone. A few individuals considered assisting the government, but they were too fearful of Capone and refused to talk. While Special Agent Malone was able to find a reporter for the *Chicago Tribune*, Jack Lingle, who had in-depth knowledge of the inner workings of Capone's organization, Lingle was murdered before IRS agents could meet with him. After Capone put out a contract to have Special Agent Wilson also murdered, the federal government was forced to provide 24-hour security for Wilson (Law Library, "Al Capone Trial").

Finally, in 1931, the federal government issued two indictments related to Capone's failure to pay income taxes from 1924 to 1929 and another indictment for conspiring to engage in the sale and distribution of alcohol in violation of the Volstead Act. Capone was facing 34 years in prison if convicted on all counts related to the three indictments. Federal prosecutors initially arranged a deal where Capone would serve only two-and-a-half years in prison for a guilty plea. However, when Capone walked into the courtroom to enter his guilty plea, Judge James Wilkerson told Capone that the prosecutors could recommend the light sentence but, as a federal judge, Wilkerson was not obligated to honor the bargain. In other words, Wilkerson made it clear that he had the power to issue a lengthier sentence if Capone pled guilty. Wilkerson wanted to send a powerful message to Capone that the federal government was not about to negotiate with a gangster. As a result, Capone withdrew his guilty plea and the case headed for trial (Kobler 2003, 328–331).

The trial of Al Capone began on October 6, 1931, in Chicago, Illinois, in the federal courtroom of Judge Wilkerson. U.S. Attorney George Johnson was set to present the evidence gathered by the federal government and defense lawyers, Michael Ahearn and Thomas Nash, were hired to represent Capone. When it was discovered that Capone's men had tried to bribe the potential jurors, the federal government wisely switched the jury pool with that of another trial to ensure that the jury was not tainted by Capone's influence. The new jury pool was then sequestered, or isolated from contact with anyone, to prevent Capone and his people from trying to bribe the jurors (Law Library, "Al Capone Trial").

The evidence introduced against Capone during the trial by George Johnson was overwhelming. On the first day of the trial, an IRS clerk testified that Capone had not filed a tax return from 1924 to 1929. Capone's failure to file a tax return was damaging evidence considering the fact that he owned a gambling casino, the Hawthorne Smoke Shop, that secured over a half a million dollars in revenue over a two-year period. Federal prosecutors also had discovered money orders to prove Capone's connection to the profits (Iorizzo 2003, 81). The federal prosecutors then produced a large number of witnesses who testified how they had been paid by Capone for various items including tailor-made suits, diamond belt buckles, homes in Florida, and automobiles. The testimony proved that Capone had spent large sums of money that had not been taxed by the federal government (Law Library, "Al Capone Trial").

Capone's defense attorneys were disadvantaged because they had not prepared for a trial. They had counted on the plea bargain with federal prosecutors and, when they realized that the case was going to trial, they only had a few hours to prepare a strategy. Defense attorney Michael Ahearn attempted to show that Capone had no wealth because he had gambled all of his money away. Unfortunately for Capone, the defense's argument was a weak attempt at deception because, in order to lose large sums of money, a person would initially have had to possess a large amount of wealth. In his closing statement to the jury, Ahearn tried to argue that Capone did not know that profits from gambling were taxable, and he had planned to pay the taxes when he was informed that he owed the money to the federal government (Iorizzo 2003, 82).

On October 17, 1931, after nine hours of deliberation, the jury returned a verdict of guilty against Capone on several counts of tax evasion from 1925 to 1927 and for failing to file tax returns in 1928 and 1929. The federal government chose to dismiss the charges against Capone related to his violation of the Volstead Act. On October 24, 1931, Judge Wilkerson sentenced Capone to 11 years in prison, and he was ordered to pay a fine of $50,000, and $30,000 in court fees. In addition, liens were placed on Capone's properties in order to prevent the sale or transfer of assets prior to making payment on all of his taxes to the federal government (Kobler 2003, 340–346).

After the trial, Capone was denied bail and sent to the Cook County jail where he enjoyed special privileges such as his own cell and shower as well as visits from fellow gangsters. Capone was able to secure these privileges by bribing prison officials with thousands of dollars smuggled into the prison (Law Library, "Al Capone

Trial"). Capone's attorneys filed an appeal with the U.S. Court for the Seventh District on the grounds that federal prosecutors had failed to show exactly how Capone was able to evade paying any income tax. On February 17, 1932, Capone's appeal was denied by the Seventh District court and, a few months later, the U.S. Supreme Court also rejected his appeal. After his appeals were denied, Capone was transferred from the Cook County jail to a federal penitentiary in Atlanta, Georgia, where he lost many of the privileges that he had enjoyed in the Cook County jail (Iorizzo 2003, 84).

In 1934, the federal government took over control of the Alcatraz prison in San Francisco Bay, California, and Capone was ordered to Alcatraz where he would be strictly regulated in terms of his communication with the outside world. Capone was no longer able to smuggle money into prison, and his letters were censored by prison authorities. Capone's time spent in Alcatraz caused him to lose influence rapidly within the world of organized crime (Kobler 2003, 342–373).

In 1938, Capone's health began to deteriorate because of the syphilis that he had contracted as a young man. Capone was released from prison in 1939 after serving only six and a half years. His original sentence had been reduced based upon his good behavior and work credits. On January 25, 1947, Capone died of cardiac arrest in Palm Island, Florida, at the age of 48 (Kobler 2003, 374–378).

Today, Al Capone remains a legendary figure in the world of organized crime, and various books and films within American popular culture have reinforced his mythical image. However, the federal government emerged victorious in its prosecution of Capone by using federal tax laws and sent a strong message to organized crime figures that it would do whatever was necessary to end their reign of terror and violence (Iorizzo 2003, 103–109).

References

Iorizzo, Luciano J. *Al Capone: A Biography.* Westport, CT: Greenwood Publishing Group, 2003.

Kobler, John. *Capone: The Life and World of Al Capone.* Cambridge, MA: Da Capo Press, 2003.

Law Library–American Law and Legal Information. "Al Capone Trial: 1931—The St. Valentine's Day Massacre, 'Impossible to Bargain with a Federal Court'." *Notable Trials and Court Cases—1918 to 1940.* http://law.jrank.org/pages/2902/Al-Capone-Trial-1931.html. (accessed December 25, 2009).

The Massie Trials (1931–1932)

Prior to gaining statehood in 1959, Hawaii was a U.S. territory where a sensitive relationship existed between the native people of Hawaii and the American military personnel stationed on the island. The Massie trials began with the alleged rape of the wife of a naval officer by a group of Hawaiian men and ended with the kidnapping and murder of one of the suspected rapists. The two trials were significant because they exacerbated the relationship between the white elite and native inhabitants of Hawaii and probably had more influence on Hawaiian politics than any other event in the history of the state (Linder, "The Massie Trials").

On September 12, 1931, Thomas and Thalia Massie went to a nightclub called the Ala Wai Inn, near the Waikiki area of Honolulu, Hawaii. Lieutenant Thomas Massie was a naval officer who had planned to get together with fellow officers for a night of drinking alcohol. After walking away from her husband and his friends to a different part of the nightclub, Thalia Massie had a confrontation with a naval officer and supposedly slapped him in the face (Law Library, "Thomas Massie Trial").

Later in the evening, Massie left the Ala Wai Inn by herself around midnight, because she had grown tired of listening to her husband carry on with his fellow officers. As she began strolling toward the beach on Kalakaua Avenue, Massie claimed that she was abducted by a group of five men who broke her jaw when she fought back against her assailants. She was then taken to an abandoned area and sexually assaulted. About one hour later, Thalia Massie stopped a car on Ala Moana Road that was occupied by a group of people who noticed that Thalia had bruises and blood on her face. Thalia asked to be taken to her home where she spoke with her husband on the telephone and told him that she had been raped by a group of Hawaiian men (Law Library, "Thomas Massie Trial").

Another woman, Agnes Peeples, also claimed to have been assaulted on the same evening as Thalia Massie. Unlike Massie, Peeples immediately reported the assault to the Honolulu police department. Apparently, Peeples was driving her car and was almost involved in a collision with another car at an intersection. The driver of the other car got out of his car and struck Peeples in the head causing her ear to bleed. Peeples wisely recorded the license plate number of the vehicle that was driven by a young Hawaiian man who had four other men in the car with him (Linder, "The Massie Trials").

Roughly one hour after Peeples reported the assault, Thomas Massie telephoned the Honolulu police department to report the attack on his wife. Police officers traveled to the Massie house and interviewed Thalia Massie who told the investigators that she had been sexually assaulted by four or five Hawaiian men. The police investigators concluded that the attacks on Peeples and Massie were probably connected and, most likely, involved the same group of Hawaiians. Their conclusion was strengthened after Thalia gave police a license plate number almost identical to the one reported by Peeples. However, it was later learned that a friend of the Massie family had told Thalia Massie about the license plate number given to police by Peeples and Massie apparently tried to give police the same number (Linder, "The Massie Trials").

The license plate number recorded by Peeples belonged to a tan Model A Ford owned by a Japanese woman living in an impoverished area referred to as "Half Hell's Acre." On the night in question, the car had been driven by the Japanese woman's son, Horace Ida, who immediately became a suspect in the two attacks. Ida told police that he was accompanied in the car by four friends, Ben Ahakuelo, Henry Chang, David Takai, and Joe Kahahawai. Ida admitted to police that he had an altercation with Agnes Peeples at the intersection, but denied any involvement in the assault of Thalia Massie (Stannard 2005, 65–81).

The mother of Thalia Massie was Grace Fortescue, a woman from New York with social status and political connections. Fortescue arrived in Hawaii from the mainland and began to pressure naval officers to force local authorities to prosecute the young Hawaiian men (Law Library, "Thomas Massie Trial"). When white people in the community heard about the sexual assault committed by the young Hawaiian men against a white woman, they also demanded revenge. Prominent businessmen in the community offered a $5,000 reward for information leading to the conviction of the suspects (Linder, "The Massie Trials").

Detective John McIntosh, who had been heading up the investigation for the Honolulu police, was certain that he had the names of the persons who committed the assault against Peeples. However, he was not certain that the same men had committed the sexual offense against Thalia Massie. In an effort to strengthen the sexual assault case, McIntosh ordered another officer to take Ida's car and drive it in the mud near the abandoned area where Massie claimed to have been assaulted in order to leave tire marks as further evidence for police (Linder, "The Massie Trials").

A critical problem with the time line of the police investigation was the fact that the two assaults supposedly happened within 10 minutes of each other, although the two crime scenes were roughly six miles apart. Therefore, it was inconceivable that the young men could have committed both assaults. Princess Kawananakoa, the only surviving member of Hawaii's royal family, asked a leading politician and lawyer, William H. Heen, to defend the five defendants who had been arrested by authorities. After meeting with the five young men, Heen concluded that they were definitely innocent of the sexual assault charges (Linder, "The Massie Trials").

 ## The "Ala Moana Rape" Trial

On November 16, 1931, the "Ala Moana rape case" began in the courtroom of Judge Alva Steadman in Honolulu, Hawaii. The jury consisted of seven nonwhite men and five white men. In her testimony for the prosecution, Thalia Massie told the story of how she left the Ala Wai Inn on September 12 and was kidnapped by the five defendants who took her away in their car. After driving her to an abandoned area, the young men allegedly raped her (Stannard 2005, 166–168).

During cross-examination, the defense attorneys, led by Heen and William Pittman, attempted to discredit Thalia Massie, who was unable to identify her attackers or the license plate number of the car immediately after the assault. However, her memory seemed to improve during the course of the investigation. A physician who examined her at the hospital after the attack was uncertain if she had been sexually assaulted by multiple offenders based upon her condition (Stannard 2005, 168–172).

Prosecutor Griffith Wight based the government's case on the testimony of several police officers. Wight called a police officer, Claude Benton, to testify about the tire tracks found at the crime scene that matched the tires of the car driven by Horace Ida. Detective Thomas Finnegan told the jury that Thalia Massie did, in fact, identify three of the suspects on the day after the alleged assault. Finally, the prosecution called Detective McIntosh to describe how Thalia Massie gave police the license plate number of the car, although it differed by one digit from the license plate number provided by Peeples. The license plate number provided by Massie was considered by the prosecution to be the best evidence in favor of conviction (Linder, "The Massie Trials").

The defense attorneys adopted a questionable strategy of claiming that police had arrested the wrong persons who committed the rape, instead of arguing that Thalia Massie was never sexually assaulted because of a lack of medical evidence. Heen was fearful that the jury would react negatively to the defense if they accused Massie of lying about the sexual assault so he simply hoped that the jurors would be able to identify this weakness in the prosecution's case on their own (Linder, "The Massie Trials").

Several witnesses testified for the defense by providing alibis for the defendants who were seen at a dance around the time of the alleged rape of Massie. Witnesses also testified to seeing Massie walking toward the beach at about midnight and being followed by a white man. Most importantly, a police investigator, Officer Sato, admitted under oath that he was instructed by Detective McIntosh to drive Ida's car in the mud at the crime scene to create the tire tracks as evidence. By calling such critical witnesses and emphasizing the questionable time line provided by police, the defense attorneys felt confident that they had created reasonable doubt in the minds of the jurors (Linder, "The Massie Trials").

On December 1, 1931, the closing arguments for the defense were presented by William Heen who argued that the police obviously tried to frame the defendants for the sexual assault of Massie when, in fact, the young men could not have been at the crime scene given their alibis and the time line created by police investigators. Griffith Wight offered a controversial summary for the prosecution by asking the jury to find the defendants guilty as a means to protect the women of Hawaii (Linder, "The Massie Trials").

The white people in Hawaii and around the United States had anxiously looked forward to a conviction against the defendants. However, after nearly 100 hours of deliberation, the jury produced six votes in favor of conviction and six votes for an acquittal. As a result, Judge Steadman was forced to declare a mistrial in the rape case of Thalia Massie (Linder, "The Massie Trials").

 ## The Murder of Joe Kahahawai: Honor Killing or Lynching?

After the verdict, riots occurred throughout Honolulu as violence between whites and nonwhites escalated. After Horace Ida was kidnapped outside of a bar and brutally assaulted by several sailors, navy personnel were ordered to stay on the military base because authorities feared that native Hawaiians and navy men would engage in continued attacks against each other. Amazingly, serious discussions of a military takeover of Hawaii were considered as a possible option by the U.S. government (Linder, "The Massie Trials").

It became apparent that a second trial would probably produce another mistrial because the same evidence would have to be presented before a jury of, at least, a few nonwhites. Therefore, Thomas Massie, two other Navy men, and Grace Fortescue decided to kidnap Joe Kahahawai and force a confession from him. They knew that they could locate Kahahawai at a courthouse in downtown Honolulu where he was required to meet with his probation officer every morning. They planned to use a fake summons from a military court and a pistol to force Kahahawai into their car (Linder, "The Massie Trials").

The Honolulu police were given a description of a blue Buick involved in the kidnapping of Kahahawai and stopped a vehicle matching this description, but only after a high-speed chase along the coastline. The car was being driven by Grace Fortescue. When Detective George Harbottle walked toward the car, he noticed a body wrapped in a sheet in the back seat. The body was identified as Joe Kahahawai, and he had been shot and killed. Harbottle proceeded to arrest the occupants of the car, Thomas Massie, Grace Fortescue, and Edward Lord. Investigators later gathered evidence at Fortescue's house where they found a fourth suspect, Albert Jones, who was extremely intoxicated. Jones was a sailor who had also been a boxer in the navy. A search of Fortescue's home produced ropes, guns, disguises, and a towel soaked in blood. At the request of Admiral Yates Stirling of the U.S. Navy, the four defendants were detained on an inactive ship, the U.S.S. *Alton,* at Pearl Harbor where they enjoyed comfortable accommodations (Linder, "The Massie Trials").

The murder of Joe Kahahawai further intensified the bad feelings between the natives of Hawaii and whites. Over 2,000 people attended the funeral of

Kahahawai, a local prizefighter who was popular within the Honolulu community. While whites viewed the murder as an "honor killing" by Thomas Massie seeking revenge for the rape of his wife, the native Hawaiians saw the murder as a lynching (Stannard 2005, 259–262).

 ## The Massie Trial

On January 21, 1932, a grand jury indicted Thomas Massie, Grace Fortescue, Edward Lord, and Albert Jones for the murder of Joe Kahahawai. Legendary defense attorney Clarence Darrow came out of retirement at the age of 75 to defend the four white defendants. Evidently, the Great Depression had had an effect on Darrow's finances and he was in need of money. Darrow was paid $30,000 for his legal services, the largest amount in his entire career for one case. Darrow knew it was obvious that his clients committed the murder so he would have to argue for an acquittal based upon temporary insanity (Linder, "The Massie Trials").

The prosecution was led by John C. Kelley who charged the four defendants with felony murder. A felony murder charge did not require Kelley to prove which person actually shot and killed Kahahawai. Because all of the four defendants participated in the kidnapping, each was equally guilty, regardless of who committed the actual murder (Linder, "The Massie Trials").

The trial began on April 4, 1932, and was presided over by Judge Charles Davis in Honolulu, Hawaii. The jury selected for the trial included seven whites and five nonwhites. In his opening statement, Prosecutor Kelley detailed the murder of Kahahawai. Kelley then called Edward Uli'i, Kahahawai's cousin, to the witness stand. Uli'i told the jury how he witnessed the kidnapping of his cousin by Albert Jones and Grace Fortescue, who used the fake summons and pistol to force Kahahawai into a car driven by Thomas Massie, who was disguised as a chauffeur (Stannard 2005, 324–331). Kelley then called upon Detective Harbottle, who provided powerful testimony about stopping the blue Buick and discovering the body of Kahahawai wrapped in a bloody sheet in the back seat of the car. Other police officers provided testimony about their search of the car that produced Kahahawai's bloody shirt containing a bullet hole (Linder, "The Massie Trials").

In terms of the murder itself, Kelley provided colorful diagrams that portrayed the murder as having occurred while Kahahawai was seated in a chair and the shooter was standing over him. Kelley also showed the jury photographs of blood found on the floor of Grace Fortescue's home and a rope found inside the home that matched the actual rope found on the victim's body. Clearly, Kelley had established the guilt of the four defendants beyond a reasonable doubt (Linder, "The Massie Trials").

Clarence Darrow began the defense's case by calling Lieutenant Thomas Massie to the witness stand. Massie told the jury how his wife was emotionally traumatized by the sexual assault. Massie also stated that he experienced emotional problems as well, which caused him to lose sleep. When Thalia Massie became pregnant as a result of the sexual assault, Lieutenant Massie said that his wife had to have an abortion performed at the hospital. The purpose of Darrow's questioning of Massie was designed to convince the jury that Massie could have been so traumatized by the rape of his wife that he was temporarily insane at the time Kahahawai was murdered. After Massie's first day of testimony, he clearly had an impact on the female jurors who cried during his testimony (Stannard 2005, 336–340).

On Massie's second day of testimony, he described how he shot and killed Kahahawai with a .32 caliber pistol provided by Albert Jones. Massie stated that he was standing over Kahahawai who was seated in Fortescue's living room. Massie said that he was trying to get a confession out of him, but Kahahawai kept maintaining his innocence. When Kahahawai finally confessed to the crime, Massie said that he became consumed with rage as he thought about the sexual assault on his wife and he must have used Albert Jones's pistol to murder Kahahawai. Massie stated that he could not actually recall shooting Kahahawai (Stannard 2005, 342–346).

After Massie's dramatic testimony, two psychiatrists were called by Darrow to establish that Massie had experienced temporary insanity at the time of the murder. The psychiatrists concluded that Massie had experienced so much stress from the rape of his wife that he was unable to control his impulses after he heard the confession from Kahahawai. The prosecution countered Darrow's use of the psychological experts by calling two psychiatric experts of their own who concluded that Massie was sane at the time of the murder based upon a series of rational acts committed by Massie leading up to the murder (Stannard 2005, 348–369).

Darrow then drew upon the testimony of Thalia Massie to tell her version of the alleged assault. Thalia Massie had added new details to her story by telling the jury how Kahahawai would not allow her to pray prior to the attack and then struck her in the face breaking her jaw (Stannard 2005, 354–358). The prosecution's cross-examination of Thalia Massie offered more drama as Prosecutor Kelley handed Massie a psychological questionnaire that she had filled out a few years earlier when she was a student at the University of Hawaii. The questionnaire was basically a self-analysis where Thalia Massie suggested that her marriage to her husband, Thomas, was not a fulfilling relationship. When Kelley asked Massie if the handwriting on the questionnaire was hers, she became so angry that she refused to answer Kelley and tore up the questionnaire. As Massie left the witness stand, she fell into her husband's arms. Darrow called the scene one of the most dramatic courtroom events that he had ever witnessed in his career (Law Library, "Thomas Massie Trial").

In his closing arguments broadcast over the radio, Clarence Darrow reminded the jury about the pain and suffering endured by Thomas and Thalia Massie as well as Grace Fortescue, the mother of the alleged victim. During his summation, Darrow fought back tears as he talked about the possibility of the family members being placed in prison after everything they had been through in the past year. Darrow concluded his comments to the jury by predicting that the island of Hawaii would forever stand as a symbol of injustice if the defendants were convicted and sent to prison (Linder, "The Massie Trials").

Prosecutor John Kelley asked the jurors to disregard the dramatic performance of Darrow and simply find the defendants guilty because the rule of law must apply equally to everyone. Thomas Massie and his partners committed murder and, if the jury excused the murder because Massie claimed to have "forgotten" that he shot Kahahawai, then no one would be safe from a possible lynching (Stannard 2005 373–377).

On April 29, 1932, after two days of deliberations, the jury found the four defendants guilty of manslaughter with a recommendation that a lenient sentence be imposed by Judge Davis. The verdict caused a strong reaction within the United States. The U.S. Congress seriously considered passing a law to allow presidential pardons for the four defendants. The federal law would most likely have been ruled unconstitutional by the federal courts because U.S. presidents are only allowed to pardon persons convicted of federal offenses under the U.S. Constitution. In addition to the congressional reaction, President Herbert Hoover telephoned Governor Lawrence Judd of Hawaii in an effort to influence Judd, who did possess the power to pardon the defendants according to the laws of the Hawaiian territory (Stannard 2005, 378–390).

On May 4, 1932, Judge Davis ordered Thomas Massie, Grace Fortescue, Albert Jones, and Edward Lord to serve 10 years in prison performing hard labor. Shortly after Judge Davis issued the sentences, Governor Judd reduced the sentences to one hour in the custody of the sheriff on the condition that the Massie party would not pursue any charges against the other suspects in the alleged rape. Governor Judd feared that another rape trial would create more racial tension in Hawaii (Law Library, "Thomas Massie Trial"). Princess Kawananakoa publicly criticized the actions of the governor in a speech where she claimed the existence of one set of laws for the white and privileged people and another set of laws for the general population of Hawaii (Linder, "The Massie Trials").

In October 1932, the Pinkerton National Detective Agency, a legendary investigative company, issued a lengthy report on the alleged assault of Thalia Massie. The Pinkertons concluded in their investigation that Thalia Massie could not been raped by the young Hawaiian men. On February 13, 1933, Prosecutor John Kelley dismissed all of the charges of sexual assault against the remaining suspects, Horace Ida, Ben Ahakuelo, Henry Chang, and David Takai (Linder, "The Massie Trials"). In 1966, Albert Jones told a writer from *Look* magazine that Kahahawai never confessed to the rape of Thalia Massie, and Jones admitted that he was the person who actually shot Kahahawai. Jones added that it was Clarence Darrow's idea to say that Thomas Massie shot and killed Kahahawai because it would be easier to convince the jury that Massie suffered from temporary insanity (Van Slingerhand 1966, 311–325).

The Massie trials served to unify the various ethnic groups that made up the native population of Hawaii. In addition, the politics of the Hawaiian territory was transformed as nonwhites began voting in large numbers and the Hawaiian legislature became more progressive. Even today, the liberal ideals and values of Hawaiian political culture can be traced back to the Massie trials of the early 1930s when the native population of Hawaii finally challenged the white establishment that had been controlling their society (Linder, "The Massie Trials").

References

Law Library–American Law and Legal Information. "Thomas Massie Trial: 1932—Mother-in-Law Takes Charge, 'Is This Your Handwriting?'" *Great American Trials*. Vol. 1. http://law.jrank.org/pages/2905/Thomas-Massie-Trial-1932.html (accessed July 25, 2009).

Linder, Douglas O. "The Massie Trials: A Commentary." *Famous Trials*. http://www.law.umkc.edu/faculty/projects/ftrials/massie/massietrialsaccount.html (accessed July 25, 2009).

Stannard. David E. *Honor Killing: How the Infamous "Massie Affair" Transformed Hawaii*. New York: Viking, 2005.

Van Slingerland, Peter. *Something Terrible Has Happened: The Account of the Sensational Thalia Massie Affair, Which Burst From Prewar Hawaii to Incense the Nation*. New York: Harper and Row, 1966.

Scottsboro Boys Trials (1931–1937)

In 1931, nine black teenagers were accused of raping two white women on a train traveling through the state of Alabama. The accusation would produce several trials and appeals in an effort to determine whether the nine young men would be freed or found guilty and executed for their alleged crime. The "Scottsboro Boys" trials raised significant issues of due process complicated by racism within the southern culture, the involvement of the American Communist Party, and the national attention thrust upon those individuals who participated in the various trials, appeals, and retrials over the course of two decades (Linder, "Scottsboro Boys").

On March 25, 1931, a number of African American and white teenagers were riding the Southern Railroad freight train from Tennessee to Alabama in search of employment during the Depression era. It was common for young people to hop a ride on the freight trains whenever they heard that jobs might be found in other areas of the United States. As the train was traveling across the border into Alabama, a fight began between some of the white and black teenagers in a boxcar on the train. Because the black teenagers were larger in number, the whites were forcibly removed from the train. When the white teenagers reported that they had been assaulted by the black teenagers, the stationmaster wired ahead to inform authorities about the assault and the train was stopped in Paint Rock, Alabama (Linder, "Scottsboro Boys").

After the black teenagers were apprehended on assault charges, two white women, Victoria Price and Ruby Bates, who also had been riding on the train, informed authorities that they had been sexually assaulted by a number of black men after the white men had been forced off of the train (Feldman 2008, 28–29). Nine of the black teenagers were taken to a jail in Scottsboro, Alabama, to face charges of raping the two white women, which was considered a capital offense in Alabama in the 1930s. The nine black teenagers faced the real possibility of execution if found guilty of raping the white women (Linder, "Scottsboro Boys").

The trial of the Scottsboro Boys began almost immediately in the courtroom of Judge A. E. Hawkins on April 6, 1932, and the black teenagers had the misfortune of being represented by one defense attorney who was unprepared and intoxicated and another defense attorney who was so elderly that he had serious memory problems. The prosecutors chose to try the nine defendants over the course of four criminal trials because they feared that one guilty verdict for the nine teenagers might easily be reversed on appeal. During the course of the four trials, the defense attorneys proved their incompetence by failing to properly cross-examine the two women who were the alleged victims of the sexual assault, even though their testimonies contradicted each other. In addition, the defense attorneys only presented the testimony of the nine black teenagers as evidence of their innocence, and the defendants were confused and unprepared during questioning. Three of the nine black teenagers actually testified against the other six codefendants, but it was believed that they had been coerced into their testimony because of threats and physical beatings (Carter 2007, 22–48).

At the end of the four trials, eight of the nine black teenagers were found guilty and sentenced to death. One of the nine defendants was a 12-year-old named Roy Wright who had a mistrial declared in his case because, even though the prosecutors recommended a life sentence for the underage defendant, the jury still sentenced Wright to death (Linder, "Scottsboro Boys").

Interestingly, the National Association for the Advancement of Colored People (NAACP) was hesitant to provide legal representation for the black teenagers during the appeal process because the interest group feared that it would gain bad publicity from defending black men accused of raping white women in the South. Instead, the American Communist Party came to the defense of the black teenagers and assigned legal representation through its International Labor Defense fund (Linder, "Scottsboro Boys").

As expected, the Alabama Supreme Court upheld the convictions of the eight defendants, but the guilty verdicts were later overturned by the U.S. Supreme Court in *Powell v. Alabama* (1932), and the defendants were granted a new trial. Samuel Leibowitz, a well-respected defense attorney from New York City, was selected by the Communist Party as the lead attorney who would argue the case for the black teenagers in the second trials (Carter 2007, 181–182).

The second trial of one of the defendants, Haywood Patterson, began on March 30, 1933. Initially, Leibowitz attempted to get the case dismissed based upon the fact that blacks had been excluded from serving on the jury, but his motion was denied by Judge James Horton. At the beginning of Patterson's second trial, Leibowitz was allowed to cross-examine Victoria Price, one of the white women alleged to have been raped. Leibowitz immediately sought to discredit Price based upon her reputation as a prostitute and he accused her of lying about the sexual assault because she feared being arrested for violating the Mann Act, a federal law that criminalized prostitution. Based upon the testimony of the physicians who had examined Price after the alleged assault, Leibowitz noted that Price did not have any injuries consistent with the brutal rape described in her statement (Linder, "Scottsboro Boys").

In addition to discrediting the prosecution witnesses, Leibowitz called several witnesses for the defense to show that Price had lied in her testimony and to establish that no sexual assault had been committed by the black teenagers. In the most dramatic moment of the trial, Leibowitz called Ruby Bates, the other alleged victim, as a defense witness who admitted that she had lied about the rape. Apparently, Price had persuaded Bates to lie about the rape in order to deflect attention away from authorities charging the two women with prostitution (Linder, "Scottsboro Boys").

Despite the efforts of Leibowitz, the jury returned a verdict of guilty on April 8, 1933, and sentenced Haywood Patterson to death by electrocution. A few months later, Leibowitz appeared before Judge Horton to petition the court for another trial. Judge Horton had been convinced that Price had lied in her testimony and agreed that a new trial was in order. Interestingly, Judge Horton had secret knowledge of a young physician who had examined the two women after the alleged crime and found no evidence that a sexual assault had occurred. The young doctor refused to testify because he was fearful that his practice would be damaged by his testimony in favor of the black defendants. Despite political pressure from powerful officials within the state of Alabama, Judge Horton overturned the guilty judgment and death sentence. In the interest of justice, Judge Horton scheduled a third trial for Haywood Patterson to be held in November 1933 (Carter 2007, 264–269).

Because the attorney general of Alabama was angered by Judge Horton's actions, a new judge was assigned to preside over the third trial of Haywood Patterson. Judge William Callahan was chosen to assure the state of Alabama a conviction of the black teenagers in a timely fashion. Throughout the third trial of Patterson, Judge Callahan reduced the influence of the news media and ruled consistently in favor of the prosecution (Linder, "Scottsboro Boys").

In trials that lasted roughly three days, Haywood Patterson and a second defendant, Clarence Norris, were tried, convicted, and sentenced to death by a jury of 12 white men. The guilty verdicts were based largely upon testimony from a white man, Orville Gilley, who swore that he had witnessed the rape of the women on the train by the black teenagers. Interestingly, Gilley had not testified at any of the previous trials, and it was also revealed by Leibowitz during the trial that Gilley and his family had received financial support over the years from the prosecutor in the case. Leibowitz and the Communist Party appealed the convictions of Patterson and Norris to the U.S. Supreme Court, and Judge Callahan decided to suspend legal proceedings against the other defendants until a ruling was handed down by the Court (Linder, "Scottsboro Boys").

In *Norris v. Alabama* (1935), the U.S. Supreme Court ruled unanimously that the guilty verdicts of Patterson and Norris should be overturned because blacks had been systematically excluded from jury selection by the prosecution. According to the unanimous opinion written by Chief Justice Charles Evans Hughes, the two defendants were denied an equal protection of the laws under the Fourteenth Amendment to the U.S. Constitution based upon the jury selection process used by the state of Alabama (Carter 2007, 322–324).

The state of Alabama persisted in its attempts to prosecute despite the two rulings by the U.S. Supreme Court that overturned the convictions of the black teenagers. In January 1936, Haywood Patterson was given a fourth trial and again found guilty of raping the white women, but, instead of sentencing Patterson to death, the jury sentenced him to 75 years in prison. It was the first time in the history of the state of Alabama that a black man had not been sentenced to death after being found guilty of raping a white woman (Carter 2007, 339–347).

In July 1937, Clarence Norris was tried for a third time and found guilty and sentenced to death during a trial that lasted less than 48 hours (Carter 2007, 369–370). A third defendant, Andy Wright, was also found guilty in an accelerated trial and given 99 years in prison and a fourth defendant, Charlie Weems, was convicted and sentenced to 75 years (372–375). Surprisingly, prosecutors decided to drop all charges of rape against a fifth defendant, Ozie Powell, in exchange for Powell pleading guilty to assault on a deputy sheriff (375). During his incarceration, Powell had stabbed a deputy sheriff with a pocketknife and was subsequently shot in the head by the sheriff, which caused Powell to suffer severe brain damage (349–351). Powell received a 20-year sentence for his plea bargain (375).

On July 24, 1937, the remaining four defendants, Willie Roberson, Olen Montgomery, Eugene Williams, and Roy Wright, had the rape charges against them dismissed by the prosecution. Prosecutors issued a statement that they were confident Roberson and Montgomery were innocent of the rape charges, and Williams and Wright were both considered underage. Prosecutors emphasized that, even if Williams or Wright were involved in the crime, they had already served six years in prison awaiting a criminal trial and, therefore, the juveniles had been punished enough (Linder, "Scottsboro Boys").

From 1943 until 1950, Charles Weems, Ozie Powell, Clarence Norris, and Andy Wright were released from prison by a parole board (Carter 2007, 411–412). Haywood Patterson escaped from prison in 1948 and became a fugitive (413). In 1976, Governor George Wallace issued the only pardon ever granted for a member of the Scottsboro Boys when he pardoned Clarence Norris (418–427).

During their time in the Alabama prison system, the young men experienced unspeakable conditions and were repeatedly assaulted by prison guards and other prisoners. In addition, most of the prisons in Alabama were infested with rats and snakes that contaminated the food served to the inmates (Linder, "Scottsboro Boys").

The Scottsboro Boys case illustrated how difficult it was for blacks to receive a fair trial when they were charged with crimes in the South during the early 20th century, particularly black men accused of raping white women. While the case revealed the evils of white prosecutors and jurors who devalued the freedoms and lives of blacks, it also highlighted the heroism of whites such as Samuel Leibowitz, Judge James Horton, and the justices of the U.S. Supreme Court who played a significant role in saving the lives of nine innocent persons (Linder, "Scottsboro Boys").

From a historical perspective, the Scottsboro Boys case provided the U.S. Supreme Court an opportunity to take a major step toward ending racial discrimination in the area of jury selection and also allowed the Court to establish a right to an attorney for citizens charged with a capital offense and laid the foundation for nationalizing the right to an attorney upon the states in *Gideon v. Wainwright* (1963). Because of the Scottsboro Boys trials, it is less likely that a defendant might be convicted based upon the racial prejudice of a jury and also less likely that the American criminal justice system might produce a wrongful conviction because of inadequate legal counsel (Acker 2007, 195–209).

 ## Samuel Leibowitz

Samuel Leibowitz was born in Romania on August 14, 1893. He came to the United States at the age of four with his parents as Jewish immigrants. After receiving his undergraduate and law degrees from Cornell University, Leibowitz began work as a criminal defense attorney because it was one career in which he would not face discrimination as a Jewish American in the early 20th century (Linder, "Samuel Leibowitz").

By 1929, Leibowitz had become the best attorney in New York City. He credited his success to meticulous preparation and knowledge of the law. While Leibowitz participated in many important trials, he did not gain national recognition until his defense of Harry Hoffman, who worked as a motion picture operator on Staten Island. A jury had found Hoffman guilty of murdering a young woman, and he was given 20 years in prison. Leibowitz was able to secure an acquittal for Hoffman in a second trial when his ballistics research of the case revealed the possibility that another man may have committed the murder (Vile 2001, 461–462).

Leibowitz is most remembered in history for his defense of nine African American youths in Scottsboro, Alabama, who were accused of raping two white women in 1931. When the U.S. Supreme Court overturned the convictions of the black youths after their first trial because they were denied legal representation, Leibowitz was asked by the International Labor Defense, a communist organization, to represent the young men in the second trials. Interestingly, Leibowitz was a member of the Democratic Party and did not associate with communists or radicals (Linder, "Samuel Leibowitz").

Leibowitz was given little chance of winning an acquittal for the defendants because of the hostile environment in the South. Throughout the trials, Leibowitz and the black defendants needed to be protected by members of the National Guard for fear of being lynched. After a second trial for two of the defendants, Leibowitz was frustrated when an all-white jury returned guilty verdicts and death sentences. The convictions were the first cases that he had ever lost in 15 years as a criminal defense lawyer. However, in 1936, the U.S. Supreme Court overturned the convictions when Leibowitz convinced the justices that the two defendants had been denied due process because blacks had been systematically excluded from the jury. After battling for four years on the Scottsboro cases, Leibowitz finally was able to negotiate the freedom of four of the defendants in exchange for allowing the prosecution of the other defendants to proceed (Linder, "Samuel Leibowitz").

After the Scottsboro Boys trial, Leibowitz returned to New York City to continue his legal practice. Although Leibowitz lost the two cases in the Scottsboro trials, he never lost a murder case during his career. He argued a total of 78 murder cases, won 77 acquittals, and had one trial end with a hung jury (Linder, "Samuel Leibowitz"). In 1941, he was appointed to serve as a judge on the county court in Brooklyn. As a judge, Leibowitz had a reputation for handing down tough sentences and supporting the use of capital punishment. He also was a staunch opponent of organized crime and led a grand jury investigation into whether New York police officers had been corrupted by the organized crime syndicate. On January 11, 1978, Leibowitz died at the age of 84 (Vile 2001, 465).

 ## Summary of *Powell v. Alabama* (1932)

In *Powell v. Alabama* (1932), the U.S. Supreme Court voted 7–2 to overturn the convictions and death sentences of eight black defendants who had been found guilty of sexually assaulting two white women. In his majority opinion for the U.S. Supreme Court, Justice Sutherland ruled that the due process rights of the defendants under the Fourteenth Amendment had been violated because Alabama did not provide adequate legal representation for the young black men. Because the Fourteenth Amendment addressed limitations on the power of the states, it was used as a vehicle to nationalize the Sixth Amendment right to counsel in death penalty cases. As a result of *Powell v. Alabama* (1932), states were required to provide adequate legal counsel to any defendant facing the possibility of a death sentence and, therefore, the eight defendants were entitled to new trials (Carter 2007, 161–163).

References

Acker, James A. *Scottsboro and Its Legacy: The Cases That Challenged American Legal and Social Justice.* Westport, CT: Praeger Publishers, 2007.

Carter, Dan T. *Scottsboro: A Tragedy of the American South.* Baton Rouge: Louisiana University Press, 2007.

Feldman, Ellen. *Scottsboro.* New York: W. W. Norton and Company, 2008.

Horne, Gerald. *Powell v. Alabama: The Scottsboro Boys and American Justice.* New York: Franklin Watts, 1997.

Linder, Douglas O. "Samuel Leibowitz." *Famous Trials.* http://www.law.umkc.edu/fac ulty/projects/ftrials/scottsboro/SB_bLieb.html (accessed August 19, 2009).

Linder, Douglas O. "The Scottsboro Boys Trial." *Famous Trials.* http://www.law.umkc. edu/faculty/projects/FTrials/scottsboro/scottsb.htm (accessed March 17, 2009).

Vile, John R. *Great American Lawyers: An Encyclopedia.* Santa Barbara, CA: ABC-CLIO, 2001.

Justice Sutherland's opinion for the Supreme Court in *Powell v. Alabama* (1932)

Mr. Justice Sutherland delivered the opinion of the Court.

The petitioners, hereinafter referred to as defendants, are negroes charged with the crime of rape, committed upon the persons of two white girls. The crime is said to have been committed on March 25, 1931. The indictment was returned in a state court of first instance on March 31, and the record recites that, on the same day, the defendants were arraigned and entered pleas of not guilty. There is a further recital to the effect that, upon the arraignment, they were represented by counsel. But no counsel had been employed, and aside from a statement made by the trial judge several days later during a colloquy immediately preceding the trial, the record does not disclose when, or under what circumstances, an appointment of counsel was made, or who was appointed. During the colloquy referred to, the trial judge, in response to a question, said that he had appointed all the members of the bar for the purpose of arraigning the defendants, and then, of course, anticipated that the members of the bar would continue to help the defendants if no counsel appeared. Upon the argument here, both sides accepted that as a correct statement of the facts concerning the matter.

There was a severance upon the request of the state, and the defendants were tried in three separate groups, as indicated above. As each of the three cases was called for trial, each defendant was arraigned, and, having the . . . indictment read to him, entered a plea of not guilty. Whether the original arraignment and pleas were regarded as ineffective is not shown. Each of the three trials was completed within a single day. Under the Alabama statute, the punishment for rape is to be fixed by the jury, and, in its discretion, may be from ten years' imprisonment to death. The juries found defendants guilty and imposed the death penalty upon all. The trial court overruled motions for new trials and sentenced the defendants in accordance with the verdicts. The judgments were affirmed by the state supreme court. Chief Justice Anderson thought the defendants had not been accorded a fair trial, and strongly dissented. . . .

In this court, the judgments are assailed upon the grounds that the defendants, and each of them, were denied due process of law and the equal protection of the laws in contravention of the Fourteenth Amendment, specifically as follows: (1) they were not given a fair, impartial and deliberate trial; (2) they were denied the right of counsel, with the accustomed incidents of consultation and opportunity of preparation for trial, and (3) they were tried before juries from which qualified members of their own race were systematically excluded. These questions were properly raised and saved in the courts below. . . .

The record shows that, on the day when the offense is said to have been committed, these defendants, together with a number of other negroes, were upon a freight train on its way through Alabama. On the same train were seven white boys and the two white girls. A fight took . . . place between the negroes and the white boys in the course of which the white boys, with the exception of one named Gilley, were thrown off the train. A message was sent ahead, reporting the fight and asking that every negro be gotten off the train. The participants in the fight, and the two girls, were in an open gondola car. The two girls testified that each of them was assaulted by six different negroes in turn, and they identified the seven defendants as having been among the number. None of the white boys was called to testify, with the exception of Gilley, who was called in rebuttal.

Before the train reached Scottsboro, Alabama, a sheriff's posse seized the defendants and two other negroes. Both girls and the negroes then were taken to Scottsboro, the county seat. Word of their coming and of the alleged assault had preceded them, and they were met at Scottsboro by a large crowd. It does not sufficiently appear that the defendants were seriously threatened with, or that they were actually in danger of, mob violence, but it does appear that the attitude of the community was one of great hostility. The sheriff thought it necessary to call for the militia to assist in safeguarding the prisoners. Chief Justice Anderson pointed out in his opinion that every step taken from the arrest and arraignment to the sentence was accompanied by the military. Soldiers took the defendants to Gadsden for safekeeping, brought them back to Scottsboro for arraignment, returned them to Gadsden for safekeeping while awaiting trial, escorted them to Scottsboro for trial a few days later, and guarded the courthouse and grounds at every stage of the proceedings. It is perfectly apparent that the proceedings, from beginning to end, took place in an atmosphere of tense, hostile and excited public sentiment. During the entire time, the defendants were closely confined or were under military guard. The record does not disclose their ages, except that one of them was nineteen; but the . . . record clearly indicates that most, if not all, of them were youthful, and they are constantly referred to as "the boys." They were ignorant and illiterate. All of them were residents of other states, where alone members of their families or friends resided.

However guilty defendants, upon due inquiry, might prove to have been, they were, until convicted, presumed to be innocent. It was the duty of the court having their cases in charge to see that they were denied no necessary incident of a fair trial. With any error of the state court involving alleged contravention of the state statutes or constitution we, of course, have nothing to do. The sole inquiry which we are permitted to make is whether the federal Constitution was contravened, . . . and as to that, we confine ourselves, as already suggested, to the inquiry whether the defendants were in substance denied the right of counsel, and, if so, whether such denial infringes the due process clause of the Fourteenth Amendment. . . .

It thus will be seen that, until the very morning of the trial, no lawyer had been named or definitely designated to represent the defendants. Prior to that time, the trial judge had "appointed all the members of the bar" for the limited "purpose of arraigning the defendants." Whether they would represent the defendants thereafter if no counsel appeared in their behalf was a matter of speculation only, or, as the judge indicated, of mere anticipation on the part of the court. Such a designation, even if made for all purposes, would, in our opinion, have fallen far short of meeting, in any proper sense, a requirement for the appointment of counsel. How many lawyers were members of the bar does not appear, but, in the very nature of things, whether many or few, they would not, thus collectively named, have been given that clear appreciation of responsibility or impressed with that individual sense of duty which should and naturally would accompany the appointment of a selected member of the bar, specifically named and assigned. . . .

The Constitution of Alabama provides that, in all criminal prosecutions the accused shall enjoy the right to have the assistance of counsel, and a state statute requires the court in a capital case where the defendant. . .is unable to employ counsel to appoint counsel for him. The state supreme court held that these provisions had not been infringed, and with that holding we are powerless to interfere. The question, however, which it is our duty, and within our power, to decide is whether the denial of the assistance of counsel contravenes the due process clause of the Fourteenth Amendment to the federal Constitution. . . .

The fact that the right involved is of such a character that it cannot be denied without violating those "fundamental principles of liberty and justice which lie at the base of all our civil and political institutions" (*Hebert v. Louisiana* [1926]), . . . is obviously one of those compelling considerations which must prevail in determining whether it is embraced within the due process clause of the Fourteenth Amendment. . . .

While the question has never been categorically determined by this court, a consideration of the nature of the right and a review of the expressions of this and other courts, makes it clear that the right to the aid of counsel is of this fundamental character. . . .

In the light of the facts outlined in the forepart of this opinion—the ignorance and illiteracy of the defendants, their youth, the circumstances of public hostility, the imprisonment and the close surveillance of the defendants by the military forces, the fact that their friends and families were all in other states and communication with them necessarily difficult, and, above all, that they stood in deadly peril of their lives—we think the failure of the trial court to give them reasonable time and opportunity to secure counsel was a clear denial of due process. . . .

Richard "Bruno" Hauptmann Trial (1935)

The trial of Richard "Bruno" Hauptmann attracted nationwide attention because it involved the kidnapping and death of the young child of Charles A. Lindbergh Sr., the national hero who was the first pilot to fly nonstop across the Atlantic Ocean in 1927. The trial highlighted the use of scientific experts who connected Hauptmann to key evidence and the role of the media, which caused a public hysteria to develop around a crime committed against a national celebrity. The biased media coverage made it difficult to conduct a fair trial of an immigrant from a discriminated group in society. Although Hauptmann was most likely guilty of kidnapping and extortion, it remains a subject of debate even today whether sufficient evidence existed to find Hauptmann guilty of first-degree murder, and subsequently executed, for what appeared to be the accidental death of a kidnapped child (Gardner 2004, 1–4).

On the evening of March 1, 1932, in Hopewell, New Jersey, Charles A. Lindbergh Jr., the 20-month old son of Charles and Anne Lindbergh, was kidnapped from the second floor of his home. A ransom note was left near the window of the second floor room demanding $50,000. The ransom note contained several misspelled words. Police later discovered a broken ladder, a chisel, and large footprints outside of the Lindbergh home. Unfortunately, police investigators never measured the size of the footprints. In the aftermath of the kidnapping, news reporters and the public fascinated by the dramatic crime raided the Lindbergh property and took various items as souvenirs. Because police investigators had failed to secure the property as a crime scene, it was likely that valuable evidence was either tainted or removed from the Lindbergh estate (Linder, "Bruno Hauptmann").

Charles Lindbergh told the New Jersey State Police that he wanted to negotiate personally with the kidnappers and did not want law enforcement to interfere until after the ransom money was paid and the young child was returned to his parents. Charles and Anne Lindbergh broadcast a statement on NBC radio asking for the safe return of the young boy and promised not to reveal the identity of the kidnapper to the authorities (Linder, "Bruno Hauptmann").

On March 5, 1932, the Lindberghs received a handwritten note from the kidnapper who informed them that the child was safe and they would be provided information about where to deliver the $50,000 in the near future. Three days later, a letter was published in a Bronx newspaper that had been written by a retired principal named Dr. John Condon. Condon inserted himself into the case by stating in the letter that he would meet privately with the kidnapper and give them an extra $1,000 in addition to the $50,000 ransom. Condon also promised not to reveal the kidnapper's name to anyone. The following day, Condon received a letter from the kidnapper instructing him to get the money from the Lindberghs and future instructions would be provided about a place and time for the delivery of the ransom (Fisher 1994, 40–43).

Lindbergh met with Condon and the two decided to publish a message in the *New York American* newspaper to the kidnapper that the ransom money was ready to be delivered. Condon received a note to meet the kidnapper at night in a cemetery. In the cemetery, Condom met a man who spoke with a German accent and tried to cover his face with a handkerchief. The kidnapper asked Condon for the money, but Condon stated that he wanted to see the baby first. During the conversation, the kidnapper asked Condon what would happen to him if the baby was dead. Before leaving, the kidnapper seemed to suggest that others were involved in the kidnapping and that he would send the baby's sleeping outfit to Condon as a "token" (Linder, "Bruno Hauptmann").

Condon received a grey sleeping outfit worn by the Lindbergh baby in a package a couple of days after his meeting with the kidnapper. On March 31, 1932, Condon received another letter from the kidnapper asking that the money be delivered by Saturday, April 4, 1932. The Internal Revenue Service (IRS) assisted Lindbergh in putting the money together. The IRS plan would be to give the kidnapper currency with yellow seals, known as "gold notes." Because the gold notes were going to be withdrawn from circulation by the U.S. in the near future, it would make the money stand apart from other currency (Linder, "Bruno Hauptmann").

Condon received another message from the kidnapper asking to meet in a different cemetery. Condon and Charles Lindbergh went to the cemetery where Condon delivered the $50,000 to the kidnapper who provided a note with the location of the Lindbergh child. The note indicated that the Lindbergh baby was in a boat near Cape Cod along the Atlantic coast (Fisher 1994, 50). As Lindbergh took off in a plane in search of his child, a truck driver stopping along the side of the road to take a rest discovered the dead body of Charles A. Lindbergh Jr. in a wooded area in Mount Rose, New Jersey, only a few miles from where he had been kidnapped from his home. An autopsy revealed that the Lindbergh baby had died from a blow to the head, most likely when the kidnapper fell from the ladder that broke as he was climbing down from the second floor window (86–92).

During the next two years, police kept track of the locations where the gold note currency was being used and were able to determine that most of the notes were being used in the German immigrant community of Yorkville in Manhattan. Investigators received a major break when a gas station attendant in Manhattan jotted down the license plate number of a customer who had used one of the gold notes. The license plate number belonged to a German immigrant by the name of Richard "Bruno" Hauptmann. The key suspect in the Lindbergh kidnapping and murder was a 35-year old who resided in the Bronx, New York, and worked as a carpenter. In a search of Hauptmann's home, police found over $12,000 of the gold note currency in his garage, and Condon's phone number was discovered penciled on a closet door (Gardner 2004, 189–190).

On September 24, 1934, Richard "Bruno" Hauptmann was charged with extorting money from Charles Lindbergh and, on October 10, 1934, he was formally charged in the kidnapping and murder of the Lindbergh baby. The trial was scheduled to begin on January 2, 1935, in Flemington, New Jersey. The trial became an international sensation as the media, spectators, and merchants selling "Lindbergh memorabilia" flooded the small town of Flemington. Many celebrities, including Jack Benny, attended the trial (Linder, "Bruno Hauptmann").

Judge Thomas Trenchard presided over the trial, while Hauptmann was defended by Edward J. Reilly. David Wilentz, the attorney general for New Jersey, headed up the prosecution team. Wilentz opened the trial by describing how Hauptmann committed the crime and ended by remarking that the state would seek the death penalty in the case (Linder, "Bruno Hauptmann").

The prosecution called as its first witness Anne Lindbergh, who gave her personal account of the ordeal. During her testimony, Wilentz had Anne Lindbergh identify the clothes worn by her child on the night of the abduction. The defense team decided not to cross-examine Anne Lindbergh who clearly had an emotional impact on the jury (Gardner 2004, 272–275).

Charles Lindbergh was then called to the witness stand. The national hero detailed his own account of the night of the kidnapping and then stated that he heard a voice in the cemetery on the night that they delivered the money to the kidnapper. Lindbergh asserted that the voice was that of Hauptmann. During cross-examination, Hauptmann's attorney, Edward J. Reilly, suggested that the kidnapping was most likely committed by disgruntled neighbors who had recently been involved in a property dispute with the Lindberghs. Reilly then raised the possibility that one of the maids was involved in the kidnapping or perhaps Dr. Condon may have answered his own advertisement in the newspaper and was involved in a conspiracy to kidnap the Lindbergh baby (Gardner 2004, 188–203; 275–280).

The Lindbergh's maid, a Scottish immigrant named Betty Gow, testified for the prosection by recounting how she identified the baby at the morgue. Reilly's cross-examination attempted to connect Gow to organized criminals from Detroit and suggested that she was involved in the crime with a number of other individuals. Gow was so traumatized after the cross-examination that she fainted (Gardner 2004, 280–285).

The prosecution then called a number of New Jersey state troopers who testified about what they observed at the crime scene, such as the broken ladder and the footprints leading away from the Lindbergh home. The defense attorneys made fun of the state troopers for failing to measure the footprints and for not examining them closely. The state troopers were also criticized for being unable to find any fingerprints at the crime scene (Gardner 2004, 310–318).

Amandus Hochmuth, a neighbor of the Lindberghs, testified that, on the night of the kidnapping, he saw Hauptmann drive a green automobile toward the Lindbergh home with a ladder inside the vehicle (Gardner 2004, 291–296). Then, Dr. Condon provided the most dramatic testimony of the trial when he described his meetings with the kidnapper in the cemeteries and then proceeded to identify Hauptmann as the man who received the $50,000 ransom from him in exchange for the note with the whereabouts of the Lindbergh baby (Fisher 1994, 292–297).

The final witnesses for the prosecution included Colonel Norman Schwarzkopf, the superintendent of the New Jersey State Police, who discussed how Hauptmann had voluntarily provided samples of his handwriting, and then a handwriting expert followed by matching Hauptmann's samples to the ransom notes (Gardner 2004, 299–310). In perhaps the most emotional portion of the trial, a county physician provided details of the autopsy and the fractured skull of the Lindbergh child (91–92). A wood expert ended the prosecution's case by identifying a piece of wood on the broken ladder recovered from the crime scene as having come from Hauptmann's house. Apparently, Hauptmann had extended the height of the ladder by using wooden boards from his attic (310–325).

Edward J. Reilly called Hauptmann to testify as the first witness for the defense. In broken English, Hauptmann denied committing the kidnapping or authoring the handwritten notes demanding ransom. Hauptmann explained that the currency of gold notes found in his garage had belonged to a friend, Isidor Fisch, who had returned to Germany in December 1932, but had recently passed away. On cross-examination, Wilentz confronted Hauptmann with his criminal record during his early life spent in Germany, including a burglary where he used an extended ladder to gain access to a second floor window. Wilentz also asked the defendant to explain how the words spelled incorrectly on the handwriting samples that Hauptmann provided to police were the same words spelled incorrectly on the ransom notes. Wilentz continued to confront Hauptmann with additional evidence against him such as the gold notes found in his garage, the wooden board missing from his attic linked to the ladder, and Condon's phone number found in his house. In the end, Wilentz's cross-examination was a huge success in establishing the guilt of Hauptmann (Linder, "Bruno Hauptmann").

Reilly then attempted to use a number of witnesses to provide an alibi for Hauptmann; however, the prosecution discredited the witnesses because they either came forward in response to radio advertisements aired by the defense team seeking anyone who might be able to provide an alibi for Hauptmann or they were testifying in exchange for money (Linder, "Bruno Hauptmann").

In closing statements before the jury, Reilly attempted to convince the jurors that the kidnapping and murder of the Lindbergh baby was most likely the result of a conspiracy between Condor, Fisch, and one or more house servants working for the Lindberghs. Reilly suggested that the Lindbergh's dog did not bark on the night of the crime because the kidnapping probably was committed by someone inside the house (Linder, "Bruno Hauptmann"). Wilentz wrapped up the case for the prosecution by providing a lengthy discussion of the mountain of evidence against Hauptmann. Wilentz ended by saying that if the jury was convinced beyond a reasonable doubt that he was guilty, then he should receive the harshest punishment, the death penalty (Gardner 2004, 243).

The jury began deliberations on February 13, 1935, and took fewer than 12 hours to convict Hauptmann of first-degree murder. Judge Trenchard then proceeded to sentence Hauptmann to death by electrocution (Gardner 2004, 356–357). On October 9, 1935, the New Jersey Supreme Court unanimously denied an appeal from Hauptmann's lawyers. Finally, the New Jersey Board of Pardons also rejected Hauptmann's appeal by a vote of 7 to 1. The governor of New Jersey, Harold Hoffman, was the only member of the board who voted in favor of Hauptmann's appeal. Hoffman actually visited Hauptmann in prison and became convinced that the kidnapping was most likely part of a larger conspiracy. Because kidnapping was not yet a federal crime at the time of the Lindbergh abduction, the federal courts were prevented from reviewing the case. Prior to his execution, Hauptmann claimed that he was innocent and had been convicted on circumstantial evidence. On April 3, 1936, Hauptmann was electrocuted in the New Jersey State Prison (Linder, "Bruno Hauptmann").

The Lindbergh trial brought about many changes to law and society. For example, the case led to legislation that would make kidnapping a federal crime. In addition, the role of the media surfaced as a significant factor in the criminal justice process based upon the fact that Hauptmann was viewed as guilty in the court of public opinion due to the pretrial publicity. As the media has expanded into other areas besides newspaper and radio, it has created more challenges for defendants in high-profile cases to receive a fair trial and for justice to be served. In the modern era, Hauptmann probably would have been convicted of kidnapping, extortion, and involuntary manslaughter, also known as unintentionally causing death because of reckless behavior. Defendants convicted of such crimes do not even face the possibility of capital punishment in the modern era. However, because the biased media coverage caused the public to direct their fear and anger toward an immigrant from an unpopular group in society, Hauptmann was unfairly convicted of first-degree murder and executed for causing the accidental death of the child of a national hero (Gardner 2004, 1–4).

Charles Lindbergh

Charles Augustus Lindbergh was born in Detroit, Michigan, on February 4, 1902. He was the only child of Charles and Evangeline Lindbergh (Berg 1998, 26). His father served as a U.S. Congressman from 1907 to 1917 and opposed the U.S. involvement in World War I (34–38). Lindbergh developed an interest in flying airplanes at a young age and decided to study mechanical engineering at the University of Wisconsin-Madison. After withdrawing from college in 1922, Lindbergh enrolled as a student at a flying school in Lincoln, Nebraska (54–60). In 1924, Lindbergh joined the U.S. Army where he was trained at a military flight school. A year later, Lindbergh graduated first in his class as a Second Lieutenant. Lindbergh's one year of training with the army was critical to his development as a pilot (72–80).

After leaving the army, Lindbergh was hired by the Robertson Aircraft Corporation to provide air mail service from St. Louis to Chicago (Berg, 1998, 84–89). At this time, Lindbergh also began his pursuit of the Orteig Prize, a $25,000 award to be presented to the first pilot to fly nonstop across the Atlantic Ocean from New York City to Paris, France. When Lindbergh attempted his flight across the Atlantic on May 20, 1927, six famous pilots had already lost their lives attempting to win the award. It took Lindbergh roughly 33 hours to fly his plane, *The Spirit of St. Louis,* to Paris where a crowd of 150,000 people had awaited his arrival. Lindbergh gained international fame and, upon his return to the United States, he was given a hero's welcome as President Calvin Coolidge presented him with the Distinguished Flying Cross. After his record-setting flight, Lindbergh became a spokesperson for the promotion of air travel and wrote a critically acclaimed book, *We,* which documented his transatlantic flight (90–131). Lindbergh was not only an aviator but a scientist. His research on the development of an artificial heart led to his invention of a glass pump for a French surgeon. Lindbergh's invention was credited with advancing research which eventually made heart surgeries possible (221).

In 1929, Lindbergh married Anne Morrow and the couple had six children (Berg 1998, 186–202). On March 1, 1932, Charles Augustus Lindbergh Jr., the 20-month old child of Charles and Anne Lindbergh, was kidnapped from their home in New Jersey. The international media sensationalized the kidnapping as the "crime of the century." A search for the young child took place over a 10-week period while the family negotiated a ransom with the kidnapper (237–275). On May 12, 1932, the dead body of the young child was discovered in a wooded area about three miles from the Lindbergh home. Police eventually arrested Bruno Hauptmann based upon a trace of the currency used as ransom payment. In 1935, the Hauptmann trial was conducted amidst a media frenzy in which the defendant was convicted and subsequently executed in 1936 (309–335). In the aftermath of the kidnapping trial, Lindbergh took his wife and children to Europe in search of seclusion (340–341).

In the late 1930s, Lindbergh toured the aviation facilities of the French and German governments at their request and accepted the German medal of honor for which he was harshly criticized by opponents of the Nazi regime (Berg 1998, 424). In 1941, Lindbergh publicly opposed the United States involvement in World War II (386–432). After the bombing at Pearl Harbor, however, Lindbergh ended his opposition and became an aviation advisor for the U.S. military during the war. While serving as a military adviser in the Pacific, Lindbergh volunteered to fly 50 combat missions as a civilian (434–470).

In the 1950s, Lindbergh avoided the public spotlight and worked as a consultant for the U.S. Air Force and was eventually appointed by President Dwight D. Eisenhower as a brigadier general (Berg 1998, 475–488). At this time, Lindbergh was also employed as a consultant for Pan American Airways where he helped to develop the Boeing 747 jet (448). Lindbergh published another book, *The Spirit of St. Louis,* in 1953 which contained a more detailed account of his famous flight across the Atlantic. The book was awarded the Pulitzer Prize (488–491). In the 1960s, Lindbergh spoke publicly about the importance of conservation and started a campaign to protect different species of whales (526–527). On August 26, 1974, Lindbergh died of cancer at his home in Hawaii (554–560).

References

Ahlgren, Gregory, and Stephen Monier. *Crime of the Century: The Lindbergh Kidnapping Hoax.* Boston: Branden Books, 1993.

Berg, Andrew Scott. *Lindbergh.* New York: Putnam Books, 1998.

Fisher, Jim. *The Lindbergh Case.* New Brunswick, NJ: Rutgers University Press, 1994.

Gardner, Lloyd C. *The Case That Never Dies: The Lindbergh Kidnapping.* New Brunswick, NJ: Rutgers University Press, 2004.

Linder, Douglas O. "The Trial of Richard 'Bruno' Hauptmann: An Account." *Famous Trials.* http://www.law.umkc.edu/faculty/projects/ftrials/Hauptmann/AccountHauptmann.html (accessed April 4, 2009).

The Nazi Saboteurs Trial (1942)

The Nazi Saboteurs trial of 1942 highlighted the delicate balance between national security and freedom. In the aftermath of the Pearl Harbor attack, German spies were arrested for plotting attacks in major U.S. cities, and public anxiety and tension increased dramatically. In an attempt to alleviate fears and send a strong message to enemies of the United States, President Franklin D. Roosevelt issued military orders and used an unprecedented amount of power to resolve the situation quickly. The military trial and executions of six German saboteurs carried out over the course of four weeks raised serious questions about whether the United States had sacrificed the principle of due process in exchange for a sense of security and unity (Fisher 2005, 112–161).

On December 7, 1941, the United States was attacked by Japanese forces at Pearl Harbor, and the United States entered World War II by declaring war on the Axis powers, namely Japan and Germany. Six months later, in June 1942, eight German soldiers were transported by Nazi submarines to the eastern coast of the United States. The German soldiers had been trained in the techniques of sabotage in Berlin and planned to commit terrorist attacks against the United States. Four of the German soldiers—George Dasch, Ernst Burger, Richard Quirin, and Heinrich Heinck—landed at Long Island, New York, while the four other German soldiers—Edward Kerling, Herbert Haupt, Werner Thiel, and Hermann Neubauer—landed at Ponte Vedra Beach, Florida. Upon their arrival, the soldiers buried their uniforms and their explosives which were to be used to bomb facilities and industries making weapons for the U.S. military (McCann 2006, 78–80).

The German soldiers that landed at Long Island were noticed by a patrolman for the Coast Guard, John C. Cullen. The soldiers threatened Cullen but, then, proceeded to give him a bribe of $300 in an attempt to keep him quiet. Cullen accepted the bribe in order to save his life, but he returned to his station and informed his superiors about the Germans. The Long Island soldiers fled to New York City dressed in civilian clothes, while the four soldiers in Florida traveled to Jacksonville also in civilian clothes to mix with the population (McCann 2006, 80–81).

Unknown to the other German soldiers, George Dasch had never intended to participate in the attacks against the United States. Dasch had planned all along to turn himself in to the Federal Bureau of Investigation (FBI), and he convinced one of the other German soldiers, Ernst Burger, to join him. Dasch traveled to Washington, D.C., where he provided a detailed confession to the FBI. Initially, FBI officials did not believe Dasch until he showed them instructions that he had received from his Nazi commanders written in invisible ink and $85,000 in cash inside a briefcase. FBI officials quickly arrested Dasch and rounded up the other seven terrorists who were at large (McCann 2006, 81–82).

On July 2, 1942, President Franklin Roosevelt issued two military orders. The first order stated that any enemies attempting to commit sabotage against the United States were to be subject to the "law of war" and tried before a military commission, also known as a tribunal or court. The second order established the military commission for the eight Nazi saboteurs which was to be carried out quickly and secretly with no opportunity for review by the American court system. Roosevelt's orders for a military trial were based on the international "law of war." The "law of war" was an undefined area of law that allowed Roosevelt to treat the Germans as "unlawful combatants" because they secretly planned to destroy life and property within the United States. If the Germans had been "lawful combatants" who followed the rules of war by fighting on the battlefield wearing enemy uniforms, then they would have been entitled to a civil trial as prisoners of war (Cohen and Wells 2004, 74–75).

Because Congress had declared war on Germany, Roosevelt, as commander-in-chief, felt justified in exercising an unlimited amount of power based upon the need to protect the country. In essence, Roosevelt took power away from both the legislative and judicial branches of government, which would not be able to affect the military trial. Roosevelt's orders also gave himself sole power to review the final decision made by the military commission (Fisher 2005, 50–52).

President Roosevelt found it necessary to use the military court mainly because the civilian courts probably would have produced a less favorable outcome. According to congressional statute, the German spies would have been facing 30 years in prison if convicted of sabotage in a civilian court. However, the eight Germans had not yet committed any acts of violence at the time of their arrest and would have been tried simply on charges of conspiracy which carried only a maximum penalty of three years in prison (Fisher 2005, 42–68). In contrast, the military trial provided the opportunity for creating a harsher punishment, and the enemy spies would become eligible for the death penalty (Johnson 2007, 147–149).

The military court also may have been the better option because the federal government was embarrassed that the sabotage was only prevented when Dasch turned himself in to the FBI. If this fact emerged during an open and public trial, it would have made the federal government look vulnerable and perhaps encouraged Germany and Japan to order more secret attacks. A military trial conducted secretly behind closed doors gave Roosevelt control over the proceedings and the outcome of the trial (Fisher 2005, 28–65).

Seven high-ranking generals were assigned by the president to sit on the military commission and their task was to evaluate the evidence and issue a ruling concerning the fate of the eight saboteurs. At his request, George Dasch was provided his own defense counsel, Colonel Carl L. Ristine, perhaps because he had come forward to expose the plot. Others speculated that he might have turned state's evidence and struck a secret deal with the Roosevelt administration. The other seven defendants were represented by two military officers, Colonel Cassius M. Dowell and Colonel Kenneth Royall. President Roosevelt assigned U.S. Attorney General Francis Biddle to serve as the prosecuting attorney for the military trial (Johnson 2007, 149).

The military trial began on July 8, 1942, under heavy security and secrecy in a conference room in the Justice Department. Therefore, the media was given virtually no information about the proceedings other than general press releases. The attorneys participating in the trial were only allowed to make general comments to the press (McCann 2006, 83).

On the first day of the trial, Colonel Royall argued that the use of a military trial was illegal because the "law of war" was supposed to apply only to U.S. citizens caught assisting the enemy. However, General Frank R. McCoy, the leader of the commission, overruled Royall's objection. The charges against the eight defendants were then formally read in the conference room. The defendants were accused of being enemies against the United States on behalf of the German government and also of acting as spies in an attempt to destroy military facilities within the United States. After the charges were read, John Cullen of the Coast Guard was the first witness to testify. Cullen identified Dasch as the man that he encountered on the beach at Long Island, New York. Next, FBI agents were called to testify on behalf of the prosecution about the interrogation of Dasch. At this time, it was revealed that an FBI agent had promised Dasch a presidential pardon in exchange for his cooperation. Royall asked that Dasch's 254-page confession be introduced as evidence and the confession was read in its entirety by the FBI agents over the course of three days. Burger's confession also was eventually introduced as evidence as well as incriminating statements signed by the other defendants during their interrogation by FBI agents. The best evidence in favor of conviction had been provided by the defendants themselves (Johnson 2007, 161–166).

The prosecution also bolstered their case with witnesses designed to reveal the seriousness of the plot such as the FBI chemist who explained how the defendants used ammonia to read the invisible instructions provided on their handkerchiefs by their Nazi commanders. As the prosecution presented its evidence over the course of 11 days, it became apparent that the defendants were going to be found guilty. In addition to the significant amount of evidence against the defendants and the obstacles of securing an acquittal in a military trial, the fact that prosecution witnesses were allowed to discuss classified information involving national security was a bad sign for the suspects. Obviously, the generals would not have allowed the German spies to hear testimony about classified information if there was any chance that they might be found not guilty. Attorney General Biddle rested the prosecution's case on July 20, 1942 (Johnson 2007, 166–180).

In his opening statement in defense of the Nazi saboteurs, Colonel Royall argued that the defendants had not yet committed any crime when they were arrested. He asserted that simply thinking about committing a crime did not constitute a violation of the law. After Royall's introductory comments, each of the eight defendants provided testimony for the defense. Five of the defendants—Haupt, Neubauer, Thiel, Heinck, and Quirin—provided similar testimony in which they told the commission how they had been forced or tricked into participating in the sabotage operation by the Nazi government. The five defendants maintained that they had no intention of spying or committing sabotage against the United States. Each stated that they had wanted to turn themselves in to the FBI but feared the Nazi government would harm their families in Germany (Cohen, "The Keystone Commandos").

Attorney General Francis Biddle's cross-examination of the five defendants followed a similar strategy where he sought to discredit each witness. For example, Biddle referred to their membership in the Nazi party as evidence of their loyalty toward Adolf Hitler. Biddle also read the signed statements that each defendant had made to FBI officials after their arrest which demonstrated their intention to commit sabotage against American military facilities (Johnson 2007, 179–187).

Unlike the first five defendants, Edward Kerling stood out as a defiant witness who wanted to prove that he was not a coward. During his testimony, he expressed his support for Hitler and Germany and, in the process, sealed his fate with the military commission (Johnson 2007, 184–186).

Next, George Dasch testified for the defense by detailing how he participated in the operation simply to escape Germany. He emphasized that he voluntarily went to the FBI with information to expose the plot. While Dasch was very nervous during his testimony and perhaps tried too hard to convey that he did not support Hitler and the Nazi Party, he achieved some success in expressing how he had always planned to cooperate with American authorities. In addition, the depositions of the FBI agents who interrogated Dasch were entered into evidence to support his testimony. On cross-examination, Biddle tried to get Dasch to admit that he was the leader of the operation, but Dasch stated that the commanders in Germany had full control of the plot. Dasch emerged from his testimony as a powerful and truthful witness (Johnson 2007, 188–192).

Ernst Burger was the final witness for the defense. Burger discussed his decision to go along with Dasch's plan to cooperate with the FBI. Burger actually had been more helpful than Dasch in providing information to FBI agents during the interrogation process. During cross-examination, Biddle was unsuccessful at portraying Burger as a loyal Nazi, and Burger was able to convey that he participated in the operation because of his fear of Hitler. Burger had known Hitler personally in the 1920s and had spent 17 months in a Nazi concentration camp for simply criticizing Hitler in a scholarly paper. After Burger's testimony, the defense rested its case on July 27, 1942 (Johnson 2007, 192–193).

On the following day, Colonel Royall decided to file a motion in federal court that the military commission was a violation of the defendants' right to a jury trial under the Constitution. The defense counsel asserted that the eight Germans should have been tried in a civilian court, as opposed to the current military proceedings. Colonel Royall had become convinced that the trial was clearly set up to convict the defendants without a fair hearing (McCann 2006, 83). The military trial was being conducted in a manner that was clearly inconsistent with the standards of due process provided in a regular criminal court. For example, in a military trial, the burden of proof rested with the defendants. In other words, the German soldiers were guilty until proven innocent. The seven generals also had allowed evidence to be introduced against the defendants under a very lenient standard and the rules of procedure had been altered during the course of the trial, which violated federal law. In a civil trial, it would be questioned whether seven of the defendants should be represented by the same attorneys because, if one defendant appeared guilty, then it could negatively affect the fate of the other defendants. Whereas a unanimous vote was necessary to convict in a civilian trial, a two-thirds vote of the seven generals was only necessary to convict in the military trial. Finally, an appeal process had not been put in place for the German soldiers other than a review by President Roosevelt (Fisher 2005, 37–72).

The U.S. Supreme Court responded to Royall's motion by deciding to hear oral arguments immediately, and the military trial was temporarily suspended. On July 29, 1942, Royall presented his argument before the Supreme Court that the eight German soldiers should be tried before a normal criminal court with a civilian judge and jury. Royall noted that martial law had not been declared and the civilian courts were functioning properly. Royall based his argument upon the case precedent of *Ex parte Milligan* (1866) in which the Supreme Court had struck down President Abraham Lincoln's use of a military commission during the Civil War. In arguing in favor of the military trial, Attorney General Biddle argued that *Milligan* did not apply to the Germans who had violated the "law of war," which allowed for enemy spies to be shot on sight. On July 31, 1942, the U.S. Supreme Court issued its decision in *Ex parte Quirin* (1942) in which the justices unanimously agreed with Biddle and the military trial was allowed to continue (Johnson 2007, 194–195).

The closing arguments before the military commission were held on August 1, 1942. Royall provided detailed biographies of the defendants and tried to garner sympathy from the generals. Royall portrayed the Germans as men who only wanted to escape Nazi Germany but were threatened and manipulated into participating in the secret operation. Royall concluded by asking the generals not to impose a death sentence upon the men (Johnson 2007, 195).

Colonel Ristine then spoke for his client, George Dasch, by telling the generals how Dasch had left Germany, at one time in his life, and strongly opposed the Nazi regime. Ristine also reminded the generals that Dasch did not harm John Cullen, the Coast Guard patrolmen, whom he encountered on the beach at Long Island, even though he had been instructed to kill anyone that tried to interfere with the operation. Ristine concluded his closing argument by reminding the generals that Dasch never intended to carry out the operation and came forward and cooperated with the FBI to prevent the attacks against America (Johnson 2007, 195–196).

In his closing statement for the prosecution, Attorney General Biddle emphasized that the defendants came to the United States with the intent to commit sabotage. They also had planned to communicate with other spies located within the United States as well as with the German government abroad during the operation based upon the instructions written in invisible ink (Johnson 2007, 196–197).

On August 3, 1942, the seven high-ranking generals on the commission handed down their decision to President Roosevelt. Six of the Nazi saboteurs—Quirin, Heinck, Neubauer, Kerling, Haupt, and Thiel—were convicted and sentenced to death. Burger and Dasch also were also found guilty and sentenced to death, but because they had come forward on their own and cooperated with FBI officials, President Roosevelt reduced their punishments. Burger was given a life sentence of hard labor, while Dasch was given a 30-year sentence of hard labor. On August 8, 1942, the six Nazi saboteurs were executed by electrocution at the District of Columbia jail. Dasch and Burger served roughly six years in prison before President Harry Truman commuted their sentences on March 20, 1948, and deported the two men back to Germany (McCann 2006, 84).

The impact of the Nazi Saboteurs trial remains highly relevant in the 21st century. After the terrorist attacks on September 11, 2001, President George W. Bush used Roosevelt's military orders and the Supreme Court's decision in *Ex parte Quirin* (1942) to justify his actions in establishing military courts to try enemy combatants. Similar to Roosevelt, Bush used a national crisis to expand his powers as president in leading a controversial War on Terror that severely limited the personal freedoms of suspected terrorists (Fisher 2005, 135–161). Recently, however, the U.S. Supreme Court recognized limits on the powers of the president when it ruled in *Hamdan v. Rumsfeld* (2006) that the military courts used by President Bush to try detainees held at Guantanamo Bay were unconstitutional. As a result of the *Hamdan* decision, future presidents will, most likely, be forced to work with Congress and the federal courts prior to exercising power over any person suspected of being an enemy combatant (Mahler 2008, 280–301).

 ## George Dasch

George Dasch was born in Speyer, Germany, on February 7, 1903. At the age of 13, Dasch began studying to become a Catholic priest. In 1917, he fought for the Germany army in World War I. After the war, he returned to his studies at the Catholic convent but had a desire to leave Germany for America.

In 1922, Dasch escaped Germany by hiding on a steamboat as a stowaway and arrived illegally in Philadelphia, Pennsylvania (Fisher 2005, 6).

Dasch worked as a cook in New York City and obtained legal status after reporting to the Customs Office and paying a tax. Dasch applied for U.S. citizenship but never completed the paperwork. In 1927, Dasch joined the U.S. Army and served briefly in Hawaii. In 1932, he moved to Chicago and worked as a salesman before moving back to New York City where he gained employment as a waiter. Dasch had been opposed to Hitler and Nazi Germany until his mother visited him in the United States in 1939 and convinced him that conditions were good in Germany. After war broke out in Europe, Dasch returned to Germany in 1941 (Fisher 2005, 6).

In 1942, Dasch was trained for three weeks in Berlin with seven other German soldiers to commit sabotage against the United States. Dasch was secretly transported by Nazi submarines with the other spies to the eastern coast of the United States. Dasch was considered to be the leader of a group of four spies that landed at Long Island, New York. However, Dasch, along with a fellow spy, turned themselves in to the FBI, which resulted in the arrest of all of the eight Germans. Dasch and the other saboteurs were tried before a military court and sentenced to death. However, President Roosevelt reduced Dasch's punishment to 30 years in prison because he exposed the plot to the FBI. President Truman commuted his sentence in 1948, and he was released and sent back to Germany. In 1959, Dasch wrote a book, *Eight Spies Against America,* detailing his account of the sabotage operation. He worked as a travel agent and tour guide for the remainder of his life in Germany where he was treated by others as a traitor. Dasch died in 1992 (Cohen, "The Keystone Kommandos").

Herbert Hans Haupt

Herbert Hans Haupt was born on December 21, 1919, in Stettin, Germany. His father served in the Germany army during World War I and came to the United States in 1923, searching for employment in Chicago. In 1925, Herbert Haupt and his mother joined his father in the United States. Haupt and his parents became U.S. citizens in 1930. After graduating from Lane Technical High School in the late 1930s, Haupt began studying to become an optometrist (Fisher 2005, 15–32).

After World War II started, Haupt fled to Mexico and received a German passport, which allowed him to travel to Japan. He then gained employment on a German cargo ship that broke through a blockade of British ships and landed in France. When the United States declared war on Germany, Haupt was living with his grandmother in Stettin, Germany. Because Haupt had lived in America as a U.S. citizen, he was recruited by Nazi intelligence to participate in a spy operation to attack military facilities within the United States. Haupt and seven other saboteurs traveled by Nazi submarines and landed on the eastern coast of the United States. However, the plot was exposed when two of the spies turned themselves in to the FBI. On June 27, 1942, Haupt was arrested by FBI officials along with his parents in Chicago. A military trial found Haupt and the seven other spies guilty of conspiracy to commit sabotage. Haupt was executed on August 8, 1942, in Washington, D.C. Haupt's mother and father were eventually deported to Germany in 1946 and 1957, respectively (Cohen, "The Keystone Kommandos").

Ernst Burger

Ernst Peter Burger was born in Augsburg, Germany, on September 1, 1906. Burger was a member of the Nazi Party from 1923 until 1925 and participated with Adolf Hitler in the Munich Beer Hall Putsch of 1923, which was a failed attempt by Hitler to seize power in Germany. In 1927, Burger came to the United States and lived for six years, working as a machinist. Burger eventually became a U.S. citizen and served in the National Guard in Michigan and Wisconsin. During the Great Depression in 1933, Burger had trouble finding work in American and returned to Germany. Upon his return to Germany, he rejoined the Nazi Party (Samaha, Root, and Sexton, "Transcript"). However, Burger eventually joined a group known as the Storm Troopers who split with the Nazi Party. While studying at the University of Berlin in 1940, Burger wrote a paper that was critical of Hitler. He was subsequently arrested and placed in a Nazi concentration camp for 17 months for "falsifying documents." After his release from the camp, he enlisted in the German army and worked guarding prisoners of war from Britain and Yugoslavia. In June 1941, Burger volunteered for intelligence work supposedly as a way to escape Germany (Cohen, "The Keystone Kommandos").

In 1942, Burger was selected to be part of a group of eight German saboteurs that traveled by Nazi submarines to the United States. The German soldiers planned to sabotage military facilities in the United States. However, George Dasch, one of the leaders of the operation, convinced Burger that they should turn themselves in to the FBI. Burger and seven other spies were found guilty of attempting to commit sabotage against the United States and sentenced to death. Upon review of the decision, President Roosevelt reduced Burger's punishment to life in prison because of his cooperation with FBI authorities in providing information about the plot. In 1948, President Truman commuted Burger's sentence after six years. Burger was released and deported back to Germany, but then he disappeared. It was thought that

Burger fled Germany and lived the remainder of his life in Spain (Cohen, "The Keystone Kommandos").

Heinrich Heinck

Heinrich Heinck was born in Hamburg, Germany, in 1907. Heinck came to the United States illegally in 1926 and lived in New York City where he worked various jobs as a busboy, machinist, and elevator operator. He returned to Germany in 1939 at the request of the German government and began work in a Volkswagen automobile factory. Because he had lived in America for 13 years, he was recruited and trained to take part in a secret operation to attack military facilities in the United States. According to the other German spies, Heinck spoke little English, had a thick German accent, and was viewed as apathetic and lacking in confidence. After traveling secretly by Nazi submarine to the United States in June 1942, Heinck was arrested along with seven other German spies. A U.S. military court convicted Heinck of attempting to commit sabotage against the United States and he was sentenced to death. He died in the electric chair on August 8, 1942 (Cohen, "The Keystone Commandos").

Edward Kerling

Edward Kerling was born in Weisbaden, Biebrich, Germany, in 1909 (Samaha, Root, and Sexton, "Transcript"). In 1928, Kerling became one of the first 80,000 German men to join the Nazi Party. In June 1929, at the age of 19, Kerling came to the United States, while maintaining his membership in the Nazi Party. Kerling worked for a meat packing company in Brooklyn, New York, and then was employed as a butler and chauffeur in Mount Kisco, New York, and Greenwich, Connecticut, as well as parts of Florida. In 1940, Kerling returned to Germany and worked at a movie theatre where he was in charge of showing Nazi propaganda films. At the beginning of World War II, Kerlin was trained by German intelligence to participate in attacks on military facilities within the United States. Kerling was considered the leader of a group of four German spies that traveled by Nazi submarine and landed near Jacksonville, Florida. However, the plot was exposed, and Kerling was arrested and subsequently convicted and sentenced to death by a military court for attempting to commit sabotage against America. On August 8, 1942, he was electrocuted (Cohen, "The Keystone Kommandos").

Hermann Neubauer

Hermann Neubauer was born in Hamburg, Germany, in 1910. In 1931, he came to the United States where he was employed as a cook and chef in restaurants and on ships in Chicago. In 1937, Neubauer joined the Nazi Party. In 1940, Neubauer returned to Germany to visit his family and was drafted into the German army to fight on the Russian front where he was wounded in his cheek and leg by shrapnel. While Neubauer was recuperating at a hospital in Vienna, Austria, he was recruited by Nazi intelligence to participate in a secret operation for the German government. In June 1942, Neubauer was sent by Nazi submarine to the eastern coast of America with seven other spies who planned to use explosives to destroy military factories within the United States. Neubauer was arrested after the plot was exposed to FBI officials by two of his fellow spies. A military court convicted Neubauer and sentenced him to death for his part in the conspiracy. He was executed in the electric chair on August 8, 1942 (Cohen, "The Keystone Kommandos").

Richard Quirin

Richard Quirin was born in Berlin, Germany, on April 26, 1908. Quirin did not know his father and took his mother's last name. At the age of two, he was placed in a home with foster parents (Samaha, Root, and Sexton, "Transcript"). Quirin came to the United States in 1927 and worked as a maintenance worker for General Electric in Schenectady, New York. During the Great Depression, Quirin was laid off from his maintenance job. After moving to New York City, Quirin worked as a housepainter and chauffeur. In 1933, he joined an organization known as the Friends of New Germany. In 1939, Quirin returned to Germany as part of a Nazi program to return Germans to their homeland. Quirin volunteered for the sabotage operation against the United States and traveled secretly with seven other German spies by way of Nazi submarines to the eastern coast of America. After the FBI arrested Quirin, he was prosecuted before a military tribunal and sentenced to death. He was executed on August 8, 1942 (Cohen, "The Keystone Commandos").

Werner Thiel

Werner Thiel was born in Essen, Germany, on March 29, 1907. In 1927, Thiel arrived in the United States and gained employment as a machinist at the Ford automobile plant in Detroit, Michigan. From 1931 until 1934, Thiel lived in New York City and worked as a porter for the railroad and as a handy man. In 1933, he joined the Friends of New Germany and, in 1937, became a member of the Nazi Party (Samaha, Root, and Sexton, "Transcript"). During his 14 years in the United States, he lived in a variety of locations such as Illinois, Indiana, California, and Florida, mainly because work was hard to find during the Great Depression. In March 1941, Thiel returned to Germany as part of a Nazi program to return German citizens to their homeland. In 1942, Thiel was recruited and trained by Nazi intelligence to take part in a sabotage operation against the United States. In June 1942, Thiel and seven other German spies were transported by Nazi submarines to the eastern coast of America. Thiel and the other spies were arrested by the FBI and tried before a military commission. Thiel was found guilty of conspiracy to commit sabotage against the United States and he was sentenced to death. He was executed on August 8, 1942 (Cohen, "The Keystone Kommandos").

John C. Cullen

John C. Cullen was born in October 1920 in Queens, New York. He was employed at Macy's as a deliveryman before joining the Coast Guard in 1940. At 12:30 a.m. on June 13, 1942, Cullen became the first American hero of World War II. As a coast guardsman, Cullen was working foot patrol along a six-mile stretch of beach at the station at Amagansett, Long Island, when he encountered three Nazi spies who had landed on the beach by way of a submarine. Cullen asked the men what they were doing, and they said that they were fishermen from South Hampton. Cullen asked the men to walk with him to the Coast Guard station where they could wait until sunrise. However, one of the spies, George Dasch, asked Cullen his age and if he had parents. Dasch responded that he wouldn't want to have to kill him and offered Cullen a bribe of $100 for his silence. However, the young coast guardsman refused. After Dasch offered $300 as a bribe, Cullen wisely accepted the bribe to save his life (Cohen "The Keystone Commandos").

Cullen then ran to the Coast Guard station to sound the alarm. Cullen and several Coast Guard officers returned to the area with rifles where they noticed a submarine stuck on a sandbar about 20 feet out in the water. They also uncovered a package of cigarettes, Nazi uniforms, and four crates of explosives buried in the sand, which were to have been used to sabotage military facilities in the United States. The FBI was notified and the submarine and explosives were impounded. The Nazi plot to destroy American lives and property had been exposed, and the German spies only had the clothes on their back and money provided by the Nazi government (Cohen "The Keystone Commandos").

On June 14, 1942, George Dasch telephoned the FBI and eventually turned himself in a few days later. Dasch and seven other spies were tried before a military commission. John Cullen was the first witness to testify, and he identified Dasch as the person that he encountered on the beach. Cullen asked to hear the sound of Dasch's voice to provide a positive identification because the darkness and fog on the night of the encounter provided limited visibility.

Six of the eight German saboteurs were executed. The two remaining spies, including Dasch, were only given prison sentences because of their cooperation with FBI authorities (Cohen "The Keystone Commandos").

John Cullen received a promotion and the Legion of Merit award for his alertness and duty to the United States. He became a national hero and was used by the Coast Guard at rallies and recruiting sessions. During the war, Cullen was assigned as a driver for an admiral and port captain. He never worked as a beach patrolman, or "sand pounder," again. After World War II, he left the Coast Guard and worked in the dairy business in New York. Cullen and his wife had two children, a son and a daughter. After his retirement, Cullen moved with his wife to Chesapeake, Virginia. In 2007, Cullen turned 87 years old and celebrated his 64th wedding anniversary (Germanotta, "Whatever happened to . . .").

 Ex parte Quirin (1942)

In June 1942, Richard Quirin and seven other German spies entered the United States with the intent to commit sabotage against military facilities in America. After their arrests, President Roosevelt ordered a military commission to try the defendants. Toward the end of the military trial, defense attorneys for the German soldiers filed a writ of habeas corpus petition with the United States Supreme Court arguing that the defendants' Fifth and Sixth Amendment right to a trial by jury had been violated by the use of the military court. Defense attorneys also argued that the trial should have been held in a civilian court where more legal protections would have been provided (Epstein and Walker 2007, 301–302).

The justices of the Supreme Court immediately heard oral arguments during a special session over the course of two days, July 29–30, 1942. Legal counsel for the defendants argued that, according to *Ex parte Milligan* (1866), the German saboteurs were entitled to a trial before a civilian judge and jury. In *Milligan,* the Court had struck down President Lincoln's use of a military commission during the Civil War because the civil courts were functioning properly. In response to the defense counsel, Attorney General Francis Biddle argued that President Roosevelt's orders were legal because Congress had declared war on Germany, and the German spies violated the "law of war" by entering the United States secretly with the intent to commit sabotage (Law Library, "Ex parte Quirin").

On July 31, 1942, the justices voted unanimously to uphold the authority of President Roosevelt to establish the military tribunal. On August 1, 1942, the military commission convicted the defendants and sentenced each to death in the electric chair. On August 8, 1942, six of the eight defendants were executed. Two of the defendants had their death sentences commuted by Roosevelt because of their cooperation with the FBI in the investigation (Law Library, "Ex parte Quirin").

The justices did not issue a formal opinion in *Ex parte Quirin* (1942) until October 29, 1942, seven weeks after the executions. Chief Justice Harlan Stone's unanimous opinion for the Court was viewed as an attempt to justify the earlier vote to deny the petition. Otherwise, the justices feared that the reputation of the Court might be harmed as history could have portrayed the Court as simply standing by while six people were executed. In his opinion, Chief Justice Stone argued that President Roosevelt had the power as commander in chief to establish the military commission during a time of war. In addition, Congress had passed Articles of War in declaring war against Germany, and this also legitimized the actions of President Roosevelt. Although the defendants did not have a right to a jury trial in a civilian court, Stone did note in his opinion that unlawful combatants can file a writ of habeas corpus petition and appeal to a federal court, such as the Supreme Court. As a consequence, any decision handed down by a military tribunal can be reviewed by a civil court (Law Library, "Ex parte Quirin").

Chief Justice Stone drew a distinction between the *Milligan* precedent and the Court's opinion in *Quirin* by stating that the German saboteurs were "unlawful combatants" and "enemy belligerents" who secretly sought to destroy life and property. If the Germans had followed the rules pertaining to the "law of war" by fighting on a battlefield with uniforms designating themselves as enemy soldiers, then they would have been entitled to a civil trial as prisoners of war. In contrast, Lambdin P. Milligan, a Confederate sympathizer during the Civil War, was not an enemy and did not behave belligerently. A lawful combatant such as Milligan, who attempted to seize weapons from a federal armory and also sought to free Confederate prisoners, was entitled to a jury trial in a civilian court. While the Court's opinion did not define the exact boundaries of military trial jurisdiction, the justices expressed confidence that the German soldiers were clearly within the boundaries (Epstein and Walker 2007, 303–306).

References

Cohen, David B., and John W. Wells. *American National Security and Civil Liberties in an Era of Terrorism.* New York: Palgrave Macmillan, 2004.

Cohen, Gary. "The Keystone Kommandos." *Atlantic.* February 2002. http://www.theatlantic.com/doc/200202/cohen (accessed August 22, 2009).

Epstein, Lee, and Thomas Walker. *Constitutional Law for a Changing America: Institutional Powers and Constraints.* Washington, D.C.: CQ Press, 2007.

Fisher, Louis. *Nazi Saboteurs on Trial: A Military Tribunal and American Law.* Lawrence: University Press of Kansas, 2005.

Germanotta, Tony. "Whatever happened to . . . Coast Guardsman Who Helped Foil Nazi Sabotage Plot on the U.S." *Virginian-Pilot.* August 27, 2007. http://hamptonroads.com/node/317111 (accessed August 24, 2009).

Johnson, David Alan. *Betrayal: The True Story of J. Edgar Hoover and the Nazi Saboteurs Captured During WWII.* New York: Hippocrene Books, 2007.

Law Library–American Law and Legal Information. "Ex parte Quirin." *Notable Trials and Court Cases—1941 to 1953.* http://law.jrank.org/pages/13645/Ex-Parte-Quirin.html (accessed August 24, 2009).

Mahler, Jeffrey. *The Challenge: Hamdan v. Rumsfeld and the Fight over Presidential Power.* New York: Farrar, Straus and Giroux, 2008.

McCann, Joseph T. *Terrorism on American Soil: A Concise History of Plots and Perpetrators from the Famous to the Forgotten.* Boulder, CO: Sentient Publications, 2006.

Transcript of Proceedings before the Military Commission to Try Persons Charged with Offenses against the Law of War and the Articles of War, Washington, D.C. July 8–August 1, 1942. Edited by Joel Samaha, Sam Root, and Paul Sexton. Minneapolis: University of Minnesota, 2004. http://www.soc.umn.edu/~samaha/nazi_saboteurs/indexnazi.htm (accessed August 22, 2009).

A-Z Reference

Abbie Hoffman (bibliographical entry)

Al Capone Trial (1931)

"Ala Moana Rape" Trial

Alan Dershowitz (bibliographical entry)

Albert DeSalvo ("The Boston Strangler") Trial (1967)

Alger Hiss Trials (1949–1950)

Amistad Trials (1839–1841)

Andrew Johnson Impeachment Trial (1868)

Anne Hutchinson Trials (1637–1638)

Anne Hutchinson's Trial November 1637 *(primary document)*

Arnold Rothstein (bibliographical entry)

Arthur Bremer (bibliographical entry)

Arthur Bremer Trial (1972)

Assassination Attempt on President Bill Clinton (event entry)

Assassination Attempt on President Harry S. Truman (event entry)

Bartolomeo Vanzetti: Court Statement (1927) *(primary document)*

Bernhard Goetz Trial (1987)

Bobby Seale (bibliographical entry)

Boston Massacre Trials (1770)

Brown v. Board of Education of Topeka, Kansas (1954) *(case entry)*

Brown v. Board of Education, Topeka, Kansas (1954) *(primary document)*

Brown v. Board of Education of Topeka, Kansas Trial (1951)

Buck Weaver (bibliographical entry)

Carthage Conspiracy Trial (1844)

Charles Comiskey (bibliographical entry)

Charles Guiteau (bibliographical entry)

Charles Guiteau Trial (1881–1882)

Charles Lindbergh (bibliographical entry)

Charles Manson Trial (1970–71)

Chicago Black Sox Trial ("*The State of Illinois v. Eddie Cicotte et al.* 1921")

Chicago Seven Trial (1969–1970)

Chicago Seven Trial: Closing Argument for the Defendants (1970) *(primary document)*

Christopher Darden (bibliographical entry)

Cinque (bibliographical entry)

Clarence Darrow (bibliographical entry)

Clarence Darrow: Mercy for Leopold and Loeb Speech (1924) *(primary document)*

Clarence "Earl" Gideon (bibliographical entry)

Claus von Bulow Trials (1982, 1985)

Clay Shaw Trial (1969)

Clinton Impeachment Trial (1999)

Clinton v. Jones (1997) *(case entry)*

Court-Martial Trial of General William Mitchell (1925)

Dakota Conflict Trials (1862)

Dakota War of 1862 (event entry)

Dan White (bibliographical entry)

Dan White Trial (1979)

David Dellinger (bibliographical entry)

David E. Herold (bibliographical entry)

Doc Holliday (bibliographical entry)

Dr. John W. Webster (bibliographical entry)

Dr. John W. Webster Trial (1850)

Dr. Samuel Mudd (bibliographical entry)

Dred Scott Trials (1847–1857)

Dred Scott v. Sanford (1857) *(case entry)*

Ed Johnson's Appeal to the Federal Courts

Edman Spangler (bibliographical entry)

Edward Kerling (bibliographical entry)

Erik Menendez (bibliographical entry)

Ernst Burger (bibliographical entry)

Evelyn Nesbit (bibliographical entry)

Ex parte Quirin (1942) *(case entry)*

F. Lee Bailey (bibliographical entry)

Falwell v. Flynt Trial (1984)

Fatty Arbuckle Trials (1921–1922)

Impeachment (case entry)

Impeachment Trial of Samuel Chase (1805)

Ira Einhorn (bibliographical entry)

Ira Einhorn Trials (1993–2002)

Jack Kevorkian (bibliographical entry)

Jack Kevorkian Trials (1994–1999)

Jack Rubenstein (aka Jack Ruby) (bibliographical entry)

Jerry Rubin (bibliographical entry)

Jesse Timmendequas Trial (1997)

JFK (film entry)

Jim Garrison (bibliographical entry)

Joe Hill Trial (1914)

John Brown (bibliographical entry)

John Brown, The Trial of (1859)

John C. Cullen (bibliographical entry)

John Froines (bibliographical entry)

John Peter Zenger Trial (1735)

John Quincy Adams (bibliographical entry)

John W. Hinckley Jr. (bibliographical entry)

John W. Hinckley Jr. Trial (1982)

John Surratt (bibliographical entry)

John Wilkes Booth (bibliographical entry)

Johnnie Cochran (bibliographical entry)

Joseph Smith (bibliographical entry)

Manuel Noriega Trial (1991–1992)

Mapplethorpe Obscenity Trial (1990)

Marcia Clark (bibliographical entry)

Mark Fuhrman (bibliographical entry)

Mary Surratt (bibliographical entry)

Massie Trials (1931–1932)

McMartin Preschool Abuse Trials (1987–1990)

Megan's Law (1996) *(primary document)*

Menendez Brothers' Trials (1993–1996)

Michael Fortier (bibliographical entry)

Michael Jackson Trial (2005)

Michael O'Laughlen (bibliographical entry)

Mike Tyson Rape Trial (1992)

Mississippi Burning Trial (*United States v. Cecil Price and Samuel Bowers et al.*, 1967)

Missouri v. Celia, a Slave (1855)

Monica Lewinsky (bibliographical entry)

Morgan Earp (bibliographical entry)

Mountain Meadows Massacre Trials (1875–1876)

Murder of Joe Kahahawai: Honor Killing or Lynching?

My Lai Courts Martial (1970)

Nat Turner (bibliographical entry)

Nat Turner: *Confessions of Nat Turner* (1831) *(primary document)*

Nathan F. Leopold Jr. and Richard Loeb Trial (1924)

Nazi Saboteurs Trial (1942)

Ronald "Ron" Goldman (bibliographical entry)

Rosenberg Trial (1951)

Rosenberg trial statement upon sentencing (1951) *(primary document)*

Ruby Ridge Shootings (event entry)

Ruby Ridge Trial (1993)

Sacco and Vanzetti Trial (1921)

Salem Witchcraft Trials (1692)

Sam Sheppard Trials (1954 and 1966)

Samuel Arnold (bibliographical entry)

Samuel Chase (bibliographical entry)

Samuel Leibowitz (bibliographical entry)

Scopes Monkey Trial (1925)

Scopes Trial: Clarence Darrow's Examination of William Jennings Bryan (1925) *(primary document)*

Scott v. Sandford (1857) *(primary document)*

Scottsboro Boys Trials (1931–1937)

Sheppard v. Maxwell (1966) *(case entry)*

Sheriff Joseph F. Shipp (bibliographical entry)

"Shoeless" Joe Jackson (bibliographical entry)

Sirhan Sirhan (bibliographical entry)

Sirhan Sirhan Trial (1969)

Susan B. Anthony Trial (1873)

Sweet Trials (1925–1926)

Summary of Ex parte Milligan (1866) *(case entry)*

War Department, Adjutant-General's Office, Washington, November 6, 1865 *(primary document)*

Werner Thiel (bibliographical entry)

William "Big Bill" Haywood (bibliographical entry)

William Jennings Bryan (bibliographical entry)

William Kennedy Smith Trial (1991)

Wyatt Earp (bibliographical entry)

Zacarias Moussaoui Trial (2006)

Bibliography

Abernathy, Thomas. *The Burr Conspiracy*. New York: Oxford University Press, 1954.

Abrams, Dan. "Should Single Guys Trade Their Pinstripes for Prison Stripes?" *MSNBC*. January 18, 2006. http://www.msnbc.msn.com/id/12134256/from/RL.5/ (accessed August 19, 2009).

Abramson, Jeffery. *We, the Jury: The Jury System and the Ideal of Democracy*. Cambridge, MA: Harvard University Press, 2000.

Acker, James A. *Scottsboro and Its Legacy: The Cases That Challenged American Legal and Social Justice*. Westport, CT: Praeger Publishers, 2007.

Ackerman, Kenneth. *The Dark Horse: The Surprise Election and Political Murder of President James A. Garfield*. New York: Da Capo Press, 2003.

Ahlgren, Gregory, and Stephen Monier. *Crime of the Century: The Lindbergh Kidnapping Hoax*. Boston: Branden Books, 1993.

Alexander, S. L. *Media and American Courts: A Reference Handbook*. Santa Barbara, CA: ABC-CLIO, 2004.

Alexander, Shana. *Anyone's Daughter: The Times and Trials of Patty Hearst*. New York: Viking, 1979.

Amar, Akhil Reed. *The Bill of Rights: Creation and Reconstruction*. New Haven, CT: Yale University Press, 2000.

American Heritage.com: History's Homepage. "Nat Turner, Lightning Rod." *American Heritage People*. http://www.americanheritage.com/people/articles/web/20051111-nat-turner-slavery-rebellion-virginia-civil-war-thomas-r-gray-abolitionist.shtml (accessed March 7, 2009).

Anderson, Gary C. *Through Dakota Eyes: Narrative Accounts of the Minnesota Indian War of 1862*. St. Paul: Minnesota Historical Society Press, 1988.

Anspacher, Carolyn. *The Trial of Patty Hearst*. San Francisco: Great Fidelity Press, 1976.

Armstrong, Zella. *The History of Hamilton County and Chattanooga, Tennessee*. Vol. 1. Johnson City, TN: The Overmountain Press, 1992.

Arseniuk, Melissa. "O. J. Simpson Trial Goes to Jury: Prosecutor Says the Key Was 'Accountability.'" *Las Vegas Sun*. October 2, 2008. http://www.lasvegassun.com/news/2008/oct/02/attorneys-make-closing-arguments-oj-simpson-trial/ (accessed August 13, 2009).

Arseniuk, Melissa. "Several Men Involved in O. J. Simpson Hotel Raid Testify against Him." *Las Vegas Sun.* September 29, 2008. http://www.lasvegassun.com/news/2008/sep/29/several-men-involved-oj-simpson-hotel-raid-testify/ (August 13, 2009).

Asinof, Eliot, and Stephen Jay Gould. *Eight Men Out: The Black Sox and the 1919 World Series.* New York: Holt, 2000.

Associated Press. "Defense Department Settles with Linda Tripp." *USA Today.* November 3, 2003. http://www.usatoday.com/news/washington/2003–11–03-tripp-lawsuit_x.htm (accessed August 16, 2009).

Associated Press. "Harry Thaw Leaves $10,000 To Evelyn Nesbit." *Washington Post.* March 30, 1947.

Associated Press. "Last-Captured Member of '70s Radical Group Is Freed" *New York Times.* May 11, 2009, p. A15.

Avrich, Paul. *The Haymarket Tragedy.* Princeton: Princeton University Press, 1986.

Axelrod-Contrada, Joan. *The Lizzie Borden "Axe-Murder" Trial: A Headline Court Case.* Berkeley Heights, NJ: Enslow Publishers, 2000.

Bagley, Will. *Blood of the Prophets: Brigham Young and the Massacre at Mountain Meadows.* Norman: University of Oklahoma Press, 2004.

Bailey, F. Lee. *The Defense Never Rests.* New York: Signet, 1972.

Baker, Peter. "Clinton 'Adamantly' Denies Jones' Allegations." *Washington Post.* July 4, 1997, p. A1.

Baker, Peter, and John F. Harris. "Clinton Admits to Lewinsky Relationship, Challenges Starr to End Personal 'Prying.'" *Washington Post.* August 18, 1998, p. A1.

Balkin, Jack M. *What Brown v. Board of Education Should Have Said: The Nation's Top Legal Experts Rewrite America's Landmark Civil Rights Decision.* New York: NYU Press, 2002.

Ball, Howard. *Justice in Mississippi: The Murder Trial of Edgar Ray Killen.* Lawrence: University Press of Kansas, 2006.

Ball, Howard. *Murder in Mississippi: United States v. Price and the Struggle for Civil Rights.* Lawrence: University Press of Kansas, 2004.

Bardsley, Marilyn. "The Boston Strangler." *Crimelibrary.com.* http://www.trutv.com/library/crime/serial_killers/notorious/boston/index_1.html (accessed January 23, 2010).

Barra, Allen. *Inventing Wyatt Earp: His Life and Many Legends.* Lincoln: University of Nebraska Press, 2009.

Barry, Kathleen. *Susan B. Anthony: A Biography of a Singular Feminist.* Bloomington, IN: AuthorHouse, 2000.

Baseball Page.com. "Buck Weaver." *Player Pages.* http://www.thebaseballpage.com/players/weavebu01.php (accessed August 11, 2009).

Bass, Paul, and Douglas W. Rae. *Murder in the Model City: The Black Panthers, Yale, and the Redemption of a Killer.* New York: Basic Books, 2006.

Baum, Frank. *Minutes of Trial of Members of Mob Who Helped Kill Joseph Smith, the Prophet.* Handwritten manuscript of the trial proceedings. Bountiful, UT: Wilford C. Wood Museum, 1845.

BBC. "Jackson Jury Hears Final Speeches." *BBC News.* June 3, 2005. http://news.bbc.co.uk/2/hi/entertainment/4604391.stm (accessed August 20, 2009).

BBC. "Jackson Reveals Courtroom 'Hurt.'" *BBC News*. March 9, 2005. http://news.bbc.co.uk/2/hi/entertainment/4331639.stm (accessed August 20, 2009).

BBC.com. Joe Hill—"Murderer or Martyr." February 19, 2002. http://www.bbc.co.uk/dna/h2g2/A676361 (accessed August 14, 2009).

"Beauty as Evidence." *Life*. June 1981, 10–13.

Beecher, Henry Ward. "The Beecher Trial: A Review of the Evidence." *New York Times*. July 3, 1875, pp. 1–34.

Belknap, Michal. *The Supreme Court under Earl Warren, 1953–1969*. Columbia: University of South Carolina Press, 2005.

Belknap, Michal. *The Vietnam War on Trial: The My Lai Massacre and Court-Martial of Lieutenant Calley*. Lawrence: University Press of Kansas, 2002.

Bell, Rachael. "Ira Einhorn: Justice At Last." *TruTV Crime Library: Notorious Murders*. http://www.trutv.com/library/crime/notorious_murders/famous/einhorn/updates_8.html (accessed July 12, 2009).

Bell, Rachael. "Ted Bundy." *TruTV Crime Library: Criminal Minds and Methods*. http://www.trutv.com/library/crime/serial_killers/notorious/bundy/index_1.html (accessed February 2, 2010).

Belli, Melvin. *Dallas Justice: The Real Story of Jack Ruby and His Trial*. New York: David McKay Company, 1967.

Benedict, Michael Les. *The Impeachment and Trial of Andrew Johnson*. New York: W. W. Norton and Company, 1999.

Berg, Andrew Scott. *Lindbergh*. New York: Putnam, 1998.

Berger, Raoul. *Impeachment: The Constitutional Problems*. Cambridge, MA: Harvard University Press, 1999.

Biography. "George Daniel 'Buck' Weaver." *ClearBuck.com*. http://www.clearbuck.com/bio.htm (accessed August 11, 2009).

Biography Channel. "The Menendez Brothers." *Biographies*. http://www.thebiographychannel.co.uk/biography_story/717:886/1/The_Menendez_Brothers.htm (accessed August 19, 2009).

Bishop, Jim. *The Day Lincoln Was Shot*. New York: Greenwich House, 1984.

Biskupic, Joan. "Unanimous Decision Points to Tradition of Valuing Life." *Washington Post*. June 27, 1997, p. A01.

Black, Charles L. Jr. *Impeachment: A Handbook*. New Haven, CT: Yale University Press, 1974.

Blue, Rose, and Corrine J. Naden. *Dred Scott: Person or Property?* New York: Benchmark Books, 2005.

Bonnie, Richard J., John C. Jeffries Jr., and Peter W. Low. *A Case Study in the Insanity Defense: The Trial of John W. Hinckley, Jr*. New York: Foundation Press, 2008.

Booth, Cathy. "Trials: Noriega Makes His Case." *Time*. February 17, 1992. http://www.time.com/time/magazine/article/0,9171,974912,00.html (accessed January 11, 2010).

Bortnick, Barry. *Polly Klaas: The Murder of America's Child*. New York: Pinnacle Books/Kensington Publishing, 1995.

Bremer, Arthur H. *An Assassin's Diary*. New York: Harper's Magazine Press, 1973.

Briggs, L. Vernon. *The Manner of the Man That Kills*. Boston: Gorham Press, 1921.

Broder, John M., and Nick Madigan, "Michael Jackson Cleared After 14-Week Child Molestation Trial." *New York Times*. June 14, 2005. http://www.nytimes.com/2005/06/14/national/14jackson.html?_r=1&pagewanted=all (accessed August 20, 2009).

Brooks, Juanita. *The Mountain Meadows Massacre*. Norman: University of Oklahoma Press, 1991.

Brown, Arnold R. *Lizzie Borden: The Legend, the Truth, the Final Chapter*. Nashville, TN: Rutledge Hill Press, 1991.

Brown, Joe B. *Dallas and the Jack Ruby Trial: Memoir of Judge Joe B. Brown Sr.* Edited by Diane Holloway. Bloomington, IN: AuthorHouse, 2001.

Brownmiller, Susan. *Against Our Will: Men, Women, and Rape*. New York: Ballatine Books, 1993.

Buffalo History Works. "The Trial and Execution of Leon Czolgosz." http://www.buffalohistoryworks.com/panamex/assassination/executon.htm (accessed March 2, 2009).

Bugliosi, Vincent. *Outrage: The Five Reasons Why O. J. Simpson Got Away With Murder*. New York: W. W. Norton and Company, 2008.

Bugliosi, Vincent. *Reclaiming History: The Assassination of John F. Kennedy*. New York: W. W. Norton and Company, 2007.

Bugliosi, Vincent, and Curt Gentry. *Helter Skelter: The True Story of the Manson Murders*. New York: W. W. Norton and Company, 1974.

Buranelli, Vincent. *The Trial of Peter Zenger*. New York: NYU Press, 1957.

Burton, Harold H. *Ex Parte Milligan and Ex Parte McCardle: The Story of a Dramatic Case and Its Sequel in the Field of Judicial Review*. s.n., 1954.

Butterfield, Fox. "Behind the Badge: A Special Report." *New York Times*. March 2, 1996. http://www.nytimes.com/books/97/03/23/reviews/fuhrman-profile.html?_r=2 (accessed August 4, 2009).

Cable, Mary. *Black Odyssey: The Case of the Slave Ship 'Amistad.'* New York: Penguin, 2003.

Cagin, Seth, and Philip Dray. *We Are Not Afraid: The Story of Goodman, Schwerner, and Chaney, and the Civil Rights Campaign for Mississippi*. New York: Nation Books, 2006.

Camisa, Henry, and Jim Franklin. *Inside Out: Fifty Years Behind the Walls of New Jersey's Trenton State Prison*. Windsor, NJ: Windsor Press and Publishing, 2003.

Cannon, Lou. *Official Negligence: How Rodney King and the Riots Changed Los Angeles and the LAPD*. New York: Basic Books, 1999.

Caplan, Lincoln. *The Insanity Defense and the Trial of John W. Hinckley Jr.* Boston: David R. Godine, 1984.

Caporael, Linda. "Ergotism: The Satan Loosed in Salem?" *Science* 192, no. 4234 (April 1976): 21–26.

Carley, Kenneth. *The Dakota War of 1862*. St. Paul: Minnesota Historical Society Press, 2001.

Carlson, Peter. *Roughneck: The Life and Times of Big Bill Haywood*. New York: W. W. Norton and Company, 1984.

Carnes, Bill, and Troy Drew. "The Trial of Henry Wirz: A Brief Summary." *Famous Trials.* http://www.law.umkc.edu/faculty/projects/ftrials/Wirz/INTRO.HTM (accessed March 18, 2009).

Carnes, Bill, and Troy Drew. "Felix de la Baume." *Famous Trials.* http://www.law.umkc.edu/faculty/projects/ftrials/Wirz/cont1.htm (accessed March 18, 2009).

Carney, Gene. *Burying the Black Sox: How Baseball's Cover-Up of the 1919 World Series Fix Almost Succeeded.* Washington, D.C.: Potomac Books, 2006.

Carr. C. *On Edge: Performance at the End of the Twentieth Century.* Hanover, NH: Wesleyan University Press, 1993.

Carter, Dan T. *The Politics of Rage: George Wallace, the Origins of the New Conservatism, and the Transformation of American Politics.* Baton Rouge: Louisiana State University Press, 2000.

Carter, Dan T. *Scottsboro: A Tragedy of the American South.* Baton Rouge: Louisiana University Press, 2007.

Carton, Evan. *Patriotic Treason: John Brown and the Soul of America.* New York: Free Press, 2006.

Cartwright, Gary. "The Longest Ride of His Life." *Texas Monthly* 15, no. 5 (May 1987): 124–194.

Ceplair, Larry, and Steven Englund. *The Inquisition in Hollywood: Politics in the Film Industry, 1930–1960.* Berkeley: University of California Press, 1983.

Chamlee, Roy Z. Jr. *Lincoln's Assassins: A Complete Account of Their Capture, Trial, and Punishment.* Jefferson, NC: McFarland and Company, 2008.

Channing, W. "The Mental State of Czolgosz, the Assassin of President McKinley." *American Journal of Insanity* 59 (1902): 233–278.

Chermak, Stephen M., and Frankie Y. Bailey. *Crimes and Trials of the Century.* Westport, CT: Greenwood Press, 2007.

Cherny, Robert W. *A Righteous Cause: The Life of William Jennings Bryan.* Norman: University of Oklahoma Press, 1994.

Cheslaw, Irving. *John Peter Zenger and His "New York Weekly Journal."* New York: unknown publisher, 1952.

Chiasson, Lloyd. *Illusive Shadows: Justice, Media, and Socially Significant American Trials.* Westport, CT: Greenwood Press, 2003.

Chipman, Norton P. *The Tragedy of Andersonville: Trial of Captain Henry Wirz (1911).* Whitefish, MT: Kessinger Publishing, 2008.

Chomsky, Carol. "The United States—Dakota War Trials: A Study in Military Injustice." *Stanford Law Review* 43 (1990): 13–98.

Clark, James C. *The Murder of James A. Garfield: The President's Last Days and the Trial and Execution of his Assassin.* Jefferson, NC: McFarland and Company, 1994.

Clarke, James A. *Defining Danger: American Assassins and the New Domestic Terrorists.* New Brunswick, NJ: Transaction Publishers, 2007.

Cohen, David B., and John W. Wells. *American National Security and Civil Liberties in an Era of Terrorism.* New York: Palgrave Macmillan, 2004.

Cohen, Gary. "The Keystone Kommandos." *Atlantic*. February 2002. http://www.theatlantic. com/doc/200202/cohen (accessed August 22, 2009).

Cohen-Almagor, Raphael. *The Right to Die with Dignity: An Argument in Ethics, Medicine, and Law*. Piscataway, NJ: Rutgers University Press, 2001.

Cole, Donald B. *The Presidency of Andrew Jackson*. Lawrence: University Press of Kansas, 1993.

"Collazo, 80, Truman Attacker in '50." *New York Times: Obituaries*. February 23, 1994, p. A16.

Collins, Ronald L. K., and David M. Skover. *The Trials of Lenny Bruce With Audio CD: The Rise and Fall of an American Icon*. Naperville, IL: Sourcebooks Mediafusion, 2002.

Conason, Joe. "The Perils of Paula Jones." *Penthouse* 32, no. 4 (December 2000): 41–54.

Cook, Fred J. "Alger Hiss—A Whole New Ball Game." *The Alger Hiss Story: Search for the Truth*. http://homepages.nyu.edu/~th15/cookcnbrief.html (accessed April 4, 2009).

Cooper, Cynthia L., and Sam Reese Sheppard. *Mockery of Justice: The True Story of the Sheppard Murder Case*. Boston: Northeastern University Press, 1995.

Corliss, Richard, and Patrick E. Cole. "Who Killed J.F.K.?" *Time*. http://www.time.com/ time/magazine/article/0,9171,974523–1,00.html (accessed August 12, 2009).

Cotton, Doyice J., and John Wolohan, eds. *Law for Recreation and Sport Managers*. Dubuque, IA: Kendall/Hunt Publishing Company, 2006.

Cox, Hank H. *Lincoln and the Sioux Uprising of 1862*. Nashville, TN: Cumberland House Publishing, 2005.

Cozzens, James Gould. *A Rope for Dr. Webster*. Columbia, SC: Bruccoli-Clark Layman, 1976.

Crawford, Deborah. *Four Women in a Violent Time*. New York: Crown Publishers, 1970.

Crime and Investigation Network. "Biography." *Ira Einhorn; The Unicorn*. http:// www.crimeandinvestigation.co.uk/famous_criminal/119/biography/1/Ira_Einhorn_ The_Unicorn.htm (accessed July 13, 2009).

Crime and Investigation Network. "The Trial." *Ira Einhorn; The Unicorn*. http:// www.crimeandinvestigation.co.uk/famous_criminal/119/the_trial/2/Ira_Einhorn_The_ Unicorn.htm (accessed July 12, 2009).

Curriden, Mark, and Leroy Phillips Jr., *Contempt of Court: The Turn-of-the-Century Lynching that Launched a Hundred Years of Federalism*. New York: Anchor, 2001.

Darden, Christopher. *In Contempt*. New York: HarperCollins, 1996.

Davis, Don. *Bad Blood: The Shocking True Story Behind the Menendez Killings*. New York: St. Martin's Press, 1994.

Davis, Jayna. *The Third Terrorist: The Middle East Connection to the Oklahoma City Bombing*. Nashville, TN: Thomas Nelson, 2004.

Davis, Thomas J. *The "Great Negro Plot" in Colonial New York*. Amherst: University of Massachusetts Press, 1990.

Davy, William. *Let Justice Be Done: New Light on the Jim Garrison Investigation*. Reston, VA: Jordan Publishing, 1999.

DeBoer, Clara Merritt. "Blacks and the American Missionary Association." *United Church of Christ*. http://www.ucc.org/about-us/hidden-histories/blacks-and-the-american.html (accessed March 12, 2009).

DeCaro, Lou Jr. *John Brown: The Cost of Freedom*. New York: International Publishers, 2007.

Dempsey, Mark, ed. *The Jack Ruby Trial Revisited: The Diary of Jury Foreman Max Causey*. Denton: University of North Texas Press, 2000.

Denhart, Andy. "Sober House Will Follow Celebrity Rehab Cast, Andy Dick in Sober Living. *Reality Blurred*. December 19, 2008. http://www.realityblurred.com/realitytv/archives/celebrity_rehab/2008_Dec_19_sober_house_cast (accessed August 24, 2009).

Department of State: Secretary of State. "2008 Official Michigan General Candidate Listing." *Official State of Michigan Web Site*. http://miboecfr.nictusa.com/election/candlist/08GEN/08GEN_CL.HTM (accessed February 13, 2010).

Dershowitz, Alan. *The Abuse Excuse and Other Cop-Outs, Sob Stories and Evasions of Responsibility*. Boston: Back Bay Books, 2000.

Dershowitz, Alan. *America on Trial: Inside the Legal Battles that Transformed Our Nation— From the Salem Witches to the Guantanamo Detainees*. New York: Warner Books, 2004.

Dershowitz, Alan. *Reversal of Fortune*. New York: Random House, 1986.

Dershowitz, Alan. "Want to Torture? Get a Warrant." *San Francisco Chronicle*. January 22, 2002, p. A19.

DeSario, Jack P., and William D. Mason. *Dr. Sam Sheppard on Trial: The Prosecutors and the Marilyn Sheppard Murder*. Kent, OH: Kent State University Press, 2003.

"Detailed: Biographical Statement." *AlanDershowitz.com*. http://www.alandershowitz.com/detailed.php (accessed February 13, 2010).

Dimond, Diane. *Be Careful Who You Love: Inside the Michael Jackson Case*. New York: Simon and Schuster, 2009.

Dinnerstein, Leonard. *The Leo Frank Case*. Athens: University of Georgia Press, 2008.

Dixon, Barbara. *Assassinations and Assassination Attempts on American Public Officials, 1835–1972*. Washington, D.C.: Congressional Research Service, Library of Congress, 1972.

Dobson, Richard. "Fatal Addiction: Ted Bundy's Final Interview." *Pure Intimacy*. http://www.pureintimacy.org/piArticles/A000000433.cfm (accessed February 8, 2010).

Doggett, Peter. *There's a Riot Going On: Revolutionaries, Rock Stars, and the Rise and Fall of the 60s*. New York: Canongate, 2008.

Donahue, Katherine C. *Slave of Allah: Zacarias Moussaoui v. The USA*. London: Pluto Press, 2007.

Douglas, John E., and Mark Olshaker. *Journey into Darkness*. New York: Simon and Schuster, 1997.

Dubofsky, Melvyn. *"Big Bill" Haywood*. New York: Palgrave Macmillan, 1987.

Dunne, John Gregory, and Calvin Trillin. *Regards: The Selected Non-Fiction of John Gregory Dunne*. New York: Thunder's Mouth Press, 2006.

Dyer, Joel. *Harvest of Rage: Why Oklahoma City Is Only The Beginning*. New York: Basic Books, 1998.

Eberle, Paul, and Shirley Eberle. *The Abuse of Innocence: The McMartin Preschool Trial*. Buffalo, NY,: Prometheus Books, 2003.

Egelko, Bob. "Brown Asks State High Court to Overturn Prop. 8." *San Francisco Chronicle*. December 20, 2008, p. A1.

Egelko, Bob. "Death Sentence Upheld for Polly Klaas' Killer." *San Francisco Chronicle.* June 9, 2009. *http://articles.sfgate.com/2009–06–02/bay-area/17208285_1_polly-klaas-richard-allen-davis-mike-meese.* (accessed December 23, 2009).

Ehrlich, Walter. *They Have No Rights: Dred Scott's Struggle For Freedom.* Westport, CT: Greenwood Press, 1979.

Ellsberg, Robert. *All Saints: Daily Reflections on Saints, Prophets, and Witnesses From Our Time.* New York: Crossroad Publishing Company, 1997.

Encyclopedia Topics. "Charles A. Comiskey." *Reference.com.* http://www.reference.com/browse/Charles+A+Comiskey (accessed August 10, 2009).

Epstein, Lee, and Thomas Walker. *Constitutional Law for a Changing America: Institutional Powers and Constraints.* Washington, D.C.: CQ Press, 2007.

Epstein, Lee, and Thomas G. Walker. *Constitutional Law for a Changing America: Rights, Liberties, and Justice.* Washington, D.C.: CQ Press, 2006.

Ernst, Cindi. "The Bernhard Goetz Trial (1985): Selected Links." *Famous Trials.* http://www.law.umkc.edu/faculty/projects/ftrials/goetzlinks.html (accessed December 21, 2009).

Ernst, Cindi. "The Dan White (Harvey Milk Murder) Trial (1979): Selected Links & Bibliography." *Famous Trials.* http://www.law.umkc.edu/faculty/projects/ftrials/danwhitelinks.html (accessed February 10, 2010).

Ewing, Charles Patrick, and Joseph T. McCann. *Minds on Trial: Great Cases in Law and Psychology.* New York: Oxford University Press, 2006.

Fehrenbacher, Don E. *Slavery, Law, & Politics: The Dred Scott Case in Historical Perspective.* New York: Oxford University Press, 2001.

Feldman, Ellen. *Scottsboro.* New York: W. W. Norton and Company, 2008.

Finkelman, Paul. *Dred Scott v. Sanford: A Brief History With Documents.* New York: Bedford/St. Martin's, 1997.

Fisher, Jim. *The Lindbergh Case.* New Brunswick, NJ: Rutgers University Press, 1994.

Fisher, Louis. *Military Tribunals and Presidential Power: American Revolution to the War on Terrorism.* Lawrence: University Press of Kansas, 2005.

Fisher, Louis. *Nazi Saboteurs on Trial: A Military Tribunal and American Law.* Lawrence: University Press of Kansas, 2005.

Flanders, Robert. *Nauvoo: Kingdom on the Mississippi.* Champaign: University of Illinois Press, 1975.

Fleitz, David L. *Shoeless: The Life and Times of Joe Jackson.* Jefferson, NC: McFarland and Company, 2001.

Fletcher, George P. *A Crime of Self-Defense: Bernhard Goetz and the Law on Trial.* Chicago: University of Chicago Press, 1990.

Fletcher, George P., and Alan Dershowitz. *The Trial of Bernhard Goetz.* Notable Trials Library, 1991.

Fox, Richard Wightman. *Trials of Intimacy: Love and Loss in the Beecher-Tilton Scandal.* Chicago: University of Chicago Press, 1999.

Fox-Genovese, Elizabeth. *Within the Plantation Household: Black and White Women of the Old South.* Chapel Hill: University of North Carolina Press, 1988.

FOXNews.com. "Fuhrman on 'Gates-Gate' Fallout." *FOX News*. July 29, 2009. http://www.foxnews.com/story/0,2933,535343,00.html (accessed August 4, 2009).

FOXnews.com. "Monica Lewinsky Earns Master's Degree in London." *FOX News*. December 21, 2006. http://www.foxnews.com/story/0,2933,238021,00.html (accessed August 15, 2009).

FOXnews.com. "Paula Jones Talks with Sean and Alan." *FOX News*. March 10, 2005. http://www.foxnews.com/story/0,2933,150036,00.html (accessed August 16, 2009).

Frank, Gerold. *The Boston Strangler*. New York: Penguin, 1981.

Frankfurter, Felix. *The Case of Sacco and Vanzetti: A Critical Analysis for Lawyers and Laymen*. Buffalo, NY: William S. Hein and Company, 2003.

Franklin, V. P., and Julian Savage Carter. *Cultural Capital and Black Education: African American Communities and the Funding of Black Schooling*. Charlotte, NC: Information Age Publishing, 2004.

Freedland, Michael. *Hollywood on Trial: McCarthyism's War Against the Movies*. London: Anova, 2008.

French, Scot. *The Rebellious Slave: Nat Turner in Memory*, Boston: Houghton Mifflin Harcourt, 2003.

Fridell, Ron. *Gideon v. Wainwright: The Right to Free Counsel*. Tarrytown, NY: Marshall Cavendish Benchmark, 2007.

Friess, Steve. "O. J. Simpson Convicted of Robbery and Kidnapping." *New York Times*. October 4, 2008. http://www.nytimes.com/2008/10/04/world/americas/04iht-simpson.1.16687098.html?_r=1 (accessed August 13, 2009).

Fuhrman, Mark. *Murder in Brentwood*. New York: Kensington Publishing, 1997.

Fuller, Horace Williams, Sydney Russell Wrightington, Arthur Weightman Spencer, and Thomas Tileston Baldwin. *The Green Bag*. Vol. 14. Boston: Boston Book Company, 1902.

Garber, M., and Rebecca L. Walkowitz. *Secret Agents: The Rosenberg Case, McCarthyism and Fifties America*. New York: Routledge, 1995.

Gardner, Lloyd C. *The Case That Never Dies: The Lindbergh Kidnapping*. New Brunswick, NJ: Rutgers University Press, 2004.

Garrison, Jim. *On the Trail of the Assassins*. New York: Warner Books, 1988.

Geary, Rick. *The Beast of Chicago: An Account of the Life and Crimes of Herman W. Mudgett, Known to the World as H. H. Holmes*. New York: NBM Publishing, 2003.

Geluardi, John. "Dan White's Motive More about Betrayal than Homophobia." *San Francisco Weekly*. January 29, 2008. http://www.sfweekly.com/2008-01-30/news/white-in-milk/1 (accessed February 14, 2010).

Germanotta, Tony. "Whatever Happened to...Coast Guardsman Who Helped Foil Nazi Sabotage Plot on the U.S." *Virginian-Pilot*. August 27, 2007. http://hamptonroads.com/node/317111 (accessed August 24, 2009).

Gerson, Noel B. *The Trial of Andrew Johnson*. Nashville, TN: T. Nelson, 1977.

Gibbon, Guy. *The Sioux: The Dakota and Lakota Nations*. Malden, MA: Wiley-Blackwell, 2002.

Gibbs, Jewell Taylor. *Race and Justice: Rodney King and O. J. Simpson in a House Divided*. San Francisco: Jossey-Bass, 1996.

Gilman, Rhoda. *The Story of Minnesota's Past*. St. Paul: Minnesota Historical Society Press, 1991.

Ginsburg, Daniel E. *The Fix Is In: A History of Baseball Gambling and Game Fixing Scandals*. Jefferson, NC: McFarland and Company, 2004.

Glaberson, William. "Stranger on the Block: A Special Report; At Center of Megan's Law Case, A Man No One Could Reach." *New York Times*. May 28, 1996, p. A1.

Goldman Family. *If I Did It: Confessions of the Killer*. New York: Beaufort Books, 2007.

Goldstein, Amy, and Rene Sanchez, "Tripp's Curious Path to the Pentagon." *Washington Post*. February 7, 1998, p. A12.

Gordon-Reed, Annette, ed. *Race on Trial: Law and Justice in American History*. New York: Oxford University Press, 2002.

Gottlieb, Alan. "Duran the Child Nobody Knew." *Denver Post*. November 6, 1994, p. 1.

Graebner, William. *Patty's Got a Gun: Patricia Hearst in 1970s America*. Chicago: University of Chicago Press, 2008.

Gray, Thomas R. *The Confessions of Nat Turner: The Leader of the Late Insurrection in Southampton, Virginia*. Whitefish, MT: Kessinger Publishing, 2004.

Green, James. *Death in the Haymarket: A Story of Chicago, the First Labor Movement, and the Bombing that Divided Gilded Age America*. New York: Pantheon, 2006.

Greenberg, Kenneth S. *Nat Turner: A Slave Rebellion in History and Memory*. New York: Oxford University Press, 2004.

Greenburg, Jan Crawford. *Supreme Conflict: The Inside Story of the Struggle for Control of the United States Supreme Court*. New York: Penguin, 2007.

Greene, Jacqueline Dembar, and Dave Von Drehle. *Triangle Shirtwaist Factory Fire*. New York: Bearport Publishing, 2007.

Gribben, Mark. "The Claus von Bulow Case." *Crimelibrary.com*. http://www.trutv.com/library/crime/notorious_murders/family/bulow/1.html (accessed January 18, 2010).

Gutierrez, Thelma, Charles Feldman, Anne McDermott, and Matt Smith. "Los Angeles Riot Still Echoes a Decade Later." *CNN.com*. April 29, 2002. http://archives.cnn.com/2002/US/04/28/la.riot.anniversary/ (accessed August 24, 2009).

Hamilton, Arnold. "New Life, Identity Await Fortier as He Leaves Prison." *Dallas Morning News*. January 18, 2006. http://www.dallasnews.com/sharedcontent/dws/dn/latestnews/stories/011906dntexfortier.1742cf8f.html (accessed August 24, 2009).

Hammer, Richard. *The Court-Martial of Lt. Calley*. New York: Putnam, 1997.

Hanchett, William. *The Lincoln Murder Conspiracies*. Urbana-Champaign: University of Illinois Press, 1989.

Harper, Frank. *Andersonville: The Trial of Captain Henry Wirz*. Greeley: University of Northern Colorado, 1986.

Harper, Ida Husted. *The Life and Work of Susan B. Anthony*. Vol. 1. New York: BiblioLife, 2007.

Harris, T. M. *Assassination of Lincoln: A History of the Great Conspiracy Trial of the Conspirators by a Military Commission*. Boston: William Press, 2008.

Haw, James. *Stormy Patriot: The Life of Samuel Chase*. Baltimore: Maryland Historical Society, 1980.

Hayden, Tom. "Biography." *The Official Tom Hayden Web Site*. http://www.tomhayden.com/biography.htm (accessed July 28, 2009).

Hayden, Tom. *Rebel: A Personal History of the 1960s*. Granada Hills, CA: Red Hen Press, 2003.

Hayes, Henry G., and Charles J. Hayes. *A Complete History of the Life and Trial of Charles Julius Guiteau, Assassin of President Garfield*. Whitefish, MT: Kessinger Publishing, 2007.

Healy, Thomas S. *The Two Deaths of George Wallace: The Question of Forgiveness*. Montgomery, AL: Black Belt Press, 1996.

Heard, Issac. "Trials of the Prisoners." *History of the Sioux War and Massacre*. http://www.law.umkc.edu/faculty/projects/ftrials/dakota/Trials_of_Prisoners.html#Trials%20of%20The (accessed March 17, 2009).

Hearn, Charles G. *Impeachment of Andrew Johnson*. Jefferson, NC: McFarland and Company, 2007.

Heidler, David Stephen, Jeanne T. Heidler, and David J. Coles. *Encyclopedia of the American Civil War: A Political, Social, and Military History*. New York: W. W. Norton and Company, 2002.

Heller, Peter. *Bad Intentions: The Mike Tyson Story*. New York: Da Capo Press, 1995.

Hewitt, Bill. "Life and Love Behind Bars." *People*. 64, no. 19 (November 7, 2005). http://www.people.com/people/archive/article/0,,20144791,00.html (accessed August 19, 2009).

Higdon, Hal. *Leopold & Loeb: The Crime of the Century*. Urbana: University of Illinois Press, 1979.

Hill, Marvin S. "Carthage Conspiracy Reconsidered: A Second Look at The Murder of Joseph and Hyrum Smith." *Journal of the Illinois State Historical Society* 97, no. 2 (Summer 2004): 107–134.

History.com. "Hunt for Abraham Lincoln's Assassin, John Wilkes Booth." *The American Civil War*. http://www.history.com/content/civilwar/the-hunt-for-john-wilkes-booth/john-wilkes-booth-biography (accessed July 29, 2009).

Hoffer, Peter Charles. *The Great New York Conspiracy of 1741*. Lawrence: University Press of Kansas, 2003.

Hoffer, Peter Charles. *The Salem Witchcraft Trials: A Legal History*, Lawrence: University Press of Kansas, 1997.

Holmes, Paul. *Retrial: Murder and Dr. Sam Sheppard*. New York: Bantam Books, 1966.

Holmes, Paul. *The Sheppard Murder Case*, New York: David McKay Company, 1961.

Horne, Gerald. *Powell v. Alabama: The Scottsboro Boys and American Justice*. New York: Franklin Watts, 1997.

House Select Committee on Assassinations. *Final Report on the House Select Committee on Assassinations*. Ipswich, MA: The Mary Ferrell Foundation Press, 2007.

Huie, William Bradford. *Three Lives for Mississippi*. Jackson: University Press of Mississippi, 2000.

Hunter, Stephen, and John Bainbridge Jr. *American Gunfight: The Plot to Kill Harry Truman-and the Shoot-out That Stopped It.* New York: Simon and Schuster, 2005.

Iorizzo, Luciano J. *Al Capone: A Biography.* Westport, CT: Greenwood Publishing Group, 2003.

Irons, Peter. *God on Trial: Dispatches from America's Religious Battlefield.* New York: Viking, 2007.

Irons, Peter. *War Powers: How the Imperial Presidency Hijacked the Constitution.* New York: Metropolitan Books, 2005.

Ise, Claudine. "'Unicorn Killer' in the TV Spotlight." *Los Angeles Times.* http://articles. latimes.com/1999/may/08/entertainment/ca-35158 (accessed July 13, 2009).

Isenberg, Nancy. *Fallen Founder: The Life of Aaron Burr.* New York: Penguin, 2008.

Jansen, Godfrey. *Why Robert Kennedy Was Killed.* New York: Third Press, 1970.

January, Brendan. *Dred Scott Decision.* New York: Children's Press, 1998.

Jezer, Marty. *Abbie Hoffman: American Rebel.* New Brunswick, NJ: Rutgers University Press, 1993.

Johnson, David Alan. *Betrayal: The True Story of J. Edgar Hoover and the Nazi Saboteurs Captured During WWII.* New York: Hippocrene Books, 2007.

Johnson, F. Roy. *The Nat Turner Insurrection Together with Thomas R. Gray's the Confession, Trial and Execution of Nat Turner as a Supplement.* Chicago: Johnson Publishing Company, 1966.

Johnson, Mat. *The Great Negro Plot: A Tale of Conspiracy and Murder in Eighteenth Century New York.* New York: Holtzbrinck Publishers, 2007.

Jones, Howard. *The Mutiny on the Amistad: The Saga of a Slave Revolt and its Impact on American Abolition, Law, and Diplomacy.* New York: Oxford University Press, 1987.

Jones, Stephen, and Peter Israel. *Others Unknown: Timothy McVeigh and the Oklahoma Bombing Conspiracy.* New York: Public Affairs, 2001.

Kaiser, Robert Blair. *"RFK Must Die": A History of the Robert Kennedy Assassination and Its Aftermath.* New York: Dutton, 1970.

Kantor, Seth. *The Ruby Cover-Up.* New York: Kensington Publishing, 1978.

Kantor, Seth. *Who Was Jack Ruby?* New York: Everest House, 1978.

Kapp, Marshall B. *Legal Aspects of Elder Care.* Sudbury, MA: Jones and Bartlett Publishers, 2009.

Kaufman, Kenneth C. *Dred Scott's Advocate: A Biography of Roswell M. Field.* Columbia: University of Missouri Press, 1996.

Kaufman, Michael. "David Dellinger, of Chicago 7, Dies at 88." *New York Times.* May 27, 2004. http://www.nytimes.com/2004/05/27/national/27dell.html?pagewanted=1 (accessed July 28, 2009).

Kelley, Darwin N. *Milligan's Fight Against Lincoln.* Hicksville, NY: Exposition Press, 1973.

Kelly, Susan. *The Boston Stranglers.* New York: Pinnacle Books, 2002.

Kidder, Frederic. *The History of The Boston Massacre.* Highland Park, NJ: Gyphron Press, 2005.

Kilgallen, Dorothy. *Murder One*. New York: Random House, 1967.

Kimmel, Stanley. *The Mad Booths of Maryland*. Indianapolis, IN: Bobbs-Merrill, 1940.

Kisseloff, Jeff. *Generation on Fire: Voices of Protest from the 1960s, An Oral History*. Lexington: University Press of Kentucky, 2007.

Kobler, John. *Capone: The Life and World of Al Capone*. Cambridge, MA: Da Capo Press, 2003.

Koon, Stacey, and Robert Dietz. *Presumed Guilty*. Lake Bluff, IL: Regnery Gateway, 1992.

Kudlac, Christopher S. *Public Executions: The Death Penalty and the Media*. Westport, CT: Greenwood Publishing Group, 2007.

La Force, Glen W. "The War-Crimes Trial of Major Henry Wirz, C.S.A.: Justice Served or Justice Denied?" *Journal of Confederate History* (Fall 1988): 287–312.

Lambert, Patricia. *False Witness: The Real Story of Jim Garrison's Investigation and Oliver Stone's Film, JFK*. New York: M. Evans and Company, 2000.

Lange, Tom, Philip Vannatter, and Dan Moldea. *Evidence Dismissed: The Inside Story of the Police Investigation of O. J. Simpson*. New York: Pocket Books, 1997.

Langford, Gerald. *The Murder of Stanford White*. London: V. Gollancz, 1963.

LaPlante, Eva. *American Jezebel: The Uncommon Life of Anne Hutchinson, the Woman Who Defied the Puritans*. New York: HarperOne, 2005.

Larsen, Richard. *The Deliberate Stranger*. Englewood Cliffs, NJ: Prentice Hall, 1980.

Larson, Edward J. *Summer of the Gods: The Scopes Monkey Trial and America's Continuing Debate over Science and Religion*. New York: Basic Books, 2006.

Larson, Erik. *The Devil in the White City: Murder, Magic, and Madness at the Fair that Changed America*. New York: Vintage Books, 2004.

Law Library–American Law and Legal Information. "Al Capone Trial: 1931—The St. Valentine's Day Massacre, 'Impossible to Bargain with a Federal Court.'" *Notable Trials and Court Cases—1918 to 1940*. http://law.jrank.org/pages/2902/Al-Capone-Trial-1931.html. (accessed December 25, 2009).

Law Library–American Law and Legal Information. "Albert Henry DeSalvo Trial: 1967—Sanity Hearing, Final Arguments." *Notable Trials and Court Cases—1963 to 1972*. http://law.jrank.org/pages/3153/Albert-Henry-DeSalvo-Trial-1967.html (accessed January 20, 2010).

Law Library–American Law and Legal Information. "Anne Hutchinson: 1637 and 1638—General Court Summons Hutchinson." *Great American Trials*. Vol. 1. http://law.jrank.org/pages/2325/Anne-Hutchinson-Trials-1637–1638-General-Court-Summons-Hutchinson.html (accessed March 23, 2009).

Law Library–American Law and Legal Information. "Bernhard Goetz: 1987—The Defense Attacks, Effective Demonstration." *Notable Trials and Court Cases—1981 to 1988*. http://law.jrank.org/pages/3412/Bernhard-Goetz-Trial-1987.html (accessed December 21, 2009).

Law Library–American Law and Legal Information. "Billy Mitchell Court-Martial: 1925." *Notable Trials and Court Cases—1918 to 1940*. http://law.jrank.org/pages/2858/Billy-Mitchell-Court-Martial-1925.html (accessed January 4, 2010).

Law Library–American Law and Legal Information. "Brown v. Board of Education: 1954—NAACP Takes on Topeka Board of Education." *Great American Trials*. Vol. 2. http://law.jrank.org/pages/3057/Brown-v-Board-Education-1954.html (accessed August 6, 2009).

Law Library–American Law and Legal Information. "Charles Manson Trial: 1970–71—Atkins Reverses Course, A 'Helter Skelter' Scheme, Case Draws Presidential Remark, Manson Speaks." *Great American Trials*. Vol. 2. http://law.jrank.org/pages/3206/Charles-Manson-Trial-1970–71.html (accessed May 20, 2009).

Law Library–American Law and Legal Information. "Chicago Seven Trial: 1969—Seale Bound and Gagged, Star-studded Witnesses Appear, Guilty Verdicts Multiply." *Great American Trials*. Vol. 2. http://law.jrank.org/pages/3193/Chicago-Seven-Trial-1969.html (accessed July 24, 2009).

Law Library–American Law and Legal Information. "Claus von Bulow Trials: 1982 & 1985—Witness Cites Mysterious Vials, New Trial, New Evidence." *Notable Trials and Court Cases—1981 to 1988*. http://law.jrank.org/pages/3356/Claus-Von-Bulow-Trials-1982–1985.html (accessed January 18, 2010).

Law Library—American Law and Legal Information. "Dan White Trial: 1979—Double Execution, Unique Defense." *Notable Trials and Court Cases—1973 to 1980*. http://law.jrank.org/pages/3303/Daniel-James-White-Trial-1979.html (accessed February 9, 2010).

Law Library–American Law and Legal Information. "Et al. United States v. Shipp: 1907–09—An Arrest Is Made, A Near Lynching and a Trial, A Guilty Verdict and Lynching, A Long Road to Justice." *Great American Trials*. Vol. 1. http://law.jrank.org/pages/2756/United-States-v-Shipp-et-al-1907–09.html (accessed July 15, 2009).

Law Library–American Law and Legal Information. "Ex Parte Quirin." *Notable Trials and Court Cases—1941 to 1953*. http://law.jrank.org/pages/13645/Ex-Parte-Quirin.html (accessed August 24, 2009).

Law Library–American Law and Legal Information. " 'Fatty' Arbuckle Trials: 1921–1922." *Great American Trials*. Vol. 1. http://law.jrank.org/pages/2839/-Fatty-Arbuckle-Trials-1921–22.html (accessed April 12, 2009).

Law Library–American Law and Legal Information. "Gideon v. Wainwright—Further Reading." *Great American Court Cases*. Vol. 8. http://law.jrank.org/pages/12948/Gideon-v-Wainwright.html (accessed March 13, 2009).

Law Library–American Law and Legal Information. "The Great Negro Plot Trial: 1741." *American Law Encyclopedia*. Vol. 2. http://law.jrank.org/pages/2351/Great-Negro-Plot-Trial-1741.html (accessed March 1, 2009).

Law Library–American Law and Legal Information. "Harry Thaw Trials: 1907–08—Evelyn Nesbit Comes to New York, Thaw Is Tried For Murder, Suggestions for Further Reading" *Great American Trials*. Vol. 1. http://law.jrank.org/pages/2751/Harry-Thaw-Trials-1907–08.html (accessed June 23, 2009).

Law Library–American Law and Legal Information. "Haymarket Trial: 1886— Chicago: Hotbed of Radicalism, Police Arrest Eight Anarchists." *Great American Trials*. Vol. 1. http://law.jrank.org/pages/2683/Haymarket-Trial-1886.html (accessed July 16, 2009).

Law Library–American Law and Legal Information. "Hollywood Ten Trials: 1948–50—Hollywood Divided Into Two Camps, The Right to Remain Silent, I Would Hate Myself in the Morning." *Notable Trials and Court Cases—1941 to 1953*. http://law.jrank.org/pages/3012/Hollywood-Ten-Trials-1948–50.html (accessed January 6, 2010).

Law Library–American Law and Legal Information. "Ira Einhorn Trial: 1993—An Abusive Relationship Leads To Murder, Defendant Flees the Country, A Trial Without

A Defendant Present." *Great American Trials*. Vol. 2. http://law.jrank.org/pages/3582/ Ira-Einhorn-Trial-1993.html (accessed July 12, 2009).

Law Library–American Law and Legal Information. "Jack Kevorkian Trials: 1994–1999— The Public Debate Over Assisted-Suicide Begins, Michigan Suspends Kevorkian's License, The Severely Ill Ask Kevorkian for Help." *Notable Trials and Court Cases—1989 to 1994*. http://law.jrank.org/pages/3609/Jack-Kevorkian-Trials-1994–99.html (accessed January 26, 2010).

Law Library–American Law and Legal Information. "Jesse Timmendequas Trial: 1997— Clues and Conflicting Stories Point to Suspect, Timmendequas Convicted, Defense Pleads Mitigating Factors." *Notable Trials and Court Cases—1995 to present*. http:// law.jrank.org/pages/3734/Jesse-Timmendequas-Trial-1997.html (accessed January 9, 2010).

Law Library–American Law and Legal Information. "Joe Hill Trial: 1914— Circumstantial Evidence But No Motive." *Great American Trials*. Vol. 1. http://law.jrank.org/ pages/2799/Joe-Hill-Trial-1914.html (accessed August 14, 2009).

Law Library–American Law and Legal Information. "Lenny Bruce Trial: 1964." *Great American Trials*. Vol. 2. http://law.jrank.org/pages/3133/Lenny-Bruce-Trial-1964.html (accessed April 15, 2009).

Law Library–American Law and Legal Information. "Leo Frank Trial: 1913—Little Mary Phagan Murdered, Prosecutors Emphasize Frank's Nervousness, Prosecution Clinches Their Case, Frank Convicted, Commuted, and Lynched." *Great American Trials*. Vol. 1. http://law.jrank.org/pages/2793/Leo-Frank-Trial-1913.html (accessed May 27, 2009).

Law Library–American Law and Legal Information. "Leopold and Loeb Trial: 1924." *Great American Trials*. Vol. 1. http://law.jrank.org/pages/2852/Leopold-Loeb-Trial-1924.html (accessed April 11, 2009).

Law Library–American Law and Legal Information. "Lizzie Borden Trial: 1893." *Great American Trials*. Vol. 1. http://law.jrank.org/pages/2708/Lizzie-Borden-Trial-1893. html (accessed April 8, 2009).

Law Library–American Law and Legal Information. "Los Angeles Police Officers Trials: 1992 & 1993." *Great American Trials*. Vol. 2. http://law.jrank.org/pages/3533/ Los-Angeles-Police-Officers-Trials-1992–1993.html (accessed May 23, 2009).

Law Library–American Law and Legal Information. "Manuel Noriega Trial: 1991—Cartel Contact Revealed, Judge Taken Ill." *Notable Trials and Court Cases—1989 to 1994*. http://law.jrank.org/pages/3489/Manuel-Noriega-Trial-1991.html (accessed January 11, 2010).

Law Library–American Law and Legal Information. "The Mapplethorpe Obscenity Trial: 1990—Obscenity or Art?" *Notable Trials and Court Cases—1989 to 1994*. http://law.jrank. org/pages/3469/Mapplethorpe-Obscenity-Trial-1990.html (accessed December 29, 2009).

Law Library–American Law and Legal Information. "Marcia Clark." *American Law Encyclopedia*. Vol. 2. http://law.jrank.org/pages/5265/Clark-Marcia-Rachel.html (accessed August 3, 2009).

Law Library–American Law and Legal Information. "McMartin Preschool Trials: 1987– 90—Mother Calls In The Police, Parents Demand Action, Rewarded for "right" answers, Paranoid Schizophrenic, Bail After Five Years, Acquittals and Deadlocks." *Great*

American Trials. Vol. 2. http://law.jrank.org/pages/3424/McMartin-Preschool-Trials-1987–90.html (accessed July 10, 2009).

Law Library–American Law and Legal Information. "Menendez Brothers' Trial: 1993–1994 & 1995–1996—Testimonials of Sexual Abuse, Cold-Blooded Killers? Battle Over Incriminating Tape, Closing Arguments, Costly Trial." *Great American Trials.* Vol. 2. http://law.jrank.org/pages/3575/Menendez-Brothers-Trials-1993–94–1995–96.html (accessed July 19, 2009).

Law Library–American Law and Legal Information. "Mike Tyson Trial: 1992— Brutal Attack." *Notable Trials and Court Cases—1989 to 1994.* http://law.jrank.org/pages/3530/Mike-Tyson-Trial-1992.html (accessed December 28, 2009).

Law Library–American Law and Legal Information. "Price and Bowers Trial: 1967—Defense Tactics Fail, Jury Reaches Tough Decision." *Great American Trials.* Vol. 2. http://law.jrank.org/pages/3163/Price-Bowers-Trial-1967.html (accessed April 26, 2009)

Law Library–American Law and Legal Information. "Randall Adams Trial: 1977—Surprise Witnesses Emerge." *Notable Trials and Court Cases—1973 to 1980.* http://law.jrank.org/pages/3278/Randall-Adams-Trial-1977.html (accessed January 30, 2010).

Law Library–American Law and Legal Information. "Randy Weaver Trial: 1993—A Fugitive from Justice, A Gunfight in the Woods, Prosecution Witnesses Help the Defense." *Notable Trials and Court Cases—1989 to 1994.* http://law.jrank.org/pages/3563/Randy-Weaver-Trial-1993.html (accessed January 2, 2010).

Law Library–American Law and Legal Information. "Richard Allen Davis: 1996—A Sorid Past, Anger in the Courtroom, Suggestions for Further Reading." *Notable Trials and Court Cases—1995 to present.* http://law.jrank.org/pages/3703/Richard-Allen-Davis-Trial-1996.html (accessed December 22, 2009).

Law Library–American Law and Legal Information. "Samuel Chase: The Samuel Chase Impeachment Trial." *American Law Encyclopedia. Vol. 2.* http://law.jrank.org/pages/5152/Chase-Samuel.html (accessed March 1, 2009).

Law Library–American Law and Legal Information. "Sweet Trials: 1925–26—Menacing Crowd Gathers, Darrow for the Defense." *Great American Trials.* Vol. 1. http://law.jrank.org/pages/2866/Sweet-Trials-1925–26.html (accessed July 13, 2009).

Law Library–American Law and Legal Information. "Theodore Robert Bundy Trials: 1976 & 1979—Bundy Forgoes Jury, On The Run and Deadly, Testimony That Could Kill." *Notable Trials and Court Cases—1973 to 1980.* http://law.jrank.org/pages/3268/Theodore-Robert-Bundy-Trials-1976–1979.html (accessed February 1, 2010).

Law Library–American Law and Legal Information. "Thomas Massie Trial: 1932—Mother-in-Law Takes Charge, 'Is This Your Handwriting?' " *Great American Trials.* Vol. 1. http://law.jrank.org/pages/2905/Thomas-Massie-Trial-1932.html (accessed July 25, 2009).

Law Library–American Law and Legal Information. "Tilton v. Beecher: 1875—Plymouth Church Clears, Mrs. Tilton Never Testifies." http://law.jrank.org/pages/2629/Tilton-v-Beecher-1875.html. *Notable Trials and Court Cases—1833 to 1882* (accessed January 12, 2010).

Law Library–American Law and Legal Information. "Triangle Shirtwaist Fire Trial: 1911—Harris and Blanck Go Free." *Great American Trials.* Vol. 1. http://law.jrank.org/

pages/2772/Triangle-Shirtwaist-Fire-Trial-1911-Blanck-Harris-go-Free.html (accessed April 6, 2009).

Law Library–American Law and Legal Information. "William "Big Bill" Haywood Trial: 1907—The Coeur D'Alene Strike, Haywood's Fate Rests on Orchard's Credibility." *Great American Trials.* Vol. 1. http://law.jrank.org/pages/2760/William-Big-Bill-Haywood-Trial-1907.html (accessed July 5, 2009).

Law Library–American Law and Legal Information. "William Calley Court-Martial: 1970—Some Refused Orders." http://law.jrank.org/pages/3208/William-Calley-Court-Martial-1970.html (accessed July 22, 2009).

Law Library–American Law and Legal Information. "William Kennedy Smith: 1991—Tabloid Interview Nets $40,000, Defendant Remains Cool, Suggestions for Further Reading." *Notable Trials and Court Cases—1989 to 1994.* http://law.jrank.org/pages/3509/William-Kennedy-Smith-Trial-1991.html. (accessed December 23, 2009).

Law Library–American Law and Legal Information. "Wyatt Earp Trial: 1881—A Mysterious Stagecoach Robbery, Trouble Brewing, Shootout, The Hearing, Aftermath." *Notable Trials and Court Cases—1833 to 1882.* http://law.jrank.org/pages/2659/Wyatt-Earp-Trial-1881.html (accessed July 17, 2009).

Lawrence, Richard. *Shooting at the President!: The remarkable trial of Richard Lawrence, self-styled "King of the United States," "King of England and of Rome," …the event, not before known to the public.* London: W. Mitchell, 1835.

Lawson, John Davison, and Robert Lorenzo Howard. *American State Trials: A Collection of the Important and Interesting Trials Which Have Taken Place in the United States from the Beginning of Our Government to the Present Day.* St. Louis, MO: Thomas Law Books, 1917.

Lee, Henry C., and Frank Tirnady. *Blood Evidence: How DNA is Revolutionizing the Way We Solve Crimes.* New York: Basic Books, 2003.

Leen, Jeff. "Lewinsky: Two Coasts, Two Lives, and Two Images." *Washington Post.* January 24, 1998, p. A1.

Leonard, Elizabeth D. *Lincoln's Avengers: Justice, Revenge, and Reunion after the Civil War.* New York: W. W. Norton and Company, 2004.

Lepore, Jill. *New York Burning: Liberty, Conspiracy, and Slavery in Eighteenth Century Manhattan.* New York: Knopf, 2006.

Lessenberry, Jack. "Death Becomes Him." *Vanity Fair* 57 (July 1994): 102–106.

Levinson, Jill S., David A. D'Amora, and Andrea L. Hern. "Megan's Law and Its Impact on Community Re-entry for Sex Offenders." *Behaviorial Sciences and the Law* 25, no. 4 (2007): 587–602.

Levy, Steven. "And Justice For All." *Newsweek.* October 18, 2002. http://www.newsweek.com/id/65190/page/1 (accessed July 12, 2009).

Levy, Steven. *The Unicorn's Secret: A Murder in the Age of Aquarius.* New York: Penguin, 1990.

Lewis, Anthony. *Clarence Earl Gideon and the Supreme Court.* New York: Random House, 1972.

Lewis, Anthony. *Freedom for the Thought that We Hate: A Biography of the First Amendment.* New York: Basic Books, 2008.

Lewis, Anthony. *Gideon's Trumpet*. New York: Random House, 1964.

Lief, Michael S., and H. Mitchell Caldwell. *The Devil's Advocate: Greatest Closing Arguments in Criminal Law*. New York: Scribner, 2007.

Linder, Douglas O. "The Amistad Case." *Famous Trials*. http://www.law.umkc.edu/faculty/projects/ftrials/amistad/AMI_ACT.HTM (accessed March 1, 2009).

Linder, Douglas O. "The Big Money Behind the Fix: Arnold Rothstein." *The Black Sox Trial: Biographies of Key Figures*. http://www.law.umkc.edu/faculty/projects/ftrials/blacksox/biographies.html (accessed August 12, 2009).

Linder, Douglas O. "Biographies: Christopher Darden." *Famous Trials*. http://www.law.umkc.edu/faculty/projects/FTrials/Simpson/Darden.htm (accessed August 3, 2009).

Linder, Douglas O. "Biographies: F. Lee Bailey." *Famous Trials*. http://www.law.umkc.edu/faculty/projects/ftrials/Simpson/Bailey.htm (accessed August 4, 2009).

Linder, Douglas O. "Biographies: Johnnie Cochran." *Famous Trials*. http://www.law.umkc.edu/faculty/projects/FTrials/Simpson/cochran.htm (accessed August 3, 2009).

Linder, Douglas O. "Biographies: Lance Ito." *Famous Trials*. http://www.law.umkc.edu/faculty/projects/ftrials/simpson/ito.htm (accessed August 4, 2009).

Linder, Douglas O. "Biographies: Mark Fuhrman." *Famous Trials*. http://www.law.umkc.edu/faculty/projects/ftrials/Simpson/Fuhrman.htm (accessed August 4, 2009).

Linder, Douglas O. "Biographies: Ronald Goldman." *Famous Trials*. http://www.law.umkc.edu/faculty/projects/ftrials/Simpson/Goldman.htm (accessed August 3, 2009).

Linder, Douglas O. "Biographies of Key Figures in the Chicago Seven Trial: Abbie Hoffman." *Famous Trials*. http://www.law.umkc.edu/faculty/projects/ftrials/Chicago7/hoffmanA.htm (accessed July 28, 2009).

Linder, Douglas O. "Biographies of Key Figures in the Chicago Seven Trial: Bobby Seale." *Famous Trials*. http://www.law.umkc.edu/faculty/projects/ftrials/Chicago7/SealeB.htm (accessed July 28, 2009).

Linder, Douglas O. "Biographies of Key Figures in the Chicago Seven Trial: David Dellinger." *Famous Trials*. http://www.law.umkc.edu/faculty/projects/ftrials/Chicago7/DellingerD.htm (accessed July 28, 2009).

Linder, Douglas O. "Biographies of Key Figures in the Chicago Seven Trial: Jerry Rubin." *Famous Trials*. http://www.law.umkc.edu/faculty/projects/ftrials/Chicago7/RubinJ.htm (accessed July 28, 2009).

Linder, Douglas O. "Biographies of Key Figures in the Chicago Seven Trial: John Froines." *Famous Trials*. http://www.law.umkc.edu/faculty/projects/ftrials/Chicago7/FroinesJ.htm (accessed July 28, 2009).

Linder, Douglas O. "Biographies of Key Figures in the Chicago Seven Trial: Lee Weiner" *Famous Trials*. http://www.law.umkc.edu/faculty/projects/ftrials/Chicago7/WeinerL.htm (accessed July 28, 2009).

Linder, Douglas O. "Biographies of Key Figures in the Chicago Seven Trial: Rennie Davis." *Famous Trials*. http://www.law.umkc.edu/faculty/projects/ftrials/Chicago7/DavisR.htm (accessed July 28, 2009).

Linder, Douglas O. "Biographies of Key Figures in the Chicago Seven Trial: Tom Hayden." *Famous Trials*. http://www.law.umkc.edu/faculty/projects/ftrials/Chicago7/HaydenT.htm (accessed July 28, 2009).

Linder, Douglas O. "The Black Sox Trial: An Account." *Famous Trials.* http://www.law. umkc.edu/faculty/projects/ftrials/blacksox/blacksoxaccount.html (accessed March 2, 2009).

Linder, Douglas O. "The Boston Massacre Trials: An Account," *Famous Trials.* http://www. law.umkc.edu/faculty/projects/ftrials/bostonmassacre/bostonaccount.html (accessed March 1, 2009).

Linder, Douglas O. "The Charles Manson (Tate-LaBianca Murder) Trial." *Famous Trials.* http://www.law.umkc.edu/faculty/projects/ftrials/manson/mansonaccount.html (accessed May 20, 2009).

Linder, Douglas O. "The Chicago Seven Conspiracy Trial." *Famous Trials.* http://www.law. umkc.edu/faculty/projects/ftrials/Chicago7/Account.html (accessed July 23, 2009).

Linder, Douglas O. "Cinque." *Famous Trials.* http://www.law.umkc.edu/faculty/projects/ ftrials/amistad/AMI_BCIN.HTM (accessed August 25, 2009).

Linder, Douglas O. "The Dakota Conflict Trials." *Famous Trials.* http://www.law.umkc. edu/faculty/projects/ftrials/dakota/Dak_account.html (accessed March 1, 2009).

Linder, Douglas O. "The Dr. Sam Sheppard Trial." *Famous Trials.* http://www.law.umkc. edu/faculty/projects/ftrials/sheppard/sheppardaccount.html (accessed March 16, 2009).

Linder, Douglas O. "The Earp-Holliday Trial: An Account." *Famous Trials.* http:// www.law.umkc.edu/faculty/projects/FTRIALS/earp/earpaccount.html (accessed July 17, 2009).

Linder, Douglas O. "The Falwell v. Flynt Trial (1984)." *Famous Trials.* http://www.law. umkc.edu/faculty/projects/ftrials/falwell/trialaccount.html (accessed March 17, 2009).

Linder, Douglas O. "The Haymarket Riot and Subsequent Trial." *Famous Trials.* http:// www.law.umkc.edu/faculty/projects/FTRIALS/haymarket/haymktaccount.html (accessed July 16, 2009).

Linder, Douglas O. "How Fair Were The Dakota Conflict Trials." *Famous Trials.* http:// www.law.umkc.edu/faculty/projects/ftrials/dakota/dakfairness.html (accessed March 13, 2009).

Linder, Douglas O. "An Introduction to the My Lai Courts-Martial." *Famous Trials.* http://www. law.umkc.edu/faculty/projects/ftrials/mylai/Myl_intro.html (accessed July 22, 2009).

Linder, Douglas O. "The Impeachment Trial of Andrew Johnson." *Famous Trials.* http:// www.law.umkc.edu/faculty/projects/ftrials/impeach/imp_account2.html (accessed March 1, 2009).

Linder, Douglas O. "The Impeachment Trial of William Clinton." *Famous Trials.* http:// www.law.umkc.edu/faculty/projects/FTRIALS/clinton/clintontrialaccount.html (accessed March 9, 2009).

Linder, Douglas O. "The Leopold and Loeb Trial: A Brief Account." *Famous Trials.* http:// www.law.umkc.edu/faculty/projects/ftrials/leoploeb/Accountoftrial.html (accessed April 10, 2009).

Linder, Douglas O. "The Leonard Peltier Trial." *Famous Trials.* http://www.law.umkc.edu/ faculty/projects/ftrials/peltier/peltieraccount.html (accessed March 28, 2009).

Linder, Douglas O. "Lincoln Assassination Conspirators: David E. Herold." *Famous Trials.* http://www.law.umkc.edu/faculty/projects/ftrials/lincolnconspiracy/herold.html (accessed July 29, 2009).

Linder, Douglas O. "Lincoln Assassination Conspirators: Dr. Samuel Mudd." *Famous Trials*. http://www.law.umkc.edu/faculty/projects/ftrials/lincolnconspiracy/mudd.html (accessed July 31, 2009).

Linder, Douglas O. "Lincoln Assassination Conspirators: Edman Spangler." *Famous Trials*. http://www.law.umkc.edu/faculty/projects/ftrials/lincolnconspiracy/spangler. html (accessed July 31, 2009).

Linder, Douglas O. "Lincoln Assassination Conspirators: George Atzerodt." *Famous Trials*. http://www.law.umkc.edu/faculty/projects/ftrials/lincolnconspiracy/atzerodt. html (accessed July 31, 2009).

Linder, Douglas O. "Lincoln Assassination Conspirators: John Surratt." *Famous Trials*. http://www.law.umkc.edu/faculty/projects/ftrials/lincolnconspiracy/surrattj.html (accessed July 30, 2009).

Linder, Douglas O. "Lincoln Assassination Conspirators: John Wilkes Booth." *Famous Trials*. http://www.law.umkc.edu/faculty/projects/ftrials/lincolnconspiracy/booth.html (accessed July 29, 2009).

Linder, Douglas O. "Lincoln Assassination Conspirators: Lewis Powell." *Famous Trials*. http://www.law.umkc.edu/faculty/projects/ftrials/lincolnconspiracy/powell.html (accessed July 29, 2009).

Linder, Douglas O. "Lincoln Assassination Conspirators: Mary Surratt." *Famous Trials*. http://www.law.umkc.edu/faculty/projects/ftrials/lincolnconspiracy/surrattm.html (accessed July 30, 2009).

Linder, Douglas O. "Lincoln Assassination Conspirators: Samuel Arnold." *Famous Trials*. http://www.law.umkc.edu/faculty/projects/ftrials/lincolnconspiracy/arnold.html (accessed July 30, 2009).

Linder, Douglas O. "Lincoln Assassination Conspirators: Michael O'Laughlen." *Famous Trials*. http://www.law.umkc.edu/faculty/projects/ftrials/lincolnconspiracy/olaughlin. html (accessed July 29, 2009).

Linder, Douglas O. "The Massie Trials: A Commentary." *Famous Trials*. http://www.law.umkc. edu/faculty/projects/ftrials/massie/massietrialsaccount.html (accessed July 25, 2009).

Linder, Douglas O. "The McMartin Preschool Abuse Trials: A Commentary." *Famous Trials*. http://www.law.umkc.edu/faculty/projects/ftrials/mcmartin/mcmartinaccount. html (accessed July 10, 2009).

Linder, Douglas O. "The Mississippi Burning Trial." *Famous Trials*. http://www.law.umkc. edu/faculty/projects/ftrials/price&bowers/Account.html (accessed April 26, 2009).

Linder, Douglas O. "The Mountain Meadows Massacre of 1857 and the Trials of John D. Lee: An Account." *Famous Trials*. http://www.law.umkc.edu/faculty/projects/FTRI ALS/mountainmeadows/leeaccount.html (accessed July 20, 2009).

Linder, Douglas O. "The Oklahoma Bombing Conspirators." *Famous Trials* http://www. law.umkc.edu/faculty/projects/FTrials/mcveigh/conspirators.html (accessed March 12, 2009).

Linder, Douglas O. "The Oklahoma City Bombing and the Trial of Timothy McVeigh." *Famous Trials*. http://www.law.umkc.edu/faculty/projects/FTRIALS/mcveigh/mcveighaccount.html (accessed March 13, 2009).

Linder, Douglas O. "The Patty Hearst Trial (1976)." *Famous Trials*. http://www.law.umkc. edu/faculty/projects/ftrials/hearst/hearstdolaccount.html (accessed March 19, 2009)

Linder, Douglas O. "President of the White Sox: Charles Comiskey." *The Black Sox Trial: Biographies of Key Figures*. http://www.law.umkc.edu/faculty/projects/ftrials/blacksox/biographies.html (accessed August 10, 2009).

Linder, Douglas O. "Rodney King." *Famous Trials: Key Figures*. http://www.law.umkc.edu/faculty/projects/ftrials/lapd/Kingkeyfigures.html (accessed August 24, 2009).

Linder, Douglas O. "The Ruby Ridge (Randy Weaver) Trial." *Famous Trials*. http://www.law.umkc.edu/faculty/projects/ftrials/weaver/weaveraccount.html (accessed January 1, 2010).

Linder, Douglas O. "Samuel Leibowitz." *Famous Trials*. http://www.law.umkc.edu/faculty/projects/ftrials/scottsboro/SB_bLieb.html (accessed August 19, 2009).

Linder, Douglas O. "The Scottsboro Boys Trial." *Famous Trials*. http://www.law.umkc.edu/faculty/projects/FTrials/scottsboro/scottsb.htm (accessed March 17, 2009).

Linder, Douglas O. "Sheriff Joseph F. Shipp." *Famous Trials*. http://www.law.umkc.edu/faculty/projects/ftrials/shipp/shippbiog.html (accessed August 25, 2009).

Linder, Douglas O. "State v. John Scopes (The Monkey Trial)." *Famous Trials*. http://www.law.umkc.edu/faculty/projects/ftrials/scopes/evolut.htm (accessed March 23, 2009).

Linder, Douglas O. "Stephen Spielberg's 'Amistad' (1997)." *Famous Trials*. http://www.law.umkc.edu/faculty/projects/ftrials/amistad/AMI_MOVI.HTM (accessed August 25, 2009).

Linder, Douglas O. "Supreme Court Decision: Sheppard v. Maxwell." *Famous Trials*. http://www.law.umkc.edu/faculty/projects/FTRIALS/sheppard/sheppardvmaxwell.html (accessed August 6, 2009).

Linder, Douglas O. "The Sweet Trials: An Account." *Famous Trials*. http://www.law.umkc.edu/faculty/projects/FTRIALS/sweet/sweetaccount.HTM (accessed July 13, 2009).

Linder, Douglas O. "The Testimony of Lori Fortier in the Timothy McVeigh Trial." *Famous Trials*. http://www.law.umkc.edu/faculty/projects/ftrials/mcveigh/lorifortiertestimony.html (accessed August 25, 2009).

Linder, Douglas O. "The Treason Trial of Aaron Burr." *Famous Trials*. http://www.law.umkc.edu/faculty/projects/ftrials/burr/burraccount.html (accessed March 1, 2009).

Linder, Douglas O. "The Trial of John Brown: A Commentary." *Famous Trials*. http://www.law.umkc.edu/faculty/projects/FTRIALS/johnbrown/brownaccount.html (accessed March 1, 2009).

Linder, Douglas O. "The Trial of John Peter Zenger: An Account." *Famous Trials*. http://www.law.umkc.edu/faculty/projects/ftrials/zenger/zengeraccount.html (accessed March 1, 2009).

Linder, Douglas O. "The Trial of John W. Hinckley, Jr." *Famous Trials*. http://www.law.umkc.edu/faculty/projects/ftrials/hinckley/hinckleyaccount.html (accessed March 16, 2009).

Linder, Douglas O. "The Trial of Joseph Shipp et al.: An Account." *Famous Trials*. http://www.law.umkc.edu/faculty/projects/ftrials/shipp/trialaccount.html (accessed July 15, 2009).

Linder, Douglas O. "The Trial of Leo Frank: An Account." *Famous Trials*. http://www.law.umkc.edu/faculty/projects/ftrials/frank/frankaccount.html (accessed May 27, 2009).

Linder, Douglas O. "The Trial of the Lincoln Assassination Conspirators." *Famous Trials*. http://www.law.umkc.edu/faculty/projects/ftrials/lincolnconspiracy/lincolnaccount.html (accessed March 1, 2009).

Linder, Douglas O. "The Trial of Lizzie Borden." *Famous Trials.* http://www.law.umkc.edu/faculty/projects/ftrials/LizzieBorden/bordenaccount.html (accessed April 8, 2009).

Linder, Douglas O. "The Trial of Orenthal James Simpson." *Famous Trials.* http://www.law.umkc.edu/faculty/projects/ftrials/Simpson/Simpsonaccount.htm (accessed March 11, 2009).

Linder, Douglas O. "The Trial of Richard 'Bruno' Hauptmann: An Account." *Famous Trials.* http://www.law.umkc.edu/faculty/projects/ftrials/Hauptmann/AccountHauptmann.html (accessed April 4, 2009).

Linder, Douglas O. "Trial of the Rosenbergs: An Account." *Famous Trials.* http://www.law.umkc.edu/faculty/projects/ftrials/rosenb/ROS_ACCT.HTM (accessed March 31, 2009).

Linder, Douglas O. "The Trial of Sacco and Vanzetti." *Famous Trials.* http://www.law.umkc.edu/faculty/projects/ftrials/SaccoV/s&vaccount.html (accessed March 26, 2009).

Linder, Douglas O. "The Trial of Susan B. Anthony for Illegal Voting." *Famous Trials.* http://www.law.umkc.edu/faculty/projects/ftrials/anthony/sbaaccount.html (accessed March 1, 2009).

Linder, Douglas O. "The Trial of William "Big Bill" Haywood." *Famous Trials.* http://www.law.umkc.edu/faculty/projects/ftrials/haywood/HAY_ACCT.HTM (accessed July 5, 2009).

Linder, Douglas O. "The Trial of Zacarias Moussaoui: An Account." *Famous Trials.* http://www.law.umkc.edu/faculty/projects/ftrials/moussaoui/zmaccount.html (accessed March 17, 2009).

Linder, Douglas O. "The Trials of Alger Hiss: A Commentary." *Famous Trials.* http://www.law.umkc.edu/faculty/projects/ftrials/hiss/hissaccount.html (accessed April 3, 2009).

Linder, Douglas O. "The Trials of Harry Thaw for the Murder of Stanford White." *Famous Trials.* http://www.law.umkc.edu/faculty/projects/ftrials/thaw/Thawaccount.html (accessed June 23, 2009).

Linder, Douglas O. "The Trials of Lenny Bruce." *Famous Trials.* http://www.law.umkc.edu/faculty/projects/ftrials/bruce/bruceaccount.html (accessed April 14, 2009).

Linder, Douglas O. "The Trials of the Los Angeles Police Officers' in Connection with the Beating of Rodney King." *Famous Trials.* http://www.law.umkc.edu/faculty/projects/ftrials/lapd/lapdaccount.html (accessed May 23, 2009).

Linder, Douglas O. "The Triangle Shirtwaist Factory Trial." *Famous Trials.* http://www.law.umkc.edu/faculty/projects/ftrials/triangle/triangleaccount.html (accessed April 5, 2009).

Linder, Douglas. "Were There More OKC Conspirators?" *Famous Trials.* http://www.law.umkc.edu/faculty/projects/FTRIALS/mcveigh/moreconspirators.html (accessed March 13, 2009).

Linder, Douglas O. "William D. Haywood." *Famous Trials.* http://www.law.umkc.edu/faculty/projects/ftrials/haywood/HAY_BHAY.HTM (accessed July 7, 2009).

Linder, Douglas O. "William Jennings Bryan (1860–1925)." *Famous Trials.* http://www.law.umkc.edu/faculty/projects/ftrials/scopes/bryanw.htm (accessed August 18, 2009).

Linder, Douglas O. "The Witchcraft Trials in Salem: A Commentary." *Famous Trials.* http://www.law.umkc.edu/faculty/projects/ftrials/salem/SAL_ACCT.HTM (accessed March 1, 2009).

Lippman, Matthew. *Contemporary Criminal Law: Concepts, Cases, and Controversies.* Thousand Oaks, CA: Sage, 2009.

Liptak, Adam. "Johnnie L. Cochran, Jr., Trial Lawyer Defined by O. J. Simpson Case, Is Dead at 67." *New York Times.* March 30, 2005. http://www.nytimes.com/2005/03/30/national/30cochran.html?pagewanted=1 (accessed August 3, 2009).

Locy, Toni. "Duran Convicted of Trying to Kill President Clinton." *Washington Post.* April 5, 1995, p. D1.

Lowenthal, John. "What the FBI Knew and Hid." *The Alger Hiss Story: Search for the Truth.* http://homepages.nyu.edu/~th15/lowenthaltyp.html (accessed April 4, 2009).

Lubet, Steven. *Murder in Tombstone: The Forgotten Trial of Wyatt Earp.* New Haven, CT: Yale University Press, 2006.

Lukas, J. Anthony. *Big Trouble: A Murder in a Small Western Town Sets Off a Struggle for the Soul of America.* New York: Simon and Schuster, 1997.

MacDonald, Carlos F. "The Trial, Execution, Autopsy, and Mental Status of Leon F. Czolgosz, Alias Fred Nieman, the Assassin of President McKinley." *The American Journal of Insanity* 58 (January 1902): 369–386.

Mahler, Jeffrey. *The Challenge: Hamdan v. Rumsfeld and the Fight over Presidential Power.* New York: Farrar, Straus and Giroux, 2008.

Maksel, Rebecca. "The Billy Mitchell Court-Martial." *Air & Space* 24, no. 2 (July 1, 2009): 46–49.

Maltz, Eric. M. *Dred Scott and the Politics of Slavery.* Lawrence: University Press of Kansas, 2007.

Mann, Abby. *Shocking True Story of the McMartin Child Abuse Trial.* New York: Random House, 1993.

Marrs, Jim. *Crossfire: The Plot That Killed Kennedy.* New York: Basic Books, 1989.

Martin, Gus. *Understanding Terrorism: Challenges, Perspectives, and Issues.* Thousand Oaks, CA: Sage, 2009.

Martin, John Barlow. "The Master of Murder Castle: A Classic of Chicago Crime." *Harper's Weekly* (December 1943): 76–85.

Matoesian, Gregory M. *Law and the Language of Identity: Discourse in the William Kennedy Smith Trial.* New York: Oxford University Press, 2001.

McCaleb, Walter F., and Charles A. Beard. *The Aaron Burr Conspiracy.* Whitefish, MT: Kessinger Publishing, 2006.

McCann, Joseph T. *Terrorism on American Soil: A Concise History of Plots and Perpetrators from the Famous to the Forgotten.* Boulder, CO: Sentient Publications, 2006.

McCann, Michael W. "Reform Litigation on Trial." *Law and Social Inquiry* 17 (1992): 715–743.

McHale, John. *Dr. Samuel A. Mudd and the Lincoln Assassination.* Southampton, NY: Heritage Books, 2000.

McLaurin, Melton A. *Celia: A Slave: A True Story of Violence and Retribution in antebellum, Missouri.* Athens: University of Georgia Press, 1999.

McRae, Donald. *The Last Trials of Clarence Darrow.* New York: William Morrow and Company, 2009.

" 'Megan's Law" Killer Escapes Death under N.J. Execution Ban." *CNN.com.* December 17, 2007. http://www.cnn.com/2007/POLITICS/12/17/death.penalty/index.html (accessed January 9, 2009).

Melnick, Jeffrey. *Black-Jewish Relations on Trial: Leo Frank and Jim Conley in the New South.* Oxford: University of Mississippi Press, 2000.

Melton, Buckner. *Aaron Burr: Conspiracy to Treason.* New York: Wiley, 2001.

Messerschmidt, Jim. *The Trial of Leonard Peltier.* Boston: South End Press, 1983.

Meyer, Roy. *History of the Santee Sioux: United States Indian Policy on Trial.* Lincoln: University of Nebraska Press, 1967.

Michaud, Stephen G., and Hugh Aynesworth. *The Only Living Witness: The True Story of Serial Sex Killer* Ted Bundy. Irving, TX: Authorlink, 1999.

Michel, Lou, and Dan Herbeck. *American Terrorist: Timothy McVeigh and the Tragedy at Oklahoma City.* New York: Regan Books, 2002.

Mooney, Michael M. *Evelyn Nesbit and Stanford White: Love and Death in the Gilded Age.* New York: William Morrow and Company, 1976.

Morris, Richard B. *Fair Trial: Fourteen Who Stood Accused, From Anne Hutchinson to Alger Hiss.* New York: Harper and Row, 1967.

Morrisroe, Patricia. *Mapplethorpe: A Biography.* New York: Da Capo Press, 1997.

Morton, Andrew. *Monica's Story.* New York: Macmillan, 1999.

Mosk, Matthew, and Carla Hall. "Victim Thrived on Life in Fast Lane, His Friends Recall." *Los Angeles Times.* June 15, 1994. http://www.latimes.com/entertainment/news/la-oj-anniv-goldman,0,3366898.story (accessed August 3, 2009).

Moussaoui, Abd Samad, and Florence Bouquillat. *Zacarias Moussaoui: The Making of a Terrorist.* London: Serpent's Tail. 2003.

"Mr. Beecher On Trial; Remarkable Testimony from Mrs. Moulton." *New York Times: Archives.* February 20, 1875. http://query.nytimes.com/gst/abstract.html?res=9505EED A133EE43BBC4851DFB466838E669FDE (accessed January 13, 2010).

MSNBC News Services. "Kevorkian Released from Prison after 8 Years: Promises Not to Help Anyone Commit Suicide; Will Work for Legalization." *msnbc.com.* http://www.msnbc.msn.com/id/18974940/ (accessed January 29, 2010).

Myers, Walter Dean. *Amistad: A Long Road to Freedom.* New York: Puffin, 2001.

Nagel, Paul C. *John Quincy Adams: A Public Life, a Private Life.* Cambridge, MA: Harvard University Press, 1999.

Nathan, Debbie and Michael Snedeker. *Satan's Silence: Ritual Abuse and the Making of a Modern American Witch Hunt.* Lincoln, NE: IUniverse, 1996

National Endowment for the Arts 1965–2000: A Brief Chronology of Federal Support for the Arts. Washington, D.C.: National Endowment for the Arts, 2000.

Neely, Mark E. *The Fate of Liberty: Abraham Lincoln and Civil Liberties.* New York: Oxford University Press 1992.

Neff, James. *The Wrong Man: The Final Verdict on the Dr. Sam Sheppard Murder Case.* New York: Random House, 2002.

Nevins, Allen. "The Case of the Copperhead Conspirator." *Joel Samaha, University of Minnesota: Cases and Other Sources.* http://www.soc.umn.edu/~samaha/cases/milligan_copperhead_conspirator.htm (accessed March 18, 2009).

Nicol, Neal, and Harry Wylie. *Between the Dying and the Dead: Dr. Jack Kevorkian's Life and the Battle to Legalize Euthanasia.* Madison: University of Wisconsin Press, 2006.

Norton, Mary Beth. *In the Devil's Snare: The Salem Witchcraft Crisis of 1692.* New York: Vintage Books, 2002.

Oaks, Dallin H., and Marvin S. Hill. *Carthage Conspiracy: The Trial of the Accused Assassins of Joseph Smith.* Urbana: University of Illinois Press, 1979.

Oates, Stephen B. *The Fires of Jubilee: Nat Turner's Fierce Rebellion.* New York: Harper Perennial, 1990.

Oderman, Stuart. *Roscoe "Fatty" Arbuckle: A Biography of the Silent Film Comedian, 1887–1933.* Jefferson, NC: McFarland and Company, 2005.

Olasky, Marvin and John Perry. *Monkey Business: The True Story of the Scopes Trial.* Nashville TN: Broadman and Holman Publishing Group, 2005.

O'Neal, Bill. *Encyclopedia of Western Gunfighters.* Norman: University of Oklahoma Press, 1991.

Osagie, Iyunolu Folayan. *The Amistad Revolt: Memory, Slavery, and the Politics of Identity in the United States and Sierra Leone.* Athens: University of Georgia Press, 2000.

Ostling, Richard, and Joan K. Ostling. *Mormon America.* New York: HarperOne, 2007.

O'Sullivan, Shane. *Who Killed Bobby? The Unsolved Murder of Robert F. Kennedy.* New York: Union Square Press, 2008.

Owens, William. *Slave Mutiny: The Revolt on the Schooner Amistad.* Baltimore, MD: Black Classic Press, 1953.

Pace, Eric. "Jerry Rubin, 1960s Radical and Yippie Leader, Dies at 56." *New York Times.* November 29, 1994. http://www.nytimes.com/1994/11/29/obituaries/jerry-rubin-1960-s-radical-and-yippie-leader-dies-at-56.html (accessed July 28, 2009).

Packard, Jerrold M. *American Nightmare: The History of Jim Crow.* New York: St. Martin's Griffin, 2003.

Padilla, Lana, and Ron Delpit. *My Blood Betrayed: My Life with Terry Nichols and Timothy McVeigh.* New York: HarperCollins, 1995.

Page, James, Madison and Michael Joachim Haley. *The True Story of Andersonville Prison: A Defense of Major Henry Wirz.* Scituate, MA: Digital Scanning, 2006.

Pawlak, Debra. "American Gothic: The Strange Life of H. H. Holmes." *The Media Drome.* http://www.themediadrome.com/content/articles/history_articles/holmes.htm (accessed December 31, 2009).

PBS. "Chronology of Dr. Jack Kevorkian's Life and Assisted Suicide Campaign." *Frontline: The Kevorkian Verdict.* http://www.pbs.org/wgbh/pages/frontline/kevorkian/chronology.html (accessed February 13, 2010).

PBS. "Joseph Smith." *American Prophet.* http://www.pbs.org/americanprophet/joseph-smith.html (accessed March 11, 2009).

PBS. "Legal Rights and Government: Missouri v. Celia." *Slavery and the Making of America.* http://www.pbs.org/wnet/slavery/experience/legal/feature2c.html (accessed March 1, 2009).

PBS. "Missouri Slave Code of 1804." *Slavery and the Making of America.* http://www.pbs.org/wnet/slavery/experience/legal/p_feature2_law1.html (accessed March 1, 2009).

PBS. "Missouri Statute of 1845, article 2, section 29." *Slavery and the Making of America.* http://www.pbs.org/wnet/slavery/experience/legal/p_feature2_law1.html (accessed March 1, 2009.

PBS. "People & Events: Dred Scott's Fight for Freedom (1846–1857)." *Africans in America.* http://www.pbs.org/wgbh/aia/part4/4p2932.html (accessed February 28, 2009).

PBS. "People & Events: John White Webster (1793–1850)." *Murder at Harvard.* http://www.pbs.org/wgbh/amex/murder/peopleevents/p_webster.html (accessed February 27, 2009).

PBS. "People & Events: The Murder of Dr. Parkman." *Murder at Harvard.* http://www.pbs.org/wgbh/amex/murder/peopleevents/e_murder.html (accessed February 27, 2009).

PBS. "Portrait of an Assassin: Arthur Bremer." *American Experience.* http://www.pbs.org/wgbh/amex/wallace/sfeature/assasin.html (accessed March 6, 2009).

Pellowski, Michael J. *The Charles Manson Murder Trial: A Headline Court Case.* Berkeley Heights, NJ: Enslow Publishers, 2004.

Pergament, Rachel. "The Menendez Brothers: Erik." *TruTV Crime Library: Notorious Murders.* http://www.trutv.com/library/crime/notorious_murders/famous/menendez/erik_8.html (accessed July 23, 2010).

Pergament, Rachel. "The Menendez Brothers: The First Trial." *TruTV Crime Library: Notorious Murders.* http://www.trutv.com/library/crime/notorious_murders/famous/menendez/trial_16.html (accessed July 19, 2009).

Pergament, Rachel. "The Menendez Brothers: Lyle." *TruTV Crime Library: Notorious Murders.* http://www.trutv.com/library/crime/notorious_murders/famous/menendez/lyle_7.html (accessed July 23, 2010).

Pergament, Rachel. "The Menendez Brothers: The Second Trial." *TruTv Crime Library: Notorious Murders.* http://www.trutv.com/library/crime/notorious_murders/famous/menendez/trial_17.html (accessed July 19, 2009).

Peterson, Merrill D. *John Brown: The Legend Revisited.* Charlottesville: University of Virginia Press, 2004.

Phillips, Rich. "Courts Try to Decide What to Do with Manuel Noriega." *CNN.com.* January 14, 2009. http://www.cnn.com/2009/CRIME/01/14/noriega.prison/index.html (accessed January 11, 2010).

Pietrusza, David. *Rothstein: The Life and Times, and Murder of the Criminal Genius Who Fixed the 1919 World Series.* New York: Carroll and Graf Publishers, 2004.

Pitts, Leonard. "For Lewinsky, Fame the Same as Notoriety." *Miami Herald.* April 20, 2000.

Plummer, William. "California Dreamer." *People* 42, no. 5 (August 1, 1994): 60–61.

Pogash, Carol. "Myth of the 'Twinkie Defense.'" *San Francisco Chronicle.* November 23, 2003, p. D1.

Posner, Gerald. *Case Closed: Lee Harvey Oswald and the Assassination of JFK.* New York: Anchor, 1993.

Powers, Ashley, and Harriet Ryan. "O. J. Simpson Sentenced to Lengthy Prison Term." *Los Angeles Times*. December 6, 2008. http://articles.latimes.com/2008/dec/06/nation/na-oj-sentencing6 (accessed August 13, 2009).

Prentzas, G. S., and Tim McNeese. *Gideon v. Wainwright: The Right to Free Legal Counsel*. New York: Chelsea House Publications, 2007.

Presidential Determination on Major Illicit Drug Transit or Major Illicit Drug Producing Countries for Fiscal Year 2010. http://www.gpoaccess.gov/presdocs/2009/DCPD-200900728.pdf (accessed January 12, 2010).

Press, Joy. "TCA Press Tour: Al Pacino Takes on Dr. Jack Kevorkian for HBO." *Los Angeles Times: Entertainment*. January 14, 2010. http://latimesblogs.latimes.com/showtracker/2010/01/tca-press-tour-al-pacino-takes-on-dr-death-for-hbo-.html (accessed February 13, 2010).

Public Report of the White House Security Review. http://www.fas.org/irp/agency/ustreas/usss/t1pubrpt.html (accessed January 7, 2010).

Putnam, William Lowell. *John Peter Zenger and the Fundamental Freedom*. Jefferson, NC: McFarland and Company, 1997.

Radosh, Ronald, and Joyce Milton. *The Rosenberg File: A Search for the Truth*. New York: Holt, Rinehart and Winston, 1983.

Ramsland, Katherine. "H. H. Holmes: Master of Illusion." *TruTV Crime Library: Criminal Minds and Methods*. http://www.trutv.com/library/crime/serial_killers/history/holmes/index_1.html (accessed December 31, 2009).

Rauchway, Eric. *Murdering McKinley: The Making of Theodore Roosevelt's America*. New York: Hill and Wang, 2004.

"The Records of the Assassination Records Review Board." National Archives. http://www.archives.gov/research/jfk/review-board/ (accessed August 12, 2009).

Rehnquist, William. *Grand Inquests: The Historic Impeachments of Justice Samuel Chase and President Andrew Johnson*. New York: Quill, 1993.

The Report of the Commission on Obscenity and Pornography, September 1970. Washington, D.C.: Government Printing Office, 1970.

Reston, Maeve. "Rodney King shot while riding bike—He tells police that he was wounded by would-be cycle thieves." *Los Angeles Times*. November 30, 2007. http://articles.latimes.com/2007/nov/30/local/me-king30?pg=1 (accessed August 24, 2009).

Reynolds, David S. *John Brown Abolitionist: The Man Who Killed Slavery, Sparked The Civil War and Seeded Civil Rights*. New York: Vintage, 2006.

Rimer, Sara. "Few Knew of White House Suspect's Turmoil," *New York Times*. November 7, 1994, p. A14.

Roberts, Randy, and J. Gregory Garrison. *Heavy Justice: The Trial of Mike Tyson*. Fayetteville: University of Arkansas Press, 2000.

Roberts, Sam. *The Brother: The Untold Story of Atomic Spy David Greenglass and How He Sent His Sister, Ethel Rosenberg, to the Electric Chair*. New York: Random House, 2001.

"Ron Goldman Foundation for Justice." *RonGoldmanFoundation.org*. http://www.rongoldmanfoundation.org/about_us.html (accessed August 3, 2009).

Roscoe, Theodore. *The Web of Conspiracy*. Englewood Cliffs, NJ: Prentice Hall, 1960.

Rosemont, Franklin. *Joe Hill: The IWW & the Making of a Revolutionary Working Class Counterculture*. Chicago: Charles H. Kerr, 2003.

Rosenberg, Charles. *The Trial of the Assassin Guiteau: Psychiatry and the Law in the Gilded Age*. Chicago: University of Chicago Press, 1995.

Rosenberg, Gerald. N. *The Hollow Hope: Can Courts Bring About Social Change?* Chicago: University of Chicago Press, 2008.

Ross, Edmund Gibson. *History of the Impeachment of Andrew Johnson: And His Trial by the Senate for High Crimes and Misdemeanors in Office*. Charleston: Forgotten Books, 2008.

Rubin, Jerry. *Growing Up at Thirty-Seven*. New York: M. Evans and Company, 1976.

Ruhlman, R. Fred. *Captain Henry Wirz and Andersonville Prison: A Reappraisal*. Knoxville: University of Tennessee Press, 2006.

Russell, Francis. *Sacco & Vanzetti: The Case Resolved*. New York: Harper and Row, 1986.

Rutherfurd, Livingston. *John Peter Zenger, His Press, His Trial, and a Bibliography of Zenger Imprints*. New York: Dodd, Mead and Company, 1904.

Rutherford, Mildred Lewis. *Andersonville Prison and Captain Henry Wirz's Trial*. Plains, GA: United Daughters of the Confederacy, 1983.

Sagart, Kelly Boyer. *Joe Jackson: A Biography*. Westport, CT: Greenwood Publishing Group, 2004.

Sanday, Peggy Reeves. *A Woman Scorned: Acquaintance Rape on Trial*. Berkeley: University of California Press, 1997.

Saunders, Debra J. "Richard Allen Davis: Safe on Death Row." *Townhall.com: Where Your Opinion Counts*. http://townhall.com/columnists/DebraJSaunders/2009/03/12/richard_allen_davis_safe_on_death_row?page=full&comments=true (accessed December 23, 2009).

"The Scandal: Susan B. Anthony's Statement Contradicted." *Brooklyn Daily Eagle*. July 27, 1874. http://eagle.brooklynpubliclibrary.org/Repository/getFiles.asp?Style=OliveXLib:ArticleToMailGifMSIE&Type=text/html&Path=BEG/1874/07/31&ID=Ar00201&Locale=&ChunkNum=0 (accessed January 13, 2010).

Schama, Simon. *Dead Certainties: Unwarranted Speculations*. New York: Vintage, 1992.

Schindehette, Susan. "To Live and Die in L. A." *People* 42, no. 5 (August 1, 1994): 54–59.

Schmidt, Susan, and Paul W. Valentine, "Grand Jury Hears Currie; Official Defends Tripp Probe" *Washington Post*. July 23, 1998, p. A4.

Schultz, Duane. *Over The Earth I Came: The Great Sioux Uprising of 1862*. New York: St. Martin's Griffin, 1993.

Scott, Gini Graham. *Homicide by the Rich and Famous: A Century of Prominent Killers*. Westport, CT: Greenwood Publishing Group, 2005.

Seale, Bobby. "Bobby Seale Black Panther Party—Personnel Files Collection." *Bobby Seale: From the Sixties to the Future ...*" http://www.bobbyseale.com/bio.htm (accessed July 29, 2009).

Seibert, Jeffrey W. *"I Done My Duty": The Complete Story of the Assassination of President McKinley.* Bowie, MD: Heritage Books, 2002.

Serrano, Richard. *One of Ours: Timothy McVeigh and the Oklahoma City Bombing.* New York: W. W. Norton and Company, 1998.

Sharp, Thomas C. *Trial of the Persons Indicted in the Hancock Circuit Court for the Murder of Joseph Smith.* June 27th, 1844.

Sherman, Casey. *A Rose for Mary: The Hunt for the Real Boston Strangler.* Boston: Northeastern University Press, 2003.

Sherr, Lynn. *Failure Is Impossible: Susan B. Anthony in Her Own Words.* New York: Three Rivers Press, 1996.

Shilts, Randy. *The Mayor of Castro Street: The Life and Times of Harvey Milk.* New York: Macmillan, 2008.

Shipp, E. R. "Tyson Gets 6-Year Prison Term For Rape Conviction in Indiana" *New York Times.* March 27, 1992, p. B12.

Simon, David R. *Elite Deviance.* New York: Allyn and Bacon, 1999.

Skipp, Catherine, and Arion Campo-Flores. "Arthur Bremer Is Alone." *Newsweek.* November 19, 2007. http://www.newsweek.com/id/69547 (accessed March 6, 2009).

Smith, Bruce. "Linda Tripp Plans More Public Life after Charges Dismissed." *Independent.* June 4, 2000. http://www.independent.co.uk/news/world/americas/linda-tripp-plans-more-public-life-after-charges-dismissed-712486.html (accessed August 16, 2009).

Smith, Clay J., ed. *Rebels in Law: Voices in History of Black Women Lawyers.* Ann Arbor: University of Michigan Press, 2000.

Smith, Elbert B. "President Harry S. Truman: Survived Assassination Attempt at Blair House." *American History* (May/June 1998).

Smith, Gibbs M. *Joe Hill.* Layton, UT: Gibbs Smith Publishing, 1984.

Smith, Kenneth. *The Truman Assassination Attempt in the American Consciousness.* Master's Thesis, Department of History, Central Connecticut State, 2003.

Smith, Maria. "Ministry Takes in Shooter." *Cumberland Times-News.* November 17, 2007. http://www.times-news.com/local/local_story_319001802.html (accessed March 6, 2009).

Smolla, Rodney. *Jerry Falwell v. Larry Flynt: The First Amendment on Trial.* Champaign: University of Illinois Press, 1990.

Soble, Ron, and John H. Johnson. *Blood Brothers: The Inside Story of the Menendez Murders.* New York: Onyx, 1994.

Sosa, Ninette. "O.J. Simpson Appeals Conviction." *CNN.com.* May 26, 2009. http://www.cnn.com/2009/CRIME/05/26/oj.simpson.appeal/ (accessed August 15, 2009).

Spitzer, Robert. "Clinton's Impeachment Will Have Few Consequences for the Presidency." *PS: Political Science and Politics* 32, no. 3 (September 1999): 541–545.

Stannard. David E. *Honor Killing: How the Infamous "Massie Affair" Transformed Hawaii.* New York: Viking, 2005.

Starr, Kenneth, W. *The Starr Report: The Finding of Independent Counsel Kenneth W. Starr on President Clinton and the Lewinsky Affair.* New York: Public Affairs, 1998.

Starr, V. Hale, and Mark McCormick. *Jury Selection.* New York: Aspen Publishers, 2000.

Steers, Edward Jr. *Blood on the Moon: The Assassination of Abraham Lincoln*. Lexington: University Press of Kentucky, 2001.

Steers, Edward Jr. *The Trial: The Assassination of President Lincoln and the Trial of the Conspirators*. Lexington: University Press of Kentucky, 2003.

Stein, Irving. *The Ginger Kid: The Buck Weaver Story*. Dubuque, IA: Brown and Benchmark, 1992.

Sullivan, Robert. *The Disappearance of Dr. Parkman*. Boston: Little, Brown and Company, 1971.

Swanson, James, and Daniel Weinberg. *Lincoln's Assassins: Their Trial and Execution*. New York: Harper Perennial, 2008.

Sward, Susan. "Moscone's Time Was Anything But Quiet: His Election, Style Reflected S. F.'s Changing Demographics." *San Francisco Chronicle*. November 26, 1998, A1.

Tanner, Karen Holliday, and Robert K. Dearment. *Doc Holliday: A Family Portrait*. Norman: University of Oklahoma Press, 2001.

Tefertiller, Casey. *Wyatt Earp: The Life Behind the Legend*. New York: Wiley, 1999.

Thomson, Helen. *Murder at Harvard*. New York: Houghton Mifflin, 1971.

Toobin, Jeffrey. *The Run of His Life: The People v. O. J. Simpson*. New York: Touchstone, 1997.

Toobin, Jeffrey. *A Vast Conspiracy: The Real Story of a Sex Scandal That Nearly Brought Down a President*. New York: Random House, 2000.

Transcript of Proceedings before the Military Commission to Try Persons Charged with Offenses against the Law of War and the Articles of War, Washington, D.C. July 8–August 1, 1942. Edited by Joel Samaha, Sam Root, and Paul Sexton. Minneapolis: University of Minnesota, 2004. http://www.soc.umn.edu/~samaha/nazi_saboteurs/indexnazi.htm (accessed August 22, 2009).

Trefousse, Hans L. *Impeachment of a President: Andrew Johnson, the Blacks, and Reconstruction*. Bronx, NY: Fordham University Press, 1999.

"Trial at the Court of Newton. 1637." *Anne Hutchinson: The Trial*. http://www.annehutchinson.com/anne_hutchinson_trial_011.htm (accessed March 22, 2009).

"Trial of Richard Lawrence." In *Assassination and Insanity: Guiteau's Case Examined and Compared with Analogous Cases From the Earlier to the Present Times*, ed. William R. Smith, Washington, D.C.: William R. Smith, 1881.

Tsang, Steve Yui-Sang. *Intelligence and Human Rights in the Era of Global Terrorism*. Westport, CT: Greenwood Publishing Group, 2007.

Tucker, Ken, *Scarface Nation: The Ultimate Gangster Movie and How It Changed America*. New York: St. Martin's Griffin, 2008.

Turner, William, and Jonn Christian. *The Assassination of Robert F. Kennedy: The Conspiracy and Cover-Up*. New York: Carroll and Graf Publishers 2006.

"Tyson Settles Civil Suit With Woman." *New York Times*. June 22, 1995, p. B12.

UNC University Libraries. "Gideon's Trumpet." *Media Resources Center*. http://www.lib.unc.edu/house/mrc/films/full.php?film_id=1957 (accessed March 13, 2009).

United States v. Francisco Martin Duran. No. 95–3096, U.S. Court of Appeals for the District of Columbia Circuit (1996). http://www.ll.georgetown.edu/federal/judicial/dc/opinions/95opinions/95-3096a.pdf (accessed January 7, 2010).

Uruburu, Paula. *American Eve: Evelyn Nesbit, Stanford White: The Birth of the "It" Girl and the Crime of the Century*. New York: Riverhead, 2008.

U.S. Department of Justice. *Attorney General's Commission on Pornography: Final Report; July, 1986*. Washington, D. C.: Government Printing Office, 1986.

Van Slingerland, Peter. *Something Terrible Has Happened: The Account of the Sensational Thalia Massie Affair, Which Burst From Prewar Hawaii to Incense the Nation*. New York: Harper and Row, 1966.

Vercammen, Paul. "O. J. Simpson Guilty of Armed Robbery, Kidnapping." *CNN.com/crime*. October 4, 2008. http://www.cnn.com/2008/CRIME/10/04/oj.simpson.verdict/ (accessed August 13, 2009).

Vile, John R. *Great American Lawyers: An Encyclopedia*. Santa Barbara, CA: ABC-CLIO, 2001.

Vine, Phyllis. *One Man's Castle: Clarence Darrow in Defense of the American Dream*. New York: Harper, 2005.

Viorst, Milton. *Fire in the Streets: America in the 1960s*. New York: Simon and Schuster, 1979.

Walker, Ronald W., Richard E. Turley, and Glen M. Leonard. *Massacre at Meadows Mountain*. New York: Oxford University Press, 2008.

Waller, Douglas C. *A Question of Loyalty: Gen. Billy Mitchell and the Court-Martial that Gripped the Nation*. New York: HarperCollins, 2004.

Walter, Jess. *Ruby Ridge: The Truth and Tragedy of the Randy Weaver Family*. New York: Harper Perennial, 2002.

Ward, Geoffrey, and Ken Burns. *Not For Ourselves Alone: The Story of Elizabeth Cady Stanton and Susan B. Anthony*. New York: Knopf, 1999.

Weil, Martin. "Alexander Feklisov, 93; Key Soviet Spy in U.S." *Washington Post: Obituaries*. http://www.washingtonpost.com/wp-dyn/content/article/2007/11/02/AR2007110202071.html (accessed April 2, 2009).

Weiner, Jon. *Conspiracy in the Streets: The Extraordinary Trial of the Chicago Eight*. New York: W. W. Norton and Company, 2006.

Weinstein, Allen. *Perjury: The Hiss-Chambers Case*. New York: Random House, 1997.

Weiss, Mike. "Killer of Moscone, Milk Had Willie Brown on List," *San Jose Mercury News*. September 18, 1998, p. A1.

Wesley, John A. *The Man Who Shot McKinley*. South Brunswick, NJ: A. S. Barnes and Company, 1970.

"Where Are They Now: The Clinton Impeachment: Linda Tripp." *Time*. http://www.time.com/time/specials/packages/article/0,28804,1870544_1870543_1870553,00.html (accessed August 16, 2009).

White, G. Edward. *Alger Hiss's Looking-Glass Wars: The Covert Life of a Soviet Spy*. New York: Oxford University Press, 2005.

White, Welsh S. *The Death Penalty in the Nineties: An Examination of the Modern System of Capital Punishment*. Ann Arbor: University of Michigan Press, 1991.

Wilson, James Q., and David Q. Wilson. *Moral Judgment: Does the Abuse Excuse Threaten Our Legal System?* New York: Basic Books, 1998.

Winerip, Michael. "Ken Starr Would Not Be Denied." *New York Times*. September 6, 1998. http://www.nytimes.com/1998/09/06/magazine/ken-starr-would-not-be-denied. html?sec=&spon=&pagewanted=all (accessed August 17, 2009).

Woodman, Sue. *Last Rites: The Struggle over the Right to Die*. New York: Da Capo Press, 2001.

Wright, Stuart A. *Patriots, Politics, and the Oklahoma City Bombing*. New York: Cambridge University Press, 2007.

Yallop, David A. *The Day the Laughter Stopped*. New York: St. Martin's Press, 1976.

Yant, Martin. "Adams v. The Death Penalty." *Columbus Alive*. November 15, 2001. http://www.truthinjustice.org/adams.htm (accessed February 1, 2010).

Yool, George Malcolm. *1692 Witch Hunt: A Layman's Guide to the Salem Witchcraft Trials*. New York: Heritage Books, 1992.

Yost, Peter. "Rosenberg Transcripts Raise Possibility of Perjury." *ABC News*. http://abcnews.go.com/US/wireStory?id=5786138 (accessed April 2, 2009).

Zabelle-Derounian-Stodola, Kathryn, *The War in Words: Reading the Dakota Conflict Through the Captivity Literature*. Lincoln: University of Nebraska Press, 2009.

Zagorin, Adam. "Charlie's an Angel?" *Time*. February 3, 1997. http://www.time.com/time/magazine/article/0,9171,985852–2,00.html (accessed August 4, 2009).

Zgoba, Kristen, Melissa Dellasandro, Bonita Veysey, and Philip Witt. "Megan's Law: Assessing the Practical and Monetary Efficacy." *The Research and Evaluation Unit Office of Policy and Planning, New Jersey Department of Corrections*. December 2008. http://www.ncjrs.gov/pdffiles1/nij/grants/225370.pdf (accessed January 9, 2010).

Zinn, Howard. *The Twentieth Century: A People's History*. New York: HarperCollins, 2003.

Zobel, Hiller B. *The Boston Massacre*. New York: W. W. Norton and Company, 1996.

Index